The Hagiographical Experiment

Supplements to Vigiliae Christianae

TEXTS AND STUDIES OF EARLY CHRISTIAN LIFE AND LANGUAGE

VOLUME 158

The titles published in this series are listed at *brill.com/vcs*

The Hagiographical Experiment

Developing Discourses of Sainthood

Edited by

Christa Gray
James Corke-Webster

TUTA SUB AEGIDE PALLAS
1683

BRILL

LEIDEN | BOSTON

Library of Congress Cataloging-in-Publication Data

Names: Gray, Christa, 1982- editor. | Corke-Webster, James, editor.
Title: The hagiographical experiment : developing discourses of sainthood / edited by Christa Gray, James Corke-Webster.
Description: Leiden ; Boston : Brill, 2020. | Series: Supplements to vigiliae christianae, 0920-623X ; volume 158 | Includes bibliographical references and index.
Identifiers: LCCN 2019054207 (print) | LCCN 2019054208 (ebook) | ISBN 9789004421325 (hardback) | ISBN 9789004421332 (ebook)
Subjects: LCSH: Christian hagiography–History and criticism. | Christian literature–History and criticism.
Classification: LCC BX4662 .H3175 2020 (print) | LCC BX4662 (ebook) | DDC 235/.209–dc23
LC record available at https://lccn.loc.gov/2019054207
LC ebook record available at https://lccn.loc.gov/2019054208

Typeface for the Latin, Greek, and Cyrillic scripts: "Brill". See and download: brill.com/brill-typeface.

ISSN 0920-623X
ISBN 978-90-04-42132-5 (hardback)
ISBN 978-90-04-42133-2 (e-book)

Contents

Preface

This volume had its origins in a conference entitled 'Hagiography as Literature', which was organised in Edinburgh in May 2015 by Christa Gray, Lucy Grig, and Thomas Tsartsidis. We are grateful to everyone who submitted abstracts for this conference, and to all those present. The conference was generously supported by the Classical Association and by the University of Edinburgh. In its wake, a Small Research Grant from the British Academy and Leverhulme Foundation made it possible for Christa Gray and James Corke-Webster to organise a range of panels at the North American Patristic Conference and at the International Medieval Congress, as well as a further workshop hosted and supported by Durham University.

We would like to thank the anonymous reader for VCS, who provided many helpful comments. We are extremely grateful to Zara Chadha for preparing the index and proof-reading the final manuscript, and to King's College, London and the University of Reading for providing the funds for this work. Most of all, however, we are indebted to the contributors of this volume, not only for their individual chapters but for the stimulating and constructive conversation they have sustained with us and with one another over the years. The many cross-references only give a small indication of the quality of this conversation.

Abbreviations

Abbreviations of authors and titles of ancient and Byzantine texts follow those of the fourth edition of the *Oxford Classical Dictionary* (OCD) wherever possible. For those texts not listed there we follow the conventions of Liddell, Scott, and Jones, *A Greek Lexicon*, and the *Thesaurus Linguae Latinae*. Abbreviated titles of journals follow those used in *L'Année Philologique*. Other abbreviations will be explained in their context.

Introduction

James Corke-Webster and Christa Gray

1 Saints and Scholars

> These extravagant tales, which display the fiction, without the genius, of poetry, have seriously affected the reason, the faith, and the morals, of the Christians. Their credulity debased and vitiated the faculties of the mind; they corrupted the evidence of history; and superstition gradually extinguished the hostile light of philosophy and science. Every mode of religious worship which had been practised by the saints, every mysterious doctrine which they believed, was fortified by the sanction of divine revelation, and all the manly virtues were oppressed by the servile and pusillanimous reign of the monks. If it be possible to measure the interval, between the philosophical writings of Cicero and the sacred legend of Theodoret, between the character of Cato and that of Simeon, we may appreciate the memorable revolution which was accomplished in the Roman empire within a period of five hundred years.[1]

This book is about a central pillar of Christian culture: stories about men and women who were considered extraordinary, not (or at least not primarily) because of their birth, status, or physical beauty, but for their exemplary devotion to God. These texts about saints, or hagiographies, began to appear in the early Roman imperial period, but their production exploded in late antiquity and the early Middle Ages and continued long afterwards.

This abundant hagiographical writing has occupied a liminal position in scholarship. Dismissal of its literary quality has sat uneasily alongside enthusiasm for what it can offer the historian. When Gibbon blamed the fall of Rome on the sapping effect that Christianity had on the empire, his caustic tongue singled out the new faith's 'extravagant tales' for special vitriol—in particular, stories about miracles and exorcisms performed by ascetics. On the other hand, he had no qualms about using texts by saints or about saints as sources for his historical narrative when it suited his argument. So, for example, he closely follows Pontius' *Life of Cyprian*, which he judges to be 'consistent … with proba-

1 Edward Gibbon, *The History of the Decline and Fall of the Roman Empire*, vol. 4: *The End of the Roman Empire* (London: Allan Lane, 1994), 428–429 (ch. 37).

 | DOI:10.1163/9789004421332_002

bility'.[2] And more than once he can be caught paraphrasing the more lurid and prurient stories of hagiography, like that of the martyr tortured by seduction in Jerome's *Life of Paul*.[3]

Gibbon's ambivalence—part derision, part exploitation—set the agenda for much later hagiographical study.[4] The suspicion of anything in the hagiographical tradition that is not unambiguously tied to a specific name, place, and cult is embedded in the approach of the Bollandists, who since the seventeenth century have been classifying hagiographical texts and rendering them accessible and usable.[5] In separating the historical wheat from the fictional chaff, their primary motivation has been theological (and perhaps apologetic), their method philological, and their interest historical.[6] But this emphasis on historical authenticity means that the literary qualities of hagiographical texts are for the Bollandists at best a pleasant diversion and at worst a sign of unreliability.

Nearly half a century ago, Peter Brown's seminal article "The Rise and Function of the Holy Man in Late Antiquity" marked a new era in the study of late antiquity as a new social, cultural, artistic, and religious area of study nestled between the high empire and early medieval world.[7] Since Brown identified the prominence of the Syrian 'holy man' as a key to wider shifts in the overall structures of surrounding society, it is not an exaggeration to claim that late antiquity as an area of study stands upon the shoulders of saints (some of them standing, in turn, on their pillars). The persistent return to Brown's

---

2 Gibbon, *Decline and Fall*, vol. 2, 542, n. 80. The paraphrase of the *Life and Passion of Cyprian* is on 541–545 (ch. 16).

3 Gibbon, *Decline and Fall*, vol. 2, 539, n. 65 (ch. 16); Jerome, *V. Pauli* 3.2–5.

4 For a fuller walk-through of the history of hagiographical research, see most recently Stephanos Efthymiadis, "Introduction", in idem (ed.), *Ashgate Research Companion to Byzantine Hagiography*, vol. 1 (Farnham: Ashgate, 2011), 1–14, with further bibliography.

5 Fundamental contributions are Hippolyte Delehaye, *Les légendes hagiographiques*, (Brussels: Société des Bollandistes, 1905; 2nd edition Brussels: Subsidia Hagiographica, 1927); English translation by Donald Attwater, *The Legends of the Saints; With a Memoir of the Author by Paul Peeters* (New York: Fordham University Press, 1962); Hippolyte Delehaye, *Les passions des martyrs et les genres littéraires*. (Brussels: Société des Bollandistes, 1921; 2nd edition Brussels: Subsidia Hagiographica, 1966), as well as René Aigrain, *L'hagiographie. Ses sources, ses méthodes, son histoire* (Brussels, Société des Bollandistes, 1953 (reprinted with additional bibliography in 2000)).

6 Flor van Ommeslaeghe, "The Acta Sanctorum and Bollandist Methodology", in Sergei Hackel, *The Byzantine Saint* (London: Fellowship of St. Alban and St. Sergius, 1981), 155–163. See now too Robert Godding et al., *Bollandistes, saints et légendes. Quatre siècles de recherche hagiographique* (Brussels: Société des Bollandistes, 2007).

7 Peter Brown, "The Rise and Function of the Holy Man in Late Antiquity", *JRS* 61 (1971), 80–101; reprinted in idem, *Society and the Holy in Late Antiquity* (Berkeley: University of California Press, 1982), 103–152.

article and its continuing re-evaluation point to the central position the saint holds in late antique history and our understandings of it.[8] For hagiography, the most immediate impact was the development of new investigations into the sociological and anthropological context of the veneration of saints.[9] But while this re-evaluation of the period renewed scholarly interest in late antique texts beyond the traditional boundaries of patristic theology, interest in hagiography remained fundamentally historical (with some important exceptions discussed further below).

This shared interest of the Bollandists and Brown's early work in the historical rather than the literary has a further common cause, namely a starting point that sees cultic veneration as a constitutive part of sainthood, which hagiography either served to instigate or to which it responded.[10] This recognises an important interdependence of cult and hagiography: the presence of saints' tombs, relics, or monasteries would inspire the production of texts, and these in turn could lead to the desire to identify saints or their remains in other places, as well as influencing Christian iconography. But such a prioritisation of cult has meant that research focuses on material phenomena at the expense of the

8 Including by its own author; see e.g. Peter Brown, "The Saint as Exemplar in Late Antiquity", *Representations* 2 (1983), 1–25, and idem, "Arbiters of the Holy: The Christian Holy Man in Late Antiquity", in idem, *Authority and the Sacred: Aspects of the Christianisation of the Roman World* (Cambridge: Cambridge University Press, 1995), 57–78; idem, "The Rise and Function of the Holy Man in Late Antiquity, 1971–1997", *JECS* 6.3, (1998), 352–376, as part of a special issue of that journal reflecting on Brown's original article. See too e.g. Garth Fagan, "The Pagan Holy Man in Late Antique Society", *JHS* 102 (1982), 33–59.

9 Again, see the seminal work by Peter Brown, *The Cult of the Saints: Its Rise and Function in Latin Christianity* (Chicago: University of Chicago Press, 1981); and on its influence James Howard-Johnston and Paul A. Hayward (eds.), *The Cult of the Saints in Late Antiquity and the Middle Ages: essays on the contribution of Peter Brown* (Oxford: Oxford University Press, 1999). For a good summary account of the foundational importance of sociological and anthropological approaches to late antique studies, see Dale Martin, "Introduction", in Dale Martin and Patricia Cox Miller (eds.), *The Cultural Turn in Late Ancient Studies: Gender, Asceticism and Historiography* (Durham, NC/London: Duke University Press, 2005), 1–21, at 4–5.

10 See e.g. Aigrain, *L'hagiographie*, 7–8: 'le saint est un homme qui, par sa correspondance à la grâce divine, a été constitué en état supernaturel de sainteté, mais il faut, pour que l'hagiographe ait à s'occuper de ce qui le concerne, que cet état de sainteté, avec les vertus héroïques qu'il comporte, ait été reconnu par l'autorité de l'Église, reconnaissance qui entraîne comme conséquences les manifestations d'un culte liturgique et public'. In this model, the sequence starts with the saint's sanctity, which reaches its recorded form in hagiography only through the medium of official recognition and ecclesiastical cult. While Brown's model of cult does not hinge on the church's official authority, hagiography is still conceived as secondary to cult, whether official, private, or popular.

literary.[11] And it has also in practice narrowed the literary range of what was studied, since texts that share some features of hagiography—and which might otherwise be counted as hagiographical in form or content—but which have no connection with contemporary cults have been neglected.[12] For this range of reasons, then, our sense of the social and cultural history of late antique sainthood is much richer than our aesthetic understanding of its hagiography.[13]

This literary neglect is in some ways entirely understandable. Despite changing scholarly interests and tastes, hagiography has consistently been perceived as credulous (and hence incredible), repetitive, and stridently ideological. Such perceptions are not entirely groundless. First, some of the subtleties of hagiographical texts are bound up with their theological and moral distinctions, which can be difficult to relate to modern literary concerns. Further, it is essentially part of the definition of hagiography that the characters it portrays are more or less perfectly matched in their thoughts and actions with a presupposed set of criteria, namely Christian values.[14] This has consequences for our attitudes as readers: reading a narrative text as hagiographical requires the assumption that it has some sort of moral and didactic agenda and seeks to edify its readers accordingly. At the very least, we must usually believe that the text is designed for the readers to admire the subject of the tale, usually as a type

11 The ERC-funded project "The Cult of the Saints", launched in 2014 under the direction of Bryan Ward-Perkins, includes a database of texts in its outputs, but these text are analysed as evidence for cult, not as works of literature; see http://cultofsaints.history.ox.ac.uk/ [last accessed 19/06/2019].

12 The recent conference "*Culte des saints et littérature hagiographique: accords et désaccords*", 25–26 September 2015, Centre d'Histoire et Civilisation de Byzance, Paris, specifically investigated those occasions when cultic practices and literary production do not align. The papers from this conference are set to be published as Vincent Déroche, Bryan Ward-Perkins, and Robert Wiśniewski (eds.), *Culte des saints et littérature hagiographique*, Centre de recherche d'Histoire et Civilisation de Byzance, Monographies (Leuven: Peeters, in press).

13 It is also true that a nuanced and contextualised literary assessment of hagiography has the potential to further our understanding of the role that these texts played in the cult of saints.

14 The construction of a *Life* on the scaffold of a pre-existing set of values is exemplified by Marius of Neapolis' *Life of Proclus*, where the author 'explicitly sets out to show how his hero, Proclus, exemplified all the virtues in the Neoplatonic canon from the lowest to the highest (*V. Procl.* 2–3), and this colours his whole approach to his subject' (John Dillon, "Holy and Not So Holy: On the Interpretation of Late Antique Biography", in Brian McGing and Judith Mossmann (eds.), *The Limits of Ancient Biography* (Swansea: Classical Press of Wales, 2006), 155–167, at 160). In our texts this hagiographic expectation can itself be the subject of literary play: see, for example, Staat in this volume on the ethical flaws of the protagonist of Jerome's *Life of Malchus*.

of role model.[15] Finally, the shared alignment with a particular set of Christian values means that, even if these do vary, repetition often follows, even if different hagiographical texts select and emphasise different virtues depending on their distinctive persuasive aims.[16]

The influence of the linguistic or cultural turn in the classical disciplines, however, has as elsewhere begun a sea change in the mainstream study of hagiography.[17] Over the last few decades, monographs have begun to appear in much greater number addressing literary aspects of hagiography.[18] The most recent achievement is the two-volume *Ashgate Research Companion to Byzantine Hagiography*, whose insistence on the literary value of hagiography is an important corrective to centuries of neglect. As its title suggests, the scope of this volume is limited to the Greek tradition of the Byzantine period, with a noticeably synchronic approach to the literary issues discussed in the second volume. Our collection seeks to supplement this work by introducing Latin texts into the discussion, though Greek, Syriac, and Coptic traditions are also represented, and by focusing for the most part on the development of hagiography in the late antique period. Unlike in the later Byzantine period, where

---

15 The centrality of this criterion means, of course, that hagiography arguably does not even need to be narrative, but can include any type of representation of an admirable Christian person or set of persons—provided it is evident that their holiness is bound up with their personality, rather than vested in external attributes such as the holding of a priesthood or episcopal see. See the contributions of Williams, Yuzwa, and Wiśniewski in this volume.

16 In a wide-ranging analysis of commonplaces in Byzantine hagiography, Thomas Pratsch found that no two *Lives* are actually identical: it is never the case that they are distinguishable only by means of differently named protagonists. 'Selbst in denjenigen Fällen, in denen eine jüngere Vita eines Heiligen nachweislich von der älteren Vita eines anderen Heiligen abhängt, also von dieser über weite Strecken abgeschrieben wurde, sind die durch Überarbeitung und Variation entstandenen Unterschiede zwischen der jüngeren und der älteren Vita so groß, daß jeweils von einer eigenen Vita gesprochen werden kann. Mithin besitzt also jede einzelne Vita ihren eigenen, individuellen Charakter': Thomas Pratsch, *Der hagiographische Topos. Griechische Heiligenviten in mittelbyzantinischer Zeit.* Millenium Studies 6 (Berlin/New York: De Gruyter, 2005), 408.

17 On its rising importance in late antique studies, see Martin, "Introduction", 5–9.

18 The bibliography amassed before the turn of the new millennium is collected in Christian Høgel, "Literary Aspects of Greek Byzantine Hagiography: A Bibliographical Survey", *SO* 72 (1997), 164–171, but considering only studies of texts produced after AD 500. In many of the fifty-nine titles that Høgel lists, literary approaches (defined as 'studies of texts or relations between texts … that concentrate on such phenomena as narrative structures, genres, thematic elements, author and audience, stylistics etc.') play only a subordinate role. More works have appeared since, many of which are referenced in the footnotes that follow, but trenchantly anti-literary historical approaches also persist, for example in Timothy D. Barnes, *Early Christian Hagiography and Roman History.* Tria Corda 5 (Tübingen: Mohr Siebeck, 2010 (2nd edition 2016)).

hagiography became an increasingly (although not entirely) stable and recognisable genre, late antique hagiography had not yet settled into fixed patterns, and instead explored a range of innovative combinations of literary form, content, and style. This makes late antiquity a particularly promising field for thinking about the literary aspects of writing about saints.

2 Definition and Development of Hagiography

The question of how to define hagiography is a notoriously thorny one.[19] The problem with many definitions is that they are inherently exclusionary—i.e., like the cult-based approaches to hagiography, they necessarily exclude interesting texts that lack these elements but nevertheless in some way, we think, participate in the 'hagiographical'. Those that look, for example, for a cradle-to-grave narrative obviously omit texts that only partially cover a holy life, or which use forms other than the narrative.[20] Accounts focused on the miraculous omit those works of hagiography that deal with the more mundane.[21] And even looser definitions too, such as the idea that hagiographies are those texts that emerge from and seek to enhance religious devotion to saints, presuppose too much about authorial intention, and exclude texts whose purpose is rather murkier.[22]

Our approach instead is founded on a sense of family resemblances. There was, we argue, no fixed template—in late antiquity, at least—for writing about saints; rather, diverse authors reacted to diverse aspects of earlier writings and appropriated, interpreted, and altered them to shape their own view on holi-

19 The problem has been reviewed recently by Claudia Rapp, "The Origins of Hagiography and the Literature of Early Monasticism: Purpose and Genre between Tradition and Innovation", in Richard Flower, Christopher Kelly, and Michael Stuart Williams (eds.), *Unclassical Traditions. Alternatives to the Classical Past in Late Antiquity*, vol. 1. Cambridge Classical Journal Supplements 34 (Cambridge: Cambridge University Press, 2010), 119–130. Her functionalist solution privileges didacticism and the *chreia* as the classical form behind hagiography. But it is still one based on common purpose, and thus to some extent exclusionary.

20 Note, for example, that "Hagiography" and "The literature of the monastic movement" are treated as separate chapters in Frances Young, Lewis Ayres, and Andrew Louth (eds.), *The Cambridge History of Early Christian Literature* (Cambridge: Cambridge University Press, 2004), at 358–361 and 373–381 respectively.

21 Moses Hadas and Morton Smith, *Heroes and Gods: Spiritual Biographies* (New York: Harper and Row, 1965).

22 For the latter definition, see e.g. Delehaye, *Les légendes hagiographiques*, 2. Delehaye also in practice ignores most of the earliest texts, on which this volume focuses in particular.

ness in their Christian heroes.[23] Since authors made use of some of the same characteristics and some different, early works of hagiography would resemble each other in some ways and not in others. Moreover, as the numbers of such Christian works increased they could echo each other. The resulting collection of works about 'saints'—subjects considered holy in some sense by their authors—[24] need have no one shared feature, but rather are all part of a family that each share some features with each other. Such a definition has the benefit of allowing for the consideration of a wider range of potential texts and authors in discussions of hagiography.

It also serves to promote a wide rather than a narrow interpretation of the literary origins of hagiography. These 'family resemblances' come from a wide range of earlier Christian and non-Christian works. The stage at which these turned into 'hagiography' is unclear. Classical biography represented a long tradition of life-writing which crossed from the Greek to the Latin tradition, but which by late antiquity was (increasingly) popular in both.[25] Religion—or, better, the relationship of their protagonist with the divine—had always been fundamental to both Greek and Roman examples of the genre, and was also the central element in Hellenistic *theios aner* literature. The late Republic and early empire also saw the emergence of the Greek novels, which follow their protagonists through the life-defining adventures of their early adulthood (and sometimes their childhood, e.g. Longus) and also place particular emphasis on their relationship with the divine.[26] As the high empire progressed into late antiq-

23 *Contra* Simon Swain, "Biography and the Biographic in the Literature of the Roman Empire", in Mark Edwards and Simon Swain (eds.), *Portraits: Biographical Representation in the Greek and Latin Literature of the Roman Empire* (Oxford: Clarendon Press, 1997), 1–37, at 36.

24 Concomitantly, and deliberately, we do not offer a precise and unequivocal definition of hagiography's central figure, the saint, or the holy woman or man, since that definition itself was continually shaped by the literary development we seek to investigate. The subjects of our texts are martyrs and ascetics, monks and bishops, and their ideas of what it means to follow Christ cover a wide range, including dying for one's faith, giving up all worldly claims and possessions, taking social responsibility for the good of the Christian community, working miracles, and attacking intransigent pagans and heretics.

25 Swain, "Biography and Biographic", as well as the other essays in that collection. An excellent overall treatment of the biographical tradition is Tomas Hägg, *The Art of Biography in Antiquity* (Cambridge: Cambridge University Press, 2012).

26 Merkelbach went so far as to characterise the novels as 'Mysterientexte': Reinhold Merkelbach, *Roman und Mysterium in der Antike* (Munich/Berlin: Beck, 1963). For subsequent discussions see e.g. Tomas Hägg, *The Novel in Antiquity* (Oxford: Blackwell, 1983), 26–27, 101–104; Froma Zeitlin, "Religion in the Ancient Novel", in Tim Whitmarsh (ed.), *The Cambridge Companion to the Greek and Roman Novel* (Cambridge: Cambridge University Press, 2008), 91–108.

uity this increasingly became the central focus, exemplified by Philostratus' mid-third-century *Life of Apollonius of Tyana*,[27] or philosophical biographies like Porphyry's *Life of Plotinus* or Iamblichus' *Life of Pythagoras*.[28] Into this mix we must add panegyric, the non-narrative mode of praise that evolved into the standard form of address to emperors, and in which divine favour for the ruler in question played an ever more important part.

At the same time, the distinctive book culture of Christianity also produced a new array of writings all concerned in some way with the lives of holy individuals. The Gospels, both canonical and non-canonical, have been the subject of many scholarly works interested in their debts to earlier forms of both pagan and Jewish life-writing.[29] The *Acts of the Apostles*, a continuation of the *Gospel of Luke* by the same author, has an equally intriguing relationship to previous examples of collective biography.[30] Next, the martyr literature of the second and third centuries cast a spotlight on the exemplary deaths of Christian men and women, and itself drew upon earlier biographers' interest in their subjects' deaths, Christian, pagan, and Jewish.[31] The same period saw the emergence of

27 See in particular Marc Van Uytfanghe, "La vie d'Apollonius de Tyane et le discours hagiographique", in Kristoffel Demoen and Danny Praet (eds.), *Theios Sophistès: Essays on Flavius Philostratus' Vita Apollonii*. Mnemosyne Supplements 305 (Leiden: Brill, 2008), 335–374.

28 See in particular Patricia Cox [Miller], *Biography in Late Antiquity: A Quest for the Holy Man*. The Transformation of the Classical Heritage 5 (Berkeley: University of California Press, 1983).

29 For example Dirk Frickenschmidt, *Evangelium als Biographie. Die vier Evangelien im Rahmen antiker Erzählkunst*. Texte und Arbeiten zum neutestamentlichen Zeitalter 22 (Tübingen: Francke, 1997); Richard A. Burridge, *What Are the Gospels? A Comparison with Graeco-Roman Biography*. Monograph Series Society for New Testament Studies 70 (Cambridge/New York: Cambridge University Press, 1992 (2nd edition with a foreword by W. Stanton, Grand Rapids, MI: W.B. Eerdmans, 2004)); Dale Miller and Patricia J. Miller, *The Gospel of Mark as Midrash on Earlier Jewish and New Testament Literature*. Studies in the Bible and Early Christianity 21 (Lewiston: E. Mellen Press 1990); Claude Goldsmid Montefiore, *Rabbinic Literature and Gospel Teachings* (London: Macmillan, 1930); and Daniel Boyarin, *The Jewish Gospels: The Story of the Jewish Christ* (New York: New Press, 2012).

30 E.g. Justin Taylor, "The Acts of the Apostles as Biography", in McGing and Mossmann, *The Limits of Ancient Biography*, 77–88, discussing, inter alia, the formal affinities of *Luke–Acts* with Diogenes Laertius' *Lives of the Philosophers* as postulated by Charles H. Talbert, *Literary Patterns, Theological Themes and the Genre of Luke–Acts*. Society of Biblical Literature Monograph Series 20 (Missoula: Society of Biblical Literature, 1974).

31 See e.g. William H.C. Frend, *Martyrdom and Persecution in the Early Church: A Study of Conflict from the Maccabees to Donatus* (Oxford: Blackwell, 1965); but cf. Glen Bowersock, *Martyrdom and Rome* (Cambridge: Cambridge University Press, 1995), arguing that Christian ideas of martyrdom were largely without precedent.

apocryphal *Acts*, dramatic tales of love and travel that were in close conversation with the themes of the Greek novels, as well as the *Pseudo-Clementine Recognitions*, a 'Christian novel'.[32]

Such, then, was the richness of the literary landscape as, from the third century on, the Roman Empire moved into the late antique period. It is at this point that we start to see the texts normally treated as the first works of hagiography. Pontius' mid-third-century *Life of Cyprian*, for example, written in Latin, seems to mediate between traditional life-writing and the martyr *acta* in describing not only the death but also the life of its episcopal protagonist.[33] In the Greek world, Eusebius of Caesarea's lost *Life of Pamphilus*, written in the late third century, and his mini 'Life of Origen', preserved in Book 6 of his *Ecclesiastical History*, are similar life-and-death accounts of exceptional Christian heroes specially favoured by divine providence. Athanasius' mid-fourth-century Greek *Life of Antony*, his famous account of the desert-bound ascetic hero, is most often seen as the starting point for Christian hagiography. In the Latin west, Jerome's triptych of fictional saints' lives—the *Life of Paul*, the *Life of Malchus*, and the *Life of Hilarion*—spark a production line of related accounts that would last for centuries.

Our interest in the current volume is neither to identify one such Ur-text as the origin of hagiography, and thus pinpoint the latter's birth, nor to dictate on that basis which earlier genre of writing, Christian or not, had the greatest influence upon hagiography, and thereby offer a conventional literary history of formal and thematic categories. We are also not seeking to explain hagiography's birth via either a specific model (or set of models) or a particular historical concatenation of motivating factors. The point is rather that the fact and process of evolution are interesting in themselves. We are concerned with the *ongoing* process by which works on hagiography came into being; that is, the decisions that authors of successive hagiographical works made about writing, selecting, arranging, and presenting their material. We have thus called this a study of development rather than of origins, and of an experiment, rather than of an established genre. Many of the key 'transitional texts' of late antiquity are represented—Eusebius' biographical writings, Athanasius' *Life of Antony*, Jerome's narrative trilogy—but others are less well known, and come not just from the late antique but also the medieval period (since development, as opposed to origins, continues well beyond hagiography's formative centuries).

32 Hägg, *The Novel in Antiquity*, 162–164.

33 These third-century texts are a particular problem for the traditional thesis that Christian cradle-to-death tales depended on the rise of desert monasticism.

This volume's contribution to the literary study of hagiography is as an analysis of the processes through which hagiography and hagiographies came into being. It takes into account the whole range of Aristotelian causes: material, formal, efficient, and final. We seek to shed light on how particular texts—and more broadly the 'type' of text they represent, in so far as such an affiliation exists—came to exist in terms of inspiration, aesthetics, intertextuality, structure, rhetorical strategy, etc. As such, the essays collected here ultimately explore what hagiography is—not because they explicitly ask what counts as hagiography, but because they help reveal the people, forms, and techniques that created it.

3 Who, What, and How

Works of hagiography were produced by, with, and for a variety of subjects, authors, and audiences, appeal to and employ a range of models and forms, and mobilise a range of strategies and techniques. Some of these came from earlier literature, both Christian and non-Christian; others were novel, or represented new combinations or twists on classical themes. That exciting diversity is, we argue, characteristic of hagiography in general, and it is the neglected and surprising influences and developments in these three areas—persons, forms, and strategies—that the specific papers in this volume aim to explore.

3.1 *Part 1: The Persons of Hagiography*

The essays in Part 1 consider *who* is involved in hagiographical construction as the subject(s), author, or audience. Each considers some combination of these three. The first of these—the saints—have, unsurprisingly, traditionally been the main focus of hagiographical scholarship. Even if their historicity was the subject of debate, accounts which presented saints' names together with a geographical location and, ideally, an approximate date made the subject of the story a much more solid object of investigation than the often anonymous or pseudonymously recorded author. When it comes to their literary assessment, however, neither saint nor author nor audience has received much praise. Momigliano, for example, saw the characterisation of classical biography—based upon 'the interchange between individual ambitions and political circumstances'—as being replaced by 'mystical experiences and contacts with divine beings' in both Christian and non-Christian later biography.[34]

34 Arnaldo Momigliano, "Ancient Biography and the Study of Religion in the Roman Empire", in idem, *On Pagans, Jews, and Christians* (Middletown, CT: Wesleyan University Press, 1987), 159–177, at 176.

Increasingly, what was important for both authors and readers was the extent to which the individuals partook in the divine.

Momigliano was of course part of a world still generally committed to a model of late antique decline.[35] While it is true that such characterisation is common to much hagiography,[36] this blanket judgement ignores an extraordinary variety of material that actually contains a very mixed company of unusual and confusing leading men and women. Different ideas about the most important aspects of divinity and devotion, and the different ways in which these ideas interact, mean hagiography is much more diverse than this model suggests. In fact hagiographic texts are themselves often aware of the dangers of homogenised characterisation, and can be caught playing with such expectations in ways that appear to prioritise being thought-provoking and entertaining over on-message ideology. In the extant hagiographical corpus the clean-cut saint of popular imagination rubs shoulders with cavorting, incompetent, petulant, and even murderous saints.

The first paper in the collection, that of James Corke-Webster, considers differing approaches to characterisation in some of the earliest attempts to write up the lives of Christian heroes. It argues that Athanasius' famed portrait was produced in response to the earlier hagiographical efforts of Athanasius' opponent in the theological sphere, Eusebius of Caesarea. Their protagonists differ on two crucial points—their education and their interaction with others. Where Athanasius' unlettered Antony spends his life seeking ever greater isolation, Eusebius' portraits of Pamphilus, Origen, and others emphasise their depth of Christian and non-Christian learning, and how they mobilised them to the benefit of their wider communities. These two approaches reveal a debate over the nature of sanctity from the earliest days, played out in a literary arena, by two innovating specialists in the written word, who had an eye on both posterity and their own immediate circumstances.

Another promising approach to the untapped potential of the characters in hagiography is narratology (the approach which has produced the best results in raising the ancient novel to literary respectability).[37] A recent case study by Annelies Bossu, Koen De Temmerman, and Danny Praet has demonstrated the

35 It is worth remembering that this article was essentially an appendix to his monograph, *The Development of Greek Biography*. Carl Newell Jackson Lectures (Cambridge, MA/London: Harvard University Press, 1971).

36 See above 4–5 for the role of Christian values in shaping a saint's character.

37 The definitive account of characterisation in the ancient novel is Koen De Temmerman, *Crafting Characters: Heroes and Heroines in the Ancient Novel* (Cambridge: Cambridge University Press, 2014).

suitability of hagiographical material for such analysis.[38] Their examination of the *Passion of Caecilia* refutes the idea that characterisation in hagiography relies on stereotypes, demonstrating instead that this text paints a complex picture of its heroine by echoing but inverting earlier tropes of erotic narrative.

The second paper, that of Julie Van Pelt, combines such a narratological approach with equally innovative approaches to hagiographical authorship. Traditional work on the latter has tended to focus on known individuals and their motivations for writing.[39] Derek Krueger's influential *Writing and Holiness*, however, has ushered in a more sophisticated appraisal of the relationship between hagiographers and their protagonists. Krueger argues that hagiography's novel approach to authorship was one of its defining features.[40] Since hagiographies captured the essence of their sacred and thus authoritative subjects, they and their authors gained authority. Writing itself became a salvific activity. In other words, the exercise of writing hagiography produced new ways of thinking about the literary process. Another important work, Williams' *Authorised Lives in Early Christian Biography*, investigates, against the backdrop of their common purpose to re-enact Scripture, the intrusion of Eusebius, Gregory of Nyssa, Athanasius, and Augustine into the texts they authored.[41] Most recently, Claudia Rapp has investigated the interwoven roles of audience, author, and text in the process of making saints present in texts.[42]

---

38 Annelies Bossu, Koen De Temmerman, and Danny Praet, "The Saint as an Astute Heroine: Rhetoric and Characterization in the *Passio Caeciliae*", *Mnemosyne* 69.3 (2016), 433–452. Koen De Temmerman has recently completed an ERC-funded research project at Ghent University, "Novel Saints: Studies in Ancient Fiction and Hagiography", which pursues these questions further across a wide range of hagiographical texts: see http://www.novelsaints.ugent.be [last accessed 19/06/2019]. Two members of the project, Julie Van Pelt and Klazina Staat, present their research in this volume.

39 Most famous, of course, is Athanasius' authorship of the *Life of Antony*, a text for imitation by other monks that was simultaneously its author's weapon against Arianism, his tool to co-opt the saint's charismatic authority to shore up his own institutional authority, and the foundation of an entire vision of the Christian *politeia*. The bibliography here is extensive; see in particular David Brakke, *Athanasius and the Politics of Asceticism* (Oxford: Clarendon Press, 1995).

40 Derek Krueger, *Writing and Holiness: The Practice of Authorship in the Early Christian East* (Philadelphia: University of Pennsylvania Press, 2004).

41 Michael Stuart Williams, *Authorised Lives in Early Christian Biography: Between Eusebius and Augustine* (Cambridge/New York: Cambridge University Press, 2008).

42 Claudia Rapp, "Author, Audience, Text and Saint: Two Modes of Early Byzantine Hagiography", *Scandinavian Journal of Byzantine and Modern Greek Studies* 1 (2015), 111–129, at 115.

Rapp posits a parallel relationship between the holy man and his followers on the one hand and between a hagiographical text and its audience on the other.

Van Pelt takes that same parallel in a new direction while employing a narratological approach. She uses the relationship between a common figure in hagiographies, the holy fool, and the crowds with whom he interacts as a lens to consider possible parallels in the relationship between the author and audience of the hagiography. Both, she argues, are engaged in a careful balancing act between misrepresentation—the fool's feigned idiocy; the author's use of fiction—and communication. Van Pelt argues that the character of the fool and his interactions with an intratextual audience are 'good to think with'[43] to help us understand better the various forms of masking used by hagiographic authors as strategies of authorisation, and the complicit role of the audience in making them effective.

Robert Wiśniewski's paper, the third in this first section, considers the characterisation of saints in clerical hagiography—the lives of bishops and presbyters, conceived against monastic hagiography dealing with the lives of monks—alongside their intended audiences. In recognising that these lives are neutral or even negative about the clerical profession's contribution to sanctity, and that clerical hagiographies rarely try to construct a consistent model for life, he problematises the idea that they were designed as straightforward models for imitation. Here again then the literary approach reveals something indirectly about evolving ideas of sanctity—in this case, that it could not be reached via the clerical life.

3.2 *Part 2: The Forms of Hagiography*

The essays in Part 2 consider *what* hagiography is, in the sense of the forms and structures chosen to shape and reshape the material presented. It is now generally agreed that discussions of genre in terms of literary categories with well-defined rules for including and excluding texts are not particularly helpful in antiquity. To yield productive results, analysis in terms of genre can be used only to study the expectations associated with particular types of writing, which ancient authors and readers could employ, exploit, or frustrate as they chose.[44] This insight has been well-applied to hagiography by, among others,

---

43 For the phrase cf. Claude Lévi-Strauss on animals in *Le totémisme aujourd'hui* (Paris: Presses universitaires de France, 1962), 128.

44 An important case study is Averil Cameron, "Apologetics in the Roman Empire—A Genre of Intolerance?", in Jean-Michel Carrié and Rita Lizzi Testa (eds.), *Humana Sapit: études d'Antiquité tardive offertes à Lellia Cracco Ruggini* (Turnhout: Brepols, 2002), 219–227.

Marc Van Uytfanghe, who advocated moving away from the idea that hagiography is a class of texts with particular formal structures by using the term 'hagiographic discourse' instead.[45]

This is the background to this section's first contribution, that of Alan Ross, which considers the key role played by traditional satire in the early development of hagiographic discourse. Comparing Jerome's *Life of Paul*, a text that samples numerous different genres, with Athanasius' earlier *Life of Antony*, Ross details how the former uses traditional satire to systematically elevate its protagonist at the expense of the latter's. Paul, not Antony, is set up as the first eremitic monk, in a move that also critiques Athanasius as hagiographer. In simultaneously imitating and satirising this early attempt at writing a saint's life, Ross suggests that Jerome made a deliberate and important intervention in the earliest stages of the creation of hagiographic discourse. That intervention on the location of true sanctity was achieved here via a novel experiment with form.

Such experimentation with genre was in fact characteristic of the period more generally. While some traditional forms of writing persisted or even became more prevalent, new forms also emerged, and, most intriguingly, various hybrids emerged. Where once this too was seen as one more sign of Rome's cultural decline, the rehabilitation of the period has sparked a surge of interest in these distinctively late antique generic developments.[46] So a 2007 volume on late antique intellectual culture examines the use and reuse of older texts and models in late antique literature, and the exciting collection of essays that stemmed from the 2013 Shifting Frontiers conference is entitled *Shifting Genres in Late Antiquity*. But though remarkably wide-ranging, the former addresses hagiography only tangentially (via the *Instituta Aegyptorum* of John Cassian) and the latter omits it entirely.[47] But experimentation with, and sophistication

45 Marc Van Uytfanghe, "L'hagiographie: un 'genre' chrétien ou antique tardif?", *AB* 111 (1993), 135–188. A parallel point has been made by Mark Edwards, "Biography and the Biographic", in Edwards and Swain, *Portraits*, 227–234, where 'the biographic' is a trait that can appear in various types of text.

46 See e.g. Jacques Fontaine, "Unité et diversité du mélange des genres et des tons chez quelques écrivains latins de la fin du IVe siècle: Ausone, Ambroise, Ammien", in Manfred Fuhrmann (ed.), *Christianisme et formes littéraires de l'antiquité tardive en Occident*. Entretiens sur l'Antiquite Classique 23 (Geneva: Fondation Hardt, 1977), 425–482.

47 J.H.D. Scourfield (ed.), *Texts and Culture in Late Antiquity: Inheritance, Authority, and Change* (Swansea: The Classical Press of Wales, 2007); Geoffrey Greatrex and Hugh Elton (eds.), *Shifting Genres in Late Antiquity* (Farnham/Burlington, VT: Ashgate, 2015), acknowledging the absence of hagiography at 1. Similarly, in the important collection of essays edited by Lieve Van Hoof and Peter Van Nuffelen (eds.), *Literature and Society in the Fourth Century AD: Performing Paideia, Constructing the Present, Presenting the Self*

of, form in hagiographical writing more than matches that of other late antique literature. This has been well demonstrated by the various modes of interplay between hagiography and historiography revealed in Arietta Papaconstantinou's collection of essays, *Writing 'True Stories'*; but the interplay between hagiography and other genres repays further attention.[48]

The next two papers take up this challenge. Zachary Yuzwa analyses the parts played by epistolographic and dialogic forms in Sulpicius Severus' attempts to write about Martin of Tours. Interactions between epistolography and hagiography are of particular importance, since many of the proto-hagiographical martyr *acta* are preserved as letters (e.g. *The letters of the churches in Lyons and Vienne to the church in Smyrna*, or the letters of Dionysius of Alexandria, all preserved in Eusebius' *Ecclesiastical History*). And the archetypal hagiography, the *Life of Antony*, is also framed as a letter. Yuzwa starts from the important observation that the *Life of Saint Martin*—the traditional narrative form of hagiography—lacks an ending, in that there is no account of Martin's death. That absence of closure prompts various 'appendices' to Sulpicius' *vita* in a series of letters and the dialogue *Gallus*. This deliberate and repeated delay in describing Martin's death, Yuzwa suggests, frustrates readers' expectations and allows and even insists upon a process of rewriting and rereading that Sulpicius suggests is itself salvific.

Michael Stuart William's paper follows Yuzwa's in considering the hagiographical correspondence of Paulinus of Nola and Sulpicius Severus. In contrast to the death-less *Life of Saint Martin*, there is no hagiographical *Life of Paulinus*, just a letter by the presbyter Uranius entitled *On the Death of Paulinus*. The letter correspondence itself, Williams suggests, can be read as part of a hagiographical discourse. These authors engage in the mutual eulogy often seen as typical of hagiography, while ostentatiously denying their own right to praise. Considering the implicit sincerity or humour of these epistolary exchanges, and the debt owed to classical models of elite correspondence, Williams argues that the essential dialectical nature of the format was key to their strategy. Read in isolation, any individual letter is misleading; only when read as part of an ongoing correspondence, where each could rely on his interlocutor reciprocating the praise, can the true dynamic of the autohagiography on display here be understood. This 'unusual' hagiographical form is thus only

(Leiden: Brill, 2015), texts concerning saints features only incidentally, mainly in the contributions by Morwenna Ludlow, "Texts, Teachers and Pupils in the Writings of Gregory of Nyssa", 83–102, and Sigrid Mratschek, "A Living Relic for the Bishop of Rome: Strategies of Visualization in a Civil Case", 134–156.

48 Arietta Papaconstantinou (ed.), *Writing 'True Stories': Historians and Hagiographers in the Late Antique and Medieval Near East* (Turnhout: Brepols, 2010).

explicable via traditional forms of elite discourse. In both these papers, then, form is manipulated in the service of the evolving debate over the nature of sanctity.

An understanding of the forms of hagiography can also benefit from changing scholarly approaches to late antique aesthetics more generally. Building on the work of Hans Peter L'Orange, Michael Roberts identified a peculiarly late antique concern for alternate repetition and variation in late antique poetry.[49] Part of this 'jeweled style' was the increasing value ascribed to the collection and arrangement of smaller items, which he dubbed an 'aesthetics of discontinuity'.[50] What Roberts observed for non-Christian poetry has been identified by Patricia Cox Miller as characteristic too of prose works and, most importantly for our purposes, Christian authors.[51] Interestingly, one of Cox Miller's chosen case studies is the late antique cult of the relics.[52] However, the significance of this aesthetic for the literary side of the cult of the saints, hagiography, has been as yet little explored.[53]

The final paper in this section develops the hypothesis that hagiographical intention can be expressed through a strategy of multiplication. Todd French considers the predilection for collective hagiography in late antiquity. Distinguishing mere florilegia from more deliberately crafted collections, French suggests that this newly favoured form was not simply one dictated by practicalities—the availability of information, for example—but a deliberate aesthetic choice. Taking as his particular subject John of Ephesus' mid-sixth-

49 Michael Roberts, *The Jeweled Style: Poetry and Poetics in Late Antiquity* (Ithaca, NY: Cornell University Press, 1989), inspired by Hans Peter L'Orange, *Art Forms and Civic Life in the Late Roman Empire*. Translated by Dr and Mrs Berg (Princeton, NJ: Princeton University Press, 1965).

50 Roberts, *The Jeweled Style*, 61.

51 Patricia Cox Miller, "'Differential Networks': Relics and Other Fragments in Late Antiquity", *JECS* 6 (1998), 113–138.

52 That suggestion is taken up by Jaś Elsner in his discussion of the Arch of Constantine: Jaś Elsner, "From the Culture of Spolia to the Cult of Relics: The Arch of Constantine and the Genesis of Late Antique Forms", *PBSR* 68 (2000), 149–184, at 175. Elsner sees the Arch as the first step in a process that would eventually lead to Constantine's burial in a mausoleum surrounded by twelve coffins, representative of the twelve apostles, which was itself the stimulus for the growth of the cult of the saints.

53 Miller, "Differential Networks", 133–137, does briefly consider some works of collective hagiography (Prudentius' *Peristephanon* and the *Historia Monachorum* in particular). Her fuller treatment of collective hagiography, "Strategies of Representation in Collective Biography: Constructing the Subject as Holy", in Tomas Hägg and Philip Rousseau (eds.), *Greek Biography and Panegyric in Late Antiquity*. The Transformation of the Classical Heritage 31 (Berkeley: University of California Press, 2000), 209–254, is concerned more with questions of characterisation (and essentially affirms Momigliano's judgement; see above n. 34).

century *Lives of the Eastern Saints*, French argues that the value of the collective work is the space it allows for multiple perspectives to be offered by the same author. That polyphony made such texts a literary space in which audiences could find and engage with multiple viewpoints.

3.3 *Part 3: The Strategies of Hagiography*

Part 3 considers *how* hagiography achieves its effects, in particular their oft-claimed purpose of combining edification with entertainment, via rhetorical, emotional, and even manipulative devices. While this question is to a certain extent implicit in the two previous sections, here we consider means of eliciting response other than character or form.

In an important monograph, *Biography in Late Antiquity*, Patricia Cox Miller explored the different experimental biographical efforts of two late antique authors, Eusebius and Porphyry, to portray the holy man.[54] Eusebius' portrait of Origen was, she suggests, Janus-faced, painting Origen as a divinely-inspired Christian scholar and Hellenised *theios anēr* carefully constructed to appeal to both a Christian and a pagan audience. Porphyry, on the other hand, employs a series of arcane motifs in his presentation of the pagan 'saint'. That pioneering work demonstrated the variety of approach with which even the earliest 'proto-hagiographers' went about their literary mission.

In a critical response to that book, John Dillon suggests that some hagiographies are in fact rather more like what he calls 'straight' biography, and that we would do well to think of a 'sliding scale between theoretical extremes of factuality and fantasy'.[55] He concludes with Damascius' *Life of Isidore*, and in noting with surprise the elements of criticism and even comedy it includes ('It is rather as if an ancient gold-encrusted icon of some whiskery old saint looked out at one from the iconostasis of late antiquity—and *winked*') Dillon surmises that 'Damascius has written something much more interesting than a hagiography'.[56] That desire to exclude from hagiography interesting literary strategies—a self-fulfilling prophecy, of course—is resisted in this section. The papers here show that such hagiographical winks are numerous enough that we perhaps do not need to push the texts in which they appear closer to biography, but rather adjust our expectations of hagiographical writing.

Christa Gray begins this section with indecision. The possibility that saints might change their minds does not fit easily with the image of a saint as an embodied catalogue of perfect virtues. Yet such flexibility is at the heart of

54 Cox [Miller], *Biography in Late Antiquity*.
55 Dillon, "Holy and Not So Holy", 156 and 164.
56 Dillon, "Holy and Not So Holy", 164.

Jerome's hagiographical writings, where saints can be swayed through supplication. Gray investigates the significance of these scenes and posits that supplication, although it played little role in ancient handbooks of rhetoric, was used by Jerome not just as a tool of characterisation but as a structural device to drive the plot in his three saints' lives. Again, implicit parallels with Athanasius' *Life of Antony*—as discussed also in Corke-Webster and Ross' papers—suggest that Jerome deliberately adopts this unusual literary strategy as part of a literary debate over sanctity and the proper means of its memorialisation.

A more serious challenge to the notion of the saint as immutably perfect comes in the rather unexpected form of hagiographical humour. There is a tradition that sees laughter as contrary to the entire Christian, and especially monastic, way of life: after all, Benedict of Nursia appears to outlaw it entirely in his *Rule*.[57] But while humour can be difficult to diagnose with certainty in any type of literature, it is possible to find—even in texts that appear hagiographical—incongruities where expectations are set up in a narrative and then deflated. This causes a sense of unease which laughter can help to dissipate. Humorous intentions appear more probable when the incongruities involve physical acts or parts of the body. It is hardly surprising to find the holy protagonists' evil opponents as the targets of such humour, as hagiographers were happy to use this tactic to prevent readers from empathising with their villains. But in some hagiographical texts there is a real risk that the reader may be made complicit in laughing at, rather than with, the saint him- or herself. Reviewing the antics of one Macarius, the protagonist of a sixth-century Coptic hagiographical compilation, and a dirty, ignorant, bungler of a saint, Konstantin Klein finds a different kind of holy fool from the famous Symeon (considered also in Van Pelt's paper). Klein likens the farcical humour of this text to that typical of *mimus* performances, a regular form of entertainment dis-

57 *Rule of Benedict* ch. 4 (a list of 'instruments of good works'), 53–54: *Verba vana aut risui apta non loqui. Risum multum aut excussum non amare* ('Not to speak useless words or words that move to laughter. Not to love much or boisterous laughter.'); ch. 6.6: *Scurrilitates vero vel verba otiosa et risum moventia aeterna clausura in omnibus locis damnamus et ad talia eloquia discipulum aperire os non permittimus* ('But as for coarse jests and idle words or words that move to laughter, these we condemn everywhere with a perpetual ban, and for such conversation we do not permit a disciple to open [his] mouth.'); ch. 7.59: *Decimus humilitatis gradus est, si non sit facilis ac promptus in risu, quia scriptum est: Stultus in risu exaltat vocem suam* ('The tenth degree of humility is that he be not ready and quick to laugh, for it is written, "The fool lifts up his voice in laughter" (Eccles. 21:23)'). The Latin text is from the Biblioteca Benedictina Intratext: http://www.intratext.com/X/LAT0011.HTM (last accessed 19/06/2019), and the English translation is by Leonard J. Doyle OblSB, last revised in 2001, taken from the official website of the Order of St Benedict: http://archive.osb.org/rb/text/toc.html (last accessed 19/06/2019).

missed as vulgar by many elite sources. Combining entertainment with edification, this hagiography serves ultimately to shed light on the sanctity of another, Shenoute, who enjoys regular cameos.

Another unexpected element in hagiography is eroticism, which can reveal, rather startlingly, how conceptually complex the hagiographer's task could be. Building on earlier work on the novel (note again the parallel with characterisation above), Virginia Burrus' pioneering work has confounded typical views of hagiography as prudish, revealing instead how they harnessed a 'countereroticism'.[58] Erotic thoughts and relationships in some hagiographies do not merely feature negatively in the context of suppression, as one would conventionally expect; instead the dynamic structures of erotic fantasies are part of the narrative's positive framework. In other words, desires familiar from the sexual sphere are turned into a vehicle for the reader's enjoyment of the tale. Burrus' approach has inspired a rich body of work on the hagiographical appeal to its readers' sexual instincts that continues apace today.[59]

Developing this investigation of eroticism in hagiography, Klazina Staat's essay in this volume considers the impact of the motif of secrecy on plot construction as she looks at the treatment of the problematic phenomenon of chaste marriage in two works of hagiography, Jerome's *Life of Malchus* and the lesser-known *Life of Amator* by Stephen of Africa. Both texts' unpredictable and at times uneasy use of concealment and revelation is designed, Staat suggests, to mould audience reception. But the degree to which the audience is let in on the secret or kept in the dark compared to the text's internal audience, varies, and is determined by very different social contexts. This not only contributes to both edification and pleasure in the reading experience, but can involve readers—through the ascetic limitation of knowledge—in the sanctity of subject and text.

The last essay in the volume, that of Anne Alwis, uses two later hagiographies to investigate metaphrasis, a process common in Byzantine hagiography which created new versions of earlier texts by systematically revising their originals. Alwis' analysis of the Byzantine metaphrasis of the martyrdom of Tatiana argues that the author makes systematic changes not simply as a stylistic exercise or a demonstration of his literary skill but as a means, via heightened characterisation and clearer plot development, of eliciting an emotive response from the audience. An analogous analysis of the sixth- or seventh-century *vita*

---

58 Virginia Burrus, *The Sex Lives of Saints: An Erotics of Ancient Hagiography* (2nd edition, Philadelphia: University of Pennsylvania Press, 2007).

59 See, for example, Sarah Schäfer-Althaus, "Painful Pleasure: Saintly Torture on the Verge of Pornography", *Mirabilia* 18 (2014), 151–159.

of Mary of Egypt demonstrates how such changes could be used to explore and alter the balance between fiction and reality. This late Byzantine focus reveals simultaneously the traditional and innovative ways in which hagiographies continued to be brought into being.

4 The Aims of the Volume

Recent classical scholarship has been obsessed with rehabilitation. The demonstration of a dismissed ancient author's hidden genius has become the bread and butter of doctoral monographs, while neglected forms of writing previously on the margins of scholarship are prime fodder for conferences and grant proposals. In some cases this has led to the birth of entirely new scholarly industries.[60] Hagiography is in the midst of such a rehabilitation (though it remains to be seen whether it will catalyse a similar explosion of interest). This volume also celebrates hagiography's weirder and more wonderful corners. But its contributors take hagiography's literary value for granted. They thus look beyond rehabilitation, to try to take stock of where the study of hagiography has got to, and attempt to lay out lines for future research.

We are the first to admit that this treatment is neither comprehensive nor definitive. There are obvious neglected areas (notably, for example, Georgian, Armenian, and Arabic hagiography, and the relationship with non-Christian hagiography).[61] The question of transmission and reception would have deserved its own focus: the liturgical use of hagiography means that its dissemination tends to be different from other types of literature.[62] Furthermore, the three sections overlap considerably with each other, though we consider this a strength. We have encouraged our contributors to identify and explore shared thematic interests, though we have not imposed terms or criteria upon them, as will be obvious in their different approaches. The selection of topics and methodologies reveals a rich literary variety in hagiographical writings. But they are united, we believe, in revealing the importance of literature—and the flexibility of its construction—to an evolving discussion of what sanctity meant through late antiquity and beyond. Hagiographical writings were the

60 The rapid rise of the ancient novel—long dismissed as the ancient equivalent of Mills and Boon literature, now recognised as a repository for some of the most sophisticated Greek literary reflection on the nature of empire—is perhaps the best example.

61 Well treated in Efthymiadis' *Ashgate Research Companion*.

62 On the questions raised by this subject see Marc Van Uytfanghe, "L'hagiographie antiqué tardive: une littérature populaire?", *Antiquité Tardive* 9 (2001), 201–218.

arena in which that important debate took place, and these essays reveal something of the ways—via person, form, and technique, and whether traditional, innovative, or both—in which their authors brought them into being, and how they thereby contributed to that ongoing debate. Sainthood, in other words, was constructed less of criteria than of conversation.

The consequences of that literary arena were of course not just felt on the page. It is now generally accepted that how texts are written has repercussions not just for literary studies but also for historical work. Texts do not merely reflect but construct reality. Stories are not so much prima facie evidence of real-world conditions and events, but attempts to make sense of experiences through narrative (rather than philosophical-scientific) logic. Hagiography was no exception. Saintly stories provided a space for interpreting and communicating Christian theological and moral teaching as it developed, and for imaginatively exploring the consequences of adopting these convictions in one's life, as well as what that life should look like more broadly. Moreover, group identity—political, tribal, or, most pertinently, religious—is articulated not only through abstract beliefs but through the stories in which these beliefs are encoded and the rituals in which the stories are enacted.[63] Careful, sensitive analysis of such stories can thus provide important insights into the experiences, values, and convictions of the groups that produced and consumed them. Our papers constantly return to this interplay between life and art. We hope therefore that this volume can serve as a spur to future work on hagiography's place in the evolution of literary narrative and contribute to wider understandings of sanctity, through the 'classical' world, the Middle Ages, and Byzantium. With that in mind, a brief Postscript by Lucy Grig draws together some of the principal insights gained from the collection and points out possible directions for these next steps.

Acknowledgments

Our thanks to the volume's contributors for their thoughts and suggestions on this Introduction.

---

63 This model corresponds to Emile Durkheim's account of religion as made up of beliefs, rituals, and experiences: Emile Durkheim, *The Elementary Forms of the Religious Life* (2nd English edition London: Allen and Unwin, 1976) (first published as *Les Formes élémentaires de la vie religieuse: le système totémique en Australie* (Paris: Alcan, 1912)).

Bibliography

Aigrain, René, *L'hagiographie. Ses sources, ses méthodes, son histoire* (Brussels, Société des Bollandistes, 1953 (reprinted with additional bibliography in 2000)).

Barnes, Timothy D., *Early Christian Hagiography and Roman History*. Tria Corda 5 (Tübingen: Mohr Siebeck, 2010 (2nd edition 2016)).

Bowersock, Glen, *Martyrdom and Rome* (Cambridge: Cambridge University Press, 1995).

Boyarin, Daniel, *The Jewish Gospels: The Story of the Jewish Christ* (New York: New Press, 2012).

Brakke, David, *Athanasius and the Politics of Asceticism* (Oxford: Clarendon Press, 1995).

Brown, Peter, "The Rise and Function of the Holy Man in Late Antiquity", *JRS* 61 (1971), 80–101; reprinted in idem, *Society and the Holy in Late Antiquity* (Berkeley: University of California Press, 1982), 103–152.

Brown, Peter, "The Saint as Exemplar in Late Antiquity", *Representations* 2 (1983), 1–25.

Brown, Peter, "Arbiters of the Holy: The Christian Holy Man in Late Antiquity", in idem, *Authority and the Sacred: Aspects of the Christianisation of the Roman World* (Cambridge: Cambridge University Press, 1995), 57–78.

Brown, Peter, "The Rise and Function of the Holy Man in Late Antiquity, 1971–1997", *JECS* 6.3 (1998), 352–376.

Brown, Peter, *The Cult of the Saints: Its Rise and Function in Latin Christianity* (Chicago: University of Chicago Press, 1981).

Bossu, Annelies, Koen De Temmerman, and Danny Praet, "The Saint as an Astute Heroine: Rhetoric and Characterization in the *Passio Caeciliae*", *Mnemosyne* 69.3 (2016), 433–452.

Burridge, Richard A., *What Are the Gospels? A Comparison with Graeco-Roman Biography*. Monograph Series Society for New Testament Studies 70 (Cambridge/New York: Cambridge University Press, 1992 (2nd edition with a foreword by W. Stanton, Grand Rapids, MI: W.B. Eerdmans, 2004)).

Burrus, Virginia, *The Sex Lives of Saints: An Erotics of Ancient Hagiography* (2nd edition, Philadelphia: University of Pennsylvania Press, 2007).

Cameron, Averil, "Apologetics in the Roman Empire—A Genre of Intolerance?", in Jean-Michel Carrié and Rita Lizzi Testa (eds.), *Humana Sapit: études d'Antiquité tardive offertes à Lellia Cracco Ruggini* (Turnhout: Brepols, 2002), 219–227.

Cox [Miller], Patricia, *Biography in Late Antiquity: A Quest for the Holy Man*. The Transformation of the Classical Heritage 5 (Berkeley: University of California Press, 1983).

Cox Miller, Patricia, "'Differential Networks': Relics and Other Fragments in Late Antiquity", *JECS* 6 (1998), 113–138.

Cox Miller, Patricia, "Strategies of Representation in Collective Biography: Constructing the Subject as Holy", in Tomas Hägg and Philip Rousseau (eds.), *Greek Biography and*

Panegyric in Late Antiquity. The Transformation of the Classical Heritage 31 (Berkeley: University of California Press, 2000), 209–254.

De Temmerman, Koen, *Crafting Characters: Heroes and Heroines in the Ancient Novel* (Cambridge: Cambridge University Press, 2014).

Delehaye, Hippolyte, *Les légendes hagiographiques* (Brussels: Société des Bollandistes, 1905; 2nd edition Brussels: Subsidia Hagiographica, 1927); English translation by Donald Attwater, *The Legends of the Saints; With a Memoir of the Author by Paul Peeters* (New York: Fordham University Press, 1962).

Delehaye, Hippolyte, *Les passions des martyrs et les genres littéraires* (Brussels: Société des Bollandistes, 1921; 2nd edition Brussels: Subsidia Hagiographica, 1966).

Déroche, Vincent, Bryan Ward-Perkins, and Robert Wiśniewski (eds.), *Culte des saints et littérature hagiographique*. Centre de recherche d'Histoire et Civilisation de Byzance, Monographies (Leuven: Peeters, in press).

Dillon, John, "Holy and Not So Holy: On the Interpretation of Late Antique Biography", in Brian McGing and Judith Mossmann (eds.), *The Limits of Ancient Biography* (Swansea: Classical Press of Wales, 2006), 155–167.

Durkheim, Emile, *The Elementary Forms of the Religious Life* (2nd English edition London: Allen and Unwin, 1976) (first published as *Les Formes élémentaires de la vie religieuse: le système totémique en Australie* (Paris: Alcan, 1912)).

Edwards, Mark, "Biography and the Biographic", in Edwards and Swain, *Portraits*, 227–234.

Edwards, Mark and Simon Swain (eds.), *Portraits: Biographical Representation in the Greek and Latin Literature of the Roman Empire* (Oxford: Clarendon Press, 1997).

Efthymiadis, Stephanos, "Introduction", in idem (ed.), *Ashgate Research Companion to Byzantine Hagiography*, vol. 1 (Farnham: Ashgate, 2011), 1–14.

Elsner, Jaś, "From the Culture of Spolia to the Cult of Relics: The Arch of Constantine and the Genesis of Late Antique Forms", *PBSR* 68 (2000), 149–184.

Fagan, Garth, "The Pagan Holy Man in Late Antique Society", *JHS* 102 (1982), 33–59.

Frend, William H.C., *Martyrdom and Persecution in the Early Church: A Study of Conflict from the Maccabees to Donatus* (Oxford: Blackwell, 1965).

Fontaine, Jacques, "Unité et diversité du mélange des genres et des tons chez quelques écrivains latins de la fin du IVe siècle: Ausone, Ambroise, Ammien", in Manfred Fuhrmann (ed.), *Christianisme et formes littéraires de l'antiquité tardive en Occident*. Entretiens sur l'Antiquité Classique 23 (Geneva: Fondation Hardt, 1977), 425–482.

Frickenschmidt, Dirk, *Evangelium als Biographie. Die vier Evangelien im Rahmen antiker Erzählkunst*. Texte und Arbeiten zum neutestamentlichen Zeitalter 22 (Tübingen: Francke, 1997).

Gibbon, Edward, *The History of the Decline and Fall of the Roman Empire*, vol. 4: *The End of the Roman Empire* (London: Allan Lane, 1994)

Godding, Robert, Bernard Joassart, Xavier Lequeux, François de Vriendt, and Joseph van der Straeten, *Bollandistes, saints et légendes. Quatre siècles de recherche hagiographique* (Brussels: Société des Bollandistes, 2007).

Goldsmid Montefiore, Claude, *Rabbinic Literature and Gospel Teachings* (London: Macmillan, 1930).

Greatrex, Geoffrey and Hugh Elton (eds.), *Shifting Genres in Late Antiquity* (Farnham/Burlington, VT: Ashgate, 2015).

Hadas, Moses and Morton Smith, *Heroes and Gods: Spiritual Biographies* (New York: Harper and Row, 1965).

Hägg, Tomas, *The Novel in Antiquity* (Oxford: Blackwell, 1983).

Hägg, Tomas, *The Art of Biography in Antiquity* (Cambridge: Cambridge University Press, 2012).

Høgel, Christian, "Literary Aspects of Greek Byzantine Hagiography: A Bibliographical Survey", *SO* 72 (1997), 164–171.

Howard-Johnston, James and Paul A. Hayward (eds.), *The Cult of the Saints in Late Antiquity and the Middle Ages: Essays on the Contribution of Peter Brown* (Oxford: Oxford University Press, 1999).

Krueger, Derek, *Writing and Holiness: The Practice of Authorship in the Early Christian East* (Philadelphia: University of Pennsylvania Press, 2004).

Lévi-Strauss, Claude, *Le totémisme aujourd'hui* (Paris: Presses universitaires de France, 1962).

L'Orange, Hans Peter, *Art Forms and Civic Life in the Late Roman Empire*, trans. Dr and Mrs Berg (Princeton: Princeton University Press, 1965).

Louth, Andrew, "Hagiography", in Young, Ayres, and Louth, *The Cambridge History of Early Christian Literature*, 358–361.

Louth, Andrew, "The Literature of the Monastic Movement", in Young, Ayres, and Louth (eds.), *The Cambridge History of Early Christian Literature*, 373–381.

Ludlow, Morwenna, "Texts, Teachers and Pupils in the Writings of Gregory of Nyssa", in Van Hoof and Van Nuffelen, *Literature and Society*, 83–102.

Martin, Dale, "Introduction", in Dale Martin and Patricia Cox Miller (eds.), *The Cultural Turn in Late Ancient Studies: Gender, Asceticism and Historiography* (Durham, NC/London: Duke University Press, 2005), 1–21.

Merkelbach, Reinhold, *Roman und Mysterium in der Antike* (Munich/Berlin: Beck, 1963).

Miller, Dale and Patricia J. Miller, *The Gospel of Mark as Midrash on Earlier Jewish and New Testament Literature*. Studies in the Bible and Early Christianity 21 (Lewiston: E. Mellen Press, 1990).

Momigliano, Arnaldo, *The Development of Greek Biography*. Carl Newell Jackson Lectures (Cambridge, MA/London: Harvard University Press, 1971).

Momigliano, Arnaldo, "Ancient Biography and the Study of Religion in the Roman

Empire", in idem, *On Pagans, Jews, and Christians* (Middletown, CT: Wesleyan University Press, 1987), 159–177.

Mratschek, Sigrid, "A Living Relic for the Bishop of Rome: Strategies of Visualization in a Civil Case", in Van Hoof and Van Nuffelen, *Literature and Society*, 134–156.

Papaconstantinou, Arietta (ed.), *Writing 'True Stories': Historians and Hagiographers in the Late Antique and Medieval Near East* (Turnhout: Brepols, 2010).

Pratsch, Thomas, *Der hagiographische Topos. Griechische Heiligenviten in mittelbyzantinischer Zeit*. Millenium Studies 6 (Berlin/New York: De Gruyter, 2005).

Rapp, Claudia, "The Origins of Hagiography and the Literature of Early Monasticism: Purpose and Genre between Tradition and Innovation," in Richard Flower, Christopher Kelly, and Michael Stuart Williams (eds.), *Unclassical Traditions. Alternatives to the Classical Past in Late Antiquity*, vol. 1. Cambridge Classical Journal Supplements 34 (Cambridge: Cambridge University Press, 2010), 119–130.

Rapp, Claudia, "Author, Audience, Text and Saint: Two Modes of Early Byzantine Hagiography", *Scandinavian Journal of Byzantine and Modern Greek Studies* 1 (2015), 111–129.

Roberts, Michael, *The Jeweled Style: Poetry and Poetics in Late Antiquity* (Ithaca, NY: Cornell University Press, 1989).

Schäfer-Althaus, Sarah, "Painful Pleasure: Saintly Torture on the Verge of Pornography", *Mirabilia* 18 (2014), 151–159.

Scourfield, J.H. David (ed.), *Texts and Culture in Late Antiquity: Inheritance, Authority, and Change* (Swansea: The Classical Press of Wales, 2007).

Swain, Simon, "Biography and the Biographic in the Literature of the Roman Empire", in Edwards and Swain, *Portraits*, 1–37.

Talbert, Charles H., *Literary Patterns, Theological Themes and the Genre of Luke-Acts*. Society of Biblical Literature Monograph Series 20 (Missoula: Society of Biblical Literature, 1974).

Taylor, Justin, "The Acts of the Apostles as Biography", in McGing and Mossmann, *The Limits of Ancient Biography*, 77–88.

Van Hoof, Lieve and Peter Van Nuffelen (eds.), *Literature and Society in the Fourth Century AD: Performing Paideia, Constructing the Present, Presenting the Self* (Leiden: Brill, 2015).

Van Uytfanghe, Marc, "L'hagiographie: un 'genre' chrétien ou antique tardif?", *AB* 111 (1993), 135–188.

Van Uytfanghe, Marc, "L'hagiographie antiqué tardive: une littérature populaire?", *Antiquité Tardive* 9 (2001), 201–218.

Van Uytfanghe, Marc, "La vie d'Apollonius de Tyane et le discours hagiographique", in Kristoffel Demoen and Danny Praet (eds.), *Theios Sophistès: Essays on Flavius Philostratus' Vita Apollonii*. Mnemosyne Supplements 305 (Leiden: Brill, 2008), 335–374.

Van Ommeslaeghe, Flor, "The Acta Sanctorum and Bollandist Methodology", in Sergei Hackel (ed.), *The Byzantine Saint* (London: Fellowship of St. Alban and St. Sergius, 1981), 155–163.
Williams, Michael Stuart, *Authorised Lives in Early Christian Biography: Between Eusebius and Augustine* (Cambridge/New York: Cambridge University Press, 2008).
Young, Frances, Lewis Ayres, and Andrew Louth (eds.), *The Cambridge History of Early Christian Literature* (Cambridge: Cambridge University Press, 2004).
Zeitlin, Froma, "Religion in the Ancient Novel", in Tim Whitmarsh (ed.), *The Cambridge Companion to the Greek and Roman Novel* (Cambridge: Cambridge University Press, 2008), 91–108.

PART 1

The Persons of Hagiography

CHAPTER 1

The First Hagiographies: The *Life of Antony*, the *Life of Pamphilus*, and the Nature of Saints

James Corke-Webster

1 Introduction

The *Life of Antony* (herafter *Antony*) is usually seen in the *communis opinio* as the first hagiography. That privileged status is based in part on its impressive and immediate impact. The *Antony* was translated and reproduced multiple times almost straight away after its production soon after AD 356,[1] and many of the fourth- and fifth-century hagiographies that follow it both name-check and echo its example.[2] But it is also true, and has been recognised since antiquity, that even in his own hagiography, Antony is not given credit as the first monastic saint. And surveys of ancient biography's development and transformation into hagiography often acknowledge earlier 'proto-hagiographies'.[3] This interest has been aided by an increasing recognition of both the crumbling of generic categories in late antiquity and the prevalence of hybrid texts that demonstrate features of numerous forms of ancient writing.[4]

It is perhaps not surprising that one of the most intriguing discussions of the *Antony* and its forerunners came from one of the pioneers of this innovative approach to ancient genre.[5] At the turn of the millennium, Averil Cameron

1 On the difficulty of pinpointing the date, see Brian R. Brennan, "Dating Athanasius' *Vita Antonii*", *VChr* 30 (1976), 52–54, critiquing the attempt of Leslie W. Barnard, "The Date of S. Athanasius' *Vita Antonii*", *VChr* 27 (1974), 169–175, to date it to late AD 357/early AD 358.

2 See the discussion of the hagiographic efforts of Jerome and others in Michael Stuart Williams, *Authorised Lives in Early Christian Biography. Between Eusebius and Augustine* (Cambridge: Cambridge University Press, 2008), 101–147.

3 See most recently, for example, the appendix to Tomas Hägg, *The Art of Biography* (Cambridge: Cambridge University Press, 2012), 380–389, at 381–382; and for an older treatment Dieter Hoster, "Die Form der frühesten lateinischen Heiligenviten von der *Vita Cypriani* bis zur *Vita Ambrosii*." Ph.D. diss., Cologne (1963). See too the "Introduction" to this volume, 7–9.

4 See in this volume "Introduction", 13–15.

5 See e.g. Averil Cameron, "Apologetics in the Roman Empire—A Genre of Intolerance?", in Jean-Michel Carrie and Rita Lizzi Testa (eds.), *Humana Sapit: études d'Antiquité tardive*

 | DOI:10.1163/9789004421332_003

suggested that the *Antony* could have been written as a response to Eusebius' *Life of Constantine* (hereafter *Constantine*), the first Christian historian's unusual account of the first Christian emperor.[6] Cameron pointed out that the probable author of the *Antony*, the bishop Athanasius, was well aware of Eusebius' literary output.[7] Moreover, these two texts, she argued, share a number of

---

offertes à Lellia Cracco Ruggini. Bibliothèque de l'antiquité tardive 3 (Turnhout: Brépols, 2002), 219–227.

6 Averil Cameron, "Form and Meaning: the *Vita Constantini* and the *Vita Antonii*", in Tomas Hägg and Philip Rousseau (eds.), *Greek Biography and Panegyric in Late Antiquity* (Berkeley: University of California Press, 2000), 72–88. Cameron had floated the comparison a few years earlier in Averil Cameron, "Eusebius' *Vita Constantini* and the Construction of Constantine", in Mark Edwards and Simon Swain (eds.), *Portraits: Biographical Representation in the Greek and Latin Literature of the Roman Empire* (Oxford: Clarendon Press, 1997), 145–174, at 169–172. The suggestion was echoed, on typological grounds, by Williams, *Authorised Lives*, 102.

7 Cameron, "Form and Meaning", 73. Cameron, at e.g. 75, acknowledges the dispute over Athanasian authorship, though on balance considers it probable (84). It has long been argued that the Greek *Antony* was not the original but rather a modification of an earlier account, probably in Copticising Greek; see both Martin Tetz, "Athanasius und die *Vita Antonii*. Literarische und theologische Relationen", *ZNTW* 73 (1982), 1–30 and René Draguet, *La vie primitive de S. Antoine conservée en syriaque*. 2 vols. Corpus Scriptorum Christianorum Orientalium 417–418 (Leuven: Peeters, 1980). Other scholars have argued further that the modifications were not Athanasian; see most famously Timothy D. Barnes, "Angel of Light or Mystic Initiate? The Problem of the Life of Antony", *JThS* 37 (1986), 353–368. Andrew Louth, "St. Athanasius and the Greek *Life of Antony*", *JThS* 39 (1988), 504–509, accepts the former argument but not the latter, and the linguistic arguments of Draguet that underlie Barnes and Louth's arguments about priority have been critiqued by Luise Abramowski, "Vertritt die syrische Fassung die ursprüngliche Gestalt der Vita Antonii? Eine Auseinandersetzung mit der These Draguets", in René-Georges Coquin (ed.), *Mélanges Antoine Guillaumont. Contributions à l'étude des christianisme orientaux*. Cahiers d' orientalisme 20 (Genève: Patrick Cramer, 1988), 47–56 and Rudolf Lorenz, "Die griechische Vita Antonii und ihre syrische Fassung", *ZKG* 100 (1989), 77–84. For the positive case for Athanasian authorship see most fully David Brakke, "The Greek and Syriac Versions of the Life of Antony", *Muséon* 107.1–2 (1994), 29–53; David Brakke, "The Authenticity of the Ascetic Athanasiana", *Orientalia* 63 (1994), 17–56; and Gerhard J.M. Bartelink (ed.), *Athanasius: Vie d'Antoine*. Sources chrétiennes 400 (Paris: Les Éditions du Cerf, 1994), 27–42. Timothy D. Barnes, *Early Christian Hagiography and Roman History*. Tria Corda 5 (Tübingen: Mohr Siebeck, 2010), 160–170, now accepts Athanasius as the editor (and gives a good summary of the full debate); reiterated in Timothy D. Barnes, "Early Christian Hagiography and the Roman Historian", in Peter Gemeinhardt and Johan Leemans (eds.), *Christian Martyrdom in Late Antiquity: History and Discourse, Tradition and Religious Identity*. Arbeiten zur Kirchengeschichte 116 (Berlin/New York: De Gruyter, 2012), 15–33, at 20–21. Jan N. Bremmer, "Athanasius' *Life of Antony*: Marginality, Spatiality and Mediality", in Laura Feldt and Jan N. Bremmer (eds.), *Marginality, Media, and Mutations of Religious Authority in the History of Christianity* (Leuven: Peeters, 2019), 23–45, argues further that Athanasius' influence is not restricted to the text's theology. Following the consensus view, I assume Athanasius to be at the least the editor of the Greek *Antony*. But even if the text is not his, it is anyway—as

features—not only their literary self-consciousness, but also their protagonists' simplicity, gradual ascent to knowledge, wrestling with demons, experience of signs that enable them to teach, works against paganism and heretics, deference to the church, angelic appearance, anticipated death, and bequest of a model for imitation.[8]

At the root of this comparison for Cameron was a shift in the authors' relationship to political power. Eusebius, aware of the threat posed to himself and his peers by the transition of power from Constantine to his sons and the recall of the pro-Nicene Athanasius, used his proto-hagiography as a 'mirror for Princes'. Athanasius, reacting against both this image of the holy man and its author, wished to place the holy man above the dictates of the imperial will and use him in his war against Arianism in all its forms.[9] Most interesting for our purposes, however, is that on this hypothesis the explosion of late antique hagiography should be traced back not to Athanasius and the *Antony* but to Eusebius and the *Constantine*.

That conclusion makes a good deal of sense. Eusebius had a track record for such generic innovation, whether in his tabular *Chronicle*, his narrative *Ecclesiastical History* (hereafter *History*) or the apologetic diptych comprising the *Preparation for the Gospel* and *Demonstration of the Gospel*.[10] He was the heir of the martyr narratives, of which he had compiled a collection—some of which he then quoted verbatim in his *History*—and wrote his own martyrdom accounts both there and in his *Martyrs of Palestine* (hereafter *Martyrs*), a narrative account of the trials and deaths of some of Eusebius' peers in his homeland during the so-called 'Great Persecution' of the early fourth century, and produced within a proto-monastic environment, Pamphilus' Caesarean 'school'. But the *Constantine* is not the most obvious candidate as a Eusebian forerunner to the *Antony*. The features Cameron identifies as parallels are largely thematic and were not confined to the *Constantine*; instead, they were, as I have argued elsewhere, features of an ideal model of Christian leadership that Eusebius had worked out systematically in his earlier works.[11] Important here are not just the 'Life of Origen' which comprises much of Book 6 and other parts of the *History*

Barnes, "Angel of Light", 367, admits—probably the work of one in his circle, so Eusebian influence is equally probable.

8 Cameron, "Form and Meaning", 74–82.

9 Cameron, "Form and Meaning", 73–74.

10 The best overview of Eusebius' oeuvre is now Aaron P. Johnson, *Eusebius*. Understanding Classics (London: I.B. Taurus, 2014).

11 James Corke-Webster, "A Bishop's Biography: Eusebius of Caesarea's *Life of Constantine*", in Koen De Temmerman (ed.), *The Oxford Handbook of Ancient Biography* (Oxford: Oxford University Press, in press).

(and which Cameron mentions only in passing),[12] but the *Martyrs*, and Eusebius' biography of his own teacher and mentor, the *Life of Pamphilus* (hereafter *Pamphilus*).

Recently Adele Monaci Castagno has strengthened Cameron's case—which was self-consciously tentative—by considering the importance for the *Antony* of Eusebian texts more generally.[13] Monaci Castagno suggests that Athanasius' portrayal of Antony deliberately foregrounded thaumaturgy because Eusebius' earlier biographical efforts had rejected it, focusing instead on asceticism and martyrdom. Athanasius' motivation, Monaci Castagno argued, was to provide an anti-Arian emphasis upon the miraculous deeds performed by the divine Christ in the flesh. This certainly strengthens the literary ties between Athanasius and Eusebius. But while the texts perhaps have different attitudes to wonderworking,[14] asceticism and martyrdom are not the focus of Eusebius' characterisation of 'saints', and Monaci Castagno therefore misrepresents what was at stake between these two authors.

The third and most effective case has been that of Arthur Urbano, who has suggested that the *Antony* was part of Athanasius' systematic attack—including for example the *Against the Heathen* and *On the Incarnation*—on Greek *paideia*.[15] Like Monaci Castagno, he argued that Athanasius had Eusebius' 'Life of Origen' in his sightline, but for Urbano Athanasius objected in particular to Eusebius' argument that Greek elite education still had value for Christians. Athanasius' theological writings focus on the exclusive value for Christians of revelation. With Antony, Athanasius proffered biographical proof of that contention—a Christian hero who bests Greek philosophers while rejecting their cultural and social Hellenic background, and who proves his superiority via the power of miracle rather than the force of argument. Athanasius thus created an alternative, Christian, explicitly non-Greek model

12 Cameron, "Form and Meaning", 74.

13 Adele Monaci Castagno, "Le trasformazioni del discorso agiografico da Eusebio a Atanasio", *AnnSE* 23 (2006), 45–65, though without reference to Cameron.

14 Although see now Hal Drake, *A Century of Miracles: Christians, Pagans, Jews, and the Supernatural, 312–410* (Oxford/New York: Oxford University Press, 2017), 152, pointing out that the *Antony* contains relatively little material on miraculous cures—as opposed to spectacular insight or demon combat. Thus further supports my case that the main contrast between Eusebius and Athanasius' writings lies elsewhere.

15 Arthur P. Urbano, "'Read It Also to the Gentiles': The Displacement and Recasting of the Philosopher in the *Vita Antonii*", *Church History* 77.4 (2008), 877–914, and idem, *The Philosophical Life: Biography and the Crafting of Intellectual Identity in Late Antiquity*. Patristic Monograph Series 21 (Washington DC: Catholic University of America Press, 2013), 205–244, apparently independent of either Cameron or Monaci Castagno.

of *paideia*. Urbano, however, is explicitly not interested in the place of the *Antony* in Christian literature,[16] and to my mind still neglects a key element of Eusebius' portrayal of Christian heroes—communality.[17]

The case for a Eusebian precedent to the *Antony* has thus been made with increasing force over the past two decades. But the exact nature of this literary contest remains only partly explored. The key to a better understanding, I suggest, is a systematic treatment of the texts,[18] detailed literary comparison, and, finally, beginning with the work of Eusebius that is considered least by all three scholars, namely the *Pamphilus*.[19] Since that text is no longer extant, beginning there may seem rather infelicitous. But the *Pamphilus* is not totally lost to us. First, a fragment survives in later quotation. Second, Eusebius speaks of Pamphilus at a number of points in both his *History* and his *Martyrs*. Since Eusebius' tendency for self-plagiarism is well established,[20] this material is a good indication of what the *Pamphilus* contained. Third, the skeleton portrait of Pamphilus that these passages produce indicates that he was the best example of the model of Christian virtue and authority that Eusebius advocated more generally. Together, this allows us to cautiously reconstruct the *Pamphilus*. Read alongside Eusebius' other biographical material, this gives us a fresh glimpse of this earliest stage in the development of hagiography, but also better reveals the brewing debate in late-third- and early-fourth-century Christianities over the nature of sanctity that lay behind it.

16 Urbano, "'Read It Also to the Gentiles'", 894; Urbano, *The Philosophical Life*, 213–214.

17 See too the criticisms in Samuel Rubenson, "Apologetics of Asceticism: The *Life of Antony* and Its Political Context", in Blake Leyerle and Robin Darling Young (eds.), *Ascetic Culture: Essays in Honor of Philip Rousseau* (Notre Dame, IN.: University of Notre Dame Press, 2013), 75–96.

18 Urbano, for example, focuses on the childhood section and chapters 72–80 of the *Antony*.

19 Edward Watts, "Three Generations of Christian Philosophical Biography", in Scott McGill, Cristiana Sogno, and Edward Watts (eds.), *The Roman Empire from the Tetrarchs to the Theodosians: Later Roman History and Culture 284–450 CE*. Yale Classical Studies 34 (Cambridge: Cambridge University Press, 2010), 117–133, notes the differences between Eusebius' 'Life of Origen' and the *Antony*, but does not discuss any direct connection.

20 See e.g. Stuart G. Hall, "The Use of Earlier Eusebian Material in the *Vita Constantini*, I.58–59", *Studia Patristica* 24 (1993), 96–101; and Stuart G. Hall, "Eusebian and Other Sources in the Vita Constantini, I", in Hanns C. Brennecke, Ernst L. Grasmück, and Christoph Markschies (eds.), *Logos: Festschrift für Luise Abramowski*. Beihefte zur Zeitschrift für die neutestamentliche Wissenschaft und die Kunde der älteren Kirche. Band 67 (Berlin: De Gruyter, 1993), 239–263.

2 The (Lost) *Life of Pamphilus* and the Eusebian Saint

Eusebius wrote the *Pamphilus* early in his literary career, around AD 310–311.[21] He tells us a little about its form when, in the short recension of his *Martyrs*, he refers the reader to the *Pamphilus*, saying, 'the remaining good deeds that stemmed from his virtue, being longer to tell, I have passed on already at an earlier moment, in a writing in three sections, specially dedicated to his life' (*De mart. Pal.* 11.3 SR).[22] We thus start with the fact that the *Pamphilus* was in three books (see too Jerome, *De vir. ill.* 81), and treated both Pamphilus' personality and his deeds. In a similar comment in the *History* we learn a little more:

> It would be no small subject to demonstrate what kind of man he was and from where he began. But each thing about his manner of life and of the school he founded, and his conflicts during the persecution in various confessions, and the crown of martyrdom with which he was finally wreathed, I have treated in a separate work concerning him.[23]

Eusebius' interest in where Pamphilus came from suggests that this work covered at least some of Pamphilus' youth, which may seem obvious, but was not a given for ancient biography. It also tells us that Pamphilus' school—which Eusebius had attended, and which thus represented his prime point of contact with his subject—was treated in detail. Finally, it reveals that the account ended with Pamphilus' martyrdom.[24]

To that skeleton we can add some flesh. Most secure is a verbatim fragment from the third book of the *Pamphilus* preserved by Jerome in his *Apology against Rufinus*, written at the turn of the fifth century. There can be no guar-

---

21 He had probably written only the *Evangelical Canons* and the *Defence of Origen* beforehand. For a proposed timeline, see Andrew J. Carriker, *The Library of Eusebius of Caesarea*. Vigiliae Christianae Supplements 67 (Leiden: Brill, 2003), 37–38.

22 οὗ τὰ λοιπὰ τῆς ἀρετῆς κατορθώματα, μακροτέρας ὄντα διηγήσεως, ἐπ' ἰδίας τῆς τοῦ κατ' αὐτὸν ὑποθέσεως βίου γραφῇ ἐν τρισὶν ἤδη πρότερον ὑπομνήμασι παραδεδώκαμεν. Translations of the *Martyrs* and the *History* my own; Greek text from Gustave Bardy, *Eusèbe de Césarée, Histoire Ecclésiastique*. Sources chrétiennes 55 (Paris: Les Éditions du Cerf, 1952–1958 [repr. 3:1967]).

23 *Hist. eccl.* 7.32.25: ὃν ὁποῖός τις ἦν καὶ ὅθεν ὁρμώμενος, οὐ σμικρᾶς ἂν γένοιτο δηλοῦν ὑποθέσεως· ἕκαστα δὲ τοῦ κατ' αὐτὸν βίου καὶ ἧς συνεστήσατο διατριβῆς, τούς τε κατὰ τὸν διωγμὸν ἐν διαφόροις ὁμολογίαις ἀγῶνας αὐτοῦ καὶ ὃν ἐπὶ πᾶσιν ἀνεδήσατο τοῦ μαρτυρίου στέφανον, ἐν ἰδίᾳ τῇ περὶ αὐτοῦ διειλήφαμεν ὑποθέσει.

24 By no means a given; see Yuzwa in this volume.

antee that Jerome has preserved it accurately, and we must remember that what has survived is a Latin translation of Eusebius' Greek. These qualifications notwithstanding, the fragment, with Jerome's introductory remarks, reads:

> For Eusebius himself, lover, publicist, and companion of Pamphilus, wrote three very elegant books containing the life of Pamphilus, in which he proclaims other qualities with extraordinary praises and extols to high heaven his humility. But in the third book he adds this: 'Who among those devoted to learning was not a friend of Pamphilus? If he saw that they required the things necessary for living, he would provide abundantly what he could. He used also to distribute the sacred Scriptures willingly, not only for reading but also for keeping, and not just to men, but also to women who he had noted as dedicated to reading. He thus prepared many copies so that when circumstance demanded, he might bestow them on those so desiring. And he himself indeed wrote nothing whatever of his own, excepting perhaps the letters that he used to send to his friends, so far had he cast himself down in humility. But he used to read the treatises of old writers very studiously, and was constantly mulling them over in contemplation.'[25]

Jerome's interest here is in Pamphilus' lack of publications; one of his goals seems to be proving that the *Defence* Rufinus had controversially translated was entirely the work of the Arian Eusebius rather than the revered martyr Pamphilus (in fact Jerome was wrong). But the quotation reveals rather more. First, it is clear that Eusebius' Pamphilus is, regardless of his publication habits, a literary figure. In the references to both his willingness to give away texts and his store of manuscripts we also glimpse his role in manuscript production. We learn that he devoted time and energy to his own studies, and Eusebius

25 Jer. *Contr. Ruf.* 1.9: *Ipse enim Eusebius, amator et praeco et contubernalis Pamphili, tres libros scripsit elegantissimos vitam Pamphili continentes, in quibus cum cetera miris laudibus praedicaret humilitatemque eius ferret in caelum, etiam hoc in tertio libro addidit: Quis studiosorum amicus non fuit Pamphili? Si quos videbat ad victum necessariis indigere, praebebat large quae poterat. Scripturas quoque sanctas non ad legendum tantum, sed et ad habendum tribuebat promptissime, nec solum viris, sed et feminis quas vidisset lectioni deditas. Vnde et multos codices praeparabat, ut, cum necessitas poposcisset, volentibus largiretur. Et ipse quidem proprii operis nihil omnino scripsit, exceptis epistulis quas ad amicos forte mittebat, in tantum se humilitate deiecerat. Veterum autem scriptorium tractatus legebat studiosissime et in eorum meditatione iugiter versabatur.* Translation my own; Latin text from Pierre Lardet (ed.), *Saint Jerome, Apologie contre Rufin*. Sources chrétiennes 303 (Paris: Les Éditions du Cerf, 1983).

highlights his attention to 'the treatises of old writers', an ambiguous phrase that probably refers to classical texts. However, the real thrust of this passage in its original Eusebian context was clearly Pamphilus' relationships with others.[26] It begins by emphasising his intimacy with the learned, and theirs with him. As well as reading materials, he also provided material assistance, which must refer to charitable giving generally.[27] And Pamphilus' failure to publish is mitigated in his penchant for letter writing, the most personal kind of literary output. Books, study, and above all care for and support of others all emerge strongly from this fragment.

To this we can add other scattered Eusebian comments on Pamphilus. The *History* introduces him as 'Pamphilus, that very eloquent man' (*Hist. eccl.* 7.32.25).[28] In the *Martyrs*, in which Pamphilus is the climactic protagonist, Eusebius privileges his God-given 'intelligence and wisdom' (*De mart. Pal.* 11.1d LR).[29] We also find here confirmation that Pamphilus' intellectual interests included non-Christian material (as hinted by 'the treatises of the old writers' above): he 'latched on in no small degree to that education honoured by the Greeks, and he trained in that connected to the divine ordinances and the inspired writings as, if I can speak rather boldly, but nevertheless accurately, one could say of no other of his contemporaries' (*De mart. Pal.* 11.1d LR; see too 7.4 LR).[30] Eusebius notes further that he had been through the schools at Berytus (*De mart. Pal.* 11.3 LR); such an elite education would be expected for one 'drawn from a noble family' (*De mart. Pal.* 11.1e).[31] It is thus very probable that the *Pamphilus*' early sections focused on his early life as an elite Roman citizen educated in the traditional syllabuses of that demographic stratum. Confirmation of this Eusebian valorisation of Christian and non-Christian learning can be found throughout Eusebius' writing, most famously in the 'Life of Origen', where in an account of Origen's education Eusebius notes: 'his father, in addition to a general education, had made these things [the Scriptures] no trivial matter for him. Ahead of everything then, before attention to Greek learnings,

26 This element is missing from Monaci Castagno, "Le trasformazioni del discorso agiografico da Eusebio a Atanasio", which does not consider this fragment of the *Pamphilus* in Jerome.

27 This distinction is elided in the translation of William H. Fremantle in Philip Schaff and Henry Wace (eds.), *Nicene and Post-Nicene Fathers*, Second Series, vol. 3. (Buffalo, NY: The Christian Literature Company, 1892), which omits Jerome's '*quoque*'.

28 τοῦτον ἐλλογιμώτατον.

29 σύνεσίν τε καὶ σοφίαν.

30 παιδείας γὰρ οὗτος τῆς παρ' Ἕλλησι θαυμαζομένης οὐ μετρίως ἧπτο τῇ τε κατὰ τὰ θεῖα δόγματα καὶ τὰς θεοπνεύστους γραφάς, εἰ χρή τι θρασύτερον, πλὴν ἀληθὲς εἰπεῖν, ὡς οὐδ' ἕτερον ἔχει τις φάναι τῶν κατ' αὐτόν, ἤσκητο.

31 ἐξ εὐπατριδῶν κατάγοντος.

he used to urge him to train in holy subjects of instruction, exacting from him each day thorough learnings and recitals' (*Hist. eccl.* 6.2.7–8; also 6.2.1).[32]

A further reference to the *Pamphilus* in the *History* reveals a concern with Pamphilus' book-collecting activities. While describing Origen's prolific literary output, Eusebius says:

> But why is it necessary for a precise catalogue of the man's works to be made in the present work, which would require its own study? I did compose one in my description of the life of the holy martyr Pamphilus of my day, in which, showing how great was Pamphilus' eagerness for divine matters, I supplied the tables of the library of the writings of Origen and of other ecclesiastical writers brought together by him.[33]

This provides further confirmation of the *Pamphilus*' focus on textual activity, despite Pamphilus' own lack of writing, as well as Origen's importance in this work (Pamphilus' school stood in the same Caesarean-Alexandrian intellectual tradition).[34] Elsewhere in the *History* we find Pamphilus described as 'truly philosophical in his lifestyle' (*Hist. eccl.* 7.32.25),[35] and in the *Martyrs* as 'sharing in inspired philosophy through the most patient training' (*De mart. Pal.* 11.3 LR),[36] and as 'distinguished through his entire life in every virtue'.[37] Pamphilus' asceticism is thus characterised by Eusebius as intellectual and philosophical.

Again, however, the most striking thing about Eusebius' diverse references to Pamphilus is the central importance of communality. We find, for example, further reference to his altruism: 'giving up his inheritance to those destitute, he distributed it all among the disabled and the dispossessed, and himself lived a life of poverty, seeking inspired philosophy through most patient training' (*De*

---

32 οὐ μετρίως γοῦν καὶ περὶ ταύτας πεπόνητο, τοῦ πατρὸς αὐτῷ πρὸς τῇ τῶν ἐγκυκλίων παιδείᾳ καὶ τούτων οὐ κατὰ πάρεργον τὴν φροντίδα πεποιημένου. ἐξ ἅπαντος γοῦν αὐτὸν πρὸ τῆς τῶν Ἑλληνικῶν μαθημάτων μελέτης ἐνῆγεν τοῖς ἱεροῖς ἐνασκεῖσθαι παιδεύμασιν, ἐκμαθήσεις καὶ ἀπαγγελίας ἡμέρας ἑκάστης αὐτὸν εἰσπραττόμενος.

33 *Hist. eccl.* 6.32.3: τί δεῖ τῶν λόγων τἀνδρὸς ἐπὶ τοῦ παρόντος τὸν ἀκριβῆ κατάλογον ποιεῖσθαι, ἰδίας δεόμενον σχολῆς; ὃν καὶ ἀνεγράψαμεν ἐπὶ τῆς τοῦ Παμφίλου βίου τοῦ καθ' ἡμᾶς ἱεροῦ μάρτυρος ἀναγραφῆς, ἐν ᾗ τὴν περὶ τὰ θεῖα σπουδὴν τοῦ Παμφίλου ὁπόση τις γεγόνοι, παριστῶντες, τῆς συναχθείσης αὐτῷ τῶν τε Ὠριγένους καὶ τῶν ἄλλων ἐκκλησιαστικῶν συγγραφέων βιβλιοθήκης τοὺς πίνακας παρεθέμην.

34 See e.g. Elizabeth C. Penland, "Eusebius Philosophus?", in Sabrina Inowlocki and Claudio Zamagni (eds.), *Reconsidering Eusebius: Collected Essays on Literary, Historical and Theological Issues*. Vigiliae Christianae Supplements 107 (Leiden: Brill, 2011), 87–97.

35 αὐτῷ τε βίῳ φιλόσοφον ἀληθῆ.

36 δι' ἀσκήσεως καρτερικωτάτης τὴν ἔνθεον μετιὼν φιλοσοφίαν.

37 παρ' ὅλον αὐτοῦ τὸν βίον ἀρετῇ πάσῃ διαπρέψας.

mart. Pal. 11.3 LR).[38] Indeed, a Eusebian gloss on Pamphilus' name—literally 'all-loving'—may indicate a focus on this quality in the work dedicated to him (*De mart. Pal.* 11.2 LR). The brief description in the *History* highlights that he was 'judged worthy of the presbyterate of that community' (*Hist. eccl.* 7.32.25).[39] Further, Pamphilus' service, like his intellectual interests, expanded beyond the confines of the Christian community, since he was also 'eminent in the government of his homeland' (*De mart. Pal.* 11.1e).[40]

Communality seems to have been the focus of the *Pamphilus*' pedagogical material too. Material in the *Martyrs* fleshes out that concern for the learning of others highlighted in the Jerome fragment. A number of other protagonists described in the *Martyrs* are pupils of Pamphilus—Apphianus, Aedesius, and Porphyry. Porphyry is also a slave of Pamphilus, as is another character, Theodulus. In both cases the text celebrates the intimacy of the relationship between teacher and student or master and slave. So, for example, Porphyry is described as 'seemingly a household slave of Pamphilus, but in disposition differing not at all from a brother or rather a true son, and lacking nothing as a reflection of his master in all things',[41] and subsequently as 'a true nursling of Pamphilus' (*De mart. Pal.* 11.15 LR).[42] His admirable behaviour in the persecution is described as typical of one 'educated by such a great man'.[43] The pedagogical material thus also emphasises the ties between Pamphilus and those around him. And this is characteristic of the *History* too, which is not only full of information about Origen's interactions with his pupils (*Hist. eccl.* 6.3.3; see also 6.3.7, 6.3.13, 6.19.12), but focuses throughout on connections between protagonists.[44]

Finally, regarding the *Pamphilus*' discussion of its protagonist's sufferings and death, two points bear emphasis. First, in the *Martyrs*, when Pamphilus is first brought before a governor, Eusebius emphasises that the trial was primarily a test of his intellectual abilities (*De mart. Pal.* 7.5 LR). Second, Pamphilus'

38 ἀποδόμενος γέ τοι τὰ εἰς αὐτὸν ἐκ προγόνων ἥκοντα γυμνοῖς, πηροῖς καὶ πένησιν τὰ πάντα διένειμεν, αὐτὸς δὲ ἐν ἀκτήμονι διῆγε βίῳ, δι' ἀσκήσεως καρτερικωτάτης τὴν ἔνθεον μετιὼν φιλοσοφίαν.

39 πρεσβείου τῆς αὐτόθι παροικίας ἠξιωμένον.

40 ταῖς κατὰ τὴν πατρίδα πολιτείαις διαπρέψαντος.

41 τὸ μὲν δοκεῖν τοῦ Παμφίλου γεγονὼς οἰκέτης, διαθέσει γε μὴν ἀδελφοῦ καὶ μᾶλλον γνησίου παιδὸς διενηνοχὼς οὐδὲν ἢ ἐλλείπων τῆς πρὸς τὸν δεσπότην κατὰ πάντα μιμήσεως.

42 θρέμμα γνήσιον Παμφίλου.

43 ὑπὸ τηλικῷδε ἀνδρὶ συνησκημένος. This familial imagery is discussed in James Corke-Webster, "Author and Authority: Literary Representations of Moral Authority in Eusebius of Caesarea's *The Martyrs of Palestine*", in Gemeinhardt and Leemans, *Christian Martyrdom in Late Antiquity*, 51–78.

44 See James Corke-Webster, *Eusebius and Empire: Constructing Church and Rome in the* Ecclesiastical History (Cambridge: Cambridge University Press, 2019), 217–226.

last days in the same text are overshadowed by those of his companions.[45] Pamphilus dies together with a group of eleven others—five unnamed Egyptians,[46] Porphyry, Paul, Seleucus, Julian, Valens, and Theodulus (*De mart. Pal.* 11).[47] Pamphilus is celebrated as 'like a certain source of a light shining by day among the phosphorescent stars, my master, flashing as with lightning, was conspicuous in their midst' (*De mart. Pal.* 11.1d LR).[48] But we hear much more about the others' trials and deaths than we do those of Pamphilus.[49] It is of course possible that Eusebius did not want to repeat what he had already treated in an earlier work. But this strategy also serves to highlight the collective rather than the individual. Pamphilus' importance is not lessened by the lack of material on his death; attention is merely shifted to his relationship with and support for others. Eusebius' focus on the group is clear when he says 'they encompassed a complete replica in miniature of the ecclesiastical body' (*De mart. Pal.* 11.1f LR; see too 11.1h LR).[50] In fact, in the *History* too, martyrdom, though regularly celebrated, is often somewhat muted in favour of a focus on literary and community accomplishments, as when Origen's suffering and death is dealt with in a single sentence (*Hist. eccl.* 6.39.5).[51] It is these connections—which make up the Christian community—about which Eusebius most cared.

This survey of Eusebius' biographical efforts, centred on his mentor Pamphilus, allow us to nuance our picture of Eusebian hagiography. Asceticism and martyrdom are indeed recurring themes, but they are not the most important. Both are celebrated in so far as they further Christians' interactions with

---

45 This is noted too by Joseph Verheyden, "Pain and Glory: Some Introductory Comments on the Rhetorical Qualities and Potential of the *Martyrs of Palestine* by Eusebius of Caesarea", in Johan Leemans (ed.), *Martyrdom and Persecution in Late Ancient Christianity: Festschrift Boudewijn Dehandschutter*. Bibliotheca Ephemeridum Theologicarum Lovaniensium 241 (Leuven: Peeters, 2010), 353–392, at 390–391.

46 On this group see Erica Carotenuto, "Five Egyptians Coming from Jerusalem: Some Remarks on Eusebius, *De Martyribus Palestinae* 11.6–13", CQ 52.2 (2002), 500–506.

47 There is perhaps an interesting comparison here with Constantine's plan, recorded in Eusebius' *Constantine*, to be buried surrounded by twelve coffins memorialising the twelve apostles (*V. Const.* 4.60).

48 οἷα δέ τις ἐν ἀποστίλβουσιν ἄστροις ἡμεροφανὴς φωστὴρ ἐν μέσοις διέπρεπεν ἐξαστράπτων ὁ ἐμὸς δεσπότης.

49 Corke-Webster, "Author and Authority", 65–66.

50 αὐτοὺς ὁλόκληρον ἐν βραχεῖ τύπον ἐκκλησιαστικοῦ συστήματος περιειληφέναι.

51 Monachi Castagno, "Le trasformazioni del discorso agiografico da Eusebio a Atanasio", 3, sees martyrdom as interwoven through Eusebius' account of Origen's life; in fact it recurs only because it is avoided in the interests of the Christian community, who can benefit more from Origen's life than his death. This is explored in more detail—along with Eusebius' nuanced attitude towards martyrdom more generally—in Corke-Webster, *Eusebius and Empire*, 175–211.

others.[52] This is perhaps most obvious with Pamphilus, whose asceticism is linked to his intellectual pursuits and charitable giving, and whose martyrdom is an opportunity to celebrate the strength he gave others in theirs. But it is true too of Origen and Eusebius' other Christian heroes.[53] What emerges most strongly from the *Pamphilus*—and what I have argued elsewhere is the key to the *History*—is the celebration of ties between individuals and of saints' contribution to the Christian community and wider society, both of which are enabled by intellectual pedigree. It is this, I argue, which lies at the heart of Eusebius' and Athanasius' literary contest.

3 The *Life of Antony* and the Athanasian Saint

At the core of Athanasius' *Antony* are these same two principles, education and community. But where Eusebius embraces both, Athanasius rejects them. This is clear from the start. Athanasius' early promise to provide 'a life of the blessed Antony'[54] that included 'how he started his training and who he was before that and how he concluded his life' (*V. Anton.* pr.2) perhaps echoes Eusebius' summary of the *Pamphilus* (*Hist. eccl.* 7.32.25) only because they reproduce the standard structure of ancient life-writing.[55] But the same cannot be said of the details that follow:

---

52 Interestingly, in the *Constantine*, while there is focus on intellectual abilities and contribution to the community via pedagogy and orthodoxy, there is almost no material on asceticism or martyrdom.

53 Monaci Castagno, "Le trasformazioni del discorso agiografico da Eusebio a Atanasio", 6, does speak more widely of Eusebius' key themes being "Paideia, ascesi, studio della Scrittura, volontà di martirio", but it is the second and fourth on which she focuses. In her discussion of Constantine (who is of course not martyred), Monaci Castagno speaks of him as a witness in his life rather than his death (50–53), which implicitly recognises that Eusebius' general treatment of martyrdom shifts focus away from traditional violent martyrdom.

54 περὶ τῆς πολιτείας τοῦ μακαρίου Ἀντωνίου. Translations of the *Antony* from Tim Vivian and Apostolos N. Athanassakis (trans.), *Athanasius of Alexandria, The Life of Antony: The Coptic Life and the Greek Life*. Cistercian Studies Series 202 (Kalamazoo, MI: Cistercian Publications, 2003); Greek text from Bartelink, *Athanasius: Vie d'Antoine*.

55 πῶς τε ἤρξατο τῆς ἀσκήσεως, καὶ τίς ἦν πρὸ ταύτης, καὶ ὁποῖον ἔσχε τοῦ βίου τὸ τέλος. In what follows I have heeded the warning of Marc Van Uytfanghe, "L'hagiographie: un 'genre' chrétien ou antique tardif?", *AB* 111 (1993), 135–188, at 167, about over-interpreting trite parallels; discussed in relation to the *Antony* at Hägg, *Art of Biography*, 382–385. The remarkable closeness and thematic consistency of the parallels here highlighted I hope tells against such an interpretation.

> Antony was an Egyptian by birth. His parents were well-born and possessed enough property to be self-sufficient. Because they were Christians, Antony was also brought up as a Christian. As a child he was raised by his parents, knowing nothing besides them and life at home. As a result, when the child grew and advanced in age, he did not continue learning his letters, wishing to stand apart from the normal activities of children. His whole desire was, as it is written [concerning Jacob],[56] to live at home, unaffected by the outside world; he would, however, join his parents in church. He was neither reckless as a child nor, when he got older, was he ever contemptuous of his parents but always obeyed them. He also listened attentively to the readings from Scripture, and kept in his heart what was profitable from them … After the death of his parents, Antony was left alone with a very small sister, and when he was around eighteen or twenty years old he had to care for his home and his sister.[57]

This opening, I suggest, was a deliberate response to Eusebius. The material in the *Pamphilus* on its protagonist's childhood must, as suggested above, have focused on precisely that education that Antony rejects. And in the mini-biography of Origen—also an Egyptian in Alexandria—in the *History*, Eusebius began with his subject's education at his parents' hands at home, making a point of emphasising, as with Pamphilus, that classical, rather than simply Christian, material was studied. He also included a tale about Origen's early abortive desire for martyrdom, foiled only by his mother's faintly farcical decision to hide his clothes. Where Antony was 'neither reckless as a child nor …

56 This latter phrase is omitted in the Vivian and Athanassakis translation.

57 *V. Anton.* 1.3–2.1: Ἀντώνιος γένος μὲν ἦν Αἰγύπτιος, εὐγενῶν δὲ γονέων καὶ περιουσίαν αὐτάρκη κεκτημένων, καὶ Χριστιανῶν αὐτῶν ὄντων, Χριστιανικῶς ἀνήγετο καὶ αὐτός. Καὶ παιδίον μὲν ὢν, ἐτρέφετο παρὰ τοῖς γονεῦσι, πλέον αὐτῶν καὶ τοῦ οἴκου μηδὲν ἕτερον γινώσκων· ἐπειδὴ δὲ καὶ αὐξήσας ἐγένετο παῖς, καὶ προέκοπτε τῇ ἡλικίᾳ, γράμματα μὲν μαθεῖν οὐκ ἠνέσχετο, βουλόμενος ἐκτὸς εἶναι καὶ τῆς πρὸς τοὺς παῖδας συνηθείας· τὴν δὲ ἐπιθυμίαν πᾶσαν εἶχε, κατὰ τὸ γεγραμμένον περὶ τοῦ Ἰακὼβ, ὡς ἄπλαστος οἰκεῖν ἐν τῇ οἰκίᾳ αὐτοῦ. Συνήγετο μέντοι μετὰ τῶν γονέων ἐν τῷ Κυριακῷ· καὶ οὔτε ὡς παῖς ἐῤῥᾳθύμει, οὔτε ὡς τῇ ἡλικίᾳ προκόπτων κατεφρόνει· ἀλλὰ καὶ τοῖς γονεῦσιν ὑπετάσσετο, καὶ τοῖς ἀναγνώσμασι προσέχων, τὴν ἐξ αὐτῶν ὠφέλειαν ἐν ἑαυτῷ διετήρει … Μετὰ δὲ τὸν θάνατον τῶν γονέων, αὐτὸς μόνος κατελείφθη μετὰ μιᾶς βραχυτάτης ἀδελφῆς· καὶ ἦν ἐτῶν ἐγγὺς δέκα καὶ ὀκτὼ, ἢ καὶ εἴκοσι γεγονὼς, αὐτός τε τῆς οἰκίας καὶ τῆς ἀδελφῆς ἐφρόντιζεν. See Bremmer, "Athanasius' *Life of Antony*", 31–36, for a discussion of how Athanasius has misrepresented reality here. I note that Bremmer thinks this is 'for reasons that are not wholly clear—perhaps just to make his biography more entertaining or more persuasive?'; I hope this article serves as at least partial explanation.

ever contemptuous of his parents', Origen had 'leapt at the chance to be in danger and rushed forward eagerly to enter the contest' (*Hist. eccl.* 6.2.3).[58] He ignores his mother when 'at first, beseeching him, she begged him to spare her maternal disposition towards him' (*Hist. eccl.* 6.2.5),[59] then 'rises to a more vehement pitch'[60] and eventually becomes 'entirely consumed by his impulse for martyrdom'.[61] And like Antony, Origen is also left with a family to support in his late teens (*Hist. eccl.* 6.2.12–13). Athanasius thus begins with an explicit reaction to Eusebius biographical efforts.[62]

Antony repeatedly revels in his lack of *grammata*, as when he declares that 'none of us is considered blessed because he has learnt and has come to know' (*V. Anton.* 33.5; see too 20.4, 72.1, 73.1–3, 78.1, 81.4, 93.4).[63] This culminates in his famed conversations with philosophers (*V. Anton.* 72.1–80.7). Numerous non-Christian intellectuals come to debate with Antony. But he simply refuses to engage with them on their terms, responding to their classic debating techniques with the simplicity of revealed knowledge and power: 'we will not offer proof by means of "plausible Greek wisdom", as our teacher said, but will persuade by means of the faith that is clearly outpacing your wordy fabrications' (*V. Anton.* 80.1; see too 77.1–78.5; 80.6).[64] This stands in sharp contrast to Eusebius' Christian heroes. They too best non-Christian intellectuals. But they do so on the latter's own terms. So, for example, Eusebius tells us of Origen that 'many others of education … went to him in order to engineer a trial of that man's pro-

58 ὁμόσε τοῖς κινδύνοις χωρεῖν προπηδᾶν τε καὶ ὁρμᾶν ἐπὶ τὸν ἀγῶνα προθύμως ἔχειν.

59 αὕτη γοῦν τὰ μὲν πρῶτα λόγοις ἱκετεύουσα, τῆς περὶ αὐτὸν μητρικῆς διαθέσεως φειδὼ λαβεῖν παρεκάλει.

60 σφοδρότερον δ' ἐπιτείναντα θεασαμένη.

61 ὅλος ἐγίνετο τῆς περὶ τὸ μαρτύριον ὁρμῆς. Origen's thirst for education and his treatment of his parents are also linked when his incessant questions to his father meant that the latter 'seemingly rebuked him to his face, exhorting him to seek nothing beyond his age or beyond the plain meaning (τῷ μὲν δοκεῖν εἰς πρόσωπον ἐπέπληττεν αὐτῷ, μηδὲν ὑπὲρ ἡλικίαν μηδὲ τῆς προφανοῦς διανοίας περαιτέρω τι ζητεῖν παραινῶν)' (*Hist. eccl.* 6.2.10).

62 It is possible also to see in Athanasius' comment on Antony that 'From the time he was a youth until great old age he kept the same zeal for ascetic discipline (ὁ ἐκ νεωτέρου μέχρι τῆς τοσαύτης ἡλικίας ἴσην τηρήσας τὴν προθυμίαν τῆς ἀσκήσεως)' (*V. Anton.* 93.1) a swipe at Origen's varying attitudes to asceticism (see e.g. *Hist. eccl.* 6.8.1). Similarly, Antony's straightforward interpretation of the instruction in Matthew 19.21 to give away one's possessions compares interestingly with Origen's interpretation of Matthew 19.12 in 'too simple and too impetuous a way (ἁπλούστερον καὶ νεανικώτερον)' (*Hist. eccl.* 6.8.2), castrating himself, especially in the light of the allegorical, Alexandrian readings that Origen favoured subsequently.

63 Οὐδεὶς γὰρ ἡμῶν κρίνεται διὰ τί οὐκ οἶδε, καὶ οὐδεὶς μακαρίζεται, ὅτι μεμάθηκε καὶ ἔγνω.

64 Ἡμεῖς μὲν οὐκ ἐν πειθοῖς σοφίας Ἑλληνικῆς λόγοις, ὡς εἶπεν ὁ διδάσκαλος ἡμῶν, ἀποδείκνυμεν· τῇ δὲ πίστει πείθομεν ἐναργῶς προλαμβανούσῃ τὴν ἐκ τῶν λόγων κατασκευήν.

ficiency in the sacred writings' (*Hist. eccl.* 6.18.2).[65] He then notes that 'many of the most notable philosophers eagerly paid attention to him, being educated by him not only in divine matters but also in those of the outside philosophy' (see too *Hist. eccl.* 6.18.3, 6.19.5–6, 6.19.12, 6.30.1).[66] Interactions with non-Christian philosophers are the proving grounds for both Eusebius' and Athanasius' subjects, but their approaches are diametrically opposed.

Athanasius' opening rejection in the *Antony* is not just of learning, however, but of learning with others. This too is programmatic. Antony is constantly celebrated for his desire for isolation.[67] After visiting the existing monks, who all live in proximity to towns (*V. Anton.* 3.3–4), Antony withdraws to the tombs near his home village (*V. Anton.* 8.1), then to the mountain (*V. Anton.* 11.2), near which he dwells for twenty years (*V. Anton.* 12.3, 14.1), and finally, after a brief visit to Alexandria (*V. Anton.* 46.1–4), to the outer mountain—the desert where he finds his proper home (*V. Anton.* 49.1, 49.4).[68] This journey ever further from civilisation is motivated by a lifelong quest for solitude, which was Antony's preferred and natural state: 'Antony, as was his custom, would withdraw by himself to his monastic cell' (*V. Anton.* 45.1; see too 9.1, 48.1, 49.1, 71.3, 84.6).[69] This self-isolation has divine support. Antony's final withdrawal is in response to divine guidance, and it is only with divine aid that he finds the route (*V. Anton.* 49.2–5; 50.1).

It is of course true that Antony remains in periodic contact with other monks. And he is regularly depicted as a kind of guide and teacher for them. But it is a role to which he seems ill-suited, and Athanasius plays up his discomfort. Such visits are presented as brief and as unwelcome interludes from Antony's proper place alone in the wilderness (e.g. *V. Anton.* 15.1, 54.1–55.1). When with the monks, he avoids eating with them if possible (*V. Anton.* 45.3). And though Antony regularly teaches them, Athanasius reminds the reader

---

65 καὶ ἄλλοι δὲ πλείους τῶν ἀπὸ παιδείας ... ᾔεσαν ὡς αὐτόν, πεῖραν τῆς ἐν τοῖς ἱεροῖς λόγοις ἱκανότητος τἀνδρὸς ληψόμενοι.

66 φιλοσόφων τε τῶν μάλιστα ἐπιφανῶν οὐκ ὀλίγοι διὰ σπουδῆς αὐτῷ προσεῖχον, μόνον οὐχὶ πρὸς τοῖς θείοις καὶ τὰ τῆς ἔξωθεν φιλοσοφίας πρὸς αὐτοῦ παιδευόμενοι.

67 Indeed Raffaella Cribiore, *Libanius the Sophist: Rhetoric, Reality, and Religion in the Fourth Century* (Ithaca, NY: Cornell University Press, 2013), 67–68, argues that Antony rejected not education but travelling away from home for higher education, which meant socialising with others.

68 On this wilderness, see Dag Ø. Endsjø, '"The truth is out there": Primordial lore and ignorance in the wilderness of Athanasius' *Vita Antonii*', in Laura Feldt (ed.), *Wilderness in Mythology and Religion: Approaching Religious Spatialities, Cosmologies, and Ideas of Wild Nature* (Berlin: De Gruyter, 2012), 113–129.

69 Αὐτὸς μέντοι συνήθως καθ' ἑαυτὸν ἀναχωρῶν ἐν τῷ ἑαυτοῦ μοναστηρίῳ.

both that this is not book learning, and that such teaching was not Antony's first inclination: 'I wanted to remain silent and not say anything about myself but to be satisfied with the foregoing remarks alone' (*V. Anton.* 39.1; see too 66.7).[70] It is again tempting to see this rejection of education and communality as an explicit response to Eusebius' hagiographical efforts, since the latter centre around heroes based in schools, defined by their relationship with pupils, and active in an exegetical pedagogical community until their deaths.

If Antony maintains loose ties to monks, his links with and contributions to wider society are even weaker. He receives consistent solicitation for healing and advice, painted as a constant irritation to him. After his first twenty-year isolation, when his friends visit he will not allow them inside (*V. Anton.* 13.1), and he only emerges when they 'forcibly tore down his door and forced him to come out' (*V. Anton.* 14.1).[71] His further attempts to retreat are motivated by the ongoing attentions of the general public: 'Since the crowds do not allow me any peace and quiet, I want to go to the Upper Thebaid on account of the numerous distractions taking place here' (*V. Anton.* 49.1).[72] His first response to people's requests is almost always to ignore or refuse them: 'Antony, however, turned away the petitioners and declined the invitations of those who journeyed to see him' (*V. Anton.* 84.4; see too 48.1, 48.3, 84.2, 84.4).[73] And as with his visits to the monks, when he does respond to these requests, it is often grudgingly.[74]

Despite his unchanging unwillingness to perform miracles,[75] Antony does heal and does give advice. But it is striking how the text emphasises how many of those acts require distance to be effective. This is most apparent in three stories Athanasius presents together. In the first, Antony tells Fronto, a sick court official, 'Go, and you will be healed' (*V. Anton.* 57.2),[76] and again in response to

70 Ἐβουλόμην μὲν οὖν σιωπῆσαι, καὶ μηδὲν ἐξ ἐμαυτοῦ λέγειν, ἀρκεῖσθαι δὲ μόνοις τούτοις.

71 βίᾳ τὴν θύραν καταβαλόντων καὶ ἐξεωσάντων.

72 Ἐπειδὴ οὐκ ἐπιτρέπουσί μοι ἠρεμεῖν οἱ ὄχλοι, διὰ τοῦτο βούλομαι ἀνελθεῖν εἰς τὴν ἄνω Θηβαΐδα, διὰ τὰς πολλὰς τῶν ὧδέ μοι γινομένας ἐνοχλήσεις.

73 αὐτὸς μὲν οὖν ἐξετρέπετο καὶ παρῃτεῖτο τὰς πρὸς τούτους ὁδούς οἱ δὲ ἐπέμενον, καὶ μᾶλλον τοὺς ὑπευθύνους ὄντας ὑπὸ στρατιώτας προσέπεμπον.

74 On this trope, see Gray's paper in this volume.

75 Towards the end of the work we do read, 'Then, although some thought that he was being bothered by the crowds and therefore turned everyone away from him, he himself was not bothered and said, "There are no more people here than the demons with whom we fought on the mountain"' (Εἶτα, τινῶν νομιζόντων ἐκ τῶν ὄχλων αὐτὸν ταράττεσθαι, καὶ διὰ τοῦτο ἀποτρεπόντων ἀπ' αὐτοῦ πάντας, αὐτὸς οὐ ταραττόμενος ἔλεγε, μὴ πλείους εἶναι τούτους ἐκείνων, μεθ' ὧν ἐν τῷ ὄρει παλαίομεν δαιμόνων) (*V. Anton.* 70.4). But here people seeking aid are equated with demons as obstacles to be overcome, and anyway this passage is followed in short order by a familiar passage in which Antony refers to his solitude with relief (*V. Anton.* 71.3).

76 Ἄπελθε, καὶ θεραπεύῃ.

Fronto's protestations at being apparently so fobbed off, 'You cannot remain here and be healed'.[77] In the second, a young Busirian woman and her parents are left outside while some monks intercede with Antony (*V. Anton.* 58.1–3). He not only anticipates their request, but also refuses their wish that the family come to him, saying that the woman is already healed (*V. Anton.* 58.3–5). In the third, Antony sends water with some monks to a visitor, still some way away, dying of thirst (*V. Anton.* 59.1–4). This triptych is then followed by further stories celebrating Antony's knowledge of faraway events (the monk Amoun's death, at *V. Anton.* 60.1–11, and the arrival of visitors, at 62.1–2; see too 82.1–3) and another healing, of one Polycratia, effected from afar (*V. Anton.* 61.1). The point seems clear. The saint is best—and most effective—in isolation.

This is addressed explicitly in a saying of Antony's. In response to an attempt by officials to keep him in company longer than he wishes, Antony replies: 'Just as fish die if they stay too long on dry land, monks also grow feeble if they stay too long with you and loiter among you. Like fish hurrying back to the sea, therefore, we too must hurry back to the mountain or we will stay too long and forget what is within' (*V. Anton.* 85.3–4).[78] Antony's reluctance to socialise results from a fundamentally inward-looking mentality, which this text makes absolutely central to sanctity. So we read elsewhere that 'Antony, as was his custom, would withdraw by himself to his monastic cell, devoting himself to his ascetic discipline: each day he would sigh, reflecting in his heart on the heavenly dwellings, focusing all his desire on them, and contemplating the transitory nature of human life' (*V. Anton.* 45.1).[79] The saint is concerned with the divine rather than the human, and with heaven rather than earth.[80]

That this is key to the work as a whole is indicated by its importance in the *Antony*'s centrepiece, the long address to the monks that takes up over a quarter of the whole (*V. Anton.* 16.1–43.3). Antony begins with a twin focus on the rejection of learning and the rejection of society: 'The Scriptures are suf-

77 Οὐ δυνήσῃ μένων ὧδε θεραπευθῆναι.

78 Ὥσπερ οἱ ἰχθύες ἐγχρονίζοντες τῇ ξηρᾷ γῇ τελευτῶσιν, οὕτως οἱ μοναχοὶ βραδύνοντες μεθ' ὑμῶν, καὶ παρ' ὑμῖν ἐκδιατρίβοντες ἐκλύονται. Δεῖ οὖν, ὥσπερ τὸν ἰχθὺν εἰς τὴν θάλασσαν, οὕτως ἡμᾶς εἰς τὸ ὄρος ἐπείγεσθαι· μήποτε ἐμβραδύνοντες, ἐπιλαθώμεθα τῶν ἔνδον.

79 Αὐτὸς μέντοι συνήθως καθ' ἑαυτὸν ἀναχωρῶν ἐν τῷ ἑαυτοῦ μοναστηρίῳ, ἐπέτεινε τὴν ἄσκησιν, καθ' ἡμέραν τε ἐστέναζεν, ἐνθυμούμενος τὰς ἐν οὐρανῷ μονάς, τόν τε πόθον ἔχων εἰς αὐτάς, καὶ σκοπῶν τὸν ἐφήμερον τῶν ἀνθρώπων βίον.

80 On this connection between Antony's withdrawal and a rejection of everything 'this-worldly', see Colm Luibhéid, "Antony and the Renunciation of Society", *Irish Theological Quarterly* 52.4 (1986), 304–314, reacting to the social-historical reading of Antony's withdrawal in Peter Brown, *The Making of Late Antiquity*. Carl Newell Jackson Lectures (Cambridge, MA: Harvard University Press, 1978), 81–101. Luibhéid's reading of the *Antony*'s desire to 'have done with accommodation and flexibility' (312) fits well the idea of Athanasius reacting to Eusebius' vision of Christianity's role in the Empire.

ficient for us for instruction ...' (*V. Anton.* 16.1), before encouraging the monks in their asceticism (*V. Anton.* 16.3–8).[81] He then asserts that 'although we have contested on earth, we will not receive our inheritance here; we have promises in heaven instead' (*V. Anton.* 16.8),[82] before emphasising renunciation from the world and its contents (*V. Anton.* 17.1–5), followed by a further exhortation to ascetic strength (*V. Anton.* 18.2, 19.1). The material on demons that occupies the rest of the address (*V. Anton.* 21.1–43.3)—and which has been much remarked upon—[83] is a consequence of the focus on the heavenly plane, where the saint's battle is really fought. Asceticism is advocated to please God, rather than for the miraculous deeds it allows (see e.g. *V. Anton.* 34.1).[84] In the *Antony*, rejection of learning fuels a model of asceticism tied to a rejection of mainstream society.[85]

This is an entirely different model of sanctity from that proffered by Eusebius, whose heroes are not only celebrated as members of pedagogical communities, but as members of society more generally. Pamphilus and Origen are both rooted in wider society; they are embedded, not isolated, saints. Early in the *History*, Eusebius works hard to 'claim' as Christian a Jewish community described by Philo in his *On the Contemplative Life*, the Therapeutae.[86] Euse-

81 Τὰς μὲν Γραφὰς ἱκανὰς εἶναι πρὸς διδασκαλίαν.

82 καὶ ἐπὶ γῆς ἀγωνισάμενοι, οὐκ ἐν γῇ κληρονομοῦμεν, ἀλλ' ἐν οὐρανοῖς ἔχομεν τὰς ἐπαγγελίας.

83 See for example Wilhelm Schneemelcher, "Das Kreuz Christi und die Dämonen. Bemerkungen zur Vita Antonii des Athanasius", in Ernst Dassmann and Karl S. Frank (eds.), *Pietas. Festschrift für Bernhard Kotting*. Jahrbuch für Antike und Christentum Ergänzungsband 8 (Münster: Aschendorff, 1980), 381–392; Norman H. Baynes, "St Antony and the Demons", *JEA* 40 (1954), 7–10; Jean Daniélou, "Les demons de l' air dans la vie d' Antoine", in Basilius Steidle (ed.), *Antonius Magnus Eremita 356–1956: Studia ad Antiquum Monachismum Spectantia*. Studia Anselmiana 38 (Rome: Herder, 1956), 136–147; and more recently Plácido Alvarez, "Demon Stories in the *Life of Antony* by Athanasius", *Cistercian Studies* 23 (1988), 101–118, and David Brakke, *Athanasius and the Politics of Asceticism*. Oxford Early Christian Studies (Oxford: Clarendon Press, 1995), 216–226.

84 It is worth noting too that Antony encourages such separation from society more widely. He convinces many others to isolate themselves, leave their homes and their urban environment and set up monastic dwellings like his (*V. Anton.* 14.5), and we read that 'Others who came to meet with him he would admonish so strongly that they would immediately forget about going to court and would bless those who withdraw from this life ... numerous soldiers and many wealthy people laid aside life's burdens and from that moment became monks (τοὺς δὲ ἄλλους τοὺς πρὸς αὐτὸν ἀπαντῶντας οὕτως ἐνουθέτει, ὡς ἐπιλανθάνεσθαι παρ' αὐτὰ τοῦ δικάζειν, καὶ μακαρίζειν τοὺς ἀναχωροῦτας ἀπὸ τοῦ βίου τούτου… πολλοὺς στρατευομένους, καὶ τῶν τὰ πολλὰ κεκτημένων, ἀποτίθεοθαι τὰ τοῦ βίου βάρη, καὶ λοιπὸν γίνεοθαι μοναχούς)' (*V. Anton.* 87.1–2).

85 Williams, *Authorised Lives*, 109–111, suggests that this reflects a rejection of the modern world in favour of that of the Bible.

86 For a full discussion, with bibliography, see Corke-Webster, *Eusebius and Empire*, 103–109, 121–147; on Eusebius appropriating them as Christian see especially Sabrina Inowlocki, "Eusebius of Caesarea's 'Interpretatio Christiana' of Philo's *De vita contemplativa*", *HThR* 97.3 (2004), 305–328.

bius presents this ascetic, text-focused community as the forerunner of his own Pamphilan school tradition. The Therapeutae remove themselves from civilisation, but not far—just outside the city walls, in fact (*Hist. eccl.* 2.17.5)—and they continue to serve the community. Eusebius notes that their name refers to their 'healing and attending to the souls of those who came to them, freeing them in the manner of doctors from the sufferings that result from vice' (*Hist. eccl.* 2.17.3).[87] Contrast this with Antony's grudging healings effected intermittently and at long range. It is tempting to see in Eusebius the kind of 'local' asceticism that Antony samples but rejects. Given this, Athanasius' comments on Antony's nickname chime interestingly with Eusebius' on Pamphilus'. 'All-loving', Eusebius observes, was a suitable moniker for one so concerned with the well-being of others (*De mart. Pal.* 11.1e). Could Antony have been aware of the contrast when he wrote, 'When everyone in the village and those with whom he associated—everyone who loved what is good—saw Antony, they would call him "God-loving"' (*V. Anton.* 4.4)?[88] Athanasius' is a different kind of saint, with a different focus.

Two specific points of comparison are worth particular comment. Antony's disconnect with society is symbolised in his receipt of an imperial missive: 'Antony neither cared about the letters, nor rejoiced over receiving them' (*V. Anton.* 81.2).[89] He has no desire that the letter of Constantine, Constantius, and Constans even be read (*V. Anton.* 81.4). Nor does he want to reply (in part because he does not know how). Again, rejection of education and society are linked. Given the paucity of Christian imperial correspondence in early Christian literature, this episode may echo Eusebius' comment on Origen that 'there is preserved a letter of his to the emperor Philip himself and another to Severa, the wife of that man, and diverse others to diverse others' (*Hist. eccl.* 6.36.3).[90] Antony does eventually reply, but only to reiterate his renunciatory message by advising them 'not to regard present things as important' (*V. Anton.* 81.5).[91] And Athanasius concludes the anecdote by asserting that 'Although Antony

---

87 τὰς ψυχὰς τῶν προσιόντων αὐτοῖς τῶν ἀπὸ κακίας παθῶν ἰατρῶν δίκην ἀπαλλάττοντας ἀκεῖσθαι καὶ θεραπεύειν.

88 Πάντες μὲν οὖν οἱ ἀπὸ τῆς κώμης καὶ οἱ φιλόκαλοι, πρὸς οὓς εἶχε τὴν συνήθειαν, οὕτως αὐτὸν ὁρῶντες, ἐκάλουν θεοφιλῆ.

89 οὔτε τὰ γράμματα περὶ πολλοῦ τινος ἐποιεῖτο, οὔτε ἐπὶ ταῖς ἐπιστολαῖς ἐγεγήθει.

90 φέρεται δὲ αὐτοῦ καὶ πρὸς αὐτὸν βασιλέα Φίλιππον ἐπιστολὴ καὶ ἄλλη πρὸς τὴν τούτου γαμετὴν Σευήραν διάφοροί τε ἄλλαι πρὸς διαφόρους. We might compare too Eusebius' account of Jesus' response to a letter received from King Abgar of Edessa, on which see James Corke-Webster, "A Man for the Times: Jesus and the Abgar Correspondence in Eusebius of Caesarea's *Ecclesiastical History*", *HThR* 110.4 (2017), 563–587, with discussion and bibliography.

91 καὶ μὴ μεγάλα ἡγεῖσθαι τὰ παρόντα.

was being recognised as so great a person and was responding to the needs of those who came to meet him, he returned once more to the inner mountain' (*V. Anton.* 82.1).[92] Such a response to imperial recognition stands in stark contrast to Origen, who when summoned by the emperor Caracalla's mother Mammaea (*Hist. eccl.* 6.21.4) acquiesces and remains with her as a teacher (*Hist. eccl.* 6.21.4).

Eusebius and Athanasius' saints also deal with heretics in strikingly different ways. Both are, of course, strident in their support for 'orthodoxy' over 'heresy' (though they would have disagreed on to what those labels referred …). But Antony's isolationist mentality means that he advocates a complete rejection of heretics' company:

> Antony was completely wonderful and orthodox in his belief, for he never had fellowship with the schismatic Melitians, knowing their malice and apostasy from the beginning. Nor did he have friendly relations with Manicheans or with any other heretics except to admonish them to change to orthodoxy. Antony held and urged that friendship and association with them was harmful and destructive to the soul. Thus he also loathed the Arian heresy, urging everyone neither to go near them nor to hold their wicked beliefs. Therefore, when some Ariomaniacs came to see him one day, he questioned them and, when he discovered that they were heretics, he chased them off the mountain, saying that their words were more evil than serpents.[93]

Later he repeats the admonition: 'you are to have no fellowship with the godless and iniquitous Arians, for "light has no fellowship with darkness"' (*V. Anton.* 69.4–5; see too 82.13, 89.4, 91.4).[94] This approach is far removed from that of Eusebius' protagonists. Too little of the *Pamphilus* survives to

---

92 Τοιοῦτος δὴ οὖν γινωσκόμενος, καὶ οὕτω πρὸς τοὺς ἀπαντῶντας ἀποκρινόμενος, ὑπέστρεφε πάλιν εἰς τὸ ἔνδον ὄρος.

93 *V. Anton.* 68.1–3: Καὶ τῇ πίστει δὲ πάνυ θαυμαστὸς ἦν καὶ εὐσεβής. Οὔτε γὰρ Μελετιανοῖς τοῖς σχισματικοῖς ποτε κεκοινώνηκεν, εἰδὼς αὐτῶν τὴν ἐξ ἀρχῆς πονηρίαν καὶ ἀποστασίαν· οὔτε Μανιχαίοις, ἢ ἄλλοις τισὶν αἱρετικοῖς ὡμίλησε φιλικά, ἢ μόνον ἄχρι νουθεσίας τῆς εἰς εὐσέβειαν μεταβολῆς· ἡγούμενος καὶ παραγγέλλων τὴν τούτων φιλίαν καὶ ὁμιλίαν βλάβην καὶ ἀπώλειαν εἶναι ψυχῆς. Οὕτω γοῦν καὶ τὴν τῶν Ἀρειανῶν αἵρεσιν ἐβδελύσσετο, παρήγγελλέ τε πᾶσι μήτε ἐγγίζειν αὐτοῖς, μήτε τὴν κακοπιστίαν αὐτῶν ἔχειν. Ἀπελθόντας γοῦν ποτέ τινας πρὸς αὐτὸν τῶν Ἀρειομανιτῶν, ἀνακρίνας καὶ μαθὼν ἀσεβοῦντας, ἐδίωξεν ἀπὸ τοῦ ὄρους, λέγων ὄφεων ἰοῦ χείρονας εἶναι τοὺς λόγους αὐτῶν.

94 ὅθεν μηδὲ μίαν ἔχετε κοινωνίαν πρὸς τοὺς ἀσεβεστάτους Ἀρειανούς· Οὐδεμία γὰρ κοινωνία φωτὶ πρὸς σκότος.

know its hero's attitude toward heretics. But Eusebius' stance is clear in his other writings, where Christian intellectuals are constantly fighting schismatic and heretical fires, interacting repeatedly with the problematic Christians and their writings to try to bring them to orthodoxy. Eusebius even answers perceived criticisms of such contact, quoting a letter of Dionysius of Alexandria insisting that one should 'scrutinise and iron it out if something does not seem soundly recorded'[95] and thus that 'it is necessary for us also to argue against our brother Nepos as if against someone present' (*Hist. eccl.* 7.24.4–5).[96] Dionysius spends three days with those led astray by Nepos' heretical work until they are 'sufficiently convinced by the counterarguments' (*Hist. eccl.* 7.24.9).[97] Moreover, once the rogue sheep are back in the fold, Eusebius will even praise Nepos for 'his faith, love of work, study in the writings, and plentiful psalmody, through which many of the brothers up till now have been cheered'[98] (*Hist. eccl.* 7.24.4), and his followers for 'their steadfastness, love of truth, speed to follow and intelligence' (*Hist. eccl.* 7.24.8).[99] In Eusebius' Christian biographies, heretics and schismatics can be saved by those interactions with saints—and their learning—that Athanasius' uneducated Antony forbids.

The endings to Eusebius' and Athanasius' respective biographies are also telling. Near the close of the *Antony* Athanasius reports that after the ascetic's death 'all of them, like orphans deprived of their father, comforted each other with his memory alone, while at the same time keeping his admonitions and exhortations' (*V. Anton.* 88.3).[100] Further on, we read of his posthumous legacy that, 'Antony was known and recognised neither through written works nor through profane wisdom nor on account of any particular skill, but only through his love of God' (*V. Anton.* 93.4).[101] In his final sentences, Athanasius does speak of 'the help they [those that give glory to Christ] give to others' (*V. Anton.* 94.1).[102] But this is done through Christ. Such a conclusion again seems a deliberate echo of Eusebius' parallel material. We do not have the end

95 ἐξετάζειν δὲ καὶ διευθύνειν, εἴ τι μὴ φαίνοιτο ὑγιῶς ἀναγεγραμμένον.

96 ἀναγκαῖον καὶ ἡμᾶς ὡς πρὸς παρόντα τὸν ἀδελφὸν ἡμῶν διαλεχθῆναι Νέπωτα.

97 ἱκανῶς ὑπὸ τῶν ἀντιλεχθέντων ᾑρημένος.

98 τῆς τε πίστεως καὶ τῆς φιλοπονίας καὶ τῆς ἐν ταῖς γραφαῖς διατριβῆς καὶ τῆς πολλῆς ψαλμῳδίας, ᾗ μέχρι νῦν πολλοὶ τῶν ἀδελφῶν εὐθυμοῦνται.

99 τὸ εὐσταθὲς καὶ τὸ φιλάληθες καὶ τὸ εὐπαρακολούθητον καὶ συνετὸν … τῶν ἀδελφῶν.

100 Ἀμέλει κοιμηθέντος αὐτοῦ, πάντες, ὡς ὀρφανοὶ γενόμενοι πατρὸς, μόνῃ τῇ ἐκείνου μνήμῃ παρακαλοῦσιν ἑαυτοὺς, κατέχοντες ἅμα τὰς νουθεσίας καὶ τὰς παραινέσεις αὐτοῦ.

101 Οὐ γὰρ ἐκ συγγραμμάτων, οὐδὲ ἐκ τῆς ἔξωθεν σοφίας, οὐδὲ διά τινα τέχνην, διὰ δὲ μόνην θεοσέβειαν ὁ Ἀντώνιος ἐγνωρίσθη.

102 τὴν τῶν ἄλλων ὠφέλειαν.

of his *Pamphilus*. But even the fragment preserved emphasises, in stark contrast to the *Antony*, the value of his written correspondence. The final lines of the 'Life of Origen' are more explicit, directing the reader to 'the sorts of sayings he left behind after these things, filled with help for those in need of restoration' (*Hist. eccl.* 6.39.5; see too 6.46.6) to be found in his letters.[103] An almost identical phrase ends Eusebius' account of Dionysius: 'conversing with many others similarly through letters, he has left behind diverse aids for those still now eagerly working with his writings' (*Hist. eccl.* 6.46.5).[104] Written legacies, useful for the communities left behind that his heroes had striven to support, were a prominent feature of Eusebius' hagiographical efforts; Athanasius' Antony, having rejected education, leaves only his memory to the wider community he has always avoided.[105]

4 Eusebius, Athanasius, and the Development of Hagiography

This review of Eusebian and Athanasian early saints' lives does not prove dependency. And I am not suggesting that Eusebius' *Pamphilus*, *Martyrs*, 'Life of Origen', or *History* more generally be considered *the* model for the *Antony*. But there are a number of striking similarities (or rather, telling divergences) that make it highly plausible that Eusebius' writings were a prominent point of departure for Athanasius. Certainly the latter's model of the saint's life was the exact opposite of Eusebius' in two key ways—education and communality. Athanasius' portrait of Antony proclaims his rejection of learning and desire for isolation, which together feed a wider rejection of society. All of Eusebius' biographical offerings privilege the exact opposite principles—the central importance for Christian heroes of both Christian and classical learning, and engagement with the wider Christian and non-Christian community.

This is important, I suggest, for the literary origins of hagiography, a topic at the centre of which the *Antony* has always stood. It has long been posited that in writing it Athanasius was responding to earlier classical biography. Earlier in the twentieth century, Hans Mertel suggested that the *Antony* fol-

103 ὁποίας τε μετὰ ταῦτα καταλείπει φωνὰς καὶ αὐτὰς πλήρεις τοῖς ἀναλήψεως δεομένοις ὠφελείας.

104 καὶ ἄλλοις δὲ πλείοσιν ὁμοίως διὰ γραμμάτων ὁμιλήσας, ποικίλας τοῖς ἔτι νῦν σπουδὴν περὶ τοὺς λόγους αὐτοῦ ποιουμένοις καταλέλοιπεν ὠφελείας.

105 Cameron, "Form and Meaning", 81, compares the physical depiction of Constantine (*V. Const.* 3.10.3–4, 4.53.1) with that of Antony (*V. Anton.* 67.4–8, 93.1–2). We might compare one of Eusebius' depictions of Pamphilus (*De mart. Pal.* 11.1), where his distinctive appearance is ascribed to his education and God-given wisdom.

lowed Plutarch's model of peripatetic biography,[106] a thesis echoed in part by Anton Priessnig, who also considered the work to have Suetonian influences.[107] Johann List alternatively suggested narrative encomium as a model;[108] Samuel Cavallin Xenophon's *Agesilaus*.[109] But perhaps the most persuasive of such putative parallels were those drawn with philosophical biography. Richard Reitzenstein first noticed the similarity between Antony's emergence from the tomb (*V. Anton.* 14.2–4) and the comparable descriptions of Pythagoras in Iamblichus and Porphyry's writings (both clearly based on a lost original).[110] 'Hard' versions of this thesis—i.e., establishing any one forerunner for the *Antony* in the 'non-Christian' tradition—have proved less than compelling. The parallels identified are often structural and rather vague, and of course indirect influence on Athanasius is just as probable as direct.[111] But despite such criticism, modern scholars have remained intrigued by the connections with philosophical biography.[112]

106 Hans Mertel, "Die biographische Form der griechischen Heiligenlegenden", Ph.D. diss., München (1909).

107 Anton Priessnig, "Die biographischen Formen der griechischen Heiligenlegenden in ihrer geschichtlichen Entwicklung", Ph.D. diss., München (1924).

108 Johann List, *Das Antonius-Leben des Hl. Athanasius des Grossen. Eine literarhistorische Studie zu den Anfängen der byzantinischen Hagiographie* (Athens: P.D. Sakellarios, 1931).

109 Samuel Cavallin, *Literarhistorische und textkritische Studien zur Vita S. Caesarii Arelatensis* (Lund: Gleerup, 1934).

110 Richard Reitzenstein, *Des Athanasius Werk über das Leben des Antonius. Ein philologischer Beitrag zur Geschichte des Mönchtums*. Sitzungsberichte der Heidelberger Akadamie der Wissenschaften, vol. 5 (Heidelberg: Carl Winter Universitätsbuchhandlung, 1914), also positing the influence of Suetonius and aretalogy. See too Anton Priessnig, "Die literarische Form der spätantiken Philosophenromane", *ByzZ* 30 (1930), 23–30, and André-Jean Festugière, "Sur une nouvelle edition du *De Vita Pythagorica* de Jamblique", REG 50 (1937), 470–494. Subsequent discussions have focused on Porphyry's *Life of Plotinus*; see e.g. Anton Priessnig, "Die biographische Form der Plotinvita des Porphyrios und das Antoniosleben des Athanasios", *ByzZ* 64 (1971), 1–5. In a slight variation to the philosophical biography theory, Karl Holl, "Die schriftstellerische Form des griechischen Heiligenlebens", *Neue Jahrbücher für das klassische Altertumswissenschaft* 15 (1912), 406–427, later in *Gesammelte Aufsätze zur Kirchengeschichte. II. Der Osten* (Tübingen: J.C.B. Mohr, 1928), 249–269, critiquing Mertel (above, n. 106), saw the *Antony* as the start of a new genre but one that drew upon Philostratus' account of Apollonius of Tyana as well as Clement of Alexandria's *Who is the rich man to be saved?*

111 As suggested in Hägg, *Art of Biography*, 384.

112 E.g. Gerhard J.M. Bartelink, "Die literarische Gattung der Vita Antonii. Struktur und Motiv", *VChr* 36 (1982), 38–62, critical of all earlier attempts other than those of Reitzenstein and Holl; see too Samuel Rubenson, "Anthony and Pythagoras: A Reappraisal of the Appropriation of Classical Biography in Athanasius' Vita Antonii", in Anders-Christian Jacobsen, David Brakke and Jörg Ulrich (eds.), *Beyond Reception: mutual influences between antique*

A separate modern historiography has focused on Athanasius' attempts to correct earlier views of Antony. Traditionally this took the form of demonstrating the lack of historicity in Athanasius' account. So Hermann Dörries, as well as critiquing Reitzenstein's theory, suggested that Athanasius' Antony was a rewriting of the reclusive, Coptic Antony that we see, for example, in the *Sayings of the Desert Fathers*.[113] Samuel Rubenson, in demonstrating the authenticity of the letters of Antony, argued that the Origenist monk they depict, focused on gnosis and asceticism, was the original figure altered by Athanasius.[114] Most influentially, David Brakke has argued that the *Antony* was Athanasius' response to various contemporary constructions of his protagonist circulating at the time in Egypt—as spiritual patron and intercessor (as in the letter of Serapion), as wisdom teacher (as in the seven letters of Antony), and as the founder of anchorite monks (as in the various *Lives* of Pachomius).[115]

Brakke's picture has attracted broad support. But the interesting parallels we have identified between Athanasius' and Eusebius' hagiographical writings allow us to push it a stage further. The most important of the three earlier models of Antony against which Brakke sees Athanasius reacting (and the topic with which his discussion climaxes) was the monasticised version of Alexandrian academic Christianity, which Brakke characterises as 'the understanding of Christianity as a philosophy, centred around the study of ancient writings under the guidance of an academically trained teacher'.[116] But though Brakke sees this as a reaction against an Egyptian tradition, in fact the most influential picture of that intellectual Christianity was that produced by Eusebius of

religion, Judaism and early Christianity. Early Christianity in the Context of Antiquity (Frankfurt am Main: P. Lang, 2006), 191–208, which contains the best summary of the debate at 192–194, and expands on Reitzenstein's observations at 201–207; Tomas Hägg, "The *Life of St Antony* between Biography and Hagiography", in Stephanos Efthymiadis (eds.), *Ashgate Research Companion to Byzantine Hagiography*. vol. 1 (Farnham: Ashgate, 2011), 17–34, at 23–24; Rubenson, "Apologetics of Asceticism"; and Bremmer, "Athanasius' *Life of Antony*", 25–26.

113 Hermann Dörries, *Die Vita Antonii als Geschichtsquelle*. Nachrichten der Akademie der Wissenschaften in Göttingen 14 (Göttingen: Vandenhoeck and Ruprecht, 1949); revised edition in Hermann Dörries, *Wort und Stunde*. vol. 1: *Gesammelte Studien zur Kirchengeschichte des vierten Jahrhunderts* (Göttingen: Vandenhoeck and Ruprecht, 1966), 145–224.

114 Samuel Rubenson, *The Letters of St. Antony: Origenist Theology, Monastic Tradition and the Making of a Saint*. Bibliotheca Historico-Ecclesiastica Lundensis 24 (Lund: Lund University Press, 1990).

115 Brakke, *Athanasius*, at 208–216 in particular. In this he built on the work of Dörries, *Die Vita Antonii*.

116 Brakke, *Athanasius*, 253–265, at 254. On Athanasius' rejection (or rather, 'misrecognition') of *paideia*, and the wider landscape in which it partook, see Urbano, "'Read It Also to the Gentiles'" and idem, *The Philosophical Life*.

Caesarea, spokesman for the communal Alexandrian-Caesarean tradition that traced its roots and key elements to the exegetical traditions of Alexandria and its Christian son, Origen.

The Eusebian connection also makes sense given that a major element in Brakke's vision of that intellectual Christianity against which Athanasius was reacting was its Arian elements; namely that Arius, the 'heretic' against whose position so much of Athanasius' output was directed, stood in an esoteric intellectual tradition of Christianity in which (among others) Origen was key.[117] Indeed, as Edward Watts has pointed out, Arius himself made much of his pedagogical lineage.[118] Eusebius not only stood in that Origenistic intellectual tradition (as did Pamphilus, who had co-authored the *Defence* with Eusebius), but was also seen by Athanasius as a champion of Arius and a leading thinker among his followers. Given that, it is easy to see why he might be sceptical of Eusebius' championing of textual engagement with heretics and their writings. Eusebius had written up his brand of Christianity in a series of life narratives as a model to be imitated. Athanasius' advocacy for a diametrically opposed vision of sanctity, and his decision to memorialise it in biography, can be seen as a response not only to Eusebius' particular vision of Christianity, but to the form in which he chose to express it.[119]

The posited link between the hagiographical writings of Eusebius and Athanasius allows us to bridge the gap between literary and historical approaches to the *Antony*. Athanasius did indeed react against pre-existing models of academic Christianity, but these were not just those of Egypt but also those of Caesarea. And he also, I suggest, took issue with the narrative portraits that had heroicised that view of Christianity, namely the early hagiographical efforts of Eusebius of Caesarea. In this regard, it is interesting that Eusebius is the early Christian author interested above all others in philosophical biography. It has been long recognised that the *History*, which is difficult to

117 See especially Brakke, *Athanasius*, 145. For this portrait of Arianism, see Rowan Williams, *Arius: Heresy and Tradition* (London: Darton, Longman, and Todd, 1987). See too Edward Watts, *City and School in Late Antique Athens and Alexandria*. Transformation of the Classical Heritage (Berkeley: University of California Press, 2008), 169–181.

118 Watts, *City and School*, 174.

119 Cameron, "Form and Meaning" and Monaci Castagno, "Le trasformazioni del discorso agiografico da Eusebio a Atanasio" both also address the importance of Athanasius' anti-Arian endeavours in support of their particular theses of Eusebian influence. Brakke, *Athanasius*, 203–208, dismisses as 'dubious prospects' (203; see too 208) attempts to identify the historical Antony and source criticism on the *Antony* itself. Such judgements are legitimate, but he does not consider in detail earlier literary treatments of the Christian models he sees Athanasius as rejecting.

nail down generically, most closely resembles a combination of national history and philosophical biography.[120] Recent studies of the *Martyrs* have argued that it should be read along such philosophical lines.[121] Eusebius' project—to present Christianity as a superior intellectual group within the Graeco-Roman landscape—involved mobilising tropes from that landscape's literature. Athanasius' engagement with those same motifs is natural if he was reacting to the writings of a fellow Christian who had done similarly.[122]

It is also no coincidence that the points of disagreement between Eusebius and Athanasius, education and societal engagement, were arguably the two key elements in classical philosophical biography. The importance of learning for the philosopher perhaps goes without saying, but integration in wider society was just as important, as Pierre Hadot famously demonstrated.[123] Ancient philosophical groups were supposed to contribute to their wider community, and ideal philosophers were those whose philosophy bettered those around them. Eusebius' proto-hagiography represented broad continuity with that tradition;[124] Athanasius' a radical departure.

An explanation for that literary divide may lie in more historical considerations. Eusebius' biographical efforts, as I have argued elsewhere, were informed by his own situation in the first three decades of the fourth century.[125] Put simply, it is no coincidence that the heroes of Eusebius' biographical efforts—his Christian 'saints'—are intellectual clerics educated in the Alexandrian-Caesarean school tradition, whose authority is validated by their intelligence, their literary output, their correspondence with Roman elites, and their efforts on behalf of the Christian community. By those standards, Eusebius, educated

120 See Arnaldo Momigliano, "Pagan and Christian Historiography in the Fourth Century A.D.", in Arnaldo Momigliano (ed.), *The Conflict Between Paganism and Christianity in the Fourth Century* (Oxford: Clarendon Press, 1963), 79–99; Timothy D. Barnes, *Constantine and Eusebius* (Cambridge, MA: Harvard University Press, 1981), 128; and David DeVore, "Genre and Eusebius' *Ecclesiastical History*: Prolegomena for a Focused Debate", in Aaron Johnson and Jeremy Schott (eds.), *Eusebius of Caesarea: Traditions and Innovations* (Cambridge MA: Harvard University Press, 2013), 19–45.

121 See especially Elizabeth C. Penland, "Martyrs as Philosophers: The School of Pamphilus and Ascetic Tradition in Eusebius's 'Martyrs of Palestine' ", Ph.D. diss., Yale (2010).

122 *Contra* Monaci Castagno, "Le trasformazioni del discorso agiografico da Eusebio a Atanasio", 62–63, who treats the influence on Athanasius of Eusebius' writings and of philosophical biography as distinct.

123 Pierre Hadot, *Philosophy as a Way of Life: Spiritual Exercises from Socrates to Foucault* (Oxford: Blackwell, 1995), at e.g. 274.

124 For a more nuanced treatment of the genre and models of Eusebius' *History*, see Corke-Webster, *Eusebius and Empire*, 72–79.

125 See Corke-Webster, *Eusebius and Empire*, 280–282.

in and heir to that exact intellectual tradition, bishop of Caesarea and steward of its substantial library and author of a vast output demonstrating his depth of knowledge, was strengthened by his own portrait of Christian authority.

The same logic can, I argue, be applied to Athanasius. This may seem a counterintuitive argument; after all, Athanasius was as well educated and as literarily aware as Eusebius, and thus far removed from his portrait of Antony. But this ignores the specific circumstances in which the *Antony* was written. Though the text is difficult to date exactly, it certainly arose from Athanasius' third exile (AD 356–362), during which, removed from Alexandria by Constantius, the antagonistic bishop abided in Upper Egypt.[126] The celebration of Antony's isolation makes sense when read against Athanasius' forced withdrawal. It is interesting, for example, that one consequence of the emphasis on Antony's (self-imposed) withdrawal is that the reader sees time and again how effective he is despite the geographical distance. As was discussed above, Antony's miracles do not require face-to-face contact or even vague proximity. Similarly, his knowledge of affairs is not compromised, and in fact he often appears better informed than his conversation partners from civilisation.[127] The saint in the desert, in other words, remains a force with which to be reckoned. One could easily see in that the wishful thinking of an exiled bishop.

For both Eusebius and Athanasius then, their use of Christian biography was in part about power; and more specifically, about mobilising their literary skills to provide historical support for their own situations. Eusebius, a scholar writing in a city of political insignificance but intellectual weight, worked to write past Christians into the upper echelons of Roman society, ending with a Christian emperor excelling because of his Christianity.[128] Athanasius, spurned by imperial authority and cast out of his urban power base, perhaps saw the dangers of that model and sought a new and independent basis for Christian authority. In other words, where Eusebius' saints were knitted into the heart of traditional urban authority, Athanasius imbued his model of sanctity with independence and absence.

126 On the dating, see above n. 1.

127 It would perhaps be possible to read the *Antony*'s warnings against the dangers of rumours in this light too (see *V. Anton.* 31–33).

128 Corke-Webster, *Eusebius and Empire*, 282–301.

5 Conclusion

In writing his seminal *Antony*, Athanasius had few precedents. But amongst them was a corpus of biographical writing he knew and disliked, namely the narrative efforts of Eusebius of Caesarea. Various points in Athanasius' *Antony* seem to be direct responses to anecdotes in Eusebius' writing. And more generally, Athanasius' overall biographical project seems diametrically opposed to Eusebius' on the two issues at the core of both their narratives—the significance of learning and education, and the degree to which the saint should be engaged in his community. What Eusebius embraced, Athanasius rejected. On this basis I have suggested that we see Athanasius as reacting not simply to other contemporary Egyptian conceptions of Antony in diverse genres—letters, sayings, etc.—but also to the academic, man-of-the-world model of sanctity spread already, and in narrative form, by Eusebius, one of Athanasius' main bêtes noires.

This has a number of consequences for this volume's wider investigation into the literary development of hagiography. First, it affirms that we should see Athanasius as responding not simply to Christian prompts but specifically to earlier Christian life-writing.[129] Connections between the *Antony* and classical biography remain a staple of scholarship, but those with earlier Christian narratives are of equal importance for understanding its provenance. And it is interesting that the Christian narratives most easily identified are those with such strong affinities to philosophical biography, given the long-posited links between that genre and the *Antony*.

Second, this link between Athanasius and Eusebius makes the birth of hagiography not simply one rooted in internal Egyptian politics but a literary development on a wider scale, involving more than one centre of fourth-century Christianity. And the importance of Palestinian Christianity in that development—already key given the role of Jerome in the post-*Antony* liter-

129 As argued by Urbano, "Read It Also to the Gentiles", at e.g., 896; *The Philosophical Life*, 214. We might compare the development of apologetic, long seen as a fundamentally outside-facing literary enterprise, but now generally accepted as a means of identity construction for Christian insiders; see in this volume "Introduction", 13. Peter Gemeinhardt, "*Vita Antonii* oder *Passio Antonii*? Biographisches Genre und martyrologische Topik in der ersten Asketenvita", in Gemeinhardt and Leemans, *Christian Martyrdom in Late Antiquity*, 79–114, sees the *Antony* as an early example of a martyrological biography—see now too by the same author *Athanasius: Vita Antonii—Leben des Antonius*. Fontes Christiani (Freiburg: Herder, 2018)—though Bremmer, 'Athanasius' *Life of Antony*', 30–31, considers the focus on martyrdom exaggerated.

ary tradition—grows still more.[130] The birthplace of Christian history was also the birthplace of what would become its most prevalent literature.

Third, at this earliest stage in the development of hagiography, we find two issues at the centre of the tussle over its contents: education and community. If hagiography was a process of 'writing up' sanctity, the first questions asked seem to have concerned the source of holy words and holy deeds—worldly or heavenly? Eusebius, writing at a watershed where both the status and the place of Christianity in the world were still up in the air, leaned towards the former; Athanasius, writing half a century later when Christianity's place was more assured, the latter. And the positions of both were dictated in part by their author's particular circumstances.

This key point of contention between these authors continued to be central to hagiography throughout the fourth century and beyond.[131] Athanasius was ultimately the more successful of the two, and it was his literary effort that became the template for most hagiography. But remembering that it was only created in reaction to an earlier, alternative attempt reminds us both that the literary development of hagiography was from its outset bound into a deeper debate over the nature of Christian spirituality, and that that debate was as influenced by hagiographers' personal circumstances as it was by intrinsic beliefs about the nature of saints.

Acknowledgments

I am grateful to Christa Gray and Michael Stuart Williams for their comments on an earlier draft.

Bibliography

Abramowski, Luise, "Vertritt die syrische Fassung die ursprüngliche Gestalt der Vita Antonii? Eine Auseinandersetzung mit der These Draguets", in René-Georges Coquin (ed.), *Mélanges Antoine Guillaumont. Contributions à l'étude des christianismes orientaux*. Cahiers d'orientalisme 20 (Genève: Patrick Cramer, 1988), 47–56.

130 See the discussion of Jerome's importance in this volume in Ross' and Gray's papers.

131 See Samuel Rubenson, "Philosophy and Simplicity: The Problem of Classical Education in Early Christian Biography", in Hägg and Rousseau, *Greek Biography and Panegyric*, 110–139; and Williams, *Authorised Lives*, 101–147.

Alvarez, Plácido, "Demon Stories in the *Life of Antony* by Athanasius", *Cistercian Studies* 23 (1988), 101–118.

Bardy, Gustave, *Eusèbe de Césarée, Histoire Ecclésiastique*. Sources chrétiennes 55 (Paris: Les Éditions du Cerf, 1952–1958 [repr. 3: 1967]).

Barnard, Leslie W., "The Date of S. Athanasius' *Vita Antonii*", *VChr* 27 (1974), 169–175.

Barnes, Timothy D., *Constantine and Eusebius* (Cambridge, MA: Harvard University Press, 1981).

Barnes, Timothy D., "Angel of Light or Mystic Initiate? The Problem of the Life of Antony", *JThS* 37 (1986), 353–368.

Barnes, Timothy D., *Early Christian Hagiography and Roman History*. Tria Corda 5 (Tübingen: Mohr Siebeck, 2010).

Barnes, Timothy D., "Early Christian Hagiography and the Roman Historian", in Peter Gemeinhardt and Johan Leemans (eds.), *Christian Martyrdom in Late Antiquity: History and Discourse, Tradition and Religious Identity*. Arbeiten zur Kirchengeschichte 116 (Berlin/New York: De Gruyter, 2012), 15–33.

Bartelink, Gerhard J.M., "Die literarische Gattung der Vita Antonii. Struktur und Motiv", *VChr* 36 (1982), 38–62.

Bartelink, Gerhard J.M. (ed.), *Athanasius: Vie d'Antoine*. Sources chrétiennes 400 (Paris: Les Éditions du Cerf, 1994), 27–42.

Baynes, Norman H., "St Antony and the Demons", *JEA* 40 (1954), 7–10.

Brakke, David, "The Greek and Syriac Versions of the Life of Antony", *Muséon* 107.1–2 (1994), 29–53.

Brakke, David, "The Authenticity of the Ascetic Athanasiana", *Orientalia* 63 (1994), 17–56.

Brakke, David, *Athanasius and the Politics of Asceticism*. Oxford Early Christian Studies (Oxford: Clarendon Press, 1995).

Bremmer, Jan N., "Athanasius' *Life of Antony*: Marginality, Spatiality and Mediality", in Laura Feldt and Jan N. Bremmer (eds.), *Marginality, Media, and Mutations of Religious Authority in the History of Christianity* (Leuven: Peeters, 2019), 23–45.

Brennan, Brian R., "Dating Athanasius' *Vita Antonii*", *VChr* 30 (1976), 52–54.

Brown, Peter, *The Making of Late Antiquity*. Carl Newell Jackson Lectures (Cambridge, MA: Harvard University Press, 1978).

Cameron, Averil, "Eusebius' *Vita Constantini* and the Construction of Constantine", in Mark Edwards and Simon Swain (eds.), *Portraits: Biographical Representation in the Greek and Latin Literature of the Roman Empire* (Oxford: Clarendon Press, 1997), 145–174.

Cameron, Averil, "Form and Meaning: the *Vita Constantini* and the *Vita Antonii*", in Tomas Hägg and Philip Rousseau (eds.), *Greek Biography and Panegyric in Late Antiquity* (Berkeley: University of California Press, 2000), 72–88.

Cameron, Averil, "Apologetics in the Roman Empire—A Genre of Intolerance?", in Jean-Michel Carrie and Rita Lizzi Testa (eds.), *Humana Sapit: études d'Antiquité tardive offertes à Lellia Cracco Ruggini*. Bibliothèque de l'antiquité tardive 3 (Turnhout: Brépols, 2002), 219–227.

Carotenuto, Erica, "Five Egyptians Coming from Jerusalem: Some Remarks on Eusebius, *De Martyribus Palestinae* 11.6–13", CQ 52.2 (2002), 500–506.

Carriker, Andrew J., *The Library of Eusebius of Caesarea*. Vigiliae Christianae Supplements 67 (Leiden: Brill, 2003).

Cavallin, Samuel, *Literarhistorische und textkritische Studien zur Vita S. Caesarii Arelatensis* (Lund: Gleerup, 1934).

Corke-Webster, James, "Author and Authority: Literary Representations of Moral Authority in Eusebius of Caesarea's *The Martyrs of Palestine*", in Gemeinhardt and Leemans, *Christian Martyrdom in Late Antiquity*, 51–78.

Corke-Webster, James, "A Man for the Times: Jesus and the Abgar Correspondence in Eusebius of Caesarea's *Ecclesiastical History*", *HThR* 110.4 (2017), 563–587.

Corke-Webster, James, *Eusebius and Empire: Constructing Church and Rome in the Ecclesiastical History* (Cambridge: Cambridge University Press, 2019).

Corke-Webster, James, "A Bishop's Biography: Eusebius of Caesarea's *Life of Constantine*", in Koen De Temmerman (ed.), *The Oxford Handbook of Ancient Biography* (Oxford: Oxford University Press, in press).

Cribiore, Raffaella, *Libanius the Sophist: Rhetoric, Reality, and Religion in the Fourth Century* (Ithaca, NY: Cornell University Press, 2013).

Daniélou, Jean, "Les demons de l'air dans la vie d'Antoine", in Basilius Steidle (ed.), *Antonius Magnus Eremita 356–1956: Studia ad Antiquum Monachismum Spectantia*. Studia Anselmiana 38 (Rome: Herder, 1956), 136–147.

DeVore, David, "Genre and Eusebius' *Ecclesiastical History*: Prolegomena for a Focused Debate", in Aaron Johnson and Jeremy Schott (eds.), *Eusebius of Caesarea: Traditions and Innovations* (Cambridge MA: Harvard University Press, 2013), 19–45.

Dörries, Hermann, *Die Vita Antonii als Geschichtsquelle*. Nachrichten der Akademie der Wissenschaften in Göttingen 14 (Göttingen: Vandenhoeck und Ruprecht, 1949).

Dörries, Hermann, *Wort und Stunde*. vol. 1: *Gesammelte Studien zur Kirchengeschichte des vierten Jahrhunderts* (Göttingen: Vandenhoeck und Ruprecht, 1966).

Draguet, René, *La vie primitive de S. Antoine conservée en syriaque*. 2 vols. Corpus Scriptorum Christianorum Orientalium 417–418 (Leuven: Peeters, 1980).

Drake, Hal, *A Century of Miracles: Christians, Pagans, Jews, and the Supernatural, 312–410* (Oxford/New York: Oxford University Press, 2017).

Endsjø, Dag Ø., '"The Truth is Out There": Primordial Lore and Ignorance in the Wilderness of Athanasius' *Vita Antonii*', in Laura Feldt (ed.), *Wilderness in Mythology and Religion: Approaching Religious Spatialities, Cosmologies, and Ideas of Wild Nature* (Berlin: De Gruyter, 2012), 113–129.

Festugière, André-Jean, "Sur une nouvelle edition du *De Vita Pythagorica* de Jamblique", *REG* 50 (1937), 470–494.

Gemeinhardt, Peter, "*Vita Antonii* oder *Passio Antonii*? Biographisches Genre und martyrologische Topik in der ersten Asketenvita", in Gemeinhardt and Leemans, *Christian Martyrdom in Late Antiquity*, 79–114.

Gemeinhardt, Peter, *Athanasius: Vita Antonii—Leben des Antonius*. Fontes Christiani (Freiburg: Herder, 2018).

Hadot, Pierre, *Philosophy as a Way of Life: Spiritual Exercises from Socrates to Foucault* (Oxford: Blackwell, 1995).

Hägg, Tomas, "The *Life of St Antony* between Biography and Hagiography", in Stephanos Efthymiadis (ed.), *Ashgate Research Companion to Byzantine Hagiography*. vol. 1 (Farnham: Ashgate, 2011), 17–34.

Hägg, Tomas, *The Art of Biography* (Cambridge: Cambridge University Press, 2012).

Hall, Stuart G., "The Use of Earlier Eusebian Material in the *Vita Constantini*, 1.58–59", *Studia Patristica* 24 (1993), 96–101.

Hall, Stuart G., "Eusebian and Other Sources in the Vita Constantini, I", in Hanns C. Brennecke, Ernst L. Grasmück, and Christoph Markschies (eds.), *Logos: Festschrift für Luise Abramowski*. Beihefte zur Zeitschrift für die neutestamentliche Wissenschaft und die Kunde der älteren Kirche. Band 67 (Berlin: De Gruyter, 1993), 239–263.

Holl, Karl, "Die schriftstellerische Form des griechischen Heiligenlebens", *Neue Jahrbücher für die klassische Altertumswissenschaft* 15 (1912), 406–427.

Holl, Karl, *Gesammelte Aufsätze zur Kirchengeschichte. II. Der Osten* (Tübingen: J.C.B. Mohr, 1928), 249–269.

Hoster, Dieter, "Die Form der frühesten lateinischen Heiligenviten von der *Vita Cypriani* bis zur *Vita Ambrosii*". Ph.D. diss., Cologne (1963).

Inowlocki, Sabrina, "Eusebius of Caesarea's 'Interpretatio Christiana' of Philo's *De vita contemplativa*", *HThR* 97.3 (2004), 305–328.

Johnson, Aaron P., *Eusebius*. Understanding Classics (London: I.B. Taurus, 2014).

Lardet, Pierre, (ed.), *Saint Jerome, Apologie contre Rufin*. Sources chrétiennes 303 (Paris: Les Éditions du Cerf, 1983).

List, Johann, *Das Antonius-Leben des Hl. Athanasius des Grossen. Eine literarhistorische Studie zu den Anfängen der byzantinischen Hagiographie* (Athens: P.D. Sakellarios, 1931).

Lorenz, Rudolf, "Die griechische Vita Antonii und ihre syrische Fassung", *ZKG* 100 (1989), 77–84.

Louth, Andrew, "St. Athanasius and the Greek *Life of Antony*", *JThS* 39 (1988), 504–509.

Luibhéid, Colm, "Antony and the Renunciation of Society", *Irish Theological Quarterly* 52.4 (1986), 304–314.

Mertel, Hans, "Die biographische Form der griechischen Heiligenlegenden", Ph.D. diss., München (1909).

Momigliano, Arnaldo, "Pagan and Christian Historiography in the Fourth Century A.D.", in Arnaldo Momigliano (ed.), *The Conflict Between Paganism and Christianity in the Fourth Century* (Oxford: Clarendon Press, 1963), 79–99.

Monaci Castagno, Adele, "Le trasformazioni del discorso agiografico da Eusebio a Atanasio", *AnnSE* 23 (2006), 45–65.

Penland, Elizabeth C., "Martyrs as Philosophers: The School of Pamphilus and Ascetic Tradition in Eusebius's 'Martyrs of Palestine'", Ph.D. diss., Yale (2010).

Penland, Elizabeth C., "Eusebius Philosophus?", in Sabrina Inowlocki and Claudio Zamagni (eds.), *Reconsidering Eusebius: Collected Essays on Literary, Historical and Theological Issues*. Vigiliae Christianae Supplements 107 (Leiden/Boston: Brill, 2011), 87–97.

Priessnig, Anton, "Die biographischen Formen der griechischen Heiligenlegenden in ihrer geschichtlichen Entwicklung". Ph.D. diss., Munich (1924).

Priessnig, Anton, "Die literarische Form der spätantiken Philosophenromane", *ByzZ* 30 (1930), 23–30.

Priessnig, Anton, "Die biographische Form der Plotinvita des Porphyrios und das Antoniosleben des Athanasios", *ByzZ* 64 (1971), 1–5.

Reitzenstein, Richard, *Des Athanasius Werk über das Leben des Antonius. Ein philologischer Beitrag zur Geschichte des Mönchtums*. Sitzungsberichte der Heidelberger Akadamie der Wissenschaften, vol. 5 (Heidelberg: Carl Winter Universitätsbuchhandlung, 1914).

Rubenson, Samuel, *The Letters of St. Antony: Origenist Theology, Monastic Tradition and the Making of a Saint*. Bibliotheca Historico-Ecclesiastica Lundensis 24 (Lund: Lund University Press, 1990).

Rubenson, Samuel, "Philosophy and Simplicity: The Problem of Classical Education in Early Christian Biography", in Hägg and Rousseau, *Greek Biography and Panegyric*, 110–139.

Rubenson, Samuel, "Anthony and Pythagoras: A Reappraisal of the Appropriation of Classical Biography in Athanasius' Vita Antonii", in Anders-Christian Jacobsen, David Brakke, and Jörg Ulrich (eds.), *Beyond Reception: Mutual Influences between Antique Religion, Judaism and Early Christianity*. Early Christianity in the Context of Antiquity (Frankfurt am Main: P. Lang, 2006), 191–208.

Rubenson, Samuel, "Apologetics of Asceticism: The *Life of Antony* and Its Political Context", in Blake Leyerle and Robin Darling Young (eds.), *Ascetic Culture: Essays in Honor of Philip Rousseau* (Notre Dame, IN: University of Notre Dame Press, 2013), 75–96.

Schaff, Philip and Wace, Henry, (eds.), *Nicene and Post-Nicene Fathers*, Second Series, vol. 3. (Buffalo, NY: The Christian Literature Company, 1892).

Schneemelcher, Wilhelm, "Das Kreuz Christi und die Dämonen. Bemerkungen zur Vita Antonii des Athanasius", in Ernst Dassmann and Karl S. Frank (eds.), *Pietas.*

Festschrift für Bernhard Kotting. Jahrbuch für Antike und Christentum, Ergänzungsband 8 (Münster: Aschendorff, 1980), 381–392.

Tetz, Martin, "Athanasius und die *Vita Antonii*. Literarische und theologische Relationen", *ZNTW* 73 (1982), 1–30.

Urbano, Arthur P., "'Read It Also to the Gentiles': The Displacement and Recasting of the Philosopher in the *Vita Antonii*", *Church History* 77.4 (2008), 877–914.

Urbano, Arthur P., *The Philosophical Life: Biography and the Crafting of Intellectual Identity in Late Antiquity*. Patristic Monograph Series 21 (Washington DC: The Catholic University of America Press, 2013).

Van Uytfanghe, Marc, "L'hagiographie: un 'genre' chrétien ou antique tardif?", *AB* 111 (1993), 135–188.

Verheyden, Joseph, "Pain and Glory: Some Introductory Comments on the Rhetorical Qualities and Potential of the *Martyrs of Palestine* by Eusebius of Caesarea", in Johan Leemans (ed.), *Martyrdom and Persecution in Late Ancient Christianity: Festschrift Boudewijn Dehandschutter*. Bibliotheca Ephemeridum Theologicarum Lovaniensium 241 (Leuven: Peeters, 2010), 353–392.

Vivian, Tim, and Apostolos N. Athanassakis (trans.), *Athanasius of Alexandria, The Life of Antony: The Coptic Life and the Greek Life*. Cistercian Studies Series 202 (Kalamazoo, MI: Cistercian Publications, 2003).

Watts, Edward, *City and School in Late Antique Athens and Alexandria*. Transformation of the Classical Heritage (Berkeley: University of California Press, 2008).

Watts, Edward, "Three Generations of Christian Philosophical Biography", in Scott McGill, Cristiana Sogno, and Edward Watts (eds.), *The Roman Empire from the Tetrarchs to the Theodosians: Later Roman History and Culture 284–450 CE*. Yale Classical Studies 34 (Cambridge: Cambridge University Press, 2010), 117–133.

Williams, Michael Stuart, *Authorised Lives in Early Christian Biography. Between Eusebius and Augustine* (Cambridge: Cambridge University Press, 2008).

Williams, Rowan, *Arius: Heresy and Tradition* (London: Darton, Longman, and Todd, 1987).

CHAPTER 2

The Hagiographer as Holy Fool? Fictionality in Saints' Lives

Julie Van Pelt

He played all sorts of roles foolish and indecent, but language is not sufficient to paint a portrait of his doings. For sometimes he pretended to have a limp, sometimes he jumped around, sometimes he dragged himself along on his buttocks, sometimes he stuck out his foot for someone running and tripped him. Other times when there was a new moon, he looked at the sky and fell down and thrashed about. Sometimes also he pretended to babble, for he said that of all semblances, this one is most fitting and most useful to those who simulate folly for the sake of Christ. For this reason, often he reproved and restrained sins, and he sent divine wrath to someone to correct him, and he made predictions and did everything he wanted, only he changed his voice and (the position of) his limbs completely. And in all that he did, they believed that he was just like the many who babbled and prophesied because of demons.[1]

1 Πάντα δὲ διὰ σχημάτων σαλῶν καὶ ἀσχήμων ἐποίει, ἀλλ' οὐ δύναται ὁ λόγος τὴν τῶν πραγμάτων εἰκόνα ὑποδεῖξαι. ἦν γὰρ ποιῶν ἑαυτὸν ποτὲ μὲν κοξαρίζοντα, ποτὲ δὲ πηδῶντα, ποτὲ δὲ συρόμενον εἰς τὰ καθίσματα, ποτὲ δὲ βάλλοντα πόδα τινὶ τρέχοντι καὶ ῥίπτονα αὐτόν. πάλιν δὲ κατὰ τὴν τῆς σελήνης γένναν ἐποίει ἑαυτὸν εἰς τὸν οὐρανὸν θεωροῦντα καὶ πίπτοντα καὶ λακταρίζοντα. ἔστιν δὲ ὅτε καὶ τὸν διαλαλοῦντα προσεποιεῖτο. ἔλεγεν γὰρ πλεῖον ὅλων τῶν σχημάτων ἁρμόζειν καὶ συμβάλλεσθαι τὸ τοιοῦτον σχῆμα τοῖς προσποιουμένοις μωρίαν διὰ Χριστόν. διὰ τούτου γὰρ πολλάκις καὶ ἤλεγχεν καὶ ἀνέκοπτεν ἁμαρτίας καὶ ὀργήν τινι πρὸς διόρθωσιν ἔπεμπεν καὶ προέλεγέν τινα καὶ ὅσα ἤθελεν ἐποίει, μόνον δὲ ὅτι τὴν ἑαυτοῦ φωνὴν καὶ τὰ μέλη ἐξήλλασσεν. Καὶ ὅσαπερ ἂν ἐποίει, εἶχον αὐτὸν ὥσπερ τοὺς πολλοὺς τοὺς ἐκ δαιμόνων διαλαλοῦντας καὶ προφητεύοντας (*Life of Symeon* 89.19–90.4). For the *Life of Symeon*, I cite the edition by André Jean Festugière, *Léontios de Neapolis. Vie de Syméon le Fou et Vie de Jean de Chypre* (Paris: Librairie orientaliste Paul Geuthner, 1974). References to this edition will consist of the page in Festugière's volume followed by the number(s) of the line(s). All translations from the *Life of Symeon* are taken from Derek Krueger, *Symeon the Holy Fool: Leontius' Life and the Late Antique City* (Berkeley/Los Angeles/London: University of California Press, 1996). For the *Life of Andrew*, I cite the edition and translation by Lennart Rydén, *The Life of St Andrew the Fool Vol. II, Text, Translation and Notes*, Acta Universatis Upsaliensis, Studia Byzantina Upsaliensa 4 (Uppsala: Textgruppen i Uppsala AB, 1995). References to the text or the translation will consist of the number(s) of the line(s) in Rydén's volume.

 DOI:10.1163/9789004421332_004

A hagiographer can be described in the most basic terms as a person who writes hagiography, as the author of a hagiographical work.[2] Even if we cannot establish his (or her)[3] historical identity, every hagiographical document implies through its mere existence a hagiographer-figure who composed the text. If the composition of a hagiographical text is the task that defines the hagiographer, then it is our goal to understand this task, in all its complexities.

Scholars have shed light on different aspects of the hagiographer's task, although in general, the focus has been on the saints themselves more than on their hagiographers.[4] An important aspect that has been highlighted by Derek Krueger is the ascetic dimension of writing hagiography.[5] His study shows that late antique and early Byzantine models of authorship conceive of literary composition as a religious activity which involves the practice of humility and religious self-fashioning. Consequently, the hagiographer aligns himself with his literary subject, the saint.

In addition, Martin Hinterberger has shed further light on the literary dimension of the hagiographer and his task by pointing out that hagiographers tend to present themselves in close connection to the saint, even if this requires a serious distortion of the historical framework of the story.[6] His observations point towards a related aspect of the hagiographer's literary task that has not yet reached its full potential as an object of modern study, namely the fact that the hagiographer often writes a *fictionalised* account.[7] Indeed, it is well known that *Lives* of Saints can hardly be seen as reliable, historically accurate accounts

2 Among the many various subgenres that hagiography comprises, this chapter, when speaking about 'the hagiographer', refers primarily to authors of saints' *Lives*.

3 Although often the subject of hagiographical accounts themselves, women seldom appear to have been writers of hagiography; see Martin Hinterberger, "The Byzantine Hagiographer and his Text", in Stephanos Efthymiadis (ed.), *The Ashgate Research Companion to Byzantine Hagiography*, vol. 2 (Farnham: Ashgate, 2014), 211–246 at 215. For reasons of convenience, I will refer to the hagiographer as masculine in the rest of this chapter.

4 This is also noted by Hinterberger, "The Byzantine Hagiographer and his Text", 211. His chapter is useful starting point for any study on the figure of the hagiographer.

5 Derek Krueger, *Writing and Holiness: The Practice of Authorship in the Early Christian East* (Philadelphia: University of Pennsylvania Press, 2004). See also the chapter by Yuzwa in the present volume where it is suggested that the practice of rewriting and rereading of hagiography is itself salvific.

6 Hinterberger, "The Byzantine Hagiographer and his Text", 213–214.

7 'Fictionalised' is used in this chapter with the meaning of 'containing fictive elements'. See below, 69–71, for a theoretical discussion on the use of the terms fiction, fictionality, and fictionalisation.

of the conducts of a holy man.[8] Nevertheless, even if these biographies of presumed historical figures are full of invented elements,[9] their narrators generally claim to tell the truth and, as Peter Turner shows, go to great lengths to convince their audiences of the truthfulness of their writings.[10] As a result of this apparent contradiction, hagiography cannot easily be categorised according to the labels of fiction and nonfiction, inherent to a modern understanding of literature.[11] This difficulty has led scholars who focus on the question of historical accuracy and treat the *Acts* of Martyrs and the *Lives* of Saints as historical sources to discard many hagiographical texts due to their 'legendary' character.[12] And even if hagiography has now become the object of literary investigation,[13] which embraces rather than dismisses its fictionalised charac-

---

8 See for example Hippolyte Delehaye, *Les légendes hagiographiques* (4th edition Brussels: Société des Bollandistes, 1955), and Timothy D. Barnes, *Early Christian Hagiography and Roman History* (Tübingen: Mohr Siebeck, 2010).

9 Sometimes even the saint him-/herself is an invented character. This is the case for the *Life of Andrew*, as we will see later in this chapter. For a discussion on Leontius of Neapolis' literary creativity in writing the *Life of Symeon*, see Paul Magdalino, "'What We Heard in the Lives of Saints We Have Seen with Our Own Eyes': The Holy Man as Literary Text in Tenth-Century Constantinople", in James Howard-Johnston and Paul A. Hayward (eds.), *The Cult of Saints in Late Antiquity and the Middle Ages: Essays on the Contribution of Peter Brown* (Oxford: Oxford University Press, 1999), 83–112 at 84–85, who looks at the impact of the acknowledgement of the fictionalised nature of hagiography on a study of the holy man (rather than on the hagiographer, who is the focus of this chapter).

10 Peter Turner, *Truthfulness, Realism, Historicity: A Study of Late Antique Spiritual Literature* (Farnham: Ashgate, 2012) discusses different literary techniques hagiographers employ to convince their readers of the truthfulness of their accounts. As such, he emphasises the realistic stance of hagiography and discloses what he calls 'hagiographical realism'.

11 In this respect, the recent chapter by Koen De Temmerman on fictionality in ancient biography is useful, since it deals with similar questions ("Ancient Biography and Formalities of Fiction", in Koen De Temmerman and Kristoffel Demoen (eds.), *Writing Biography in Greece and Rome: Narrative Technique and Fictionalization* (Cambridge: Cambridge University Press, 2016), 3–25).

12 Exemplary are the studies by René Aigrain, *L'hagiographie: ses sources, ses méthodes, son histoire* (Brussels: Société des Bollandistes, 1953), and Hippolyte Delehaye, *Les passions des martyrs et les genres littéraires* (Brussels: Société des Bollandistes, 1966), as well as Herbert Musurillo, *The Acts of the Christian Martyrs* (Oxford: Clarendon Press, 1972), which contains editions of only twenty-eight texts out of hundreds of possible candidates, based on criteria of historicity.

13 Already in the 1980s, Alison G. Elliott devoted careful attention to the narrative construction of late antique saints' *Lives* in her *Roads to Paradise, Reading the Lives of the Early Saints* (London: University Press of New England, 1987). More and more scholars have picked up a literary approach to hagiography ever since, studying these texts as creative pieces of literature, the need for which has been voiced eloquently by Lennart Rydén in his chapter on "Literariness in Byzantine Saints' Lives", in Paolo Odorico and Panagiotis

ter, only very recently have scholars started to pay particular attention to the fictionality of hagiography as an object of investigation in itself, trying to voice and resolve the theoretical difficulties that are tied up with it.[14]

How can we, as a modern audience, understand the hagiographer and his puzzling task of writing hagiography, which involves practising at once holiness and fictionalisation? As its title suggests, in this chapter I would like to make a comparison between the hagiographer (meant as a generic concept rather than a concrete individual)[15] and a particular type of saint, the holy fool. This comparison is inspired by Stavroula Constantinou's reference to 'masked authors' in her chapter on the holy fool and the cross-dresser as 'actors' and 'actresses'.[16] I believe there is some mileage in pursuing the analogy between the masked fool and the author of hagiography further, since, perhaps not by their concrete actions, but rather by the intended results of those actions, the hagiographer and the fool are not entirely dissimilar to one another. In other words, an understanding of the character of the holy fool can help a modern

A. Agapitos (eds.), *Les Vies des saints à Byzance. Genre littéraire ou biographie historique? Actes du IIe colloque international philologique 'ΕΡΜΗΝΕΙΑ'* (Paris: Centre d'études byzantines, néo-helléniques et sud-est européennes, EHESS, 2004), 49–58.

14 Turner, *Truthfulness, Realism, Historicity*, made an important contribution in this respect: even though his study approaches the problem of fictionality from the opposite direction, namely as a problem of historicity, his examination of what truthfulness and realism actually meant in a late antique Christian context is revealing for the dynamics on a literary level. A recent chapter by Charis Messis on the phenomenon of 'novelisation' in hagiography also constitutes a step towards a better understanding of the problem of its fictionality: "Fiction and/or Novelisation in Byzantine Hagiography", in Efthymiadis (ed.), *Ashgate Research Companion*, vol. 2, 313–342. Finally, it is worth mentioning the volume edited by Panagiotis Roilos, *Medieval Greek Storytelling: Fictionality and Narrative in Byzantium* (Wiesbaden: Harrassowitz, 2014), which also includes discussions of late antique hagiographical material.

15 It should be clear by now that the 'hagiographer' with which this chapter is concerned, does not coincide with the extra-textual, historical author. Nor does he fully coincide with the primary narrator, as this depends on the particular narrative situation which differs from text to text. Rather, I use 'hagiographer' as an overarching term to refer to what can be called the 'implied author' (Wolf Schmid, "Implied Author", in Jan C. Meister (ed.), *The Living Handbook of Narratology* (Hamburg: Hamburg University, 2013), http://www.lhn.uni-hamburg.de/article/implied-author-revised-version-uploaded-26-january-2013 [last accessed 07/05/2018]). On the complex constellation of the historical author, implied author, and primary narrator in Byzantine hagiography, see Lennart Rydén, "Fiction and Reality in the Hagiographer's Self-Presentation", *TM* 14 (2002), 547–552, and Hinterberger, "The Byzantine Hagiographer and his Text", 212–215 (and esp. n. 5).

16 Stavroula Constantinou, "Holy Actors and Actresses: Fools and Cross-Dressers as the Protagonists of Saints' Lives", in Efthymiadis, *Ashgate Research Companion*, vol. 2, 343–362 at 356–357.

audience to acquire a better understanding of the hagiographer's task and his relation with his readership, at least with regard to one particular dimension, namely the paradoxical meeting point of fictionalisation and truth.

1 Preliminary Observations

The term 'holy fool' or 'σαλὸς διὰ Χριστόν' ('fool for Christ's sake') refers to a particular type of saint and a specific literary character type in Byzantine hagiography that remained popular from its early stages until the current day.[17] The most famous ones are probably Symeon Salos and Andrew Salos, but their stories are part of a broad religious and literary tradition of holy folly in late antiquity and beyond.[18] Vincent Déroche disentangled the history of the figure of the *salos* as the simultaneous development of two types: the active and the passive *salos*.[19] While the passive *salos* lives quietly in a monastic community and pretends to be mad as a means of reaching the virtuous state of *apatheia* ('insensibility') while avoiding worldly praise of his/her fellow monks,[20] the active *salos* usually obtains *apatheia* while living a solitary life in the desert, and then returns to the world to mock it. The goal of his feigned madness is not just to mask his own virtue, but to act on his urban environment and to save souls.[21]

My comparison between the hagiographer and the holy fool is concerned with the second type, the active *salos*. Symeon of Emesa is the prime example of this type of holy folly, but apart from his *Life*, written by Leontius of Neapo-

17 Constantinou, "Holy Actors", 343–345.

18 Lennart Rydén provides a nice overview of the type of the holy fool in Greek hagiography: "The Holy Fool", in Sergei Hackel (ed.), *The Byzantine Saint* (London: Fellowship of St. Alban and St. Sergius, 1981), 106–113. Krueger traces the shared context of stories of holy folly and concealed sanctity in late antique and early Byzantine culture (*Symeon the Holy Fool*, ch. 4).

19 This distinction corresponds to the geographical opposition between Syria and Egypt and the religious opposition between eremitism and coenobitism; see Vincent Déroche, *Études sur Léontios de Néapolis*. Acta Universitatis Upsaliensis, Studia Byzantina Upsaliensa 3 (Uppsala: Textgruppen i Uppsala AB, 1995), 177. On this distinction, see also José Grosdidier de Matons, "Les thèmes d'édification dans la vie d'André Salos", *TM* 4 (1970), 277–328.

20 A famous example is the anonymous nun in Palladius' *Lausiac History* (34, 1).

21 Déroche, *Études sur Léontios de Néapolis*, 176: 'La différence avec le type précédent tient à l'utilisation de la folie feinte: au lieu d'être un simple moyen de masquer sa vertu et de progresser dans l'humiliation, la folie provocante peut aussi être un moyen d'agir sur le monde et de sauver des âmes.'

lis in the seventh century (BHG 1677), two other texts deal with a holy fool of his kind: the *Life of Paul the Corinthian* (BHG 2362) and the *Life of Andrew Salos* (BHG 115z), written by a certain Nikephoros, most likely in the tenth century.[22] Since the *Life of Paul* has not been transmitted in full,[23] this chapter will focus on the *Lives* of Symeon and Andrew.

Both Symeon and Andrew spend a lifetime pretending to be mad; while hiding their true identities as holy men and displaying subversive behaviour, they edify the people of the city. They eat insatiably, deal with base women, pretend to be drunk, walk around naked, and relieve themselves publicly, but they also perform miracles. More importantly, their narratives address questions concerning truth, falsehood, belief, and deception. On the one hand, the image of holy folly can serve as a metaphor for the task of the hagiographer in general: just like the holy fool edifies the people in the city by putting on a theatrical show, the hagiographer conveys a religious truth by writing a fictionalised narrative. On the other hand, the *Lives* of Symeon and Andrew may serve as concrete case studies for exploring this particular metaphorical connection. As we will see, the paradox that is involved in writing the story of a holy fool (how was the hagiographer able to write the story of a *secret* saint?), forces the hagiographer into employing all kinds of strategies to ensure his authority, aligning him with his saintly subject in unexpected ways.[24]

I would like to emphasise that holy folly as a metaphor for the hagiographer's task does not derive from contemporary evidence: in other words, I do not claim that Byzantines saw hagiographers as holy fools. The value of comparing the two lies in the fact that it allows us to circumvent the modern bias of a rigid distinction between fiction and nonfiction when thinking about the problem of fictionality in saints' *Lives*; it allows us to imagine it in a narrative language belonging to the hagiographical realm itself. At the same time, as modern read-

22 The author presents himself as Nikephoros in the epilogue of his text. However, the historical identity of the author is not certain. On the author of the *Life of Andrew*, see Lennart Rydén, *The Life of St Andrew the Fool Vol. 1, Introduction, Testimonies and Nachleben*. Acta Universatis Upsaliensis, Studia Byzantina Upsaliensa 4 (Uppsala: Textgruppen i Uppsala AB, 1995), 57. On the date of the *Life*, see Lennart Rydén, "Date of the 'Life of Andreas Salos'", *DOP* 32 (1978), 127–155.

23 On the *Life of Paul* and its textual tradition, see Sergei Ivanov, "St Paul the Corinthian, Holy Fool", in E. Kountoura-Galake (ed.), *The Heroes of the Orthodox Church. The New Saints, 8th–16th C.* (Athens: Institute for Byzantine Research, 2004), 39–46.

24 I cautiously hypothesise that what will be argued for the *Lives* of Symeon and Andrew and their hagiographers holds general significance for the writing of saints' *Lives* and applies to 'the hagiographer' in the broader sense. To fully support this claim, I would like to extend this study by testing the validity of the analogy on a larger corpus of *Lives* in a later stage of research.

ers, we can never entirely shake off these categories and the mental concepts they are tied up with. In fact, it will be helpful to attempt to define what scholars understand nowadays by 'fiction' and 'nonfiction', before venturing into the world of hagiography.

The past decades have produced an abundance of literature on theories of fiction, in which different approaches have generated different definitions of the notions of fiction, nonfiction, and their relation to other theoretical concepts such as fictionality, fictiveness, and fictionalisation.[25] However, bearing in mind the difficulties of applying the modern framework of fiction and nonfiction to hagiography, I would like to focus on ideas that are well suited to be transferred to the world of ancient, late antique, and early medieval literature because they allow a broad understanding of these concepts. In this respect, Marie-Laure Ryan's 1997 article "Postmodernism and the Doctrine of Panfictionality" is extremely useful, where she defines fiction and nonfiction in terms of specific sets of game rules.[26]

According to Ryan, the rules of nonfiction 'specify that the text is to be evaluated in terms of truth'.[27] As a result, the text enters into a polemical relation with other representations that share the same frame of reference, which is the real world in which we live.[28] By contrast, the rules of fiction specify that the

25 Most influential are speech act theory (John Langshaw Austin, *How to Do Things with Words* (2nd edition Cambridge, MA: Harvard University Press, 1975), and John Searle, *Speech Acts: An Essay in the Philosophy of Language* (Cambridge: Cambridge University Press, 1969)), fictional worlds theory (Thomas Pavel, *Fictional Worlds* (Cambridge, MA: Harvard University Press, 1986), and Marie-Laure Ryan, "Possible Worlds in Recent Literary Theory", *Style* 26.4 (1992), 528–554), fiction as make-believe (Kendall Walton, *Mimesis as Make-believe. On the Foundations of the Representational Arts* (2nd edition Cambridge, MA: Harvard University Press, 1990)) and fiction(ality) as rhetoric (Wayne Booth, *The Rhetoric of Fiction* (2nd edition Chicago/London: University of Chicago Press, 1983), and Richard Walsh, *The Rhetoric of Fictionality. Narrative Theory and the Idea of Fiction* (Columbus: Ohio State University Press, 2007)).

26 Four years earlier, John Morgan already talked about fiction in terms of game rules in his contribution on the fictionality of the ancient Greek novel: "Make-Believe and Make Believe: The Fictionality of the Greek Novels", in Christopher Gill and Timothy P. Wiseman (eds.), *Lies and Fiction in the Ancient World* (Exeter: University of Exeter Press, 1993), 175–229 at 186, 194, and 210. Although he does not pursue an actual theory of fiction based on the notion of game rules, he shows that the idea is suitable to be applied to pre-modern literature. The idea of fiction as a game goes back to Walton's famous study, *Mimesis as Make-believe*.

27 Marie-Laure Ryan, "Postmodernism and the Doctrine of Panfictionality", *Narrative* 5.2 (1997), 165–187 at 166.

28 On theory of frames of reference, see also Benjamin Harshaw, "Fictionality and Fields of Reference. Remarks on a Theoretical Framework", *Poetics Today* 5.2 (1984), 227–251.

text 'makes no claim to external truth but rather guarantees its own truth'.[29] This truth is called the 'fictional truth'; it is only truth within the unique fictional world generated by the text that functions as its frame of reference.[30] This unique fictional world of reference can, to a certain degree, present overlap with the real world in which we live. Thus, reading fiction is 'a form of double-think, a game of truth ... in which the ordinary rules of truth and falsehood are both simulated and suspended'.[31]

Defining fiction and nonfiction as a set of game rules has advantages. For instance, it acknowledges that fiction and nonfiction are not ontological categories; that a novel, for example, is not inherently fictional, but is *regarded* as such and read as such, because both author and reader approach it according to the same game rules (i.e. those of fiction, described above).[32] However, this means also that it is perfectly possible that one person would place a certain book in the nonfiction-section of a library, while another person would place the same book in the fiction-section. The problem with hagiography is precisely that we do not know on what shelf the *Life of Symeon*, for instance, was thought to belong.

Finally, scholars have made an important distinction, one that I would like to adopt, pointing out that the term 'fiction' can in fact be employed to refer to two different things: that which is 'fictitious' or 'fictive' (i.e. which is not true, a lie), and that which is 'fictional' (i.e. which, in line with Ryan's definition of fiction, is not susceptible to truth-judgement, such as a modern novel).[33] The former use of 'fiction' is the one at work in studies like those by Hippolyte Delehaye and Timothy Barnes,[34] who are concerned with finding out to what extent a

---

29 Ryan, "Postmodernism and the Doctrine of Panfictionality", 167.

30 Cf. Dorrit Cohn, *The Distinction of Fiction* (Baltimore/London: John Hopkins University Press, 1999), 13: 'A work of fiction itself creates the world to which it refers by referring to it.'

31 Michael Wood, "Prologue", in Gill and Wiseman, *Lies and Fiction*, xiii–xviii at xvi.

32 The idea that the fictional status of a text relies on a mutual awareness of both author and reader that what is written is outside of truth-judgement is expressed by many critics. Examples are Walsh, *The Rhetoric of Fictionality*, 36; Morgan, "Make-Believe", 180; and Northrop Frye, *The Secular Scripture. A Study of the Structure of Romance* (Cambridge, MA/London: Harvard University Press, 1976), 17. The same idea is evoked by the concept of fiction as a communicative contract between author and (implied) reader, put forward, among others, by Stein Haugom Olsen and Peter Lamarque, *Truth, Fiction, and Literature: A Philosophical Perspective* (2nd edition Oxford: Clarendon Press, 1996).

33 On this distinction see Calin Andrei Mihailescu and Walid Hamarneh, "Introduction: Under the Jealous Gaze of Truth", in iidem (eds.), *Fiction Updated. Theories of Fictionality, Narratology, and Poetics* (Toronto/Buffalo: University of Toronto Press, 1996), 3–18 at 8; Cohn, *The Distinction of Fiction*, 3; Jean-Marie Schaeffer, *Pourquoi la fiction?* (Paris: Seuil, 1999); and De Temmerman, "Ancient Biography and Formalities of Fiction", 5.

34 Cf. n. 8.

hagiography is historically reliable. However, if hagiographies are to a certain extent 'fictions' in the sense of 'not historically accurate' (i.e. the first meaning of fiction described above), but at the same time engage in claims of truthfulness, and if we take these claims seriously (as Turner suggests we should),[35] then they are not to be straightforwardly identified with 'fiction' in the second sense of the term. As a result, we must distinguish 'fiction' from 'fictionality' and 'fictionalisation'.[36] While fictionality refers to the use of make-believe, fictionalisation refers to the hagiographer's deliberate shaping of the narrative according to criteria other than historicity, his literary fashioning. The point is that these do not automatically turn the whole narrative into literary 'fiction' as defined by Ryan; they do not necessarily place it outside of truth-judgement.

The rest of this chapter will further tease out the analogy between the holy fool and the hagiographer. First, using the metaphor of the fool's mask, I look at the way the hagiographer presents himself (with a particular focus on the more covert strategies of authentication which hagiographers could employ in addition to explicit truth claims). Second, I examine how the fool's/hagiographer's self-presentation reflects upon the expected relation with his audience. Comparing the performance of the fool in the city with the literary performance of the hagiographer will hopefully help to make sense of the 'contract' between the hagiographer and his readership that is promoted by his text, of the rules that govern its game.

2 The Mask of the Holy Fool/Hagiographer

> And wanting him to refresh his body, John said to him playfully, 'Come take a bath, Fool!' And Symeon said to him, laughing, 'Yes, let's go, let's go!' And with these words, he stripped off his garment and placed it on his head, wrapping it around like a turban. And Deacon John said to him, 'Put it back on, brother, for truly if you are going to walk around naked, I won't go with you.' Abba Symeon said to him, 'Go away, idiot, I'm all ready. If you won't come, see, I'll go a little ahead of you.' And leaving him, he kept a little ahead.[37]

35 Turner, *Truthfulness*, 43.

36 Simona Zetterberg Gjerlevsen and Henrik Skov Nielsen defend this view in a forthcoming chapter in the *Narratologia* series entitled "Distinguishing Fictionality".

37 … βουληθεὶς ὡς ἐν τάξει παιγνιδίου ἀνακτήσασθαι αὐτοῦ τὸ σῶμα λέγει αὐτῷ· 'ἔρχῃ λούῃ, Σαλέ;' λέγει αὐτῷ ἐκεῖνος γελῶν· 'ναί, ἄγωμεν ἄγωμεν' καὶ σὺν τῷ λόγῳ ἀποδύεται τὸ ἱμάτιον αὐτοῦ καὶ ἐπιτίθει αὐτὸ εἰς τὴν κεφαλὴν αὐτοῦ δήσας αὐτὸ εἰς αὐτὴν ὡς φακιόλιν. καὶ λέγει αὐτῷ ὁ

As is illustrated in this passage, during his act of pretended folly Symeon makes sure to dress in the appropriate costume (or should we say 'undress'?). Stavroula Constantinou discusses 'the mask of the holy fool', behind which he hides his true identity.[38] The mask or the disguise of the holy man consists of few clothes: it is his nakedness in particular which marks his position of fool.[39] Constantinou points out that the mask of the saint is more than just a means to hide his identity: 'costume serves a twofold function: it directs the wearer's actions, and it generates a specific set of expectations.'[40] Thus, the nakedness of the saint is part of his public spectacle and contributes to the construction of his reputation as a madman. Besides the mask of nudity, Symeon adopts other costumes as well. When entering the city of Emesa, he binds the corpse of a dead dog to his belt and drags it along.[41] Apart from the symbolic significance of the deed,[42] this very first act of foolishness turns out to be extremely effective in portraying an image and creating a first impression: once the schoolchildren see him running around like this, they immediately start calling him a 'crazy abba'.[43] Thus, the so-called 'mask of foolishness'[44] that is adopted by the holy fool turns out to be a theatrical costume, crucial to the success of his performance in the city.

The hagiographer, like the holy fool, also hides behind a mask in his writing in order to provoke a specific set of expectations in his audience. As Constantinou observes, often 'hagiographers hide their real identities and intentions

κύρις Ἰωάννης· 'φόρεσον, ἀδελφέ, ἐπεὶ ὄντως ἐὰν γυμνὸς περιπατεῖς, ἐγὼ μετὰ σοῦ οὐκ ἔρχομαι'. λέγει αὐτῷ ὁ ἀββᾶς Συμεών· 'ὕπαγε, ἔξηχε, ἐγὼ ἔργον πρὸ ἔργου ἐποίησα. εἰ δὲ οὐκ ἔρχῃ, ἴδε ἐγὼ προλαμβάνω σε μικρόν.' καὶ ἀφεὶς αὐτὸν προεποίησεν ὀλίγον (*Life of Symeon* 82.24–83.3).

38 Constantinou, "Holy Actors", 348–352.

39 Symeon appears naked in lines 82.27 (cf. the passage quoted above) and 90.18–19. Andrew appears to walk around nearly naked the whole time due to extreme poverty, as becomes clear from the passage about the severe winter storm (lines 422–442). His nakedness is explicitly mentioned in lines 86, 276, 332, 1039, and 1452.

40 Constantinou, "Holy Actors", 349.

41 *Life of Symeon* 79.19–25.

42 The dragging of the dead dog has been interpreted as a symbolic act by Constantinou, "Holy Actors", 351, and others, e.g. Krueger, *Symeon the Holy Fool*, 90 on its link with the Cynic tradition and Vincent Déroche, *Syméon Salos, le fou en Christ* (Paris: Paris-Méditerranée, 2000), 59–60.

43 ἀββᾶς μωρός (*Life of Symeon* 79.24–25). The very first act of foolishness performed by Andrew, which also has the desired effect of constituting his false identity of fool, consists of ripping up his clothes. Again the symbolic function of the act (referring to the naked state of the fool for Christ's sake in this case) coexists with its immediate effectiveness.

44 For the 'Maske der Verrückheit', see Ernst Benz, "Heilige Narrheit", *Kyrios* 3 (1938), 1–55, Walter Nigg, *Der christliche Narr* (Stuttgart: Artemis-Verlag, 1956), and Peter Hauptmann, "Die 'Narren um Christi Willen' in der Ostkirche", *Kirche im Osten* 2 (1959), 27–49.

behind their fictitious protagonists and their own pen names (Nikephoros, Eulogia) or anonymity'.[45] However, hagiographers found other ways to mask themselves as well. As Lennart Rydén notes, saints' *Lives* are generally characterised by a complex relation between the historical author, implied author, primary narrator, and protagonist, resulting in 'several degrees of visibility' in which the hagiographer can appear.[46] In the *Lives* of the fools, we find examples of various techniques employed to complicate this constellation of narrative voices, resulting either in a higher or a lower degree of visibility of the hagiographer. However, as we shall see, in both cases, these techniques aim at masking the hagiographer's deliberate shaping of the narrative and are intended to authenticate his narration.

A well-established way of disguising authorship among hagiographers is to present the *Life* of a saint as an eyewitness report, a technique that has been identified by Hippolyte Delehaye as 'la fiction littéraire du témoin bien informé'.[47] Often, the 'well informed witness' is one of the characters of the story. This happens in the *Life of Symeon Salos*, where Leontius claims to have heard the story from John the Deacon, who is presented as a close friend of Symeon and a reliable source. When Leontius has narrated the beginning of Symeon's story, he suddenly comments:

> All this Symeon narrated in Emesa, where he pretended to be a fool, to a certain deacon of the holy cathedral church of the same city of Emesa, an excellent and virtuous man, who, by the divine grace which had come to him, understood the monk's work, and it was on his behalf that this most blessed Symeon performed a wonderful marvel, which we shall recall in its proper place. This aforementioned John, beloved of God, a virtuous deacon, narrated for us almost the entire life of that most wise one, calling on the Lord as witness to his story, that he had written nothing to add to the narrative, but rather that since that time he had forgotten most things.[48]

45 Constantinou, "Holy Actors", 356.

46 Rydén, "Fiction and Reality", 547. See also n. 15.

47 Delehaye, *Les passions des martyrs et les genres littéraires*, 182.

48 Ταῦτα δὲ πάντα ἐξηγήσατο ὁ ἐνάρετος Συμεὼν τινι ἐν Ἐμέσῃ, ἔνθα καὶ τὸν σαλὸν προσεποιήσατο, διακόνῳ τῆς ἁγίας καθολικῆς ἐκκλησίας τῆς αὐτῆς Ἐμεσηνῶν πόλεως, ἀνδρὶ θαυμαστῷ καὶ ἐναρέτῳ, ὃς καὶ ἐκ τῆς προσούσης αὐτῷ θείας χάριτος ἐνόησεν τὴν ἐργασίαν τοῦ γέροντος, εἰς ὃν καὶ θαῦμα φοβερὸν ἐποίησεν οὗτος ὁ μακάριος Συμεών, οὕτινος θαύματος ἐν τῷ ἰδίῳ τόπῳ μνημονεύσομεν. ὁ εἰρημένος οὖν θεοφιλὴς Ἰωάννης, ὁ ἐνάρετος διάκονος, αὐτὸς ἡμῖν τὸν ἅπαντα βίον σχεδὸν τοῦ πανσόφου διηγήσατο, τὸν κύριον προβαλλόμενος τῶν λεγομένων μάρτυρα, ὡς

From now on the story is presented to the reader through the filter of John's trustworthy testimony (as indicated by φησίν ('so he said') appearing on the next line). Thus, while the first half of the *Life*, which takes place in the desert in the absence of John the Deacon, is accounted for by the assuring words that 'all this Symeon narrated [to him] in Emesa', the second half, set in Emesa, is accounted for by the fact that John was present himself to witness everything from close by. Moreover, since John is the only one living in the city who is aware of Symeon's real identity and of his holiness from the beginning, he is the ideal source for the hagiographer's information on the secret saint.[49]

It has often been assumed that Leontius' claim to John's testimony is no more than a literary construction, as it would be highly unlikely that Leontius (who lived in the seventh century) met a contemporary of Symeon (who lived in the sixth).[50] Krueger, on the other hand, argues that there is no reason to assume that Leontius did not intend to convey the idea that he used a written source by John the Deacon, rather than an oral account.[51] Either way, the point is that Leontius skilfully validates his claims concerning the reliability of his sources through the way in which he works them into his narrative.[52] In the passage quoted above, mentioning the fact that John admits to his own forgetfulness bolsters his image as a reliable source, as it shows him to be self-aware about his own fallibility and, consequently, that he can be trusted on what he transmits. A later passage confirms once again that Symeon 'told him [John] his whole life'.[53] The scene evokes a situation in which John can ask the saint all kinds of questions and thereby has access to a first-hand account of the saint's personal experiences, once again representing him as a reliable source. By pre-

ὅτι οὐδὲν κατὰ προσθήκην ἐπέγραψεν τῷ διηγήματι ἀλλὰ μᾶλλον καὶ τὰ πλεῖστα ἐκ τοῦ χρόνου ἐπελάθετο (*Life of Symeon* 59.16–24).

49 In addition to John the Deacon, other characters are presented as sources for Symeon's sanctity as well in order to deal with the paradox of writing the life of a secret saint: whenever a character witnesses a miracle (s)he is forced to keep it silent (see below when 'the audience of the holy fool/hagiographer' is discussed), a motif that goes back to the gospel of Mark. However, the texts always specifies that the silence must be kept as long as the saint is alive, but that after his death, the character in question proclaims the story openly (e.g. *Life of Symeon* 98.13 and 102.27–29).

50 See for example Festugière, *Léontios de Neapolis*, 14.

51 Krueger, *Symeon the Holy Fool*, 23–24.

52 On how Leontius manipulates the chronology of Symeon's life to fit the proposed picture, see also Lennart Rydén, "Introduzione", in P. Cesaretti (ed.), *Leonzio di Neapoli. Niceforo prete di Santa Sofia. Vite dei Saloi Simeone e Andrea* (BHG *1677, 115z*)*. Premessa di Augusta Acconcia Longo. Introduzione di Lennart Ryden*. Testi e studi bizantino-neoellenici 19 (Roma: Dipartimento di scienze dell'antichità 'Sapienza', 2014), 33–54 at 40–41.

53 ὅτε ὅλον τὸν βίον αὐτοῦ ἐξεῖπεν αὐτῷ (*Life of Symeon* 83.10).

senting the narrative as coming from John, who heard it from Symeon himself, the hagiographer not only establishes a direct connection with the saint, imbuing his own persona with authority, but also succeeds in layering on top of his own authorship two trustworthy narrative voices, which makes his own deliberate fashioning of the narrative move quietly to the background.

Another option, which can be perceived in the *Life of Andrew Salos*, is that the hagiographer presents *himself* as the 'well informed witness', thus promoting himself to the forefront instead of lingering in the background of the narrative.[54] In the *Life of Andrew*, now and then the hagiographer steps onto the stage as a character in the story, thus creating the illusion that he was a close friend of the saint and witnessed everything he tells us from close by. Since it has been argued convincingly that the *Life of Andrew* was written in the tenth century, while the saint, according to the text, supposedly lived in the fifth or the sixth century, the author's claim that he himself was present at that time can certainly be revealed as a literary construction.[55] In fact, Andrew himself must be an invented character.[56]

The first time the hagiographer appears as a character is in lines 89–95, right after the detailed description of a dream of the saint in which he sees himself battling a demon:

> In the morning he came to me, unworthy though I am, telling me in confidence what he had seen. As I listened I was amazed, for a fragrance as from a very costly ointment issued invisibly from him. Having jointly considered the matter we decided that he should expose himself to public ridicule in the guise of one possessed by a demon and mad for the sake of him who said, 'Be a fool for my sake and you will enjoy many good things in my kingdom.' For otherwise he could not escape from his earthly master.[57]

---

54 As Rydén points out (*Life of St Andrew*, vol. 1, 28), the narrative situation of the *Life of Andrew* becomes even more complex when a second figure who functions as 'témoin bien informé' is introduced: Epiphanius, the young disciple of the saint. Thus, in the epilogue the hagiographer can claim authority twice over, saying that he wrote in his book 'partly what I have seen with my own eyes, partly what I have learnt from the renowned Epiphanius who became bishop here' (*Life of Andrew* 4396–4397: ἃ μὲν καὶ οἰκείοις ὀφθαλμοῖς ἑώρακα, ἃ δὲ καὶ παρὰ τοῦ ἀοιδίμου Ἐπιφανίου τοῦ γεγονότος ἐνθάδε ἀρχιερέως μεμάθηκα).

55 On the date of the *Life of Andrew*, see Rydén, "Date of the 'Life of Andreas Salos'", and on its 'chronological fiction', see Rydén, *Life of St Andrew*, vol. 1, 38.

56 Rydén, *Life of St Andrew*, vol. 1, 143. There is a long tradition of pseudepigraphy in (Judaeo-)Christian writings. I thank James Corke-Webster for this observation.

57 Πρωΐας δὲ γενομένης ἔρχεται πρός με τὸν ἀνάξιον καὶ θαρρεῖ μοι τὴν ὅρασιν. Ἐγὼ δὲ ἀκούσας ἐξέστην· εὐωδία γὰρ ἐξήρχετο ἐξ αὐτοῦ ἀοράτως ὥσπερ μύρου πολυτίμου. Σκεψάμενοι δὲ ἀμφότεροι

In order to understand the appearance of the first person in this passage we must look at what precedes. The *Life of Andrew* starts out in a way not uncommon for a hagiographical text; after the prologue, in which the hagiographer speaks in the first person, presenting his story ('I want to describe to you …'[58]) and imploring the audience to pay attention, the actual story begins in what appears to be a third-person narration by an omniscient narrator.[59] However, in the passage quoted above, the hagiographer suddenly speaks in the first person again, this time representing himself as a character in the story next to the saint. After this passage, the third-person perspective appears to be resumed when the hagiographer picks up again his role as an omniscient narrator.[60] Such sudden intrusions of the hagiographer in the story are found a couple of times hereafter and they do not occur randomly. The passage quoted above explains how the hagiographer was able to narrate the saint's dream (a private experience that would normally not be accessible to him): it was the saint who told him in detail what he had seen. Other occasions when the hagiographer suddenly enters the stage of the narrative are also related to the narration of dreams and visions or to the narration of miraculous events (namely lines 408–421, where the hagiographer, while secretly observing Andrew, witnesses the saint levitating, lines 429–740, which include a long account by Andrew in which he narrates his experience of rising up to paradise during a severe winter storm, and lines 1786–1790, where Epiphanius, Andrew's disciple, goes to the hagiographer after having a divine dream and tells him about it).[61] It seems,

---

ἐκρίναμεν τοῦ παραδειγματίσαι ἑαυτὸν εἰς τάξιν δαιμονῶντος καὶ μαινομένου διὰ τὸν εἰπόντα· 'Γίνου σαλὸς δι' ἐμὲ καὶ πολλῶν ἀγαθῶν ἀπολαύσεις ἐν τῇ βασιλείᾳ μου.' Ἄλλως γὰρ ἀποδράσαι τοῦ σωματικοῦ αὐτοῦ δεσπότου οὐκ ἠδύνατο.

58 βούλομαι ὑμῖν διηγήσασθαι (*Life of Andrew* 4).

59 This typical mode of narration, found in many medieval hagiographical narratives, is described by Eva von Contzen, *The Scottish Legendary: Towards a Poetics of Hagiographic Narration* (Manchester: Manchester University Press, 2016), 61.

60 This is clear, for instance, in lines 101–102: 'The cook woke up and, thinking day was dawning, went out to draw water.' (Ἔξυπνος δὲ γενόμενος ὁ μάγειρος καὶ νομίσας ὅτι πρὸς ἡμέραν ἐστὶν ἐξῆλθε τοῦ ἀντλῆσαι ὕδωρ.)

61 Apart from the four passages mentioned already, there is one other moment in which the hagiographer acts as a character in the story in the *Life of Andrew*, and where he firmly secures his role as 'témoin bien informé' by creating an intertextual parallel between himself and John the Deacon in the *Life of Symeon*. At line 224, reference is made to Symeon. Next, the hagiographer describes a situation which is reminiscent of a passage in the *Life of Symeon* (94.19–24) and clearly must be read in light of that reference: 'In the evening he came to me, unworthy though I am, as I lay sleeping alone in my room … He gave me a coherent account of everything with meekness, for only to me, O most faithful brothers, did he speak plainly and without dissimulation; to all others he feigned a deranged state of mind.' (*Life of Andrew* 225–231: Ἑσπέρας δὲ γενομένης ἔρχεται πρός με τὸν ἀνάξιον,

then, that the hagiographer appears as a first-person homodiegetic narrator in those moments when his narrative authority is questionable due to the fact that the event he is telling is either heuristically problematic or challenges the conventions of plausibility (by defying basic human capacities for instance).[62] This relates to Turner's observation regarding the use of explicit truth claims in hagiography: 'precisely because their details are challenging, miracles are often an occasion to remind readers of the hagiographer's factual integrity.'[63] Here, the hagiographer's efforts to write himself into the story on precisely those occasions presents a more covert strategy of satisfying the same literary needs.

Whereas in the previous examples from the *Life of Andrew* the sudden switch to first-person narration highlights the hagiographer's position, the same narrative technique can also be used to do the opposite, that is, to conceal the hagiographer's role from the reader's view. This effect is created when the narration suddenly switches to a first person which is not to be identified with the hagiographer, but with one of the other characters. In the *Life of Symeon* this technique is used when the experiences of one of the citizens are related, and another time when those of John the Deacon are told.[64] In both cases, the character in question, while normally being referred to in the third person, suddenly becomes a speaking 'I', a first-person narrator at the primary level of narration.[65] The reader is left with the impression that (s)he is listening directly to the personal testimony of that character, without the hagiographer's mediation intervening. The same happens in the *Life of Andrew*, first at lines 208–216, during the narration of one of Andrew's dreams, and again at line 1734, where it is Epiphanius' perspective that is taken when his divine vision is narrated. Here, the sudden switch from the third person to the first person does not aim at promoting the *hagiographer* to the forefront, as is the case elsewhere in this

---

ἐμοῦ μόνου ἔνδον τοῦ οἰκήματος καθεύδοντος, καὶ ὑπομειδιάσας μικρὸν ἤρξατο δάκρυσι τὸ τίμιον αὐτοῦ πρόσωπον καταβρέχειν. Προσπλακέντες δὲ ἐπὶ πολλὴν ὥραν καὶ ἀσπασάμενοι ἀλλήλους ἐκαθέσθημεν. Ἐπηρώτησα οὖν αὐτὸν πῶς ἐν δεσμοῖς ὢν ἀπελύθη. Ὁ δὲ καθεξῆς διηγήσατό μοι πάντα μετὰ πραότητος· ἐμοὶ γὰρ μόνῳ, ἀδελφοί μου πιστότατοι, ὡμίλει ὀρθῶς καὶ ἀδόλως, τοῖς δὲ λοιποῖς φρενήρει διαθέσει.) As Rydén notes, 'similarly, Symeon the Fool is said to have talked in an orderly manner only to his friend the deacon John' (*Life of St Andrew*, vol. 2, 307).

62 The narration of events which raise questions concerning the hagiographer's knowledge of them due to their hidden nature is also discussed by Staat in her chapter in the present volume.

63 Turner, *Truthfulness*, 27.

64 *Life of Symeon* 93.13–15, 94.12–13, and 23–24.

65 The hagiographer could have announced the direct speech of the character, using a phrase such as 'he said', in which case in would have been clear that these words belong to a second, embedded level of narration. Since such an announcement is missing, the character appears to speak directly to us, at the primary level of narration.

Life, but serves on the contrary to make him disappear in the background by promoting the voice of one of the other characters instead. The ultimate effect of both strategies is however essentially the same, and indeed, they are used within the same rather 'problematic' narrative context: the narration of a divine dream.

The hagiographer can use different strategies to mask his deliberate shaping of the narrative: he can either construct for himself a prominent position at the forefront of the narrative action by taking up the position of well-informed witness (*Life of Andrew*), or he can hide behind other reliable narrative voices by presenting other characters as 'témoin bien informé' or letting them step in as primary narrators, directly addressing his readership (*Life of Symeon* and *Life of Andrew*). Thus the mask of the hagiographer can work in two directions, focusing the reader's attention on what is a constructed façade, or directing attention away from what is actually hidden behind it.[66] The *Life of Andrew* proves that both can be present in one and the same text. Like the mask of the fool, the hagiographer's disguised self-presentation helps to direct the audience's expectations. It eases the reader into taking seriously his explicit claims of truthfulness and historicity, often found in prologues and epilogues of hagiographical narratives, just like the holy fool's nudity paves the way for the citizens to regard him as a *salos*. Thus, paradoxically, the hagiographer's literary fashioning and fictionalisation lead to authentication. It is true that the need to portray reliability resonates with the idea that fictional narrative must to some extent deny its own fictionality in order to work as fiction (what Ryan calls 'the paradox of fiction').[67] Otherwise, it would be hard for the reader to commit to the fictional game of 'make-believe'. From this perspective, it is not surprising that the hagiographer presents his narrative as a true story, even when it is not. However, the mask the hagiographer puts on betrays a deeper need for authentication and supports the idea that the game rules of hagiography are different from those of what we call fiction today: while, according to the rules of the latter, the fictional truth that is communicated needs no validation outside of its attribution to the implied author's design, the hagiographer apparently needs to perform a certain role and portray a certain character in order to earn the trust of his audience. This leads us to the next section of this chapter, which considers the (ambiguous) position of the reader and the question of belief.

66 The two directions of the hagiographer's mask described here can be related to the two modes of making the saint present that Claudia Rapp introduces and explores in a recent article: "Author, Audience, Text and Saint: Two Modes of Early Byzantine Hagiography", *SJBMGS* 1 (2015), 111–129.

67 Ryan, "Postmodernism and the Doctrine of Panfictionality", 168. See also Morgan, "Make-Believe", who discusses 'strategies of realism' in the ancient novel.

3 The Audience of the Holy Fool/Hagiographer

> One of them started a discussion, saying, 'Brothers, curse upon Satan! How could this fool predict what happened to us?' One of the others answered, 'You fool, do you not know that what the demon intends to do he tells his companion? No doubt it was the demon living with him that did this to us because we mocked him.' The first said, 'Not at all! In my opinion God punished us because we beat him pitilessly.' The other replied again, 'You fool, do you think God cares about a madman? God gave him a demon and we beat him for fun, there is nothing strange about that. Had he been a saint you would have convinced me that we were punished by God, but since he is mad God does not care.' Discussing this and other matters of concern to the young they went away.[68]

If the city is the theatre in which the holy fool performs, then the people in the city are his audience. Often, the citizens that appear in the story do not have a name (though sometimes their profession is mentioned), an indication that they are the representatives of an abstract category of people. The people in the audience, the inhabitants of the city, generally do not realise they are watching a performance (or do they?).

In any case, the holy fool does everything he can to make his audience believe in his act. Apart from wearing the appropriate costume, which I discussed above, 'it was the saint's practice, whenever he did something miraculous, to leave that neighbourhood immediately, until the deed which he had done was forgotten. He hurried on immediately elsewhere to do something inappropriate, so that he might thereby hide his perfection.'[69] His goal is to

68 Εἷς δὲ ἐξ αὐτῶν λόγον κινήσας ἔφη· 'Καταργηθῇ ὁ σατανᾶς, ἀδελφοί, πῶς τοῦτο ἡμῖν ὁ σαλὸς ἐκεῖνος προεφθέγξατο;' Λέγει ὁ ἕτερος· '"Εξηχε, οὐκ οἶδας ὅτι ὃ βούλεται ὁ δαίμων ποιῆσαι, τῷ συμπράκτορι αὐτοῦ λέγει; Τάχα γὰρ ὑπὲρ οὗ ἐνεπαίξαμεν αὐτὸν ὁ συμπεριφερόμενος αὐτῷ δαίμων ἐποίησεν ἡμῖν ταῦτα.' "Εφη ὁ ἕτερος· 'Οὐχί, μὴ γένοιτο, ἀλλ' ὡς εἰκάζω, ὑπὲρ οὗ ἐτύψαμεν αὐτὸν ἀνηλεῶς, διὰ τοῦτο ὁ θεὸς ἀνταπέδωκεν ἡμῖν.' Λέγει πάλιν ὁ ἕτερος· 'Ναί, ἔξηχε, μέλει τῷ θεῷ περὶ σαλοῦ; 'Εκεῖνος γὰρ δαίμονα αὐτῷ δέδωκε καὶ ἡμεῖς παιγνίως αὐτὸν ἐτύψαμεν, καὶ οὐδὲν θαυμαστόν. Εἰ γὰρ ἦν ἅγιος, ἔπειθες ἄν με ὅτι ὁ θεὸς ἀνταπέδωκεν ἡμῖν· ἐπεὶ δὲ ἔξηχός ἐστι. τοῦτο οὐ μέλει τῷ θεῷ.' Ταῦτα αὐτῶν λεγόντων καὶ ἄλλα τινὰ ἅ εἰσι τοῖς νέοις ἐπιτήδεια ἐπορεύοντο (*Life of Andrew* 260–271).

69 'Επετήδευσεν δὲ καὶ τοῦτο ὁ ὅσιος, ὅτι καθότι ἐποίει τίποτε παράδοξον, εὐθέως ἤλλασσεν τὴν γειτονίαν ἐκείνην, ἕως οὗ λησμονηθῇ τὸ πρᾶγμα, ὃ ἐποίησεν. ἔσπευδεν δὲ καὶ παραυτὰ σχηματίσασθαι ἄκαιρον τίποτε, ἵνα δι' ἐκείνου ἐπικαλύψῃ τὸ κατόρθωμα. (*Life of Symeon* 81.5–8). A concrete example can be found in the *Life of Symeon* 81.22–25: 'Then the tavern keeper understood that Abba Symeon had broken the wine jar for the same reason. And he was

save souls without being exposed as holy.[70] However, this enterprise involves a paradox,[71] since the edified citizen necessarily becomes aware by means of his edification that he is dealing with a saint rather than a fool. As a result, while most people in the city are convinced that he is an actual fool and treat him likewise, sometimes a citizen discovers the true nature of the holy man, who then finds himself compelled to silence him/her by force so that his secret stays hidden. This happens, for example, in the *Life of Symeon* at 87.15–17, where the lips of the two monks who experience Symeon's gift of prophecy are burnt so they cannot tell what they know.[72] In the *Life of Andrew*, force is sometimes replaced by or combined with persuasion, as in the following passage:[73]

> When the pious woman came to herself after this vision she was greatly amazed and exclaimed, 'How wonderful God is in his goodness! What luminaries he has on earth, and nobody knows it!' Often she wanted to tell some people what she had seen, but immediately a divine power prevented her, throwing her into a trembling so that henceforth she kept the miracle secret *voluntarily*. One day the righteous man met her and said, 'Keep my secret for the time being, Barbara,'—that was her name—'and do not reveal it to anybody until I have come to the place of the wondrous tabernacle, to the House of God!' She answered, 'Unfortunately I do not

---

edified and considered Symeon to be holy. Thereupon the saint wanted to destroy his edification, so that the tavern keeper would not expose him.' (τότε οὖν ἔγνω ὁ κάπηλος, ὅτι δι' αὐτὸ ἔκλασεν καὶ ὁ ἀββᾶς Συμεὼν τὸ βισσίν. καὶ οἰκοδομήθη καὶ εἶχεν αὐτὸν ἅγιον. Θέλων οὖν ὁ ὅσιος ἀναλῦσαι τὴν οἰκοδομὴν αὐτοῦ, ἵνα μὴ θριαμβεύσῃ αὐτόν.) The reason why he does not want to be exposed is given in 78.23–25: 'And his every prayer was that his works might be hidden until his departure from life, so that he might escape human glory, through which human arrogance and conceit arises, and which also made the angels fall from heaven.' (ἡ δὲ εὐχὴ αὐτοῦ ὑπῆρχεν πᾶσα τοῦ σκεπασθῆναι αὐτοῦ τὴν ἐργασίαν μέχρι τῆς αὐτοῦ μεταστάσεως ἐκ τοῦ βίου, ἵνα διαφύγῃ τὴν τῶν ἀνθρώπων δόξαν, δι' ἧς παραγίνεται τῷ ἀνθρώπῳ ὑπερηφανία καὶ οἴησις ἡ καὶ ἀγγέλους ἀπολέσασα ἐξ οὐρανῶν.)

70 *Life of Symeon* 91.12–16.

71 Further aspects of the paradox inherent in the fool's conduct (as well as the paradox of writing the story of a holy fool, which I introduced above at 68 are discussed by Youval Rotman, *Insanity and Sanctity in Byzantium. The Ambiguity of Religious Experience* (Cambridge, MA/London: Harvard University Press, 2016), 11–31.

72 Other examples are found in the *Life of Symeon* 88.16–18 and 90.20–22. The topos goes back to Mark 1:44 (cf. Matthew 8:4) and a handful of other passages in Mark and Matthew. I thank Christa Gray for this observation.

73 A similar passage is lines 1335–1346, where the boy who witnessed the levitation of Andrew is silenced.

> want to. And even if I want to tell somebody, I cannot, honourable luminary and wholly marvellous elect of the Lord, for I am prevented by an invisible power, and trembling enters my bones and my strength is troubled within me.'[74]

The element of persuasion is important not just in this passage, but in the *Life of Andrew* in general. Whereas Symeon reaches his goals through acts, Andrew generally converts the people through words.[75] Furthermore, in the *Life of Andrew* discussions often arise among the citizens concerning the nature of the holy fool (like the one in the passage quoted at the beginning of this section):[76] do his special powers arise from a pious or an evil source, and consequently, is he a saint or a possessed madman? As Rydén remarks, it is precisely in this no man's land between the realm of the angels and the realm of the demons that the holy fool can operate.[77] Such discussions among citizens concerning the nature of the fool explicitly address the question of belief on the part of the audience in the performance of the saint and are symptomatic for their ambiguous position in the paradoxical game of the fool. On the one hand, the citizens are led to believe in the act of the holy fool, who is said to deceive his audience (his performance is called *apatē*, 'deceit').[78] On the other hand, the result of this deception is edification, which means that the citizen realises that (s)he is dealing with a saint who serves a higher cause and is then forced—or willing—to play along in his game of make-believe.

---

74 Ταῦτα ὁρῶσα ἡ γυνὴ ἐκείνη ἡ θεοσεβὴς ἐξεπλήττετο σφόδρα ἐν ἑαυτῇ γενομένη καὶ ἔλεγε· 'Βαβαὶ τῆς τοῦ θεοῦ ἀγαθότητος· οἵους φωστῆρας ἔχει ἐπὶ γῆς καὶ οὐδεὶς ἐπίσταται.' Πολλάκις οὖν ἠβουλήθη τὰ ὁραθέντα αὐτῇ τισι διηγήσασθαι καὶ παραχρῆμα θεία τις δύναμις ἐκώλυεν αὐτὴν εἰς τρόμον ἄγουσα, καὶ λοιπὸν ἑκοῦσα τὸ θαῦμα ἀπέκρυπτεν. Ὅθεν ἐν μιᾷ συναντᾷ αὐτῇ ὁ δίκαιος καὶ λέγει αὐτῇ· 'Φύλαττέ μου τὸ μυστήριον ἐν τῷ τέως, Βαρβάρα,' (τοῦτο γὰρ ἦν ὄνομα αὐτῇ) 'καὶ μηδενὶ αὐτὸ ἐξείπῃς ἄρτι. ἕως οὗ ἐλεύσομαι ἐν τόπῳ σκηνῆς θαυμαστῆς ἕως τοῦ οἴκου τοῦ θεοῦ.' Ἡ δὲ πρὸς αὐτὸν ἀπεκρίνατο· 'Κακῶς καὶ οὐ θέλω· εἰ δὲ καὶ θελήσω τινὶ διηγήσασθαι, οὐ δύναμαι, τίμιε φωστὴρ καὶ ἐκλεκτὲ κυρίου πανθαύμαστε· κωλύομαι γὰρ ἀοράτῳ δυνάμει καὶ εἰσέρχεται τρόμος εἰς τὰ ὀστᾶ μου καὶ ἐν ἐμοὶ ἡ ἰσχύς μου ταράττεται' (*Life of Andrew* 3603–3614).

75 For example the monk at the Staurion (*Life of Andrew* 1952–2124).

76 Such discussions are abundant in the *Life of Andrew*, but they can also be found in the *Life of Symeon*, e.g. 90.11–13: 'There was a certain village headman living near Emesa, and when he heard about Symeon's way of life he said, "Believe me, if I saw him, I would know if he's pretending or if he really is an idiot."' (Ἦν δέ τις πλησίον Ἐμέσης μένων πρωτοκωμήτης, καὶ ὡς ἤκουσεν τὸν βίον αὐτοῦ, λέγει· 'πίστευσον, ἐὰν ἴδω, νοῶ ἐὰν προσποιητός ἐστιν καὶ ἐάν τε ἐν ἀληθείᾳ ἐστὶν ἔξηχος.')

77 Rydén, *The Holy Fool*, 110.

78 See the *Life of Symeon* 56.21 and 82.12.

Perhaps we can image the reader of hagiography to resemble the citizen when it comes to the ambiguous nature of his belief.[79] Whether readers of hagiography actually took the narrative as factual/historical truth or not remains almost impossible to reconstruct. It is not unlikely, however, that both options were simultaneously in place: that some readers literally believed what was written, while others did not (or only to a certain extent). Like the people in the city of the holy fool, then, some readers may not have realised they were reading a fictionalised story, while others did but chose to play along with the game anyway. As such, the question of whether or not the audience took the narrative to be representing historical truth would be irrelevant to the functioning of the genre, and thus to the game rules of hagiography. Indeed, another type of belief, religious in kind, is at stake in this genre. And even if sometimes readers simply turned to hagiography for entertainment, like the people in the city 'go have a drink where the Fool is' because he brings them amusement,[80] at the same time, stories about saints combine frivolous pleasure with very serious didactic purposes in a way similar to ancient myth.[81] Although this

79 This raises the complex question of who the audience of hagiography was, which requires a study in itself. Stephanos Efthymiadis and Nikos Kalogeras point out that the question of the audience of Byzantine hagiography is an understudied topic: "Audience, Language and Patronage in Byzantine Hagiography", in Efthymiadis, *Ashgate Research Companion*, vol. 2, 247–284 at 248. However, their own article also claims to trace the 'intended audience' rather than the actual one (ibidem). They point to Claudia Rapp, "Figures of Female Sanctity: Byzantine Edifying Manuscripts and Their Audience", DOP 50 (1996), 313–344, for a discussion of the historical reader.

80 See the *Life of Symeon* 81.8–11 ('πίωμεν ὅπου ὁ Σαλός') and the *Life of Andrew* 232–244, where the people in the city are said to deliberately seek out the holy fool because they find him entertaining. The analogy here is that both the holy fool and the hagiographer can win souls by first attracting them with entertainment. On the entertaining function of hagiography as the 'mass media' of its time, see Alexander Kazhdan, "Byzantine Hagiography and Sex in the Fifth to Twelfth Centuries", DOP 44 (1990), 131–143 at 131. Edification through amusement is also emphasised by Averil Cameron, *Christianity and the Rhetoric of Empire: The Development of Christian Discourse* (Berkeley: University of California Press, 1991), esp. at 47–119, and von Contzen, *The Scottish Legendary*.

81 According to Frye (*The Secular Scripture*, 22), classical mythology is 'pleasant enough to entice the more light-minded reader, but when he digests [it] he will find that [it] is really wholesome food'. The fictionality of myth is discussed by Ryan, "Postmodernism and the Doctrine of Panfictionality", 181. She writes: 'It [myth] combined the guaranteed truth of fiction with the knowledge-claim of nonfiction and its referential anchoring in a non-textual reality. But in contrast to nonfiction, it conveyed this knowledge through a mode of expression that could be interpreted as figural.' The parallel between hagiography and myth has been drawn by Alison G. Elliott (*Roads to Paradise*, 11), who states that '[fictional Lives] conform more closely to literary and mythic norms of conduct and portray the ideal rather than the actual'. See also Anthony Kaldellis, "The Emergence of Literary Fiction in

combination does not fit with our modern system of thinking, which maintains a strong division between fiction and nonfiction and associates these categories with pleasure and didacticism respectively, in the ancient narrative system, where texts often seem to float between history and fiction, such associations are not necessarily valid.[82] For example, ancient historiography used illustrative dialogue and rhetorical and dramatic modes in order to accomplish a 'dramatic re-enactment of events', while pleasure was also a 'legitimate function' of ancient historical texts.[83] Conversely, ancient fiction (such as the Greek novels) adopted historiographical techniques of authentication.[84] Thus, ancient literature was 'a vehicle for shared truth rather than for the individual imagination'.[85] Moreover, ancient biography, an important predecessor of Christian *Lives*, also blurred the line between history and fiction through its 'willingness to read poetic truth as historical fact, and vice versa'.[86] Finally, in

---

Byzantium and the Paradox of Plausibility", in P. Roilos (ed.), *Medieval Greek Storytelling. Fictionality and Narrative in Byzantium* (Wiesbaden: Harrassowitz Verlag, 2014), 115–130 at 120.

82 Ancient literary and rhetorical theory classifies texts according to three instead of two categories: *historia* (or *alēthēs*; true narrative), *fabula* (or *muthos*; narrative that is untrue nor like the truth), and *argumentum* (or *plasma*; narrative that consists of invented material but nevertheless could have happened). Although Morgan, "Make-Believe", 190, calls this famous division a 'flawed tool for thinking about fiction' because it 'lacks any element of intentionality', the tripartite scheme nonetheless reveals a fundamental difference from modern thinking about texts. The third category, *argumentum*, seems to align with what is going on in hagiographical texts. See also Claudia Rapp, "Storytelling as Spiritual Communication in Early Greek Hagiography: The Use of Diegesis", *JECS* 6.3 (1998), 431–448 at 443, on the criterion of plausibility in hagiography, a genre that does not 'make a distinction between truth and verisimilitude or like-truth'.

83 Morgan, "Make-Believe", 184. For a discussion of Byzantine historiography and 'how it explores the twilight zone between history and fiction', see also Panagiotis Agapitos, "In Rhomaian, Persian and Frankish Lands: Fiction and Fictionality in Byzantium and Beyond", in Panagiotis A. Agapitos and Lars Boje Mortensen (eds.), *Medieval Narratives between History and Fiction: From the Centre to the Periphery of Europe, c. 1100–1400* (Copenhagen: Museum Tusculanum Press, 2012), 235–268 at 258.

84 Morgan, "Make-Believe". On the hybrid nature of ancient narrative fiction, see also Niklas Holzberg, "The Genre: Novels Proper and the Fringe", in G. Schmeling (ed.), *The Novel in the Ancient World* (Leiden/New York/Köln: Brill, 1996), 11–28 at 15–19.

85 Christopher Gill and Timothy P. Wiseman, "Preface", in iidem (eds.), *Lies and Fiction in the Ancient World* (Exeter: University of Exeter Press, 1993), vii–ix at viii.

86 Patricia Cox [Miller], *Biography in Late Antiquity, A Quest for the Holy Man* (Berkeley: University of California Press, 1983), xii. On the relationship between ancient biography and Christian *Lives*, see also Marc Van Uytfanghe, "La biographie classique et l'hagiographie chrétienne antique tardive", *Hagiographica* 12 (2005), 223–248; Samuel Rubenson, "Antony and Pythagoras: A Reappraisal of the Appropriation of Classical Biography in Athanasius' Vita Antonii", in David Brakke, Anders-Christian Jacobsen, and Jörg Ulrich (eds.),

the 2012 book *How to Do Things with Fictions*, Joshua Landy explores the use of fictional stories in the Gospel of Mark, and contends that these captured the spirit of what Christianity meant for contemporaries, regardless of whether they actually happened this way.[87]

Like ancient and late antique historiography and biography, it seems, hagiography presents higher truths in a fictionalised form.[88] The following passages from the *Lives* of Symeon and Andrew seem to indicate that, like the holy fool, the hagiographer indeed serves a higher goal with his literary 'performance'. In his prologue, for instance, Leontius says that the sinner must be aroused by a divine yearning 'through the stories which are told to him',[89] and about Andrew we learn that 'he loved to read the Holy Scriptures but even more the Passions of the martyrs and the Lives of the God-bearing Fathers, so that his heart was aflame with trust in them and aroused to imitation of their good way of living'.[90] Furthermore, in lines 3788–3790, once again the hagiographer appears and assures us that 'this, my friends, I have learnt from blessed Andrew and written down for the edification of our souls, that we may consider how we lead our life in this world, for nothing escapes God and his saints'.[91] Thus, para-

Beyond Reception: Mutual Influences between Antique Religion, Judaism, and Early Christianity (Bern: Peter Lang, 2006), 191–208; and Tomas Hägg, "The Life of St Antony between Biography and Hagiography", in Stephanos Efthymiadis (ed.), *The Ashgate Research Companion to Byzantine Hagiography*, vol. 1 (Farnham: Ashgate, 2011), 17–34.

87 Joshua Landy, *How to Do Things with Fictions* (Oxford: Oxford University Press, 2012).

88 See Catherine Cubitt, "Introduction: Writing True Stories—A View from the West", in Arietta Papaconstantinou (ed.), *Writing 'True Stories'. Historians and Hagiographers in the Late Antique and Medieval Near East* (Turnhout: Brepols, 2010), 1–12 at 11. In her introduction, Cubitt also refers to the 'powerful, higher truth' of the stories explored in the volume ("Introduction", 12).

89 δι' ἀκοῆς καὶ διηγήσεως πρὸς αὐτὸν καταντώσης (*Life of Symeon* 56.7).

90 Ἠγάπα δὲ τοῦ ἀναγινώσκειν τὰς θείας γραφάς, πλεῖον δὲ τὰ τῶν ἁγίων μαρτύρια καὶ τοὺς βίους τῶν θεοφόρων πατέρων, ὥστε ἐκκαίεσθαι τὴν καρδίαν αὐτοῦ εἰς τὴν τούτων πεποίθησιν καὶ εἰς μίμησιν διεγείρεσθαι τῆς ἀγαθῆς αὐτῶν πολιτείας (*Life of Andrew* 29–33). Other examples can be found in the *Life of Andrew*, e.g. lines 731–737, where Andrew just told a story of his spiritual journey to Paradise and back: in this passage the narrator suddenly speaks in the first person, as discussed at 76, and testifies that 'Blessed Andrew's story sent my soul into a trance'. (Ταῦτα τοῦ μακαρίου Ἀνδρέου πρός με διηγουμένου εἰς ἔκστασιν φρενῶν ἤγαγε τὴν ψυχήν μου.) In another passage, the boy who witnessed the levitation of Andrew exclaims (1332–1334): 'My goodness, what a miracle! How many hidden servants God has, who lead a good way of life and have a good conscience! What we hear from the Lives of the saints we have seen with our own eyes.' ('Βαβαὶ τοῦ μυστηρίου· πόσους κρυπτοὺς δούλους ἔχει ὁ θεὸς καὶ ἀγαθῆς πολιτείας καὶ συνειδήσεως, καὶ ἅπερ ἐν τοῖς βίοις τῶν ἁγίων ἠκούομεν, ταῦτα οἰκείοις ὀφθαλμοῖς ἑωράκαμεν.')

91 Ταῦτα, ὦ φίλοι, γέγραφα, μεμαθηκὼς παρὰ τοῦ μακαρίου Ἀνδρέου, πρὸς ὠφέλειαν τῶν ἡμετέρων

doxical as it may sound, the hagiographer has no intention of deceiving his audience with his fictionalised account, but writes in order that their souls may be saved. Similarly, the holy fool, even though his performance is called *apatē* ('deceit'),[92] eventually (and paradoxically) targets religious truth. In both cases, in order to convey a specific kind of truth, moral in nature, the 'fiction' must be 'believed' in one way or another. Theorists have been struggling for decades with the question of to what extent a reader of fiction can be said to 'believe' what he reads. Critics have often interpreted the reader's position as one of a 'willing suspension of disbelief'.[93] In this regard, some have pointed at the problem of a reader's emotional involvement with a fictional text: fiction, which we know to be fiction, can nonetheless move us to actual tears.[94] In his chapter on the fictionality of the ancient Greek novel, John Morgan points out that 'if it makes sense at all to talk about believing fiction, the belief must clearly be different in kind rather than degree from that accorded to straightforwardly factual statements'.[95] When dealing with Christian literature, the question of belief becomes even more pressing when the issue of religious involvement is considered. If it is the kind of belief Morgan is referring to that is responsible for our tears when we read about the death of our favourite character in our favourite novel, then perhaps it is a similar kind of belief that is responsible for the religious involvement of the readers of saints' *Lives*, and which is targeted by the hagiographer.

4 Conclusions

According to Grosdidier de Matons, the task of the hagiographer is not to represent but to interpret; it is to present a model as perfect as possible.[96] In order to

ψυχῶν, ὅπως σκοπῶμεν πῶς περιπατῶμεν ἐν τῷ κόσμῳ τούτῳ· οὐδὲν γὰρ λανθάνει θεῷ καὶ τοῖς ἁγίοις αὐτοῦ.

92 Cf. n. 78.

93 This term was first introduced by Samuel Taylor Coleridge, *Biographia Literaria* (Oxford: Clarendon Press, 1907 (1817)). See also the chapter by Alwis in the present volume for a discussion of this term.

94 Booth, *The Rhetoric of Fiction*, discusses reader involvement in Ch. 5. The question is also addressed by Walsh, *The Rhetoric of Fictionality*, in his chapter "Why We Wept for Little Nell". See also Gregory Currie, "Emotion and the Response to Fiction", in idem, *The Nature of Fiction* (Cambridge: Cambridge University Press, 1990), 182–216, and Schaeffer, *Pourquoi la fiction?*

95 Morgan, "Make-Believe", 193.

96 Grosdidier de Matons, *Les thèmes d'édification dans la vie d'André Salos*, 277: 'La tâche

do this, fictionality/fictionalisation can be a powerful tool. Like the fool, whose theatrical performance is crucial to his mission of edifying the townsmen, the hagiographer presents a narrative that is not an accurate presentation of the historical truth so as to represent 'not the life as lived, but the life as made sense of, the life imaginatively reconstructed and rendered significant'.[97] In order to better understand the implications of such fictionalising practices for the literary contract between hagiographer and reader, I have further pursued the analogy between the hagiographer's task of writing and the performance of the holy fool. Although the comparison will probably not elucidate every aspect of the game called hagiography, at least it has led to the following observations.

Firstly, like the holy fool must wear a costume to support his performance, the hagiographer hides behind a mask to support his narrative and to authenticate it. In fact, he can use different techniques to conceal his own authorship and/or generate an opportune self-presentation, namely by appearing prominently in the text as a highly constructed or fictional persona, or, on the contrary, by disappearing from the text by promoting other narrative voices to the forefront. The double potential of the mask (i.e. to present a constructed façade and to hide what is behind it) in both cases results in a presentation of the material as reliable and trustworthy. From this it may be inferred that the rules of hagiography prescribe that all parties involved approach the hagiographical text as containing a message whose truth value is guaranteed by the authorial power of the figure of the hagiographer (in the case of his constructed appearance) or of his sources (in the case of his disappearance). In this respect, the rules of hagiography differ from those of what we regard as fiction today, since, according to the rules of modern fiction, both sender and receiver mutually agree on the fact that the message has no truth value in the world outside the text and therefore does not need any external authorisation (it 'guarantees its own truth').[98]

On the other hand, although the hagiographer, like the fool, does everything in his power to make his audience believe in his literary performance, he does not intend to deceive his reader (which does align him with writers of modern fiction),[99] since his ultimate goal is to rouse in his audience a different kind of

---

de l'hagiographe consiste, non à représenter, mais à interpréter un personnage hors série pour en faire un modèle aussi parfait que possible.'

97 Geoffrey Cubitt, "Introduction: Heroic Reputations and Exemplary Lives", in Geoffrey Cubitt and Allen Warren (eds.), *Heroic Reputations and Exemplary Lives* (Manchester: Manchester University Press, 2000), 1–26 at 3.

98 According to Ryan's definition ("Postmodernism and the Doctrine of Panfictionality", 167).

99 According to the definition provided by Morgan ("Make-Believe", 225).

belief, which is a belief in the religious rather than the historical truth of his narration. Here, it helps to compare the goal of the holy fool to edify the citizens through a theatrical show with the hagiographer's practice of edifying his reader through a fictionalised account, since both involve a paradox: like the spectator needs to believe in the feigned folly of the holy man in order to be edified and receive moral truth, the reader of hagiography needs to 'believe' the narrative of the hagiographer (regardless of whether (s)he actually takes it to be historically accurate) in order to benefit from its edifying qualities. In both cases, the 'fictiveness' of the performance is only instrumental to this higher goal. Eventually, what the hagiographer and the fool both aim at is to spread religious truth, and that despite (or is it thanks to?) their deceptions.

While this 'other' kind of belief appears to correspond rather well to the kind of belief involved in a reader's emotional engagement with modern fiction (different from the factual belief in the historicity of the events narrated), what is different here is that, given its religious nature, the truth that is proclaimed in the text has the real world as its frame of reference, while the fictional truth of the modern novel is truth only within the fictional world, which is its frame of reference.[100] This is illustrated by the fact that an author of a modern novel cannot (or should not) be held responsible for the ideological viewpoints his narrator or his characters proclaim (although there have been cases in the past where this occurred; think for instance of the trial against Gustave Flaubert or the attacks against Salman Rushdie).[101] The fact that the hagiographer does seek to establish a direct link between the ideological statements issued in his text and the concrete reality inhabited by its readers accounts for the hybrid and paradoxical nature of the hagiographer's enterprise, who wears a mask in order to imbue his narrative with reliability and authority and to disguise his literary fashioning, but without the primary intention of making his reader actually believe in the historical truth of his narrative (although this must have been the unavoidable effect in some cases). Rather than just adhering to strategies of realism to draw the reader into the text in order to achieve emotional

100 Again according to Ryan's definition ("Postmodernism and the Doctrine of Panfictionality", 167). That does not mean that a modern work of fiction cannot say something about the real world in which we live (why would certain governments otherwise have censorship policies?), but it always does so indirectly.

101 Public prosecutors brought Flaubert to court for the immoralities proclaimed in his *Madame Bovary* in 1857, while, more recently, Rushdie's highly controversial *Satanic Verses* (1988) was the object of a violent storm of critiques. In both cases, the discrepancy between the rules according to which the prosecutors approach the literary work in question and the rules according to which the authors (and presumably also the modern-day public) conceive of it resulted in painful misunderstandings with severe consequences.

involvement, the hagiographer must create for himself a more profound narrative as well as ideological authority for his audience to become religiously involved.

The hagiographer is then indeed like the saint he is writing about (as Derek Krueger proposed) since his practice of humility results in the edification of others, and, more particularly, he is like the type of the *salos*, since this practice is inextricably connected to a kind of performance that is well compared to that of the holy fool, who also, in his nakedness and self-degrading, practises humility and fictionalisation at once. Moreover, shedding light on the fictionalising dimension of the hagiographer's task has allowed us to reflect on the intricate role of the hagiographer for the construction of the hagiographical text: he reflects onto his saintly subject a certain authority while at the same time the saintly subject reflects religious authority onto the hagiographer, all of which is achieved through his own narrative crafting, which establishes a complex but profound link between the hagiographer and the saint.[102]

Acknowledgments

I would like to thank the organisers and participants of the 2015 colloquium on Hagiography as Literature held at the University of Edinburgh and the editors of this volume for their enthusiasm and inspiring feedback on early versions of this article. I am also grateful to Koen De Temmerman and Kristoffel Demoen for providing me with useful remarks and feedback. This article was made possible by the support of both the ERC Starting Grant 'Novel Saints' at Ghent University (Grant Agreement 337344) and the FWO Flanders.

Bibliography

Agapitos, Panagiotis A., "In Rhomaian, Persian and Frankish Lands: Fiction and Fictionality in Byzantium and Beyond", in Panagiotis A. Agapitos and Lars Boje Mortensen (eds.), *Medieval Narratives between History and Fiction: From the Centre to the Periphery of Europe, c. 1100–1400* (Copenhagen: Museum Tusculanum Press, 2012), 235–268.

Aigrain, René, *L'hagiographie: ses sources, ses méthodes, son histoire* (Brussels: Société des Bollandistes, 1953).

102 See also Williams in this volume for an illustration of conspicuous modesty involved in hagiographical writing.

Austin, John Langshaw, *How to Do Things with Words* (2nd edition Cambridge, MA: Harvard University Press, 1975).

Barnes, Timothy D., *Early Christian Hagiography and Roman History* (Tübingen: Mohr Siebeck, 2010).

Benz, Ernst, "Heilige Narrheit", *Kyrios* 3 (1938), 1–55.

Booth, Wayne, *The Rhetoric of Fiction* (Chicago/London: University of Chicago Press, 1983²).

Cameron, Averil, *Christianity and the Rhetoric of Empire: The Development of Christian Discourse* (Berkeley: University of California Press, 1991).

Cohn, Dorrit, *The Distinction of Fiction* (Baltimore/London: John Hopkins University Press, 1999).

Coleridge, Samuel Taylor, *Biographia Literaria* (Oxford: Clarendon Press, 1907 (1817)).

Constantinou, Stavroula, "Holy Actors and Actresses: Fools and Cross-Dressers as the Protagonists of Saints' Lives", in Stephanos Efthymiadis (ed.), *The Ashgate Research Companion to Byzantine Hagiography*, vol. 2 (Farnham: Ashgate, 2014), 343–362.

Cox [Miller], Patricia, *Biography in Late Antiquity: A Quest for the Holy Man*. The Transformation of the Classical Heritage 5 (Berkeley: University of California Press, 1983).

Cubitt, Catherine, "Introduction: Writing True Stories—A View from the West", in Arietta Papaconstantinou (ed.), *Writing 'True Stories': Historians and Hagiographers in the Late Antique and Medieval Near East* (Turnhout: Brepols, 2010), 1–12.

Cubitt, Geoffrey, "Introduction: Heroic Reputations and Exemplary Lives", in Geoffrey Cubitt and Allen Warren (eds.), *Heroic Reputations and Exemplary Lives* (Manchester: Manchester University Press, 2000), 1–26.

Currie, Gregory, "Emotion and the Response to Fiction", in idem (ed.), *The Nature of Fiction* (Cambridge: Cambridge University Press, 1990), 182–216.

De Temmerman, Koen, "Ancient Biography and Formalities of Fiction", in Koen De Temmerman and Kristoffel Demoen (eds.), *Writing Biography in Greece and Rome: Narrative Technique and Fictionalization* (Cambridge: Cambridge University Press, 2016), 3–25.

Delehaye, Hippolyte, *Les légendes hagiographiques* (4th edition Brussels: Société des Bollandistes, 1955).

Delehaye, Hippolyte, *Les passions des martyrs et les genres littéraires* (Brussels: Société des Bollandistes, 1966).

Déroche, Vincent, *Études sur Léontios de Néapolis*, Acta Universitatis Upsaliensis, Studia Byzantina Upsaliensa 3 (Uppsala: Textgruppen i Uppsala AB, 1995).

Déroche, Vincent, *Syméon Salos, le fou en Christ* (Paris: Paris-Méditerranée, 2000).

Efthymiadis, Stephanos and Nikos Kalogeras, "Audience, Language and Patronage in Byzantine Hagiography", in Stephanos Efthymiadis (ed.), *The Ashgate Research Companion to Byzantine Hagiography*, vol. 2 (Farnham: Ashgate, 2014), 247–284.

Elliott, Alison G., *Roads to Paradise: Reading the Lives of the Early Saints* (London: University Press of New England, 1987).

Festugière, André Jean, *Léontios de Neapolis. Vie de Syméon le Fou et Vie de Jean de Chypre* (Paris: Librairie orientaliste Paul Geuthner, 1974).
Frye, Northrop, *The Secular Scripture: A Study of the Structure of Romance* (Cambridge, MA/London: Harvard University Press, 1976).
Gill, Christopher and Timothy P. Wiseman, "Preface", in iidem (eds.), *Lies and Fiction in the Ancient World* (Exeter: University of Exeter Press, 1993), vii–ix.
Grosdidier de Matons, José, "Les thèmes d'édification dans la vie d'André Salos", *TM* 4 (1970), 277–328.
Hägg, Tomas, "The Life of St Antony between Biography and Hagiography", in Stephanos Efthymiadis (ed.), *The Ashgate Research Companion to Byzantine Hagiography*, vol. 1 (Farnham: Ashgate, 2011), 17–34.
Harshaw, Benjamin, "Fictionality and Fields of Reference: Remarks on a Theoretical Framework", *Poetics Today* 5.2 (1984), 227–251.
Hauptmann, Peter, "Die 'Narren um Christi Willen' in der Ostkirche", *Kirche im Osten* 2 (1959), 27–49.
Hinterberger, Martin, "The Byzantine Hagiographer and his Text", in Stephanos Efthymiadis (ed.), *The Ashgate Research Companion to Byzantine Hagiography*, vol. 2: (Farnham: Ashgate, 2014), 211–246.
Holzberg, Niklas, "The Genre: Novels Proper and the Fringe", in Gareth L. Schmeling (ed.), *The Novel in the Ancient World* (Leiden/New York/Köln: Brill, 1996), 11–28.
Ivanov, Sergei, "St Paul the Corinthian, Holy Fool", in Eleonora Kountoura-Galake (ed.), *The Heroes of the Orthodox Church: The New Saints, 8th–16th C.* (Athens: Institute for Byzantine Research, 2004), 39–46.
Kaldellis, Anthony, "The Emergence of Literary Fiction in Byzantium and the Paradox of Plausibility", in Panagiotis Roilos (ed.), *Medieval Greek Storytelling: Fictionality and Narrative in Byzantium* (Wiesbaden: Harrassowitz Verlag, 2014), 115–130.
Kazhdan, Alexander, "Byzantine Hagiography and Sex in the Fifth to Twelfth Centuries", *DOP* 44 (1990), 131–143.
Krueger, Derek, *Symeon the Holy Fool: Leontius' Life and the Late Antique City* (Berkeley/Los Angeles/London: University of California Press, 1996).
Krueger, Derek, *Writing and Holiness: The Practice of Authorship in the Early Christian East* (Philadelphia: University of Pennsylvania Press, 2004).
Landy, Joshua, *How to Do Things with Fictions* (Oxford: Oxford University Press, 2012).
Magdalino, Paul, "'What We Heard in the Lives of Saints We Have Seen with Our Own Eyes': The Holy Man as Literary Text in Tenth-Century Constantinople", in James Howard-Johnston and Paul A. Hayward (eds.), *The Cult of Saints in Late Antiquity and the Middle Ages: Essays on the Contribution of Peter Brown* (Oxford: Oxford University Press, 1999), 83–112.
Messis, Charis, "Fiction and/or Novelisation in Byzantine Hagiography", in Stephanos Efthymiadis (ed.), *The Ashgate Research Companion to Byzantine Hagiography*, vol. 2 (Farnham: Ashgate, 2014), 313–342.

Mihailescu, Calin Andrei and Walid Hamarneh, "Introduction: Under the Jealous Gaze of Truth", in iidem (eds.), *Fiction Updated: Theories of Fictionality, Narratology and Poetics* (Toronto/Buffalo: University of Toronto Press, 1996), 3–18.

Morgan, John, "Make-Believe and Make Believe: The Fictionality of the Greek Novels", in Christopher Gill and Timothy P. Wiseman (eds.), *Lies and Fiction in the Ancient World* (Exeter: University of Exeter Press, 1993), 175–229.

Musurillo, Herbert, *The Acts of the Christian Martyrs* (Oxford: Clarendon Press, 1972).

Nigg, Walter, *Der christliche Narr* (Stuttgart: Artemis-Verlag, 1956).

Olsen, Stein Haugom and Peter Lamarque, *Truth, Fiction, and Literature: A Philosophical Perspective* (2nd edition Oxford: Clarendon Press, 1996).

Pavel, Thomas, *Fictional Worlds* (Cambridge, MA: Harvard University Press, 1986).

Rapp, Claudia, "Figures of Female Sanctity: Byzantine Edifying Manuscripts and Their Audience", *DOP* 50 (1996), 313–344.

Rapp, Claudia, "Storytelling as Spiritual Communication in Early Greek Hagiography: The Use of Diegesis", *JECS* 6.3 (1998), 431–448.

Rapp, Claudia, "Author, Audience, Text and Saint: Two Modes of Early Byzantine Hagiography", *SJBMGS* 1 (2015), 111–129.

Roilos, Panagiotis (ed.), *Medieval Greek Storytelling: Fictionality and Narrative in Byzantium* (Wiesbaden: Harrassowitz, 2014).

Rotman, Youval, *Insanity and Sanctity in Byzantium: The Ambiguity of Religious Experience* (Cambridge, MA/London: Harvard University Press, 2016).

Rubenson, Samuel, "Antony and Pythagoras: A Reappraisal of the Appropriation of Classical Biography in Athanasius' Vita Antonii", in David Brakke, Anders-Christian Jacobsen, and Jörg Ulrich (eds.), *Beyond Reception. Mutual Influences between Antique Religion, Judaism, and Early Christianity* (Bern: Peter Lang, 2006), 191–208.

Ryan, Marie-Laure, "Possible Worlds in Recent Literary Theory", *Style* 26.4 (1992), 528–554.

Ryan, Marie-Laure, "Postmodernism and the Doctrine of Panfictionality", *Narrative* 5.2 (1997), 165–187.

Rydén, Lennart, "Date of the 'Life of Andreas Salos'", *DOP* 32 (1978), 127–155.

Rydén, Lennart, "The Holy Fool", in Sergei Hackel (ed.), *The Byzantine Saint* (London: Fellowship of St. Alban and St. Sergius, 1981), 106–113.

Rydén, Lennart, *The Life of St Andrew the Fool*, 2 vols., Acta Universatis Upsaliensis, Studia Byzantina Upsaliensa 4 (Uppsala: Textgruppen i Uppsala AB, 1995).

Rydén, Lennart, "Fiction and Reality in the Hagiographer's Self-Presentation", *TM* 14 (2002), 547–552.

Rydén, Lennart, "Literariness in Byzantine Saints' Lives", in Paolo Odorico and Panagiotis A. Agapitos (eds.), *Les Vies des saints à Byzance. Genre littéraire ou biographie historique? Actes du IIe colloque international philologique 'EPMHNEIA'* (Paris: Centre d'études byzantines, néo-helléniques et sud-est européennes, EHESS, 2004), 49–58.

Rydén, Lennart, "Introduzione", in P. Cesaretti (ed.), *Leonzio di Neapoli. Niceforo prete di Santa Sofia. Vite dei Saloi Simeone e Andrea* (BHG *1677, 115z*). *Premessa di Augusta Acconcia Longo. Introduzione di Lennart Ryden.* Testi e studi bizantino-neoellenici 19 (Roma: Dipartimento di scienze dell'antichità 'Sapienza', 2014), 33–54.

Schaeffer, Jean-Marie, *Pourquoi la fiction?* (Paris: Seuil, 1999).

Schmid, Wolf, "Implied Author", in Jan C. Meister (ed.), *The Living Handbook of Narratology* (Hamburg: Hamburg University, 2013), Website http://www.lhn.uni-hamburg .de/article/implied-author-revised-version-uploaded-26-january-2013 [last accessed 07/05/2018].

Searle, John, *Speech Acts: An Essay in the Philosophy of Language* (Cambridge: Cambridge University Press, 1969).

Turner, Peter, *Truthfulness, Realism, Historicity: A Study of Late Antique Spiritual Literature* (Farnham: Ashgate, 2012).

Van Uytfanghe, Marc, "La biographie classique et l'hagiographie chrétienne antique tardive", *Hagiographica* 12 (2005), 223–248.

von Contzen, Eva, *The Scottish Legendary: Towards a Poetics of Hagiographic Narration* (Manchester: Manchester University Press, 2016).

Walsh, Richard, *The Rhetoric of Fictionality: Narrative Theory and the Idea of Fiction* (Columbus: Ohio State University Press, 2007).

Walton, Kendall, *Mimesis as Make-Believe: On the Foundations of the Representational Arts* (2nd edition Cambridge, MA: Harvard University Press, 1990).

Wood, Michael, "Prologue", in Christopher Gill and Timothy P. Wiseman (eds.), *Lies and Fiction in the Ancient World* (Exeter: University of Exeter Press, 1993), xiii–xviii.

Zetterberg Gjerlevsen, Simona and Henrik Skov Nielsen, "Distinguishing Fictionality", *Narratologia* (forthcoming).

CHAPTER 3

Clerical Hagiography in Late Antiquity

Robert Wiśniewski

This chapter deals with late antique *vitae* whose heroes belonged to the clergy, and particularly with the questions of for whom and for what these texts were written. In order to introduce this issue, however, I will begin with monastic hagiography. While this volume argues that it would go too far to say that the lives of holy monks gave rise to the very idea of writing the stories of the Christian saints, there is not much doubt that they started the interest in those personages whose merits lay in their life, and not in their martyrdom. What was the purpose of these writings? Hippolyte Delehaye, whose name we still quote with reverence and justly so, defined hagiography as literature written in order to launch, promote, or maintain the cult of a saint.[1] Interestingly, this definition does not fit well with the majority of the earliest lives of holy monks. In the *Life of Antony*, written most probably in the AD 360s, which set the rules for the genre, we find neither an exact date of its hero's death nor the localisation of his grave which, as the author tells us, remains hidden.[2] Thus two pieces of information essential for the development of the cult, two *coordonnées hagiographiques*, as Delehaye calls them, are missing. Moreover, there are only a few miracles in this text and none of them is posthumous.[3] Thus, the *Life of Antony* was certainly not written to start a cult. Athanasius tells about his purpose directly—he writes in order to provide an example of virtue and *askēsis* to be followed by those who entered upon a noble rivalry with the monks of Egypt.[4] And the contents of the *Life of Antony*, including a long sermon addressed to his pupils, show that this was really the goal that the author had in mind.[5] The cultic ambitions, which can be found in several early martyrdoms, are absent from other early *vitae* as well. There is no trace of them in Jerome's lives of Paul and Malchus, both written not long after the *Life of Antony*.[6] Only in

1 Hippolyte Delehaye, *Les légendes hagiographiques* (2nd edition Brussels: Société des Bollandistes, 1955), 2.

2 Athan. *V. Anton.* 90–92.

3 Athan. *V. Anton.* 54–65.

4 Athan. *V. Anton.* 1 and 94.

5 Athan. *V. Anton.* 16–43 (about a third of the length of the *vita*).

6 For Paul see Pierre Leclerc, "Antoine et Paul: métamorphose d' un héros", in Yves-Marie Duval (ed.), *Jérôme entre l'Occident et l'Orient. XVIe centenaire du départ de saint Jérôme de Rome et de*

 | DOI:10.1163/9789004421332_005

the last of his monastic *vitae*, that of Hilarion, dating from the early AD 390s, does Jerome try to construct the cult of his hero, but even here the parenetic function is dominant.[7] It does not mean that the lives of the holy men of the desert were composed just for the training of the monks, but the monks were certainly an important, intended, and real audience which sought this kind of literature. It suffices to mention the *Rule of Benedict*, which recommended them to read the *vitae patrum*, which are 'the instruments whereby well-living and obedient monks attain to virtue'.[8]

In this chapter, I want to raise the question of whether the lives of saintly clerics had a similar function; whether they were written in order to provide their colleagues or followers with a role model. The writing of clerical *vitae* started quite early. The first life of a bishop, the *Vita Cypriani*, was composed probably shortly after its protagonist's death in AD 258 and so somehow preceded the heyday of hagiography by over a hundred years. Its author, Pontius of Carthage, explains that he aims to describe the life of a man who, not only in his death, but also in his life was an incomparable example to others.[9] Pontius emphasises the priesthood of his hero and claims that since Cyprian was a martyr and bishop he should be honoured more than those martyrs who were simply lay people and catechumens.[10] Still, Cyprian did suffer martyrdom and we can wonder whether his life would have been written at all had he died in peace. Also, the *Vita Cypriani* is a specific text because of its particular goal. It aims to explain why its hero survived the persecution of Decius in AD 250 in hiding and died only in that of Valerian in AD 258, and it is partly this delay of martyrdom which made the author focus on the years which had preceded Cyprian's glorious death. Two other texts which also belong to the pre-history of clerical hagiography, Eusebius of Caesarea's lives of Origen and Pamphilus, the latter now lost, also present stories of the men who suffered and died dur-

son installation à Bethléem. Actes du colloque de Chantilly, Sept. 1986 (Paris: Études augustiniennes, 1988), 256–265; for Malchus: Christa Gray, *Jerome, Vita Malchi: Introduction, Text, Translation, and Commentary* (Oxford: Oxford University Press, 2015), 12–14.

7 Jer. *V. Hilarion*. 32–33; see also the ending of Jerome's *Letter* 108 (or the *Vita Paulae*) in which the author expresses his belief in her intercession, names the place in which she was buried and gives the date of her death, all these elements were important for the cult: Jer. *Ep.* 108.33–34.

8 … *bene viventium et oboedientium monachorum instrumenta virtutum*, *Regula Benedicti* 73, see also 42, de Vogüé, Adalbert (ed.), *La Règle de saint Benoît*, 2 vols. Sources chrétiennes 181–182 (Paris: Les Éditions du Cerf, 1972).

9 Pont. *V. Cypr.* 1; see Hugo Montgomery, "Pontius' *Vita S. Cypriani* and the Making of a Saint", *SO* 71 (1996), 195–215.

10 Pont. *V. Cypr.* 1.2 and 19. 1–4.

ing (or shortly after) persecutions.[11] Even if Pontius or Eusebius thought about their heroes as role models for the clergy, this model was not fully applicable in post-Constantinian Christianity.

The interest in the lives of clerics who did not die martyrs began closer to the end of the fourth century. The earliest safely dated *vita* of this kind is Gregory of Nyssa's *Life of Gregory Thaumaturgus*, which praises the deeds of the third-century bishop of Neocaesarea in Pontus with whom Gregory's family was closely linked. Moreover, after the death of his brother, Basil, bishop of Caesarea, Gregory described his life in his *Sermon* 43, also known as the *Eulogy for Basil*. Not much later, Sulpicius Severus wrote the *Life of Martin* (c. AD 396) and the *Dialogues* (c. AD 406), which recounted and defended the life and virtues of their hero, bishop and monk, not entirely popular among the Gallic episcopate. These were followed by the *vitae* of Ambrose by Paulinus, deacon of the church of Milan (c. AD 422), Augustine by Possidius, bishop of Calama (in the AD 430s), then by the lives of two successive bishops of Arles, Honoratus and Hilary, both formerly monks at Lérins, and the *Life of Germanus of Auxerre* by Constantius of Lyon.[12] In Greek literature the situation was slightly more complicated. The early *Dialogue on the Life of John Chrysostom*, written still in his lifetime at the very beginning of the fifth century by Palladius, is a text on the margins of the genre as it is an apology of the bishop rather than a proper *vita*. A few other lives of early bishops at least contain the material from the late fourth or early fifth century, but are very difficult to date with any precision. The *Life of Aberkios*, supposedly second-century bishop of Hierapolis, which

11 Eus. *Hist. eccl.* 6.1–39 (Origen) and *Hist. eccl.* 6.32.3 (mentioning the *Life of Pamphilus*); see Joseph Verheyden, "Origen in the Making: Reading between (and behind) the Lines of Eusebius' *Life of Origen* (*Hist. eccl.* 6)", in Sylwia Kaczmarek and Henryk Pietras (eds.), *Origeniana Decima: Origen as Writer* (Leuven: Peeters, 2011), 713–726, and James Corke-Webster in this volume.

12 Gregory of Nyssa, *Vita Gregorii Thaumaturgi*: ed. Günter Heil, *Gregorii Nysseni Opera* 10.1 (Leiden: Brill, 1990); Gregory of Nyssa, *In Basilium fratrem*: Jean Bernardi (ed.), *Grégoire de Nazianze, Discours 42–43*, Sources chrétiennes 384 (Paris: Les Éditions du Cerf, 1992); Sulpicius Severus, *Vita Martini* and *Epistulae*: Jacques Fontaine (ed.), *Sulpice Sévère, Vie de saint Martin*. Sources chrétiennes 133–135 (Paris: Les Éditions du Cerf, 1967–1969); ibid., *Dialogi*: *Sulpice Sévère, Gallus. Dialogues sur les 'vertus' de saint Martin*, Sources chrétiennes 510 (Paris, Éditions du Cerf, 2006); Paulinus of Milan, *Vita Ambrosii*: Antoon A.R. Bastiaensen (ed.) *Vite dei santi*, vol. 3 (Milan: Mondadori, 1975); Possidius, *Vita Augustini*: *ibidem*; Honoratus, *Vita Hilarii*: Samuel Cavallin (ed.), Paul-André Jacob (comm.), *Honorat de Marseille, La Vie d'Hilaire d'Arles*, Sources chrétiennes 404 (Paris: Les Éditions du Cerf, 1995); Hilary, *Sermo de vita sancti Honorati*: Marie-Denise Valentin (ed.), *Hilaire d'Arles, Vie de saint Honorat*, Sources chrétiennes 235 (Paris: Les Éditions du Cerf, 1977); Constantius of Lyon, *Vita Germani*: René Borius (ed.), *Constance de Lyon, Vie de saint Germain d'Auxerre*, Sources chrétiennes 112 (Paris: Les Éditions du Cerf, 1965).

presents his travels and adventures in various parts of the Mediterranean, is probably a fictitious development of an Aberkios' (not necessarily Christian) tomb inscription. Two other *vitae* of bishops active at the end of the fourth and the beginning of the fifth century had an even more complex history. The *Life of Epiphanius of Salamis* presumably contains some notes of eyewitnesses (members of his clergy), but was edited by a later compiler who may have worked as late as the sixth century. The *Life of Porphyry of Gaza*, also most probably based on a fifth-century account, was certainly reworked over a century later. We encounter a similar problem when dealing with the less well-known *Life and Martyrdom of Athenogenes of Pedachthoe*, whose fifth-century author, a certain Anysios, probably made use of an earlier story.[13]

One hardly needs to state that the protagonists of all these lives were bishops. There are no late antique lives of deacons or clerics holding lower ecclesiastical offices. The lives of presbyters are few. It is worth repeating that Origen and Pamphilus, both holding this rank, were both victims of the persecutions.[14] The same can be said about the untypical 'Life of Felix', contained in Poems 15 and 16 of Paulinus of Nola, which presents its hero as a confessor rather than a presbyter, for Felix too did suffer during the persecution.[15] Presbyters living

13 Palladius: Anne-Marie Malingrey and Philippe Leclercq (eds.), *Palladius, Dialogue sur la vie de Jean Chrysostome*, Sources chrétiennes 341 and 342 (Paris: Les Éditions du Cerf, 1988); *Sancti Abercii Vita*, Theodor Nissen (ed.) (Leipzig: Teubner, 1912); the *Life of Epiphanius* (BHG 596–599) does not have a critical edition and has to be consulted in PG 41.23–116, see Claudia Rapp, "Epiphanius of Salamis, the Church Father as Saint", in Anthony A. Bryer and George S. Georghallides (eds.), *The Sweet Land of Cyprus: Papers Given at the Twenty-Fifth Jubilee Spring Symposium of Byzantine Studies, Birmingham, March 1991* (Nicosia: The Cyprus Research Centre for the Society for the Promotion of Byzantine Studies, 1993), 169–187, at 178–179; Mark the Deacon: Anna Lampadaridi (ed.), *La Conversion de Gaza au christianisme. La Vie de S. Porphyre par Marc le Diacre* (*BHG 1570*). *Edition critique, traduction, commentaire* (Brussels: Société des Bollandistes, 2016); Athenogenes of Pedachthoe: P. Maraval (ed.), *La Passion inédite de S. Athénogène de Pédachthoè en Cappadoce* (*BHG 197b*) (Brussels: Société des Bollandistes, 1990).

14 The ecclesiastical status of Origen is not entirely clear. He was ordained presbyter, but his ordination was contested. It is possible that when he moved to Caesarea he did not perform liturgical duties, but certainly was a member of the clergy whom the bishop invested with the authority to preach.

15 Willy Evenepoel, "The *Vita Felicis* of Paulinus Nolanus", in Marc Van Uytfanghe and Roland Demeulenaere (eds.), *Aevum inter utrumque: Mélanges offerts à Gabriel Sanders, professeur émérite à l'Université de Gand* (The Hague: Nijhoff International, 1991), 143–152. But see Michael Stuart Williams, "Always Already a Martyr? Felix of Nola as Martyr and Confessor", in Vincent Déroche, Bryan Ward-Perkins, and Robert Wiśniewski (eds.), *Culte des saints et littérature hagiographique: accords et désaccords* (Leuven: Peeters, 2019), 151–183, who argues that Paulinus wanted to create a more complex image of Felix, consciously downplaying his martyrdom.

in the post-Constantinian period had little chance to have their own *vita*, and probably the only early text of this kind in which the priesthood of the protagonist plays an important role is a short fifth- or sixth-century Gallic *Life of Romanus, presbyter at Blaye*.[16] The preponderance of the bishops over presbyters in hagiography is hardly surprising. It reflects their superior position in real life and the stronger interest in their story after their death: their cult, important for the identity of the local community, inspired this interest in a natural way. Also, we can suppose that in most cases their life was more attractive from the literary point of view, since their activity was more varied and usually more spectacular than that of lower clerics. This situation was not dissimilar to that of the monastic hagiography which usually tells us about either hermits or abbots, and not normal rank-and-file coenobitic monks. If the latter drew the interest of hagiographers it is because for some reason they turned out to be not entirely normal coenobites, but e.g. women disguised as monks.[17] Of course, one can wonder whether the lives of bishops were attractive as exemplary lives for the presbyters, the main working force of the clergy. But we have to remember that the presbyters could easily identify with the bishops, both because they were usually considered as belonging to the same group of the *hiereis* or *sacerdotes* (unlike deacons and lower clerics)[18] and because many of them could hope that one day they would attain the supreme grade of priesthood.

Although above I have listed most of the early *vitae* of the bishops, and in what follows I will refer to a few later texts, this article is very far from providing a complete catalogue of the late antique clerical hagiography. Neither does it analyse all the motives which drove late antique authors to writing these texts, and which, as the examples quoted above show, differed. It focuses on the question of whether the lives of the bishops were written to provide a model to be imitated by their clerical audience. This question is important not only for a better understanding of the beginnings of an important hagiographical subgenre. It is also important for the study of the history of clergy which in this period was emerging as a distinct social group. In the early fourth century it

16 Gottfried Vielhaber (ed.), *Sancti Romani Vita Prima* (BHL 7305), *AB* 26 (1907), 52–56. *Vita Secunda* (BHL 7306): *AB* 5 (1886), 178–191. See also Bruno Krusch (ed.), *Vita Memorii*, MGH SRM 3 (Hannover: Hahn, 1896), 10–104, but Memorius of Troyes was both a presbyter and martyr.

17 Evelyne Patlagean, "L'Histoire de la femme déguisée en moine et l'évolution de la sainteté féminine à Byzance", *Studi Medievali*, Third Series 17 (Spoleto: CISAM, 1976), 597–623. The only exceptions I know (both thanks to Vincent Déroche) are the *Life of Dositheos*, a young coenobite who did not perform miracles or any other deeds, written by his monastic superior, Dorotheus of Gaza (BHG 2117), and the *Life of Paulus Hypotacticus* (BHG 2363).

18 See e.g. Isid. *Etymol.* 7.12.20–21.

was hardly possible to identify a cleric as such in the street and it was not easy to describe a way of life specific for clerics.[19] But then the situation began to change. Clerics slowly started to differ from the lay people in their clothes and hairstyle. Synodal canons forbade them to carry out several extra-ecclesiastical professional activities or participate in wedding feasts, and even tried to keep them out of public places. Even more importantly, the no-sex life or celibacy became more and more widespread, at least as an ideal.[20] All this took time, but we can see in the evidence a conscious effort of shaping distinct customs of clergy.[21] And this is why I wonder whether hagiography played a role in this process. Did the hagiographers write for clerics? Did they aim to provide them with a model of priestly life, and, if so, what did this model consist in?

1 Lives of Monks-Clerics

As one can suspect, the answer is complex. We certainly cannot say that all lives of presbyters and bishops were written with a clerical audience in mind and aimed to provide it with role models. The purposes of the authors, the audiences which they targeted, and the types of clerical life that they presented varied.

A distinct type of clerical lives were those whose heroes were at the same time priests and monks. An obvious starting point to study the function of such hagiographies are the Martinian writings of Sulpicius Severus, which created a pattern of the monk-bishop. According to Sulpicius Severus, Martin started his saintly career as a monk, or a soldier desiring to be a monk, but the episcopal ordination was an important caesura in his life. 'I shall therefore set about writing the life of St Martin, and shall narrate both what he did previous to his episcopate, and what he performed as a bishop',[22] says the author at the

19 Still in AD428 Pope Celestine claims that the priests should differ from other people by their customs, and not by their clothes: Celestine I, *Ep.* 4 (*Cuperemus quidem*) 1.2, see Stanislaw Adamiak, in the database *Presbyters in the Late Antique West* (http://www.presbytersproject.ihuw.pl/, henceforward PLAW [last accessed 6/08/2019]) ER1792; but in 506 the synod of Agde forbids clerics to wear unsuitable clothes and orders them to be tonsured: *Concilium Agathense*, can. 20, see Jerzy Szafranowski, PLAW ER929.

20 See David Hunter, *Marriage, Celibacy, and Heresy in Ancient Christianity: The Jovinianist Controversy* (Oxford: Oxford University Press, 2007), 243–284.

21 This process can be seen in diverse types of evidence, but especially in synodal canons. See William E. Klingshirn, "Christian Divination in Late Roman Gaul: The *Sortes Sangallenses*", in Sarah I. Johnston and Peter T. Struck (eds.), *Mantikê: Studies in Ancient Divination* (Leiden: Brill, 2005), 99–128, at 114–115.

22 *Igitur sancti Martini vitam scribere exordiar ut se vel ante episcopatum vel in episcopatu gesserit* (Sulp. Sev. *V. Mart.* 1.7).

outset. However, he makes it clear that Martin's sanctity was not upgraded in any way by his episcopal ordination. Quite the contrary—if the sanctity is to be measured by the power to perform miracles, Martin lost part of it when he became a bishop. As Sulpicius Severus puts it, 'Martin used to say to you, Sulpicius, that such an abundance of power was by no means granted him while he was a bishop, as he remembered to have possessed before he obtained that office'.[23] Of course, paradoxically, being a bishop contributed to Martin's holiness, but only in this way that living in the world, among 'quarrelsome clerics and furious bishops',[24] made holiness more difficult to attain. Consequently, this holiness is more praiseworthy than in the case of monks who passed their life in easier conditions. Thus, there is a link between Martin's episcopate and sanctity, but he was a saint in spite and not because of being a bishop. When his hagiographer says that he raised two men from the dead as a monk, and only one as a bishop, he suggests that Martin must have been a very exceptional saint, if being a bishop he resuscitated anybody at all.[25] The implication, of course, is that normally bishops do not do this. Admittedly, in the end Sulpicius Severus presents Martin as an ideal bishop, but his sanctity, and indeed also his episcopal authority, is based on his monastic or ascetic life, his desire for martyrdom, and his virtues equal to those of the martyrs. The *Life* and the *Dialogues* clearly propose a new model of priesthood, founded upon monastic experience. In order to be a good cleric one has to be a monk. The 'new model clergy', trained in Martin's community in Marmoutier, should replace the clerical and particularly episcopal establishment which Sulpicius Severus criticises almost on every page of his writings.[26]

Such a conscious effort to construct a clerical model upon the monastic one is rarely as strong as in Sulpicius Severus, but we can find it in many other *vitae*. Let us take a look at the *Life of Honoratus*, the founder of the monastic community in the Lérins Islands at the beginning of the fifth century and then the bishop of Arles from AD 428 to AD 430. In this text, written by Hilary, Honoratus' successor at the episcopal see of Arles, the latter is presented as predestined to be a bishop. He is described as exercising a 'private episcopate' (*privatus … episcopatus gerebatur*) and being a mentor of several bishops already at the

23 *Illud autem animadverti saepe, Sulpici, Martinum tibi dicere solitum, nequaquam sibi in episcopatu eam virtutum gratiam suppetisse, quam prius se habuisse meminisset* (Sulp. Sev. *Dial.* 2.4.1).

24 *… inter clericos dissidentes, inter episcopos saevientes* (Sulp. Sev. *Dial.* 1.24.2).

25 Sulp. Sev. *Dial.* 2.4.3, see also *V. Mart.* 7.

26 The bishops trained in Martin's monastery: *V. Mart.* 10.9.

beginning of his monastic life, long before his ordination.[27] Then, when he is a presbyter, Honoratus is treated as equal, or better, by the bishops.[28] Finally, as a bishop, he is praised for being at the same time stern and gentle, successful in making the sinners repent and bringing peace to the divided church of Arles. His priesthood does matter. But his episcopal activity is presented very briefly, in just four chapters out of thirty-nine.[29] Admittedly, it is partly justified by the fact that he was a bishop for only two years, while he spent many more as a monk. However, in the *vitae* the length of the successive stages of the saint's career does not necessarily reflect the length of the corresponding periods of his real life. In this case, the episcopal period of the *vita* is consciously kept brief and the author does not tell us about any episode from this period, which suggests that he did not feel a need to treat this part of Honoratus' activity in any detail. And this is interesting, because the *Life of Honoratus*, or *Sermo de vita sancti Honorati*, was not addressed to a monastic audience. It was delivered by Honoratus' relative and fellow-monk in Lérins, but above all, his successor at the episcopal see, probably on the first anniversary of his death. It was preached in Arles and the audience consisted of the inhabitants of this city. And yet, Hilary was talking to them about Honoratus' monastic life—probably because it was this life, and not the episcopate, which made him a saint. Hilary's aim was to praise the bishop because he was a holy monk, not to show how exactly the episcopal office should be held.

Some Lives show the priesthood as an even more unimportant episode in the lives of their heroes. According to his Life, Daniel the Stylite, for instance, living in the suburbs of Constantinople in the mid fifth century, was ordained priest from a distance, because he did not allow the archbishop to mount the ladder, and so the latter was not able to reach the top of the column on which the saint was standing.[30] The only function of this episode is to show that the holy monk wanted to avoid the glory of priesthood—we cannot see him exercising any priestly duties.

Still other *vitae* depict the clerical life as a dirty business that monks should keep out of as far as possible. Two interesting examples of Lives of this kind come, perhaps symptomatically, from the seventh century. The first of them is the *Life of St Aemilianus of Berceo*. It tells about an excellent monk whose piety

27 Hil. Arelat. *V. Honor.* 9.4. I am grateful to Jerzy Szafranowski for drawing my attention to this passage and discussing with me several issues concerning the life of the monks-clerics.

28 Hil. Arelat. *V. Honor.* 16.3.

29 Bishop: Hil. Arelat. *V. Honor.* 25–28; death and burial; 29–36.

30 *V. Daniel.* 42–43.

did not pass unnoticed by a local bishop and who consequently was ordained presbyter. The passage which describes the priestly period of his life runs as follows:

> Finally, he was unwillingly compelled to obey, and so performed the office of presbyter in the church of Berceo. Then setting aside those things to which men of that order, the men, that is, of our day, are accustomed to dedicate themselves, he imparted his holy care on this life to which he had been dragged back. In this, however, through continual prayer, week-long fasts, perpetual vigils, true discernment, sure hope, great frugality, kindly righteousness, firm endurance, in short with the greatest austerity he tirelessly kept himself from all evil things.[31]

All that the author has to say about Aemilianus' life after ordination is that he did not behave like a cleric, but as a monk, apparently following the example of Martin presented above. The catalogue of his virtues is partly generic, partly monastic: long fasts, continual prayer, perpetual vigils, and discernment are frequently referred to in monastic stories from Egypt. Even more interestingly, the clerical period of Aemilianus' life ends abruptly. Other clerics ('of the worst sort!', as the author presents them) accuse him of alienating church property, his bishop dismisses him, and Aemilianus returns to the monastic life.[32] This episode might be interpreted as written with monks in mind, warning them against the dangers of the clerical life. However, the *Life of Aemilianus* was not written for monks. It was dedicated to a presbyter, a certain Fronimianus,[33] and so it cannot be taken as a piece of monastic literature. Moreover, it was

---

31 *Tandemque coactus est invitus obedire quapropter in ecclessia Vergegio presbiterii est functus officio. Tunc relictis quibus deditii solent esse istius ordinis, nostri quidem homines temporis, sanctam impertiebat curam in hanc in quam retractus fuerat vitam in quo tamen continuatae preces, hebdomadarum inedia, iugis vigilia, discretio vera, spes certa, frugalitas magna, iustitia blanda, patientia solida, et ut breviter dicam ab omni omnino re mala indefesse persitebat parsimonia maxima* (Braul. *V. Aemil.* 12), Luis Vázquez de Parga, *Sancti Braulionis Caesaraugustani episcopi Vita S. Emiliani* (Madrid: Instituto Jerónimo Zurita, 1943). Translated by Andrew T. Fear, *Lives of the Visigothic Fathers* (Liverpool: Liverpool University Press, 1997), 24–25.

32 Braul. *V. Aemil.* 13.

33 See Braul. *V. Aemil.* 1. Fronimianus probably later became an abbot of the monastery of St Aemilanus, but nothing in the *vita* suggests his monastic status. Also, the fact that Braulio refers to him as his brother should not be taken at face value—this is not an unusual way for a bishop to address presbyters, contrary to what Claude W. Barlowe, *Iberian Fathers*, vol. 2 (Washington DC: CUA Press, 1969), 35 n. 1, claims.

not only written for a cleric, it also was written by a bishop. Its author, Braulio, was the metropolitan bishop of Saragossa. Admittedly, the general unflattering remarks about contemporary clerics, 'the men of that order, the men, that is, of our day', can be read as an admonition directed to contemporary priests; such admonitions can be found in some other hagiographical stories in which the protagonist of a *vita* has to face the jealousy or hatred of depraved monks or worldly clerics. But the thing is that in the lives which show an example to follow such stories usually have a happy ending—bad men are converted, punished or at least ashamed, and the saint shows what the things should and can look like.[34] This text does not bring any positive message, at least for clerics—the hypothetical clerical reader of the *Vita Aemiliani* is left perplexed. Even if he learnt that a good presbyter should pray, fast, keep vigils, and be renowned for discernment, hope, frugality, righteousness, endurance, and austerity, the message is not really encouraging as far as the clerical career is concerned, since the good man who became a priest finally had to leave the ranks of the clergy.

Another hagiographic text in which the clerical period of the protagonist's life is obviously downplayed is the anonymous *Vita sancti Fructuosi*, also written in seventh-century Spain.[35] Its author, probably a monk writing for monks,[36] essentially ignores the fact that his hero was a priest and presents him as a hermit and a founder of monasteries. After seventeen chapters devoted to this activity, a very short Chapter 18 just mentions Fructuosus' ordination to an unnamed bishopric, which he, according to the convention, fiercely resisted. This is not an uncommon motif in the life of a bishop. Ambrose of Milan, Hilary of Arles, or Germanus of Auxerre, to name just a few, did not want to accept the honour of the bishopric either.[37] But their Lives, having described this resistance, duly present their activity as bishops. It is not so with the *Life of Fructuous*, whose hero dies in Chapters 19–20. Now, this narrative hardly

34 See e.g. Sulp. Sev. *V. Mart.* 9.3–7 and *Dial.* 3.15; Greg. Mag. *Dial.* 2.3.1–6. Interestingly, a close parallel to the *Life of Aemilianus* can be found in contemporary Greek lives of bishops, which also focus on their monastic, not clerical, activity, see Stephanos Efthymiadis, "The Place of Holy and Unholy Bishops in Byzantine Hagiographical Narrative (Eighth–Twelfth Centuries)", in John S. Ott and Trpimir Vedriš (eds.), *Saintly Bishops and Bishops' Saints* (Zagreb: Hagiotheca, 2012), 169–182, on 177–178.

35 *Vita Fructuosi*, in Fear, *Lives of the Visigothic Fathers*, 123–144.

36 Formerly the author of this *vita* was identified with Valerius of Bierzo. This identification has been rejected by the new editor of the *Life of Fructuosus*, but the monastic character of the milieu in which it was written is well visible throughout the text, see Manuel C. Díaz y Díaz, *La Vida de San Fructuoso de Braga* (Braga: Diário do Minho, 1974), 15–20.

37 Paulin. Mediol. *V. Ambr.* 6–9; Honor. Mass. *V. Hilar.* 9; Const. *V. Germ.* 2.

reflects the real story of his life. We know that Fructuosus was a bishop of Dumio, and then of Braga, a metropolitan see, for about ten years, and before that he was a presbyter.[38] But the *vita* does not say anything about it. The only piece of information about Fructuosus' life as a bishop is that he 'spent the rest of his life dispensing alms and in construction of monasteries', otherwise sticking to his former monastic habits.[39] Apparently the only merit in being a bishop is that one can live as if one was not one (which is a heroic feat) and have more resources that can be spent to satisfy the needs of the poor and monks. In all, Fructuosus followed the path of Aemilianus, even if only up to a point. He was certainly more successful, but strangely enough this does not seem to be of much interest to the author. One meagre chapter devoted to priesthood against seventeen devoted to monastic life is hardly likely to make clerical readers enthusiastic about their vocation.

A similar phenomenon of downplaying the priestly career of hagiographical heroes can be seen in Byzantine hagiography. Stephanos Efthymiadis shows that, from the end of the seventh century on, the lives of bishops become rare, and even in those few that were written in this period references to the episcopal career of their heroes are brief and insignificant, while the emphasis is put on their monastic experience. Efthymiadis attributes this 'monasterization of sanctity'[40] to the dwindling of the cities and city-based episcopal power due to the crisis of the seventh century. But in seventh-century Spain the position of the bishops did not really dwindle.[41] Thus, we are possibly dealing with a more profound phenomenon. The monastic model of the holy life was growing in attractiveness at the expense of the clerical model, at least at the literary level.

38 See Luis A. García Moreno, *Prosopografía del reino visigodo de Toledo* (Salamanca: Ediciones Universidad, 1974), no. 383; for his presbyterial ordination see Marta Szada, PLAW PR155.

39 *Residuum vitae suae tempus in elemosinarum dispensatione atque monasteriorum consumavit aedificatione* (*V. Fruct.* 18).

40 The term was coined by Rosemary Morris, "The Political Saint of the Eleventh Century," in Sergei Hackel (ed.), *The Byzantine Saint* (London: Fellowship of St. Alban and St. Sergius, 1981), 43–50, at 50.

41 Efthymiadis, "The Place of Holy and Unholy Bishops", 171. For the position of bishops in seventh-century Spain see Rebecca Devlin, "Separating the Secular from the Spiritual: Wives, Sons and Clients of the Clergy in Late Antique *Hispania*", *Sacris Erudiri* 58 (2019), 339–359.

2 Non-monastic *Vitae*

The situation is different with the lives of clerics who did not have a monastic past before ordination or whose clerical career was not much influenced by it. To this category belong for instance the lives of Gregory Thaumaturgus, Porphyrios of Gaza, John the Almsgiver, Ambrose of Milan, Germanus of Auxerre, and Romanus of Blaye.

In most of them the clerical status of their heroes was an essential element of their literary image. They were truly clerical saints in the sense that their sanctity was closely related to their priesthood. Their *vitae* quickly pass over the years preceding their ordination, focus on the period of priesthood, and often try to show elements of idealised clerical life which is independent of, although not necessarily untouched by, monastic experience.

A good example of such hagiographies is the *Life of Germanus of Auxerre*, written by Constantius, presbyter in Lyon, in the AD 470s, on the request of Patiens, the bishop of this city.[42] It virtually starts with the episcopal ordination of the protagonist, ignoring his earlier life. Germanus is introduced as the future successor of the Apostles, that is, a bishop, already at the beginning of Chapter 1, and becomes one in Chapter 2. In the following forty-six chapters he is a bishop, although the author also mentions his ascetic way of life.[43] Germanus performs a number of miracles. We follow him to Britain (twice), where he confounds the Pelagians and commands the Britons fighting against the Picts and Saxons; to Arles, where he visits the prefect of the Gauls with a mission from his city; and to Ravenna, where he intercedes at the imperial court on behalf of the inhabitants of his region. We can see him as he appeases Goar, the king of the Alans, and imperial officials. In all, he acts as a patron of his city, defender of Gaul and Britain, and champion of orthodoxy.[44] As such he is a good example of the expanded role of the bishops who protected and represented their communities, or at least were depicted in this way.[45]

Yet it is far from certain whether this image was drawn in order to show clerics how to be a good bishop, for in his *vita* we can hardly meet Germanus in Auxerre. We can see him just once as he celebrates the mass in his city, which is indeed a priestly act, but the author mentions it only as a setting of a mir-

42 See René Borius, in his introduction to *Vie de Saint Germain d'Auxerre*, Sources chrétiennes 112 (Paris: Les Éditions du Cerf, 1965), 44–46.

43 Const. *V. Germ.* 3 and 9.

44 Const. *V. Germ.* 19, 24 and 46.

45 Raymond Van Dam, *Leadership and Community in Late Antique Gaul* (Berkeley: University of California Press, 1985), 45–46.

acle.[46] All of Germanus' preaching activity is summarised in a half of a short sentence.[47] In one episode we can see him giving alms, but this does not happen in Auxerre.[48]

Thus, the *Vita Germani*, from the beginning to the end, is certainly a life of a bishop, but not an instruction in how to be one. This is by no means an isolated case. There were other bishops whose sanctity was deeply clerical, but could hardly pass for an imitable model. The *Life of Porphyrios of Gaza* focuses on just one aspect of its protagonist's activity: it is a history of his struggle against pagan cult in the city. The history of this text is complicated and we are not sure when it was written, but neither in the sixth century, when it was at least edited, nor even in the fifth century, when its first version was probably composed, was the pagan cult a major issue.[49] Some people might still have called on the old gods, but their shrines were closed and in most places the pagan cult was dead or dying. Thus this *vita*, although it certainly showed a bishop in action, did not provide an obvious model to follow.

The *Life of Porphyrios* is, however, interesting because it focuses on an element which most non-monastic lives of clerics had in common. They present the life which their protagonists lead as a fight, conducted in the interest of the Christian people. It could be the fight against pagan cults: Porphyrios, Gregory Thaumaturgus, and Romanus of Blaye chased away demons from pagan shrines and statues, and converted the local population. It could be the fight against heresy or schism: Ambrose and Basil of Caesarea had to deal with Arians, Germanus of Auxerre with Pelagians, and Augustine with Arians, Donatists, Pelagians, and Manicheans. The ways in which the bishops conducted this war differed. Augustine won over the enemies in public disputes.[50] Ambrose reduced them to silence by miracles, Germanus 'poured out the floods of eloquence mingling them with thunders of the Apostle and the Gospels', and confounded the enemies by giving sight to a blind child.[51] Epiphanius and Porphyrius petitioned the emperors for the laws against heretics and pagans respectively, and Aberkios destroyed their idols.[52] But the fight is usually there. In this context

46 Const. *V. Germ.* 7.
47 Const. *V. Germ.* 32.
48 Const. *V. Germ.* 33.
49 For the history of this text see now Lampadaridi, *La Conversion de Gaza au christianisme.*
50 Poss. *V. August.* 6, 9, 14, 17, 18.
51 Paulin. Mediol. *V. Ambros.* 11 (an Arian virgin dies), 12 (a man plotting against Ambrose is sent to exile), 16 (those who disbelieve in the veracity of the relics found by Ambrose are punished), 17 (an Arian is converted by a miracle), 18 (two Arians who challenged Ambrose to a debate die); cf. Const. *V. Germ.* 14–15 and 27 (the debate and healing of a child).
52 *V. Epiph. Sal.* 105–106; Marc. Diac. *V. Porph.* 26–54, *V. Aberc.* 1–6.

it is worth repeating that it is far from certain that such a vision of priestly life was designed to show an example to follow for clerics. I suppose that it was not meant to be imitated any more than a *passio* of a martyr was imitated by a sixth-century audience. Of course, such an image could promote the theological views of the author in the same way in which Athanasius used the image of Antony who had rejected Arianism in order to strengthen his own theological position. But in the lives of bishops such function of the scenes presenting the fight against heresy or paganism was scarcely essential. In the sixth century there was not much need to convince the audience that paganism was distasteful. The motif of the fight was rather emphasised for the narrative purpose. First of all, it helped to assimilate its hero to one of the two literary models of Christian sanctity, both of them highly agonistic: the martyr and the ascetic.[53] It also often made the *vita* interesting from a literary point of view. The lives of bishops did not have other obvious elements which created their dramatic effect, with the exception of miracles. But thaumaturgy was not specific to bishops. Of course, we cannot exclude that the agonistic model of holding the office, presented in the lives of the bishops and presbyters, could have an impact on behaviours of their clerical readers. But even if it was so, it was probably not intentional.

As for the forms of piety which are presented in the lives of the holy priests, they are rarely distinctive. Admittedly, clerics prayed, kept vigils, fasted, and sometimes dressed humbly, but they were not the only ones to do it, and they did not do it in any spectacular way, since in all this they were obviously outdistanced by the monks. The bishops and presbyters had exclusive access to the celebration of the Eucharist, but this neither sanctified them nor proved their sanctity, it rather required the sanctity from the celebrant, as can be seen in frequent admonitions addressed to the priests, reminding them that they should keep constant chastity and fast before approaching the altar.[54] Also, in late antiquity, Eucharistic piety, resembling what we know from the middle ages, did not yet exist.[55] Consequently, the clerical lives only rarely show their heroes

53 The motif of the bloodless martyrdom or desire for martyrdom can be found in several lives of bishops: Sulp. Sev. *Ep.* 2.9–12; Paulin. Mediol. *V. Ambros.* 52; Const. *V. Germ.* 4.19–21.

54 See e.g. Siricius, *Ep.* 1.9–10 (S. Adamiak, PLAW ER1466); Innocent, *Ep.* 6.2 (S. Adamiak, PLAW ER1612); *Concilium Carthaginense a. 390*, can. 2 (S. Adamiak, PLAW ER132); *Concilium Carthaginense a. 419*, can. 3–4 (S. Adamiak, PLAW ER227); *Concilium Turonense a. 461*, can. 1 (J. Szafranowski, PLAW ER813).

55 Godefridus J.C. Snoek, *Medieval Piety from Relics to the Eucharist. A Process of Mutual Interaction* (Leiden: Brill, 1995).

performing this most essential act of their ritual activity. In Sulpicius Severus' writings, for instance, there is one episode in which we can see Martin preparing for the Mass and then celebrating it. It shows him staying apart from the chatting clergy, sitting on a simple stool, and not a throne, giving secretly his own tunic to a beggar, and ultimately having a globe of fire over his head. But the episode is focused rather on Martin's charity, rewarded during the sacrifice, than on the Eucharist itself.[56]

Some *vitae* mention other devotional practices of their heroes, such as the veneration of relics, but this rarely plays an important role in the narrative. The notable exception is the *Life of Ambrose*, which recounts the discovery of the bodies of the martyrs Gervasius and Protasius, Vitalis and Agricola, and Nazarius.[57] The *Life of Germanus* emphasises only his personal piety toward relics.[58] But that is all. Interestingly, the cult of saints is entirely absent from the *Life of Augustine*, whose subject in fact organised the transfer of the relics of St Stephen to Hippo, advertised their power, and encouraged people to make written accounts of the miracles that they had experienced.[59]

Some attention can be paid to preaching, an essential task of the bishop. The late-fourth- or fifth-century *Life of Aberkios*, for instance, mentions several times his successful sermons which converted a number of pagans. Still, Aberkios, like Germanus of Auxerre, preached mostly far away from his home city.[60] Also, the sermons often did not serve so much to present the episcopal rhetorical skills of the hero as to express the views which the author of the *vita* found important. It suffices to remember that the long sermons appear already in the *Life of Antony*, a monastic saint, not a cleric.[61]

Another element which can be found in several lives of clerics is a description of their generosity and almsgiving. This was always an essential element of their real activity and self-representation. The funerary inscriptions which tell us anything at all about the activity of the bishops usually emphasise their care for the poor.[62] In hagiography, however, almsgiving is usually described briefly

56 Sulp. Sev. *Dial.* 2.2.1–2.

57 Paulin. Mediol. *V. Ambros.* 15–16 (Gervasius and Protasius), 29 (Vitalis and Agricola), and 32–33 (Nazarius).

58 Const. *V. Germ.* 4 and 15.

59 August. *Serm.* 318.1 (deposition of relics), *Serm.* 319–324, and *Civ.* 22.8 (miracles and written accounts advertising them).

60 *V. Aberc.* 7–11, 24–30, 74–75.

61 Athan. *V. Anton.* 16–43, 73–80, 89–90. Similar function of the sermon: Honor. Mass. *V. Hilar.* 14, 18, and 26. See also Paulin. *V. Ambros.* 17; Const. *V. Germ.* 32; for Augustine: see above.

62 Pere Maymó i Capdevila, "Actuación social e ideario episcopal en los 'carmina Latina epigraphica' hispanos: una propuesta de análisis", *Cassiodorus* 6/7 (2000/2001), 215–229;

and rarely is a leading thread of the story. Admittedly, in the *Life of Epiphanius of Salamis*, we can see the bishop taking care about the needy, both in Cyprus where he redeems a captive with money from the church chest, and, more interestingly, in Jerusalem, thus far outside his jurisdiction, where he sells bishop John of Jerusalem's silver plates to support the poor.[63] Even more specific from this point of view are two seventh-century lives of John the Almsgiver, the patriarch of Alexandria, whose author focuses precisely on the bishop's charity.[64] Almsgiving was a feature which certainly could be imitated, but only within certain limits. As I have already mentioned, Aemilianus of Berceo is praised by the author of his *Life*, Bishop Braulio of Saragossa, for distributing wealth belonging to the church. But Braulio, who wrote this text in the AD 630s, knew well the synodal canons, including those of the councils of Toledo in AD 598 and 638 (he participated in the latter), which prohibited alienation of the church property, even if they agreed to it in the case of urgent needs.[65] In real life, giving away what belonged to the church was not necessarily a laudable act. Interestingly, the *vitae* of two bishops of Arles, Hilary and Caesarius, in which we can see their protagonists selling liturgical vessels in order to free captives, mention this fact in a somewhat apologetic tone. In the latter, written by a group of clerics from Arles, we can read what follows:

> For the man of God said that no rational man who had been redeemed by the blood of Christ should, as punishment for having lost his freedom, become perhaps an Arian or a Jew, or a slave instead of a free man or a slave of man rather than of God.[66]

---

similarly in Gaul, but not in Italy: Adam Izdebski, "Bishops in Late Antique Italy: Social Importance vs. Political Power", *Phoenix* 66 (2012), 158–175, at 171.

63 *V. Epiph. Sal.* 63–67 (Cyprus), 77–78 (Jerusalem), see also 96–98 (Epiphanius' intervention during a famine in Cyprus).

64 For the editions of these two *vitae* see: Gelzer, Heinrich (ed.), *Leontius von Neapolis, Leben des heiligen Johannes des Barmherzigen Erzbischofs von Alexandrien* (Freiburg and Leipzig: J.C.B. Mohr, 1893); Hippolyte Delehaye, "Une Vie inédite de saint Jean l'Aumonier", *AB* 45 (1927), 5–74. For the same phenomenon in the later era see Efthymiadis, "The Place of Holy and Unholy Bishops", 175. Other lives mentioning this issue, e.g. Honor. Mass. *V. Hilar.* 11; Const. *V. Germ.* 33.

65 *Concilium Toletanum III* (*a. 589*), can. 3, see M. Szada, PLAW ER345; *Concilium Toletanum V* (*a. 638*), can. 5, see M. Szada, PLAW ER498.

66 ... *hoc vir Dei dicens: Ne rationabilis homo sanguine Christi redemptus, perdito libertatis statu, pro obnoxietate aut Arrianus forsitan efficiatur aut Iudaeus aut ex ingenuo servus aut ex Dei servo hominis*; *V. Caesar. Arel.* 1.32; B. Krusch, *MGH SRM* 3 (Hannover: Hahn, 1896), 469; trans. W.E. Klingshirn, *Caesarius of Arles: Life, Testament, Letters* (Liverpool: Liverpool University Press, 1994); for its authors see *V. Caes.* 1.1–2 and 2.1; see also Honor. Mass. *V. Hilar.* 11.

Even more interestingly, Paulinus of Milan, the author of the *Life of Ambrose*, who claims that his hero fulfilled his duties toward the poor and prisoners, omits altogether a similar episode, although we know that Ambrose at least once happened to sell sacred vessels.[67] Such activity was evidently ambiguous, at least in the eyes of the local clergy which in hagiography should be duly punished for their greed: in the *Life of Epiphanius*, a deacon who opposed Epiphanius' generosity dies, and Bishop John becomes blind in one eye. Even the lives of John the Almsgiver should not be taken as a real model which can be put into life. As Ewa Wipszycka has demonstrated, they present an *économie miraculeuse* which had very little in common with the real world: the amount of money that the hero distributes was in fact inaccessible even for such a rich bishop as the patriarch of Alexandria.[68] And it was not so because its author did not have any idea about ecclesiastical economy—Leontius of Neapolis was a bishop himself and knew the Alexandrian Church very well. It is because in this life, generous almsgiving plays a persuasive role which in other lives is played by thaumaturgy—it overwhelms the reader with wonder (*thauma*). Interestingly, in the other life written by Leontius, that of Symeon the Holy Fool, also almost devoid of miracles, the same role is played by the extremely eccentric behaviour of the hero.[69]

3 Positive Examples

Among the early *vitae* of bishops there is, however, at least one whose author deliberately constructed an image which was meant to be imitated by his clerical readers. The life in question is that of Augustine, already mentioned above, written by his pupil and friend Possidius of Calama. Interestingly, Possidius was active in the same region, period, and milieu as Paulinus, deacon of the church of Milan, who administered its estates in Africa, where he wrote the *Life of Ambrose*.[70] Yet one has an impression that these two authors, who almost cer-

67 Paulin. Mediol. *V. Ambros.* 38.4; Ambros. *Off.* 2.136–143. See Pauline Allen, Bronwen Neil, and Wendy Mayer, "Reading the Texts: a Methodology of Approach to Genre", in eaedem (eds.), *Preaching Poverty in Late Antiquity. Perception and Realities* (Leipzig: Evangelische Verlagsanstalt, 2009), 35–68, at 57.

68 Ewa Wipszycka, "L'Économie du patriarchat alexandrin à travers les vies de saint Jean l'Aumonier", in Christian Decobert and Jean-Yves Empereur (eds.), *Alexandrie médiévale*, vol. 2 (Cairo: IFAO, 2002), 61–81.

69 I am grateful to Przemysław Nehring for attracting my attention to this issue. See also Julie Van Pelt's article in this volume.

70 Emilien Lamirande, "La Datation de la *Vita Ambrosii* de Paulin de Milan", *REAug* 27

tainly knew each other, lived in two completely different realities. The world of Paulinus is full of demons, miraculous healings, God-sent visions, and miracles punishing those who plotted against, disagreed with, or offended Ambrose. Possidius, on the contrary, does not say anything about God's direct interventions in the course of human life, with the exception of one miracle that is just mentioned, not really described.[71]

More importantly, the two Lives differ very much in the way in which they present the daily episcopal duties of their heroes. In his *Life of Ambrose*, Paulinus, writing at the request of Augustine, then elderly bishop of Hippo, tells a lot about Ambrose's struggle against the Arians, his relations with emperors, the relics of martyrs that he discovered, and above all about his miracles. But he describes all episcopal activities and religious practices of his hero in a single chapter (out of fifty-six).[72] In all, Paulinus presents Ambrose as a holy bishop, but hardly shows how a normal bishop should act.

Possidius' picture of Augustine's episcopal activity is far more developed and definitely aims at providing a role model for the clergy. Already in the preface Possidius emphasises that he is a bishop and writes the life of a priest (*sacerdos*).[73] And that is what he really does. He omits the early period of Augustine's life and summarises all that happened before his presbyterial ordination, including his 'conversion' in Milan, in three chapters (out of thirty-one), simply referring his reader to the *Confessions*.[74] But he describes in relative detail Augustine's dress, meals, and his care for the sick. He writes a lot about the bishop's household. Possidius emphasises that no woman was allowed to live there, even if she was related to Augustine. This may seem a secondary issue in the *vita*, but the problem of women living in clerical houses vividly interested clerics and was much discussed at several councils.[75] Possidius refers directly to these discussions, remarking that the rules which Augustine set for his household exceeded the requirements imposed by the synods.[76] Also, he adds that Augustine regularly frequented the gatherings of bishops.[77] That is obviously

(1981), 44–55; Brigitta Stoll, "Die *Vita Augustini* des Possidius als hagiographischer Text", *Zeitschrift für Kirchengeschichte* 102 (1991), 1–13.

71 Poss. *V. August.* 29.4–5.

72 Paulin. Mediol. *V. Ambros.* 38.

73 Poss. *V. August.* praef. 1–3. The word *sacerdos* can be used in regard to presbyters, but more frequently it means 'bishop'; see the database *Presbyters in the Late Antique West.*

74 Poss. *V. August.* praef. 5–6.

75 In Africa see: *Concilium Carthaginense a. 345/348*, can. 3; *Concilium Hipponense a. 393*, can. 16; see S. Adamiak, PLAW ER64 and ER212.

76 Poss. *V. August.* 26.1.

77 Poss. *V. August.* 21.1; see also 8.6 and 18.2.

what most bishops did, but other hagiographers do not mention it. Possidius tells even more about a sphere which for Augustine himself was not particularly interesting, namely administrative activity. The longest passage in the entire *vita* is devoted to the rules of accepting donations for the Church.[78]

Possidius evidently tries to show in this text how to deal with the matters which he considers important for himself and other clerics. This is also why he includes in the *vita* a letter to bishop Honoratus of Thiabe, in which Augustine explains how the clerics should behave facing the danger of the Vandal invasion.[79] This long letter, the only text of Augustine quoted *in extenso*, brutally breaks the narration about his illness and death, and seems totally out of place in the *vita*. But Possidius thinks differently. He writes for clerics, and finds it equally important to provide them with a pattern of clerical life and to make them familiar with the views of his hero, an exemplary bishop, on the most burning issue for the clergy of his days—the *vita* was written in the early AD 430s when the Vandal conquest of Africa had not yet been completed.

In this effort to instruct its readers how to fulfil clerical duties the *Life of Augustine* is by no means commonplace in late antique hagiography. There is, however, another narrative text which, on a limited scale, sought to provide the audience with a pattern of good episcopacy and focused on the bishop's duties. I am thinking about the *Liber Pontificalis*, a series of very short biographies of the bishops of Rome, written originally in the AD 530s, reedited shortly after, and later continued up to the ninth century. This interesting and curious text cannot be easily counted as hagiography. It had some cultic ambitions, since, unlike many lives of saints, it constantly provides two essential *coordonnées hagiographiques*,[80] the date of death and place of burial of the popes. Also, most of its heroes are presented as decent and pious people. Yet only a few of them, except martyrs, can be fully qualified as saints, and some lives, like that of Anastasius II, who is punished by God by sudden death, present heroes whom the authors consider to be simply bad bishops.[81]

As far as the bishops of the first three centuries are concerned, the original author registers their decisions concerning liturgy, administration, and customs, but these are normally not presented as the glorious deeds proving holiness. The life of the early-third-century bishop Callixtus for instance informs us

---

78 Poss. *V. August.* 24.

79 Poss. *V. August.* 30.

80 Hippolyte Delehaye, *Cinq leçons sur la méthode hagiographique* (Brussels: Société des Bollandistes, 1934), 13–14.

81 *Lib. Pont.* 52 (Anastasius II), see also 57 (Boniface II), and 60 (Silverius, only in the first part of his life; the second part, by another author, presents him as a saint).

that 'he decreed that on Saturdays three times a year there should be a fast from corn, wine and oil according to the prophecy'.[82] The purpose of such remarks is rather to justify a custom contemporary to the author than to give credit to a specific pope. More importantly, the author notes churches and other buildings which were constructed by or during the pontificate of specific popes, although even such pieces of information are provided in a very matter-of-fact tone, and one can wonder whether the author really aimed to praise the builders or simply mentioned the buildings out of chronicler's duty.

For our purpose the most interesting section is a later part of the *Liber Pontificalis*, containing slightly longer lives of the seventh-century popes, usually written not long after their death by anonymous clerics of Rome, the continuators of the original authors. They show a certain model of holding the episcopal office and do it from an evidently clerical perspective. They often mention the fight of their heroes against heresies, though they do not tell anything about their prayers, vigils, fasts, or—with a single exception—miracles.[83] But the popes are truly praised when they care about the welfare of the clergy. The life of Boniface IV (d AD 615) for instance presents him in the following way:

> Blessed Boniface was the most mild and compassionate of all men. He loved his clergy and gave them an entire stipend (*roga*) … On his death he was buried in St Peter's; for his funeral he left an entire stipend to all the clergy.[84]

A similar passage can be found in the life on Eugene I (d AD 657):

> He was kind, mild, meek, courteous to all, and of remarkable holiness. He gave the customary stipend to the clergy and supplied alms to the needy, so that he ordered the full priestly allowances to be distributed to the poor, the clergy, and the household even on the day he passed away.[85]

---

82 *Hic constituit ieiunium die sabbati ter in anno fieri, frumenti, vini et olei, secundum prophetiam* (*Lib. Pont.* 17.2).

83 *Lib. Pont.* 76.8 (Pope Martin).

84 *Erat enim beatissimus Bonifatius mitissimus super omnes homines et misericors. Hic clerum amavit. Roga integra clero suo dedit* (*Liber Pontificalis* 71.1), L. Duchesne (ed.), *Liber Pontificalis* (Paris: Ernest Thorin, 1886); trans. Raymond Davis, *The Book of Pontiffs* (*Liber Pontificalis*), *The Ancient Biographies of the First Ninety Roman Bishops to AD 715* (Liverpool: Liverpool University Press, 1989).

85 *Benignus, mitis, mansuetus, omnibus affabilis et sanctitatis praeclarior. Rogam clero solitam tribuit et indignentibus elemosynam subministravit, ut etiam die transitus sui pauperibus vel clero seu familiae praesbyteria in integro erogari praeceperit* (*Liber Pontificalis* 77.1).

Another element which seems to be important for the authors of the *Liber Pontificalis* is the clerical background of the bishops—clerical and not monastic. In the seventh century many popes were former monks, but only one of them, Adeodatus, is mentioned as such, whereas we can quite frequently learn about clerical ancestors of and lower orders taken by the future popes.[86] Eugene I, for instance, is proudly called 'a cleric from his cradle'.[87]

The message of the *Liber Pontificalis* for the future bishops is quite clear. Firstly, climb the grades of clerical hierarchy slowly and certainly do not jump from the monastery to the episcopal see (such an 'undue leap' being frequently condemned in church canons).[88] Secondly, once you are elected, respect the clergy, that is to say, grant them offices and money. This is a very real example to follow, but we will hardly find it in the lives of holy bishops, including that of Augustine. The examples of the *Life of Augustine* and of the *Liber Pontificalis* were different in the sense that while in the former a bishop sets a model for his colleagues and especially lower clerics, in the latter it is the lower clergy that constructs an image of a good superior.

The evidence presented above shows that clerical hagiographies sometimes tried to construct a consistent model of life, which could be followed specifically by clerics, but they did it rarely. Sometimes they avowed this openly. In Gregory's of Nyssa *Encomium of Basil* we can see a protagonist who is explicitly presented as an example to imitate, but hardly as a model for clerics. Although Basil was a presbyter for about ten years and a bishop for eight, Gregory tells little about his priestly functions. In this case, however, it does not result from the fact that Basil is presented as a monk who just happened to become a bishop, similar to the hagiographical heroes named above. Basil definitely is a leader of his people. Gregory compares him to Moses, because he saved the people from heresy like Moses saved the Israelites from Egypt. But as Michael Stuart Williams rightly argues, in Gregory's eyes Moses is not a particularly priestly or episcopal figure.[89] His *Life of Moses* shows what the Christian, and not just clerical, life should look like; and even if Gregory admits that this example is difficult to follow, it should be followed by all Christians, not just by clerics, and the same is true of the example of Basil.

86 *Lib. Pont.* 79.1 (*ex monachis*).

87 *Lib. Pont.* 77.1 (*clericus a cunabulis*).

88 See e.g. Boniface, *Ep.* 5.4, S. Adamiak, PLAW ER1784.

89 Michael Stuart Williams, *Authorised Lives in Early Christian Biography* (Cambridge: Cambridge University Press, 2008), 82–88.

4 Conclusion

Clerical hagiography certainly played a role similar to the monastic one in the sense that it provided clerics with heroes to be proud of. But unlike monastic *vitae*, the lives of clerics rarely show how exactly their heroes can be followed otherwise than by fighting against pagans and heretics (who were not always available), adopting a firm position when dealing with rulers or by performing miracles and distributing alms (which could be difficult or problematic). The *Life of Augustine*, which also presented the daily business of the bishop, specific for this office, is exceptional in this respect.

I would argue that the lack of a fully developed model of clerical sanctity resulted mostly from a widely shared conviction that, unlike monasticism, priesthood was not really a way to holiness. Claudia Rapp is certainly right when she says that the division between the charismatic holy men and the hierarchical clergy is false.[90] There were holy bishops in late antiquity who just happened to be so but they were not holy *because* they were bishops. One could become a saint by choosing the life of a hermit, but hardly that of a cleric. The relation between priesthood and holiness was opposite. Ideally, one was made a cleric because one was a saint already, and not the other way round. Consequently, there was no specific hagiographical model of clerical life, or, to put it more cautiously, such a model was not complete. It consisted mostly of two features, care for the poor and the fight against paganism and heresy, the latter being definitely more prominent in most *vitae*, probably because it was attractive from the literary point of view. The almsgiving could be imitated, the fight against the adversaries of the faith not necessarily so.

Needless to say, the real life of a bishop was hardly limited to these two activities. It consisted also of maintaining relations with other bishops, attending councils, supervising clergy, preaching, celebrating Eucharist and baptism, teaching catechumens, overseeing church property, and administering justice.[91] All this is only occasionally referred to in hagiography. I have mentioned above Possidius' unusual remark about Augustine's eagerness to attend the councils. The lack of similar remarks in other *vitae* is sometimes puzzling. Caesarius of Arles, as a metropolitan bishop, convened a series of councils which played a very important role in the life of the Church in Gaul. He considered this aspect of his episcopal activity essential, and yet no council is mentioned in his life, although it was written by Caesarius' clerics.

---

90 Claudia Rapp, *Holy Bishops in Late Antiquity* (Berkeley: University of California Press, 2005), *passim*.

91 See Rapp, *Holy Bishops*, 246.

This is not to say that a model of clerical life did not exist at all. It certainly did, but it was being shaped mostly by letters, didactic treatises, collections of questions and answers, and synodal canons. As for the *vitae* of holy presbyters and bishops, even those written with clerical audiences in mind, they had diverse functions. They promoted the cult of a local bishop, advocated the monastic way of life, defended the doctrinal position of the author, and above all provided the local community with a heroic past. They also fashioned *esprit de corps* among the clergy. But they rarely taught them how to be a good and pious priest.

Acknowledgments

The research on this article has been supported by a grant from the National Science Centre (Poland, DEC-2013/10/E/HS3/00202) and by the ERC Advanced Grant *The Cult of Saints: a Christendom-wide study of its origins, spread and development up to 700* (COS) run by Bryan Ward-Perkins at the University of Oxford with partnership at the University of Warsaw.

Bibliography

Allen, Pauline, Bronwen Neil, and Wendy Mayer, "Reading the Texts: A Methodology of Approach to Genre", in eaedem (eds.), *Preaching Poverty in Late Antiquity. Perception and Realities* (Leipzig: Evangelische Verlagsanstalt, 2009), 35–68.

Barlowe, Claude W. (trans.), *Iberian Fathers*, vol. 2 (Washington DC: CUA Press, 1969).

Bastiaensen, Antoon A.R. (ed.), *Vite dei santi*, vol. 3 (Milan: Mondadori, 1975).

Bernardi, Jean (ed.), *Grégoire de Nazianze, Discours 42–43*. Sources chrétiennes 384 (Paris: Les Éditions du Cerf, 1992).

Borius, René (ed.), *Constance de Lyon, Vie de saint Germain d'Auxerre*, Sources chrétiennes 112 (Paris: Les Éditions du Cerf, 1965).

Cavallin, Samuel (ed.), *Honorat de Marseille, La Vie d'Hilaire d'Arles*, Sources chrétiennes 404 (Paris: Les Éditions du Cerf, 1995).

Davis, Raymond (trans.), *The Book of Pontiffs (Liber Pontificalis): The Ancient Biographies of the First Ninety Roman Bishops to AD 715* (Liverpool: Liverpool University Press, 1989).

de Vogüé, Adalbert (ed.), *La Règle de saint Benoît*, 2 vols. Sources chrétiennes 181–182 (Paris, Les Éditions du Cerf, 1972).

Delehaye, Hippolyte, "Une Vie inédite de saint Jean l'Aumônier", *AB* 45 (1927), 5–74.

Delehaye, Hippolyte, *Cinq leçons sur la méthode hagiographique* (Brussels: Société des Bollandistes, 1934).

Delehaye, Hippolyte, *Les Légendes hagiographiques* (2nd edition Brussels: Société des Bollandistes, 1955).

Devlin, Rebecca, "Separating the Secular from the Spiritual: Wives, Sons and Clients of the Clergy in Late Antique Hispania", *Sacris Erudiri* 58 (2019), 339–359.

Díaz y Díaz, Manuel C. (ed.), *La Vida de San Fructuoso de Braga* (Braga: Diário do Minho, 1974).

Duchesne, Louis (ed.), *Liber Pontificalis* (Paris: Ernest Thorin, 1886).

Efthymiadis, Stephanos, "The Place of Holy and Unholy Bishops in Byzantine Hagiographical Narrative (Eighth–Twelfth Centuries)", in John S. Ott and Trpimir Vedriš (eds.), *Saintly Bishops and Bishops' Saints* (Zagreb: Hagiotheca, 2012), 169–182.

Evenepoel, Willy, "The *Vita Felicis* of Paulinus Nolanus", in Marc Van Uytfanghe and Roland Demeulenaere (eds.), *Aevum inter utrumque: Mélanges offerts à Gabriel Sanders, professeur émérite à l'Université de Gand* (The Hague: Nijhoff International, 1991), 143–152.

Fear, Andrew T. (trans.), *Lives of the Visigothic fathers* (Liverpool: Liverpool University Press, 1997).

Fontaine, Jacques (ed.), *Sulpice Sévère: Vie de Martin*, 3 vols., Sources chrétiennes 133–135 (Paris: Les Éditions du Cerf, 1967–1969).

Fontaine, Jacques (ed.), *Sulpice Sévère: Gallus ou Dialogues sur les "vertus" de Saint Martin*, Sources chrétiennes 510 (Paris: Les Éditions du Cerf, 2006).

García Moreno, Luis A., *Prosopografía del reino visigodo de Toledo* (Salamanca: Ediciones Universidad, 1974).

Gelzer, Heinrich (ed.), *Leontius von Neapolis, Leben des heiligen Johannes des Barmherzigen Erzbischofs von Alexandrien* (Freiburg/Leipzig: J.C.B. Mohr, 1893).

Gray, Christa, *Jerome, Vita Malchi: Introduction, Text, Translation, and Commentary* (Oxford: Oxford University Press, 2015).

Heil, Günther (ed.), *Gregorii Nysseni Opera* 10.1 (Leiden: Brill, 1990).

Hunter, David, *Marriage, Celibacy, and Heresy in Ancient Christianity: The Jovinianist Controversy* (Oxford: Oxford University Press, 2007).

Izdebski, Adam, "Bishops in Late Antique Italy: Social Importance vs. Political Power", *Phoenix* 66 (2012), 158–175.

Klingshirn, William E. (trans.), *Caesarius of Arles: Life, Testament, Letters* (Liverpool: Liverpool University Press, 1994).

Klingshirn, William E., "Christian Divination in Late Roman Gaul: The *Sortes Sangallenses*", in Sarah I. Johnston and Peter T. Struck (eds.), *Mantikê: Studies in Ancient Divination* (Leiden: Brill, 2005), 99–128.

Krusch, Bruno (ed.), *Vita Caesarii Arelatensis* SRM 3 (Hannover: Hahn, 1896), 457–501.

Krusch, Bruno (ed.), *Vita Memorii*, MGH SRM 3 (Hannover: Hahn, 1896), 102–104.

Lamirande, Emilien, "La Datation de la *Vita Ambrosii* de Paulin de Milan", *REAug* 27 (1981), 44–55.

Lampadaridi, Anna, *La Conversion de Gaza au christianisme. La Vie de S. Porphyre par Marc le Diacre* (BHG *1570*). *Edition critique, traduction, commentaire* (Brussels: Société des Bollandistes, 2016).

Leclerc, Pierre, "Antoine et Paul: métamorphose d'un héros", in Yves-Marie Duval (ed.), *Jérôme entre l'Occident et l'Orient. XVIe centenaire du départ de saint Jérôme de Rome et de son installation à Bethléem. Actes du colloque de Chantilly, Sept. 1986* (Paris: Études augustiniennes, 1988), 256–265.

Malingrey, Anne-Marie and Philippe Leclercq (eds.), *Palladios, Dialogue sur la vie de Jean Chrysostome*, Sources chrétiennes 341 and 342 (Paris: Les Éditions du Cerf, 1988).

Maraval, Pierre, *La Passion inédite de S. Athénogène de Pédachthoè en Cappadoce* (*BHG 197b*) (Brussels: Société des Bollandistes, 1990).

Maymó i Capdevila, Pere, "Actuación social e ideario episcopal en los 'carmina Latina epigraphica' hispanos: una propuesta de análisis", *Cassiodorus* 6/7 (2000/2001), 215–229.

Montgomery, Hugo, "Pontius' *Vita S. Cypriani* and the making of a saint", *SO* 71 (1996), 195–215.

Morris, Rosemary, "The Political Saint of the Eleventh Century", in Sergei Hackel (ed.), *The Byzantine Saint* (London: Fellowship of St. Alban and St. Sergius, 1981), 43–50.

Nissen, Theodor (ed.), *Sancti Abercii Vita* (Leipzig: Teubner, 1912).

Patlagean, Evelyne, "L'Histoire de la femme déguisée en moine et l'évolution de la sainteté féminine à Byzance", *Studi Medievali*, Third Series 17 (Spoleto: CISAM, 1976), 597–625.

Rapp, Claudia, "Epiphanius of Salamis, the Church Father as Saint", in Anthony A.M. Bryer and Georgios S. Georghallides (eds.), *The Sweet Land of Cyprus: Papers Given at the Twenty-Fifth Jubilee Spring Symposium of Byzantine Studies, Birmingham, March 1991* (Nicosia: The Cyprus Research Centre for the Society for the Promotion of Byzantine Studies, 1993), 169–187.

Rapp, Claudia, *Holy Bishops in Late Antiquity* (Berkeley: University of California Press, 2005).

Sancti Romani Vita Secunda (BHL 7306), *AB* 5 (1886), 178–191.

Silva-Tarouca, Carlo (ed.), *Collectio Thessalonicensis: epistularum Romanorum Pontificum ad vicarios per Illyricum aliosque episcopos*, Textus et Documenta. Series Theologica 23 (Rome: Pontifica Universitas Gregoriana, 1937).

Snoek, Godefridus J.C., *Medieval Piety from Relics to the Eucharist: A Process of Mutual Interaction* (Leiden: Brill, 1995).

Stoll, Brigitta, "Die *Vita Augustini* des Possidius als hagiographischer Text", *Zeitschrift für Kirchengeschichte* 102 (1991), 1–31.

Valentin, Marie-Denise (ed.), *Hilaire d'Arles, Vie de saint Honorat*, Sources chrétiennes 235 (Paris: Les Éditions du Cerf, 1977).

Van Dam, Raymond, *Leadership and Community in Late Antique Gaul* (Berkeley: University of California Press, 1985).

Vázquez de Parga, Luis (ed.), *Sancti Braulionis Caesaraugustani episcopi Vita S. Emiliani* (Madrid: Instituto Jerónimo Zurita, 1943).

Verheyden, Joseph, "Origen in the Making: Reading between (and behind) the Lines of Eusebius' *Life of Origen* (*Hist. eccl.* 6)", in Sylwia Kaczmarek and Henryk Pietras (eds.), *Origeniana Decima: Origen as Writer* (Leuven: Peeters, 2011), 713–726.

Vielhaber, Gottfried (ed.), *Sancti Romani Vita Prima* (BHL 7305), *AB* 26 (1907), 52–56.

Williams, Michael Stuart, *Authorised Lives in Early Christian Biography* (Cambridge: Cambridge University Press, 2008).

Williams, Michael Stuart, "Always Already a Martyr? Felix of Nola as Martyr and Confessor", in Vincent Déroche, Bryan Ward-Perkins, and Robert Wiśniewski (eds.), *Culte des saints et littérature hagiographique: accords et désaccords* (Leuven: Peeters, 2019) 151–183.

Wipszycka, Ewa, "L'Économie du patriarchat alexandrin à travers les vies de saint Jean l'Aumônier", in Christian Decobert (ed.), *Alexandrie médiévale*, vol. 2 (Cairo: IFAO, 2002), 61–81.

PART 2

The Forms of Hagiography

CHAPTER 4

Eremitic *aemulatio*: Genesis of Genre in Jerome's *Vita Pauli*

Alan J. Ross

1 Jerome, 'Writer of Satire in Prose'

> You drink from jewelled cups, but he [Paul] was satisfied with the cupped hands that nature had given him. You weave gold into your tunics, but he did not even have the shabbiest garment belonging to your slave. But then paradise lies open to him, poor as he was, while hell will welcome you in your golden clothes. He was clothed with Christ despite his nakedness: you who are dressed in silks have lost the garment of Christ. Paul who lies covered in the vilest dust will rise again in glory: heavy stone tombs press down upon you, you who will burn together with your wealth. Have a care, I ask you, for yourselves, have a care at least for the riches you love. Why do you wrap your dead in cloths of gold? Why does your ostentation not cease amidst the grief and tears? Or are the corpses of the rich unable to rot except in clothes of silk?[1]
>
> *V. Pauli* 17.2–4

With a string of pithy comparisons, accusatory second-person pronouns, threats of hellish damnation, and a congeries of detail about their luxurious life (jewelled cups, golden tunics, silken fabrics, elaborate tombs) Jerome constructs the imagined audience for his first hagiographic work, the *Life of Paul*

1 *vos gemma bibitis, ille [Paulus] concavis manibus naturae satisfecit. vos in tunicis aurum texitis, ille ne vilissimi quidem mancipi vestri indumentum habuit sed e contrario illi pauperculo paradisus patet, vos auratos gehenna suscipiet. ille Christi vestem, nudus licet, servavit; vos vestiti sericis indumentum Christi perdidistis. Paulus vilissimo pulvere opertus iacet resurrecturus in gloria: vos operosa saxis sepulcra premunt cum vestris opibus arsuros. parcite, quaeso, vos, parcite saltem divitiis quas amatis. cur et mortuos vestros auratis obvolvitis vestibus? cur ambitio inter luctus lacrimasque non cessat? an cadavera divitum nisi in serico putrescere nesciunt?* Translations of the *V. Pauli* are taken, often adapted, from Carolinne White, *Early Christian Lives* (London: Penguin, 1998). The text of the *V. Pauli* cited in this chapter is that of Morales, published in Pierre Leclerc, Edgardo Martín Morales, and Adalbert de Vogüé, *Trois vies de moines (Paul, Malchus, Hilarion)* (Paris: Les Éditions du Cerf, 2007).

 | DOI:10.1163/9789004421332_006

of Thebes (*V. Pauli*). Whoever these aristocratic, Latin-speaking Christian readers may have been, they were in need of cajoling into a more ascetic lifestyle through the example of Paul's simple existence. A heady Juvenalian or Lucilian sense of indignation hangs around these epigrammatic sketches with their vivid detail, and moralising contrasts between an ascetic ideal (Paul) and the degenerate addressees, expressed with rhetorical questions and prodding second-person verbs.[2] Indeed, the style here is familiar from Jerome's wider corpus. This paragraph at the conclusion to the *V. Pauli* could easily be added to the body of evidence that later prompted some to accuse Jerome of being a *satiricum scriptorem in prosa* (*Epist.* 40.2.3)[3]—a writer of satire in prose.

Satire in the fourth century had indeed moved away from its traditional roots in poetry and entered the world of prose.[4] Not only were Christians reading the likes of Lucilius, Juvenal, and Persius, but they adopted their style (though not their metre) and deployed their satiric barbs against new targets: pagans, heretics, as well as the traditional victims, those whom the satirist believed to be examples of immoral behaviour.[5] Tertullian uses irony and overly detailed description (the hallmarks of satire) to satirise pagan festivals;[6] Arnobius ridicules the pagan gods in a series of explicit *reductiones ad absur-*

2 Although allusion may be to other satiric passages: David Wiesen, *St. Jerome as a Satirist: A Study in Christian Latin Thought and Letters* (Ithaca, NY: Cornell University Press, 1964), 49 notes that the phrase *gemma bibitis* alludes to Virgil's 'satiric denunciation of urban luxury' at *Georgics* 2.506 *ut gemma bibat.* See Susannah Morton Braund, *Juvenal, Satires I* (Cambridge: Cambridge University Press, 1996), 17–29 for typical satiric tropes used by Juvenal.

3 Or more accurately, it is a charge that Jerome imagines could be levelled against him by his detractors; it is therefore a form of self-definition. *Letter* 40 is dated to AD 385. The *V. Pauli* was composed around a decade earlier when Jerome was in Syria, possibly during his stay with Evagrius of Antioch after a period experiencing ascetic life with eastern monks. See Adalbert de Vogüé, "La Vita Pauli de saint Jérôme et sa datation. Examen d'un passage clé (ch. 6)", in Gerhard J.M. Bartelink, Anton Hilhorst, and Corneille H. Kneepkens (eds.), *Eulogia. Mélanges offerts à Antoon A.R. Bastiaensen à l'occasion de son soixante-cinquième anniversaire* (Steenbrugge: Abbatia S. Petri, 1991), 395–406, and Stefan Rebenich, *Hieronymus und sein Kreis. Prosopographische und sozialgeschichtliche Untersuchungen* (Stuttgart: Steiner, 1992), 86–98.

4 Danuta Shanzer, "Latin Literature, Christianity and Obscenity in the Later Roman West", in Nicola McDonald (ed.), *Medieval Obscenities* (Woodbridge: York Medieval, 2006), 179–202, at 188.

5 See Shanzer, "Latin Literature" for the development of Christian satire, and Cristiana Sogno, "Persius, Juvenal, and the Transformation of Satire in Late Antiquity" in *A Companion to Persius and Juvenal*, Susannah Morton Braund and Josiah Osgood (eds.) (Malden, MA: Wiley-Blackwell, 2012), 363–385 for satire in the fourth century more generally. Wiesen, *Jerome* provides the classic study of Jerome's use of satire.

6 *Apol.* 35.2. Discussed in Sogno, "Persius", 366. Cf. Timothy D. Barnes, *Tertullian: A Historical and Literary Study* (Oxford: Oxford University Press, 1971), 107.

dum that mock them for their all-too-human sexual habits.[7] Jerome has not just left us examples of his satiric style, but also his theorising on its use and purpose. In the rest of the letter in which he refers to himself as a *scriptor satiricus*, Jerome outlines his satiric programme: to cure the pompous and hypocritical of their shortcomings, as a doctor would cure his patient.[8] As Sogno notes, 'this and other passages suggest that Jerome views satire … as socially beneficial, but appreciates the unpleasantness of the satirical process.'[9] Indeed, among Jerome's later targets for his satirical barbs were monks whom he judged to be guilty of the crime that was most likely to rile a satirist: hypocrisy. In a letter dated to 411, Jerome attacks those who have adopted the title but not the true lifestyle of monasticism: 'Though they drink from glass and eat from plates of earthenware, it is gold they swallow, and amidst crowds of servants swarming round them they claim the name of hermit.'[10] Unlike Tertullian and Arnobius, Jerome willingly turns his satiric pen against his fellow Christians, and even certain holy men of the desert of whom he disapproves.

It is difficult to know how unpleasant Jerome's early readers might have found the epilogue of the *V. Pauli*. Perhaps, if they were perusing the codex of Jerome's latest work in one hand whilst sipping out of a *gemma* with the other, they squirmed uncomfortably at the recognition of themselves in Jerome's depiction. Just as likely, they appreciated the clearly satiric flourish at the conclusion of a witty literary work that throughout mixes together the qualities of many other generic types:[11] the novel, encomium, travel-aretalogy, and biography, to name a few.[12] For, as Rebenich has noted, the *V. Pauli* marks the genesis

7 Books 3–5 of the *Adversus Nationes* contain sustained, satirical attacks upon the pagan gods for their human form and the human urges and immorality that come with it.

8 *Epist.* 40.1. Cf. the similar sentiments (and imagery) in *Epist.* 117.2.

9 Sogno, "Persius", 384, discussing Jer. *Epist.* 125.5.

10 *in vitro et patella factili aurum comeditur et inter turbas et examina ministrorum nomen sibi vindicant solitarii*, Jer. *Epist.* 125.16.1. The vocabulary may be different, but there is clear thematic and stylistic similarity to the attack upon the imagined readers of the *V. Pauli*. The detailed description and sense of indignation in this *Letter* are also joined by those accusatory second-person forms (*putes* … 'you would think that …') and more epigrammatic sketches in the rest of the paragraph.

11 Those satiric attacks in the epilogue are at least sufficiently general in nature, addressed to *vos* rather than a named individual, that any reader may not feel as personally insulted as Onasus of Segesta, the subject of *Epist.* 40, quoted above.

12 Richard Reitzenstein, *Hellenistische Wundererzählungen* (Leipzig: Teubner, 1906), 63; Julius Plesch, *Die Originalität und literarische Form der Mönchsbiographien des hl. Hieronymus* (Munich: Kgl. Hof- und Universitäts-Buchdruckerei von C. Wolf, 1910), 35; Herbert Kech, *Hagiographie als christliche Unterhaltungsliteratur. Studien zum Phänomen des Erbaulichen anhand der Mönchsviten des hl. Hieronymus* (Göppingen: Kümmerle, 1977),

of ascetic monastic *belles-lettres*.[13] Nonetheless, beyond the epilogue, the presence of polemic satire has rarely entered modern discussions of the *V. Pauli*, yet, as I will argue here, it provides a generic tenor that suffuses the whole of the *V. Pauli*, even if it appears in a less biting and aggressive form as it does in the conclusion to the *V. Pauli* and in *Letter* 125. Indeed, because Jerome's polemic often relies on allusive engagement with the only other monastic hagiography likely then in existence, Athanasius' *Vita Antonii*, this allusive polemic plays a key role in Jerome's conception of a new hagiographic genre.

2 'A Certain Paul of Thebes Was the Originator of This Practice': The *Vita Pauli* and the *Vita Antonii*

Despite the plethora of subtle allusions to classical and Christian texts throughout the *V. Pauli*, one work is identified prominently, if obliquely, in the preface:

> Seeing, then, that an account of Antony has been recorded in both Greek and Latin, I have decided to write a few things about the beginning and end of Paul's life.[14]
>
> *V. Pauli* 1.4

A life of the Egyptian monk Antony had been written by Athanasius of Alexandria around AD 362 and was subsequently translated into Latin twice, on the latter occasion in AD 373 by Jerome's friend and host in Antioch, Bishop Evagrius.[15]

266; Susan Weingarten, *The Saint's Saints: Hagiography and Geography in Jerome* (Leiden: Brill, 2005), 42–74. Cf. Stefan Rebenich, "Inventing an Ascetic Hero: *Jerome's Life of Paul the First Hermit*", in Andrew Cain and Josef Lössl (eds.), *Jerome of Stridon: His Life, Writings and Legacy* (Farnham: Ashgate, 2009), 13–28 at 18–20. Jerome continued his rich blending of genre in his next hagiographical work, the *Vita Malchi* (for which see Christa Gray, *Jerome, Vita Malchi: Introduction, Text, Translation, and Commentary* (Oxford: Oxford University Press, 2015), 14–42).

13 Stefan Rebenich, *Jerome* (London: Routledge, 2002), 25.

14 *igitur quia de Antonio tam Graeco quam Romano stilo diligenter memoriae traditum est, pauca de Pauli principio et fine scribere disposui.*

15 There is some doubt over the nature of Athanasius' authorship (or editorship) of the *Vita Antonii*: see Averil Cameron, "Form and Meaning: The *Vita Constantini* and the *Vita Antonii*", in Tomas Hägg (ed.), *Greek Biography and Panegyric in Late Antiquity* (Berkeley: University of California Press, 2002), 72–86 at 75, and Timothy D. Barnes, *Early Christian Hagiography and Roman History* (Tübingen: Mohr Siebeck, 2010), 160–170. Importantly for my argument, Jerome certainly believed that Athanasius was the author, *Vir. Ill.* 88 (as did his contemporary Gregory of Nazianzus, *Or.* 21.5). For the earlier Latin transla-

The existence of the original Greek *Vita Antonii* (*V. Anton.*), and the new Latin version or versions now in circulation, are acknowledged by Jerome as the major prompt for his composition of the *V. Pauli*.[16] The first sentence of the *V. Pauli* proclaims that there was doubt among many people about who the first eremitic monk may have been (*V. Pauli* 1.1). Although the common opinion suggests that it was Antony, Jerome sets out to demonstrate that Paul of Thebes in fact deserved this title, and had indeed been acknowledged as such by Antony himself.[17] The mention of Greek and Latin accounts of Antony sets up the *V. Anton.* as a well-marked and sustained intertext for the *V. Pauli*, the full implications of which for the genesis of a hagiographical genre will be explored in the final section of this chapter. Yet there are distinct divergences between these two earliest monastic *vitae*: whereas Athanasius had set out to document the deeds of Antony in a lengthy work that thematically narrates Antony's progress further and further into the desert, his battles with demons and the devil, confrontations with pagans, and miracle cures of those who came to visit him, Jerome in the *V. Pauli* succinctly narrates only Paul's early life and death (*V. Pauli* 4–6 and 10–17).[18] The central section of the text (*V. Pauli* 7–9), where one might have expected to read details of Paul's life, is instead devoted to Antony.

A brief summary of the *V. Pauli* may help locate my later discussions of specific sections within the wider contours of the text. After the prologue, Jerome sets the beginning of Paul's monasticism at the time of the persecutions by Decius and Valerian (the AD 250s), under whom the bishops Cornelius of Rome and Cyprian of Carthage were martyred (*V. Pauli* 2). Jerome offers two further, detailed examples of martyrdom (*V. Pauli* 3) before turning to Paul's youth and

---

tion see Henricus Hoppenbrouwers, *La plus ancienne version latine de la vie de S. Antoine par S. Athanase* (Nijmegen: Dekker and Van de Vegt, 1960) and Gerhard J.M. Bartelink and Christine Mohrmann, *Vita di Antonio* (Milan: Mondadori, 1974); for the date of Evagrius' translation, see Pascal Bertrand, "Die Evagriusübersetzung der *Vita Antonii*", Ph.D. diss., Utrecht (2005), 27. Bertrand provides the first modern critical edition of Evagrius' text. Now Bertrand and Lois Gandt have published editions of both texts: Lois Gandt and Pascal H.E. Bertrand (eds.), *Vitae Antonii versiones latinae: Vita beati Antonii abbatis Evagrio interprete; Versio vetustissima*. CCSL 170 (Turnhout: Brepols, 2018).

16 I argue here that Jerome read specifically the version by Evagrius, as attested by his allusions. Contextual information supports this view: the two men were good friends and Jerome was present in Antioch soon after the completion of Evagrius' translation. Cf. Barnes, *Hagiography*, 161.

17 'It is not so much that [Antony] came before all others, but rather that he inspired everyone with a commitment to this way of life' (*V. Pauli* 1.2).

18 Stated as his purpose in the preface: 'I have decided to write a few things (*pauca*) about the beginning and end (*principio et fine*) of Paul's life' (*V. Pauli* 1.4).

early life (*V. Pauli* 4–5). Like Antony, his parents died early, and he was left with the care of a sister.[19] His new brother-in-law threatens to betray him to the persecutors, and thus Paul flees further and further into the desert before finding a cave, open to the sky with a palm tree and pool fed by a spring inside. It is here that Paul spends the rest of his life.

Meanwhile, upon receiving a vision that he is not alone in the desert nor the only perfect monk, Antony sets out on a journey to visit his monastic colleague (*V. Pauli* 7.1–3). At first unsure where to look, he is actively helped by two desert creatures, a centaur (*V. Pauli* 7.3–6), who cannot speak an intelligible language, but helps nonetheless by pointing the way; and a faun (*V. Pauli* 8), who makes a startling revelation about pagan worship. Antony finally finds Paul's cave by following a thirsty she-wolf which made its way towards Paul's spring (*V. Pauli* 9). After an initial rebuff, Antony is admitted to Paul's abode (*V. Pauli* 9.5–6) and the two converse for a day, sharing a god-sent loaf of bread (*V. Pauli* 10–11.2), before Paul announces that he is soon to die and that God had sent Antony to ensure that his body would be buried. Instructing Antony to return to his mountain and fetch a cloak (*pallium*) given to him by Athanasius to use as his burial shroud, Paul dies alone (*V. Pauli* 11.3–13). Upon his return the distraught Antony buries Paul's body, which he had found in a position of prayer, with the help of two lions who excavate a grave with their paws (*V. Pauli* 14–16). The text concludes with the reproach to Jerome's imagined readers, quoted at the head of this chapter (*V. Pauli* 17–18), and his instruction that they should follow Paul's ascetic example.

As Barnes notes, Jerome 'narrates the visit of Antony to Paul as a forgotten episode in the life of Antony'.[20] Antony's journey fills the central section of the text, where we may have expected to find details of Paul's life had Jerome not already excused himself for narrating only Paul's *principium* and *finis*.[21] Summarised in this neutral way, the story of this forgotten episode could appear to be one of pious reverence towards both monks. Antony is undoubtedly the junior partner, the younger monk, the one who makes a pilgrimage to revere his master, but Jerome demonstrates Antony's blessed nature via the help he receives from the creatures of the desert, and at the narrative's conclusion he is established as a true disciple through the act of burying Paul's body. Nonetheless, if Jerome presents the core of his narrative as a supplement to the *V. Anton.*, the detail and style of his narrative ensure that it is a far from flattering addition.

19 Whereas Antony sends his sister to live among a group of female ascetics, Paul's is quickly married.

20 Barnes, *Hagiography*, 180.

21 *V. Pauli* 1.4. Cf. above.

Modern scholarship has often commented on the relationship between these two texts, noting that Jerome consciously sets Paul up as not just the earlier but also the superior monk, and thus seeks to supplant Antony with Paul as the truer example of asceticism.[22] In a succinct and perfunctory article entitled 'the metamorphosis of a hero', Leclerc catalogues several instances in which Paul trumps Antony within the narrative of the *V. Pauli*. Although Leclerc does not draw the distinction, there are in fact two Antonys that form the basis of the metamorphosis of his title; Jerome's Antony (the character within the *V. Pauli*) and Athanasius' Antony (the hero of the *V. Anton.*). In terms of a direct comparison between the two monks *within* the narrative of the *V. Pauli*, Jerome makes Antony thirteen years younger than Paul, and thus Antony is not just a later arrival in the desert but he is also the junior figure (*V. Pauli* 7.1);[23] Antony stumbles at the entrance to Paul's cave and initially has the door slammed in his face (*V. Pauli* 10.4);[24] during their conversation, only Paul is granted *oratio recta* by Jerome, Antony remains silent, and Paul's questions cast Antony as a worldly character, the source of information about what has been going on in the outside world in terms of new buildings, new rulers, and the fate of paganism (*V. Anton.* 10.1).[25]

Equally, some of Leclerc's observations draw on a comparison between Jerome's Paul of the *V. Pauli* and Athanasius' ideal monk as represented by Antony in *V. Anton.*: Antony is ill-educated, but Paul is educated in Greek and Egyptian literature. Antony initially wished to be a blood martyr (*V. Anton.* 23), whereas Paul avoids persecution by fleeing to the desert (*V. Pauli* 5.1). Antony's desert is forbidding and full of demons, whereas Paul's is presented as a *locus amoenus*. Antony's journey in the *V. Anton.* had been one towards personal perfection; in the *V. Pauli* it is one of pilgrimage to Paul. Athanasius stresses the physical robustness of Antony (*V. Anton.* 14), Jerome his age and infirmity (*V. Anton.* 7.2). Paul is given bread daily as a gift of God (brought to him, as to

22 E.g. most recently Jan N. Bremmer, "Athanasius' Life of Antony: Marginality, Spatiality and Mediality", in Jan N. Bremmer and Laura Feldt (eds.), *Marginality, Media, and Mutations of Religious Authority in the History of Christianity* (Leuven: Peeters, 2019), 33–67 at 62–64.

23 Pascal Leclerc, "Antoine et Paul: métamorphose d'un héros", in Yves-Marie Duval (ed.), *Jérôme entre l'Occident et l'Orient. XVIe centenaire du départ de saint Jérôme de Rome et de son installation à Bethléem. Actes du colloque de Chantilly, Sept. 1986* (Paris: Études augustiniennes, 1988), 256–265 at 261.

24 Leclerc, "Antoine et Paul", 262–263. Wolpers had noted that this scene is reminiscent of the paraclausithyron of love elegy, with Antony playing the part of the pining *exclusus amator*. Theodor Wolpers, *Die englische Heiligenlegende des Mittelalters* (Tübingen: Niemeyer, 1964), 51.

25 Leclerc, "Antoine et Paul", 263.

Elijah, by a raven) whereas Antony has to grow his own food (*V. Anton.* 11, 21, 25; *V. Pauli* 10.2). Jerome's Antony exclaims that he bears the title of monk falsely and acts as Paul's pupil (*V. Pauli* 13.1).[26]

Leclerc's catalogue reveals Jerome's construction of an agonistic relationship between the two monks, the purpose of which, according to Leclerc, is to cast Jerome's principal character as the greater monk through the 'dévalorisation' of Antony and by establishing Paul as the true innovator and inventor of the ascetic life.[27] Leclerc has identified an important strand in the complex literary weave that is the *V. Pauli*, but I would suggest this agonistic thread is more integral to the fabric of Jerome's text than Leclerc allows. In the next section, I wish to suggest that Jerome does not just seek to make Paul superior to Antony (as Leclerc suggests) but he also polemically denigrates Athanasius' Antony of the *V. Anton.* in comparison to his Antony of the *V. Pauli* (a relationship that did not form part of Leclerc's study). Furthermore, this satirical polemic extends to the original author of the *V. Anton.* himself. This agonistic relationship is constructed not just between the two 'historical' figures of the monks themselves, but between their textual representations, in other words between the two *vitae* as literary objects. In so doing, for all the polemic and satire, Jerome actually codifies and defines the generic content of not just the ideal ascetic life, but the literary form in which it should be 'recorded', disseminated, and used as an *exemplum*.[28] As the next section will also show, Evagrius' Latin translation often stands at an important medial and mediating point in this intertextual relationship.[29]

---

26 Leclerc, "Antoine et Paul", 260–264.

27 Leclerc's original and convincing observations on Jerome's 'revision' of Antony have been unduly overlooked by later scholars. More recently Rebenich, in a piece that seeks to explain why the *V. Pauli* achieved such popularity in antiquity and the middle ages concludes that 'Athanasius' *Vita Antonii* served Jerome as a literary model for his first *vita* but he also tried to imitate its success'. Rebenich talks of the *V. Pauli* as a 'response' to the *V. Anton.*, and Jerome as offering 'corrections' to Athanasius' ideal of the ascetic monk: Rebenich "Inventing an Ascetic", 22. The examples he adduces do not necessarily imply negative criticism of Antony, rather an updating of the ideal by Jerome: e.g. that Paul embraces traditional classical education, whereas Antony revels in his lack of any sort of education.

28 By 'recorded' I do not suppose that the *V. Pauli* is anything other than Jerome's fiction (a view shared by Barnes, *Hagiography*), merely that the text itself claims to present events that actually happened. Jerome uses historiographical motifs (reference to sources 1.2; his aim of preserving events that will otherwise be forgotten 1.4; and the use of digressions 7.1) to bolster his claim that he records actual events. See Van Pelt in this volume for these and other methods of constructing authority that were available to the hagiographer.

29 Leclerc compares actions, details, and themes, but does not interrogate the text of the *V. Pauli* or *V. Anton.* I argue here that Evagrius' Latin version is the main text (rather than

3 '"I Wrongly Bear the Name of Monk"': Jerome's Antony vs Athanasius' Antony

> As to how he lived during the middle years of his life or what attacks of Satan he endured, no one knows anything for certain.[30]
>
> *V. Pauli* 1.4

In the prologue of the *V. Pauli*, Jerome states that he writes only about Paul's 'beginning and end' because no-one knew exactly what had happened in the middle of Paul's life, though this does not prevent Jerome from supposing that Paul must have endured 'the attacks of Satan'. This programmatic statement is a potent denigration of Athanasius and his Antony. A principal lesson that the reader unfamiliar with the Egyptian desert would take away from Athanasius' *V. Anton.* is that it is a place full of demons, who torment, ridicule, and physically abuse monks like Antony, testing their devotion to Christ and their ascetic lifestyle.[31] These physical and mental battles with demons provide the majority of the subject matter of the *V. Anton.* and justify Athanasius' argument that asceticism in the form of eremitic monasticism was the new martyrdom.[32] The description and explanation of demonology thus is a fundamentally important aspect of Athanasius' narrative, and combating demons was, according to Athanasius, a skill unique to Antony.[33] Jerome's elision of the middle part of Paul's life, whilst acknowledging that demonic torment nonetheless probably took place, simultaneously undercuts the importance of Antony's demonic struggles and Athanasius' confidence in being able to report them in so much detail.[34]

---

the Greek *V. Anton.* or the earlier Latin version) that Jerome engages with: hence I quote it primarily in my discussions, noting any variations with the Greek or the other Latin version. *V. Anton.* refers to the chapter divisions shared by all three versions of the *Vita Antonii*; *V. Anton.-Ev.* to Evagrius' Latin version, and *V. Anton.-Lat.* to the earlier Latin translation.

30 *quomodo autem in media aetate vixerit, aut quas Satanae pertulerit insidias, nulli hominum compertum habetur.*

31 Gerhard J.M. Bartelink, *Vie d'Antoine*. Sources chrétiennes 400 (Paris: Les Éditions du Cerf, 2004), 54–56.

32 Tomas Hägg, "The *Life of St. Antony* between Biography and Hagiography", in Stephanos Efthymiadis (ed.), *The Ashgate Research Companion to Byzantine Hagiography*, vol. 1 (Farnham: Ashgate, 2013), 17–34, at 22. See also Plácido Alvarez, "Demon Stories in the Life of Antony by Athanasius", *Cistercian Studies* 23 (1988), 101–118, and Peter Brown, *The Body and Society: Men, Women, and Sexual Renunciation in Early Christianity* (New York: Columbia University Press, 1988), 213–240.

33 *V. Anton.* 88.

34 Jerome seems to have harboured suspicions about monks' credentials as demon-fight-

Furthermore, by purporting only to narrate Paul's *principium* and *finis*, Jerome draws our attention to a lacuna at the centre of the saint's life (*in media aetate*), which corresponds to an absence of Paul himself at the centre of the textual *Life*, at *V. Pauli* 7–9. That textual lacuna is filled by Antony, alone in the desert, where he confronts those two strange creatures, the centaur and the faun, and asks them for help, then follows the she-wolf into the cave. Those first two creatures are well-known in the literary landscape of pagan letters. The centaur was symbolic of hyper-sexualised masculine barbarism, perhaps best known for running amok through the civilised conventions of marriage.[35] The faun, as another animal-human crossbreed, typically represented a similar mix of charged animalistic sexuality; or as White puts it, the faun is 'little more than ambulatory genitalia'.[36] The she-wolf too fits this pattern: as Goldberg has recently pointed out, the term for she-wolf, *lupa*, was also a slang term for prostitute.[37] In the context of the *V. Pauli*, the sudden appearance of all three might cast the astute reader's mind back to the opening of the *V. Pauli* and the description of blood martyrdom under Decius and Valerian, in which a pious

ers. In the letter in which he satirises hypocritical monks, he praises good monks as those 'who have no skill—as some foolish fellows have—in inventing monstrous stories of their struggles with demons, tales invented to excite the admiration of the ignorant mob and to extract money from their pockets' (*Epist.* 125.9.3). Although written more than thirty years after the *V. Pauli*, this letter hints at Jerome's prejudice against the sort of demonology originally set out in the *V. Anton.*

35 Hom. *Il.* 1.262–269, *Od.* 21.295–304 (the centaurs' drunken rape of the bride at Perithous' wedding). Roger Bartra, *Wild Men in the Looking Glass: the Mythic Origins of European Otherness*. Translated by Carl T. Berrisford (Ann Arbor: University of Michigan Press, 1994), 16. See Patricia Cox Miller, "Jerome's Centaur: A Hyper-Icon of the Desert", *JECS* 4 (1996), 209–233 at 225–227 for the suggestion that Jerome includes these two creatures in order to construct an ambivalent view of the desert as hostile or primitively Arcadian. I suggest Jerome loads the reader's initial expectation towards the former interpretation, while the creatures' actions may suggest the latter. Underlying both scenes, however, is a sustained commentary on similar episodes in Athanasius' *V. Anton.*

36 Hayden White, "The Forms of Wildness: Archaeology of an Idea", in Edward Dudley and Maximilian Novak (eds.), *The Wild Man Within: An Image in Western Thought from the Renaissance to Romanticism* (Pittsburgh: University of Pittsburgh Press, 1972), 3–38 at 24.

37 Goldberg also notes that the sexual tension invoked by the *lupa* is transferred to Antony when he arrives at Paul's door, Charles Goldberg, "Jerome's She-Wolf", *JECS* 21 (2013), 625–628. Both Antony and the wolf pant after what they desire: *lupam sitis ardoribus anhelantem* 9.2; *anhelitu temperato, callidus explorator* [*Antonius*] *ingressus est* 9.3. *anhelo* and *ingredior* both carry sexual overtones, and the latter especially was used metonymically for sexual penetration in the Latin Vulgate (J.N. Adams, *The Latin Sexual Vocabulary* (London: Duckworth, 1982), 176 and 195 with examples from Firm. Mat. *Math.* 1.10.10 and Vulg. *Gen.* 6.4).

Christian was lashed naked to a luxurious bed of feathers by garlands of flowers.[38] Into this sensuous place enters a beautiful prostitute (recalled later by the *lupa*) who masturbates the victim and attempts to mount him. To preserve his chastity, he bit off his tongue and spat it in her face as she kissed him, 'and so the sense of lust was overcome by the sharp pain that replaced it' (*V. Pauli* 1.3).[39] If Athanasius had argued that the monk's resistance of demonic temptation was the new equivalent of blood martyrdom, perhaps Antony's encounter with these creatures, who were traditionally representative of bestial hypersexuality, was to allow Jerome's Antony the opportunity to show that he had the ability to withstand such temptation. It is not the case. As noted above, these potential symbols of sexual excess help Antony in his search for Paul.

Several scholars have read these episodes as Jerome's means of revising the definition of the desert that he found in the *V. Anton.*: no longer is it an inhospitable place full of threatening demons, but a *locus amoenus* where such potentially threatening creatures are themselves Christianised and become helpers of the monk.[40] Such interpretations rightly assume a strong intertextual connection between the *V. Anton.* and the *V. Pauli*, but if we investigate these connections in terms of the human protagonist within the desert land-

38 An observation also made by Virginia Burrus, *The Sex Lives of Saints: An Erotics of Ancient Hagiography* (Philadelphia: University of Pennsylvania Press, 2004), 28, and Goldberg, "Jerome's She-Wolf", 626.

39 For Jerome's rich blend of allusion here (including Virgil, Ovid, and a trope of philosophers tortured by tyrants), see Barnes, *Hagiography*, 178–179. Also Burrus, *Sex Lives*, 24–31.

40 'In this scenario, the centaur embodies the monk's trust in God', Cox Miller, "Jerome's Centaur", 220. Cf. also John Kelly, *Jerome, his Life, Writings, and Controversies* (New York: Harper and Row, 1974), 60; Antoine Guillaumont, "La conception du désert chez les moines d'Egypte" *RHR* 188 (1975), 3–21 at 10. More recently Robert Wiśniewski, "*Bestiae Christum loquuntur* ou des habitants du désert et de la ville dans la *Vita Pauli* de saint Jérôme", *Augustinianum* 40 (2000), 105–144 has argued that Jerome drew inspiration from the contemporary commentary tradition on Isaiah 34 (in which the prophet describes the destruction of Edom and, once deserted, its subsequent inhabitation by a range of wild creatures including ravens and goat-devils, which Wiśniewski equates with the centaur in the *V. Pauli*) to present Paul's Egyptian desert as a place of salvation in counterpoint to the hostility of cities and specifically Alexandria. Wiśniewski rightly identifies one intertextual layer in Jerome's complex web, but here I argue for a connection (between *V. Anton.* and *V. Pauli*) closer to home, and more clearly marked by the explicit reference to the *V. Anton.* in *V. Pauli*.1.4. I concur that Jerome presents Alexandria in a negative light, but, unlike Wiśniewski (141–142), I do not shy away from suggesting that this hostility extends also to the city's bishop, Athanasius (see Section 4 below).

scape, then Jerome's alterations make Antony seem all the more out of place. We should remember, of course, that the desert of the *V. Anton.* and the desert of the *V. Pauli* are supposed to be one and the same (even though Paul and Antony dwell in different, though not so distant, parts of it). Any change in Jerome's presentation is necessarily a *correction* of how it had been presented by Athanasius.

Despite the unexpected reversal in the role allotted to these desert creatures in the *V. Pauli*, the centaur and faun nonetheless still provide a point of intertextual engagement with Antony's encounters and interactions with demons in the *V. Anton.* Specifically, I suggest, they are used in the *V. Pauli* to undermine Athanasius' demonological expertise as presented in the *V. Anton.* First, then, how did the Antony of the *V. Anton.* deal with demons and the devil? Having survived the devil's temptation in his dreams (*V. Anton.* 5–6), and physical beatings carried out both by the devil (*V. Anton.* 8) as well as by demons who adopt the shape of wild animals (*V. Anton.* 9), Antony was in an authoritative position to provide advice on how to identify and combat such enemies in the desert. In a lengthy speech, delivered to an internal audience of other monks at *V. Anton.* 16–43, Antony sets out his demonology and offers two relatively simple solutions for those who may find themselves confronted with a demon: one should boldly question the creature about who it is and from where it comes, and also make the sign of the cross.[41] Both techniques will result in the instant disappearance of the tormenting demon.[42] Athanasius provides his reader with an illustration of the efficacy of these techniques slightly later in the narrative: disturbed while making a wicker basket, Antony looks up to see a beast, half horse and half human (clearly a centaur, though Athanasius does not use the term). Keeping his cool, Antony puts the theory that he has just proposed into practice:

> Antony made the sign of the cross on his own forehead and just said 'I am the servant of Christ (*Christi servus*): if you have been sent to me, I shall

41 The main theme of the speech is that skills in 'discerning spirits' are essential to the ascetic lifestyle. Richard M. Peterson, "'The Gift of Discerning Spirits' in the *Vita Antonii* 16–44", *Studia Patristica* 17 (1982), 523–527.

42 *Audacter requirite quis sit ille et unde venerit … si vero diaboli fuerit oblata tentatio, fidelis animae percunctationibus evanescet* ('demand boldly what it is and where it comes from … if it really is a temptation offered by the devil, it will vanish when the faithful soul interrogates him', *V. Anton.-Ev.* 43); *quae omnia ad primum quoque signum crucis evanescunt* ('all these [shape-shifting demons] vanish as soon as the sign of the cross is made', *V. Anton.-Ev.* 23).

> not run away'. There was not a moment of delay: at once the hideous monster fled with its attendant evil spirits, and as it rushed in headlong flight it was destroyed.[43]
>
> *V. Anton.-Ev.* 53

The procedure has direct and potent effect. Athanasius' inclusion of this episode neatly reinforces Antony's demonological credentials: experience leads the monk to formulate a strategy that can be learned by others, and this strategy is endorsed for the reader by the example of its application by Antony against the demonic centaur.

Jerome's Antony of *V. Pauli* is not nearly as astute. Firstly, one should note that, in addition to the classical associations of sexual excess and violence associated with the centaur, the creature's appearance in the *V. Pauli* also alludes to Antony's interaction with the same creature in the *V. Anton.*[44] When Jerome's Antony meets the centaur he dutifully makes the sign of the cross as he had (or would?) in the *V. Anton.*, but neglects the rest of his routine. Antony does indeed question this strange creature, but he forgets (or has not yet learned?) the correct procedure for dealing with monstrous apparitions in the desert. Instead he unthinkingly asks it for help ('And he said, "Hey you, where does the servant of God live"?'[45]), a question to which the centaur (perhaps surprisingly for the reader of *Vita Antonii*) gives an answer by pointing the way with his arm. There are other structural parallels with the scene at *V. Anton.-Ev.* 53: Antony's statement in the *V. Anton.* that he is the *Christi seruus* has been transposed into a question that identifies Paul (not Antony) as the *Dei seruus* in the *V. Pauli*; the centaur likewise runs off at speed (*ac sic patentes campos uolucri transmittens fuga*) and vanishes (*evanuit*) as it had done in the *V. Anton.* Jerome admits that he (and Antony) do not know exactly what this creature is: perhaps it was the devil or perhaps it was a creature that naturally appears in the desert (*V. Pauli* 7.6); if this is an especially tame version of the centaur that had appeared in the *V. Anton.*, it is not altogether clear why its temperament

43 *Vexillum crucis in fronte sua pingens hoc tantum ait: 'Christi servus sum; si ad me es missa, non fugio'. Nullum in medio spatium et statim informe prodigium quantocius cum satellitum turba fugit, et in medio cursu ruens exstinctum est.* He uses the same procedure against the devil at *V. Anton.* 41.

44 This does not rule out Wiśniewski's identification of allusion to Isaiah 34 and its commentary tradition, but the structural similarity to the same scene-type in the *V. Anton.* and the opening reference to a Life of Antony at *V. Pauli* 1.3 promotes the intertext with the *V. Anton.* above any other.

45 *et heus tu, inquit, quanam in parte dei servus hic habitat?* (*V. Pauli* 7.4).

has changed. But there have been hints that Antony should really have been more suspicious. Instead of speaking, the centaur 'gave (*infrendens*) some sort of barbaric grunt, grinding out (*frangens*) the words rather than pronouncing them'[46] (*V. Pauli* 7.5). That grinding speech is a trademark of Athanasius' devil and his demons, who repeatedly 'ground their teeth (*fremebant dentibus suis*)' (*V. Anton.-Ev.* 9) to show their frustration with Antony.[47]

There is a twofold undermining of Athanasius and his Antony here. On one level, the natural hostility of the desert as the abode of the devil is questioned and Jerome injects some narratorial uncertainty about his subject matter (*incertum habemus*) in contrast to the more authoritative Athanasian narrator. Moreover, this uncertainty about the identity of the centaur casts Antony as no longer the astute combatant of demons, well-versed in their ways and suspicious of their tricks to the extent of paranoia.[48] Instead he is credulous and only too willing to accept their help.

Battling with demons is a significant (perhaps the most significant) theme of Athanasius' *V. Anton.* A close second is Antony's refutation of paganism, best illustrated by his conversation with the pagan philosophers at *V. Anton.* 72–80, in which he castigates pagan divinities for adopting animal form (*V. Anton.* 74) and for the immoral acts they perform (*V. Anton.* 75), whilst the pagans themselves are vilified for treating demons as gods (*V. Anton.* 80). Whereas Athanasius is not clear whether Antony's conversation brings about the pagans' conversion, the philosophers certainly depart enlightened and impressed by Antony's exorcism of a demon from a possessed Christian (*V. Anton.* 81). Again, Athanasius' Antony exhibits a well-reasoned response to pagan critics (and one that is quite typical of Christian apologetic of the mid fourth century).[49]

The scene finds its parallel in the second of the encounters that Jerome's Antony has during his journey to Paul. Chancing upon a *homunculus* with a hooked nose and horns on his forehead, Antony receives a confession from the creature:

> **Antonius**, et **quisnam esset interrogans**, hoc ab eo responsum accepit: '**mortalis ego sum**, et unus ex accolis eremi, quos vario delusa **errore**

---

46 *barbarum nescio quid infrendens, et frangens potius verba quam proloquens.*

47 *stridens dentibus* (*V. Anton.-Ev.* 6); *frendebat dentibus suis* (*V. Anton.-Ev.* 52).

48 *Et ille Scripturarum doctus eloquio, multas esse daemonum captiones, solerti propositum labore servabat*, 'And Antony, knowing from what the Bible says that the wiles of the devil are numerous, maintained his commitment firm by means of skilful effort' (*V. Anton.-Ev.* 7).

49 Cf. Arnobius *Adv. nat.* 2–4, Firmicus Maternus *de errore* 1–5; Augustine *Civ.* 4.10.16, 716.24.

> **gentilitas**, Faunos, Satyrosque, et Incubos colit. Legatione fungor **gregis mei**. Precamur ut pro nobis communem Dominum depreceris; **salutem mundi** olim **venisse** cognovimus, et in universam terram exiit sonus eius.'
>
> *V. Pauli* 8.3

> **Antony, questioning him as to who it was**, received this reply: '**I am a mortal creature**, one of the inhabitants of the desert whom the **pagans**, deluded by various **errors**, worship, calling them fauns, satyrs and incubi. I am acting as envoy **for my tribe**. We ask you to pray for us to the Lord we share, for we know **He came** once **for the salvation of the world**, and His sound has gone out over the whole earth'.

The readers of the *V. Anton.* again have their expectations undermined: Antony's same question received a far more sinister reply elsewhere in the *V. Anton.*:

> Quem [puerum horridum et nigrum] cum **interrogaret Antonius quisnam esset** qui talia loqueretur, ait: '**ego sum fornicationis amicus**'.[50]
>
> *V. Anton.-Ev.* 6

> When **Antony asked** him [an ugly black boy] **who it was** who was saying this, he replied: '**I am the friend of fornication.**'

This little black boy was, once again, the devil in disguise, and the Antony in the *V. Anton.* was thus right to be suspicious. The faun's reply to the same question that it is in fact a mortal overturns the response expected by the reader of the *V. Anton.* (We should note here that the allusion works only with Evagrius' translation; the earlier Latin translation, as had the Greek original, used a direct question: *deinde Antonio interrogante 'quis es tu ut talia loqueris apud me?'*, *V. Anton.-Lat.* 6).[51] Furthermore, Antony in the *V. Anton.* had preached at those doubting pagan philosophers by defining Christian doctrine thus: 'Christian belief states that God **has come for the salvation of the world** (*Christiana credulitas **pro salute mundi** Deum suum **venisse** testatur*)' (*V. Anton.-Ev.* 74)—

50 This allusion was first identified by Susana González Marín, "Relaciones intertextuales entre la *Vita Pauli* de Jerónimo y la *Vita Antonii* de Atanasio", in Vicente Bécares, Francisca Pordomingo Pardo, and Rosario Cortés Tovar (eds.), *Intertextualidad en las literaturas griega y latina*, (Madrid: Ediciones Clásicas, 2000), 319–336, at 329.

51 Cf. εἶτα τοῦ Ἀντωνίου· Τίς εἶ σὺ ὁ τοιαῦτα λαλῶν παρ' ἐμοί; εὐθὺς ἐκεῖνος οἰκτρὰς ἠφίει φωνάς· Ἐγὼ τῆς πορνείας εἰμὶ φίλος (*V. Anton.* 6).

the phrase with which the faun now defines its belief in Christ. Again, the allusion operates only with Evagrius' translation, not the earlier Latin one.[52] The dense pocket of allusions here to Evagrius' Latin version of the *V. Anton.* also suggests that the faun's description of paganism as *vario delusa **errore gentilitas*** and his statement about his mission (*legatione fungor **gregis mei***) allude to Antony's claim upon converting pagans just before his conversation with the philosophers: *quanti etiam ab **errore gentilium** retracti **nostro** iuncti sunt **gregi**!*, 'How many have been saved from the **error of the pagans**, and added to **our flock**!' (*V. Anton.-Ev.* 70).

In the *V. Pauli*, then, there is a distinct role reversal—it is the faun who instructs Antony about the true nature of pagan demons (which turn out not to be pagans at all, but Christians). Antony is denied the opportunity to convert this creature—he cannot question it further before it happily and without prompting confesses that it is *already* a member of the Christian flock. Indeed, the faun professes Christian doctrine in terms that Antony would use himself to convert those pagan philosophers at *V. Anton.* 74.[53] Reading the *V. Pauli* back onto the *V. Anton.* (and it seems very much that Jerome wanted his work to be viewed as the prequel to Athanasius' text), then it appears, comically, that Athanasius' Antony gets the information for his attacks on the pagans directly from the horse's (or in this case faun's) mouth—the mouth of a 'misunderstood' demon—and not from his direct experience of battling such creatures.

Through a series of allusions to the Latin text of Evagrius' version of the *V. Anton.*, Jerome undermines two of the major characteristics of Athanasius' Antony, his demon-fighting credentials and the source of his Christian apologetics. Jerome's technique, moreover, verges on the satirical. Those allusions to the *V. Anton.* raise the expectations of the reader, only to dash them in a comic reversal of the Athanasian prototype.

4 The Denigration of Athanasius, 'Inheritor of the Blessed Antony'

Evagrius' Latin version of the *V. Anton.* serves as an important intertext for Jerome's *V. Pauli*. The more comical and polemic aspects of Jerome's detraction of Antony rely upon a knowledge of Evagrius' text. Jerome elsewhere is

52 The earlier Latin version had rendered this sentence *illa enim nostra fides adventum Christi asserit propter salutem generis humani esse factum* (*V. Anton.-Lat.* 74.7), rather more closely representing the original: Ἡ μὲν γὰρ ἡμετέρα πίστις ἐπὶ σωτηρίᾳ τῶν ἀνθρώπων τὴν τοῦ Χριστοῦ παρουσίαν λέγει.

53 The faun also manages to quote a psalm (*in omnem terram exivit sonus eorum*, Ps. 18.5).

complimentary about Evagrius as a translator, however, praising his philosophy of translation, and particularly the statement Evagrius made in his preface to the *V. Anton.* that he translated sense not words.[54] In this section, I suggest that Jerome's detraction of Antony extends to Athanasius as the figure who claimed proximity to Antony, and who thereby created authority not just for rendering Antony's life into text, but for his own clerical status. Ironically, however, that inheritance was partly due to Evagrius' loose approach to translation.

Athanasius had appeared obliquely as a character within the *V. Anton.* during Antony's death scene, but in a way that importantly established him as a successor of Antony. Being close to God, Antony was able to foresee his imminent death, and he informed his fellow monks. In this final speech he also provided some instructions for what should happen to his few possessions:

> Melotem et pallium tritum cui superiaceo Athanasio episcopo date, quod mihi novum ipse detulerat; Serapion episcopus aliam accipat melotem.
>
> *V. Anton.-Ev.* 91

> Please give to Athanasius this sheepskin and the worn cloak on which I am lying, because he gave it to me when it was new. Let bishop Serapion receive the other sheepskin.

The cloak (*pallium*) makes a brief reappearance a few sections later in an authorial interjection by Athanasius as the primary narrator:

> Legatarius autem Antonii benedicti qui tritum pallium cum melote imperio eius meruerat accipere, Antonium in Antonii muneribus amplectitur et tamquam magna haereditate ditatus laetanter per vestimentum recordatur imaginem sanctitatis.
>
> *V. Anton.-Ev.* 92

> The inheritor of the blessed Antony who has been deemed worthy of receiving the worn cloak and the sheepskin according to Antony's orders, embraces Antony in Antony's gifts: the garment causes him to remember with joy the paragon of holiness as if a large inheritance had made him wealthy.

---

54 *non verba, sed sententias transtulisse* (*Epist.* 57.6).

The cloak has become a potent symbol of Athanasius' inheritance of Antony's ascetic authority. The term used to refer to Athanasius, *legatarius*, is legalistic Latin and designates the recipient of a legacy via the terms of a will.[55] The idea of Athanasius as Antony's legatee is reinforced by the simile of *haereditas* in the following sentence. This passage, however, is not all it seems. It is one of those moments when Evagrius has translated sense not words, and in the process has made a significant alteration to the original. The subject of this sentence in the Greek version had referred not just to Athanasius:

> Καὶ τῶν λαβόντων δὲ ἕκαστος τὴν μηλωτὴν τοῦ μακαρίου Ἀντωνίου καὶ τὸ τετριμμένον παρ' αὐτοῦ ἱμάτιον, ὡς μέγα χρῆμα φυλάττει. Καὶ γὰρ καὶ βλέπων αὐτά, ὡς Ἀντώνιόν ἐστι θεωρῶν· καὶ περιβαλλόμενος δὲ αὐτά, ὡς τὰς νουθεσίας αὐτοῦ βαστάζων ἐστὶ μετὰ χαρᾶς.
>
> And each of those who received a sheepskin from Anthony, and the cloak that he wore out, guards it like a treasure. For looking upon it is like seeing Antony, and wearing it is like taking up his counsels with great joy.

In the Athanasian original, both Athanasius and Serapion treasure Antony's former possessions, and there is no reiteration of Antony's command about who should receive (and deserve—*meruerat*) the cloak. The definition of both men as οἱ λαβόντες does not carry the legalistic overtones of *legatarius*. The earlier Latin translation of this passage follows the Greek more closely, and uses a plural to ensure the reader knows that both bishops formed the subject, and does not use the term *legatarius*.[56] In comparison, Evagrius cuts Serapion out of Antony's inheritance, and makes Athanasius the sole heir, as symbolised by the *pallium*. Not only does Athanasius deservedly possess this 'relic' of Antony, but it provides him with spiritual sustenance, and it plays a further role in connecting the subject of the *V. Anton.* with the text's author: Athanasius is clearly imbued with ascetic authority as well as the authority, and indeed the right, to become Antony's hagiographer.

Although unnamed as the author of the *V. Anton.* in the preface of the *V. Pauli*, the bishop of Alexandria appears within the narrative of the *V. Pauli* itself, and in a similar scene type in the lead-up to Paul's death:

---

55 First attested in Suet. *Galba* 5.2, and subsequently frequently in the jurists (Gai. *Inst.* 2, 195 and 200). OLD s.v. *legatarius*.

56 *Et **illi** autem qui melotas acceperunt beatissimi Antonii et tritum stratorium, quasi magnam facultatem **custodiunt**.*

> 'quamobrem, perge, quaeso, nisi molestum est, et pallium quod tibi Athanasius episcopus dedit ad obvolvendum corpusculum meum defer.' hoc autem beatus Paulus rogavit, non quod magnopere curaret, utrum tectum putresceret cadaver, an nudum—quippe qui tanti temporis spatio, contextis palmarum foliis vestiebatur—sed ut a se recedenti moeror suae mortis levaretur.
>
> *V. Pauli* 12.2–3

> 'And so I beg you to go back, unless it is too much trouble, and bring me the cloak which bishop Athanasius gave you and wrap it around my poor body.' The blessed Paul asked this not because he was particularly bothered whether his corpse was naked or clothed as it decomposed (had he not for a long time been dressed in woven palm leaves?) but so that by going away Antony might be spared the grief caused by Paul's death.

The death scene is clearly modelled on that of Antony in the *V. Anton.* Again comical reversals are apparent: Antony similarly gives instructions to those around him immediately prior to his death, and tells his audience that he is confident that his body will remain incorrupt (*resiliet incorruptum, V. Anton.* 91), whereas Paul (according to his private thoughts, reported by Jerome) expects his to rot (*putresceret*). Athanasius' cloak, which Paul requests, plays an important role in taking Antony off-scene at the crucial moment of Paul's death, allowing Paul to die as a true monk, alone.[57] Jerome is not explicit regarding Antony's completion of Paul's order—the description of later preparations for Paul's burial suggest that he did use the cloak: the body is wrapped (*obvoluto ... corpore, V. Anton.-Ev.* 16), although nothing is explicitly named as the thing *in which* the body is wrapped. Nonetheless, Antony has been presented as a scrupulous follower of Paul's orders during this scene, not least in making the arduous journey back to his cave to fetch the cloak in the first place, so it is difficult to imagine him disobeying Paul's final request (*V. Pauli.* 13.1).

The scene has been read positively by Rebenich: 'This is an exceptionally symbolical act because by handing over the pallium to Paul, Antony acknowledges Paul's precedence and legitimises Jerome's Life of the first hermit.'[58] Yet, reading Evagrius' version of the *V. Anton.* one can be in no doubt that Athanasius' cloak ended up back in the hands of Antony at the time of his own death, and ultimately with Athanasius as a sign of the bishop's inheri-

57 Leclerc, "Antoine et Paul", 264.

58 Rebenich, "Inventing an Ascetic", 22; cf. Kech, *Hagiographie*, 45.

tance of Antony's possessions and his *sanctitas*. Perhaps Jerome has made a slip in his otherwise careful dovetailing of details between the *V. Anton.* and *V. Pauli*, but given his care elsewhere we should instead view this as a conscious disruption of the links between the *V. Pauli* and the *V. Anton.* and another form of polemic against Athanasius. The cloak, which is so clearly a symbol of ascetic authority in the *V. Anton.*, Jerome implies, never returned with Antony to his mountain retreat, and thus never back to Athanasius.[59] It cannot fulfil the role of ensuring Athanasius' authority in becoming Antony's hagiographer. Jerome thus questions the accuracy of Athanasius'/Evagrius' account; and in any case, the role that Antony makes the *pallium* play in the *V. Pauli*—to act as a shroud for Paul—was entirely against Paul's wishes. Paul's interest in the *pallium* was feigned, and merely a ruse (albeit a well-intentioned one) to remove Antony from the scene of his death. Antony may think that he dutifully performs Paul's orders, but Paul had no intrinsic interest in the cloak, indeed he dismisses it as a worldly object of no use for a true monk: why should his body be covered in death when in life it had been clad only with palm leaves?

Athanasius appears as a character in one other place in his *V. Anton.*, in his own see in Alexandria during Antony's visit to the city at the behest of the bishops (*V. Anton.* 69–71).[60] There, he confounded Arians, converted pagans, and exorcised demons. Athanasius makes use of a single first-person plural verb to indicate his presence among the crowd that witnessed Antony's expulsion of a demon from a possessed girl.[61] The Alexandria of the *V. Anton.* is not just the scene of the meeting of the monk and his future hagiographer, but is a place that grows in its Christianity because of Antony's presence.

Jerome swiftly overturns this view of Alexandria in the *V. Pauli*. After the faun's startling revelation that he is no pagan demon but a devoted Christian,

59 We should note that the exchange of cloaks which is being suggested (and frustrated) here is influenced as much by the conventions of Jerome and his fellow Christian intellectuals as by what desert monks themselves may be doing. Williams' discussion in this volume of Paulinus' gift-exchange with Sulpicius illustrates how on the one hand the gift of a cloak had an established symbolic meaning in bringing the receiver into an ascetic tradition; whereas it was also possible to play with those conventions and expectations to introduce some humour. Here too, we may see expectations frustrated: the ascetic link between Paul and Athanasius is broken by the disappearance of the cloak.

60 Dated to AD 337 or AD 338, i.e. the period between Athanasius' first and second exiles. Bartelink, *Vie d'Antoine*, 317 n. 1.

61 *accidit etiam ut cum eum redeuntem circa portam prosequeremur* … ('it happened that when we escorted him back near the gate …' *V. Anton.-Ev.* 71.1).

Antony exclaims: '"Woe to you, Alexandria, for worshipping monsters instead of God. Woe to you, you whore of a city, to which demons from all over the world have flocked in great numbers"' (*V. Pauli* 8.5).[62] As Wiśniewski has argued, this exclamation may be part of Jerome's promotion of desert Christianity over its urban counterpart.[63] Yet the specificity of Antony's outburst comes as rather a surprise: the faun had not suggested where these pagans might be, certainly not that they were in a city, and least of all Alexandria. The exclamation does neatly break the connection between Athanasius and Antony, however, reversing the image of Alexandria as an increasingly Christian city to its very opposite, a demonic centre. It is difficult to resist the conclusion that Jerome's attack on Athanasius extends not just to his role as Antony's hagiographer but even as bishop of Alexandria.[64]

5 'Recorded for Posterity': Imitation, Competition, and the Creation of a Genre

To return to my opening discussion, one may now ask whether the *V. Pauli* is satire. The answer is certainly not formally, but there are clear satirical elements within the text. We may not find the sense of outrage, the vivid descriptions, and the second-person apostrophes, which appear in the conclusion addressed to the imagined readers, in the body of the narrative. Nevertheless, there is a sense that Jerome attempts to deflate the rather self-regarding tone of the *V. Anton.*, and that many of the tropes within the *V. Pauli* recall similar themes and episodes in the 'serious' hagiography of the *V. Anton.*, only for the expected outcomes of these episodes to be overturned in a comic inversion.[65] By a series of comic yet polemic inversions of the Athanasian prototype, then, Jerome not only rams home his point that Paul really was the first monk (and not simply chronologically, but as the practitioner of a more ideal form of ascetic existence), but he also denigrates Athanasius, the figure who helped spread

62 '*vae tibi Alexandria, quae pro Deo portenta veneraris; vae tibi, civitas meretrix, in qua totius orbis daemonia confluxere*'. The reference to a *meretrix* recalls the agent of martyrdom at the opening of the life, *V. Pauli* 3.3, and confirms the view that Alexandria is a place hostile to Christians.

63 Wiśniewski, "*Bestiae*", 133–136.

64 A point that Wiśniewski entertains briefly as one conclusion, but dismisses on historical grounds, "*Bestiae*", 141–142. See my discussion in the next section.

65 Parodying of 'serious' genres, especially epic, was typical of classical satire, and is a constant theme in Juvenal. See Braund, *Juvenal*, 21–24.

Antony's (mis-held) reputation.[66] What does Jerome's satirical and polemic attitude towards his predecessor mean for our question of the literary origins of hagiography? It may seem that the moment of genesis for ascetic hagiography was also a moment of literary destruction: Jerome sets out to supplant the example of Antony with the example of Paul. But it is important to note that Jerome does not seek to wipe out the memory of Antony, this is not literary *damnatio memoriae*. Quite the opposite, Jerome perpetuates the textual depiction of Antony by drawing his reader's attention to the fact that the Greek and Latin versions of the *V. Anton.* have ensured that the story of Antony 'has been recorded for posterity' (*memoriae traditum est, V. Pauli* 1.1). It is the existence of the *V. Anton.* that prompts Jerome to compose the *V. Pauli*, a phenomenon that the astute reader is not allowed to forget, as appreciation of the witty polemic relies on knowledge of the *V. Anton.*, and specifically the *V. Anton.* of Evagrius. Jerome does not just recognise Athanasius as his predecessor, he *makes* him his predecessor, a necessary first step in creating a genre. Although Athanasius did not single-handedly invent hagiography,[67] Jerome appears to have detected the novelty of the *V. Anton.*'s literary form of ascetic life, and thus by engaging with it, and even parodying some of its conventions, helps to define its formal characteristics.

Jerome thus treads a careful balance between *aemulatio* and *imitatio*, the two ways of engaging with a literary predecessor that between them define a new contribution to a genre. Literary *imitatio* perhaps speaks for itself, but *aemulatio*, a stance of polemic competition, is rhetorically often the first step to asserting that one makes a new (better) addition to a genre, whilst being a marker and defining aspect of a genre itself. To take the example of historiography, Tacitus opens his *Histories* by praising his distant predecessors and attacking all those who had attempted to write imperial history more recently.[68] And

66 This attitude extends to other of Jerome's works. In the *Chronicon* (322b, s.a. 356), Jerome simultaneously denies Athanasius the role of Antony's hagiographer, whilst promoting himself as Paul's: *Antonius monachus* CV *aetatis anno in heremo moritur. solitus multis ad se venientibus de Paulo quodam Thebaeo mirae beatitudinis viro referre, cuius nos exitum brevi libello explicuimus* ('Anthony the monk dies in his 105th year in the desert. He was accustomed to recount to many who came to him about a certain man Paul the Theban of wonderful blessings, whose death we have ourselves explained in a brief book'). Antony has been historicised by Jerome as the source of the story of Paul, not primarily as a monastic figure (and less still the subject of hagiography) in his own right.

67 See Corke-Webster in this volume.

68 *Nam post conditam urbem octingentos et viginti prioris aevi annos multi auctores rettulerunt, dum res populi Romani memorabantur, pari eloquentia ac libertate: postquam bellatum*

Jerome's contemporary, Ammianus, similarly places himself in a tradition of historiographical writers by beginning the (now lost) first book of the *Res Gestae* where Tacitus had left off in AD 96, whilst simultaneously damning contemporary exponents of breviary history.[69] Indeed, by the Roman period, such polemic had itself become a tradition of historiography, and one that was itself open to imitation.[70] Jerome is rather different in that he identified only one predecessor with whom to engage in both *imitatio* and *aemulatio*, and thus he connects his *V. Pauli* to the *Life of Antony* whilst also denigrating some of its claims. To complicate this situation, however, one should note that the crucible for the genesis of the ascetic hagiography, where *imitatio* and *aemulatio* collide and shower the reader with the fiery sparks of polemic satire, is Latin literature: Jerome's polemic allusion relies on the existence specifically of Evagrius' Latin *V. Anton.*

This observation raises one final question, of a more historical than literary nature. Did Jerome risk offending his patron by creating a monastic figure that so clearly undermined the depiction of Antony in the *V. Anton.*, to which Evagrius had just lent his name? This is not a question I propose to answer definitively at the end of an already-lengthy chapter and in a volume that is primarily interested in literary causes; but we might note that both Evagrius' translation and the *V. Pauli* are securely dated to around AD 373 and AD 374,[71] and thus in the immediate aftermath of Athanasius' death in May AD 373. Might we imagine Jerome instituting a competitive literary game with Evagrius over the literary legacy of the recently deceased Athanasius; especially since Evagrius

---

apud Actium atque omnem potentiam ad unum conferri pacis interfuit, magna illa ingenia cessere; simul veritas pluribus modis infracta ('Many historians have treated of the earlier period of eight hundred and twenty years from the founding of Rome, and while dealing with the Republic they have written with equal eloquence and freedom. But after the battle of Actium, when the interests of peace required that all power should be concentrated in the hands of one man, writers of like ability disappeared; and at the same time historical truth was impaired in many ways', Tac. *Hist.* 1.1.) Cf. John Marincola, "Tacitus' prefaces and the decline of imperial historiography", *Latomus* 58 (1999), 89–96.

69 For Ammianus' attacks on writers of breviary, such as Eutropius, at 15.1.1, see Gavin Kelly, *Ammianus Marcellinus* (Cambridge: Cambridge University Press, 2008), 240.

70 'Nearly every ancient historian seeks to portray himself as a lonely seeker of truth, as the only one who has somehow understood the historian's proper task, while his predecessors (as he will frequently remind us) failed in the effort', John Marincola, *Authority and Tradition in Ancient Historiography* (Cambridge: Cambridge University Press, 1999), 217; 217–237 provide a study of the uses of polemic from the earliest Greek historians to Ammianus.

71 For the dating of Evagrius' translation see Bertrand, "Evagriusübersetzung", 27.

had given a more prominent role to Athanasius as the legatee of Antony? At least with the bishop's death, Jerome risked no personal backlash from Alexandria, which would have been fully justifiable given the help that Athanasius offered the supporters of Evagrius and Paulinus during the Melitian schism in Antioch.[72] Whatever the personal relationship between Evagrius and Jerome as *littérateurs*, it remains a moot point whether we would have had a *Vita Pauli* (indeed whether the Catholic Church would have had a St Paul of Thebes),[73] were it not for Evagrius' decision to translate and therefore popularise Athanasius' *Life of Antony*.

Acknowledgments

An earlier version of this chapter was delivered at the Late Roman Seminar, Oxford and at the Constructed Sainthood Workshop, Durham. It is my pleasure to thank both audiences, together with the editors and Jan Bremmer, who read a draft, for their insightful and helpful comments. All remaining shortcomings are my own.

Bibliography

Adams, James N., *The Latin Sexual Vocabulary* (London: Duckworth, 1982).
Alvarez, Plácido, "Demon Stories in the Life of Antony by Athanasius", *Cistercian Studies* 23 (1988), 101–118.
Barnes, Timothy D., *Tertullian: a Historical and Literary Study* (Oxford: Oxford University Press, 1971).
Barnes, Timothy D., *Athanasius and Constantius* (Berkeley: University of California Press).
Barnes, Timothy D., *Early Christian Hagiography and Roman History* (Tübingen: Mohr Siebeck, 2010).
Bartelink, Gerhard J.M., *Vie d'Antoine*. Sources chrétiennes 400 (Paris: Les Éditions du Cerf, 2004).
Bartelink, Gerhard J.M. and Christine Mohrmann, *Vita di Antonio* (Milan: Mondadori, 1974).

72 Timothy D. Barnes, *Athanasius and Constantius* (Berkeley: University of California Press), 44–45. Rebenich, *Hieronymus*, 7.
73 At least until the Second Vatican Council, when his feast day (15 January) was removed from the calendar. Rebenich, "Inventing an Ascetic", 16.

Bartra, Roger, *Wild Men in the Looking Glass: the Mythic Origins of European Otherness*. Translated by Carl T. Berrisford (Ann Arbor: University of Michigan Press, 1994).

Bertrand, Pascal H.E., "Die Evagriusübersetzung der *Vita Antonii*", Ph.D. diss., Utrecht (2005).

Bertrand, Pascal H.E. and Lois Gandt, *Vitae Antonii versiones latinae: Vita beati Antonii abbatis Evagrio interprete; Versio vetustissima*, CCSL 170 (Turnhout: Brepols, 2018).

Braund, Susannah Morton, *Juvenal, Satires 1* (Cambridge: Cambridge University Press, 1996).

Bremmer, Jan N., "Athanasius' Life of Antony: Marginality, Spatiality and Mediality", in Jan N. Bremmer and Laura Feldt (eds.), *Marginality, Media, and Mutations of Religious Authority in the History of Christianity* (Peeters: Leuven, 2019), 33–67.

Brown, Peter, *The Body and Society: Men, Women, and Sexual Renunciation in Early Christianity* (New York: Columbia University Press, 1988).

Burrus, Virginia, *The Sex Lives of Saints: An Erotics of Ancient Hagiography* (Philadelphia: University of Pennsylvania Press, 2004).

Cameron, Averil, "Form and Meaning: The *Vita Constantini* and the *Vita Antonii*", in Tomas Hägg (ed.), *Greek Biography and Panegyric in Late Antiquity* (Berkeley: University of California Press, 2002), 72–86.

Cox Miller, Patricia, "Jerome's Centaur: A Hyper-Icon of the Desert", *JECS* 4 (1996), 209–233.

de Vogüé, Adalbert, "La Vita Pauli de saint Jérôme et sa datation. Examen d'un passage clé (ch. 6)", in Gerhard J.M. Bartelink, Anton Hilhorst, and Corneille H. Kneepkens (eds.), *Eulogia. Mélanges offerts à Antoon A.R. Bastiaensen à l'occasion de son soixante-cinquième anniversaire* (Steenbrugge: Abbatia S. Petri, 1991), 395–406.

Goldberg, Charles, "Jerome's She-Wolf", *JECS* 21 (2013), 625–628.

González Marín, Susana, "Relaciones intertextuales entre la *Vita Pauli* de Jerónimo y la *Vita Antonii* de Atanasio", in Vicente Bécares, Francisca Pordomingo Pardo, and Rosario Cortés Tovar (eds.), *Intertextualidad en las literaturas griega y latina*, (Madrid: Ediciones Clásicas, 2000), 319–336.

Gray, Christa, *Jerome, Vita Malchi: Introduction, Text, Translation, and Commentary* (Oxford: Oxford University Press, 2015).

Guillaumont, Antoine, "La conception du désert chez les moines d'Egypte", *RHR* 188 (1975), 3–21.

Hägg, Tomas, "The *Life of St. Antony* between Biography and Hagiography", in Stephanos Efthymiadis (ed.), *The Ashgate Research Companion to Byzantine Hagiography*, vol. 1 (Farnham: Ashgate, 2013), 17–34.

Hoppenbrouwers, Henricus, *La plus ancienne version latine de la vie de S. Antoine par S. Athanase* (Nijmegen: Dekker and Van de Vegt, 1960).

Kech, Herbert, *Hagiographie als christliche Unterhaltungsliteratur. Studien zum Phä-*

nomen des Erbaulichen anhand der Mönchsviten des hl. Hieronymus. Göppinger Arbeiten zur Germanistik (Göppingen: Kümmerle, 1977).

Kelly, Gavin, *Ammianus Marcellinus* (Cambridge: Cambridge University Press, 2008).

Kelly, John N.D., *Jerome, his Life, Writings, and Controversies* (New York: Harper and Row, 1974).

Leclerc, Pierre, "Antoine et Paul: métamorphose d'un héros", in Yves-Marie Duval (ed.), *Jérôme entre l'Occident et l'Orient. XVIe centenaire du départ de saint Jérôme de Rome et de son installation à Bethléem. Actes du colloque de Chantilly, Sept. 1986* (Paris: Études augustiniennes, 1988), 256–265.

Leclerc, Pierre, Edgardo Martín Morales, and Adalbert de Vogüé, *Trois vies de moines (Paul, Malchus, Hilarion)*. Sources chrétiennes 508 (Paris: Les Éditions du Cerf, 2007).

Marincola, John, *Authority and Tradition in Ancient Historiography* (Cambridge: Cambridge University Press, 1999).

Marincola, John, "Tacitus' prefaces and the decline of imperial historiography", *Latomus* 58 (1999), 89–96.

Peterson, Richard M., "'The Gift of Discerning Spirits' in the *Vita Antonii* 16–44", *Studia Patristica* 17 (1982), 523–527.

Plesch, Julius, *Die Originalität und literarische Form der Mönchsbiographien des hl. Hieronymus* (Munich: Kgl. Hof- und Universitäts-Buchdruckerei von C. Wolf, 1910).

Rebenich, Stefan, *Hieronymus und sein Kreis. Prosopographische und sozialgeschichtliche Untersuchungen* (Stuttgart: Steiner, 1992).

Rebenich, Stefan, *Jerome* (London: Routledge, 2002).

Rebenich, Stefan, "Inventing an Ascetic Hero: Jerome's Life of Paul the First Hermit", in Andrew Cain and Josef Lössl (eds.), *Jerome of Stridon: His Life, Writings and Legacy* (Farnham: Ashgate, 2009), 13–28.

Reitzenstein, Richard, *Hellenistische Wundererzählungen* (Leipzig: Teubner, 1906).

Shanzer, Danuta, "Latin Literature, Christianity and Obscenity in the Later Roman West", in Nicola McDonald (ed.), *Medieval Obscenities* (Woodbridge: York Medieval, 2006), 179–202.

Sogno, Cristiana, "Persius, Juvenal, and the Transformation of Satire in Late Antiquity", in Susannah Morton Braund and Josiah Osgood (eds.), *A Companion to Persius and Juvenal* (Malden, MA: Wiley-Blackwell, 2012), 363–385.

Weingarten, Susan, *The Saint's Saints: Hagiography and Geography in Jerome* (Leiden: Brill, 2005).

Wiesen, David, *St. Jerome as a Satirist: A Study in Christian Latin Thought and Letters* (Ithaca, NY: Cornell University Press, 1964).

Wiśniewski, Robert, "*Bestiae Christum loquuntur* ou des habitants du désert et de la ville dans la *Vita Pauli* de saint Jérôme", *Augustinianum* 40 (2000), 105–144.

White, Carolinne, *Early Christian Lives* (London: Penguin, 1998).

White, Hayden, "The Forms of Wildness: Archaeology of an Idea", in Edward Dudley and Maximilian Novak (eds.), *The Wild Man Within: An Image in Western Thought from the Renaissance to Romanticism* (Pittsburgh: University of Pittsburgh Press, 1972), 3–38.

Wolpers, Theodor, *Die englische Heiligenlegende des Mittelalters* (Tübingen: Niemeyer, 1964).

CHAPTER 5

A *Life* Beyond Measure: Sulpicius, Martin, and the Possibilities of Perpetual Discourse

Zachary Yuzwa

Sulpicius Severus' *Life of Martin* comes to a sudden conclusion. The author, having recounted his journey to meet Martin and learn the facts of his life, declares: 'Now my book demands its end.'[1] The *Life* ends without the saint's death. It is an unexpected turn in the narrative, an ending that comes just as the author meets his subject for the first time. And the text itself encourages the sense of surprise. Sulpicius is praising Martin's virtues, his wisdom, when he abruptly calls his narrative to a close. It is a precipitous conclusion to a narrative that had been piling miracle upon miracle, with little sign of ceasing. But this decision to postpone the saint's death will allow Sulpicius the opportunity to rewrite Martin, to revalue and reinscribe the meaning of his *Life*. Sulpicius writes a saint whose life exceeds the boundaries of his hagiography. Because there is yet no death to end Martin's virtuous *Life*, the saint's story remains unfinished. Sulpicius conceives the need for further supplement. He will write first an end to Martin's life in a series of letters and then a literary afterlife for the saint in a dialogue called the *Gallus*.

In this article, I attend especially to Sulpicius' attempts to negotiate the narrative problem of closure in the Martinian corpus. A reader of Sulpicius' writings on Martin will realise that—even in this ostensibly paradigmatic hagiographical corpus—the author resists the traditional bounds of biographical

1 Sulpicius Severus, *Vita Martini*, 26.1, *Sed iam liber finem postulat*. The standard modern edition is Jacques Fontaine (ed.), *Sulpice Sévère, Vie de saint Martin*, 3 vols. (Paris: Les Éditions du Cerf, 1967–1969), hereafter *Mart.* Fontaine's edition of the *Life* also includes Sulpicius' three letters on the death of Martin, hereafter *Epist.* 1, *Epist.* 2, and *Epist.* 3. Fontaine has also produced the standard edition of Sulpicius' final Martinian text, the *Gallus*: Jacques Fontaine, (ed.), *Gallus: Dialogues sur les 'vertus' de saint Martin* (Paris: Les Éditions du Cerf, 2006), hereafter *Dial.* Recently published is Philip Burton (ed.), *Sulpicius Severus' Vita Martini* (Oxford: Oxford University Press, 2017). The edition of the text of the *Life* is substantially similar to that of Fontaine, but included with it are a lucid translation and an immensely useful commentary. A recent English translation of Sulpicius' entire corpus can be found in Richard Goodrich, *Sulpicius Severus: The Complete Works* (New York: Newman Press, 2015). All translations herein are my own unless otherwise noted.

 | DOI:10.1163/9789004421332_007

literature. The *Life* ends without its expected ending, Martin's death delayed indefinitely. The letters that follow depict multiple deaths—a near death, potential and exemplary deaths, even a dreamed death—all while continuing to postpone the real thing. The inevitability of Martin's death in the narrative of his life is keenly felt by the reader of these letters, but the saint's natural end is diverted and delayed until the last possible moment. Then, having finally laid Martin to rest, Sulpicius revives the saint in a dialogue whose hagiographical narrative lacks a natural beginning and end. The *Gallus* reanimates Martin after his death and writes the holy man into a narrative whose own parameters are potentially boundless.

I argue that this play at closure, its frustration and eventual fulfillment, is for Sulpicius a means of defying the parameters of biographical narrative.[2] In fact, the multi-volume and multi-genre nature of the corpus represents the essential content of Sulpicius' innovation on earlier *Lives* and other ancient texts that participate in what Uytfanghe has termed 'discours hagiographique'.[3] The *Life of Martin* has long been read as an archetype of late ancient saints' lives, but what makes Sulpicius' depiction of Martin so compelling is this trajectory that carries the reader through a *Life*, a series of letters, and a literary dialogue. Sulpicius, standing near the beginning of the hagiographical tradition in the Latin west, writes the life of a saint beyond the *Life* itself.[4] And of course, it is the explicit recognition of such innovation that most obviously justifies prolonged scholarly attention to an already well-studied corpus.

The *Gallus*, in particular, offers a revision of the earlier *Life*, taking up stories and themes that echo Sulpicius' original but inserting them into a narrative framework that allows for perpetual discourse. Like the *Letters*, the *Gallus* addresses itself to the problem of closure, but rather than postponing, delaying, and prolonging, this dialogue imagines a literary performance altogether

2 The problems of closure have been given some attention by scholars of ancient literature. Cf. Deborah H. Roberts, Francis M. Dunn, and Robert Fowler (eds.), *Classical Closure: Reading the End in Greek Literature* (Princeton, NJ: Princeton University Press, 1997); Don Fowler, *Roman Constructions: Readings in Postmodern Latin* (Oxford: Oxford University Press, 2000); Tim Whitmarsh, *Narrative and Identity in the Ancient Greek Novel: Returning Romance* (Cambridge: Cambridge University Press, 2011). Don Fowler, "Second Thoughts on Closure", *Classical Closure* (Princeton, NJ: Princeton University Press, 1997), 3–22 explores the tension between narrative closure and 'aperture' in classical literature, a question whose contours were first outlined in Kermode's discussion of *peripeteia* ('the falsification of one's expectation of the end'); Frank Kermode, *The Sense of an Ending* (Oxford: Oxford University Press, 1967), 18.

3 Marc Van Uytfanghe, "L'hagiographie: un 'genre' Chrétien ou antique tardif?", *AB* 111 (1993), 135–188. Uytfanghe's description usefully allows for the possibility of a discourse held in common without the elision of generic difference.

4 Cf. Williams in this volume on the formal variety of early hagiographical literature.

unbounded by an ending. The dialogue launches Martin's story *in medias res* and advances thematically rather than chronologically. The narrative is governed not by a temporal movement towards Martin's death: the experienced reader knows that this death has always already come. Rather, the paratactic structure of the work, replete with episode and digression, seems to compel the reader to admit the possibility of a life without end.

Walter Benjamin writes of the authority that death confers on the act of storytelling: '… not only a man's knowledge or wisdom, but above all his life—and this is the stuff that stories are made of—first assumes transmissible form at the moment of his death. This authority is at the very source of the story … Death is the sanction of everything that the storyteller can tell. He has borrowed his authority from death.'[5] Death is what gives a life its closure. This is the case in the most mundane sense of the term, but it is also holds more broadly: our ability to understand and interpret a life depends on the nature of that life's end. Death is the end that determines the means. In narrative terms, death resolves the tensions of plot; it is the 'modification of structure that makes *stasis*'.[6] D.A. Miller puts it this way: 'Everything in a narrative exists in view of the hidden necessity determined by its final configuration of event and meaning.'[7] In a life, and likewise in the story of a life, death is that necessity.

We should of course be wary of the assumption that hagiographical literature is biography in some strict sense, but we can nevertheless recognise the biographical functions that comprise a central element of the texts in this corpus. Don DeLillo observes: 'All plots tend to move deathward.'[8] We might therefore say that the death of the central character is one common figure through which a reader perceives closure in a text, particularly in a text like the *Life of Martin*. But what is it that we talk about when we talk about closure? Following Hamon, I understand closure as an effect of reading as much as it is the product of writing.[9] It is a sense that develops in the reader through a 'retrospective patterning', an activity of constituting and reconstituting meaning as more narrative information is presented.[10] It is primarily a question of function, justifying to the reader the cessation of narrative and completing the meaning

5 Walter Benjamin, "The Storyteller", in *Illuminations*. Translated by Harry Zohn (New York: Schocken, 1968), 94.
6 Barbara H. Smith, *Poetic Closure* (Chicago: University of Chicago Press, 1968), 34.
7 D.A. Miller, *Narrative and Its Discontents: Problems of Closure in the Traditional Novel* (Princeton, NJ: Princeton University Press, 1981), xiii.
8 Don DeLillo, *White Noise* (New York: Viking, 1985), 26.
9 Philippe Hamon, "Clausules", *Poetique* 6 (1975), 495–526.
10 Smith, *Poetic Closure*, 12–13.

of what has gone before.[11] 'Closure allows the reader to be satisfied by the failure of continuation, or put another way, it creates in the reader the expectation of nothing.'[12]

Sulpicius shows himself to be keenly aware of his readers' expectations. In his third letter, he imagines a reader whose expectations for the *Life* were explicitly frustrated by the omission of Martin's death.[13] His mother-in-law Bassula, the addressee of his third letter, has complained to Sulpicius that 'he ought to have narrated the blessed passing of that man'.[14] Though the *Life* may have ended, Sulpicius' task can end only when he has brought Martin's life to its close. Of course, there is precedent for a *Life* whose sense of closure is produced by something other than the death of the central character: Jerome's *Life of Malchus* ends with the monk's death made implicit but never explicitly narrated.[15] Nepos' *Life of Atticus* seems to have been written before the subject's death (then later edited).[16] The opposite extreme might be those *Lives* of Plutarch that extend well beyond the unavoidable death of the subject; a prominent example is the *Life of Caesar*, whose narrative tensions are not resolved until Brutus' story is finished as well.[17] Nevertheless, the contemporary texts that most directly inform Sulpicius' *Life of Martin*—early hagiographical literature like the *Vita Antonii* and Jerome's *Vita Hilarionis*—regularly foreground scenes of death and burial as a means of obtaining closure in the narrative,[18] and the saint's death scene will become a standard trope in late ancient hagiographies.[19] Fontaine acknowledges as much when he comments on Sulpicius' decision not to narrate Martin's death in the *Life*: 'Que

11 Miller, *Narrative and Its Discontents*, xi.

12 Smith, *Poetic Closure*, 34.

13 *Epist.* 3.3–4.

14 *Epist.* 3.4 *Namque accepi litteras tuas, quibus scribis in eadem, qua de obitu sancti Martini fecerim mentionem, ipsum beatum viri transitum exponere debuisse.*

15 Jerome, *V. Malchi* 11, *haec mihi senex Malchus adulescentulo rettulit; haec ego vobis narravi senex*. The narrator situates his telling long after Malchus' death, but the death itself is left unwritten. Cf. also Jerome's *Epist.* 24 on the life of Asella, Theodoret's *Life of Symeon*, or the many early martyrologies that end with the martyr being led away for execution but elide the execution proper, e.g. Justin Martyr's account of the martyrdom of Ptolemaeus and Lucius in *Apol.* 2.2 or Eusebius on Marinus *Hist. eccl.*, 7.15.

16 Cf. Timothy D. Barnes, *Early Christian Hagiography and Roman History* (Tübingen: Mohr Siebeck, 2010), 210.

17 Christopher B.R. Pelling, "Is Death the End? Closure in Plutarch's *Lives*", in Roberts, Dunn, and Fowler (eds.), *Classical Closure*, 228–250.

18 Athanasius, *V. Anton.* 92; Jerome, *V. Hilarion.* 45.

19 Cf. Pierre Boglioni, "La scène de la mort dans les premières hagiographies latines", in Claude Sutto (ed.), *Le sentiment de la mort au moyen age* (Montréal: L'Aurore, 1978), 183–210.

l'on se réfère aux traditions païennes ou chrétiennes de la biographie antique, la lacune était grave.'[20] Of course, Sulpicius himself signals his awareness of readerly expectations when he writes Bassula's complaint into his account of Martin's death. In writing a reader like Bassula—a reader who demands Martin's death as the only means of obtaining closure in Martin's *Life*—Sulpicius acknowledges that this was a *Life* interrupted rather than brought to its natural end.

1 The Conclusion to the *Life of Martin*

We must therefore ask why Sulpicius' *Life of Martin* produces in this imagined reader the sense that closure was not obtained in that text. If a satisfying sense of closure comes from an end that is in some ways predicted (if not entirely predictable) from the text,[21] then we should be able to adduce cues that encourage the imagined readers of Sulpicius' *Life* to form certain expectations of the narrative. Why does Bassula expect Martin's death? After a prefatory letter and extended prologue, the *Life* describes where the saint was born and raised, the status and religion of his parents, his induction into the Christian faith, and his early desire for a life of ascetic withdrawal.[22] The parallels with the introduction to the *Life of Antony* are well-documented, but this subject matter is common to other prominent early hagiographical texts.[23] In this biographical narrative, the major chronological milestones are twofold: the saint's earliest vision of Christ and then his election as bishop.[24] The former is occasioned by that famous act of saintly humility, Martin's cutting of his cloak to clothe a beggar outside the gates at Amiens.[25] The vision is presented as a formative experience for the holy man—his later baptism is a footnote by comparison[26]—and sets in motion

20 Fontaine, *Vie de saint Martin*, 1263.

21 See Hamon, "Clausules", 513.

22 *Mart.* 2. 1–4.

23 Cf. Burton, *Vita Martini*, 146–147, which outlines the characteristics that the introduction to the *Life* shares 'more or less in common with various others'. The list includes 'place of birth', 'parents' social status', 'parents' religion', 'early spiritual experiences', 'gradual process of separation from worldly affairs', and 'decisive step into anchoretic life'. Burton adduces parallels with the *Vita Antonii*, Jerome's *Vita Hilarionis*, and the Greek *Vita Pachomii*, among others.

24 Cf. Clare Stancliffe, *St. Martin and His Hagiographer: History and Miracle in Sulpicius Severus* (Oxford: Clarendon Press, 1983), 86–107.

25 The vision is recounted at *Mart.* 3.3–4. The scene outside the gates occurs just before, *Mart.* 3.1–2.

26 A single clause: *cum esset annorum duodeviginti ad baptismum convolavit* (*Mart.* 3.5).

Sulpicius' account of the saint's miraculous deeds and holy virtues. From this point in the text, consistent temporal signposts suggest to the reader the narrative's forward movement through time. Sulpicius signals a shift to each new section of his *Life* with temporal markers: 'next', 'shortly thereafter', 'at the same time'.[27]

The standard template for a *Life* points us towards death as a logical end, but even as Sulpicius' narrative marches us forward in time, the reader recognises in Martin a special power over death itself. In fact, there is a marked tension between the narrative patterns that condition the reader to expect the saint's eventual death and the conspicuous ability of the saint to postpone death in this world. A miraculous surrender saves him from a battle in which he planned to court an almost certain death.[28] Later faced with axe-wielding brigands, Martin is spared only when one of the thieves restrains the other mid-blow.[29] Martin eventually retreats to an ascetic life on an island where his diet includes a nearly fatal ration of hellebore; he prays for and obtains his recovery.[30] He resurrects from the dead a catechumen struck by a sudden fever.[31] Then he resurrects a slave who had hanged himself.[32] Every chapter of the *Life* between Martin's vision and his election as bishop shows him mastering death in some way. Although there is no indication that Martin's ability to control the limits of natural life is predictive of Sulpicius' attempts to extend the parameters of his literary programme, nevertheless the persistent deferral of death in this *Life* serves to produce an ongoing discursive pattern that in retrospect seems analogous to the rhetorical problems posed by the radical abundance of the saint's miraculous virtue.

In the section that follows Martin's election as bishop, Sulpicius explains: 'it is beyond my abilities to describe his excellence'.[33] This is no mere trope, at

27 The narrative proper begins at *Mart.* 2.1, *igitur Martinus ... oriundus fuit*. Regular temporal markers—some absolute, some relative—situate the narrative throughout the first section of the *Life* up to Martin's election as bishop: *Mart.* 2.6, *triennium fere ante baptismum*; *Mart.* 3.1, *quodam itaque tempore*; *Mart.* 3.3, *nocte igitur consecuta*; *Mart.* 4.1, *interea inruentibus intra Gallias barbaris*; *Mart.* 5.1, *exinde relicta militia*; *Mart.* 5.3, *nec multo post*; *Mart.* 6.1, *igitur Martinus inde*; *Mart.* 6.4, *dehinc cum haeresis Arriana per totum orbem et maxime intra Illyricum pullulasset*; *Mart.* 7.1, *cum iam Hilarius praeterisset*; *Mart.* 8.1, *nec multo post*; *Mart.* 9.1, *sub idem fere tempus*. Each chapter begins with some indication of the temporal framework, consistently indicating to the reader a logical movement through time.

28 *Mart.* 4.

29 *Mart.* 5.

30 *Mart.* 6

31 *Mart.* 7.

32 *Mart.* 8.

33 *Mart* 10.1, *Iam vero, sumpto episcopatu qualem se quantumque praestiterit, non est nostrae facultatis evolvere.*

least not in this *Life*. The ineffable quality of Martin's virtue becomes a theme for Sulpicius in this corpus, and what follows in the *Life* seems an attempt to express in narrative terms the saint's utter inexpressibility.[34] After this second milestone in the chronology of Martin's life, the motivating impulse of the narrative seems no longer to be the forward movement of time. Instead, the miracles are grouped by kind: Martin's dealings with pagans, his healing miracles, his victories over the devil. Miracle collections do have a propensity to become unmoored from time,[35] and the temporal signposts that characterised the first half of the *Life* become less marked and eventually fall away altogether. The natural end to the *Life* recedes from view. What could possibly end the life of a holy man with such tangible power over death?

That Martin's death is not narrated in the *Life* is regularly explained by an appeal to historical context.[36] Quite simply: Martin was alive when Sulpicius wrote and published the work.[37] This fact demands attention, but we should

34 Cf. John 21:25, *sunt autem et alia multa quae fecit Iesus quae si scribantur per singula nec ipsum arbitror mundum capere eos qui scribendi sunt libros amen.*

35 Jerome's *Life of Hilarion* displays a similar tendency, with the saint's miracles in Palestine showing no obvious temporal sequence, their abundance increasing with Hilarion's fame. Cf. Stancliffe, *St. Martin and His Hagiographer*, 95; Goodrich, *Sulpicius Severus*, 251.

36 Cf. Stancliffe, *St. Martin and His Hagiographer*, 72; Fontaine *Vie de saint Martin*, 18.

37 The traditional dating assigns Martin's death to November AD 397. The primary witness comes from Gregory of Tours (*Virt. Mart.* 1.3, *Hist.* 1.48), who is supposed to have access to episcopal records at Tours; cf. Stancliffe, *St. Martin and His Hagiographer*, 115. This dating is supported by internal (though largely circumstantial) evidence from Sulpicius' writings; e.g., Martin's death is said to follow closely on that of Clarus, who was already dead when the *Life* was written. *Mart.* 23.1, *Clarus quidam adulescens nobilissimus, mox presbyter, nunc felici beatus excessu, cum, relictis omnibus, se ad Martinum contulisset, brevi tempore ad summum fidei virtutumque omnium culment enituit.* Cf. Stancliffe, *St. Martin and His Hagiographer*, 72. Barnes, however, has questioned the traditional dating of Martin's death, suggesting he might have died as late as November AD 401. See Timothy D. Barnes, "The *Historia Augusta* and Christian Biography", in François Paschoud (ed.), *Historiae Augustae Colloquium Genevense* (Bari: Edipuglia, 1999), 37. There are many inconsistencies that make this claim defensible, but the preponderance of evidence for AD 397 makes it unlikely. Burton, in his recent edition of the *Life*, offers a comprehensive review of the evidence for the chronology of Martin's life. See Burton, *Vita Martini*, 9–22. There is much that is unclear and some evidence that is downright contradictory, but Burton regards the saint's death in AD 397 as 'the single most secure date in the chronology of the life of Martin'; see Burton, *Vita Martini*, 12.

The completion of the *Life* should be dated between late AD 396 and spring AD 397, especially on the basis of evidence from Paulinus' epistolary corpus. Paulinus writes to Sulpicius that he has received a copy of the *Life*. The dating of this letter (*Epist.* 11) to AD 397 was first proposed by Paul Reinelt, *Studien über die Briefe des hl. Paulinus von Nola* (Breslau: Druck von R. Nischkowsky, 1903), 11, and taken up by Pierre Fabre, *Essai sur la*

be careful how we frame Sulpicius' decision. The suggestion that 'this situation creates a serious problem for the hagiographer'[38] ignores the fact that the hagiographer has expressly chosen to present the *Life* on these terms. Scholars have proposed a number of external factors that could motivate such an ostensibly problematic decision.[39] In particular, the ecclesiastical tensions still simmering among the Gallic clergy in the long aftermath of the Priscillian controversy are for Sulpicius an ongoing concern.[40] The author is keen to defend the ascetic programme of Martin against accusations that would make the bishop sympathetic to Priscillianism. And of course this is all part of a larger debate, especially prevalent in Gaul, about the emerging prominence of ascetic practice in the Christian church.[41] A published *Life* is therefore an opportunity for Sulpicius to address the *obtrectatores* that continue to oppose Martin and the community he founded. But instead of asking how Sulpicius copes with the problem of writing a *Life* that cannot include the death of its subject,[42] we might rather ask what opportunities Sulpicius creates by choosing to publish his text in this form. How does Sulpicius write an end to this *Life* and what does he accomplish by supplanting so natural a marker of literary closure?

What finally signals the close of the narrative is the appearance of its author as a character within the text. This is a third milestone in the *Life*: the moment when Sulpicius meets Martin for the first time. Sulpicius burns with a desire to meet Martin and makes a pilgrimage to see him.[43] Sulpicius seeks out Martin to support the biographical project he has undertaken, and the narrator enters

Chronologie de l'oeuvre de Saint Paulin de Nole (Paris: Belles Lettres, 1948), 23–27. Recent scholarship has supported this conclusion; cf. Dennis Trout, *Paulinus of Nola: Life, Letters, Poems* (Berkeley: University of California Press, 1999), 127 and Sigrid Mratschek, *Der Briefwechsel des Paulinus von Nola* (Göttingen: Vandenhoeck and Ruprecht, 2002), 457–458. Burton is more circumspect: 'Whether Martin was still alive when [the *Life*] was published is unclear,' Burton, *Vita Martini*, 4. It is possible that the *Life* was a 'work in progress' as Burton claims, but the language of Paulinus' *Epist.* 11 makes clear that Sulpicius has sent his friend a copy of the *Life*. This would seem to constitute publication in our context.

38 Christian Tornau, "Intertextuality in Early Latin Hagiography: Sulpicius Severus and the *Vita Antonii*", *Studia Patristica* 35 (2001), 158–166, at 162.

39 Stancliffe, *St. Martin and His Hagiographer*, 73; Dieter von der Nahmer, *Die Lateinische Heiligenvita* (Darmstadt: WBG, 1994), 69.

40 Stancliffe, *St. Martin and His Hagiographer*, 278–296 describes the ecclesiastical context at length.

41 Cf. David Hunter, "Vigilantius of Calagurris and Victricius of Rouens: Ascetics, Relics, and Clerics in Late Roman Gaul", *JECS* 7 (1999), 401–430.

42 Tornau, "Intertextuality in Early Latin Hagiography", 162.

43 *Mart.* 25.1, *Nam cum olim, audita fide eius, vita atque virtute, desiderio illius aestuaremus, gratam nobis ad eum videndum peregrinationem suscepimus.*

the frame of the text as a character.[44] Fontaine in his commentary marks off the final three chapters of the *Life* (*Mart.* 25–27) as a kind of epilogue to the text.[45] Tornau, however, notes the clear narratological differences that mark *Mart.* 25 as distinct from the sections that follow it.[46] Sulpicius writes the story of Martin's life up to that point at which he himself enters it. We are still within the narrative proper as Sulpicius reports the content of their conversation. But in the next section the text turns from narrating this meeting between saint and hagiographer, and Sulpicius as narrator draws attention to the inadequacy of the narrative itself.[47] 'How insignificant is this panegyric compared to the virtues of Martin!'[48] In no way can this text equal that saint. He claims that no one could possibly describe Martin's inner life and his daily conduct or that mind of his ever intent on heaven.[49] Homer could not do Martin justice, Sulpicius claims: 'Truly I confess that not even Homer himself, were he to ascend from the underworld, could explain it; so great were all things in Martin, that they could not possibly be grasped in words.'[50]

Sulpicius employs this inexpressibility topos at key junctures in the narrative. His *Life* cannot suitably contain the life of Martin; only a text without limits could describe a saint who transcends human nature.[51] We have already seen the similar claim that immediately follows Martin's election as bishop.[52] Here, the comparison to Homer recalls the first chapter of the *Life*, where Sulpicius opposes the value of a text that invokes imitation of Hector to one that invokes imitation of Martin.[53] The author adduces not just the inadequacy of his lan-

---

44 *Mart.* 25.1–2.

45 Fontaine, *Vie de saint Martin*, 1043.

46 Tornau, "Intertextuality in Early Latin Hagiography", 159.

47 We might say, following the formulations of Genette, that the text moves from the intradiegetic to the extradiegetic level of narrative discourse. See Gérard Genette, *Narrative Discourse: An Essay in Method*. Translated by Jane E. Lewin, Foreword by Jonathan Culler (Ithaca, NY: Cornell University Press, 1983). Original publication: "Discours du récit", in *Figures III* (Paris: Seuil, 1972).

48 *Mart.* 25.8, *Quamquam in Martini virtutibus quantula est ista laudatio!*

49 *Mart.* 26.2: *interiorem vitam illius et conversationem cotidianam et animum caelo semper intentum nulla umquam, vere profiteor, nulla explicabit oratio.*

50 *Mart.* 26.3, *Vere, fatebor, non si ipse, ut aiunt, ab inferis Homerus emergeret, posset exponere; adeo omnia maiora in Martino sunt, quam ut verbis concipi queant.* Cf. Jerome's similar claim at the beginning of his *Vita Hilarionis*: *mihi tanti ac talis viri conversatio vitaque dicenda est, ut Homerus quoque si adesset, vel invideret materiae, vel succumberet* (*Hilar.* 1).

51 *Mart.* 2.7, *ultra humanum modum*; *Mart.* 27.1, *extra naturam hominis*; *Dial.* 2.4.2, *humanam substantiam supergressus.*

52 *Mart.* 10.1. See above, n. 33.

53 *Mart.* 1.3–6.

guage but the absolute impossibility of recounting Martin's life sufficiently. 'In no way,' he writes, 'could I get at all of his deeds.'[54] For Martin in his humility tried to hide his virtues.[55] Moreover, Sulpicius has omitted a great number of his deeds, assuming it enough to record only his most impressive powers.[56] And finally the reader, Sulpicius fears, might suffer *fastidium* were he to tell every last one of Martin's deeds.[57] In the end, however, it is not the reader, but rather Sulpicius himself who grows weary, who succumbs to the burdens imposed by the virtues of Martin. The author in his conclusion takes up this conceit from the first chapter of the *Life* and revises it, ostensibly as a means of bringing closure to his work. Sulpicius' recognition of his work's radical and inevitable insufficiency compels an interruption in the narrative.

Sulpicius therefore calls Martin's *Life* to a close: 'Now my book demands its end. Our discourse must be closed.' Martin's life has not ended, but the *Life* must. Tornau notes the intense break signalled by this pleonastic formulation and suggests an echo of the conclusion to the *Life of Anthony*.[58] In recalling the archetypal saint's *Life*, Sulpicius writes an ending that potentially conforms to the expectations of readers familiar with the conventions of the still nascent genre of hagiographical life-writing. Indeed, we should not presume that—in the absence of Martin's death—Sulpicius altogether avoids the use of closural techniques here at the end of the *Life*. The metaleptic intervention of the narrator into the narrative space of the text is itself one means of signalling an end: the author, by writing himself into the work, alerts the reader to its textual nature and draws attention to the extent of its limits. What is more, Sulpicius finds a body to substitute for that of the saint: the *Life* must end 'not because all those things that should be said of Martin have been exhausted, but because I, like inexpert poets grown negligent at the end of their work, succumb, crushed by the burden of my subject matter'.[59] The hagiographer has been conquered by this saint 'who cannot be conquered by death'.[60]

The abrupt conclusion is likewise a long-established topos (Fontaine notes the Ciceronian echoes).[61] But when so employed, such a closural technique can

54 *Mart.* 1.7, *nequaquam ad omnia illius potuerim pervenire.*

55 *Mart.* 1.7.

56 *Mart.* 1.8, *si tantum excellentia notaretur.*

57 *Mart.* 1.8.

58 Tornau, "Intertextuality in Early Latin Hagiography", 162–163.

59 *Mart.* 26.1, *sed iam finem liber postulat, sermo claudendus est, non quod omnia, quae de Martino fuerint dicenda, defecerint, sed quia nos, ut inertes poetae extremo in opere neclegentes, victi materiae mole succumbimus.*

60 *Epist.* 3.14, *nec morte vincendum.*

61 Fontaine, *Vie de saint Martin*, 1079–1080. Cf. also Ernst R. Curtius, *European Literature in*

be expected to end a work. Sulpicius, upon declaring this end, instead keeps writing. Even before Sulpicius writes a letter or dialogue as a supplement to the *Life*, that text itself offers an internal supplement. The narrative of Martin's life has ended, but the *Life* appends a *vita* of a new sort, one that describes not the *facta et virtutes* but the *vita interior* of Martin, what Fontaine calls 'un portrait spirituel'.[62] And no matter how apparently inexpressible, Sulpicius enumerates Martin's ascetic feats: his abstinence from food and from sleep; his ceaseless prayer; his patience and his generosity, even to those who would revile him.[63] Sulpicius describes Martin's indescribable inner life, if briefly, and thereby adds the first of many supplements to a hagiographical corpus that will only grow.

Even with such a (seemingly final) description in the books, Sulpicius continues. The text at last writes its end by offering a sort of readers' guide as its conclusion, an ostensibly foolproof hermeneutical strategy for any who would read of Martin. Sulpicius first condemns those who 'hated in [Martin] what they did not see in themselves'.[64] On the other hand, those who would not just read but would actually believe Sulpicius' work, they will have a reward from God.[65] The phrase used here repeats exactly the wording Sulpicius had used to describe the reward he expects for writing this *Life*.[66] It is a work written as absolute truth.[67] Indeed, Sulpicius is unflinching about the veracity of his work, no matter how improbable, a veracity which becomes for him all the more essential because of that very improbability.[68]

Sulpicius, long after ending the narrative of Martin's life, continued to supplement his work. The first supplement serves as a sort of literary doubling, recounting not Martin's *Life*—that is to say, his deeds—but his inner life, and beginning with the same inexpressibility topoi he used at the very outset of the *Life* proper. The second supplementary section is yet one step further removed from narrative, inasmuch as it comments directly on the work just finished. It becomes a guide for how to read the text, a text that of course has already been

the Latin Middle Ages. Translated by W.R. Trask (Princeton, NJ: Princeton University Press, 1953), 83–84.

62 Fontaine, *Vie de saint Martin*, 95.

63 *Mart.* 26.4–27.2.

64 *Mart.* 27.3, *qui in illo oderant quod in se non videbant.*

65 *Mart.* 27.7, *paratumque, ut spero, habebit a Deo praemium, non quicumque legerit, sed quicumque crediderit.*

66 Cf. *Mart.* 1.6, *sed aeternum a Deo praemium exspectemus.* See below, 163.

67 *Mart.* 1.9, 27.7.

68 Cf. Virginia Burrus, *The Sex Lives of Saints* (Philadelphia: University of Pennsylvania Press, 2004), 92–93. On the narrative function of fictionality in hagiography, cf. Van Pelt in this volume.

read. These supplements serve as the first indication of a life still in the process of being written, still in the process of being read. Sulpicius seems to tell himself and the reader: there is much left to write and to read. This is how—that is, both truthfully and credibly—we should go about it. The need for supplement allows Sulpicius to define readerly expectations, allows him to manage the experience of his readers and set the terms on which they encounter the text. By writing a text that not only admits of but truly demands a sequel, Sulpicius constructs a text that imagines the possibility of perpetual discourse on Martin, discourse that might offer salvation to those who read and who write the life of this holy man into their own.

2 Life and Death in Sulpicius' *Letters*

The subsequent movement from *Life* to letters is marked by a further devolution of narrative structure. The *Life* begins straightforwardly and continues just so, one deed of Martin following the next according to a logical order. When, however, that order is subverted and the paratactic structure of the narrative is abandoned, Sulpicius delays the *Life*'s expected end beyond the bounds of the work. The choice to write Martin's death outside the *Life* becomes a literary enactment of Martin's saintly abundance. The letters that follow each take up the subject of Martin's inevitable death, but the death itself proves elusive. There are three genuine letters extant in Sulpicius' corpus.[69] All three address the possibility of Martin's death in some way. Over the course of these letters, we instead read a near death, a vision of Martin's ascent to heaven, reports of his death, accounts of exemplary deaths that the saint could have suffered (but did not), Martin's own prediction of his approaching end, even a debate over the merits of a death that seems like it may never come. The very existence of these letters advertises the radical abundance of Martin's life and deeds, his

69 Seven letters spuriously attributed to Sulpicius are also extant. Of the three genuine letters, the traditional order is attested in our earliest extant manuscript; cf. Fontaine, *Vie de saint Martin*, 216. Stancliffe, *St. Martin and His Hagiographer*, 79–80 argues that the traditional arrangement reflects the order of composition. Barnes argues for a different order of composition (*Epist.* 2 and *Epist.* 3 immediately following Martin's death, then *Epist.* 1 sometime thereafter); see Barnes, *Early Christian Hagiography*, 216. His assertion is defensible but nevertheless takes for granted that Sulpicius 'placed' the first letter in that position and almost certainly intended them to be collected and read in the sequence reproduced in modern editions. For more on this, see Zachary Yuzwa, "Reading Genre in Sulpicius Severus' Letters", *Journal of Late Antiquity* 7.2 (2014), 329–350, at 333.

mastery over death, his ability to overfill the limits of a traditional biography; their content implicitly reinforces that fact.[70]

The first letter takes up the claim voiced at the end of the *Life*: certain *obtrectatores* do not believe that Martin could possess the powers described by Sulpicius.[71] One such critic, the author hears, has pointed out that the saint was once nearly burned alive by fire. How could he save others from death, when he could scarcely save himself?[72] Sulpicius presents this as a criticism not only of Martin but also of the *Life* as he wrote it: the author presumably omitted this story because it reflects poorly on his subject.[73] Sulpicius repeats a familiar refrain in response. Martin's 'deeds are not so few that they could be altogether contained [in that work]'.[74] Sulpicius' omission is not evidence against Martin. Rather, Martin is so great that the sum of his deeds exceeds the capacity of the *Life*. But the author resolves to narrate this story here, so no critic can further impugn the saint.

The body of the letter recounts a dramatic near-death experience. It is winter. A fire has been lit and a bed of straw has been prepared for the saint's comfort. Accustomed to sleeping on the bare ground, Martin finds the bed too great a luxury to bear. He discards the straw and falls into sleep. The bedding catches fire and Martin awakes to find himself surrounded by deadly flames. His first instinct is to flee, but he finds the door bolted. His robe catches fire. Facing certain death, the saint recovers himself and resorts at last to prayer. The fire is driven back by God and Martin sits surrounded by a circle of now harmless flames.[75] This first supplement to the *Life* again draws our attention to Martin's mastery over death. It dramatises the saint's ability to defer death and displays conspicuously the author's ability to write a saint beyond the bounds of biography. Sulpicius makes this clear in the text: 'No one should wonder that I omitted this from that work I wrote about his life: I admitted in that very same book that it did not include all of his deeds, because if I wanted to set forth everything, I would have produced a boundless volume (*inmensum volumen*) for my readers.'[76] The saint's power over death in the text is again linked to the radical

70 For more on the function of genre and the role of the reader in these letters, see Yuzwa, "Reading Genre", 337–346.

71 *Mart.* 27.3–4. See above n. 64.

72 *Epist.* 1.2.

73 *Epist.* 1.8.

74 *Epist.* 1.8, *neque enim sunt tam parua quae gessit ut omnia potuerint comprehendi.*

75 *Epist.* 1.10–14.

76 *Epist.* 1.8, *Ceterum omissum hoc a me libello illo, quem de vita illius scripsimus, nemo miretur, cum ibidem sim professus me non omnia illius facta conplexum, quia, si persequi universa voluissem, inmensum volumen legentibus edidissem.*

inability of hagiographical narrative to comprehend and contain the saint himself: any narrative of Martin's deeds that attempts to be comprehensive would need to be *inmensus*, literally beyond measure.

In the second letter, Sulpicius acknowledges Martin's death, but the details of that death are obscured, the saint's passing mediated by the haze of a dream or the third-hand report of a household servant. Martin in this letter is again 'indescribable'.[77] Sulpicius recounts a dream vision in which Martin appears aflame, eyes shining, hair purple, but 'impossible to look at'.[78] Sulpicius is nevertheless able to recognise the saint.[79] He sees Martin hold up and smile upon the *Life* Sulpicius had written, before the saint ascends to heaven. The author is then woken from the fog of sleep by a household servant bearing news of Martin's death. But even that report comes at far remove from the source: two monks have come from Tours; they pass a message to a household servant at Primuliacum; that servant relays the message to Sulpicius. All this is recounted in a letter where Sulpicius himself is giving the news to his correspondent, the deacon Aurelius (and likewise to readers of the Martinian corpus). Then, the narrative shifts again. This seems a natural place to narrate the saint's passing, but Sulpicius postpones Martin's death further: in its place he recites the various martyrdoms Martin could have suffered but did not.[80] Here in this letter, Martin's death is marked by a series of absences: a vision discerned in the altered reality of a dream, a succession of reports spoken and written, a catalogue of deaths suffered by others. These signs all point to the death, without showing the death itself. The natural end to Martin's life is acknowledged, but again deferred to a subsequent text. The letter ends, Sulpicius writes, because his page is full.[81]

In the third letter, we do finally read an end to Martin's life. Sulpicius constructs an epistolary setting in which his reader and correspondent, frustrated by the apparent lack of closure in the narrative thus far, demands a proper end. We have already seen that this imagined reader clearly defines her expectations of Sulpicius as author of Martin's *Life*: he must narrate the saint's passing.[82] Sulpicius acquiesces, but here in the third and final letter, even this end is drawn out at length: Martin had long known the time of his eventual death,[83]

77 *Epist.* 2.14, *ineffabilem virum.*

78 *Epist.* 2.3, *non possit aspici.*

79 *Epist.* 2.3.

80 *Epist.* 2.9–13.

81 *Epist.* 2.18, *Simul iam pagina inpleta non recipit.* This closural technique is common enough in ancient letters. Cf. Cic. *Att.* 13.34, *complere paginam volui.*

82 *Epist.* 3.4. See above nn. 13–14.

83 *Epist.* 3.6, *Martinus igitur obitum suum longe ante praescivit.*

but Sulpicius' account of it does not come readily. Before he writes Martin's death, he recounts the saint's journey to a not-so-nearby church; he reports a miracle performed on the road; he describes the 'considerable length of time' Martin spent at the church.[84] After accomplishing his aims, Martin senses his health failing him. Here, then, is the *transitus* that Sulpicius has promised Bassula. But even after all these preliminaries, Sulpicius stages a lengthy debate over Martin's death. The retinue of monks that surrounds Martin begs him to tarry still on this earth, a plea that seems to be reflected in Sulpicius' own persistent literary deferrals. Martin, though conflicted, gives himself over to God's will. Sulpicius exclaims: 'O man, whom no language can describe, unconquered by toil, and unconquerable even by death, who showed no personal preference for either alternative, and who neither feared to die nor refused to live!'[85] Sulpicius here repeats language from the second letter: Martin is a *vir ineffabilis*.[86] At the very moment of Martin's passing, the author again proclaims the inexpressibility of the saint's virtue. Indeed, Sulpicius fashions a direct link between the saint's ability to overcome death and the author's inability to express his virtue in words: Martin is at once a man 'indescribable' and 'unconquerable by death'. Martin lingers feverishly for a few days,[87] his death subject to seemingly endless delay. Finally, though, Sulpicius gives up the ghost, so to speak, and allows the moment of Martin's death to arrive at last. Martin speaks his last words and Sulpicius writes the words he had so long postponed: 'With that utterance, therefore, [Martin] returned his spirit to heaven.'[88] The final section of this third letter describes the funerary rites performed for the saint, measuring them against a triumph. Martin's body is accompanied not by the conquered, but rather by those who themselves conquered the world;[89] Martin is applauded not by a mob, but by divine psalms and heavenly hymns;[90] Martin is received not into Tartarus but into the bosom of Abraham, a pauper on earth who enters heaven as a rich man.[91]

84 *Epist.* 3.9, *Aliquandiu ergo in vico illo vel in ecclesia ad quam ierat commoratus.*

85 *Epist.* 3. 14, *O virum ineffabilem, nec labore victum nec morte vincendum, qui in nullam se partem pronior inclinaverit, nec mori timuerit nec vivere recusarit!*

86 Cf. n. 77 above.

87 *Epist.* 3.14, *per aliquot dies.*

88 *Epist.* 3.17, *Cum hac ergo voce spiritum caelo reddidit.*

89 *Epist.* 3.21, *Ducant illi prae curribus suis vinctos post terga captiuos; Martini corpus hi, qui mundum ductu illius vicerant prosequuntur.*

90 *Epist.* 3.21, *Illos confusis plausibus populorum honoret insania; Martino divinis plauditur psalmis, Martinus hymnis caelestibus honoratur.*

91 *Epist.* 3.21, *Illi post triumphos suos in tartara saeva trudentur; Martinus Abrahae sinu laetus excipitur, Martinus pauper et modicus caelum dives ingreditur.*

But this literary production promises more than just a triumphant end for the saint himself. Sulpicius compels his reader to acknowledge that a final end to Martin-focused discourse is not only unwanted but impossible. Throughout the corpus, Sulpicius describes the benefits that redound not just to the saint himself but also to those who would write, read, and talk about Martin.[92] In a preface to the *Life*, Sulpicius writes:

> For this reason, I will have a prize for my effort, if I write the life of a most holy man to serve in the future as an example to others ... In this, we take account of our own benefit as well, so that we might await not the empty remembrance of men, but the eternal reward of God.[93]

Here, before any account of Martin's life is even begun, Sulpicius promises a text that accomplishes some salvific end—*a deo praemium*—for those who would participate in its production and its consumption. That claim is echoed at the end of the *Life*, when Sulpicius extends the same reward to those who read his *Life* faithfully: 'whoever would not just read but would actually believe will have a reward from God.'[94] In his second letter, Sulpicius further advances the notion that the act of writing and reading hagiographical literature is a means of making the saint present, a means of obtaining his intercession. By writing Martin, Sulpicius renders the saint explicitly present to himself and to his readers: 'He will not be absent from us, believe me, he will not be absent. He will be present among us as we discuss him, he will stand beside us as we pray.'[95] Literary reproductions will allow the writer and his readers to experience the saint's presence: so long as they continue to talk about the saint, Martin will be with them. Sulpicius reiterates this in the last words of his final letter, as he consoles Bassula over Martin's death: 'as a guardian he looks back on me as I write and you as you read.'[96]

---

92 I discuss this at length in Yuzwa, "Reading Genre", *passim* but esp. 337–346. Derek Krueger has shown the way hagiographical writing is seen to produce holiness in the author: 'By representing the saints, authors hoped to resemble them.' See Derek Krueger, *Writing and Holiness* (Philadelphia: University of Pennsylvania Press, 2004), 94.

93 *Mart.* 1.6, *Unde facturus mihi operae pretium videor, si vitam sanctissimi viri, exemplo aliis mox futuram, perscripsero ... In quo ita nostri quoque rationem commodi ducimus, ut non inanem ab hominibus memoriam, sed aeternum a Deo praemium exspectemus.*

94 *Mart.* 27.7, *paratumque, ut spero, habebit a Deo praemium, non quicumque legerit, sed quicumque crediderit.*

95 *Epist.* 2.16, *non deerit nobis ille, mihi crede, non deerit: intererit de se sermocinantibus, adstabit orantibus.*

96 *Epist.* 3.21, *custodiens me haec scribentem respicit, te legentem.*

Sulpicius' readers, before coming to the *Gallus*, are made fully aware of the possibilities of writing and reading about Martin. A hagiographical narrative not limited by some natural end constantly admits of more literary production, and texts that continue beyond measure allow the author and his audience to participate again in the salvation that Martin offers. So long as there remains a need for further discussion of Martin, there will remain more opportunities to seek his guardianship, more opportunities to obtain the potentially salvific benefits of writing and reading the deeds of this holy man. Sulpicius, therefore, would create the conditions for a work that is potentially limitless, *inmensus*.

3 Episode and Digression in the *Gallus*

The *Gallus* follows nearly ten years after Sulpicius has written Martin's death and burial.[97] This literary dialogue writes a conversation between three interlocutors: Sulpicius, Postumianus, who has recently returned from a journey to the eastern deserts, and Gallus, a disciple of Martin. They discuss the virtues of holy men in the east and later Martin himself. The text consists in three *orationes perpetuae*. The first and longest occupies the first half of the first day, as measured by the passing of time in the outermost narrative frame. In this speech (conventionally labelled the first of three books in the dialogue), Postumianus recounts at length his journey to the deserts of the east, his encounters with the monks there, and the stories he heard from them. In the second *oratio perpetua*, which fills the second part of that first day, Gallus (at the urging of his interlocutors) satisfies the demand for more miracles and sayings of Martin, so as to add to those already compiled by Sulpicius in his *Life* and letters. That section of dialogue (the second book in Fontaine's critical edition) ends when at sunset a domestic interrupts the literary idyll the three interlocutors had been composing. That servant had come to announce the arrival of a fellow-monk and partisan of Martin, a certain Refrigerius. The three interlocutors make a temporary end to their dialogue and retire for the night. The monk's evening

97 Sulpicius writes this last text in the Martinian corpus most likely in AD 404 or thereabouts. External evidence provides a *terminus ante quem* of AD 411 for the *Gallus*: Jerome cites the text in his *Commentary on Ezekiel*. On the dating of this commentary, see John N.D. Kelly, *Jerome: His Life, Writings, and Controversies* (New York: Harper and Row, 1975), 304–308. The dramatic action of the dialogue (whether properly 'historical' or not) is set c. AD 404: it is near the start of Postumianus' three-year journey that he arrives in Alexandria in the very midst of the Origenist controversy. Cf. Burton, *Vita Martini*, 4–5.

advent portends the events of the following morning, when a *turba monachorum* press for entrance into their company. They had heard that Martin was the topic of conversation. The final *oratio perpetua* (the third and shortest of the books) begins on the morning of the second day, Gallus picking up where he left off the previous evening, though with a markedly larger audience. He continues to pile the account of one miraculous deed upon the other, in a display of unceasing narrative abundance. Gallus' growing collection of salutary tales ends only when the press of night demands it. In fact, Postumianus is just asking after another anecdote when Sulpicius interrupts him, pointing to the sinking sun and declaring the day over. A Martinian narrative is inevitably abounding, as Sulpicius' character makes explicit. Nearly the last we hear of Martin in the text is Sulpicius' avowal: 'There is no point in waiting for someone to reach an end when talking about Martin. He spreads too widely to be bound by the limits of any conversation.'[98]

In fact, we see that such ostensibly natural conversation, with its concomitant potential for unstructured, even endless, discourse is particularly suitable for comprehending Martin as fully as possible. Unlike biography, a genre seemingly bounded by a fundamentally teleological structure (though even this basic tenet Sulpicius ignores, or at least avoids), dialogue seems to admit readily of anecdote and episode, digression and interruption.[99] Or rather, we might better say that dialogue *as Sulpicius writes it* consistently displays such narrative tendencies. A conversation can very well last for days, as this one does.

If the *Life* and the letters in some way represent a meditation on the end of Martin's life, then the *Gallus* dramatises the possibilities of a literary afterlife unbounded by temporal parameters,[100] rendering a discursive world in which Martin's deeds can be told ever and again. With the *Gallus*, Sulpicius finds the means of rendering this death meaningless in narrative terms; he finds the means of reanimating Martin, not in body of course, but in this still expand-

98 *Dial.* 3.17.1, *De Martino autem exspectare non debes ut ulla sit meta referenti: latius ille diffunditur quam ut ullo valeat sermone concludi.*

99 Averil Cameron, *Dialoguing in Late Antiquity* (Cambridge, MA: Harvard University Press, 2014) challenges the scholarship that has disregarded or denigrated the robust tradition of literary dialogue among Christians in late antiquity and continues a debate most recently restarted by Simon Goldhill (ed.), *The End of Dialogue in Antiquity* (Cambridge: Cambridge University Press, 2008). Whether Christian literature admits openness or is necessarily 'totalizing' and whether Christians can 'do' dialogue in the robust sense intended by Goldhill is outside the scope of this paper. For Sulpicius, however, the narrative setting of this literary dialogue offers the possibility of continued and open discourse on Martin.

100 Cf. Whitmarsh, *Narrative and Identity*, especially Chapter 6, "Limen", 214–252.

ing literary corpus. Though Martin has died, discourse on the saint can continue without end. The *Gallus*, by the peculiarities of its narrative structure, will dramatise the boundlessness of Martin and Martin-directed literary practice.

Of course, at the outset of the text there is no explicit indication that the conversation here depicted will ever eventually address Martin at all. We read that the interlocutor Gallus reminds Sulpicius of Martin, having been one of the saint's disciples;[101] however, that character's presence (and by extension Martin's) is quickly obscured by the arrival of a certain Postumianus, a dear friend just returned from his travels in the eastern deserts. Sulpicius, himself a character, requests an *historia peregrinationis*. Postumianus obliges and the text at first reads like a monastic travelogue, somewhat reminiscent of the nearly contemporary *Historia Monachorum* and evincing no obvious occupation with the deeds of Martin.

But even at this point we see that Sulpicius has made some innovation on his previous attempts at writing holy men: the narrative of saintly deeds—depicting not a single *Life* but a collection of interlocking anecdotes about multiple monks—is rendered in an essentially episodic structure, one constantly interrupted and diverted.[102] We might explain this by adducing the apparent demands of the subject: a text that depicts numerous holy men will naturally exhibit a sort of episodic or anecdotal structure, it seems reasonable to suggest. But the constant shifting of subject in the internal narrative is punctuated by the dialogic interruptions of the interlocutors in the outermost narrative frame. Indeed, the dialogue form creates conditions suitable for the sort of structural divagation which is engendered by multiple and in some ways competing authorial voices within the narrative world of the text. Gallus' narrative undermines the basic teleological assumptions of biography: it begins *in medias res*, at some middle point in Martin's life, and continues not according to an obvious chronological order, but seemingly at random, one anecdote obliquely suggesting the next.

The episode with which the character Gallus begins his account of Martin reflects the author's self-conscious engagement with the potential of recursive narrative. For though its place in Martin's life is intermediate, even chronologically indeterminate, its significance in the context of Sulpicius' literary project is explicitly foregrounded. In a sort of *captatio benevolentiae*, with which he begins his speech, Gallus makes explicit his intention to avoid repeating what

101 *Dial.* 1.1.1, *propter Martini memoriam.*

102 Cf. French on collective biography in this volume.

Sulpicius has already written of Martin; his narrative, however, begins with a condensed reimagining of the most famous deeds from the *Life*. Gallus' first anecdote about Martin is a double of the saint's famous encounter with a pauper outside the gates at Amiens. In fact, the entire series of episodes that begin Gallus' account is linked not by chronology nor even by theme, but rather by the common tendency to repeat and reinscribe the most famous deeds of Sulpicius' earlier *Life*. In addition to this reduplicated act of charity, Gallus tells of miraculous healings and even another resurrection.[103] Such repetition immediately structures a narrative that admits of constant retelling. Martin's miraculous *virtus*—as Sulpicius has described it—engenders ever more miracles and the subsequent discourse necessary to describe them.

Running counter to this reduplicative tendency is the recurring sense in the dialogue that one exemplary episode or one particular series of exemplary episodes ought to satisfy the desires of the audience. The few ought to stand in for the many. So Postumianus claims, when he has finished his narrative: 'Let it be enough for you to know these things about the virtues of the Lord, virtues which he has accomplished in his servants either for the purpose of imitation or of avoidance.'[104] As recompense for so satisfying his interlocutors, Postumianus asks to hear more of Martin.[105] The character Sulpicius immediately picks up on this notion of sufficiency: 'Was my book not enough for you?'[106] Here we mark a fundamental characteristic of Martinian narrative: it is never enough; one text can never fully comprehend that holy man. Postumianus replies, 'This task was given me by many monks, that if ever I should return to this country and find you well, I should compel you to supply those particulars about the virtues of the blessed man which you claimed to pass over in that book of yours.'[107]

And indeed, Gallus, having been chosen to tell of these overlooked episodes, adduces a similar tendency. He recounts a spectacular series of holy and miraculous deeds, then claims: 'Already I have narrated so many things to you that

103 Referring respectively to *Mart.* 16 and *Mart.* 7–8.

104 *Dial.* 1.22.5, *Haec vos de virtutibus Domini, quas in servis suis vel imitanda operatus est vel timenda, scire sufficiat.*

105 *Dial.* 1.22.6, *Sed quia satisfeci vestris auribus, immo etiam verbosior fui fortasse quam debui, tu modo, ad me loquebatur, debitum faenus exsolve, ut te de Martino tuo, ut es solitus, plura referentem, iam pridem in hoc desideriis meis aestuantibus, audiamus.*

106 *Dial.* 1.23.1, *Quid? inquam, tibi de Martino meo liber ille non sufficit, quem ipse tu nosti me de illius vita atque virtutibus edidisse?*

107 *Dial.* 1.23.7, *a multis fratribus haec mihi iniuncta legatio est, ut, si umquam terras istas te incolumi contigissem, ea te supplere conpellerem, quae in illo tuo libro de virtutibus beati viri professus es praeterisse.*

my discourse ought to have satisfied your desires.'[108] It has not, of course. 'But because I cannot disregard your will, I will speak for what remains of the day.'[109] This makes the point even more explicitly, in that Gallus recognises his inability to fully comprehend Martin in speech: his only limit is the setting sun.

It is with this declaration that the narrative reins of Gallus' account are completely loosed: the possibility of sufficient speech having been precluded, Gallus' subsequent narrative reproduces a discourse of abundance. Each episode suggests the next only obliquely, and the series evinces no constraining pattern, whether chronological or otherwise. One miracle is heaped on the next. This random parataxis dominates Gallus' narrative in the dialogue's second book. The result is a text that depicts a sort of endless middle to Martin's life, its telling not limited by the traditional constraints of biographical literature. Sulpicius, having already written Martin's death, is free to write a narrative without the structuring principles demanded by a proper ending. The narrator Gallus jumps from one story to the next, each quite literally an episode (in the etymological sense), a sort of sidetrack that 'join[s] the main route from an unexpected angle'.[110]

The series of passages that ends the second book demonstrates this episodic arrangement quite explicitly. When Gallus agrees to speak for what remains of the day, he notices straw beds being prepared for the three interlocutors (*Dial.* 2.8). This suggests to him a story about Martin and blessed straw. The story which follows happened 'around the same time' as that which preceded it (*Dial.* 2.9). This story about a demonic cow seemingly suggests another animal story (*Dial.* 2.9). That pair of animal stories is followed by sayings of Martin, themselves illustrated by animal parables (*Dial.* 2.10). The last of these sayings is a long parable about virginity, fornication, and marriage (*Dial.* 2.10), which occasions a story about a monk who wants to live in celibate companionship with his wife (*Dial.* 2.11). The conclusion to this episode is an aphorism about the separation of men from women in the monastic life (*Dial.* 2.11). That saying naturally suggests the highest example of sequestered virginity experienced by Martin: the committed virgin who refused even to see the holy man himself (*Dial.* 2.12). Gallus so highly praises her virginity because it is said that even angels would discourse with Martin. The preceding occasions a discussion of Martin's visitation with angels (*Dial.* 2.13). The miracu-

108 *Dial.* 2.8.5, *iam quidem vobis, inquit, tanta narravi ut satisfacere studiis vestris meus sermo debuerit.*

109 *Dial.* 2.8.5, *Sed quia voluntati vestrae non obsecundare mihi non licet, quantum adhuc diei superest loquar.*

110 Whitmarsh, *Narrative and Identity*, 235.

lous result of this is Martin's ability to prophesy future events (*Dial.* 2.13). As the sun finally sets, conversation proceeds in turn to Martin's visions of the Apocalypse (*Dial.* 2.14). It is with this subject that the conversation will end for the day, a coincidence which seems almost to suggest a correspondence between the furthest extremes of historical time and the final limits of Martinian discourse. This is a self-consciously literary evocation of the contours of oral conversation—one story always suggests another—but it likewise foregrounds the possibilities of perpetual discourse. Because Martin's deeds are beyond measure, there will always be one more *exemplum* to add, one more miracle to tell.

Really what constrains Gallus' speech is the arrival of a servant boy. In the very midst of his speech, Gallus is interrupted. He had yet to finish what he set out to relate, when there entered a boy from the household. This servant is decidedly out of place, a disturbing presence who does in fact derail the discussion. Of course, the unexpected entrance of uninvited guests, slaves, and other such characters is not so unexpected given the generic context. We naturally think of the sudden and disruptive entrance of Alcibiades, flute-girl on his arm and surrounded by revelers, in Plato's *Symposium* (212c–213b). Though perhaps the *coup de théâtre* is here less dramatic, still it marks a dramatic change in context and sudden end to discourse. For the boy announces that the priest Refrigerius is standing at the door. His looming presence immediately cools the conversation. The participants are unsure: should they keep listening to Gallus or attend to their friend outside? Gallus himself makes the decision for them, adducing the approach of night: 'Even if not on account of the arrival of that most holy priest, we would have had to leave off this speech, for night compels us to finish the discourse so far advanced. Though in no way has it been possible to tell everything about Martin's virtues, this will have to be enough for today.'[111] This is a not uncommon topos among ancient authors for bringing a text to its close. Cicero's *De Oratore* does similar.[112] For Sulpicius, the only limits to discourse on Martin are external constraints.

On the second day of conversation in the *Gallus*, the narrative on Martin is again bound not by internal concerns, rather only by the passing of time in the uppermost level of the text.[113] But acknowledging this as a literary

111 *Dial.* 2.14.7–8, *Etiamsi non ob adventum sanctissimi sacerdotis relinquenda nobis haec esset oratio, nox ipsa cogebat hucusque prolatum finire sermonem. Verum quia de Martini virtutibus nequaquam explicari universa potuerunt, haec vos hodie audisse sufficiat.*

112 Cic. *De or.*, 3.209.

113 *Dial.* 3.17.1, *Dies, inquam, abiit, Postumiane, surgendum est; simul studiosis auditoribus cena debetur.*

commonplace—and perhaps one especially suited to dialogue[114]—allows us to see the possibilities that this particular genre and this particular trope might offer Sulpicius in his depiction of Martin. Sulpicius makes explicit the fact that no narrative can contain Martin; no speech is enough to represent him fully; there can be no end to any discussion of him.[115] Attempts to comprehend Martin in speech and in literature are by definition endless. In his literary afterlife, the possibility of closure is denied outright. There is always cause for still more narrative.

The way these stories about Martin end highlights the formal diversity of early hagiographical literature. Krueger's recognition that Christian writing in late antiquity becomes for authors a manifestation of ascetic discipline of course extends to the writing of hagiography. In Sulpicius' Martinian corpus, the salvific potential of writing (and reading) Martin serves to mediate the narrative structure, even the generic form of hagiographical literature. Sulpicius, compelled to produce a 'text without end',[116] experiments across a series of texts and writes his story of Martin in a life, a series of letters, and finally a dialogue. Sulpicius explores the manifold possibilities of genre and narrative in the context of a still nascent and constantly developing literary project of hagiographical remembering. In the earliest examples of Latin 'hagiography', we read texts that engage diverse generic forms even as they employ hagiographical discourse; we read texts that experiment with how to write the figure of the saint and moreover how to inscribe the role of the reader in the work. A study of literary closure allows us to see how Sulpicius writes a *Life* beyond measure and creates for himself and his readers the possibility of perpetual discourse.

4 The Problem of Closure in the Martinian Corpus: An Epilogue

The *Gallus* ends with Sulpicius, as interlocutor, imagining the reception of this text in the far distant lands to which he expects Postumianus will travel, in an effort to spread the *nomen et gloria Martini*. In a comment that subtly elides the distinction between oral conversation—still ongoing in the narrative world of the *Gallus*—and the literary dialogue presented to external readers,

114 Curtius, *European Literature*, in his treatment of concluding topoi in ancient literature, points out that this is a technique that 'befits only an outdoor conversation', 90.

115 *Dial.* 3.17.1, *De Martino autem exspectare non debes ut ulla sit meta referenti: latius ille diffunditur quam ut ullo valeat sermone concludi.*

116 *Epist.* 1.8, *volumen inmensum.*

the interlocutor Sulpicius characterises their discourse in the language of writing, instructing his friend to 'unroll the volume of our speech.'[117] This elision allows Sulpicius, as an author speaking through his eponymous interlocutor, the opportunity for metatextual commentary; allows him quite explicitly to consider the potential reception of his work. As Postumianus returns eastward, he will bear with him a record of their conversation. Postumianus' easterly journey will take him to Italy, where Paulinus will not refuse to compare Martin to his Felix.[118] It will take him to Africa, whose people will venerate not only Cyprian, who consecrated the city of Carthage by the blood he spilled as a martyr, but Martin also.[119] It will take Postumianus—if he veers just a little out of his way—to Greece, where he might remind the people that Plato was no wiser, Socrates no braver, than Martin.[120] Nor did Paul's preaching at Corinth mean that Christ has forsaken Gaul, because the latter can claim Martin as its own.[121] Postumianus will finally return to Egypt, which will recognise that Europe, on account of Martin, will not yield to its *virtus*.[122]

I think we are compelled to take quite seriously Sulpicius' frequent claims about the impossibility of narrating Martin's deeds in their totality. This holy man, in Sulpicius' telling, frustrates the possibility of closure. Armine Mortimer, in her work on narrative closure, adopts a fitting phrase: she describes the narrative text as 'une paysage inépuisable', an inexhaustible landscape.[123] We have already seen how exhausted Martin leaves his hagiographer. But the resonance

---

117 *Dial.* 3.17.3, *primum sermonis nostri, quod vel hesterno confecimus vel hodie diximus volumen evolve*. Fontaine, *Gallus*, 358 n. 1, glosses the phrase, explaining that *sermonis nostri volumen* refers to 'une copie complète du dialogue.' Of course, this is what Sulpicius alludes to, but the simple equation of speech to text ignores the complex movements of production and reception that are collapsed in Sulpicius' metatextual remark. The interlocutors—as Sulpicius the author represents them—are highly aware of their participation in a written, textual production. Cf. also Gallus' earlier remark that the text is arranged in the 'form of a dialogue', *Dial.* 3.5.6, *speciem dialogi*.

118 *Dial.* 3.17.5, *ille, Martini non invidus, gloriarum sanctarumque in Christo virtutum piisimus aestimator, non abnuet praesulem nostrum cum suo Felice conponere*.

119 *Dial.* 3.17.5, *licet iam, prout ipse dixisti, virum noverit, tamen nunc praecipue de eo plura cognoscat, ne solum ibi Cyprianum martyrem suum, quamvis sancto illius sanguine consecrata, miretur*.

120 *Dial.* 3.17.6, *iam si ad laevam Achaiae sinum paululum devexus intraveris, sciat Corinthus, sciant Athenae non sapientiorem in Academia Platonem nec Socraten in carcere fortiorem*.

121 *Dial.* 3.17.6, *felicem quidem Graeciam, quae meruit audire Apostolum praedicantem, sed nequaquam a Christo Gallias derelictas, quibus donaverit habere Martinum*.

122 *Dial.* 3.17.7, *cum vero ad Aegyptum usque perveneris, quamquam illa suorum sanctorum numero sit et virtutibus superba, tamen non dedignetur audire quam illi vel universae Asiae in solo Martino Europa non cesserit*.

123 Armine Mortimer, *La Clôture Narrative* (Paris: Corti, 1985), 228.

extends also to the metaphor of physical geography: Martinian discourse will extend to the very ends of the Roman world. At each stop, Postumianus will occasion discourse on Martin and this abundance of insufficient speech will continue, as Sulpicius hopes, without end.

The primary aim of Postumianus' renewed travel will be to spread once more stories of Martin; that is, explicitly to bear the text we readers have in our hands out into the world.[124] But Sulpicius adds one further destination: the shores of Ptolemais, where a certain Pomponius is buried. Here, at the end of the *Gallus*, Sulpicius again substitutes one death for another: this Pomponius was a wayward disciple of Martin, now buried on the shores of a foreign land.[125] He has lost his monastic community, is separated not only from his home but also from Sulpicius (and from this particular gathering of Martinian monks). By refusing the Martin-centred discourse that Sulpicius constructs, Pomponius likewise abandons the promise of salvation inherent to that particular practice of *sermo*.

Most striking, however, is the decidedly final sense that the mention of Pomponius conveys. The text ends: 'We grieved over these things in an especially mournful voice, and while the tears of everyone were drawn out by our laments, with great admiration of Martin but no less sorrow from our weeping, we scattered.'[126] The *discessum est* is a pleasing parallel to the *convenissemus* with which the dialogue began, a clear marker of literary closure;[127] at the same time, however, the departure is definitive and troubling. If the lament here is sincere, the *discessus* is revealing. It marks first of all a real dispersal of the community so recently gathered to hear and tell of Martin. It does not necessarily signal the final end of Martinian discourse: this conversation has produced a great deal of material for Postumianus to convey eastward, thereby perpetuating the exemplary loop constructed around Martin's *virtus*. In other ways, however, the end remains all too real. We do not travel with Postumianus once more to the East, do not hear the discourse that Martin and Martinian narratives engen-

124 *Dial.* 3.17.2, *ista interim de illo viro portabis Orienti, et dum recurris diversasque oras, loca, portus, insulas urbesque praeterlegis, Martini nomen et gloriam sparge per populos.*

125 *Dial.* 3.18.2–3, *dices tamen illi, sed non aspere, non acerbe, conpatientis alloquio, non exprobantis elogio. Quod si vel te quondam vel me semper audire voluisset, et Martinum magis quam illum quem nominare nolo fuisset imitates, numquam, a me tam crudeliter disparatus, ignoti pulveris syrte tegeretur, naufragi sorte praedonis passus in medio mari mortem, et vix in extremo nanctus litore sepulturam.*

126 *Dial.* 3.18.5, *haec cum maxime flebili voce gemeremus, omnium lacrimis per nostra lamenta commotis, cum magna quidem Martini admiratione, sed non minore ex nostris fletibus dolore discessum est.*

127 *Dial.* 1.1.1, *cum in unum locum ego et Gallus convenissemus.*

der. We remain in Gaul, at Primuliacum, where the conversation has reached its definitive end. The now complete biography of Martin ends not with the saint's death, but with the death of a wayward disciple. It likewise ends with the possibility of community precluded, at least in the narrative world of the text. The gathered monks depart.

Here we move into the realm of speculation: we have seen that the *Gallus* constructs a discursive reality, in which salvation can be achieved through literary practice, but then its final passage seems to suggest—if only as a hint—that these literary monuments are the only real possibility that remains. The community of monks at Primuliacum departs. Is it for the last time? Could we go so far as to say that Sulpicius constructs this discursive practice because literature is now his only recourse? We hear Sulpicius often lamenting the fact that the community of Martinians is especially beleaguered in Gaul.[128] Indeed, despite the persistent popularity of cultic practice centred on Martin throughout the middle ages, there is evidence to suggest that the cult consists not so much in continuous and centralised devotional practice, but rather in diverse, localised reinventions.[129] It is tempting to speculate that Sulpicius writes this ascetic practice of eulogising Martin because the communal practice of asceticism is no longer a possibility for him. And so, the literary remembrance of the saint becomes quite a bit more than that. The practice of literature, of reading and of writing, may well be for Sulpicius the only means of practising Martinian asceticism, the only means of participating in his saintly *virtus*.

Bibliography

Barnes, Timothy D., "The *Historia Augusta* and Christian Biography", in François Paschoud (ed.), *Historiae Augustae Colloquium Genevense* (Bari: Edipuglia, 1999), 33–41.

128 Cf. the story of Brice, Martin's successor in the episcopal see at Tours, *Dial.* 3.15. The tensions between traditionalist and ascetic factions among the clergy in fourth-century Gaul are made clear in Stancliffe, *St. Martin and His Hagiographer*, 278–296 and more recently Hunter, "Vigilantius of Calagurris", 401–430.

129 The standard work remains Charles Pietri, *La Ville de Tours du IVe au VIe siècle: naissance d'une cité chrétienne* (Rome: École Française de Rome, 1983), 89–169. Sharon Farmer, *Communities of Saint Martin: Legend and Ritual in Medieval Tours* (Ithaca, NY: Cornell University Press, 1991), gives an account of the competing interests which mark the cult of Martin at Tours later in its development. For a study that focuses on Martin's cult in the period immediately following his death, see Allan S. McKinley, "The First Two Centuries of Saint Martin of Tours", *Early Medieval Europe* 14.2 (2006), 173–200.

Barnes, Timothy D., *Early Christian Hagiography and Roman History* (Tübingen: Mohr Siebeck, 2010).

Benjamin, Walter, "The Storyteller", in *Illuminations*. Translated by Harry Zohn (New York: Schocken, 1968), 83–110.

Boglioni, Pierre, "La scène de la mort dans les premières hagiographies latines", in Claude Sutto (ed.), *Le sentiment de la mort au moyen age* (Montréal: L'Aurore, 1978), 183–210.

Burrus, Virginia, *The Sex Lives of Saints: An Erotics of Ancient Hagiography* (2nd edition Philadelphia: University of Pennsylvania Press, 2007).

Burton, Philip, *Sulpicius Severus' Vita Martini* (Oxford: Oxford University Press, 2017).

Cameron, Averil, *Dialoguing in Late Antiquity* (Cambridge, MA: Harvard University Press, 2014).

Curtius, Ernst Robert, *European Literature in the Latin Middle Ages*. Translated by Willard R. Trask (Princeton, NJ: Princeton University Press, 1953).

DeLillo, Don, *White Noise* (New York: Viking, 1985).

Fabre, Pierre, *Essai sur la Chronologie de l'oeuvre de Saint Paulin de Nole* (Paris: Belles Lettres, 1948).

Farmer, Sharon, *Communities of Saint Martin: Legend and Ritual in Medieval Tours* (Ithaca, NY: Cornell University Press, 1991).

Fontaine, Jacques, *Sulpice Sévère: Vie de Martin*, 3 vols., Sources chrétiennes 133–135 (Paris: Les Éditions du Cerf, 1967–1969).

Fontaine, Jacques, *Sulpice Sévère: Gallus ou Dialogues sur les "vertus" de Saint Martin*, Sources chrétiennes 510 (Paris: Les Éditions du Cerf, 2006).

Fowler, Don, "Second Thoughts on Closure", in Roberts, Dunn, and Fowler, *Classical Closure*, 3–22.

Fowler, Don, *Roman Constructions: Readings in Postmodern Latin* (Oxford: Oxford University Press, 2000).

Genette, Gérard, *Narrative Discourse: An Essay in Method*. Translated by Jane E. Lewin, Foreword by Jonathan Culler (Ithaca, NY: Cornell University Press, 1983). Original publication: "Discours du récit" in *Figures III* (Paris: Seuil, 1972).

Goldhill, Simon (ed.), *The End of Dialogue in Antiquity* (Cambridge: Cambridge University Press, 2008).

Goodrich, Richard, *Sulpicius Severus: The Complete Works* (New York: Newman Press, 2015).

Hamon, Philippe, "Clausules", *Poetique* 6 (1975), 495–526.

Hunter, David G., "Vigilantius of Calagurris and Victricius of Rouens: Ascetics, Relics, and Clerics in Late Roman Gaul", *JECS* 7 (1999), 401–430.

Kelly, John N.D., *Jerome: His Life, Writings and Controversies* (New York: Harper and Row, 1975).

Kermode, Frank, *The Sense of an Ending* (Oxford: Oxford University Press, 1967).

Krueger, Derek, *Writing and Holiness: The Practice of Authorship in the Early Christian East* (Philadelphia: University of Pennsylvania Press, 2004).

McKinley, Allan S., "The First Two Centuries of Saint Martin of Tours", *Early Medieval Europe* 14.2 (2006), 173–200.

Miller, D.A., *Narrative and Its Discontents: Problems of Closure in the Traditional Novel* (Princeton, NJ: Princeton University Press, 1981).

Mortimer, Armine, *La Clôture Narrative* (Paris: Corti, 1985).

Mratschek, Sigrid, *Der Briefwechsel des Paulinus von Nola. Kommunikation und soziale Kontakte zwischen christlichen Intellektuellen* (Göttingen: Vandenhoeck and Ruprecht, 2002).

Pelling, Christopher B.R., "Is Death the End? Closure in Plutarch's *Lives*", in Roberts, Dunn, and Fowler, *Classical Closure*, 228–250.

Pietri, Charles, *La Ville de Tours du IVe au VIe siècle: naissance d'une cité chrétienne* (Rome: École Française de Rome, 1983).

Reinelt, Paul, *Studien über die Briefe des hl. Paulinus von Nola* (Breslau: R. Nischkowsky, 1903).

Roberts, Deborah H., Francis M. Dunn, and Robert Fowler (eds.), *Classical Closure: Reading the End in Greek Literature* (Princeton, NJ: Princeton University Press, 1997).

Smith, Barbara H., *Poetic Closure* (Chicago: University of Chicago Press, 1968).

Stancliffe, Clare, *St. Martin and His Hagiographer: History and Miracle in Sulpicius Severus* (Oxford: Clarendon Press, 1983).

Tornau, Christian, "Intertextuality in Early Latin Hagiography: Sulpicius Severus and the *Vita Antonii*", *Studia Patristica* 35 (2001), 158–166.

Trout, Dennis, *Paulinus of Nola: Life, Letters, Poems* (Berkeley: University of California Press, 1993).

Van Uytfanghe, Marc, "L'hagiographie: un 'genre' Chrétien ou antique tardif?", *Analecta Bollandiana* 111 (1991), 135–188.

Whitmarsh, Tim, *Narrative and Identity in the Ancient Greek Novel: Returning Romance* (Cambridge: Cambridge University Press, 2011).

Yuzwa, Zachary, "Reading Genre in Sulpicius Severus' Letters", *Journal of Late Antiquity* 7.2 (2014), 329–350.

CHAPTER 6

The Perils of Paulinus: Letters as Hagiography in the Correspondence of Paulinus of Nola and Sulpicius Severus

Michael Stuart Williams

Paulinus of Nola was one of the most celebrated Christians of his day. His status as an example of ascetic renunciation was magnified by the wealth he had disposed of as a member of the Roman senatorial elite.[1] His fame in his lifetime was arguably comparable to that of Martin of Tours, in whose *Life*—written by their mutual friend Sulpicius Severus—Paulinus makes a cameo appearance.[2] And yet aside from this passing mention that brings them together, Paulinus' presence in hagiographical literature may seem to present an almost total contrast to that of Martin. As Zachary Yuzwa argues elsewhere in this volume, Sulpicius' writings present a Martin whose death is constantly deferred: his *Life* appears in his lifetime, and in his supplementary letters Sulpicius continues to postpone Martin's passing for as long as he dares.[3] In stark contrast, there is no hagiographical *Life of Paulinus* deserving of the name, but instead only an account of his death: a letter by the presbyter Uranius, styled *De obitu Paulini*, which as that title reveals is quite unlike Sulpicius' letter on Martin in getting rapidly to the point, bringing the reader promptly to Paulinus' deathbed.[4] The letter is brief and unambitious, contenting itself with the report of the dying man's miraculous vision of the dead Martin and the martyred Januarius of Naples, and a short panegyric on his virtues.[5] It is striking that so famous an ascetic, one coupled even in his dying moments with Martin, should have attracted no hagiography, nor even the kind of respectful biography that was accorded to other prominent churchmen of

1 Dennis E. Trout, *Paulinus of Nola: Life, Letters, Poems* (Berkeley/Los Angeles: University of California Press, 1999), 10–15 similarly emphasises Paulinus' contemporary and enduring fame as a compelling example of ascetic renunciation.

2 Sulp. Sev. *Mart.* 19; although note that Paulinus is also offered by the narrator at this point, and subsequently (at 25) by Martin himself, as an example to all Christians.

3 See Yuzwa in this volume.

4 Uran. *Epist.* 12.2–4.

5 Uran. *Epist.* 12.3, 5–12.

 | DOI:10.1163/9789004421332_008

his generation—figures such as Ambrose of Milan or Augustine of Hippo, than whom Paulinus was no less extraordinary.[6]

Yet the example of Augustine may allow us to recover this 'missing' hagiography of Paulinus of Nola by inspiring us to look elsewhere: that is, to his own writings. Possidius' biography of Augustine emphasises his subject's actions in the church, but if we are looking for insight into Augustine's renunciation of the world and his spiritual life we turn naturally to his *Confessions*.[7] Paulinus, often credited with inspiring Augustine to write the *Confessions*, evidently had a similar interest in self-analysis and self-disclosure, even though he produced nothing comparable to that work.[8] Yet his copious writings about his spiritual patron Felix of Nola, and especially his verse account of that saint's life and miracles, have been interpreted as in some ways disguised autobiography.[9] But Paulinus wrote about himself more explicitly in his letters, at least some of which evidently circulated widely, and which provide a detailed and authoritative account of his spiritual lifestyle, his aims and intentions, and his successes and failures.[10] It may be possible, then, in the spirit of exploring definitions of the genre and its boundaries, to see in these letters a kind of autohagiography, in which Paulinus represents his own ascetic project and constructs himself—albeit implicitly, and not without irony—as something resembling a saint.

---

6 This is unlikely to be an example of the phenomenon noted by Wiśniewski in this volume, by which clerics *qua* clerics are uncommon subjects of hagiography: extraordinary figures such as Ambrose and Augustine received biographies which looked beyond their clerical duties, as also did the fifth-century ascetic bishops of Gaul, whose *Lives* are rarely stuffed with miraculous events. For discussion of how such lives could nevertheless become the stuff of hagiography, see Peter Turner, *Truthfulness, Realism, Historicity: A Study in Late Antique Spiritual Literature* (Farnham: Ashgate, 2012), 44–61.

7 For the contrast in these terms between this text and the *Confessions*, see Erika Hermanowicz, *Possidius of Calama: A Study of the North African Episcopate in the Age of Augustine* (Oxford: Oxford University Press, 2008), 17–42.

8 For discussion of Paulinus' role in the genesis of the *Confessions*, see James J. O'Donnell, *Augustine: Confessions*, vol. 2, (Oxford: Clarendon Press, 1992), 360–362.

9 Argued in most detail in Gennaro Luongo, *Lo specchio dell'agiografo* (Naples: Nuove Edizioni Tempi Moderni 1992) and accepted in e.g. Trout, *Paulinus of Nola*, 167–169.

10 That these letters anticipated a wider audience than a single recipient, and were vehicles of deliberate self-representation, is recognised at both Sigrid Mratschek, *Der Briefwechsel des Paulinus von Nola: Kommunikation und soziale Kontakte zwischen christlichen Intellektuellen* (Göttingen: Vandenhoeck and Ruprecht, 2002), 408–414 and Catherine Conybeare, *Paulinus Noster: Self and Symbols in the Letters of Paulinus of Nola* (Oxford: Oxford University Press, 2000), 19–40; that they did indeed circulate is evident from August. *Epist.* 186.39–41, in which Augustine and Alypius cite and even quote back to him some of Paulinus' letters to Sulpicius Severus.

There is no doubt that hagiography can be written in epistolary form, whether we cite its prehistory in letters reporting the deaths of martyrs (echoed in Uranius' letter, mentioned above, on the death of Paulinus) or in the defining example of the *Life of Antony*, also framed by its author as a letter. Letters of course can be vehicles for narrative and especially anecdote, forms which are fundamental to hagiography insofar as it purports to present its audience with other lives and experiences; and they often had a didactic and even edifying purpose, providing moral advice and examples whether from a Roman philosopher such as Seneca the Younger or from desert ascetics such as Antony and Shenoute.[11] Moreover, letters in the classical tradition were tightly bound up with the presentation of the self: indeed, self-fashioning in antiquity is often seen at its most dynamic, and arguably at its most deliberate and self-conscious, in elite exchanges of letters.[12] But if these elements seem to offer the prospect of understanding letters as a mode of (auto)hagiography, there remains a significant difficulty, for Christian authors more than for most: that is, the strong expectation that the subject of the hagiography will be openly praised. The precise relationship between hagiography and panegyric is too broad a topic to broach here, but the overlap between them can be seen in texts ranging from Eusebius of Caesarea's *Life of Constantine*, supposed by some to combine outright panegyric with historical narrative, to the minor example of Uranius listing the virtues of Paulinus after telling of his death.[13] The most perti-

---

11 The letters of Antony of Egypt receive their fullest discussion in Samuel Rubenson, *The Letters of St Antony: Monasticism and the Making of a Saint* (Minneapolis, MN: Fortress Press, 1995); those of Shenoute in Caroline T. Schroeder, *Monastic Bodies: Discipline and Salvation in Shenoute of Atripe* (Philadelphia: University of Pennsylvania Press, 2007); for a recent account of the didactic purpose of Seneca's *Epistulae Morales*, see John Schafer, "Seneca's *Epistulae Morales* as Dramatized Education", *CPh* 106 (2011), 32–52.

12 For some examples of this self-consciousness across the range of Latin letter-writing, see Jon Hall, *Politeness and Politics in Cicero's Letters* (Oxford: Oxford University Press, 2009), Stanley E. Hoffer, *The Anxieties of Pliny the Younger* (New York: Oxford University Press, 1999), Andrew Cain, *The Letters of Jerome: Asceticism, Biblical Exegesis, and the Construction of Christian Authority in Late Antiquity* (Oxford: Oxford University Press, 2009), and Jennifer Ebbeler, *Disciplining Christians: Correction and Community in Augustine's Letters* (Oxford: Oxford University Press, 2012).

13 Uran. *Epist.* 12.5–12. For Eusebius, see Timothy D. Barnes, "Panegyric, History and Historiography in Eusebius' *Life of Constantine*", in Rowan Williams (ed.), *The Making of Orthodoxy: Essays in Honour of Henry Chadwick* (Cambridge: Cambridge University Press, 1989), 94–123, and its amplification in Timothy D. Barnes, "The Two Drafts of Eusebius' *Vita Constantini*", in idem, *From Eusebius to Augustine: Selected Papers 1982–1993* (Aldershot: Variorum, 1994), XII; the argument is reviewed and extended in Averil Cameron, "Form and Meaning: The *Vita Constantini* and the *Vita Antonii*", in Tomas Hägg and Philip Rousseau (eds.), *Greek Biography and Panegyric in Late Antiquity* (Berkeley/Los Angeles: University

nent illustration is perhaps the *Gallus*, a series of dialogues by Sulpicius Severus in which the narrative of the life of Martin of Tours is revisited purely in the form of anecdotes swapped between the speakers, and which affords an opportunity for extravagant praise of the exemplary saint. But where the praises of another might be multiplied—perhaps endlessly, as Yuzwa again points out in this connection—it is a different matter with praise of oneself.

Even classical letter-writers such as Pliny the Younger are wary of seeming to invite approval of their actions, and often take care to restrict themselves to reporting the words or actions of others.[14] For Christians, for whom excessive pride was a sin, there was even more reason to be conspicuously modest.[15] Augustine was well aware of the danger in his *Confessions* and takes great pains to disavow any hint of self-praise—although some have still read it as culminating in a smug self-portrait of the author as a model of spiritual progress.[16] Likewise the letters of Antony and Shenoute focus strictly on the advice they give to others, and largely forego any effort to establish their own moral authority through self-description or even self-reference. But as Romans from a social and educational elite began to take up ascetic lifestyles, and in a way which did not lead them wholly to abandon existing assumptions and practices, it is

of California Press, 2000), 72–88. The volume in which the latter appears offers broader discussion of the relationship between biography—including hagiography—and panegyric in late antiquity; see also the "Introduction" to this volume.

14 Thus Plin. *Epist.* 1.8 explicitly discusses the difficulties of self-praise; at 4.5 and 9.23 he negotiates the risks by reporting the reception given to his speeches on various occasions, but is careful not to grant them excessive significance.

15 Vainglory, more specifically, was widely recognised as an occupational hazard for the ascetic: it can be found in Joh. Chrys. *Inan. glor.* in the mid AD 380s and, in the West, in e.g. Cassian. *Inst.* books 11 (on vainglory) and 12 (on pride): the latter specifically concerns itself with pride as the foundation of all sin and a particular temptation for those who would be perfect. The same point would also be made by Augustine of Hippo, in e.g. August. *Serm.* 340A.1, and August. *Nat. et grat.* 33; for discussion see John C. Cavadini, "Pride", in Allan D. Fitzgerald (ed.), *Augustine Through the Ages: An Encyclopedia* (Grand Rapids, MI: Eerdmans, 1999), 679–684.

16 Thus John Freccero, "Autobiography and Narrative", in Thomas C. Heller, Morton Sosna, and David E. Wellbery (eds.), *Reconstructing Individualism: Autonomy, Individuality, and the Self in Western Thought* (Stanford, CA: Stanford University Press, 1986), 16–29, at 16–18, reading the story in the *Confessions* as 'claim[ing] to be true, definitive, and concluded' and Augustine as representing himself as having 'seen the light, never to sin again'; see also Sidonie Smith and Julia Watson, *Reading Autobiography: A Guide for Interpreting Life Narratives* (Minneapolis, MN: University of Minnesota Press, 2010), 105 on Augustine's 'loss of self' in his self-portrait as narrator, but cf. Michael Stuart Williams, "Augustine's *Confessions* as Autobiography", in Koen De Temmerman (ed.), *The Oxford Handbook of Ancient Biography* (Oxford: Oxford University Press, forthcoming) on the more provisional character of Augustine's achievement.

possible to see the contortions that might be required by this need to avoid self-praise. In this chapter I therefore examine the correspondence between Paulinus of Nola and Sulpicius Severus as occupying precisely this point of overlap between polite self-representation and a desire to advertise and praise their common ascetic enterprise. The emphasis is necessarily on Paulinus, since it is only his letters that survive, but there is sufficient reference to the content of the letters of Sulpicius to establish the broad nature of his contribution.[17] But I hope to show that these letters, while not in themselves transgressing against the demands of appropriate modesty, nevertheless open up the space for a kind of hagiographical discourse.

In part the opening up of this space emerges from the nature of correspondence, both for authors and readers. Letters are always incomplete: not only in the sense that, in antiquity at least, it was expected that the words of a letter would often be supplemented by an additional report from its carrier, but also because a letter anticipates a certain interpretation by its recipient. The existence of a correspondence thus invites or presumes a relationship between the parties involved, and this relationship consists as much in what is left unsaid as in what is down in black and white on the page. The context must be reconstructed by the reader, and much of the character of a correspondence is derived from what is taken for granted by the correspondents. This is what allows for irony and humour, both of which go beyond any 'objective' meaning of the text and require instead a readiness to read between the lines. And it is in this realm of irony and humour, and of tacit understandings, that the correspondence of Paulinus and Sulpicius hints at something more than the conventional modesty on open display, and allows the letters to be read as hagiographical discourse. In their letters each represented the other as impeccably holy and themselves as impossibly abject, just as modesty required. But the character of the correspondence, between ostensibly equal partners engaged in a common ascetic enterprise, allows the praise of one to be reflected directly back on to the other, even as it was disavowed. The effect is not unlike that of collective hagiographies, as observed by Todd French elsewhere in this volume, in which an overall picture emerges which may not be extractable from any individual text.[18] Similarly in a correspondence, no single letter can be interpreted in isolation, but each must be read according to how it is situated in the relationship as a whole.

17 The letters under discussion are therefore those from Paulinus of Nola to Sulpicius Severus as they survive in Paulinus' collection, numbered 1, 5, 11, 17, 22, 23, 24, 27–32.

18 Thus French in this volume.

Allowances must be made, then, for these letters to be saying something other than what they appear to mean on the surface. The two main modes in which this can be achieved are irony and humour, but there must of course be some justification for identifying these in a given passage or text. This is a difficult business, as the contribution of Konstantin Klein in this volume makes clear: irony and humour exist either in the eye of the beholder, and are therefore disputable, or rely on the intention of the author, and are therefore unrecoverable.[19] What strikes a modern reader as funny or ironic may not have been intended that way; and if, as in the case of Paulinus' correspondence with Sulpicius, we have the original letters but none of the responses, it becomes very fraught indeed. But we may perhaps approach irony and humour by focusing first on what is most obviously sincere. The correspondence between Paulinus and Sulpicius is underpinned from its beginning by a readiness to pursue a life of ascetic perfection even in the face of criticism from others around them. We first encounter Paulinus responding to Sulpicius' anxiety on this score with an unrelenting firmness of purpose, warning his friend to shun questioners and critics whose flawed understanding will see them consigned to the flames.[20] No doubt is here permitted regarding the essential value of their common ascetic project, nor of the sincerity of their commitment to it. And it is in this context that we should interpret the way Paulinus later plays down his own ascetic efforts and achievements. The very failings to which he admits in his letters draw attention to the exalted status for which he strives; and they must be read against the praise from Sulpicius, which he acknowledges as he deflects it. The conspicuous modesty employed by Paulinus implies not indifference to praise but an awareness of the problem it presents; and it sits awkwardly with his refusal to accept any such deflections from Sulpicius in turn. The anecdotes he tells against himself do indeed undermine any claim to ascetic perfection. But we should not be too quick to suppose that Paulinus believed his achievements to be so minimal as he pretends.

It is perhaps most illuminating to say that Paulinus was no less, and no more, sincere in rejecting this praise from Sulpicius as he was in praising Sulpicius in return as an example of ascetic perfection. The point is not to calibrate it precisely, but to recognise that irony and self-deprecation allowed such potentially awkward claims to be kept at a comfortable distance. This was especially advantageous at a time when the development of Christian ascetic norms was still at an early stage, in which controversy was rarely far away. Paulinus was a reluc-

19 Klein in this volume.

20 Paul. Nol. *Epist.* 1.4.

tant theorist and yet a high-profile practitioner of asceticism, whose practices and principles could not but position him in what Dennis Trout calls 'a vital but still fluid western religious movement', and who might easily attract censure; Sulpicius, for his part, found his hero Martin of Tours subjected to criticism to which he felt obliged to respond.[21] Moreover, both were embedded in a social network which included individuals whose ascetic ideas would become a matter of intense and often hostile debate: it is enough to mention Jerome, Vigilantius, Jovinian, and Julian of Eclanum, and to recall that the Pelagian controversy was already brewing at the turn of the fifth century.[22] In these circumstances a civilised irony helped defuse the risk of controversy; and half-serious denials might prepare the way for an unambiguous declaration if that should ever be required.[23] Paulinus and Sulpicius could each praise the other for outstanding ascetic achievements, and could each dwell at length on their own limitations. But the extravagance of the praise on the one hand, and the apparent humour in the passages of self-deprecation on the other, may suggest that neither praise nor self-censure was offered—or ought to be taken—entirely seriously.

1 Conspicuous Modesty

In discussing the interaction of Paulinus and Sulpicius Severus, Dennis Trout pointed to the way in which they made use of contemporary exemplars to reflect on their own aspirations and identities. The image of Martin of Tours in the works of Sulpicius Severus, and Paulinus' own appearance in the *Life of Martin*, plus Paulinus' own account in a letter to Sulpicius of a visit of Melania the Elder to his establishment at Nola, are put forward by Trout as externalised portraits of the kind of ascetic life envisaged by the two friends for

---

21 Trout, Paulinus of Nola, 121; for the controversies over Martin of Tours, see Clare Stancliffe, *St Martin and His Hagiographer: History and Miracle in Sulpicius Severus* (Oxford: Clarendon Press, 1983), 249–261.

22 Some commentary on these connections may be found in Stancliffe, *St Martin*, 265–312; Elizabeth Clark, *The Origenist Controversy: The Cultural Construction of an Early Christian Debate* (Princeton, NJ: Princeton University Press, 1992), 200–202; David G. Hunter, "Vigilantius of Calagurris and Victricius of Rouen: Ascetics, Relics, and Clerics in Late Roman Gaul", *JECS* 7 (1999), 401–430; Trout, *Paulinus of Nola*, 121–132; and Mratschek, *Der Briefwechsel*, 517–547. August. *Epist.* 186, from AD 416, expresses concern about Paulinus' links to those involved in the Pelagian controversy; according to the uncertain report in Genn. *uir. ill.* 19, Sulpicius was later supposed to have been 'deceived by the Pelagians': see Stancliffe, *St Martin*, 15–16.

23 I would like to thank Christa Gray for helping me to refine this point.

themselves.[24] We must keep in mind, however, that exemplarity is not a simple matter, and that these portraits are not simply self-portraits; at most, as Trout is careful to say, they allow Sulpicius and Paulinus to offer 'fragments and reflections of their own auto-biographies'.[25] It is important therefore to take seriously the distance both authors insist upon between their own lives and achievements and those of the saints they describe. Sulpicius is not only modest regarding his eloquence in the preface to the *Life of Martin*, but appears in the story itself as tongue-tied and inadequate in the presence of Martin and Paulinus; for his part, Paulinus deflects the attempts of Sulpicius to equate him with Martin—and even to have Martin openly praise him—and, famously, makes a show of his reluctance to be coupled with Martin as a pair of actual portraits on the walls of the baptistery planned by Sulpicius.[26]

At the same time, taking these protestations seriously need not mean accepting them at face value. In the last example, Catherine Conybeare presents Paulinus as merely 'affect[ing] a tone of horror' at the intended compliment of being memorialised next to Martin. As this suggests, the character of his response is rather more complex than a simple refusal: he gives Sulpicius his blessing to go ahead with the portraits, and readily provides the accompanying verses for which he had been asked. His contribution is to draw the contrast sharply between himself and Martin, in terms which are ostensibly humble but which are so overdrawn as to amount to a kind of comic irony—as Conybeare too seems to recognise, in adding an exclamation mark to her paraphrase: 'Obviously Martin's face is there as an example, and his own as a terrible warning!'[27]

Hence it is important to remain alive to the humour and ambivalence of this exchange, and this might be extended to the correspondence as a whole. In particular, it should be noted that we see the same dynamic from both sides: Sulpicius not only praises Paulinus to the skies, only for Paulinus to deflect the praise, but Paulinus in turn is extravagant in his praise for Sulpicius, who is

24 Dennis E. Trout, "*Amicitia, Auctoritas*, and Self-fashioning Texts: Paulinus of Nola and Sulpicius Severus", *Studia Patristica* 28 (1993), 123–129, at 125: these episodes 'served to legitimate Severus's own conversion by appealing to the personal influence and persuasive examples of both Martin and Paulinus'; cf. 126: Paulinus' portrait of Melania 'overtly and subtly promoted the author and his friends together with the work's subject'. A similar emphasis on these two characters as exemplars of the ascetic life may be found in Conybeare, *Paulinus Noster*, 17.

25 Trout, "*Amicitia*", 123.

26 Sulp. Sev. *Mart.* 25; Paul. Nol. *Epist.* 32.5. Sulpicius' modesty is read as submissiveness in Virginia Burrus, *The Sex Lives of Saints: An Erotics of Ancient Hagiography* (Philadelphia: University of Pennsylvania Press, 2004), 94–96, 102.

27 Conybeare, *Paulinus Noster*, 108, 109; Paul. Nol. *Epist.* 32.3–4.

implied in the replies to his letters to be equally modest in response. Their relationship is built out of this kind of back-and-forth, which is visible throughout but receives explicit comment in the opening of Paulinus' *Letter* 24:

> Whether I call to mind your comments about yourself, as you seek with false censure to lessen your burdens, or those about me, as you increase my burdens with unjustified praise, I shall convict you of sinning against charity from motives of charity. ... As I have said, the palm of perfection would be apposite for yourself; so why should you presume to ascribe it to me as though the contest were already fought and I were victorious ...?[28]

Paulinus consistently positions himself in this way: he praises to the skies the achievements of others—whether the famous desert ascetics, as in his early letter to Ausonius, or friends and even strangers such as Amandus and Augustine—while denying that he himself deserves the praise that continues to come his way.[29] It does not constitute an insistence that perfection cannot be achieved by mere mortals: after all, Sulpicius is offered the palm. He simply refuses to claim it for himself, or to allow it to be attributed to him.

The apparent humility of Paulinus here has regularly inspired debate, in particular over whether or not it is sincere. For a long time its sincerity was insisted upon: most influentially by Pierre Fabre, who specifically read disavowals such as that above as the mark of a disappointed man who had found ascetic progress more difficult than he imagined.[30] W.H.C. Frend also saw these letters as both painfully sincere and 'deeply self-revelatory'.[31] But doubts about the true extent of Paulinus' humility have increasingly been raised. Dennis Trout, in relation to Paulinus' refusal of ordination and his expressed desire to start at the lowest level of the clerical hierarchy, makes the cautious obser-

28 Paul. Nol. *Epist.* 24.1: *sive enim ea reputem quae de te, sive illa quae de nobis loqueris, onera nostra iniustis laudibus cumulans, tua falsis vituperationibus minuens, arguam te in caritatem de caritate peccare. ... quae te apud te ipsum, ut dixi, conveniat, cur audeas nobis ut decertato agone victoribus palmam perfectionis adscribere ...* Elsewhere, Paulinus rejects Sulpicius' praise and turns it back on its source on numerous occasions: e.g. Paul. Nol. *Epist.* 5.4 and 23.3. Translations of Paulinus taken from Patrick G. Walsh, *Letters of St. Paulinus of Nola* (Westminster, MD: Newmann Press/London: Longmans, Green, and Co., 1966–1967).

29 Trout, *Paulinus of Nola*, 129–123, plus 181–182 on Paul. Nol. *Carm.* 10.181–184, in response to Ausonius.

30 Pierre Fabre, *Saint Paulin de Nole et l'Amitié chrétienne* (Paris: E. de Boccard, 1949), 287, 307–308.

31 William H.C. Frend, "The Two Worlds of Paulinus of Nola", in James W. Binns (ed.), *Latin Literature of the Fourth Century* (London: Routledge and Kegan Paul, 1974), 100–133, at 119.

vation that 'Paulinus's humility was not necessarily disingenuous ...'—which is of course to concede that at first glance it looks very much as though it was.[32] Other scholars have questioned the sincerity of Paulinus' ascetic renunciation precisely on the basis of his acknowledged failure to achieve it. Sigrid Mratschek, for instance, observes that Paulinus led an 'abstemious but not strongly ascetic way of life', and has demonstrated that he continued to operate in elite circles of visitation and patronage.[33] This is developed by Richard Goodrich into something close to a charge of hypocrisy: emphasising the presence of slaves in the household, he argues that Paulinus was not only far from the ascetic model as we might imagine it, but had in fact scarcely broken free from his previous aristocratic way of life.[34] Either way, Paulinus stands accused of pretending either that he is in serious pursuit of perfection, or else that his chosen lifestyle would not stand in the way of that pursuit.

Mratschek concludes that Paulinus' rejection of praise was a deliberate pose, better understood as 'a modesty topos' than as true self-criticism.[35] But the point is not simply to replace humility (presumably genuine) with modesty (presumably false), and so to convict Paulinus on the charge of hypocrisy, but to understand his use of the topos in the context of a classical letter-exchange. Indeed, the very fact that Paulinus' living conditions at Nola, like those of Sulpicius at Primuliacum, combined a considerable austerity with 'long-familiar patterns of elite behavior' is a clue to the possibility of understanding this attitude in relation to correspondence in a classical mode.[36] In this connection, I think it is necessary to qualify the view of David Konstan that these letters in particular articulate and enact a new Christian understanding of literary friendship,

32 Trout, *Paulinus of Nola*, 94.

33 Mratschek, *Der Briefwechsel*, 109: 'ein enthaltsames, aber kein streng asketisches Leben'; cf. esp. Sigrid Mratschek, "*Multis enim notissima et sanctitas loci*: Paulinus and the Gradual Rise of Nola as a Center of Christian Hospitality", *JECS* 9 (2001), 511–554; and Sigrid Mratschek, "A Living Relic for the Vicar of Rome: Strategies of Visualization in a Civil Case", in Lieve Van Hoof and Peter Van Nuffelen (eds.), *Literature and Society in the Fourth Century AD: Performing Paideia, Constructing the Present, Presenting the Self* (Leiden: Brill, 2015), 134–156.

34 Richard J. Goodrich, *Contextualizing Cassian: Aristocrats, Asceticism, and Reformation in Fifth-Century Gaul* (Oxford: Oxford University Press, 2007), 192–197.

35 Mratschek, *Der Briefwechsel*, 425: 'Die Abwehr der *falsa praeconia* ... war ... eher ein Bescheidenheitstopos, um christliche Demut zu zeigen, als echte Selbstkritik'.

36 Trout, *Paulinus of Nola*, 135; cf. 145: 'Paulinus endorses a partial détente between an ascetic impulse perceived as subversive of traditional elite values and aristocratic families still deeply imbued with those values'. See also Joseph T. Lienhard, *Paulinus of Nola and Early Western Monasticism* (Cologne/Bonn: Peter Haustein, 1977), 98: Sulpicius 'does not appear to have undertaken a life of poverty so severe as Paulinus's' (!).

in which the ostensible equality of classical correspondents—often achieved by open condescension—is replaced by an abject self-abasement.[37] Certainly there are many ostentatious displays of humility in these letters, especially from Paulinus, who at times indeed presents himself as hopelessly inferior to his correspondents and wholly dependent on their charity in even including him in their circle. But we can suspect, as Konstan does, that Paulinus did not himself take this stance too seriously, and that his correspondents were no less capable readers than we are today.[38] The new language in which Christian authors talked about friendship, especially in the abstract, should not lead us to disregard the continuities in their practice.

And what we see is in fact a model of epistolary exchange which appears to presume a basic equality, or at least reciprocity.[39] What this means is that Paulinus' show of humility did not establish a permanent position as his correspondent's inferior; as we have seen, Sulpicius responded by adopting the same rhetoric in turn, so that he praised Paulinus while making himself in turn an abject sinner. The result is an exchange in which both parties take it in turns to take on the inferior role, only to return to the superior role when they receive the reply. Thus it is through the exchange of letters, rather than in any single letter, that each is able to assure the other of their essential virtue. The overall effect is not of abjection but, as in so many classical correspondences, of a mutual admiration society. It is a civilised game of one-upmanship—or rather one-downmanship—recognisable to any reader of Stephen Potter, and it is certainly not without precedent in the classical world.[40] We might see it in Pliny the Younger's representation of his relationship to Tacitus; it is also reminiscent of the letters between Cicero and Pae-

37 Thus David Konstan, "Problems in the History of Christian Friendship", *JECS* 4 (1996), 87–113, esp. 101: 'Christian humility ... disrupts the classical ideal of friendship based on equality of virtue'.

38 Konstan, "Problems", 100: 'To the extent that Paulinus takes seriously his protestations of his unworthiness ...'—a concession which allows us to suppose that the change may be merely to the *rhetoric* of friendship.

39 Conybeare, *Paulinus Noster*, 66–67; cf. 90, noting that Paulinus all the same 'never uses hierarchical language in addressing those whom he considers to be his friends'; although the point is not that classical authors used hierarchical language but that they condescended to their inferiors—lowering their own status in recognition of the permanently low status of their correspondents. In these letters, on the contrary, both parties aim to lower their own status while raising that of their correspondent. For this language of status in analysing interactions in dramatic scenes, see the discussion of Keith Johnstone, *Impro: Improvisation and the Theatre* (London: Methuen, 1979), 33–74.

40 Some relevant techniques are conveniently set out in Stephen Potter, *One-Upmanship* (London: Rupert Hart-Davis, 1952).

tus.[41] Cicero there engages in ready philosophical banter, and in general represents his correspondent as (generally) far more learned and committed to his philosophical views than Cicero himself.[42] But we should certainly not suppose that Cicero imagined himself to be greatly deficient as a philosopher, or that he was uncommitted to his philosophical interests; and we should probably suppose that Paetus wrote equally playful and equally flattering letters in return.[43]

This jokey one-upmanship, in Cicero and Pliny as much as in the letters of Paulinus, relies on the fundamental point that the correspondents are engaged in a common project, to which their commitment can be taken for granted. The sense of this common project is palpable in Paulinus' letters to Sulpicius, as well as elsewhere in his correspondence: for example, in his eagerness to have himself included in the circles of Jerome and Augustine and other like-minded figures.[44] To Jerome he presented himself as a literary man and a keen student of scripture, before seeking advice on the question of whether he could serve as both priest and monk.[45] Similarly, he would later flatter Augustine by styling him as his spiritual superior and guide.[46] In neither case was the approach well received: Jerome seems to have resented his recruitment into Paulinus' (potentially dubious) project, while Augustine in his response explicitly rejected what he seems to have interpreted as false modesty: thus 'you answered quite well if it were not for the fact that you chose to consult me about what you either are ignorant about along with me or know along with

41 Pliny's relationship to Tacitus focuses less on serious matters than on those he preferred to treat with disdain: hunting in Plin. *Epist.* 1.6, and literary fame in Plin. *Epist.* 9.23 (not to Tacitus, but with Pliny coupling their names). Note in this connection Christopher Whitton, "'Let us tread our path together': Tacitus and the Younger Pliny", in Victoria E. Pagán (ed.), *A Companion to Tacitus* (Chichester: Blackwell, 2012), 345–368, esp. 347 on the modern 'vindication of epistolography as a genre, and of Pliny as a writer, where professions of humility are not to be taken literally'.

42 Thus Cic. *Fam.* 9.18 compares the idea of his teaching *principia* to Paetus to the proverbial pig teaching Minerva; 9.20 disclaims the praise of his guests; 9.15 offers extravagant praise of Paetus.

43 For these letters as serious in intent, see Sean McConnell, *Philosophical Life in Cicero's Letters* (Cambridge: Cambridge University Press, 2014), 162, esp. n. 9, identifying Cicero's 'exploitation of indirect and subtle modes of drawing attention to and discussing frankly serious matters'.

44 Thus Conybeare, *Paulinus Noster*, 6–7 notes Paulinus' range of contacts, as well as the 'political adroitness' that allowed him to remain on terms simultaneously with both Jerome and Rufinus of Aquileia.

45 These approaches from Paulinus do not survive, but the content of the correspondence can be inferred from the replies of Jerome, *Epp.* 53, 58: see Trout, *Paulinus of Nola*, 90–101.

46 Paul. Nol. *Epist.* 45.4 [= August. *Epist.* 94.4].

me or perhaps know better than I do'.[47] What Dennis Trout calls the 'curiosities and ambivalences' of Jerome's response, and the not untypically pained sincerity of Augustine's reply to Paulinus, throw into relief the relaxed and civilised tone of the correspondence with Sulpicius. Whereas Sulpicius rejects the praises applied to himself but nevertheless returns them in kind, Jerome and Augustine both direct Paulinus towards the difficulties and dangers of the pursuit of ascetic perfection. Their understanding of the aim of the game was riddled with qualifications and doubts, and hence they were less willing to play along.

In fact, the carefully modulated and non-specific claims made as part of the exchange between Paulinus and Sulpicius may represent a more subtle stance than that envisaged by Jerome in his admonition to Paulinus: that 'to be a Christian is the great thing, not merely to seem one', and that 'there is nothing great in wearing a sad or disfigured face, in simulating and in showing off fasts, or in wearing a cheap cloak while you retain a large income'.[48] The lesson may well have been taken on board by Paulinus, who avoids these clichés of the aristocratic ascetic by inverting them: as we shall see, he frankly admits to his comfortable lifestyle, his difficulty in fasting, even his enjoyment of a lambswool tunic; and he repeatedly points up his struggles to commit wholeheartedly to the life of a monk. Rather than claiming to be more virtuous than he was, he claimed to be *less* virtuous: in the knowledge, perhaps, that to claim too much is to invite the reader's doubts, whereas to claim too little is to recruit their sympathies. It would be a rare reader who took the conspicuous modesty of Paulinus as a sign of his inadequacy as an ascetic. On the contrary, the vignettes in which he shows off his failings are better read as examples of irony and humour.

47 August. *Epist.* 95.2: *sed bene mihi respondisti, ... nisi quod me consulere voluisti, quod aut mecum nescis, aut mecum scis, aut magis quam ego forsitan scis*; cf. 95.5, in which Augustine qualifies his implicit praise of Paulinus' ascetic achievements by extending to him the uncertainty and provisionality of which he is very aware in his own efforts: *inde ergo interrogavi quid sentias, quasi huius vitae recta regula retenta atque servata iam securi simus, cum in tam multis, maximeque in his quae breviter, ut potui, commemoravi, periculosissime laborare me sentiam.* Translation from Roland J. Teske, *The Works of Saint Augustine: A Translation for the 21st Century. Letters* (New York: New City Press, 2001).

48 Jer. *Epist.* 58.7 (tr. NPNF): *esse Christianum grande est, non videre*; 58.2: *nihil est enim grande tristi et lurida facie uel simulare uel ostentare ieiunia, possessionum reditibus abundare et vile iactare palliolum.* For discussion of this letter see Trout, *Paulinus of Nola*, 96.

2 Gentleman Amateurs

The wittiness of Paulinus' letters to Sulpicius has previously been remarked by Catherine Conybeare, although her observations are largely restricted to instances of wordplay—which is admittedly the form of wit most easily identified in a literary text.[49] But even in the very letters she cites for the wittiness of their language and allusion, it seems possible to see in addition an element of humour: actual jokes, intended not just to be appreciated, but to make the reader laugh. Thus Paulinus' *Letter* 23 reports to Sulpicius on the presence of Victor, a monk from Sulpicius' establishment, and a former companion of Martin and his great disciple Clarus. Victor here is famously compared not only to Martin and Clarus but also to Christ, and we must suppose that this is very far from a joke, and may indeed seem forbiddingly serious.[50] But the extravagant comparison also serves as the set-up for self-deprecation, as Paulinus finds himself placed in a seemingly subordinate role in his ascetic community; and yet one which ironically reinforces his social superiority in the household as traditionally composed. The scene begins from Paulinus' admission that Victor, in true imitation of Christ, insisted on serving him, and indeed requested to wash his feet and even his sandals.[51] This was an act with real resonance for both Paulinus and Sulpicius, recalling as it did not only the actions of Christ but those of Martin when Sulpicius had first met him: and on that occasion too Sulpicius reports that he had lacked the will to resist, and had even supposed that it might be an insult to do so.[52]

Paulinus, perhaps with this uncomfortable example in mind, feels likewise obliged to apologise for his acceptance of this service from Victor; and although he explicitly justifies it as enabling Victor's own virtuous action, and by recasting himself not as the master of the household but instead as a mere disciple, it is hard to believe that the social comedy entirely escapes him:

> But I confess that once (and once only) I followed the example of the apostles in the washing of feet. I have read that they offered their feet to be washed by the Lord who attended them. ... [Indeed,] once they had

49 Conybeare, *Paulinus Noster*, 109, 123, in both of which the example is the excursus on hair in Paul. Nol. *Epist.* 23.

50 Paul. Nol. *Epist.* 23.3; see Conybeare, *Paulinus Noster*, 123 and Mratschek, *Der Briefwechsel*, 304, 322.

51 Paul. Nol. *Epist.* 23.4.

52 Sulp. Sev. *Mart.* 25.3: *ad vesperum autem pedes nobis ipse abluit, nec reniti aut contra ire constantia fuit; ita auctoritate oppressus sum, ut nefas putarem, si non acquievissem.*

> understood the mystery of this great gift and realised the greatness of the blessing, those who had hesitated to proffer their feet when He first prepared to minister to them finally asked that not only their feet but their whole bodies be washed from head to foot. I too revered the Lord Jesus in my brother Victor, for every faithful soul is of God, and he who is humble in heart is the heart of Christ; and I confess that to heal my weakness I begged my fellow servant, a better man than me, to rub me with oil or water. …[53]

Baldly understood, this presents Paulinus as at first resistant to having his feet washed, but eventually conceding and finding a good biblical precedent for his predicament. Left at that, this might have been a story of Victor's virtue enabled by Paulinus; but some doubts might be raised by the rapidity with which he overcomes his reluctance and submits to a full-body massage, which immediately receives a glowing review: 'I did not fail to obtain the anticipated help, for the oil, as if invested with healing properties by his holy hands, seeped into my marrow all the more smoothly because of the gentleness of the application, and the bones that had been humbled rejoiced'.[54] This may suggest a stunning lack of self-awareness, or perhaps a rather sly irony. Richard Goodrich prefers the first, looking askance at the scene and commenting wryly that Paulinus 'frequently cultivated merit in this way'.[55] But the search for a biblical justification, and the hedging around and confessional language, suggests self-consciousness more than obliviousness; and hence neither true humility nor entitled arrogance, but a kind of comic self-deprecation.

This impression is further reinforced by the anecdote which immediately follows, and which Paulinus explicitly links with the comment that it will show how Victor tended to his bodily needs. Victor has taken over the duties of chef and has produced a millet gruel which met his own high standards of frugality; and which Paulinus praises, while admitting that he could barely stomach

53 Paul. Nol. *Epist.* 23.5: *sed de pedibus lavandis tantum semel fateor apostolico me exemplo cessisse, quos legeram pedes suos lavandos servienti domino praebuisse. … unde perspecto muneris tanti mysterio et intellecta boni magnitudine qui primo ministrantis apparatu pedes offerre trepidaverant iam non pedes tantum sed totos se usque ad caput perlui rogaverunt. et ego dominum Iesum in fratro Victore, quia omnis anima fidelis ex deo et humilis corde cor Christo est, fateor, ad remedium infirmitatis, ut oleo me vel aqua melior conservus adtingeret.*

54 Paul. Nol. *Epist.* 23.5: *nec inritus fui praesumptae opis; nam quasi medicatum manibus piis oleum de ipsi unguenti mansuetudine mihi lenius in medullas perlapsum est, et exultaverunt ossa humiliata.*

55 Goodrich, *Contextualizing Cassian*, 195.

this unappetising meal.[56] The letter makes a point of the proper frugality of the dish, and of Victor's status as 'a truly spiritual cook, more expert in feeding the inner man'—for which purpose he took care to remove all the more appealing elements of the recipe.[57] It also follows the pattern of the foot washing scene by appealing to scriptural precedent, specifically in the hotch-potch cooked by Ezekiel at God's command; and notes the small mercy that Victor did not quite follow the divine recipe, for the unaccustomed mix of ingredients would have led the pot itself to rebel and crack from side to side.[58] The comic tone is all but unmistakeable, as indeed others have remarked.[59] One final extract from this story will give the flavour:

> [H]e filled a large pot ... and brought in to me steaming bowls emitting a strong smell, smoking out with the stinking vapour not only the surroundings of my modest board but also the whole area of my little room. To increase the blessing conferred on me, he bestowed on my table the meal of another prophet as well, for he brought to me the pot of Eliseus into which he had put some meal [*farinam*]. No poisonous herb had he boiled in it, but the seasoning of salvation, carrying out each of his actions in the name of the Lord; hence I felt safe and untroubled, and I did not cry out to him: *Death is in the pot, O man of God* ...[60]

The language is elevated, but it is difficult to escape the sense that Paulinus is poking fun at himself for his failure to live up to his ideals as effectively as his guest. There is some good-natured teasing of Victor, and of the old rustic who helps in the kitchen and who loves this sort of simple fare; and as for Pauli-

56 Paul. Nol. *Epist.* 23.6–9.

57 Paul. Nol. *Epist.* 23.6: *verum spiritalis coquus interiorem hominem cibare doctius.*

58 Paul. Nol. *Epist.* 23.7: *nam homo sanctus fideli cautione metuisset aliquid nobis de scriptura sancta subtrahere, et ut totum iuxta dei verbum confectionem prophetici panis inpleret, lentem quoque et hordeum et viciam miscuisset in crumilum, ut aestuantibus extra sui labra fervoribus dissimilum sibi fructuum quasi repugnante coctura fatiscens rimis olla crepitaret.*

59 Thus Mratschek, *Der Briefwechsel*, 322 recognises the humour of the situation, which 'ihn aber derart amüsierte, daß er ihr drei lange Kapitel eines Briefe widmete'; cf. Frend, "Two Worlds", 121 on Victor as providing 'an element of comic relief in Paulinus' correspondence'.

60 Paul. Nol. *Epist.* 23.7 (tr. Walsh): *nihilominus tamen de paucioribus frugibus testam capacem replens intulit nobis multo nidore catina fumantia totumque non solum mensulae nostrae ambitum sed et cellulae nostrae spatium olida caligine vaporavit atque ut multiplicaret nobis benedictionem, alterius quoque prophetae prandium cenulae nostrae contulit, ut Elisaei nobis ollam inferret, in quam misit farinam; nec herbam veneni sed condimentum salutis incoxit, in nomine domini gerens omne quod agebat. quo tuti atque securi non exclamavimus ad eum: 'homo dei, mors in olla'* ...

nus himself, the portrait is not self-lacerating but lightly ironic. He presents himself, in comparison to Victor, as merely a dilettante; his pose is that of a gentleman amateur confronted with a true professional. And given that the regimes at Nola and Primuliacum were not too dissimilar, we may suppose that he expected some sympathy from Sulpicius. Paulinus—in the letters—does not really bemoan his inability to lead an ideal ascetic existence: what he offers instead is merely the recognition that he is by his nature bound to come up short.

A final example of how Paulinus' self-deprecation may not be meant too seriously comes in the letter he sends to Sulpicius reporting Melania's visit. He begins by acknowledging a gift of camel-hair cloaks Sulpicius has sent him, designed to be as uncomfortable as possible. Paulinus, quite typically, gives in response an extended exegesis of biblical stories related to camels and camel-hair garments, from David to John the Baptist to the camel who could not pass through the eye of a needle.[61] More than that, he expresses gratitude to Sulpicius for such a gift which ensures that he will be constantly pricked and prompted towards humility; and he notes that such a reminder is an essential guard against the sin of pride, and an essential push towards self-accusation.[62] After four paragraphs of this, he notes that he is sending a gift in return: a tunic, which 'suits your blameless life, being woven from soft lambswool which soothes the skin with its touch'.[63] Commentary on this episode has usually focused on the fact that this gift was from Melania herself, and that Paulinus has already worn it; as such, it serves to incorporate Sulpicius into an authoritative ascetic tradition.[64] It is quite possible that it alludes to the famous example of the passing of an ascetic mantle between Antony and Athanasius in the *Life of Antony*, which in turn was intended to bring to mind the prophet Elisha's taking up of the mantle of Elijah.[65]

But as presented by Paulinus it surely has the form of a joke. Paulinus exchanges the lambswool tunic he has been wearing for a camel-hair cloak, in order to be reminded constantly of his imperfections; and he passes it on

61 Paul. Nol. *Epist.* 29.1–2.

62 Paul. Nol. *Epist.* 29.3.

63 Paul. Nol. *Epist.* 29.5: *nam vel hoc innocentiae tuae congruit, quod de tenero agnorum vellere contexta blanditur adtactibus.*

64 Conybeare, *Paulinus Noster*, 30–31 notes the exchange but makes nothing of the difference in the gifts; Mratschek, *Der Briefwechsel*, 427–432 notes that both the camel-hair cloak and Melania's tunic incorporate the receiver into the wider ascetic community, but does not comment on the imbalanced exchange in this instance.

65 2 Kings 2:13; Athan. *V. Anton.* 91; see also the comments on this tradition by Ross in this volume.

to Sulpicius, who has no need of such a reminder, being already perfect. The dynamic of extravagant praise, on the one hand, and self-deprecation on the other, is neatly encapsulated in this exchange. Sulpicius' gift allows Paulinus to own his ascetic ideals, and to confess, apparently shamefacedly, that he has not been living up to them; on the other hand, he is glad to acknowledge Sulpicius—wholly seriously, it seems—as an ascetic whose status does not require that he wear an uncomfortable garment.[66] The gift-exchange is undoubtedly sincere, and so are the ascetic ideals; but Paulinus can still poke fun at his aristocratic lifestyle without abandoning it entirely—Sulpicius, after all, is conclusive proof that it is no barrier to ascetic perfection.

3 Conclusion

By adopting this playful and ironic tone, Paulinus could disarm criticism of his failure to live up to his ideals, but without ever quite abandoning those ideals. The pose of a gentleman amateur, after all, allows for a real commitment to fundamental principles and values, even if these are laughed off in conversation. Cicero's letters to Paetus provide a very similar example: in a manner reminiscent of Paulinus, Cicero confesses that his stomach is far too sensitive to tolerate the philosophical diet of Paetus, which in theory he approves.[67] But this should hardly lead us to suppose that he was not sincere in his philosophy—nor, we should keep in mind, that he believed his limitations to be as great as he pretends. Paulinus too is taking advantage of the privilege of a gentleman to take serious matters lightly: to approach them, at least in public, in a spirit of ironic detachment. The fact that he jokes about them does not preclude his being genuinely conscious of his flaws; but, at the same time, we should not imagine that this is the voice of despair, as Fabre supposed. His failures did not inspire him—as they did Augustine—to question whether the pursuit of perfection was really the proper aim. On the contrary, Paulinus remained (as Frend called him) a 'seeker after perfection', as his exhortations to Sulpicius and himself attest.[68] And his letters make clear that he was well aware

66 Thus Mratschek, *Der Briefwechsel*, 432: 'Die Übergabe an Sulpicius Severus machte diesen auch ohne unangenehme Selbstkasteiung zum anerkannten Asketen'.

67 Thus Cic. *Fam.* 9.16.

68 Frend, "Two Worlds", 127; for examples of Paulinus' commitment to the pursuit of perfection, see e.g. Paul. Nol. *Epist.* 1.9; 11.12–13; 23.18; 24.5–7, 15, 21; in the latter case note also the comment of Mratschek, *Der Briefwechsel*, 425 n. 61, that only at the end of this long letter 'bezeichnete sich Paulinus definitiv als "*non perfectus*"'.

that even the limited austerity of his chosen lifestyle stacked up well against his peers. Thus he aligns himself with Melania, in his account of her visit to Nola, against her other relatives who admired her and yet clung to their luxurious lifestyles and appurtenances.[69] We see it also in his disdain for monks in name only, such as Marracinus, a letter-carrier known to both Paulinus and Sulpicius, who comes in for vitriolic criticism: a criticism which of course only implies that they themselves are proving more successful in their asceticism.[70]

Nevertheless, this pursuit of perfection was kept apart from the dangers of self-praise by Paulinus' refusal to affirm any exalted status for himself. Praise of his chosen lifestyle is instead displaced on to others, both in his praise of Sulpicius and other contemporaries and in the praise he receives from them. The strategy of praising others in order that this might be reflected back on oneself can be found in Pliny the Younger, for whom 'whether your own performance is better or worse or on a par, you should show your appreciation; for if your superior does not meet with applause neither will you, and it is in your own interest that anyone you equal or surpass should be well received.'[71] As for the praise he receives, even his rejection of it draws attention to it: given the loss of Sulpicius' letters, we would never know about his praises of Paulinus if the latter did not regularly refer to it. But he can acknowledge it while displaying a proper modesty in rejecting it, leaving the reader stranded between the ascetic perfection claimed for Paulinus by others, and the catalogue of failings he offers up to show how far he remains from that ultimate aim. A charitable reader (such as Augustine) could conclude that Paulinus knew well that perfection was impossible to achieve.[72] But this is to look at Paulinus' presentation of himself in isolation, and to overlook his praise of Sulpicius precisely as having achieved perfection. The effect of the correspondence as a whole

69 Paul. Nol. *Epist.* 29.12: 'the rich marvelled at this poor saint whilst our poverty mocked them'; Melania as 'my sister in poverty'; cf. 13 and the emphasis on the difference between the two types of guest.

70 Paul. Nol. *Epist.* 22.

71 Plin. *Epist.* 6.17.4: *sive plus sive minus sive idem praestas, lauda vel inferiorem vel superiorem vel parem: superiorem quia nisi laudandus ille non potes ipse laudari, inferiorem aut parem quia pertinet ad tuam gloriam quam maximum videri, quem praecedis vel exaequas.* Translation from Betty Radice, *The Letters of the Younger Pliny* (West Drayton: Penguin, 1975). Note the comments of Roy K. Gibson, "Pliny and the Art of (In)offensive Self-Praise", *Arethusa* 36 (2003), 235–254, at 251–252, although I am bound to disagree with his assertion (at 237) that 'self-effacement is not regarded as a virtue at any stage of pagan classical culture'—itself undermined in his footnote by the suspicion of irony in the cited source.

72 This is the reading proposed in August. *Epist.* 186.40, which cites Paulinus' letters back to him as a way of assuring him of distance from the ideas of Pelagius.

is found in this double voice, and in the reader's reconstruction of the reality behind the insistent self-deprecation. Perhaps the praise was excessive on both sides; so too, perhaps, was its ritual rejection. But in proffering both, Paulinus and Sulpicius committed themselves to neither. And in an age in which ascetic claims were very much open to contest, this was perhaps what allowed them to keep their own lifestyles, for the most part, free of criticism and controversy.

The edifying anecdote is arguably the basis of hagiography, and in the letters between Paulinus and Sulpicius we see plenty of anecdotes which promote the saintliness of others. Yet it seems more difficult to claim these letters as examples of autohagiography, given that many of the anecdotes Paulinus tells about himself are at least unflattering if not unedifying. It might also perhaps be objected that scattered stories do not constitute a hagiography, which seems to demand a more continuous narrative. But if this is the effect of reading individual letters, it may be proposed that something different occurs when we read them as a collection—which in this case means overcoming the absence of Sulpicius' letters and imagining as best we can the implicit relationship constituted by the whole correspondence.[73] To do this allows the reader to look beyond the unedifying surface of each individual anecdote and to glimpse the overall effect: of two correspondents fiercely committed to their common ascetic project, modest in assessing their own achievements but generous in praising the other, and in this way living up precisely to the demands of a life of renunciation. As it is in the *Life of Martin*, Paulinus' saintliness is something of an informed attribute: in his passing appearance there, Paulinus does nothing to draw attention to himself, and his status as an example to all relies on his being praised as such by the narrator and subsequently by Martin.[74] The hagiography of Paulinus emerges only in the contrast between his modest appearance and his celebrated status. It is his refusal to act in a way that openly invites approbation that, perversely, entitles him to it.

---

73 Some remarks on such an enterprise are offered in Greg Woolf, "Pliny/Trajan and the Poetics of Empire", *CPh* 110 (2015), 132–151, at 147: in particular, it is worth noting that a correspondence develops themes more disparately and implicitly than might be the case in a narrative form both less disjointed and more under a single author's control. I am grateful to James Corke-Webster for pointing out this reference.

74 Sulp. Sev. *Mart.* 19, 25.

Bibliography

Barnes, Timothy D., "Panegyric, History and Historiography in Eusebius' *Life of Constantine*", in Rowan Williams (ed.), *The Making of Orthodoxy: Essays in Honour of Henry Chadwick* (Cambridge: Cambridge University Press, 1989), 94–123.

Barnes, Timothy D., "The Two Drafts of Eusebius' *Vita Constantini*", in idem, *From Eusebius to Augustine: Selected Papers 1982–1993* (Aldershot: Variorum, 1994), XII.

Burrus, Virginia, *The Sex Lives of Saints: An Erotics of Ancient Hagiography* (Philadelphia: University of Pennsylvania Press, 2004).

Cain, Andrew, *The Letters of Jerome: Asceticism, Biblical Exegesis, and the Construction of Christian Authority in Late Antiquity* (Oxford: Oxford University Press, 2009).

Cameron, Averil, "Form and Meaning: The *Vita Constantini* and the *Vita Antonii*", in Tomas Hägg and Philip Rousseau (eds.), *Greek Biography and Panegyric in Late Antiquity* (Berkeley/Los Angeles: University of California Press, 2000), 72–88.

Cavadini, John C., "Pride", in Allan D. Fitzgerald (ed.), *Augustine Through the Ages: An Encyclopedia* (Grand Rapids, MI: Eerdmans, 1999), 679–684.

Clark, Elizabeth, *The Origenist Controversy: The Cultural Construction of an Early Christian Debate* (Princeton: Princeton University Press, 1992).

Conybeare, Catherine, *Paulinus Noster: Self and Symbols in the Letters of Paulinus of Nola* (Oxford: Oxford University Press, 2000).

Ebbeler, Jennifer, *Disciplining Christians: Correction and Community in Augustine's Letters* (Oxford: Oxford University Press, 2012).

Fabre, Pierre, *Saint Paulin de Nole et l'amitié chrétienne* (Paris: E. de Boccard, 1949).

Freccero, John, "Autobiography and Narrative", in Thomas C. Heller, Morton Sosua, and David E. Wellbery (eds.), *Reconstructing Individualism: Autonomy, Individuality, and the Self in Western Thought* (Stanford, CA: Stanford University Press, 1986), 16–29.

Frend, William H.C., "The Two Worlds of Paulinus of Nola", in James W. Binns (ed.), *Latin Literature of the Fourth Century* (London: Routledge and Kegan Paul, 1974), 100–133.

Gibson, Roy K., "Pliny and the Art of (In)offensive Self-Praise", *Arethusa* 36 (2003), 235–254.

Goodrich, Richard J., *Contextualizing Cassian: Aristocrats, Asceticism, and Reformation in Fifth-Century Gaul* (Oxford: Oxford University Press, 2007).

Hall, Jon, *Politeness and Politics in Cicero's Letters* (Oxford: Oxford University Press, 2009).

Hermanowicz, Erika, *Possidius of Calama: A Study of the North African Episcopate in the Age of Augustine* (Oxford: Oxford University Press, 2008).

Hoffer, Stanley E., *The Anxieties of Pliny the Younger* (New York: Oxford University Press, 1999).

Hunter, David G., "Vigilantius of Calagurris and Victricius of Rouen: Ascetics, Relics, and Clerics in Late Roman Gaul", *JECS* 7 (1999), 401–430.

Johnstone, Keith, *Impro: Improvisation and the Theatre* (London: Methuen, 1979).

Konstan, David, "Problems in the History of Christian Friendship", *JECS* 4 (1996), 87–113.

Lienhard, Joseph T., *Paulinus of Nola and Early Western Monasticism* (Cologne/Bonn: Peter Haustein, 1977).

Luongo, Gennaro, *Lo specchio dell'agiografo* (Naples: Nuove Edizioni Tempi Moderni 1992).

McConnell, Sean, *Philosophical Life in Cicero's Letters* (Cambridge: Cambridge University Press, 2014).

Mratschek, Sigrid, "*Multis enim notissima et sanctitas loci*: Paulinus and the Gradual Rise of Nola as a Center of Christian Hospitality", *JECS* 9 (2001), 511–554.

Mratschek, Sigrid, *Der Briefwechsel des Paulinus von Nola. Kommunikation und soziale Kontakte zwischen christlichen Intellektuellen* (Göttingen: Vandenhoeck and Ruprecht, 2002).

Mratschek, Sigrid, "A Living Relic for the Vicar of Rome: Strategies of Visualization in a Civil Case", in Lieve Van Hoof and Peter Van Nuffelen (eds.), *Literature and Society in the Fourth Century AD: Performing Paideia, Constructing the Present, Presenting the Self* (Leiden: Brill, 2015), 134–156.

O'Donnell, James J., *Augustine: Confessions*, 3 vols. (Oxford: Clarendon Press, 1992).

Potter, Stephen, *One-Upmanship* (London: Rupert Hart-Davis, 1952).

Radice, Betty, *The Letters of the Younger Pliny* (West Drayton: Penguin, 1975).

Rubenson, Samuel, *The Letters of St Antony: Monasticism and the Making of a Saint* (Minneapolis, MN: Fortress Press, 1995).

Schafer, John, "Seneca's *Epistulae Morales* as Dramatized Education", *CPh* 106 (2011), 32–52.

Schroeder, Caroline T., *Monastic Bodies: Discipline and Salvation in Shenoute of Atripe* (Philadelphia: University of Pennsylvania Press, 2007).

Smith, Sidonie and Julia Watson, *Reading Autobiography: A Guide for Interpreting Life Narratives* (Minneapolis, MN: University of Minnesota Press, 2010).

Stancliffe, Clare, *St Martin and His Hagiographer: History and Miracle in Sulpicius Severus* (Oxford: Clarendon Press, 1983).

Teske, Roland J., *The Works of Saint Augustine: A Translation for the 21st Century. Letters* (New York: New City Press, 2001).

Trout, Dennis E., "*Amicitia, Auctoritas*, and Self-fashioning Texts: Paulinus of Nola and Sulpicius Severus", *Studia Patristica* 28 (1993), 123–129.

Trout, Dennis E., *Paulinus of Nola: Life, Letters, Poems* (Berkeley/Los Angeles: University of California Press, 1999).

Turner, Peter, *Truthfulness, Realism, Historicity: A Study in Late Antique Spiritual Literature* (Farnham: Ashgate, 2012).

Walsh, Patrick G. *Letters of St. Paulinus of Nola* (Westminster, MD: Newmann Press/London: Longmans, Green, and Co., 1966–1967).

Whitton, Christopher, "'Let us tread our path together': Tacitus and the Younger Pliny", in Victoria E. Pagán (ed.), *A Companion to Tacitus* (Chichester: Blackwell, 2012), 345–368.

Williams, Michael Stuart, "Augustine's *Confessions* as Autobiography", in Koen De Temmerman (ed.), *The Oxford Handbook of Ancient Biography* (Oxford: Oxford University Press, forthcoming).

Woolf, Greg, "Pliny/Trajan and the Poetics of Empire", *CPh* 110 (2015), 132–151.

CHAPTER 7

Hagiographical Compilation as Literature: Receiving Saints, Recrafting Heroes, Redeploying Theologies

Todd E. French

From the earliest standalone *vita*, organised to explore the details of an extraordinary person, hagiography underwent a significant shift to rather unwieldy collections of saintly material in the fourth through the early seventh centuries. This chapter examines how and why compilatory strategies were popularised in late antiquity. Building on the work of Patricia Cox Miller that explores the concept of collective biography as literature, this research will focus on the authorial advantages of compilatory practice and on the polyphonic possibilities that emerge in these late antique hagiographical sources.[1]

As the amount of saintly literature grew, so too did new communities of readers and hearers who thrived on the narratives of saints. The fascination with the desert and its offering of hidden sanctity and perceived holiness struck a chord with late antique Christians. Stories of those who had given all, as Jesus had suggested to the Rich Young Man, circulated broadly, capturing the imaginations of those who only seemed capable of giving a little.[2] The move to the desert is well-documented and profoundly interesting.[3] If the notion of *anachōrēsis* was 'in the air' of the third century in Egypt, the tales of holy persons were equally 'in the minds' of subsequent generations. Narratives that crafted and promulgated new subjectivities dominated Christian literary traditions.[4]

---

1 Patricia Cox Miller, "Strategies of Representation in Collective Biography: Constructing the Subject as Holy", in Tomas Hägg and Philip Rousseau (eds.), *Greek Biography and Panegyric in Late Antiquity* (Berkeley: University of California Press, 2000), 209–254. On exploring the influence and connection between the Christian and Greco-Roman forms of *vita*, see Averil Cameron, *Christianity and the Rhetoric of Empire: The Development of Christian Discourse* (Berkeley: University of California Press, 1991), 15–88.

2 Mark 10:21, Matthew 19:21, quoted prominently e.g. in Athanasius' *Life of Antony*, ch. 2.

3 Derwas J. Chitty, *The Desert a City: An Introduction to the Study of Egyptian and Palestinian Monasticism Under the Christian Empire* (Yonkers, NY: St Vladimir's Seminary Press, 1995).

4 On the notion of creating new subjectivities, see Richard Valantasis, "A Theory of the Social Function of Asceticism", in Vincent L. Wimbush and Richard Valantasis (eds.), *Asceticism* (New York: Oxford University Press, 1995), 549–550.

 | DOI:10.1163/9789004421332_009

As the stories proliferated of Christians willing to sacrifice all, so did the interest in recording and compiling their histories. This was mirrored by a burgeoning interest among late antique writers who hoped to capture histories, narratives, philosophies, laws, medical knowledge, etc., through encyclopaedic methods.[5] These often functioned in two ways, either a propaedeutic way or as a means of helping the reader to comprehend and order the world.[6] Encyclopaedic texts, like Pliny's *Naturalis Historia* or Vitruvius' *De Architectura*—to name just a few early examples—explore affinities for the wealth of knowledge available to their civilisation. These modes of compiling and structuring continue in all manner of subject areas over many centuries, eventually leading to the later medieval Christian figures Hildegard of Bingen and her *Physica* and *Causae et Curae*, and Hugh of Saint-Victor with his treatment of the arts in *Didascalicon*.[7] A general interest in collecting material from bygone eras appeared to be contagious.[8] Compilations of material had become a fashionable way of accumulating knowledge for various purposes ranging from medical inquiry to religious practice, and seem to have been the primary method for dealing with any topic that was not focused on the present.[9] Although the impetus varied

---

5 Note, for instance, the sustained effort of collection that was undertaken in law by Justinian and his legal staff. There is much more work to be done on the interaction between Justinian's law and the promulgation of saintly literature in the Byzantine empire. See Caroline Humfress, "Law and Legal Practice in the Age of Justinian", in Michael Maas (ed.), *The Cambridge Companion to the Age of Justinian* (Cambridge: Cambridge University Press, 2005), 161–184.

6 Many do both. See Marco Formisano, "Late Latin Encyclopaedism: Towards a New Paradigm of Practical Knowledge", in Jason König and Greg Woolf (eds.), *Encyclopaedism from Antiquity to the Renaissance* (Cambridge: Cambridge University Press, 2013), 201.

7 Several excellent bibliographies relating to encyclopaedism are readily available online. See the "Medieval Encylopedias, Bestiaries, Lapidaries, and Herbals" entry from ARC Humanities Press; the online journal, *Spicae, Cahiers de l'Atelier Vincent de Beauvais*; and the *Atelier Vincent de Beauvais*: "Bibliographie sur les encyclopédies médiévales". Editions of Hildegard's works: Reiner Hildebrandt and Thomas Gloning (eds.), *Physica: Liber Subtilitatum Diversarum Naturarum Creaturarum: Textkritische Ausgabe* (Berlin: De Gruyter, 2010); Laurence Moulinier (ed.), *Beate Hildegardis Cause et cure* (Berlin: Akademie Verlag, 2003). For Hugh of Saint-Victor see Thilo Offergeld (ed.), *Hugo von St Viktor. Didascalicon de studio legendi* (*Studienbuch*) (Freiburg i.B.: Herder, 1997).

8 The book culture and reading styles of early Christianity are another facet of this story and very interesting, especially as it relates to Augustine. Guy Stroumsa, "On the Status of Books in Early Christianity", in Carol Harrison, Caroline Humfress, and Isabella Sandwell (eds.), *Being Christian in Late Antiquity: A Festschrift for Gillian Clark* (Oxford/New York: Oxford University Press, 2014), 57–89.

9 Alexander Meeus, "Compilation or Tradition? Some Thoughts on the Methods of Historians and Other Scholars in Antiquity", *Sacris Erudiri* 56 (2017), 398. Meeus also points out that Momigliano has repeatedly made this same claim. See Arnaldo Momigliano, *Essays in Ancient and Modern Historiography* (Middletown, CT: Wesleyan University Press, 1977), 142;

from author to author, these collections expanded the possibilities for building imagined and real communities, deploying theologies and social movements, and prescribing social relations for subsequent centuries.

Alongside this fascinating history of encyclopaedic knowledge, florilegia and compilations of lives also proliferated. The non-Christian precursors include Plutarch's *Parallel Lives*, Philostratus' *Lives of the Sophists*, Diogenes Laertius' *Lives of Eminent Philosophers*, Eunapius' *Lives of the Philosophers and Sophists*, and Damascius' *Philosophical History*.[10] Rather than an attempt to collect all information on a given subject, these authors engaged in the plucking of a few of the most beautiful or compelling narratives from history. This model certainly had appeal for hagiographers who accessed a wealth of stories, some more interesting than others. Whether these can be strictly considered florilegia, or a hybrid of styles, is part of the interest of this chapter. Certain authors, like John of Ephesus, moved easily between what we might term 'genres', calling into question whether the notion of genre works at all for these texts.[11] There appears to be some innovation in what these compiling authors achieved.

Several compilations emerge in the fourth to seventh century period directly following the surge in popularity of desert monasticism. There was significant interest in collecting the stories of the fabled saints for emulation as well as commemoration. The hagiographical technique of combining multiple saints into a single document was a function of several factors. What could be done with hundreds of pithy sayings that had been handed down from previous generations? These shorter narratives and aphorisms were in danger of being lost if not recorded. Several authors toured the monasteries of Egypt, Palestine, and Syria, collecting the bits of material that could not support an entire *vita*, but were valuable to continuing practitioners and historians alike. Intentions varied in this enterprise, including personal interest and connection, justification

Arnaldo Momigliano, *The Classical Foundations of Modern Historiography* (Berkeley: University of California Press, 1990), 106–107.

10 Muriel Debié, "Writing History as 'Histoires': The Biographical Dimension of East Syriac Historiography", in Arietta Papaconstantinou and Hugh Kennedy (eds.), *Writing 'True Stories': Historians and Hagiographers in the Late Antique and Medieval Near East* (Turnhout: Brepols Publishers, 2010), 48.

11 A recent symposium at the 2018 American Academy of Religion, Denver, CO, organised by Massimo Rondolino, spent significant time debating the notion of genre and whether it is helpful for thinking about hagiography, especially as hagiography goes beyond strict formats of ancient Western paradigms. Debié notes that the notion of genre has also been helpfully critiqued by Marc Van Uytfanghe, "L'hagiographie: un 'genre' chrétien ou antique tardif?", *Analecta Bollandiana* 111 (1993), 135–188; Debié, "Writing History as 'Histoires'", 44. See the "Introduction" to this volume, 13–15.

of theological heritage, preservation, emulation, and even promotion of the cult of saints. This would be enough to signal the multiplicity of readings we might attempt in these works. If we consider political, social, and authorial factors, we are left with even more possibilities for reading these compilations.

This chapter will focus on the rich and intriguing compilation of John of Ephesus, illustrating the fascinating political and religious landscape that is reflected in his work. John's work is one of only a few prominent compilations that emerged in this period. Five other compilers known by name are Palladius of Galatia, Theodoret of Cyrrhus, Cyril of Scythopolis, Gregory of Tours, and John Moschus. Two collections have been transmitted anonymously: first, the *Historia Monachorum*, which chronicles a trip by seven monks from Rufinus' monastery in AD 394–395, and second, the *Apophthegmata Patrum*, a late-fifth- to early-sixth-century collection of sayings and stories. All these compilations attempt a sustained treatment of the ascetic life in their collections. Palladius, the pupil of Evagrius of Pontus, writes his collection around AD 419 using his work to explore the Egyptian monastic life with varying levels of detail. Theodoret's work on the monks of Syria, the *Historia Religiosa*, was written around AD 440 and supplies narrative as well as commentary on a number of lives in his collection. Cyril's work, which ends with the death of John the Hesychast in AD 558, focuses on the lives of the Palestinian monks in the time of the Origenist controversy, chronicling religious communities alongside his own theological development.[12] Gregory of Tours (d. AD 594) wrote twenty *Lives* in his *Liber Vitae Patrum*, and he recorded the deeds of the previous eighteen bishops next to his own at the end of his *Historia Francorum* (10.31).[13] The *Pratum Spirituale* of John Moschus (d. AD 619) is the latest compilation from our time period; his work is a florilegium characterised by great variety.[14] All of these compilations emerge as interesting sites of polyphonic history, carrying

12 John Binns and Richard Price, *Cyril of Scythopolis, Lives of the Monks of Palestine* (Kalamazoo, MI: Cistercian Publications, 1991), xi.

13 Edward James, *Gregory of Tours: Life of the Fathers* (Liverpool: Liverpool University Press, 1991), xi.

14 Debié includes the five martyrdoms by Abgar here as well, which we will bracket based on the number of collected texts and on the subject matter. Sebastian P. Brock, *A Brief Outline of Syriac Literature* (Kottayam: St. Ephrem Ecumenical Research Institute, 1997), 35; Paul Devos, "Abgar, hagiographe perse méconnu (début du ve siècle)", *Analecta Bollandiana* 83 (1965), 303–328. Numerous martyr compilations emerge in later Syriac sources. Brock notes, 'A particularly fascinating collection of lives are those of the Persian martyrs, dating from the fourth to the seventh centuries, throughout which period the Church of the East suffered intermittent persecution from the Sassanid authorities, normally at the prompting of the Zoroastrian clergy.' Sebastian P. Brock, *An Introduction to Syriac Studies* (Piscataway, NJ: Gorgias Press LLC, 2017), 9.

forward a range of voices that a single *Life* could not. The author as guide, or perhaps, as Patricia Cox Miller has put it, as a 'threshold' or 'prism' to the figures they represent, is a useful way of beginning to think about the way these works were intended to be received and with which communities the writers were in conversation.[15] For John of Ephesus, we will explore how his work operates somewhere between encyclopaedia and florilegium, purporting to encompass the detail of the monk's Syrian world, as well as carefully selecting those vignettes that could work with the author's agenda. In particular, John's close relationship to Justinian I and Theodora provides a significant context, rendering a vivid example of polyphony in the late antique compilation.[16] John tells us marvellous and intimate stories while maintaining a semblance of distance between the figures and his own position.

Several aspects of polyphony in the compilation will drive this chapter. Beginning with the variety of external motives that drive the compilatory process, I shall explore the possibility of its internal functions in the text, the variety of authorial voices, the author's agency in selection of narratives, the functionality of the compilation in various frames of storytelling, and finally the literary sophistication at work in these texts. I argue that compilations can serve a range of literary functions due to their variegated nature and should not be simply characterised by categories like florilegium or encyclopaedia. Our authors exhibit significant agency in their choice of style and utilised it in a number of ways. Finally, I maintain that late antique compilations are particularly polyphonic and should be read as such.

1 John of Ephesus

Born around AD 507 in the territory of Ingiliene, which was under the jurisdiction of Amida, John of Ephesus wrote fascinating histories about the monks of his Syrian homeland.[17] His Miaphysite community, a persecuted sect of Christianity that believed in one nature (*mia physis*) of Christ, had suffered severe treatment under the Emperor Justin I, who belonged to the dominant Chalcedonian group, affirming the dual nature of Christ as restated by the

15 Patricia Cox [Miller], *Biography in Late Antiquity: A Quest for the Holy Man* (Berkeley: University of California Press, 1983), 145–146. Cf. Debié, "Writing History as 'Histoires'", 47.

16 The literary differences between the three volumes of John's compilation and the dates we ascribe to them are problems that still need a fair amount of scholarly attention.

17 Susan Ashbrook Harvey, *Asceticism and Society in Crisis: John of Ephesus and the Lives of the Eastern Saints* (Berkeley: University of California Press, 1990), 28.

Council of Chalcedon in AD451. John was fully aware of the social fallout that could emerge from subscribing to a different theological party from the ruler. His stories range from recorded tales to personal experiences, including the stories from his own childhood in the monasteries of the stylite Maro, and John Urtaya at Amida. Ordained deacon by John of Tella, John travelled widely in Syria and as far as Palestine and Egypt. After John spent a short stint in Constantinople, Justinian selected him for a post geared towards converting pagans in Asia. John, an avowed Miaphysite, would have seemed a strange choice for the position, given Justinian's own support of the Chalcedonian community; but Justinian's wife, the Empress Theodora, was an ardent supporter of the Miaphysites. We can only speculate on the curious relationship that John must have maintained between his Miaphysite community, the Emperor, and Theodora. Was he an agent of Justinian meant to play both sides toward reconciliation? Was he a concerned Christian bishop, bent on recording the deeds of the holy ascetics? Was he focused on emulating the saints through his own commemoration of their deeds? Or was he actively promoting the cause of the Miaphysite community? The only evidence we have of John's role is from his own hand. Questions multiply in the examination of this text.

Other factors, extending beyond the quantity and type of natures in Christ, also emerge as possible factors of interpretation for the polyphony of these works, in particular, the problem of figures considered heretical, such as Origen, and their lingering influence on Christian theology. While the history of Origen's theological influence and eventual hereticisation has been eloquently addressed by historians, the ways in which hagiographical texts relate to him and the later Origenist movement has received unequal attention, and is significant for our work here.[18] During John's tenure in Constantinople, Justinian took on an instrumental role in orchestrating a synodical condemnation of Origen in AD543, a move focused on the Origenist monks and their non-mainstream theologies, such as apokatastasis, the notion that souls would be restored.[19] There are two fascinating connections to our work on compilation in John of Ephesus. The first is the compilatory work in law already being undertaken by Justinian, and from there the promulgation of a particular style of justice that

18 Elizabeth A. Clark, *The Origenist Controversy: The Cultural Construction of an Early Christian Debate* (Princeton, NJ: Princeton University Press, 1992).

19 Brooks thinks that John lived in Constantinople from AD540 to some time between AD542 and AD546, when he took a villa in Sycae (modern Galata) across the Golden Horn to the North, until AD578. Brooks, E.W. (ed.), *John of Ephesus: Lives of the Eastern Saints*. Patrologia Orientalis 82 (Turnhout: Brepols, 2003), vi.

is rendered in his compilations and directly related to Origen's condemnation. A brief look at these themes will begin our discussion of the polyphonic nature of John's work.

Justinian commissioned the *Corpus Iuris Civilis*, a compilation of updated jurisprudence. This legal work is often highlighted as his crowning achievement as an emperor, with lines of influence to contemporary civil and ecclesiastical legal systems. Justinian gained control when his uncle Justin I died. From the time he assumed full imperial power, just four months after his uncle Justin I appointed him co-emperor in AD 527, it took less than two years to publish the *Codex Justinianus*.[20] The *Digest* (or *Pandects*) produced in AD 530, as well as the *Institutes*, were the result of some 2,000 works from earlier Roman jurists.[21] It is worth noting that if the digest was a systematisation (*digerere*) of law, the name 'Pandects' (πανδέκτης) literally means 'all-receiver' or encyclopaedia.[22]

In the first book of Justinian's *Institutes*, under the heading of *De Iustitia et Iure*, we read a simple definition of Justice: 'Justice is the constant and perpetual wish to render everyone his due.'[23] The definition of justice is interesting in the context of compilation. How could one mete out justice properly if all pertinent laws were not collected so as to adequately understand what precedents were available and properly 'render everyone his due?' The definition of justice is also fascinating when put in conversation with the condemnation of Origen, who had promulgated a notion of justice that was restorative and had none of the retributive flavour that a late Roman emperor might desire on this earth. For Origen, the judgement of one's deeds was accomplished by their own memory and conscience. He explains that 'receiving by divine power into the memory all those things of which it had stamped on itself certain signs and forms at the moment of sinning', and seeing 'a kind of history, as it were, of all the foul, and shameful, and unholy deeds which it has done', the soul would

20 Michael Maas, "Roman Questions, Byzantine Answers: Contours of the Age of Justinian", in idem (ed.), *The Cambridge Companion to the Age of Justinian* (Cambridge: Cambridge University Press, 2005), 6.

21 Maas, "Roman Questions", 6. For a broad view of the development of the Roman law from 1000 BC through modern Europe, see George Mousourakis, *A Legal History of Rome* (London: Routledge, 2007).

22 McGuckin notes that 'Digest (derived from the Latin *digerere*) meant "systematization;" *Pandects* (derived from the Greek *pan dexesthe*) meant "encyclopedia."': John Anthony McGuckin, *The Ascent of Christian Law: Patristic and Byzantine Formulations of a New Civilization* (Yonkers, NY: St. Vladimir's Seminary Press, 2012), 245 n. 10.

23 '*Iustitia est constans et perpetua voluntas ius suum cuique tribuens*': Paul Krueger et al., *Corpus juris civilis*, 1.1. Translated by Thomas Collett Sandars, *The Institutes of Justinian with English Introduction, Translation and Notes* (7th edition London: Longmans, Green, and Co., 1917).

become 'an accuser and a witness against itself'.[24] Ultimately leading to 'a solidification undoubtedly into a firmer structure ... and a restoration' that would be effected.[25] Punishments abound in Justinian's legal code, raising the question of whether Origen's condemnation was simply politically and theologically driven or triggered by some ideological concerns Justinian had over how Christian imperial power was conceptualised in jurisprudence: specifically, how a legal code could work without temporal punishments as retribution.[26]

The theme of retributive justice is prominent in both legal and hagiographical texts. The ascetic, depicted as wielding God's power in judgement of a wrongdoer, or acting as judge or mediator between two parties, is a central aspect of John's hagiographies. As we consider how stories were selected and crafted by the author of the compilation, certain themes become signposts for theological positions and political frameworks. How the saint—and his author—navigate the terrain of a given topic, like retribution, highlights the impact of the author on the hagiographical enterprise. The intimate connection between 'restoration' and 'retribution' in legal and theological works adds considerable texture to a compilation like John's *Lives of the Eastern Saints*. What type of justice a monk engages in is a useful means by which to discern the author's voice and its relationship to the prevailing culture. It begins to situate his community, his political outlook, and his theological predilections.

I have argued elsewhere that John of Ephesus' hagiographies take on a particularly retributive aspect because of his situation in the capital.[27] My work here develops that theme further in the context of the compilation. Whether an author included a story, or not, could be dictated by their political leanings on a theological dispute. Moreover, the text could attempt to prescribe a particular style of comportment in society as their protagonists were revered and emulated by subsequent generations. It is impossible to know precisely what an author thought, but we can begin to 'shade' the outline of our authorial figures based on what they chose to include in their compilation, as situated in the context we can glean historically. As Cox Miller aptly states, we have to look at the author's intent 'not only as a way of imagining his work's context, but also as a reflection of the author's deep sense of himself', for in the 'creative moment,

24 Origen, *De Principiis* 2.10.4. Translated by Philip Schaff, *ANF* 4.

25 Origen, *De Principiis* 2.10.5.

26 See Ilaria Ramelli, *The Christian Doctrine of Apokatastasis: A Critical Assessment from the New Testament to Eriugena* (Leiden: Brill, 2013), 724–738, and Henry Chadwick, *The Church in Ancient Society: From Galilee to Gregory the Great* (Oxford: Oxford University Press, 2001), 612–627.

27 Todd E. French, "Just Deserts: Origen's Lingering Influence on Divine Justice in the Hagiographies of John of Ephesus", *Studia Patristica* 92 (2017), 105–113.

it is not only the depths of the cultural situations that are sounded, but also the soulful depths of the author'.[28] Although Cox Miller argues that the biographies of Origen and Plotinus were not 'exercises in literary dexterity' and that the 'biographers were not manipulating their prisms', I think we should be open to the possibility that there were a range of motivations at work in crafting compilations.[29] Should we pre-emptively exclude some literary and political aspects to preserve a perceived or superimposed, and possibly anachronistic, integrity in an author? I think there is room for both readings. The polyphonic nature of these texts allows for the depth of authorial character as well as shrewd literary stylings. Both shine through in John of Ephesus' compilation.

As we attempt to understand how John's work functions as literature, details about which antagonists receive punitive justice (pagans) and which receive a more restorative form (Chalcedonians), signal the socio-political factors influencing John's work. There are ample examples of social conflict in John's text, and unlike the many saints depicted by Theodoret and Cyril, whose protagonists apply immediate punishment followed by restoration and often didactic explanations, John's saints regularly engage in behaviour that cannot be reversed. A notable example is the story about Simeon the Mountaineer, who, upon reaching a small town filled with uninformed, pagan-leaning inhabitants, realises he has a duty to admonish them.[30] Setting up his headquarters in a dilapidated old chapel, Simeon takes it upon himself to forcibly tonsure a portion of the town's children, setting them apart for service to God. When the parents of two boys baulk at his actions, he gives them a fair warning about how their shortsighted actions will be punished. He explains that neither of the boys will make it to the next week if they are reclaimed by their parents.[31] Within three days both boys are dead. The parents are repentant, but there is no reversal. The inhabitants of the town live out their years in fear of further retribution for not heeding Simeon's advice. I propose that this style of punishment fits perfectly with an anti-Origenian, law-orientated theology that was coming into fashion under the rule of Justinian. It is focused on the pagan, rather than the divided sects of Christianity, and functions partially, approximating how Cox Miller understood the 'Life of Origen' to operate, in closing 'the rift, to heal internal wounds in order to present a united front to the pagan enemy'.[32] John's

---

28 Cox [Miller], *Biography in Late Antiquity*, 135–136.

29 Cox [Miller], *Biography in Late Antiquity*, 134–135.

30 The text refers to them as living like wild animals, a well-attested framing of the pagan in hagiographical texts. See Cox Miller, "Strategies of Representation", 227.

31 John of Ephesus, *Lives* 16, *PO* 17: 244–245, 247.

32 Cox [Miller], *Biography in Late Antiquity*, 138. At 70 she points out that Eusebius' work

choice to include or render the saint as retributive and the judgement as final in the case of the pagan town communicates a stance on Origen's theology as well as a reconciling undercurrent in sectarian Christianity. This is made possible not just in the rendering of the story, as would necessarily be the case in a single *vita* like that of Eusebius, but in the structuring of polyphony through multiple stories in the collection. John's work is capable of carrying a more complex range of positions.

A problem arises when we seek this type of retributive flavour in the whole of John's work. John's saints readily engage in retribution when they are correcting the pagans in the countryside. When it comes to Christians of the Chalcedonian variety, however, retribution falls off sharply. This is certainly in keeping with John's position at court with Theodora and his role under Justinian. It would clearly have been a mistake to record only stories of confounded Chalcedonian persecutors—indeed most of John's stories avoid these interactions altogether. The paucity of extant Miaphysite histories also plays a role here.[33] Given the lengthy period of persecution, it seems likely that there were hagiographical stories that ridiculed and condemned Chalcedonian figures. Why would John have avoided collecting or manufacturing these, and yet include numerous stories about the persecution of his party?

We gain insight into authorial intentions through contemplating how active the authors were in selecting and rejecting various stories.[34] Here I would draw a distinction between a florilegium of the type we see in John Moschus or in the *Apophthegmata Patrum*, where it appears that only the most poignant and sometimes outrageous narratives were 'plucked' from the field of beautifully flowering stories.[35] Other compilations read as more deliberate, exploring themes of theological controversy and social animosities in more carefully

'addresses two different communities and attempts to be faithful to two major orientations.' See also James Corke-Webster's compelling work on Eusebius that reappraises the *Ecclesiastical History* in terms of 'Eusebius' new vision of the Christian church responding to elite suspicions' by constructing the Christians as 'intellectuals of the highest calibre' and demonstrating 'the full range of traditional Roman virtues': James Corke-Webster, *Eusebius and Empire: Constructing Church and Rome in the Ecclesiastical History* (Cambridge: Cambridge University Press, 2019), 76.

33 Jan Jacob van Ginkel, *John of Ephesus: A Monophysite Historian in Sixth-Century Byzantium* (Groningen: Rijksuniversitet, 1995), 43.

34 Cox Miller, "Strategies of Representation", 231, notes that Theodoret saw the 'pretense of completeness' as no longer necessary. Cf. John of Ephesus, *Lives*, Prologue.

35 Here Moschus' treatment of one monk's vision of a river of fire in which he is standing upon a bishop's head. John Wortley, *John Moschus: The Spiritual Meadow* (Kalamazoo, MI: Cistercian Publications, 1992), 44.

crafted collections.[36] John of Ephesus appears more intentional, and his utilisation of this genre is a profoundly interesting development in the history of literary composition and saintly commemoration.[37] John's work lies somewhere between encyclopaedia, which I think attempts to capture the broadest range of examples, and florilegium, which selects only those examples that support the author's aims. His approach is selective, and yet he goes beyond capturing just the most colourful of the works available to him. His work does several things at once. It is personal, without being dominated by local details. It is political, but even-handed, exploring both Miaphysite and Chalcedonian figures. It is reconciliatory, bringing sects together against a common pagan opponent, while acknowledging the persecutions of the Miaphysite community. It is expansive, covering three volumes and fifty-eight lives in total. And it is commemorative, recording lives of saints that would be lost if not for John's work. It is the epitome of polyphonic, both in scope and in application. Pliny's encyclopaedic *Naturalis Historia* yields some fascinating parallels. As Trevor Murphy comments in his introduction with regard to whether authorial statements can be used to secure Pliny's authorial voice, 'There is more than one "Pliny", that is, more than one perspective on Nature authorised by the text. Any reading that isolates a single passage from the *Natural History* and says of it "this is what Pliny thought in his heart" risks limiting what is really a many-voiced text.'[38] It is the same for John of Ephesus.

Authors of compilations allowed their theological and political leanings to impact on their work, yielding a style that is as prescriptive as it is commemorative, and as intriguing as it is entertaining. Beyond serving as a repository for historical narrative, the compilation can function itself as a complicated narrative.[39] Although saints' lives can be compiled, constructed, and promulgated

36 Cyril of Scythopolis and Theodoret of Cyrrhus both come to mind.

37 Debié argues that the compilation functions as a type of historical summary, confusing some later editors. Muriel Debié, "Writing History as 'Histoires'", 49–50.

38 Trevor Morgan Murphy, *Pliny the Elder's Natural History: The Empire in the Encyclopedia* (Oxford: Oxford University Press, 2004), 11.

39 I have argued elsewhere, in Todd E. French, "Many Truths, One Story: John of Ephesus's Lives of the Eastern Saints", in Rico Monge, Kerry San Chirico, and Rachel Smith (eds.), *Hagiography and Religious Truth* (London: Bloomsbury Academic, 2016), 153–167, that many 'truths' are available to the reader of John's hagiography. Whereas that article broached the idea that compilations can be polyphonic, this research builds upon these possibilities, asking how the compilation could be strategically developed, deployed as literature, and intentionally veil the author's intents. The result is a perspective on compilation that opens up greater possibilities of interpretation—asking again how the author intended for this to be received, whether that mattered to his contemporaries, and how it should matter to us now.

along particular political and theological vectors, they can be interpreted in a number of ways, signalling the malleability of this literary form.

2 Florilegia and Compilatory Strategies

Palladius' extensive travels yielded more material than he could hope to include in his *Lausiac History*. He states: 'I leave you an account now, an epitome as it were, of merely the outstanding ascetic practices and miracles of the noble athletes and great men.'[40] These extant stories of saints and their miracles, however, range from spectacular and amazing to questionably miraculous and mostly forgettable. When there were too many stories of monks from a region or monastery, the author was required to make decisions. This process was most likely simple and geared toward collecting the most remarkable, absurd, funny, or educational examples. A further example of the florilegium comes from John Moschus, who begins his prologue with a description of the meadow of possible narrative flowers. He states, 'From among these I have plucked the finest flowers of the unmown meadow and worked them into a crown which I now offer to you, most faithful child; and through you, to the world at large'.[41] He goes further to describe himself as a wise bee, who gathers up the deeds of the fathers that are spiritually beneficial.[42] This classical metaphor can be traced back to Plato's *Ion*, and remains a vibrant theme in subsequent Christian literature.[43] This is put into practice at times through hilarious moments, like visions of monks in the afterlife putting down their superiors.[44] John Moschus

---

40 ἐνέβην εἰς τοὺς ἀγῶνας τοῦ σκάμματος, καὶ ὡς ἐν ἐπιτομῇ τῶν γενναίων ἀθλητῶν καὶ μεγάλων ἀνδρῶν τὰ ἔπακρα μόνον ἆθλά τε καὶ σημεῖα ἀναγραψάμενος: Palladius, *The Lausiac History* Foreword 4; Greek text from Edward Cuthbert Butler, *The Lausiac History of Palladius* (Cambridge: Cambridge University Press, 1898), p. 4, lines 15–17; translation from Robert T. Meyer, *Palladius: The Lausiac History* (Westminster, MD: Newman Press/London: Longmans, Green, and Co., 1965).

41 ἐξ ὧν τὰ καλὰ δρεψάμενος ἄνθη πλεκτὸν στέφανον ἀκηράτου λειμῶνος λαβὼν, προσφέρω σοι, τέκνον πιστότατον, καὶ διὰ σοῦ τοῖς πᾶσι: John Moschus, *The Spiritual Meadow*, Prologue 3, *PG* 87C, 2852; trans. John Wortley (Kalamazoo, MI: Cistercian Publications, 1992).

42 John Moschus, *The Spiritual Meadow*, Prologue.

43 See Corke-Webster, *Eusebius and Empire*, 14–15.

44 Going into a trance the elder saw 'a river of fire with a multitude [of people] in the fire itself. Right in the middle was the brother, submerged up to his neck. The elder said to him: "Was it not because of this retribution that I called on you to look after your own soul, my child?" The brother answered and said to the elder: "I thank God, father, that there is relief for my head. Thanks to your prayers I am standing on the head of a bishop"' (Καὶ δὴ θεωρεῖ ἐν ἐκστάσει γενόμενος ποταμὸν πυρὸς, καὶ πλῆθος ἐν αὐτῷ τῷ πυρὶ, καὶ μέσον

and Palladius operate under the guiding principle that they should be trusted to assemble the most beautiful bouquet of texts—we, the readers, benefit from their judicious selection. Although this is certainly a well-worn path in antiquity, contemporary readers will ask what other factors were at play in the selecting of particular themes and stories.

It is possible to read through the veil of St Antony's *vita*, recognising the anti-Arian, Emperor-snubbing tone of its author (or redactor?), Athanasius. This is more difficult in works which compile many stories of many figures, which can be tethered to specific historical events or comprised of free-floating musings on the saintly life. The search for a unifying idea in these works is quite complicated. They have been read a number of ways by historians in antiquity and contemporary devotees, as well as modern scholars of ancient history, and they continue to be read in contemporary Christian communities for devotional purposes.[45] As a result, historians have often been satisfied to take the writers at their word when examining them.[46] One could easily be tempted to follow an author's stated intent and interpret these texts as commemorating the saint and chronicling the wonderful deeds of these otherwise unknown ascetics. While this certainly supplies a particular viewpoint on the texts, it leaves a wealth of data unexplored. Why and how and when these texts were compiled is as interesting as the 'who' these texts purport to be about.

Whereas any text can be read for the author's voice as much as historical detail, the hagiographical compilations offer another layer to the medium. Since many stories in the compilation carry the caveat of being collected from others, they stand a further step removed from the author.[47] The compiler, as

---

τὸν ἀδελφὸν βεβαπτισμένον ἕως τραχήλου. Τότε λέγει αὐτῷ ὁ γέρων· Οὐ διὰ ταύτην τὴν τιμωρίαν παρεκάλουν σε, ἵνα φροντίσῃς τῆς ἰδίας ψυχῆς, τέκνον; Ἀπεκρίθη ὁ ἀδελφὸς, καὶ εἶπεν τῷ γέροντι· Εὐχαριστῶ τῷ Θεῷ, Πάτερ, ὅτι κἂν ἡ κεφαλή μου ἄνεσιν ἔχει. Κατὰ γὰρ εὐχάς σου ἐπάνω κορυφῆς ἵσταμαι ἐπισκόπου). John Moschus, *The Spiritual Meadow*, 44 (PG 87 [1863], 2900).

45 For example, the preface by the Metropolitan Anthony of Sourozh to Benedicta Ward, *The Sayings of the Desert Fathers: The Alphabetical Collection* (London: Mowbrays, 1975; 2nd edition Kalamazoo, MI: Cistercian Studies, 1986), ix, calls on the reader to 'approach them with veneration'.

46 See Chitty, who explains: 'While Cyril is a typical Palestinian of his day, full of naïve superstition (which makes his work of all the more value to the modern scholar), he never gives us the impression that he is embroidering or enlarging on what he himself has heard or seen … We have little impression of originality in Cyril's personal religion.' Chitty, *The Desert a City*, 131.

47 For example, Theodoret explains in section 11 of his Preface to the *Historia Religiosa*: Τῶν δὲ λεχθησομένων ἐνίων μὲν αὐτόπτης ἐγενόμην ἐγώ ὅσα δὲ μὴ τεθέαμαι, παρὰ τῶν ἐκείνους τεθεαμένων ἀκήκοα, ἀνδρπῶν ἀρετῆς ἐραστῶν καὶ τὴς ἐκείνων θέας καὶ διδασκαλίας ἠξιωμένων ('Of

author, has a freer hand in crafting the work since it would be nearly impossible to personally witness a collection of events and figures that spanned such geographical and temporal distances.[48] He necessarily relies on the stories of others and in so doing introduces some distance between his rendering and the actual events. John portrays this distance, in similar hagiographical style to Palladius, as the limitation of his ability to relate the wonderful deeds of the saints with his inadequate language.[49] We should ask if this is the required, and/or feigned, humility of a historian writing about saints, or acknowledgment of his impact on the process of recording this material?[50] Both aspects could be at play in the author's rendering of his work.

As a result, the compilation provides an air of anonymity. The reader is not told every saint's name and full life story in the compilation. Many saints emerge from obscurity in their local context, proffering only their exemplary action, and return to anonymity as the compiler moves on to the next saint. It is rare to have a full *vita* of an anonymous saint, and stories that circulated anonymously were sometimes applied to specific figures after the fact.[51] It is enough for the compilation to select the pertinent details that the reader might benefit from, or that might propel the author's agenda(s) in his work.

---

some of what I shall tell I was myself the eye-witness; whatever I have not seen I have heard of from those who have seen these men, those who as lovers of virtue were counted worthy to see them and be taught by them'). Translated by Richard M. Price, *Theodoret of Cyrrhus: A History of the Monks of Syria* (Kalamazoo, MI: Cistercian Publications, 1985), 8.

48 Even though this is precisely what he claims in the prologue.

49 Palladius, *Lausiac History*, Foreword 4; Butler, *The Lausiac History of Palladius*, p. 4, lines 7–9, states: 'Untutored as I am in the use of language, and having but slight knowledge of the spiritual, I myself felt unequal to the task of cataloguing the holy fathers in the spiritual life. I feared the magnitude of the undertaking' ('Εγὼ τοίνυν ὁ καὶ τῇ γλώττῃ ἀπαίδευτος καὶ πνευματικῆς γνώσεως ἀκροθιγῶς πως γευσάμενος καὶ τοῦ καταλόγου τῶν ἁγίων πατέρων πνευματικοῦ βίου ἀνάξιος, δεδοικὼς τὸ ὑπὲρ ἐμὲ ἄμετρον τῆς ἐπιταγῆς μέγεθος). John of Ephesus, *Lives of the Eastern Saints*. Translated by Ernest W. Brooks, Patrologia Orientalis 82 (Turnhout: Brepols, 2003) 1, *PO* 17: 2: 'By means [of] the vile and common pigments of our poor words' (*byd smmn' šyṭ' wšḥym' dmltn msknt'*).

50 Krueger argues that this claim to be 'witless and unskilled' aligns the author with the humility of the saint. Derek Krueger, "Early Byzantine Historiography and Hagiography", in Arietta Papaconstantinou and Hugh Kennedy (eds.), *Writing 'True Stories': Historians and Hagiographers in the Late Antique and Medieval Near East* (Turnhout: Brepols Publishers, 2010), 15.

51 A prime counterexample to the anonymous saint is the story of the Man of God of Edessa. He proves the latter point about application and conflation of stories onto specific saints after the fact. His story later gets bound up with the St Alexius tradition. See Robert Doran, *Stewards of the Poor: The Man of God, Rabbula, and Hiba in Fifth-Century Edessa* (Kalamazoo, MI: Cistercian Publications, 2006).

The author of the compilation regularly purports to collect material for a range of purposes, including admonishing the faithful, revering the heroic, and memorialising the saints in historically accurate forms—or as John states, committing them 'to the memorial of my handwriting.'[52] John's project can be read as commemorative of the heroes of the Miaphysite community in the face of widespread persecution from Christian leaders that were intent on seeing the theological precepts of the Council of Chalcedon, including a two-natured Christ, supported broadly in churches and monasteries. Theodoret engages similarly with the preface to his work on the monks of Syria by offering several pages of support for his project on the basis that hearing of a saint might be as valuable as seeing a saint.[53] In reality, the aims of the author may go well beyond these honoured traditions.

The single *vita* often relies on the proximity of the author to the subject, i.e., pains are taken to show that the author knew their subject intimately, as in the case of St Antony.[54] The compilation, which by nature covers numerous figures in a range of times and locations, increases distance through its style. Although some, like John, may declare that they have borne witness to the events they depict, the educated reader sees an additional layer of complication to the narratives. It is no longer the story told by the author, but rather the stories collected by the author, as told by the sources.[55] The compilation can serve as a platform that promotes more immediate trust in the veracity of the narrative details, since a non-critical reader might believe the material, with its variation in theme and style, was simply brought together by the author with few adjustments. This style serves as an ideal format for distancing the author from the message. That is to say that one *could* conclude that the author is recording material without personal interest.

The relationship of the compiling author to the authors of the constituent parts is quite interesting in these texts. The compiling author, our hagiogra-

52 John of Ephesus, *Lives* 1, PO 17: 3: *lʿwhdnʾ dktbt ʾydy lʾ ʾtl.*

53 Theodoret of Cyrrhus, *A History of the Monks of Syria*, Prologue: Price, *History of the Monks*, 3–9.

54 The *Life of Antony* begins with the author's declaration that what he writes is gleaned from 'what I myself know (for I have seen him often) and what I was able to learn from him when I followed him more than a few times and poured water over his hands' (διὰ τοῦτο ἅπερ αὐτός τε γινώσκω (πολλάκις γὰρ αὐτὸν ἑώρακα) καὶ ἃ μαθεῖν ἠδυνήθην παρὰ τοῦ ἀκολουθήσαν τος αὐτῷ χρόνον οὐκ ὀλίγον καὶ ἐπιχέαντος ὕδωρ κατὰ χειρὸς αὐτοῦ): Athanasius, *V. Anton.*, pr. 5.

55 The claim of authority and impartiality has an important history in classical literature. See John Marincola, *Authority and Tradition in Ancient Historiography* (Cambridge: Cambridge University Press, 1997), 158–174.

pher, may or may not have drafted the saintly literature that he compiles in his text. We recognise some ambiguity in voice on this most basic level. Likewise, the relationship of the narrator to the reader is also of considerable importance. Whether the narrator presents himself as a disembodied voice or an active participant in the narrative makes considerable difference in how the text is received. Several unique possibilities emerge: the narrator can be a character in the story he tells (homodiegetic), or the main protagonist, 'giving an account of an adventure he was personally involved in', (autodiegetic), or completely dissociated from the protagonist (heterodiegetic).[56] An author might choose to engage with any of these styles to tell their narrative. Our authors of compilation regularly engage with all three. John of Ephesus easily moves from the explanation of his role as eyewitness on this journey of exploration (autodiegetic), to stories about his own life and healing by a saint (homodiegetic), to the relation of narrative dissociated from his role (heterodiegetic).[57] The result is a text that can utilise a number of rhetorical strategies in its discursive toolbox. The reader is brought into the adventure of the author as he travels and explores, collecting the hidden bits of wisdom for posterity's sake. As reader, one is engaged in the captivating mental image of ancient monks relating treasured tales. This has two functions. It distances the author from the narrative, foregrounding a notion of the author as a disinterested collector. It also validates the text by providing some provenance and authenticity. Likewise, the reader is exposed to texts that locate the narrator as a central figure in the story, like John's personal healing from a saint. This functions to validate the story—depending on whether one trusts the author. The reliability of the narrator is another interesting factor as it opens up the possibility of outside influences on the author-reader relationship.[58]

Some compilations, like the *Apophthegmata Patrum*, not only exist without a stated author, but leave considerable amounts of material unconnected to a named character, hindering the reader from grounding the wisdom of a saint in any specific historical context.[59] Other compilations attempt clearer lines

56 Monika Fludernik, *An Introduction to Narratology* (London/New York: Routledge, 2009), 31.

57 These will be explored in more detail below.

58 Although narratologists have argued that unreliable narration 'must always have existed', it has been analysed mainly in works from 1800 to 1950. Fludernik, *Introduction to Narratology*, 113.

59 Cox Miller, "Strategies of Representation", 230: 'Students of the *Historia monachorum* and allied collections such as Palladius' *Lausiac History* and Theodoret's *Historia religiosa* have frequently noted that the individual units of the collections are biographical sketches that often omit conventional biographical data like ancestry, place of birth and death, main

of provenance, ascribing deeds and sayings to famous figures. John of Ephesus works in both styles, encompassing a wide range of saints from the famous, like Jacob Baradaeus, Severus, and Anthimus, to the local holy men and women, like Susan, Abraham, and Maro.

When examining a compilation such as John's, the structure is as significant as the content. We should consider why John decides to start his work with Habib, a saint that few would know, who is surrounded mostly by nameless interlocutors. Perhaps even more striking is that John never mentions this first saint's theological leanings, or puts him in conversation with the heresies swirling about in this region.[60] If John had set out to craft an apologetically orientated treatise, he would likely have mentioned specifics about Habib's community.[61] Instead, the saint that is displayed is one that is reluctant to interact with society, yet understands his duty to justice. Habib's narrative begins with a focus on social justice: an old man from the community is accused of plundering his fellow townspeople.[62] The cheated villagers tell the local holy man, Habib, and he takes the matter up for them. Asking God to hinder the people from ever seeing the man again, the deed is accomplished and the man dies the same night. He does not trick a Chalcedonian or admonish his seekers to consider their views on Christology. He is a model 'Holy Man', subduing wrongdoers, judiciously solving economic disputes, and humbly silencing critics who point out his outwardly focused lifestyle.[63] Habib also appears to embody an immediate and absolute justice that is worth considering in its broader theological context. The narrative, removed from any descriptive element about who the transgressor was or where he was from, is conveniently devoid of historical moorings. In this style, specific details beyond the holy person's name only served to complicate the form and impact of the narrative. In reality it did

---

achievements, and so on.' She cites Samuel Rubenson, *The Letters of St. Antony: Monasticism and the Making of a Saint* (Minneapolis, MN: Fortress Press, 1995), 177; Pierre Canivet, *Le monachisme syrien selon Théodoret de Cyr* (Paris: Editions Beauchesne, 1977), 69; Harvey, *Asceticism and Society in Crisis*, 34–37. See also Patricia Cox Miller, "Desert Asceticism and 'The Body from Nowhere'", *JECS* 2 (1994), 143–144.

60 It is possible here that John is simply modelling 'sanctity for those non-Chalcedonians persecuted by the imperial authorities': Debié, "Writing History as 'Histoires'", 52.

61 Jan van Ginkel affirms this point: 'The central aim is not to convert Chalcedonians, but to incite the monks to persevere and to prevent the masses from wavering. A recurrent theme is the resolve of the saints in enduring the persecution.' Van Ginkel, *John of Ephesus*, 44.

62 *w'p hn' b'z hw' lsgi''*: John of Ephesus, *Lives* 1, *PO* 17: 8.

63 Peter Brown, "The Rise and Function of the Holy Man in Late Antiquity", *JRS* 61 (1971), 80–101. Habib calls forth judgement on a man who exclaims, 'Will not this fellow go and sit in his monastery and be quiet? For see! He comes out and wanders about to eat and drink' (*dl' 'zl hn' ytb bdyrh wšl' dh' npq ph' dn'kwl wnšt'*): John of Ephesus, *Lives* 1, *PO* 17: 9.

not matter what deed holder in what village of the countryside had engaged in these actions and reaped his recompense. What did matter was that the narrative could be easily related, with the brunt of its providentially linked message about social justice still intact. The quintessential form of hagiographical vignette was one that was impactful, insightful, funny, or compelling, with just enough detail to contextualise the figure. All the while, this should be divorced from any hard details that might get in the way of the story's long-term effect. This model was far easier to achieve in a compilatory framework. There was no need to link the moment to a broader storyline, and if the author did—as in the case of some of John of Ephesus' figures—it was to necessarily increase the legitimacy of the frame.[64]

3 The Prologue—a Topos of Hagiography?

Thoughtful writers often make space outside of their text to foreground some ideas and provide a context to their work. In contemporary literature, writers use this as an opportunity to thank foundations and friends, inform the reader of their own interest in the topic, and even gesture towards some methodological underpinnings. Our ancient hagiographers were similarly interested in the prologue, the importance of which was paramount for a text that would be perceived as not the author's own, but a collection of others', stories. Much fruitful work has been done on prefaces, not only of literary texts but also in the context of canon law—an interesting parallel to hagiography in that the only impact a later reader might assume the copyist of a legal work could have on these 'static' texts was their introduction and contextualising remarks.[65] Like canon

64 John comments that he has determined in his mind 'Not to be a witness with my handwriting except only of things confirmed by the sight of my eyes as well as the written record, and not to repeat in writing what I have only heard, but the things that I have both heard and also seen' (*dl' 'hw' bktbt 'ydy 'l' blḥwd d'ylyn dḥzt' d'yny 'm ktybt' mšrrn*): John of Ephesus, *Lives* 4, PO 17: 71–72.

65 Cox Miller, "Strategies of Representation", 210. Eva Riad, *Studies in the Syriac Preface* (Uppsala: Uppsala University, 1988). Claude Aziza, *Vivre l'Antiquité: Recueil de Préfaces et Autres Textes* (Bordeaux: Ausonius éditions, 2016); Robert Somerville and Bruce Clark Brasington, *Prefaces to Canon Law Books in Latin Christianity: Selected Translations, 500–1245* (New Haven, CT: Yale University Press, 1998); Justin Lake, *Prologues to Ancient and Medieval History* (Toronto: University of Toronto Press, 2013); Laura Jansen (ed.), *The Roman Paratext: Frame, Texts, Readers* (Cambridge: Cambridge University Press, 2014); Peter van Nuffelen, *Orosius and the Rhetoric of History* (Oxford: Oxford University Press, 2012); Aaron Pelttari, *The Space That Remains: Reading Latin Poetry in Late Antiquity* (Ithaca, NY: Cornell University Press, 2014).

law, which certainly maintained an air of continuity and rigidity, hagiography was often produced in the frame of accurately recorded, rigid accounts, while proving sufficiently malleable over time in the creative hands of the hagiographer.

As mentioned above, the distance of the author from the narratives in the style of compilation is intriguing on a number of levels, not the least of which is the fact that we rarely hear, and perhaps are expected not to presume, the author's voice in the narratives themselves.[66] This makes the prefatory statements of the author, as disinterested collector, all the more necessary. And from the historian's perspective, they are equally informative as they carry what might be called veiled insights about the author's aims. It should be noted here that these can be read *against* the author as effectively as they can be read for the author's true intentions. A perfect example of this is John of Ephesus in his preface to the *Lives of the Eastern Saints*. He states that he will not record any events that he has not personally witnessed. Brooks, the editor of the volume, comments in a footnote here that 'this statement cannot be taken literally', because one of his accounts is of Abraham Kalesh, who died before John's birth.[67] Cox Miller asserts that 'the biographer mediated the intimacy between saint and reader by asserting the intimacy between saint and biographer.'[68]

John maintains a sense of duty in recording these deeds of the Syrian holy persons. He connects a scriptural passage from Matthew 5:16 to his own work: 'Let your light so shine before men, that they may see your good deeds, and glorify your Father who is in heaven.'[69] He explains that his own work of compiling histories is to render their pattern for posterity, memorialising it in writing.[70] The signalled theme of John's work is commemoration, or the historical recording of the saints' lives in order to protect them from the deterioration of time. With the concept of polyphony in mind, the reader wonders if this is all John's work aims to accomplish.

As with all literature, the onus on the reader is to go beyond what is stated, reading for authorial intent—if there is some—and also allowing the literature new life in the context of history. John goes on to state that his goal is twofold, to expose the saints' deeds for the glorification of God, and to effect change in the life of the hearer. The light of the 'triumphs' of his saints will cause the reader

66 The notable exception is John of Ephesus' inclusion of his own childhood narrative in the story of Abraham and Maro. John of Ephesus, *Lives* 4, *PO* 17: 61–62.

67 John of Ephesus, *Lives*, Introduction, *PO* 17: 3 n. 2.

68 Cox Miller, "Strategies of Representation", 211.

69 John of Ephesus, *Lives* 1, *PO* 17: 1.

70 *bʿwhdnʾ dktybtn*: John of Ephesus, *Lives* 1, *PO* 17: 1–2.

to imitate them and 'receive their patterns in themselves'.[71] John hoped the text would have an effect on the lives of those who read it, signalling the prescriptive aspect of his work. This future-orientated dimension to John's work foreshadows another important concept about the compilation. These texts offered a wider range of possibilities for introspection and relation. Future readers would relate to the stories through their saints, but also through the power a text can have to shape cultural meaning and life.

4 John of Tella: A Polyphonic Vignette

A prime example of John's carefully worded histories comes to us in his chapter about John of Tella. He begins his chapter by noting that he was singular in every category against which he might be judged, bearing his cross daily among persecuted men, and 'a hero' and 'true martyr of the truth of his faith' when compared to other martyrs.[72] John of Ephesus tells us that the schismatic followers of Chalcedon 'became accomplishers of the saying, "They changed God's truth into a lie."'[73] In facing this trouble we might expect him to call on God's power for retribution and justice. Instead, John of Tella takes the persecution as a sign of being found worthy of suffering with Christ and returns to his former anchoritic life.[74] John of Ephesus appears to be setting up a model for viewing the Miaphysites in their persecution. Like the great martyrs of old, they persevere in their righteous action, 'rejoicing and exulting that they had been thought worthy to suffer persecution with Christ'.[75]

John proceeds to record that the Miaphysites were fearful of igniting further persecution and so refused to ordain openly.[76] This notion of the Miaphysites existing in fear is fascinating. John's depiction of the community is not one of overt strength, but rather has shifted from the power of Habib in the first chapter to a downtrodden and fearful community full of persecuted Christians.[77] The layers here are worth noting, given our theme of polyphony. John of Tella

71 *wlmsb dmwthwn bqnwmyhwn*: John of Ephesus, *Lives* 1, *PO* 17: 2.
72 *gnbr' ... shd' šryr' dḥlp šrr' dhymnwth*: John of Ephesus, *Lives* 24, *PO* 18: 311.
73 *whww mšlmn' dhy d'myr' dḥlpw šrrh d'lh' bkdbwt'*: John of Ephesus, *Lives* 24, 18: 312.
74 John of Ephesus, *Lives* 24, *PO* 18: 312–313.
75 *kd ḥdyn wrwzyn dšww d'm mšyḥ' ntrdpwn*: John of Ephesus, *Lives* 24, *PO* 18: 313.
76 John of Ephesus, *Lives* 24, *PO* 18: 314.
77 John relates that they realised their fear was unscriptural (cf. 1John 4:18): *Lives* 24, *PO* 18: 315.

took it upon himself to travel and ordain widely, and John tells us that hundreds flocked to him each day. When word spread of his work, and orders were given that he should die if he did not stop, John of Tella replied that he would continue to help those in need and would not be hindered by an earthly king from performing his duty to his heavenly king.[78] John of Ephesus displays for us a saint that was in opposition to the majority party, but who did not let that define his life of service to the Christian faithful. He wraps up his comments on John of Tella by commenting on the many persecuted figures who were exiled, imprisoned, and burnt in public.[79]

John of Ephesus closes the section with a benediction of hope that God may mercifully visit his church and expiate those who by sin have become 'sons who provoke.'[80] The tone is remarkably forgiving and mirrors his call for peace in other parts of his compilation.[81] Although impacted on by our author, the possibilities of reconciliation pass well beyond his control. Even with perfect examples of social comportment in sectarian Christian controversies, the harsh reality of political and theological struggles in late antiquity was significant. Does John expect his audience to follow in the steps of John of Tella, or is it possible to read John against himself in this text? He has recorded the fear of persecution in the same text that depicts a saint capable of wielding God's power on earth (Habib). John of Tella speaks his truth to the 'earthly king' with power, amid threats being made on his life. Are we to see the Miaphysite community as resilient or downtrodden or both, rejoicing in persecution while effecting change through social action?

Underneath whatever John might covet in a future Christian community lies the question of how accurately he represents the past. Whether John of Tella's ordinations took place as John records them, and how Miaphysites responded to persecutions, is certainly worth considering. What we can begin to be sure about is that John's work is comprised of more than one voice and should be read as such, however accurately the picture might have represented any particular moment in time. This common question of veracity in literature is worth exploring in a bit more detail.

---

78 John tells us that he ordained 170,000: *Lives* 24, PO 18: 318, 320.

79 John of Ephesus, *Lives* 24, PO 18: 322.

80 *bny' mmrmrn'*: John of Ephesus, *Lives* 24, PO 18: 324.

81 This is perhaps most poignant in the story of John of Hephaestopolis, where he says 'by whose prayers may schisms and strifes be done away from within it [the church] until the end' (*dbṣlwthwn qdyšt' nbṭlwn mn gwh sdq' wḥryn' 'dm' lḥrt' 'myn*): John of Ephesus, *Lives of the Eastern Saints*, 25, PO 18: 338.

5 Literature and History?

One could make the case that Athanasius' rendering of Antony is far more literary than historical. On the one hand, we might argue that much of Antony's life is an imaginative tableau of Athanasius, replete with anti-Arian inclusions and the markings of a bishop eager to control this burgeoning, desert asceticism.[82] On the other, it is a collection of stories about the fabled man, which had a vibrant life in the minds of later Christians.[83] A significant mark of literature is that it has a viability that extends beyond its historical details, inspiring later figures (e.g. Augustine) to emulate and interpret the document in their own contexts. Even decoupled from its mantle as history, it finds new life as a cohesive whole, whether interacting with new populations and meanings, or resituated in a veiled propagandistic style.

John of Ephesus engages in a similar style, acknowledging his own interest in the heroic figures from the surrounding districts.[84] He does so, however, in a compilatory manner, which distances him from the figures in unavoidable, yet advantageous, ways. Here literature can be deployed not simply as the fictive rendering of the saint, but rather as a freely functioning artistic form, necessarily divorced from the author's managing impetus. Junot Díaz, the acclaimed author of *The Brief Wondrous Life of Oscar Wao*, argues that if a character is too purposeful, they lose believability, causing the reader to awaken to the intentions of the author.[85] This notion is intimately related to Roland Barthes' notion of the *effet de réel* which holds that 'it is precisely the superfluity of apparently pointless detail which authenticates the text as realistic: the details would not be there if they were not an integral part of true-to-life description'.[86] Lack of purpose, or superfluity of detail, both lend a sense of believability to the text and allow the reader to imagine narrative in vivid, if inefficient, ways, mimicking much of real life.[87]

---

82 David Brakke, *Athanasius and the Politics of Asceticism* (Oxford: Clarendon Press, 1995). On the impact of literary heroising and liminalising of the saint to control the power of asceticism, see James A. Francis, *Subversive Virtue: Asceticism and Authority in the Second-Century Pagan World* (University Park, PA: Pennsylvania State University Press, 1995).

83 See Augustine, *Confessions* 8.6.14.

84 John of Ephesus, *Lives* 1, *PO* 17: 2–3.

85 This is a convenient and compelling notion, given the blatant misogyny and racism in which so many of his characters engage. Conversation at Rollins College, 10/26/17, and subsequent email correspondence on 10/27/16.

86 Fludernik, *Introduction to Narratology*, 54; Roland Barthes, "L'effet de réel", *Communications* 11.1 (1968), 84–89.

87 This in many ways is akin to what Cox Miller sees as Philostratus' 'failure to be consistent in

If we take a moment to consider literature as an art form which is capable of communicating directly with the reader, several interesting possibilities emerge in our discussion of hagiographical compilation. For most literature to come alive, to be viable in new contexts, with the power necessary to communicate directly with hearers from a variety of communities, it needs to be perceived as transcending an author's aim.[88] The internal complications of good literature draw the hearer in, beyond authorial propaganda. I argue that reading authors of hagiography as solely focused on embodied faith for emulation and devotion is an oversimplification of dynamic works like the one John of Ephesus crafts.

Does John's hagiography need to transcend his intentions, as stated in the preface to his work, to become literature? Perhaps it operates on more than one level, serving as a locus of emulation and devotion, but also a complicated, polyphonic narrative, capable of being read in a multiplicity of ways, including against itself at times, and mirroring the complications John himself faced in his roles as bishop, Justinianic official, historian, and ascetic enthusiast.[89] The compilation, in contradistinction to standalone lives, is capable of bringing forward numerous voices—many of which rest in conflict with each other.[90] Cox Miller has convincingly argued that fourth-century collective biography aims to achieve some 'sameness' even as it provides 'diversity' through particularities from individual lives.[91] She posits that 'any real sense of difference between individuals evaporates to the extent that each one exemplifies the subjectivity

---

compositional style and presentation', which is often '"exasperating" to a modern reader'. She states that this style embeds 'the individual sophists in a personalized context of social and political interaction'. Cox Miller, "Strategies of Representation", 220.

88 Here I would cite the distaste an 'Arian' would surely have had for a text like the *Life of Antony*.

89 Bakhtin's argument that the character's words 'destroy the monologic plane of the novel and calls forth an unmediated response—as if the character were not an object of authorial discourse, but rather a full valid, autonomous carrier of his own individual word', is quite applicable to these hagiographies. Mikhail M. Bakhtin, *Problems of Dostoevsky's Poetics, Theory and History of Literature*, vol. 8 (Minneapolis, MN: University of Minnesota Press, 1984), 5.

90 Farrell notes, 'The medieval compilation and commentary, on the other hand, are products of multiple authors in a much more literal way: the author(s), compiler(s), and commentator(s) may well be different individuals and may function at different historical moments, further, they may *all* function as points of intersection for a multiplicity of voices, which suggest that the manuscript text may have several "centers" or, indeed, that the manuscript text may be more radically *de*centered than any nineteenth-century novel.' Thomas J. Farrell, *Bakhtin and Medieval Voices* (Gainesville: University Press of Florida, 1995), 126.

91 Cox Miller, "Strategies of Representation", 221.

that is the heart of the collection's interest'.[92] I wonder, with a text like John's, if we can accurately describe his text's intended subjectivity. Does collective biography demand the evaporation of difference among these subjects? Moreover, can we locate John's subjectivity in relation to the text? This may be less about fourth-century versus sixth-century collections, given that Gregory of Tours' *Vita Patrum* does indeed seem to argue that the compilation is geared more toward determining a definitive 'Life' of the saints than 'Lives'.[93] And yet, John's enigmatic style suggests that there may not be one 'Life' unifying his narratives. It has the possibility of discordant polyphony, which serves a number of ends. It can be read by an array of communities, each taking away their own message, indicative of the life of the text beyond the author.[94] It also reinforces the believability of the author, since counter-examples promote trust in historical veracity. A fine example of this is found in the interpretation of the Gospels, wherein discordant or dissimilar claims support the notion that the original sources were not doctored into harmony.[95] The remaining question is whether we can conceive of late antique authors rising to such a level of literary facility. Given our examples, and their complicated histories of interpretation, I suggest that this is precisely the level of literary inquiry we should be applying to these texts.

The question of how these texts were read and how they were meant to be read draws us closer to the question of context. Considering the problems raised by the categories of humour and epistolary dialectic, as discussed in Konstantin Klein's and Michael Stuart Williams' work in this volume, we are reminded of the possibility that there may also be ways of reading compilations that are foreign to the modern historian. Communities receiving these stories at face value, as true stories of saintly character, should certainly account for at least some portion of the readership. To imagine that this was the best way to read such a text, however, would be short-sighted. I am arguing that compilations fall into a class of literature that was capable of more than the basic conveyance of narrative. Compilations can muster several concurrent operations, and not all of these fall strictly under the author's control.

We can see how texts of compilations were crafted to explore particular themes at particular times and places. They simultaneously subvert the cri-

---

92 Cox Miller, "Strategies of Representation", 221.

93 Cox Miller, "Strategies of Representation", 221; James, *Gregory of Tours*, xiv.

94 Roland Barthes, "The Death of the Author", *Aspen: The Magazine in a Box* 5+6 (1967).

95 This is commonly referred to as the 'criterion of dissimilarity' and is often used to prove the authenticity of Jesus' sayings. Paula Fredriksen, *From Jesus to Christ* (New Haven, CT: Yale University Press, 1988), 5.

tique of interested author through their polyphonic style while continuing to prescribe discursive models for ascetic life. The result is a style that could do a range of things, although not always controllable by the author. The further the text moved along the spectrum toward a disinterested form of literature, the more possibilities emerged for dissonant readings. That is to say, it could be read by divergent groups for unique conclusions.[96] In choosing the compilation as a literary style, authors such as John give their texts life that transcends apologetic discourse on a particular theme.

6 Conclusions

Given the complicated relationship between John's Miaphysite faith and his closeness to Emperor Justinian, his choice to commemorate the saints of Syria in a compilatory style becomes a fascinating point of inquiry. The compilation, by virtue of being distanced from the author's hand, can serve to shield the author from criticism, as well as leave enough room and multiplicity of voices for the author to promote particular viewpoints, prescriptions for holiness, and commemorative vignettes. His work avoids a single theme, allowing for multiple voices and multiple possibilities of reading. The compilation allows John to touch on significant issues with varying depths of specificity depending on the topic, by increasing or lessening the frame of anonymity. John utilises the prologue to his advantage, like so many before him, claiming to have witnessed everything he records, but also recording far more than he could have witnessed. This opens the reader's mind to the broader possibilities within the text. John communicates with the audience on different levels, from overt and intimate descriptions of his actions to more veiled representations of his saints as model holy persons witnessing to their faith in persecution. Even John's clearest formulae, such as the pagan conversions by Simeon, can be reinterpreted and complicated through other stories in his collection.

I have argued for a literary and polyphonic aspect in John's compilation specifically, and I believe that it can be extended to other compilations of the

96 We should note here that the opposite could be argued, since the polyphonic version of these texts could look identical to one that was truly and simply compiled with no design. One wonders if the work of John Moschus does not fall into this category, especially as he mixes the categories of retributive justice. However, some have argued well for a far more deliberate work: see Brenda Llewellyn Ihssen, *John Moschos' Spiritual Meadow: Authority and Autonomy at the End of the Antique World* (Farnham/Burlington, VT: Routledge, 2014).

period. The hagiographical narrative lends itself to being recrafted and redeployed for a range of objectives. Set in a volume of collected stories, the scope of its dynamic possibilities multiplies, giving the author significant agency that was unavailable to writers of single *vitae*. The lives of the saints take on a life of their own as they are received, interpreted, and reimagined by the author, and eventually by the reader. This is what makes the compilation such an intriguing facet of historical interpretation, functioning as 'real' literature that lives well beyond the compiler's designs.

In conclusion, this chapter offers compilations as a site of renewed interest and possibility. The author of the compilation has preserved a range of voices and ideas, leaving room for interpretation among ancient and modern readers alike. As much as any author of great literature is capable, these hagiographers manipulated their media in thoughtful and energetic ways. Drawing on a range of motives, methods, agency, and polyphony, the compilation became a powerful tool for a range of outcomes. Through projection onto the heroic and martyred saints of the past, compilations attempted to forecast and prescribe new paradigms for the future, shaping social comportment, and re-envisioning theology, reconciliation, providence, political power, and justice in the lives of the future reader.

Bibliography

Aziza, Claude, *Vivre l'antiquité: Recueil de préfaces et autres textes* (Bordeaux: Ausonius éditions, 2016).

Bakhtin, Mikhail M., *Problems of Dostoevsky's Poetics, Theory and History of Literature*, vol. 8 (Minneapolis, MN: University of Minnesota Press, 1984).

Barthes, Roland, "The Death of the Author", *Aspen: The Magazine in a Box* 5+6 (1967).

Barthes, Roland, "L'effet de réel." *Communications* 11.1 (1968), 84–89.

Brakke, David, *Athanasius and the Politics of Asceticism* (Oxford: Clarendon Press, 1995).

Brock, Sebastian P., *A Brief Outline of Syriac Literature* (Kottayam: St. Ephrem Ecumenical Research Institute, 1997).

Brock, Sebastian P., *An Introduction to Syriac Studies* (Piscataway, NJ: Gorgias Press, 2017).

Brooks, Ernest W. (ed.), *John of Ephesus: Lives of the Eastern Saints*. Patrologia Orientalis 82 (Turnhout: Brepols, 2003).

Brown, Peter, "The Rise and Function of the Holy Man in Late Antiquity", *JRS* 61 (1971), 80–101.

Butler, Dom Cuthbert, *The Lausiac History of Palladius: A Critical Discussion Together with Notes on Early Egyptian Monachism* (Cambridge: Cambridge University Press, 1898).

Cameron, Averil, *Christianity and the Rhetoric of Empire: The Development of Christian Discourse* (Berkeley: University of California Press, 1991).

Canivet, Pierre, *Le monachisme syrien selon Théodoret de Cyr* (Paris: Editions Beauchesne, 1977).

Chadwick, Henry, *The Church in Ancient Society: From Galilee to Gregory the Great* (Oxford: Oxford University Press, 2001).

Clark, Elizabeth A., *The Origenist Controversy: The Cultural Construction of an Early Christian Debate* (Princeton, NJ: Princeton University Press, 1992).

Corke-Webster, James, *Eusebius and Empire: Constructing Church and Rome in the Ecclesiastical History* (Cambridge: Cambridge University Press, 2019).

Cox [Miller], Patricia, *Biography in Late Antiquity: A Quest for the Holy Man*. The Transformation of the Classical Heritage 5 (Berkeley: University of California Press, 1983).

Cox Miller, Patricia, "Desert Asceticism and 'The Body from Nowhere'", *JECS 2.2* (1994), 137–153.

Cox Miller, Patricia, "Strategies of Representation in Collective Biography: Constructing the Subject as Holy", in Tomas Hägg and Philip Rousseau (eds.), *Greek Biography and Panegyric in Late Antiquity* (Berkeley: University of California Press, 2000), 209–254.

Debié, Muriel, "Writing History as 'Histoires': The Biographical Dimension of East Syriac Historiography", in Arietta Papaconstantinou and Hugh Kennedy (eds.), *Writing 'True Stories': Historians and Hagiographers in the Late Antique and Medieval Near East* (Turnhout: Brepols Publishers, 2010), 43–75.

Devos, Paul, "Abgar, hagiographe perse méconnu (début du ve siècle)", *Analecta Bollandiana* 83 (1965), 303–328.

Farrell, Thomas J., *Bakhtin and Medieval Voices* (Gainesville: University Press of Florida, 1995).

Fludernik, Monika, *An Introduction to Narratology* (London/New York: Routledge, 2009).

Formisano, Marco, "Late Latin Encyclopaedism: Towards a New Paradigm of Practical Knowledge", in Jason König and Greg Woolf (eds.), *Encyclopaedism from Antiquity to the Renaissance* (Cambridge: Cambridge University Press, 2013), 197–215.

Francis, James A., *Subversive Virtue: Asceticism and Authority in the Second-Century Pagan World* (University Park, PA: Pennsylvania State University Press, 1995).

Fredriksen, Paula, *From Jesus to Christ* (New Haven, CT: Yale University Press, 1988).

Gregg, Robert C. (transl.), *Athanasius: The Life of Antony and the Letter to Marcellinus*. (New York: Paulist Press, 1980).

Harvey, Susan Ashbrook, *Asceticism and Society in Crisis: John of Ephesus and the Lives of the Eastern Saints* (Berkeley: University of California Press, 1990).

Hildebrandt, Reiner and Thomas Gloning (eds.), *Hildegard von Bingen, Physica: Liber*

Subtilitatum Diversarum Naturarum Creaturarum. Textkritische Ausgabe (Berlin: De Gruyter, 2010).

James, Edward, *Gregory of Tours: Life of the Fathers* (Liverpool: Liverpool University Press, 1991).

Humfress, Caroline, "Law and Legal Practice in the Age of Justinian", in Maas, *The Cambridge Companion to the Age of Justinian*, 161–184.

Jansen, Laura (ed.), *The Roman Paratext: Frame, Texts, Readers* (Cambridge: Cambridge University Press, 2014).

Krueger, Derek, *Writing and Holiness: The Practice of Authorship in the Early Christian East* (Philadelphia: University of Pennsylvania Press, 2004).

Krueger, Derek, "Early Byzantine Historiography and Hagiography", in Arietta Papaconstantinou and Hugh Kennedy (eds.), *Writing 'True Stories': Historians and Hagiographers in the Late Antique and Medieval Near East* (Turnhout: Brepols Publishers, 2010), 13–20.

Krueger, Paul, Theodor Mommsen, Rudolf Schöll, and Wilhelm Kroll, *Corpus juris civilis* (Berlin: Weidmann, 1888).

Lake, Justin, *Prologues to Ancient and Medieval History* (Toronto: University of Toronto Press, 2013).

Lamirande, Emilien, *Theodoret. Histoire des moines de Syrie: Histoire philothée*. vol. 1. Sources chrétiennes 234 (Paris: Les Éditions du Cerf, 1977).

Llewellyn Ihssen, Brenda, *John Moschos' Spiritual Meadow: Authority and Autonomy at the End of the Antique World* (Farnham/Burlington, VT: Routledge, 2014).

Maas, Michael, "Roman Questions, Byzantine Answers: Contours of the Age of Justinian", in idem, *The Cambridge Companion to the Age of Justinian*, 3–27.

Maas, Michael (ed.), *The Cambridge Companion to the Age of Justinian* (Cambridge: Cambridge University Press, 2005).

Marincola, John, *Authority and Tradition in Ancient Historiography* (Cambridge: Cambridge University Press, 1997).

McGuckin, John Anthony, *The Ascent of Christian Law: Patristic and Byzantine Formulations of a New Civilization* (Yonkers, NY: St. Vladimir's Seminary Press, 2012).

Meeus, Alexander, "Compilation or Tradition? Some Thoughts on the Methods of Historians and Other Scholars in Antiquity", *Sacris Erudiri* 56 (2017), 395–413.

Meyer, Robert T., *Palladius: The Lausiac History* (Westminster, MD: Newman Press/London: Longmans, Green, and Co., 1965).

Momigliano, Arnaldo, *Essays in Ancient and Modern Historiography* (Middletown, CT: Wesleyan University Press, 1977).

Momigliano, Arnaldo, *The Classical Foundations of Modern Historiography* (Berkeley: University of California Press, 1990).

Moulinier, Laurence (ed.), *Beate Hildegardis Cause et cure* (Berlin: Akademie Verlag, 2003).

Mousourakis, George, *A Legal History of Rome* (London: Routledge, 2007).

Murphy, Trevor Morgan, *Pliny the Elder's Natural History: The Empire in the Encyclopedia* (Oxford: Oxford University Press, 2004).

Offergeld, Thilo (ed.), *Hugo von St Viktor. Didascalicon de studio legendi* (*Studienbuch*) (Freiburg i.B.: Herder, 1997).

Pelttari, Aaron, *The Space That Remains: Reading Latin Poetry in Late Antiquity* (Ithaca, NY: Cornell University Press, 2014).

Price, Richard M., *Cyril of Scythopolis: The Lives of the Monks of Palestine* (Kalamazoo, MI: Cistercian Publications, 1991).

Ramelli, Ilaria, *The Christian Doctrine of Apokatastasis: A Critical Assessment from the New Testament to Eriugena* (Leiden: Brill, 2013).

Riad, Eva, *Studies in the Syriac Preface* (Uppsala: Uppsala University, 1988).

Rubenson, Samuel, *The Letters of St. Antony: Monasticism and the Making of a Saint* (Minneapolis, MN: Fortress Press, 1995).

Somerville, Robert and Bruce Clark Brasington, *Prefaces to Canon Law Books in Latin Christianity: Selected Translations, 500–1245* (New Haven, CT: Yale University Press, 1998).

Stroumsa, Guy, "On the Status of Books in Early Christianity", in Carol Harrison, Caroline Humfress, and Isabella Sandwell (eds.), *Being Christian in Late Antiquity: A Festschrift for Gillian Clark* (Oxford/New York: Oxford University Press, 2014), 57–89.

Valantasis, Richard, "A Theory of the Social Function of Asceticism", in Vincent L. Wimbush and Richard Valantasis (eds.), *Asceticism* (New York: Oxford University Press, 1995), 544–552.

van Ginkel, Jan Jacob, *John of Ephesus: A Monophysite Historian in Sixth-Century Byzantium* (Groningen: Rijksuniversitet, 1995).

Van Nuffelen, Peter, *Orosius and the Rhetoric of History* (Oxford: Oxford University Press, 2012).

Van Uytfanghe, Marc, "L'hagiographie: Un 'genre' chrétien ou antique tardif?" *Analecta Bollandiana* 111 (1993), 135–188.

Ward, Benedicta, *The Sayings of the Desert Fathers: The Alphabetical Collection* (London: Mowbrays, 1975; 2nd edition Kalamazoo: Cistercian Studies, 1986).

Wortley, John, *John Moschus: The Spiritual Meadow* (Kalamazoo, MI: Cistercian Publications, 1992).

PART 3

The Strategies of Hagiography

CHAPTER 8

How to Persuade a Saint: Supplication in Jerome's *Lives* of Holy Men

Christa Gray

Among the arguments emerging from this volume is the cardinal position of Jerome in the development of hagiography in general and for ascetic biography in particular. His imaginative responses to the *Life of Antony* set the tone for later adaptations, and their popularity is attested in the vast number of surviving manuscripts.[1] Varied as his three *Lives of Holy Men* are in structure and content, close reading reveals some shared patterns of composition. This chapter identifies one such pattern and discusses its implications for the literary shaping of these hagiographical narratives. It focuses on the scenes of supplication which are found at pivotal points in all of the *Lives*: that is to say, on intense requests at moments of crisis, articulated in a sequence of actions which combine movement and speech. My discussion has three aims: firstly, to bring out the intertextual relations between the three works; secondly, to investigate the links of this pattern with earlier texts; and, thirdly (and most importantly), to consider the motivation for using supplication as a literary structure and to explore what it can tell us about Jerome's construction of sainthood.

1 Supplication: What Is It?

In this chapter I treat supplication as a particularly emphatic, ritualised method of asking someone for something. The classic object of such a plea is the life of the suppliant (for example, Lykaon in *Iliad* 21.34–135), but it is also suitable for something valued more or less than one's own life (for example, Priam suppli-

1 See Bernard Lambert, *Bibliotheca Hieronymiana Manuscripta: la tradition manuscrite des œuvres de saint Jérôme*, vol. 2 (Stenbrugis: Martinus Nijhoff, 1969), 459–514 for the figures: I count 471 manuscripts of the *Vita Pauli*, 285 of the *Vita Hilarionis* (with Edgardo M. Morales' observation that in Lambert's catalogue there is one duplication and one manuscript which does not contain the text, in Pierre Leclerc, Edgardo M. Morales, and Adalbert de Vogüé, *Trois vies de moines* (*Paul, Malchus, Hilarion*), Sources chrétiennes 508 (Paris: Les Éditions du Cerf, 2007), 114), and 349 of the *Vita Malchi*.

 | DOI:10.1163/9789004421332_010

cating Achilles for the return of his son Hector's body in *Iliad* 24). Even immortal deities can be portrayed as employing supplication (for example, Thetis in *Iliad* 1.495–513). What distinguishes supplication from a mere request is its elaborate form, which Fred Naiden has analysed as consisting of four steps: 1. 'an approach to an individual or a place'; 2. 'a distinctive gesture', usually a physical lowering of the suppliant and often involving touching or clasping a part of the body of the person supplicated; 3. 'the request for a boon', which 'is wholly verbal'; and 4. 'the response of the supplicandus' (the person to whom supplication is made).[2] According to Naiden, 'supplication emerges as a practice with legal, moral, and religious elements': in this sense, it goes to the heart of a community's most precious values. I am not concerned here with any 'original' archaic Greek beliefs about the efficacy of each of the formal elements of the supplication and their combination;[3] but Jerome's use of the form may provide some hints for the significance and meaning of supplication in a Christian context.

Supplication thus provides a promising angle from which to approach stories about saints. First of all, it represents a recognised form of communication—not even restricted to the ancient world—both in literature and in real life.[4] The ceremonial structure of supplication makes it suitable for stylised representation in literature. In fact, Kevin Crotty has argued that supplication forms a fundamental structure of both the *Iliad* and the *Odyssey*.[5] This means that the intertwining of the two strands of supplication's manifestation—historical and literary—goes back at least as far as Homer. This characteristic makes supplication a useful focal point for interpreting hagiography (in so far as it appears in hagiographical texts): after all, the problem of the relationship of a historical saint's real existence with his or her representation in biographical or liturgical texts is a particularly salient one, given that it constantly raises questions about imitability and its limits in life as well as in literature.

2 Fred S. Naiden, *Ancient Supplication* (Oxford: Oxford University Press 2006), 4.

3 John Gould, "Hiketeia", *JHS* 93, 74–103 elaborates the underlying ritual mechanics of supplication in Homer and in Greek tragedy with much insight and some plausibility. His argument is contradicted by Kevin Crotty, *The Poetics of Supplication: Homer's Iliad and Odyssey* (Ithaca, NY: Cornell University Press, 1994).

4 Naiden, *Ancient Supplication* is the standard work on the practice and presentation of supplication, with a very helpful appendix of literary and documentary sources. Unfortunately, his discussion of Christian supplication is restricted to an 'Epilogue' (276–279) based on Gregory of Tours' *Historia Francorum*, which mainly deals with supplication at altars in the presence of a member of the clergy, without reference to the phenomenon of the holy man.

5 Crotty, *Poetics of Supplication*.

2 The Rhetoric of Supplication

In Aeschylus' *Suppliants* the daughters of Danaus entreat Pelasgus, the king of Argos, to protect them from being forcibly married to their Egyptian cousins. They appeal to divine protection and to their ancestral kinship with Argos, and they threaten to commit suicide if their plea is not accepted. Pelasgus then leads an assembly of the Argive people to vote in favour of protecting the women (Aesch. *Suppl.* 605–624), and when the Egyptians arrive to carry them off, the Argives stop them (Aesch. *Suppl.* 911–951). Susanne Gödde shows that the Danaids' speeches—even though they are cast in the form of choral lyric—contain strong elements of 'an orator's line of reasoning aimed at plausibility vis-à-vis an audience' ('die auf Plausibilität bedachte Beweisführung eines Redners gegenüber einem Publikum').[6] In consequence, she argues, the play reflects an early stage of the culture of democratic oratory which was in the process of being established at Athens.[7]

Despite this close affinity between supplication and rhetoric, ancient rhetorical handbooks offer little discussion of supplication. The classical genres of oratory—forensic, deliberative, and epideictic—are not primarily geared towards the fulfilment of individual needs but towards a common good. The orator's own objective must, of course, be presented as conducive to this shared good, but it does not have logical priority. In order to achieve his aim,[8] the orator has to convince the audience by pleasing them. In Aristotle's *Rhetoric* pity is figured as a negative emotion ('a sort of pain', 2.8.2, 1385b13), arising from witnessing another's undeserved misfortune and imagining that it could be one's own. Therefore, pity must not be invoked as the primary emotion in oratory: after all, the aim of oratory is to make the audience feel good about themselves and the decision which they are being persuaded to make. Negative emotions like pity can only have a subsidiary role, especially in perorations.[9] By contrast, the ceremony of supplication at least implies, if it is not wholly based upon, the

6 Susanne Gödde, *Das Drama der Hikesie. Ritual und Rhetorik in Aischylos' Hiketiden* (Münster: Aschendorff, 2000), 179.

7 Gödde, *Drama der Hikesie*, 179.

8 Orators in the ancient world are almost always male, and rhetorical handbooks presuppose a male speaker in a misogynistic environment. By contrast, people of any kind and status performed supplications: Naiden, *Ancient Supplication*, 19.

9 Cf. David Konstan, "Rhetoric and Emotion", in Ian Worthington (ed.), *A Companion to Greek Rhetoric* (Malden, MA/Oxford: 2007), 420–421: in ancient Attic oratory, pity could only be invoked if 'the facts—or a plausible interpretation of them—had already … demonstrated the innocence of the speaker.'

evocation of pity: the suppliant acknowledges the power of the addressee and begs them to provide the benefit which the suppliant so desperately needs.

In Christian discourse pity is seen more positively. The emotion is ascribed even to God himself, and humans are taught to emulate the divine in this regard, as Jerome's contemporary Gregory of Nyssa makes clear in *On the Beatitudes* 5.2 (124.26–125.2 Callahan): 'If indeed God is called pityful (*eleēmōn*) by the divinely inspired scripture, and the Deity is itself the truly blessed, then the conclusion would appear to follow that if someone, though human, becomes pitiful, he is deemed worthy of divine blessedness.'[10] In Christian thought, at least, the merciful person comes closer to God. However, it is not the improved status of pity alone that recommends supplication to Christians; rather, it is its close affinity with prayer. At Luke 18:1–8, Jesus tells the following parable to illustrate the efficacy of praying constantly:

> Then Jesus told his disciples a parable to show them that they should always pray and not give up. He said: 'In a certain town there was a judge who neither feared God nor cared what people thought. And there was a widow in that town who kept coming to him with the plea, "Grant me justice against my adversary." For some time he refused. But finally he said to himself, "Even though I don't fear God or care what people think, yet because this widow keeps bothering me, I will see that she gets justice, so that she won't eventually come and attack me!"' And the Lord said, 'Listen to what the unjust judge says. And will not God bring about justice for his chosen ones, who cry out to him day and night? Will he keep putting them off? I tell you, he will see that they get justice, and quickly. However, when the Son of Man comes, will he find faith on the earth?'[11]

10 Translation: Stuart George Hall, "Translation of Gregory of Nyssa, *On the Beatitudes*", in Hubertus R. Drobner and Albert Viciano (eds.), *Gregory of Nyssa: On the Beatitudes. An English Version with Commentary and Supporting Studies. Proceedings of the Eighth International Colloquium on Gregory of Nyssa* (*Paderborn, 14–18 September 1998*). Vigiliae Christianae Supplements 51 (Leiden: Brill, 2000), 58. See David Konstan, *Pity Transformed* (London: Duckworth, 2001), 120.

11 Ἔλεγεν δὲ παραβολὴν αὐτοῖς πρὸς τὸ δεῖν πάντοτε προσεύχεσθαι αὐτοὺς καὶ μὴ ἐγκακεῖν λέγων· κριτής τις ἦν ἔν τινι πόλει τὸν θεὸν μὴ φοβούμενος καὶ ἄνθρωπον μὴ ἐντρεπόμενος. χήρα δὲ ἦν ἐν τῇ πόλει ἐκείνῃ καὶ ἤρχετο πρὸς αὐτὸν λέγουσα· ἐκδίκησόν με ἀπὸ τοῦ ἀντιδίκου μου. καὶ οὐκ ἤθελεν ἐπὶ χρόνον. μετὰ δὲ ταῦτα εἶπεν ἐν ἑαυτῷ· εἰ καὶ τὸν θεὸν οὐ φοβοῦμαι οὐδὲ ἄνθρωπον ἐντρέπομαι, διά γε τὸ παρέχειν μοι κόπον τὴν χήραν ταύτην ἐκδικήσω αὐτήν, ἵνα μὴ εἰς τέλος ἐρχομένη ὑπωπιάζῃ με. Εἶπεν δὲ ὁ κύριος· ἀκούσατε τί ὁ κριτὴς τῆς ἀδικίας λέγει· ὁ δὲ θεὸς οὐ μὴ ποιήσῃ τὴν ἐκδίκησιν τῶν ἐκλεκτῶν αὐτοῦ τῶν βοώντων αὐτῷ ἡμέρας καὶ νυκτός, καὶ μακροθυμεῖ ἐπ' αὐτοῖς; λέγω ὑμῖν ὅτι ποιήσει τὴν ἐκδίκησιν αὐτῶν ἐν τάχει.

The parable provides an analogue for praying to God in the relationship of two human beings. As a matter of course, one cannot request anything from God except in an attitude of supplication, given the unbridgeable difference in power. Even so, the terms in which the analogy is constructed dignify the suppliant as someone who deserves to receive what she asks for. In another gospel episode transmitted in Mark 7:24–30 and Matthew 15:21–28, Jesus himself is swayed by the arguments of a Syrophoenician (or Canaanite) woman, whose daughter he refused to heal on the basis that she is not Jewish (Mark 7:27–29):

> 'First let the children eat all they want,' he told her, 'for it is not right to take the children's bread and toss it to the dogs.' 'Lord,' she replied, 'even the dogs under the table eat the children's crumbs.' Then he told her, 'For such a reply, you may go; the demon has left your daughter.'[12]

In Matthew 15:28, Jesus specifies that the woman's repartee shows her faith, which is also the issue at stake in the Lukan parable. Neither story hinges on the evocation of pity; instead they show the value of determination and persistence.

With these developments in mind, let us now look at Jerome's *Lives*. To supplement the gaps in classical rhetorical theory where supplication is concerned, I have found it useful to take recourse to the discipline of linguistic pragmatics to understand what makes supplication effective. Particularly helpful for understanding these verbal aspects of supplication is the influential theory of 'politeness' developed by Penelope Brown and Stephen Levinson.[13] It takes its starting point from a socio-anthropological notion of 'face', a person's image which participants in social interactions construct. According to Brown and Levinson, face 'consists of two specific kinds of desires ("face-wants") attributed by interactants to one another: the desire to be unimpeded in one's actions (negative face) and the desire (in some respects) to be approved of (positive face).'[14] Further, these wants are 'satisfiable only by the actions (including expressions of wants) of others, [and therefore] it will in general be to the

πλὴν ὁ υἱὸς τοῦ ἀνθρώπου ἐλθὼν ἆρα εὑρήσει τὴν πίστιν ἐπὶ τῆς γῆς; Greek text from Nestle and Aland; NIV translation used unless otherwise stated.

12 καὶ ἔλεγεν αὐτῇ· ἄφες πρῶτον χορτασθῆναι τὰ τέκνα, οὐ γάρ ἐστιν καλὸν λαβεῖν τὸν ἄρτον τῶν τέκνων καὶ τοῖς κυναρίοις βαλεῖν. ἡ δὲ ἀπεκρίθη καὶ λέγει αὐτῷ· κύριε· καὶ τὰ κυνάρια ὑποκάτω τῆς τραπέζης ἐσθίουσιν ἀπὸ τῶν ψιχίων τῶν παιδίων. καὶ εἶπεν αὐτῇ· διὰ τοῦτον τὸν λόγον ὕπαγε, ἐξελήλυθεν ἐκ τῆς θυγατρός σου τὸ δαιμόνιον.

13 Penelope Brown and Stephen C. Levinson, *Politeness: Some Universals in Language Usage*. Studies in Interactional Sociolinguistics (Cambridge: Cambridge University Press, 1987).

14 Brown and Levinson, *Politeness*, 13.

mutual interest of two [agents] to maintain each other's face.'[15] Impositions such as requests are perceived as 'face threatening acts' ('FTAs').[16] The extent to and the ways in which they are mitigated through 'politeness strategies' seeking to minimise injury and maximise benefit to the addressee's face reveal not only the relative power and status of the participants but also show up fundamental values of the participants' society.[17] Although the details of Brown and Levinson's discussion have often been queried and refined, it presents a useful tool for describing the verbal aspects of supplication and their motivations.

3 Supplication in the *Vita Pauli*

If we follow the chronological sequence, the first extended scene of supplication in Jerome's *Lives* occurs at *Vita Pauli* 9.4–6. Antony has been searching for Paul in the Egyptian desert, guided by a centaur, a faun, and a she-wolf, and is finally making his way into the cave where Paul lives. But Paul continues to prefer his solitude: as soon as he notices Antony's approach, he bars his door against him:

> Finally [Antony] saw, through the terrifying darkness, a light in the distance. He hurried on more eagerly, hitting a stone with his foot, which made a noise. At this sound, the blessed Paul closed the door which had stood open and reinforced it with a bolt. Then Antony fell down before the door and kept asking, until the sixth hour and beyond, to be admitted. He said: 'Who I am, from where and why I have come, you know. I am aware that I do not deserve to look at you (*scio me non mereri conspectum tuum*); but unless I see you I will not withdraw. You who welcome wild beasts, why are you turning back a human being? I searched and I have

15 Brown and Levinson, *Politeness*, 60.

16 More specifically, a request is a threat to the addressee's 'negative face wants': Brown and Levinson, *Politeness*, 65–66. The heightened emotions at play in a supplication additionally threaten the addressee's positive face wants, by giving them 'possible reason to fear him or be embarrassed by him': Brown and Levinson, *Politeness*, 66. At the same time, the interaction threatens the suppliant's own positive face through the expression of 'apologies', the 'breakdown of physical control over the body', including 'falling down', and 'emotion leakage', including 'non-control of … tears': Brown and Levinson, *Politeness*, 68.

17 A successful interaction will leave both participants undamaged and perhaps even enhanced with regard to their face. This is possible wherever both parties acknowledge and cooperate in addressing each other's face wants.

> found, I am knocking so that it may be opened unto me; but if I do not gain my end, I shall die right here in front of your door posts. I'm sure that you will at least bury my corpse.' These words he spoke and stood firm, rooted to the spot without moving. And the great man gave him his reply in few words: 'No one makes a request by means of threats, no one engages in slander amid tears. And you are surprised if I should not welcome you, seeing that you have come prepared to die?' He smiled at him and opened the entrance. When it stood open, both sides shared in an embrace and they greeted one another by their own names. Together they gave thanks to the Lord.

Antony's response is that of a supplicant: he assumes a dejected pose[18] and begins his speech by emphasising Paul's superior knowledge[19] and his own humility.[20] However, he then leaves behind the conventional strategies of politeness: instead he reproaches Paul for treating him worse than an animal (that is, than the she-wolf who showed him the way). His subsequent adaptation of Christ's words in the gospel ('Seek and ye shall find; knock and it shall be opened unto you', Matthew 7:7),[21] although it highlights the shared Christian values of both participants, is designed to make a claim: Paul is obliged to keep Christ's promise.[22] Finally, Antony threatens Paul with having to bury his corpse

18 Brown and Levinson also note the role gestures play in politeness, including the pose of supplication: e.g. *Politeness*, 190, in connection with asking for forgiveness.

19 See Brown and Levinson, *Politeness*, 124–125 for the positive politeness strategies of presuming the addressee's knowledge about the context of a request.

20 Cf. Brown and Levinson, *Politeness*, 178–179 for the combination of the speaker's self-humbling and raising of the addressee as a negative politeness strategy; see also Williams in this volume, on humility in conversations between Christians.

21 Αἰτεῖτε καὶ δοθήσεται ὑμῖν, ζητεῖτε καὶ εὑρήσετε, κρούετε καὶ ἀνοιγήσεται ὑμῖν, in the King James Bible translation.

22 In this sense, the statement refers back to Antony's dogged confidence at *V. Pauli* 7.3: *nec tamen a coepto itinere deducebatur, dicens: 'Credo in Deo meo, quod servum suum, quem mihi promisit, ostendet'* ('Yet he was not diverted from his original path; he said: "I believe in my God, that he will show me his servant, whom he promised to me"')—a passage which itself alludes to the gospel, Luke 2:29 *nunc dimittis servum tuum Domine secundum verbum tuum in pace* ('Sovereign Lord, as you have promised, you may now dismiss your servant in peace'). Virginia Burrus, *The Sex Lives of Saints: An Erotics of Ancient Hagiography* (Philadelphia: University of Pennsylvania Press, 2004), 175 n. 44 also notes the relevance of further biblical passages, such as the explicitly erotic Song of Songs 5:2 *vox dilecti mei pulsantis 'aperi mihi soror mea amica mea columba mea inmaculata mea …'* ('[the voice of] my beloved, [who] is knocking: "Open to me, my sister, my darling, my dove, my flawless one …"') and Revelation 3:20 *ecce sto ad ostium et pulso si quis audierit vocem meam et aperuerit ianuam introibo ad illum et cenabo cum illo et ipse mecum* ('Here I am! I stand at the

if he dies before he is admitted.[23] Antony's speech is followed by two verses plucked from Virgil: first, Antony's stance is equated to that of Anchises as he refuses to leave Troy with his family at *Aen.* 2.650 (*talia perstabat memorans fixusque manebat*). The second line introduces the poet Musaeus' response to the Sibyl's question where she and Aeneas may find his father's spirit in the Underworld at *Aen.* 6.672 (*atque huic responsum paucis ita reddidit heros*). The intertextual relationship between the passages is not immediately satisfying: what these lines do for the *Vita Pauli* here is provide the *mots justes* for emphasising Paul's grand status and the taciturnity which appears to be an aspect of his withdrawal from the world. Their epic associations underline the sense that these two heroes are engaged in a tense battle of the wills: by giving his speech a turn away from politeness, Antony has risked the failure of his quest. Paul's response sounds like a stern rebuke of Antony's mode of framing his demands: he suggests that Antony used the wrong strategy, threatening where he should have begged and mixing his emotional appeal with misrepresentations. At the same time, his laughter defuses the tension as he gives in to Antony's demands.[24] The affection then expressed in the mutual embrace seems at odds with the hostility exhibited so far.

This scene sits almost exactly in the centre of the *Life of Paul*.[25] In its details, Antony's interaction with Paul in this passage follows the four steps which Naiden identifies for supplication: approach, gesture, verbal request, and reaction. Firstly, Antony makes his way to Paul's cave, a journey which takes several chapters to complete (*V. Pauli* 7–9). Secondly, he falls down in front of his locked door (*pro foribus conruens*, *V. Pauli* 9.5). Thirdly, there is his speech, of which the quoted words should be imagined to represent only a small part: we

---

door and knock. If anyone hears my voice and opens the door, I will come in and eat with that person, and they with me').

23 Paul in his response explicitly calls Antony's reference to his death a threat: *nemo sic petit ut minetur* ('no one pleads by way of threatening'). The strategy of using threats of suicide to blackmail the addressee is familiar from ancient Greek supplication: see Gödde, *Drama der Hikesie*, 19 on the Danaids' threat to pollute the sanctuary by hanging themselves in the sanctuary where they have taken refuge, at Aesch. *Suppl.* 455–467.

24 According to Brown and Levinson, *Politeness*, 124, '[j]oking is a basic positive-politeness technique' which serves to stress 'shared background knowledge and values.' Perhaps more importantly for our purposes, humour can be used to make a speech act less face-threatening than it actually is (*Politeness*, 229). Also relevant is the observation that 'laughter in conversation is finely attuned to the occurrence of FTAs' ('face-threatening acts') (*Politeness*, 232).

25 It is preceded by c. 1,200 and followed by c. 1,000 words. If we exclude the preface of c. 150 words, the scene appears even more central; but then it would be consistent to exclude the epilogue as well, which also contains c. 150 words.

are told that it goes on *ad sextam et eo amplius horam*, and Antony arrived at the entrance of the cave at the first light of dawn. Fourthly and finally, Paul's response, although critical and mocking, is positive: he agrees to welcome Antony into his solitude. The fact that a God-sent raven then provides a whole loaf of bread instead of the customary half-loaf signals divine approval for this decision (*V. Pauli* 10.2–3).

There is much that is intriguing about this meeting of Antony and Paul. Alan Ross in this volume mentions the important parallels between this scene and the *paraclausithyron*,[26] which support the sustained erotic interpretation of Virginia Burrus.[27] Gendered aspects, furthermore, are implicit in the practice of supplication: as Froma Zeitlin has argued, it is a sacrilege to harm people supplicating in a sacred place, and in this regard 'the virgin and the suppliant are isomorphic categories'.[28] If this insight is applied to the *Life of Paul*, Antony simultaneously plays the parts of the *exclusus amator* and the virgin in need of protection. This suggests that the patterns constructed by supplication contribute to the paradox of erotic sublimation constructed by Jerome.

Herbert Kech notes that Paul's refusal to admit Antony after a long and strenuous journey appears 'positively inhuman' ('geradezu unmenschlich')[29]—a revealing phrase for characterising the superhuman asceticism practised by Paul in this text. Kech explains Paul's behaviour by appealing to narratological concerns: it introduces a delay in the narrative and, by provoking Antony's sup-

---

26 Suggested by Pierre Leclerc, "Antoine et Paul: métamorphose d'un héros", in Yves-Marie Duval (ed.), *Jérôme entre l'Occident et l'Orient. XVIe centenaire du départ de saint Jérôme de Rome et de son installation à Bethléem. Actes du colloque de Chantilly, Sept. 1986* (Paris: Études augustiniennes, 1988), 262–263, on the basis of Theodor Wolpers' paraphrase of the encounter in *Die englische Heiligenlegende des Mittelalters: eine Formgeschichte des Legendenerzählens von der spätantiken lateinischen Tradition bis zur Mitte des 16. Jahrhunderts* (Tübingen: Max Niemeyer, 1964), 51.

27 Burrus, *Sex Lives*, 30. She also points out that the reference to the clandestine mint present in the cave (*V. Pauli* 5.2), dating from 'the time when Antony was joined to Cleopatra' (*ea tempestate qua Cleopatrae iunctus Antonius est*), invites the association of Paul with Cleopatra as 'Antony's' partner: Burrus, *Sex Lives*, 28.

28 Froma I. Zeitlin, "Patterns of Gender in Aeschylean Drama: Seven against Thebes and the Danaid Trilogy", in Mark Griffith and Donald J. Mastronarde (eds.), *Cabinet of the Muses: Essays on Classical and Comparative Literature in Honor of Thomas G. Rosenmeyer* (Atlanta: Scholars Press, 1990), 105, referring to the status of the Dainaids as virgin suppliants in Aeschylus' *Suppliants*. Cf. also Gould, "Hiketeia", 97–98, for the wife as the quintessential suppliant at her husband's hearth.

29 Herbert Kech, *Hagiographie als christliche Unterhaltungsliteratur: Studien zum Phänomen des Erbaulichen anhand der Mönchsviten des hl. Hieronymus*. Göppinger Arbeiten zur Germanistik (Göppingen: Kümmerle, 1977), 41.

plication, adds high drama to this climactic point in the plot.[30] Even so, Paul's response to Antony's pleading is awkward in its reasoning. He appears to justify his *initial* refusal by Antony's *subsequent* threats of suicide, thus inverting cause and effect.[31] Kech comments as follows:

> Mit dieser Art Logik ins Recht gesetzt, läßt er sich herab, in lächelnder Pose den ungebetenen Gast zu empfangen ... Die Kontroverse wird nicht bis zum Ende ausgetragen, sondern vorzeitig überlagert von Umgangsformen (Umarmung, Begrüßung, Danksagung), die ob ihrer Formalität und Konventionalität nichts darüber aussagen, wer wem nachgegeben hat.[32]

This interpretation of the encounter as a conflict which is not resolved but rather put aside emphasises the text's concern with saving Paul's face.[33] Antony's visit threatens his commitment to absolute solitude; but for the narrative to gain access to him, in the form of Antony and his later report to his disciples, he needs a way to make an exception without losing his ascetic credibility. For the reader, Antony's speech illustrates the effort that is necessary to get Paul to compromise his solitude. In one sense, the self-humiliation expressed through the medium of supplication expresses his inferiority to Paul. But at the same time, this expression also gives him rhetorical power over his addressee: as Susanne Gödde has observed in the case of Aeschylus' suppliants, the act of supplication makes a strength out of weakness.[34] Paul, therefore, frames his response in such a way that he appears to act not so much in response to Antony's supplication as in spite of it. He thus compounds Antony's humiliation, albeit unfairly.

Applying Brown and Levinson's concepts of 'positive' and 'negative face' to the depiction of supplication in this scene, I find that these concepts correlate

30 Kech, *Hagiographie*, 41.

31 Kech, *Hagiographie*, 42.

32 Kech, *Hagiographie*, 42.

33 For the notion of face see, besides Brown and Levinson, *Politeness*, also the useful discussion in Peter Barrios-Lech, *Linguistic Interaction in Roman Comedy* (Cambridge: Cambridge University Press, 2016), 32–34. I suggest that the self-humiliation of the petitioner in a supplication ritual may serve both to maintain the addressee's 'positive face' by acknowledging their power and to restore the threat to their 'negative face' caused by the request.

34 Gödde, *Drama der Hikesie*, 33, with reference to Danièle Aubriot-Sévin, *Prière et conceptions religieuses en Grèce ancienne jusqu'à la fin du ve siècle av. J.-C.* Collection de la Maison de l'Orient Méditerranéen 22, Série littéraire et philosophique 5 (Lyon: Bocchard, 1992), 426, who points out the (superficial) connection with the paradoxical logic of Jesus' Beatitudes (Matthew 5:3–12); cf. also 2 Corinthians 12:10: 'That is why, for Christ's sake, I delight in weaknesses, in insults, in hardships, in persecutions, in difficulties. For when I am weak, then I am strong'.

nicely with the communicative needs of the texts. The reader needs to understand that Paul deserves to be honoured for his superlative holiness (~'positive face'), and at the same time that he deserves to be left in the solitude which is the basis of his holiness (~'negative face'). Antony's visit threatens mainly the latter, and so he needs to make the highest possible amends for it, reinforcing perceptions of Paul's holiness by catering to his 'positive face'. Antony's supplication and Paul's response thus enable Paul to compromise his solitude in return for higher prestige.

4 Supplication in the *Vita Malchi*

The *Captive Monk* contains three scenes where characters try to change the protagonist's mind by means of supplications, and they take up an increasing amount of space. The first occurs close to the beginning of Malchus' first-person narrative, when his parents try to make him abandon his proposal of becoming a monk at *V. Malchi* 3.1:

> … I was the only son of my parents. When they were trying to force me to marry on the grounds that I was the representative of the line and the heir of the family, I replied that I wanted instead to be a monk. With what threats my father, with what cajoling words my mother hounded me to betray my chastity can be seen from the single fact that I fled both my home and my parents.[35]

The parents' conduct is marked from the start by coercion (*ad nuptias cogerent*). Malchus' preference is met with threats and blandishments, distributed along gender lines: the father uses threats (*minis*), the mother flatteries (*blanditiis*).[36] Both strategies reflect those used by Antony in the *Life of Paul*: he compliments Paul by acknowledging his foreknowledge and admitting that he is not worthy of his sight (*scio me non mereri conspectum tuum, V. Pauli* 9.5); and he uses the threat of his own death to gain admission regardless, on which Paul calls him out (*nemo sic petit ut minetur, V. Pauli* 9.6). Further, the parents'

35 *solus parentibus fui. qui cum me quasi stirpem generis sui et heredem familiae ad nuptias cogerent, monachum potius esse velle respondi. quantis pater minis, quantis mater blanditiis persecuti sunt ut pudicitiam proderem, haec res sola indicio est, quod et domum et parentes fugi.*

36 Note that 'flattery' is a derogatory way of referring to another's attempt at using positive politeness: cf. Brown and Levinson, *Politeness*, 73.

attempts at persuasion are classed as 'persecution' (*persecuti sunt*), aiming at a 'betrayal' (*proderem*) of Malchus' 'chastity' (*pudicitiam*, interpreted in the ascetic sense of complete sexual abstinence).[37] The pro-ascetic ethos of the *Captive Monk* endorses the judgement that Malchus' parents are in the wrong: their request that he should marry is an act of aggression which he is obliged to refuse.

Much more troubling is Malchus' reaction to his abbot's remonstrations when he proposes to leave the monastery again to return to his now-widowed mother and to his inheritance at *V. Malchi* 3.6–7:

> My abbot began to shout that this was a temptation of the devil and that under the pretext of a worthy act there lay the wiles of the old foe. This was what it meant for a dog to return to its vomit. This was the way, he said, in which many monks had been led astray; the devil never revealed himself openly. He put before me a great many examples from Scripture, among them the story that in the beginning he also tripped up Adam and Eve through the hope of divinity. And when he failed to convince me, he grovelled at my knees and entreated me not to leave him, not to lose myself, not to look behind my back while holding the plough. Woe to me, poor creature that I am! I achieved a base victory, thinking that his aim was not my best interests but his own comfort.[38]

The abbot first maintains his position of authority in trying to convince Malchus through arguments, using biblical quotations and the deterrent example of the fall of Adam and Eve. When Malchus remains indifferent, the abbot resorts to supplication. Malchus' principal transgression in the text lies in his failure to take pity on the undignified grovelling of his superior. This is marked by the switch to the narrator's perspective at *V. Malchi* 3.7: if the text is read without quotation marks indicating the change of speaker, *vae misero mihi* could at first sight be taken to be the abbot's direct speech, using the vocab-

37 In classical Rome *pudicitia* covers appropriate sexual behaviour, including virginity for unmarried girls and marital fidelity for matrons. See Rebecca Langlands, *Sexual Morality in Ancient Rome* (Cambridge: Cambridge University Press, 2006).

38 *clamare hoc coepit abbas meus diaboli esse temptationem et sub honestae rei occasione antiqui hostis astutias. hoc esse reverti canem ad vomitum suum. sic multos monachorum esse deceptos. numquam diabolum aperta fronte se prodere. proponebat mihi exempla de Scripturis plurima, inter quae illud, ab initio quod Adam quoque et Evam spe divinitatis supplantaverit. et cum persuadere non posset, provolutus genibus obsecrabat ne se desererem, ne me perderem, ne aratrum tenens post tergum respicerem. vae misero mihi! vici pessimam victoriam, reputans illum non meam utilitatem sed suum solacium quaerere.*

ulary of misery appropriate to supplication.[39] In fact, of course, it is the aged Malchus lamenting his younger self's wrong-headedness. Unlike in the conflict with Malchus' parents, the narrator here takes a different view from the protagonist.

The most extended supplication scene is *V. Malchi* 6.7–8. As in the *Vita Pauli*, this scene comes just after the arithmetic centre of the text. The protagonist-narrator Malchus, formerly a monk and now a captive of the pagan Saracens, has just consented under pressure to marry a female fellow-slave whose husband disappeared during the same raid in which they were both captured. Malchus then resolves, in a monologue, to commit suicide rather than consummate this union (*V. Malchi* 6.4–6). The woman reacts with a supplication:

> Then she rolled before my feet and said: 'I beg you in the name of Jesus, I ask you by the crisis of the present hour not to pour out your blood. Or, if you are determined to die, turn the sword against me first. Let us be united in that way instead. Even if my husband should return to me I would preserve the chastity which captivity has taught me; indeed, I would perish rather than lose it. Why are you dying to avoid being joined to me? I myself would die if you wanted to join yourself to me. Therefore take me as your partner in chastity, and love the bond of the soul more than that of the body. Let the masters think you my husband, Christ will know that you are my brother. We shall easily convince them of our marriage when they see this mutual love of ours.' I confess I was dumbfounded. I marvelled at the woman's virtue and loved her more than a spouse.[40]

The woman's point of view has been unknown (or perhaps rather ignored) until the point of her supplication. By performing the gesture of self-humiliation, she forces the self-absorbed protagonist to pay attention to her. She deftly uses the formula of the oath to surprise Malchus with a reference to his own god,

39 Such laments are appeals to pity, which form a conventional (but not ubiquitous) part of supplication: see Gödde, *Drama der Hikesie*, 118–123 (on maternal mourning in Euripides' *Suppliants*); cf. Naiden, *Ancient Supplication*, 97–100.

40 *tunc illa provoluta pedibus meis 'per ego te,' inquit, 'Iesum, per huius horae necessitatem rogo, ne effundas sanguinem tuum. uel si mori placet, in me primum verte mucronem. sic nobis potius coniungamur. etiam si vir meus ad me rediret servarem castitatem quam me captivitas docuit; vel interirem ante quam perderem. cur moreris ne mihi iungaris? ego morerer, si iungi velles. habeto me ergo coniugem pudicitiae et magis animae copulam amato quam corporis. sperent domini maritum, Christus noverit fratrem. facile persuadebimus nuptias cum nos viderint sic amare.' fateor, obstupui; et admiratus virtutem feminae coniuge plus amavi.*

Jesus, to prevent him from accomplishing his plan. Her first rhetorical move is thus claiming shared ideological ground.[41] Her next move is to retreat from her initial plea, as she permits him to go ahead with his suicide—as long as she is killed first, which would result in a union preferable to marriage. This suggestion illustrates her own commitment to sexual abstinence, which, she claims, she is prepared to uphold even in the event of recovering her original husband. Since she is in agreement with Malchus, it would be absurd for him to escape the situation by means of violence. The absurdity is expressed in a double polyptoton of *morior* and *iungo* in her reproachful pairing of question and answer: *Cur moreris ne mihi iungaris? Ego morerer, si iungi velles*. If both parties prefer death to intercourse, suicide becomes unnecessary.

The woman shows great creativity of thought in interpreting the notion of 'joining' (*iungo* and compounds/cognates): it can be achieved through death, so there is no point of using death in an attempt to avoid it. This semantic flexibility prepares the ground for her central proposal: she offers herself as a *coniunx pudicitiae*, echoing and developing a concept used by Malchus in his suicide speech: *habet et pudicitia servata martyrium suum* ('the preservation of chastity also has its own martyrdom', *V. Malchi* 6.5). *Pudicitia*, associated by Malchus with death, now replaces death, in the woman's reasoning, as a basis of union. The phrase *coniunx pudicitiae* appears as an oxymoron only if the sexual aspect is foregrounded in the definition of *coniunx*. However, if other foundations—for example, death—are admissible, a shared commitment to sexual abstinence seems no worse a basis than a shared readiness to die for its sake (even though this completely inverts the original meaning of *coniunx*). All that is required, the woman claims, is to privilege the soul over the body—in another close echo of Malchus' earlier suicide speech, where he impressed on his soul that its 'death is more to be feared than that of the body' (*V. Malchi* 6.5: *tua* ***magis*** *mors timenda est* ***quam corporis***, countered by the woman's ***magis*** *animae copulam amato* ***quam corporis***). Further, in the circumstances, this mutual love of souls is not an end in itself: a display of genuine affection will also prevent their owners from suspecting that the marriage is not, in fact, genuine.

The woman's speech is a sophistic tour de force: she combines the urgency of a supplication with acute observation of Malchus' mind and a cunning redefinition of the crucial concept of (*con*)*iungo*. It is no wonder that she leaves him flabbergasted (*V. Malchi* 6.8: *obstupui*). His admiration leads to affection, in accordance with her proposition, and as a result he not only refrains from

---

41 Cf. Brown and Levinson, *Politeness*, 103–104 for the strategy of claiming common ground.

killing himself, but is moved to enter into the relationship which makes them so distinctive as a pair.[42] Malchus' concern with his own monastic purity and solitude gives way to a narrative where the first person plural predominates as the couple agrees to escape from the Saracens.[43] In a final dramatic development, they are saved from death at the hands of their pursuing master through the action of a lioness, in a scene which serves as proof of divine recognition of their chaste union (*V. Malchi* 9). Although this event is less miraculous than the bread-bearing raven of the *Vita Pauli*, it fulfils a similar function of confirming that the protagonist's response to being supplicated was the correct one.

Each of the supplications in the *Captive Monk* represents an attempt to make Malchus connect with others. His parents want to integrate him into secular society through marriage; his abbot tries to keep him in the community of monks; and the woman proposes a chaste partnership to avoid Malchus dying in solitude, and this turns out to be the first step in rehabilitating him as a coenobitic monk (*V. Malchi* 10.3) and, eventually, as a highly respected inhabitant of the village of Maronias (*V. Malchi* 2.2–3). It appears that supplications are the narrative's favourite method for dramatising Malchus' crises of conscience and thus for making clear to the reader what is at stake in each of his decisions.

42 The primary narrator, the young Jerome, encounters them living together at *Vita Malchi* 2.2, and it is his curiosity about their way of life which prompts Malchus' autobiographical narrative: see especially Klazina Staat's chapter in this volume.

43 *Vita Malchi* 8.2 *invadimus iter … portantes*; 8.3 *pervenissemus*; *aquis nos credimus … subremigantes*; *conscenderamus*; 8.4 *bibimus … praeparantes*; 8.5 *currimus*; *aspicimus*; *promovemur*; 9.1 *respicimus*; *timemus*; *nos proditos intelligimus*; 9.2 *timentes … intravimus*; *nos foveae credimus … progredientes*; *fugimus*; *incurreremus*; *habemus* (twice); 9.3 *quid putas fuisse nobis animi?*; 9.5 *nos … protrahat*; *nostrum exspectat adventum*; 9.6 *nobis … videntibus*; 9.7 *aspicimus*; *quid tunc nobis terroris … fuit*; *spectabamus hostem nostrum*; 9.8 *nostras latebras*; 9.9 *bestia pro nobis dimicaret*; 9.10 *pavemus*; *ne movere quidem nos ausi praestolabamur … saepti*; 9.11 *nobisque cedit hospitium*; *erumpimus*; *exspectamus*; *egredi cogitantes illius semper figuramus occursum*; 10.1 *eximus*; *videmusque*; *refocilati … venimus*; 10.2 *oblati … pandimus*; *transmissi … accepimus*. Roughly every fifth word in the passage down to 10.2 contains a reference to the first person plural. For the problem of their separation at the end of the narrative, where Malchus states: 'I returned myself to the monks; this one I handed over to the virgins' (*Vita Malchi* 10.3: *me monachis reddo; hanc trado virginibus*), see Staat in this volume.

5 Supplication in the *Vita Hilarionis*

As in the other two texts, supplication plays a key part in reconciling the solitary and the communal aspects of Hilarion's holiness in the *Life of Hilarion*.[44] Like Paul, he is in danger of becoming a mere rumour thanks to his strict solitude—until a woman from Eleutheropolis makes a journey of approximately thirty miles to ask for his help in curing her infertility (*V. Hilarion*. 7.1–4):

> He had already been living in the desert for twenty-two years and was known to all, albeit only by his reputation, which had spread through all the cities of Palestine. One day a certain woman from Eleutheropolis, who found herself held in contempt by her husband on account of her infertility (in a period of fifteen years she had not produced any marital offspring), was the first who had the courage to break through to the blessed Hilarion. He had expected nothing of that kind, but she immediately fell down before his knees and said: 'Forgive my daring, forgive my desperation. Why are you turning away your eyes? Why are you shrinking from your petitioner? Do not look on me as a woman but look at my misery. This is the sex which gave birth to the Saviour. It is not the healthy who need a physician but those who are unwell.' At last he relented. Seeing a woman after such a long stretch of time, he questioned her about the reason for her coming and her weeping. And after he learned it, he lifted his eyes to heaven and asked her to have faith. He accompanied her with tears as she left, and after a year had passed he saw her with a son.[45]

44 Dieter Hoster, "Die Form der frühesten lateinischen Heiligenviten von der *Vita Cypriani* bis zur *Vita Ambrosii* und ihr Heiligenideal", Ph.D. diss., Cologne (1963), 79: 'Überhaupt geht es Hieronymus weniger darum, ein Lehrbuch für werdende Mönche zu schreiben, sondern den wunderbaren Vorgang darzutun, wie Mönche, die einsam in der Wüste leben, in aller Welt berühmt werden.'

45 *Viginti et duos iam in solitudine habebat annos, fama tantum notus omnibus, et per totas Palaestinae vulgatus urbes, cum interim mulier quaedam Eleutheropolitana, cernens despectui se haberi a viro ob sterilitatem—iam enim per annos quindecim nullos coniugii fructus dederat—prima irrumpere ausa est ad beatum Hilarionem, et nihil tale suspicanti, repente genibus eius advoluta: 'Ignosce,' inquit, 'audaciae, ignosce necessitati meae. Quid avertis oculos? Quid rogantem fugis? Noli me mulierem aspicere, sed miseram. Hic sexus genuit Salvatorem. Non habent sani opus medico, sed qui male habent.' Tandem substitit, et post tantum temporis visa muliere interrogavit causam adventus eius ac fletuum. Et postquam didicit, levatis ad caelum oculis, fidere eam iussit, euntemque lacrimis prosecutus exacto anno vidit cum filio.*

The encounter is partly inspired by the story of Hannah at 1 Samuel 1:1–20, who pours out her desperation at her infertility to God in the Temple: 'Lord Almighty, if you will only look on your servant's misery and remember me, and not forget your servant but give her a son, then I will give him to the Lord for all the days of his life, and no razor will ever be used on his head' (1Sam. 1:11). The manner of her intercession draws the ire of the High Priest Eli, who assumes that she is drunk. She corrects him and asks: 'Do not take your servant for a wicked woman; I have been praying here out of my great anguish and grief' (1Sam. 1:16). Eli responds: 'Go in peace, and may the God of Israel grant you what you have asked of him' (1Sam. 1:17). Eli's switch from disapproval to blessing is an indication that her wish will be granted: Hannah falls pregnant and names her son Samuel, 'Because I asked the Lord for him' (1Sam. 1:20).

The Eleutheropolitan woman uses supplication to negotiate a difficult encounter with a less-than-welcoming servant of God. After completing the first two steps of approaching Hilarion stealthily and surprising him by falling down at his feet, she first pre-empts a more hostile reaction by asking him to forgive her boldness (*'ignosce,' inquit, 'audaciae', V. Hilarion.* 7.1).[46] She then repeats the request, but replaces *audaciae* with *necessitati* ('need'). This substitution suggests an attempt at justifying her *audacia* by means of her *necessitas*: she would not have approached him but for her desperation.[47] Hilarion is taken aback by her request, as appears from her next speech act: *'quid avertis oculos? quid rogantem fugis?'* (*V. Hilarion.* 7.2). These two questions are both urgent and reproachful: as Rodie Risselada has shown, the use of *quid* in place of *cur* expresses dismay at another's action.[48] There is not much in these questions that can be taken as politeness: a cooperative hearer must assume that the urgency of the woman's predicament has made her dispense with good man-

46 Apologising is categorised as negative politeness: Brown and Levinson, *Politeness*, 187–190.

47 This is a switch to positive politeness, insofar as the notion of justification indicates a degree of shared understanding: cf. Brown and Levinson, *Politeness*, 103, 128.

48 See Rodie Risselada, *Imperatives and Other Directive Expressions in Latin: A Study in the Pragmatics of a Dead Language*. Amsterdam Studies in Classical Philology (Leiden: Brill/ Amsterdam: Gieben, 1993), 208–210 on the difference between 'relatively neutral' questions with *quid* or *cur* on the one hand, and on the other the 'expressive' use of interrogative *quid* 'not to obtain an explanation for the realization of a state of affairs that is (being) realized … | … but to express the speaker's (negative) emotions with respect to whatever motivation he can think of. The expressive force involved may be just surprise, but more usually it involves outright disapproval … When a *quid* interrogative is combined with a second person present tense predication, it invariably has the conventionalized implicit directive force to put an end to the behaviour that is explicitly mentioned.' The corpus to which these statements refer is Plautus.

ners.[49] She correctly identifies her gender as a main stumbling block and asks Hilarion to foreground another aspect of her person: *Noli me mulierem aspicere, sed miseram*.[50] Her conceptual division of the aspects under which she may be perceived suggests a similar sophistication as that shown by Malchus' partner, who redefined aspects of *coniugium* at *V. Malchi* 6.7.[51] Her misery is what qualifies her as a suppliant who deserves a hearing. As for her gender, she adds that it is not without merit: *Hic sexus genuit Salvatorem*. This reference makes clear that she shares Hilarion's Scriptural reference points, while at the same time hinting at the problem for which she seeks help: she wants to be able to procreate, just like the mother of Christ. In fact, there is every reason to suppose that she is Christian, especially since she caps her claim by quoting Jesus' own words: *Non habent sani opus medico, sed qui male habent*. This phrase is found in all three synoptic gospels (Matthew 9:12, Mark 2:17, Luke 5:31). Thus the woman assumes Christ's authority for her own cause: she is unwell (and, moreover, metaphorically unwell because of the inferiority of her sex). As such, her right to ask for help has been endorsed by Jesus himself. It can be argued that, among the suppliants in the *Lives*, the Eleutheropolitan woman makes the cleverest use of her material: she has come to ask for fertility, and her choice of references to birth and to sickness alludes to the nature of her suffering while she is only asking Hilarion to listen to her.[52] Hilarion only relents at the end of this speech (*Tandem substitit, V. Hilarion*. 7.3), which suggests that each of its parts is vital to persuade him to listen to her. Once he has heard her out, he answers her weeping with his own tears. As in the case of Hannah, their hard-won understanding is followed by the birth of a son in the following year.

---

49 Cf. Brown and Levinson *Politeness*, 95–96: 'In cases of great urgency or desperation, redress would actually decrease the communicated urgency.'

50 The background seems to be a rule that the holy man must remain separate from others. See Emile Durkheim, *The Elementary Forms of the Religious Life* (2nd English edition, London: Allen and Unwin, 1976; first published under the title *Les Formes élémentaires de la vie religieuse: le système totémique en Australie*, Paris: Alcan, 1912), 299–325. The woman here transgresses the demands of 'negative cult', a concept which inspired Brown and Levinson's 'negative politeness.' According to this framework, Hilarion's fasting and self-mortification has conferred ritual purity on him (cf. Durkheim, *Elementary Forms*, 310–311), which is threatened by contact with a woman, especially one who is sexually active and thus clearly 'profane' rather than 'sacred'.

51 See above, 243–244.

52 For hints and 'association clues' as aspects of politeness see Brown and Levinson, *Politeness*, 213–216: they are ways of concealing an imposition by leaving the addressee the choice of interpreting it as a request.

The Eleutheropolitan woman is the first person to elicit a healing miracle from Hilarion. She is followed immediately by a more assertive and powerful suppliant, Aristaenete, whose demands on Hilarion are even less modest, at *V. Hilarion.* 8.1–5:

> This sign, his first, was soon made more renowned by another greater sign. Aristaenete, the wife of Helpidius who later became praetorian prefect, was a very distinguished woman among her own class and even more distinguished among Christians. When she returned with her husband and her three children from the blessed Antony, she halted at Gaza because they felt unwell. For in that place, whether because of its rotten air or, as transpired later, on account of the glory of Hilarion, the servant of God, they were all seized with a semi-tertian fever, and the physicians despaired of them ... But when [Aristaenete] learned that there was a certain hermit in the neighbouring desert, she forgot the trappings of her status as a matron (she only knew herself to be a mother) and went accompanied by her maidservants and eunuchs; her husband could scarcely persuade her to make the journey riding on a donkey. And when she had reached him, she said: 'By Jesus, our most merciful God, I call on you, by his cross and his blood, to give me back my three sons; and let the name of our Lord and Saviour be glorified in the city of the gentiles, and let his servant enter Gaza, and let Marnas fall down.'[53]

The Eleutheropolitan woman had used supplication to break the first barrier, to make Hilarion listen and speak to her. Aristaenete asks for more: she needs Hilarion to leave his hermitage in the desert and to enter the nearby city of Gaza in order to heal her three children from a raging fever. Her high status allows

53 *Hoc signorum eius principium maius aliud signum nobilitavit. Aristaenete, Helpidii, qui postea praefectus praetorio fuit, uxor, valde nobilis inter suos et inter Christianos nobilior, revertens cum marito et tribus liberis a beato Antonio, Gazae propter infirmitatem eorum remorata est. Ibi enim, sive ob corruptum aerem, sive, ut postea claruit, propter gloriam Hilarionis, servi Dei, hemitritaeo pariter arrepti omnes a medicis desperati sunt. Iacebat ululans mater et quasi inter tria filiorum discurrens cadavera, quem primum plangeret, nesciebat. Agnito autem quod esset quidam monachus in vicina solitudine, oblita matronalis pompae—tantum se matrem noverat—vadit comitata ancillulis et eunuchis, vixque a viro persuasum est ut asello sedens pergeret. Ad quem cum pervenisset: 'Per eum te,' ait, 'Iesum, clementissimum Deum nostrum, obtestor, per crucem eius et sanguinem, ut reddas mihi tres filios, et glorificetur in urbe gentilium nomen Domini Salvatoris, et ingrediatur servus eius Gazam, et Marnas corruat.'*

her to elaborate the ritual of self-humiliation.[54] The first words of her speech echo those of Malchus' companion at *V. Malchi* 6.7: *per ego te ... Iesum*, and she likewise repeats *per* to appeal to a related subject, Jesus' cross and blood.[55] After this invocation, she states her request, *ut reddas mihi tres filios*, which is immediately followed by reference to the subsequent benefits for Christianity in its struggle against paganism. The use of the present subjunctive presents the possibility, or rather the wish, that Hilarion's healing presence in Gaza will cause the city's patron god Marnas to topple.[56] By implying that Hilarion is invested in this goal, she makes it appear that her appeal is helping him to obtain what he desires.[57]

Only when Hilarion refuses to act as she asks does she assume the full pose of the suppliant by prostrating herself (*V. Hilarion.* 8.6–7):

> He refused and said that he would never go out of his cell and was not in the habit of entering even a farm, let alone the town. She prostrated herself on the floor and kept shouting over and over: 'Hilarion, servant of Christ, give me back my children. Antony kept them safe in Egypt, now let them be saved by you in Syria.' All those who were present were crying, and Hilarion himself was crying as he kept refusing her request. What more is there to say? The woman only left after he promised her to enter Gaza after sunset.[58]

54 The depiction of this elaboration seems slightly parodic: although completely oblivious of her *matronalis pompa* (NB the echo of Hilarion's torments, which include hearing a *planctum quasi muliercularum* at *V. Hilarion.* 3.7, followed by a *pompa* at 3.8), Aristaenete still arrives in a procession of maidservants and eunuchs.

55 Note that a reference to Christ's blood would have confused Malchus' woman's speech, whose initial argument is concerned with whose blood should be shed. Cf. also the Eleutheropolitan woman's repetition of *ignosce* with two separate objects at *V. Hilarion.* 7.1.

56 In fact, Hilarion's victory over Marnas comes not when he finally acceded to Aristaenete's request but at a later point, in chapter 11, and even then it does not achieve the complete downfall of the god and his cult.

57 See Brown and Levinson, *Politeness*, 125 for offers and promises as a positive politeness strategy.

58 *Renuente illo et dicente numquam se egressurum de cellula nec habere consuetudinem, ut non modo civitatem sed ne villam quidem ingrederetur, prostravit se humi crebro clamitans: 'Hilarion, serve Christi, redde mihi liberos meos. Quos Antonius tenuit in Aegypto, a te serventur in Syria.' Flebant cuncti qui aderant, sed et ipse negans flebat. Quid multa? Non prius mulier recessit quam ille pollicitus est se post solis occasum Gazam introiturum.*

The sequence is the same as that observed in the request made of Malchus by his abbot,[59] and it seems to reflect the high status of the petitioner. Aristaenete's second speech is full of urgency. The complex periodic structure of the first plea gives way to simple parataxis with a bald infinitive (*redde*), followed by an analogy between Hilarion and his great mentor, Antony. As a result, everyone cries, including Hilarion; but whereas in the case of the Eleutheropolitan woman his tears only appeared after he had responded favourably to her plea, here he still holds out against Aristaenete. His tears show that pity threatens to overwhelm his resolve, but it takes more persistence on Aristaenete's part for him to abandon his refusal. The emphasis on the length of time taken up by her supplication recalls the hours Antony spent supplicating Paul at *V. Pauli* 9.5.[60] Aristaenete finally extracts a promise from Hilarion, which comes with a further delay: he only enters Gaza after sunset. By contrast, once he has arrived, his presence is immediately effective, with emphasis placed on the boys' swift recovery through temporal adverbials (*V. Hilarion*. 8.8):

> And after he arrived, he inspected each little bed and the children's burning limbs and called on Jesus. And by his wonderful power sweat immediately (*statim*) broke out simultaneously (*pariter*) as though from three springs; and within the same hour (*eadem hora*) they accepted food, recognised their grieving mother, and, blessing God, kissed the holy man's hand.[61]

Overall, Aristaenete's supplication succeeds not because of her promises and self-humiliation but thanks to her persistence. In this, her strategy is comparable to that of Antony in the *V. Pauli* passage, who threatens to besiege Paul's door until he (Antony) dies. Once Hilarion gives in to Aristaenete's tenacious begging and enters Gaza, he becomes a celebrity, not only in Palestine but in Syria and Egypt (*V. Hilarion*. 8.9–10):

> After this became known and spread about far and wide, the people of Syria and Egypt competed in running to him, with the result that many became Christians and announced that they would be monks. For at

59 See above, 242.

60 See above, 238–239.

61 *Quo postquam venit, singulorum lectulos et ardentia membra considerans, invocavit Iesum. Et, o mira virtus, statim quasi de tribus fontibus sudor pariter erupit; eadem hora acceperunt cibos, lugentemque matrem cognoscentes et benedicentes Deum sancti manus deosculati sunt.*

> that time there were no monastic establishments in Palestine and no one knew a monk before the holy Hilarion. He was the first founder and instructor of that committed way of life in this province. The Lord Jesus had the aged Antony in Egypt, and in Palestine he had the younger Hilarion.[62]

Thus it is again thanks to supplication that the holy man's exploits become known; by extension, the two women's supplications lead Hilarion to provide Jerome with the bulk of the material presented in his *Life*. In consequence, the pattern all but disappears from the narrative,[63] where Hilarion now continues to work miracles without being pressed.

6 Concluding Discussion

The preceding analysis suggests that the practice of supplication is deliberately employed throughout the three *Lives*. Particularly extended supplications addressed to the protagonist come at key points in the plot development; unlike some other instances, these set-piece scenes invariably have a positive outcome. This pattern is unlikely to be a coincidence. It appears to be inspired by various scenes in the *Life of Antony*,[64] whose Latin translation by Evagrius was the most important inspiration for Jerome's hagiographical construction, but supplication is much more prominent and elaborate in Jerome than in his model.[65] By constructing supplication in an emphatic and dramatic manner, Jerome's *Lives* convey an ambition to be considered a supremely engaging class

---

62 *Quod postquam auditum est et longe lateque percrebuit, certatim ad eum de Syria et Aegypto populi confluebant, ita ut multi Christiani fierent et se monachos profiterentur. Necdum enim tunc monasteria erant in Palaestina nec quisquam monachum ante sanctum Hilarionem in Syria noverat. Ille fundator et eruditor huius conversationis et studii in hac provincia primum fuit. Habebat Dominus Iesus in Aegypto senem Antonium, habebat in Palaestina Hilarionem iuniorem.*

63 The only exception is *V. Hilarion.* 23.2–4, where the monks of Bruchium unsuccessfully petition him (albeit in indirect speech) to stay with them. Hilarion knows that he is being persecuted by the Gazans by order of the emperor Julian, so his refusal is an act of kindness to the monks.

64 Especially chapters 48 and 71, where Antony's readiness to help is contrasted with his desire to be left alone.

65 There is no space in this chapter to elaborate on this assertion. In any case a thoroughgoing analysis of the detailed correspondences between Jerome's *Lives* and the *Life of Antony* remains a desideratum.

of literature, one which appeals not only to the theological and moral curiosity of his Christian audience but also to their appetite for a good tale.

A further point which emerges from the discussion is the close connection between the suppliants' arguments and the values of asceticism. The overwhelming commitment of Jerome's protagonists to solitude is an extreme instance of 'negative face wants' according to the terminology of Brown and Levinson.[66] In view of this fact it is only logical that the strategies of positive politeness dominate the suppliants' rhetoric: there is no point trying to minimise the extent of the imposition on one who desires most to be left in peace altogether. Positive politeness is riskier than its negative counterpart.[67] Suppliants portray themselves as having nothing to lose, and risky strategies appear in keeping with this presentation. This consideration also accounts for the elements of the suppliants' petition which cannot be analysed as polite in any sense, such as the Eleutheropolitan woman's indignant questions about Hilarion's attempts to withdraw from her. Her rudeness must necessarily be ascribed to her desperation, otherwise it would appear as shocking arrogance. Paradoxically, the use of supplication turns a person's weakness into a strength.[68] What seems an expression of abjection becomes a means of exerting force.[69] This fact may explain why women are so often chosen to perform supplication in Jerome's *Lives*: perhaps their lesser social power makes their pleas more compelling.[70]

It seems reasonable, then, to ascribe the prominence of supplication in our texts to Jerome's championing of asceticism. Compensating the protagonists for their compromises, the suppliants provide a justification for connecting both perfect exemplars like Paul and Hilarion and less perfect monks like Malchus with the needs of a wider society. In this regard, the *Lives* put a particular spin on the notion that supplication leads to reintegration into

66 Note that the terminology is adapted from Emile Durkheim's concepts of 'negative cult' and 'positive cult'. Durkheim includes asceticism in his discussion of negative cult: Durkheim, *Elementary Forms*, 299–325.

67 Brown and Levinson, *Politeness*, 73: 'Note that positive politeness precedes negative politeness in the continuum of FTA 'danger' for the following reasons. Positive politeness redresses by means of fulfilling [the hearer's] want that some others should want some particular desires of his. To pursue this strategy [the speaker] must make the assumption that he is a member of the set of these others; the efficacy of his redress is totally vulnerable to [the hearer's] concurrence in this assumption.'

68 Gödde, *Drama der Hikesie*, 33, and Aubriot-Sévin, *Prière et conceptions religieuses*, 426; see above, 240.

69 Gödde, *Drama der Hikesie*, 181, 187.

70 Brown and Levinson, *Politeness*, 29–33, only outline the complexities added by the factor of gender in analysing politeness, rather than including it systematically in their study.

society.[71] In the case of the supplicated ascetic, it is they themselves as well as their suppliants who are reclaimed for humanity at large. The fact that Paul rescues Antony from his threatened death means that his story becomes known through Antony and can be recorded by Jerome for posterity. Malchus' acquiescence to the woman's proposal is the first step towards his return and monastic reintegration. Without her, he would have perished as a renegade and suicide. Finally, the concerns of the Eleutheropolitan woman and Aristaenete with their offspring symbolises their non-ascetic affiliations. Supplication allows Hilarion to connect with them while showing his reluctance.[72] On the level of the text as a whole, supplication therefore enables the telling of at least a significant chunk of the story in the first place. In religious terms, it serves as an expiatory rite for violating the ascetic's mandatory isolation.[73] The high energy required for this ceremony illustrates the great awe in which ascetics ought to be held—including, naturally, the ascetic author of the texts himself.

Bibliography

Aubriot-Sévin, Danièle, *Prière et conceptions religieuses en Grèce ancienne jusqu'à la fin du ve siècle av. J.-C.* Collection de la Maison de l'Orient Méditerranéen 22, Série littéraire et philosophique 5 (Lyon: Bocchard, 1992).

Barrios-Lech, Peter, *Linguistic Interaction in Roman Comedy* (Cambridge: Cambridge University Press, 2016).

Brown, Penelope and Stephen C. Levinson, *Politeness: Some Universals in Language Usage*. Studies in Interactional Sociolinguistics (Cambridge: Cambridge University Press, 1987).

Burrus, Virginia, *The Sex Lives of Saints: An Erotics of Ancient Hagiography* (Philadelphia: University of Pennsylvania Press, 2004).

Crotty, Kevin, *The Poetics of Supplication: Homer's Iliad and Odyssey* (Ithaca, NY: Cornell University Press, 1994).

Durkheim, Emile, *The Elementary Forms of the Religious Life* (2nd English edition, London: Allen and Unwin 1976). Original publication: *Les Formes élémentaires de la vie religieuse: le système totémique en Australie* (Paris: Alcan, 1912).

Gödde, Susanne, *Das Drama der Hikesie: Ritual und Rhetorik in Aischylos' Hiketiden* (Münster: Aschendorff, 2000).

71 See Naiden, *Ancient Supplication*, 103, for this notion and criticism.

72 Kech, *Hagiographie*, 115, observes that the need for supplication is part of the textual strategies aiming at edification.

73 Cf. Durkheim, *Elementary Forms*, 150, on crisis situations.

Gould, John, "Hiketeia", *JHS* 93 (1973), 74–103.

Hall, Stuart G., "Translation of Gregory of Nyssa, *On the Beatitudes*", in Hubertus Drogner and Albert Viciano (eds.), *Gregory of Nyssa: On the Beatitudes. An English Version with Commentary and Supporting Studies. Proceedings of the Eighth International Colloquium on Gregory of Nyssa (Paderborn, 14–18 September 1998)*. Vigiliae Christianae Supplements 52 (Leiden/Boston/Cologne: Brill, 2000), 21–90.

Hoster, Dieter, "Die Form der frühesten lateinischen Heiligenviten von der *Vita Cypriani* bis zur *Vita Ambrosii* und ihr Heiligenideal". Ph.D diss., Cologne (1963).

Kech, Herbert, *Hagiographie als christliche Unterhaltungsliteratur: Studien zum Phänomen des Erbaulichen anhand der Mönchsviten des hl. Hieronymus*. Göppinger Arbeiten zur Germanistik (Göppingen: Kümmerle, 1977).

Konstan, David, *Pity Transformed* (London: Duckworth, 2001).

Konstan, David, "Rhetoric and Emotion", in Ian Worthington (ed.), *A Companion to Greek Rhetoric* (Malden, MA/Oxford: Wiley-Blackwell, 2007), 411–425.

Lambert, Bernard, *Bibliotheca Hieronymiana Manuscripta: la tradition manuscrite des œuvres de saint Jérôme*, vol. 2 (Stenbrugis: Martinus Nijhoff, 1969).

Langlands, Rebecca, *Sexual Morality in Ancient Rome* (Cambridge: Cambridge University Press, 2006).

Leclerc, Pierre, "Antoine et Paul: métamorphose d'un héros", in Yves-Marie Duval (ed.), *Jérôme entre l'Occident et l'Orient. XVIe centenaire du départ de saint Jérôme de Rome et de son installation à Bethléem. Actes du colloque de Chantilly, Sept. 1986* (Paris: Études augustiniennes, 1988), 256–265.

Leclerc, Pierre, Edgardo M. Morales, and Adalbert de Vogüé, *Trois vies de moines (Paul, Malchus, Hilarion)*. Sources chrétiennes 508 (Paris: Les Éditions du Cerf, 2007).

Naiden, Fred S., *Ancient Supplication* (Oxford: Oxford University Press, 2006).

Risselada, Rodie, *Imperatives and Other Directive Expressions in Latin: A Study in the Pragmatics of a Dead Language*. Amsterdam Studies in Classical Philology (Leiden: Brill/Amsterdam: Gieben, 1993).

Wolpers, Theodor, *Die englische Heiligenlegende des Mittelalters: eine Formgeschichte des Legendenerzählens von der spätantiken lateinischen Tradition bis zur Mitte des 16. Jahrhunderts* (Tübingen: Niemeyer, 1964).

Zeitlin, Froma I., "Patterns of Gender in Aeschylean Drama: Seven against Thebes and the Danaid Trilogy", in Mark Griffith and Donald J. Mastronarde (eds.), *Cabinet of the Muses: Essays on Classical and Comparative Literature in Honor of Thomas G. Rosenmeyer* (Atlanta: Scholars Press, 1990), 103–115.

CHAPTER 9

Holy Fools and Sacred Sidekicks: Comic Relief and Humorous Elements in a Hagiographical Text from Egypt

Konstantin M. Klein

At the beginning of the fifth century, Synesius of Cyrene compared man's role in the great theatre of the world with the performance of an actor: for both it was paramount to play the part well and, while doing so, to improve one's virtue and art.[1] In this comparison Synesius explicitly referred to characters of ancient tragedy; however, it is safe to assume that he knew about plays not only from his reading of learned books, but because he himself had (voluntarily or not) glimpsed actual theatrical performances staged in Cyrene or elsewhere. His contemporary Augustine distinguished between tragedy and comedy on the one hand (both barely, but somehow, tolerable), and the unbearable genre of scenic performances on the other, that is to say, lowbrow theatrical shows such as the late antique *mimus* and *pantomimus*.[2] For Synesius, it would have been even easier to watch such shows in the large city of Alexandria, where he moved in the AD 390s to study with the renowned philosopher Hypatia. Syne-

1 Synes. *Provid.* 13.9.

2 Cf. Aug. *Civ.* 2.8; on the genres of *mimus* and *pantomimus* in late antiquity in general, cf. Alexander Puk, *Das römische Spielewesen in der Spätantike* (Berlin: De Gruyter, 2014), 289–300, and particularly on the Church Fathers' knowledge of them, 297–299. Claudia Ludwig compared late antique and Byzantine saints' lives with the second-century *Vita Aesopi* elucidating similar themes, while, of course, no direct influence from this text on hagiography can be observed, cf. Claudia Ludwig, *Sonderformen byzantinischer Hagiographie und ihr literarisches Vorbild: Untersuchungen zu den Viten des Äsop, des Philaretos, des Symeon Salos und des Andreas Salos* (Frankfurt: Peter Lang, 1997), esp. 385–387. On late antique theatrical performances, cf. William Furley, "Mimos", *DNP* 8 (Stuttgart: Metzler, 2000), coll. 201–207, Lore Benz, "Pantomimos", *DNP* 9 (Stuttgart: Metzler, 2000), coll. 274–276, and Jean-Michel Carrié, "Conclusion", in Christian Landes and Jean-Michel Carrié (eds.), *Jeux et spectacles dans l'Antiquité tardive* = *AntTard* 15 (2007), 215–219, esp. 215–216. Three sixth-century circus programmes have been discovered on papyri, attesting to a wide range of activities (mimes, acrobats, tightrope walkers) which took place between the chariot races; cf. *POxy*. 2707, *PBingen*. 128, and *PHarrauer*. 56 with Charlotte Roueché, "Spectacles in Late Antiquity: Some Observations", in Christian Landes and Jean-Michel Carrié (eds.), *Jeux et spectacles dans l'Antiquité tardive* = *AntTard* 15 (2007), 59–64, esp. 62.

 | DOI:10.1163/9789004421332_011

sius arrived there in turbulent times: In AD 391, the emperor Theodosius the Great promulgated a decree that forbade entering and walking around in pagan temples.[3] In the same year, Theophilus, the bishop of Alexandria, obtained legal authority to reuse one of the abandoned temples and planned to transform it into a church. During the renovations, a riot between Christians and pagans erupted, which ended with the pagans barricading themselves inside the Serapeum which eventually was demolished by monks and Roman soldiers with imperial toleration.[4] Theodosius may not have ordered the destruction of the Serapeum; however, the events in Alexandria were inspired by his legislation, even if the Emperor did not intend—and perhaps could not foresee—its consequences. Further south in Egypt, the end of the great temple of Alexandria spurred another charismatic and resolute holy man to action: even if the ancient gods were gradually fading away, Shenoute, the abbot of the monastery of Atripe, undoubtedly helped accelerate this process.[5] The destruction of temples in Panopolis, carried out by the famous abbot and his followers,[6] however, will not be at the centre of this study, which will focus on a different monk in a different town: Macarius of Tkōou.[7] However, as much as the set of events in his saint's life (transmitted under the unusual title *Panegyricus*) differs from the actions, deeds, and achievements accomplished by the fanatic monks of Alexandria or by emblematic figures such as Shenoute, Macarius of Tkōou is styled as their contemporary and fellow-countryman, and the description of his life is modelled before a background in which Shenoute's deeds and alleged destruction of temples as well as the religious climate of late antique Egypt have a significant presence.

3 *C.Th.* 16.10.10 and 11 (a. 391); the literature on the destruction of pagan temples in late antiquity is vast, but cf. Jean Gaudement, "La condamnation des praticques païennes en 391", in Jacques Fontaine and Charles Kannengiesser (eds.), *Epektasis: FS Jean Daniélou* (Paris: Beauchesne, 1972), 597–602, on the laws of the year AD 391.

4 There is no agreement on the exact date of the destruction of the Serapeum. For a convincing argument in favour of the year AD 391, cf. Judith McKenzie, Sheila Gibson, and Andreas Reyes, "Reconstructing the Serapeum in Alexandria from the Archaeological Evidence", *JRS* 94 (2004), 73–121, esp. 108.

5 David Bell, *Besa: Life of Shenoute*, (Kalamazoo, MI: Cistercian Publications, 1983), 18–19.

6 An excellent summary of scholarship on this topic can be found in Jitse Dijkstra, "The Fate of the Temples in Late Antique Egypt", in Luke Lavan and Michael Mulryan (eds.), *The Archaeology of Late Antique 'Paganism'* (Leiden: Brill, 2011), 389–436, esp. 396–400, who convincingly argues that many of the destructive deeds attributed to Shenoute of Atripe are a mere topos of hagiography and do not represent actual destructions of a multitude of temples.

7 The Arabic versions of the text call the place Qāw, located in the tenth Egyptian *nome*. It should most likely be identified with Qāw al-Kubrā or Qāw al-Kabīr between Asyūṭ and Aḫmīn in Upper Egypt.

1 A *Panegyricus* for the Least Successful Saint

The *Panegyricus on Macarius* is attributed to the mid-fifth-century Patriarch Dioscorus of Alexandria, who also figures prominently in the first segment of the text by spending a certain amount of time in praising himself (albeit implicitly through the words of others). However, we know for sure that Dioscorus was neither the author nor the compiler of the text. The *Panegyricus* is one of the most fascinating texts of late antique Egypt, and yet it is hardly known. There are three main reasons for this: firstly, the historical information contained in the so-called *Panegyricus* is—at best—muddled and difficult to untangle. Secondly, the text is a compilation of a variety of older bits and pieces,[8] perhaps glued together in the early sixth century by a compiler who clearly was not among the most talented of his profession. Thirdly, the few studies devoted to this text published so far predominantly focus on single episodes and aim less at making sense of the text as a whole.[9]

Being a compilation, the *Panegyricus* contains not only passages on the life of Macarius but also completely unrelated other narratives, for example episodes taken from other Coptic saints' lives,[10] or an account of the events in Jerusalem in the year AD 453, when the Orthodox Patriarch, Juvenal, was reinstalled in the Holy City by imperial troops and ordered the soldiers to commit a bloodbath culminating in the rape of all Monophysite women. All these digressions describe events that are, at best, only vaguely connected with Macarius himself, who, at least nominally, is supposed to be the text's main protagonist.

8 David Johnson, *A Panegyric on Macarius Bishop of Tkôw Attributed to Dioscorus of Alexandria* (Louvain: Secretariat du CorpusSCO, 1980), 7*–8*. On the transmission of and scholarly work on the text itself cf. also Stephen Emmel, "Immer erst das Kleingedruckte lesen. 'Die Pointe verstehen' in dem koptischen Panegyrikos auf Makarios von Tkōou", in Anke Blöbaum, Joachim Kahl, and Simon Schweitzer (eds.), *Ägypten—Münster. Kulturwissenschaftliche Studien zu Ägypten, dem Vorderen Orient und verwandten Gebieten* (Wiesbaden: Harrassowitz, 2003), 91–114, esp. 91–92. See French in this volume.

9 Cf. Emmel, "Kleingedruckte", and David Frankfurter, "Illuminating the Cult of Kothos: The *Panegyric on Macarius* and Local Religion in Fifth-Century Egypt", in James Goehring (ed.), *The World of Early Egyptian Christianity: Language, Literature, and Social Context* (Washington, DC: Catholic University of America Press, 2007), 176–188; there is a recent, careful edition of the Arabic versions of the text published alongside a rather mediocre study of the *Panegyricus* (Samuel Moawad, *Untersuchungen zum Paneygyrikos auf Makarios von Tkōou und zu seiner Überlieferung* (Wiesbaden: Reichert 2010); cf. Konstantin Klein, "Review of S. Moawad (2010), *Untersuchungen zum Panegyrikos auf Makarios*, Wiesbaden", *Plekos* 16 (2014), 55–77).

10 Cf. the commentary on the narratives concerning Apa Longinos, Moawad, *Untersuchungen*, 193–199.

The main narrative tries to concern itself with the relationship between the narrator and the hero; it is then constantly interrupted, however, by other narratives attributed to other narrators. These digressions are somewhat typical for Coptic literature; most Coptic Martyrs' Acts, for example, present historical content in a blatantly unhistorical manner—a stylistic trait that has caused modern scholars to dismiss them as unworthy of serious consideration.[11] Additionally, a considerable number of Coptic martyrdoms contain passages that can be matched word for word elsewhere, and it has often been suggested that they were commissioned from professional *scriptoria* and perhaps paid for by the yard: they were padded out with literary filling material until they reached the requisite size.[12] It is possible that the *Panegyricus on Macarius* was compiled in a similar way.

There is good reason why it is worth focusing specifically on this peculiar saint about whom we know so very little (the *Panegyricus* itself is not particularly helpful for constructing anything like a conventional hagiographical biography in the Bollandist sense of the word,[13] since it contains very little information on its protagonist). Macarius functions as the connector of a variety of episodes that are all surprisingly unusual for the genre of hagiography—one could go as far to call them 'humorous'. To use this term for a piece of Christian literature is, of course, problematic: humour and laughter are always determined by the interest and perspective of the audience of a text, and while it is difficult to explain what humour means even in modern literature, it is all the more speculative to imagine how a text was perceived at a different time and place, in this case in late antique Egypt. In the following, I will set out what I perceive to be the humorous content of the text and then proceed to a more general discussion of humour in this text and in other hagiographical works.

The bottom line of all episodes on Macarius is largely the same: the holy man from Tkōou may well be the least successful saint of Coptic hagiography. This becomes obvious when one compares, for example, the descriptions of Shenoute's very successful destructions of temples in Panopolis with the shambolic attempts of Macarius to live up to these ideals. Of course, there were pagans living in the vicinity of the Bishopric of Tkōou. Not just any pagans, but rather the worst kind:[14]

11 Eve Reymond and John Barns (eds.), *Four Martyrdoms from the Pierpont Morgan Coptic Codices* (Oxford: Clarendon Press, 1973), 6.

12 Cf. Reymond and Barns, *Martyrdoms*, 2–3 and Hippolyte Delehaye, "Les Martyrs d' Égypte", *Analecta Bollandiana* 40 (1922), 5–154 and 299–364, esp. 171–173.

13 See the Introduction to this volume, 2–3.

14 *Pan. Mac.* 5.1–2: ⲛⲉⲩⲛ̄ⲟⲩϯⲙⲉ ⲙ̄ⲡⲉⲙⲛ̄ⲧ ⲙⲡⲓ̈ⲉⲣⲟ ⲉⲩϣⲙ̄ϣⲉ ⲛⲟⲩⲉⲓⲇⲱⲗⲟⲛ ⲛϩⲏⲧϥ̄ ⲉⲩⲙⲟⲩⲧⲉ

> There was a village on the west side of the river in which they worship an idol called Kothos which is mounted in the niches of their houses. And when they go inside their doors, they are accustomed to bow down and worship them. [Circumstances] being thus then, the priests of our village came and told my father everything the pagans were doing, how they were seizing the children of the Christians and slaying them for their idol, Kothos. For instance, one day they waylaid them and he saw them performing their lawless acts by slaying the little children and pouring [out] their blood upon the altar of their god, Kothos.

The pagans of this village are particularly wicked: they call out to the Christian children, deceive them with candy, slay them, and eventually make strings for ritual harps from their stretched intestines. This is a clear call to action for Macarius: he immediately sets out for the temple with some fellow-monks in order to end the bloodthirsty cult. However, since most of his companions start to run off on the way, before even attempting their heroic deed, Macarius has to enter the temple with only three others. What happens next is best described as a complete disaster, recounted by one of Macarius' three companions:[15]

> And when we had gone inside, they [the pagans] made haste and threw themselves upon us. They numbered twenty, while we were [only] four. They said: 'Your life-span stops today. Behold, your slaughtering place.' At once they leapt upon my father first. They bound him like a guileless sheep. [Afterwards], they made ready to offer us three up on the altar of their god.

Unlike any other piece of hagiography, the situation is rather hopeless for Macarius and his companions. However, while the pagans are still speaking,

---

ⲉⲣⲟϥ ϫⲉⲅⲟⲑⲟⲥ · ⲉϥⲧⲁⲗⲏⲩ ⲉϩⲣⲁï ⲉϫⲛ̄ⲛⲉⲩϣⲟⲩϣⲧ̄ ϩⲛ̄ⲛⲉⲩⲏï : ⲉⲩϣⲁⲛⲃⲱⲕ ⲇⲉ ⲉϩⲟⲩⲛ ϩⲛ̄ⲛⲉⲩⲣⲟ · ϣⲁⲩⲑⲃ̄ⲃⲓ̈ⲟϫⲱⲟⲩ ⲉⲡⲉⲥⲏⲧ ⲛ̄ⲥⲉⲟⲩⲱϣⲧ ⲛⲁϥ : ⲉⲩϣⲟⲟⲡ ⲟⲩⲛ ⲛ̄ⲧⲉⲓϩⲉ ⲁⲛⲉⲡⲣⲉⲥⲃⲩⲧⲉⲣⲟⲥ ⲙ̄ⲡ̄ϯⲙⲉ ⲉⲓ ⲁⲩⲧⲁⲩⲟ ⲉⲡⲁⲉⲓⲱⲧ ⲛ̄ϩⲱⲃ ⲛⲓⲙ ⲉⲧⲟⲩⲉⲓⲣⲉ ⲙ̄ⲙ̄ⲟⲟⲩ ⲛ̄ϭⲓⲛ̄ϩⲉⲗⲗⲏⲛ · ⲛ̄ⲑⲉ ⲉⲧⲟⲩϭⲱⲡⲉ ⲛ̄ⲛⲉϣⲏⲣⲉ ⲛ̄ⲛⲉⲭⲣⲏⲥⲧⲓⲁⲛⲟⲥ · ⲉⲩϣⲱ̄ⲱ̄ⲧ ⲙ̄ⲙ̄ⲟⲟⲩ ⲛ̄ⲅⲟⲑⲟⲥ ⲡⲉⲩⲉⲓⲇⲱⲗⲟⲛ : ⲁⲙⲉⲗⲓ̈ ⲟⲩⲛ̄ ⲁⲩϭⲱⲣϭ̄ ⲉⲣⲟⲟⲩ ⲛⲟⲩϩⲟⲟⲩ ⲁϥⲛⲁⲩ ⲉⲣⲟⲟⲩ ⲉⲩⲉⲓⲣⲉ ⲛ̄ⲧⲁⲛⲟⲙⲓ̈ⲁ ⲉⲩⲕⲱⲛⲥ̄ ⲛ̄ⲛⲉϣⲏⲣⲉ ϣⲏⲙ ⲉⲩⲥⲱⲧϥ̄ ⲙⲡⲉⲩⲥⲛⲟϥ ⲉⲧϣⲏⲩⲉ ⲙⲡⲉⲩⲛⲟⲩⲧⲉ ⲅⲟⲑⲟⲥ : The *Panegyricus* is quoted according to the edition by David Johnson (Johnson, *Panegyric*). His translation has been used throughout this chapter, with minor adaptations. The quoted passages all follow MS Morgan Codex 609.

15 *Pan. Mac.* 5.6: ⲁⲛⲟⲛ ⲇⲉ ⲛⲧⲉⲣⲉⲛⲃⲱⲕ ⲉϩⲟⲩⲛ · ⲁⲩϭⲉⲡⲏ · ⲁⲩⲧⲟⲕⲟⲩ ⲉϫⲱⲛ ⲉⲩⲉⲓ̈ⲣⲉ ⲛ̄ϫⲱⲟⲩⲧ · ⲉⲛⲣ̄ϥ̄ⲧⲟⲟⲩ ϩⲱ̄ⲱ̄ⲛ · ⲡⲉϫⲁⲩ ϫⲉⲁⲡⲉⲧⲛ̄ⲁϩⲉ ⲟⲩⲱ̄ ⲙ̄ⲡⲟⲟⲩ · ⲉⲓⲥⲡⲉⲧⲛ̄ⲙⲁ ⲛⲕⲱ̄ⲱ̄ⲛⲥ̄ · ⲛⲧⲉⲩⲛⲟⲩ ⲁⲩⲃⲟϭⲟⲩ ⲉϫⲛ̄ⲡⲁⲉⲓⲱⲧ ⲛ̄ϣⲟⲣⲡ̄ ⲁⲩⲥⲟⲛϩϥ̄ ⲛⲑⲉ ⲛⲟⲩⲉⲥⲟⲟⲩ ⲛⲃⲁⲗϩⲏⲧ · ⲙⲛ̄ⲛⲥⲱⲥ ⲁⲛⲟⲛ ϩⲱⲱⲛ ⲙ̄ⲡ̄ϣⲟⲙⲛⲧ ⲁⲩⲥⲉⲃⲧⲱⲧⲟⲩ ⲉⲧⲁⲗⲟⲛ ⲉϫⲛ̄ⲧ̄ϣⲏⲩⲉ ⲙ̄ⲡⲉⲩⲛⲟⲩⲧⲉ · On the destruction of the temple, cf. also Dijkstra, "Fate of the Temples", 397.

suddenly Besa, Shenoute's successor as abbot of the White Monastery, knocks at the door, appearing as the *deus ex machina* and preventing the impending catastrophe. Through the mere presence of Besa the doors of Macarius' temple-prison miraculously open, allowing for monastic reinforcement troops to enter the scene: Besa has fourteen monks with him, i.e. eleven more companions than Macarius. Eventually, with their help—but *only* with their help—the destruction of the temple of Kothos takes place.

If we follow the rhetoric of a large number of accounts from Egypt on this topic, the destruction of temples belonged to the standard repertoire of almost every Coptic holy man. Macarius, however, was obviously no good at this task. Therefore, one may assume that his talents lay elsewhere. A different opportunity to shine might arise from theological competence.[16] However, regarding this point various episodes from the *Panegyricus* make it more than clear that Macarius was rather unimpressive, especially since he did not understand Greek (the *Panegyricus* keeps stressing this point) and therefore was excluded from most of the debates of his age. Already the introduction takes away any chance of excelling in these matters: if saints are soldiers, Macarius is compared to an archer.[17] He is not fighting in the first line of battle, but one would find him at the rear of the hoplites, aiming his arrow at the enemy. The main reason, to quote the *Panegyricus*, why Macarius is 'not a pikeman' is that he does not understand the Greek language.[18] Apart from his linguistic incompetence, it is

16 On the question of the theological competence of monastic heroes, cf. Johannes Roldanus, "Stützen und Störenfriede: mönchische Einmischung in die doktrinäre und kirchenpolitische Rezeption von Chalkedon", in Johannes van Oort and Johannes Roldanus (eds.), *Chalkedon: Geschichte und Aktualität: Studien zur Rezeption der christologischen Formel von Chalkedon* (Leuven: Peeters, 1998), 123–146.

17 See Wiśniewski in this volume.

18 Cf. *Pan. Mac.* 1.3–5: ⲛⲑⲉ ⲅⲁⲣ ⲛ̄ⲛⲉⲛⲟϭ ⲙ̄ⲙⲁⲧⲟⲓ̈ ⲉⲧϩⲛ̄ⲛ̄ⲁⲣⲓⲑⲙⲟⲥ ⲉⲩϣⲁⲛⲛⲁⲩ ⲉⲩϣⲏⲣⲉ ϣⲏⲙ ⲉϥⲟ̄ ⲛⲁⲛⲇⲣⲁⲧⲏⲥ ϣⲁⲩϯϩⲧⲏⲩ ⲉⲧⲉϥⲅⲩⲙⲛⲁⲥⲓⲁ ϫⲉϥⲛⲁⲉⲣϣⲁⲩ ⲉⲁϣ ⲙⲡⲟⲗⲩⲙⲟⲥ ⲉϣⲱⲡⲉ ⲙⲉⲛ ⲟⲩⲕⲟⲛⲧⲟⲧⲟⲥⲡⲉ ⲡϣⲏⲣⲉ ϣⲏⲙ ⲙ̄ⲙⲁⲧⲟⲓ̈ ⲉⲧⲙ̄ⲙⲁⲩ ⲉϥⲟ̄ ⲛϫⲱ̄ⲱ̄ⲣⲉ ϣⲁⲩⲛⲟϫϥ ⲉⲑⲏ ⲙ̄ⲡⲉⲙⲗⲁϩ ⲛϥϣⲱⲡⲉ ⲉⲙⲛ̄ϭⲉ ϩⲓⲑⲏ ⲙⲙⲟϥ ⲉϣⲱⲡⲉ ⲇⲉ ⲟⲛ ⲟⲩⲇⲟⲝⲟⲧⲏⲥⲡⲉ ϣⲁⲕϩⲉ ⲉⲣⲟϥ ϩⲓⲡⲁϩⲟⲩ ⲛⲛϩⲟⲡⲗⲓⲧⲏⲥ ⲉϥϣⲱϣ ⲙ̄ⲡⲉϥⲥⲟⲧⲉ ϩⲛ̄ⲧⲉϥϭⲓϫ ⲛ̄ϩⲃⲟⲩⲣ ⲉⲣⲉⲡⲉϥⲃⲁⲗ ⲛ̄ⲟⲩⲛⲁⲙ ⲣⲁⲕⲉ ⲉϫⲛ̄ⲧⲉϥϭⲓϫ ⲛ̄ⲟⲩⲛⲁⲙ ⲉⲧⲃⲉⲡϭⲓⲛⲥⲱⲕ ϫⲉⲛⲛⲉϥⲛⲟⲩϫ ⲛ̄ⲛⲉϥⲥⲟⲧⲉ ⲉⲡϫⲓⲛϫⲏ ⲁϫⲛ̄ⲣⲉϩⲧⲟⲩⲁ ϩⲛ̄ⲛⲉϥϫⲁϫⲉ ⲉⲧⲉϥⲡⲟⲗⲩⲙⲉⲓ ⲛⲙ̄ⲙⲁⲩ · ⲛ̄ⲧⲉⲓϩⲉ ⲇⲉ ⲉϣϫⲉ ⲛ̄ⲟⲩⲕⲟⲛⲧⲟⲧⲟⲥ ⲁⲛⲡⲉ ⲙⲁⲕⲁⲣⲓⲟⲥ ⲉⲧⲉⲡⲁⲓⲡⲉ ϫⲉⲛⲛϥ̄ⲛⲟⲓ̈ ⲁⲛ ⲉϣⲁϫⲉ ⲙ̄ⲙⲛ̄ⲧⲟⲩⲁⲓ̄ⲛⲓ̈ⲛ ⲁⲗⲗⲁ ⲙⲡⲉϥϭⲱ ⲛ̄ⲟⲩⲉϣⲉⲓ̄ ⲛⲙ̄ⲙⲁⲛ ⲉⲡⲡⲟⲗⲩⲙⲟⲥ ⲛ̄ⲕⲁⲗⲭⲏⲇⲱⲛ ⲁⲩⲱ ⲛ̄ⲥⲉⲟⲡϥ ϩⲱⲱϥ ⲉⲡⲥⲟⲟⲩ ⲛϣⲉⲙⲁⲃⲧⲁϥⲧⲉ ⲛ̄ⲉⲡⲓⲥⲕⲟⲡⲟⲥ · ('For just as with military leaders who are among the ranks, when they see a brave young man, they are wont to pay attention to his exercises in order [to know] for what kind of combat he is fitted. If that young soldier is a pikeman and is strong, they place him at the front of the battle where he has no one else in front of him. Again, if he is an archer, you would find him at the rear of the hoplites, aiming his arrow with his left hand while his right eye is trained on his right hand for the purpose of shooting, lest he shoot his arrows in vain without

also surprising that the author/compiler of the *Panegyricus* is so open regarding Macarius' theological shortcomings. If we compare this with, for example, the Palestinian Saints' Lives authored by Cyril of Scythopolis, the difference is striking: Cyril knew that his monastic heroes, Euthymius the Great and Saint Sabas, were also not too well versed in dogmatic affairs, but he nevertheless managed successfully to conceal their somewhat limited knowledge of theological matters.

Despite these limitations, Macarius took part, according to the text, in the most important Church meetings of the fifth century, if only to be continuously mocked, for example at the Council of Ephesus in AD 431: 'Father, put on your clean clothes, for we are going to meet the emperor', his companions advise him.[19] Macarius only responds that the emperor's heart is ten thousand times filthier than his clothes. Of course, some things are inevitable: Macarius is stopped by the chamberlains, who refuse him entrance to the Council, to which he is only admitted after the narrator, Dioscorus of Alexandria, sneaks him into the assembly under the pretext that he is his book-carrier. Inside the Council church Macarius desires at once to speak anathema over Nestorius, but this form of participation at the Council fails as well, since the bishop of Tkōou simply cannot find any interpreter to convey his curses against the heretic.[20] Thereby the narrator, with a face-saving ploy, shifts the focus from Macarius' failure (conveyed in a parenthesis, yet still noticeable for the audience of the *Panegyricus*) on to his determination.

2 The Miracles Worked by Macarius

Macarius' talents as a destroyer of temples, as a polyglot, and therefore as a learned theologian, are found wanting; as a last resort, the performance of miracles appears as a chance to salvage his hagiographical honour. And indeed, the saint performs at least two impressive healing miracles, but again, the image we gain is somewhat tainted: when Macarius is travelling by boat to reach the Council of Ephesus, he encounters the brother of the shipowner. This brother has one good and one blind eye and—this we might conjecture from the text—

hitting any of his enemies with whom he is fighting. And thus, even if Father Macarius is not a pikeman—which is to say that he does not understand how to speak the Greek language—nevertheless he did not rest without going with us to the war of Chalcedon, and he was numbered also among the 634 bishops').

19 *Pan. Mac.* 6.3: ϫⲉⲁⲡⲁ ⲫⲟⲣⲉⲓ ⲛ̄ⲛⲉⲕϩⲟⲉⲓⲧⲉ ⲉⲧⲣⲁϩⲉ ϫⲉⲉⲛⲃⲏⲕ ⲉⲁⲡⲁⲛⲧⲁ ⲉⲡⲣ̄ⲣⲟ.

20 *Pan. Mac.* 6.5.

is quite used to his one-eyed way of life. Unfortunately for him, his good eye has caught an inflammation, so he asks Macarius to help him. The saint makes the sign of the Cross over the blind eye, clearly not realising that the sailor aimed at a cure for the seeing but diseased eye.[21] Even the reaction of the sailor upon having his previously blind eye miraculously restored to sight is not as thankful as the rules of the genre would have us expect—until Macarius rectifies his error by healing the diseased eye as well. While the underlying greatness of the miracle, an accidental healing, is clear, it is nevertheless remarkable that neither the miracle worker himself nor the one who was healed really fully perceive what has happened. The episode may be related to a similar one recorded in MS Brit. Lib. orient 7029, edited by Wallis Budge in 1915, in which two Nubians, one of them blind in one eye, are doubting the miraculous healing powers of Apa Aaron in the desert eastwards of Philae. Immediately, the half-blind man experiences the healing of his blind eye, while, unfortunately, the previously healthy eye turns blind. Only when they approach Apa Aaron are both eyes healed.[22] Here, however, in stark contrast to the episode in the *Panegyricus on Macarius*, the Nubians are eventually more than thankful for the miracle.

Something similar happens in a different hagiographical text that seems—at least at a first glance—important for a discussion of the *Panegyricus on Macarius*: the *Life of Symeon the Holy Fool* authored by the Cypriot Bishop Leontius of Neapolis. Symeon's attitude to miracles seems fairly similar to that of Macarius, though Symeon's camouflage appears much more intentional and deliberate according to Leontius' account:[23]

---

21 *Pan. Mac.* 3.1–4. The biblical precedent of a healing miracle restoring sight and performed in two steps is Mark 8:22–26.

22 Cf. Ernest Alfred Wallis Budge, *Coptic Texts v: Miscellaneous Coptic Texts in the Dialect of Upper Egypt* (London: Trustees of the British Museum, 1915), no. 123; cf. Konstantin Klein, "Invisible Monks, Human Eyes and the Egyptian Desert in Late Antique Hagiography", in Hans Barnard and Kim Duistermaat (eds.), *The History of the Peoples of the Eastern Desert* (Los Angeles: University of California Press, 2012), 298–311. See also Van Pelt in this volume.

23 *V. Sym.* 147: Ἐπετήδευσεν δὲ καὶ τοῦτο ὁ ὅσιος, ὅτι καθότι ἐποίει τίποτε παράδοξον, εὐθέως ἤλλασσεν τὴν γειτονίαν ἐκείνην, ἕως οὗ λησμονηθῇ τὸ πρᾶγμα, ὃ ἐποίησεν. The *Vita Symeonis* is quoted according to the edition by Lennart Rydén in André-Jean Festugière (ed.), *Vie de Syméon le Fou et Vie de Jean de Chypre* (Paris: Geuthner, 1974). The translation by Derek Krueger, *Symeon the Holy Fool: Leontius's Life and the Late Antique City*, (Berkeley: University of California Press, 1996), has been used throughout this study with minor adaptations. On holy fools (with a strong emphasis on the later Byzantine and Old Russian hagiographic literature), cf. Sergey Ivanov, *Holy Fools in Byzantium and Beyond* (Oxford: Oxford University Press, 2006), esp. 1–10 for a definition of the phenomenon of holy foolery.

> It was also the saint's practice, whenever he did something miraculous, to leave that neighborhood immediately, until the deed which he had done was forgotten. He hurried on immediately elsewhere to do something inappropriate, so that he might thereby hide his perfection.

Healing of eyes plays an important part in the *Life of Symeon* too: one miracle occurs when some teenage girls mock the saint, and he consequently curses them so that God makes them cross-eyed. Only after they beg him to be healed does he decide to kiss some of them, and thus restore their sight. However, he leaves some others cross-eyed as a reminder of their sin, and also, as Leontius of Neapolis comments, since otherwise they would have exceeded all the women of Syria in debauchery.[24] Differently to Macarius, here the healing happens very much as a conscious deed of the saint.

However, in one of the more humorous episodes in Symeon's *Life* (which includes a mockery of the clergy's liturgical dresses) another healing miracle of diseased eyes takes place:[25]

> For sometimes when Sunday came, [Symeon] took a string of sausages and wore them as a [deacon's] stole. In his left hand he held a pot of mustard, and he dipped [the sausages in the mustard] and ate them from morning on … Wherefore also a certain rustic, who had leucoma in his two eyes, came to make fun of him. Symeon anointed his eyes with mustard. The man was nearly burned to death, and Symeon said to him, 'Go wash, idiot, with vinegar and garlic, and you will be healed immediately.' As it seemed a better thing to do, he ran immediately to the doctors instead and was completely blinded.

Only when the man remembered Symeon's advice to wash his eyes with vinegar and garlic are his eyes healed. The way the miracle is described is just as witty as the passage with the half-blind sailor in the *Panegyricus on Macarius*.

---

24 *V. Sym.* 157–158, cf. Vsévolod Rochcau, "Saint Syméon Salos, ermite palestinien et prototype des 'Fous-pour-le-Christ'", *Proche-Orient Chrétien* 28 (1978), 209–219, and Ludwig, *Sonderformen*, 381–382.

25 *V. Sym.* 160–161: ἔστιν γὰρ ὅτε καταλαμβανούσης τῆς ἁγίας κυριακῆς λαμβάνειν αὐτὸν σειρὰν σαλσικίων καὶ φορεῖν αὐτὰ ὡς ὠράριον καὶ κρατεῖν ἐν τῇ ἀριστερᾷ αὐτοῦ χειρὶ σίνηπι καὶ οὕτως βάπτειν καὶ τρώγειν ἀπὸ πρωΐ… ὅθεν καὶ τις ἐλθὼν προσπαῖξαι αὐτῷ χωρικός, ἔχων ἐν τοῖς δυσὶν ὀφθαλμοῖς αὐτοῦ λευκώματα ἄσπρα, ἐχρίσθη ὑπ' αὐτοῦ ἐκ τοῦ σινήπεως εἰς τοὺς ὀφθαλμοὺς αὐτοῦ. τοῦ δὲ στυφθέντος ἕως θανάτου λέγει αὐτῷ· «ὕπαγε νίψαι, ἔξηχε, εἰς ὄξος καὶ εἰς σκόρδα καὶ εὐθὺς ὑγιαίνεις». ἐκεῖνος δὲ ὡς δοκῶν τι ποιεῖν εὐθὺς εἰς ἰατροὺς ἔδραμεν καὶ πλέον ἐτυφλώθη.

However, despite many similarities there is a fundamental difference: Symeon, according to the author, may do foolish things, but is still always in control of the situation. He is always and ultimately right. Macarius, on the other hand, is a saintly person with certain healing powers of which he is not at all aware. To put it differently: Symeon is a holy fool, Macarius is holy, but a fool.[26]

The second miracle in the *Panegyricus* is quite similar to this first one. It takes place in the city of Constantinople, where Macarius stays while attending the Council of Chalcedon in AD 451. The wife of a pious lawyer suffers from leprosy. Unable to find the actual saint, who only incidentally has met her husband, the sick woman grasps the latter's hand (that had previously touched the saint) and immediately experiences a full healing. When she and the husband later approach Macarius in order to thank him for the miracle, Macarius, once again, simply does not understand what has happened.[27] The motif of slow-wittedness appears very often in early Christian Egyptian martyrdoms. However, in these texts, this attitude is usually assigned to the pagan governors, who, as a rule, are irascible and stupid.[28] This might be so since it has only recently been recognised that Coptic martyrdoms, a genre that Hippolyte Delehaye had described as *cette misérable littérature*,[29] show not only the influence of the latecomer among Greek literary forms, the prose romance, but also of Greek drama—especially with Coptic martyrdoms' tendency for stock character types.[30] A good example is the Coptic *Passion of St Shenoufe and his Brethren*, in which the governor witnesses how Shenoufe is not harmed by the fire underneath a gridiron on which the martyr was placed. Consequently, the

26 Cf. also the discussion in Katrina Triezenberg, "Humor in Literature", in Victor Raskin (ed.), *The Primer of Humor Research* (Berlin/New York: De Gruyter; 2008), 523–542, esp. 532: Symeon fits the (modern) description of the fool, whose behaviour runs against social norms, whereas Macarius simply is a target of laughter. On the boundaries of Symeon's foolery, cf. Vincent Déroche, *Études sur Léontios de Néapolis* (Uppsala: Acta Universitatis Upsaliensis, 1995), 163–164.

27 *Pan. Mac.* 12,3–5.

28 Reymond/Barns, *Martyrdoms*, 2, Jill Harries, "Constructing the Judge: Judicial Accountability and the Culture of Criticism in Late Antiquity", in Richard Miles (ed.), *Constructing Identity in Late Antiquity* (London: Routledge, 1999), 214–233, and James Corke-Webster, "Author and Authority: Literary Representations of Moral Authority in Eusebius of Caesarea's The Martyrs of Palestine", in Peter Gemeinhardt and Johan Leemans (eds.), *Martyrdom in Late Antiquity (300–400 AD): History and Discourse, Tradition and Religious Identity*, (Berlin: De Gruyter, 2012), 51–78. See also Alwis in this volume on the changing characterisation of persecutors.

29 Delehaye, "Les Martyrs", 148.

30 Cf. Reymond and Barns, *Martyrdoms*, 1–2.

governor wants to ascertain the matter and receives serious burns in the face.[31] In a few texts, slow-wittedness appears also as a sign of sanctity, as is the case with St Thecla in the Coptic *Passion of St Paese and Thecla*: Thecla, Paese's sister, who is travelling down the Nile to join her brother in martyrdom, boards a ship steered by the archangels Raphael and Gabriel with the Virgin Mary and Elizabeth, no less, as fellow passengers. Even though Mary and Elizabeth make their identity abundantly clear, Thecla does not understand any of their hints, as, for example, when the Virgin tells Thecla that her son was set upon a wooden cross. Thecla goes on to ask the noble women to which city they belong. Even the answer 'Jerusalem' does not suffice to make the slow-witted Thecla recognise Mary and Elizabeth.[32]

The prototype of such saintly slow-wittedness can be found in the Bible, in the *First Letter to the Corinthians*, a passage often quoted in Coptic martyrdom accounts:[33] 'We are fools for the sake of Christ' (1 Cor 4:10) or 'God chose what is foolish in the world to shame the wise' (1 Cor 1:27). The importance of these lines is also apparent from Leontius of Neapolis' preface to his *Life of Symeon the Holy Fool*:[34]

> For we know that to the most senseless and disdainful we seem to be relating something incredible and worthy of laughter. But if they had listened to the words, 'If one wishes to be wise in this age, let him be a fool, that he may become wise', and again, 'We are fools for Christ's sake', and again, 'For the foolishness of God is wiser than men', they would not consider

31 Cf. *Martyrdom of Shenoufe and His Brethren* 111R.i–ii, (in Reymond and Barns, *Martyrdoms*).

32 *Martyrdom of Paese and Thecla* 69R.ii–69V.i (in Reymond and Barns, *Martyrdoms*). Cf. *Pan. Mac.* 6.1 for a similar vision, in which, however, the saint (John the Baptist), as for safety's sake, clarifies that he is the son of Zechariah, and that his mother is Elizabeth, the relative of Mary, the mother of the Lord (ⲡⲉϫⲁϥ ⲛⲁⲓ̈ ϫⲉⲁⲛⲟⲕⲡⲉ ⲓⲱϩⲁⲛⲛⲏⲥ ⲡϣⲏⲣⲉ ⲛ̄ⲍⲁⲭⲁⲣⲓⲁⲥ · ⲧⲁⲙⲁⲁⲩⲧⲉ ⲉⲗⲓⲥⲁⲃⲉⲧ ⲧⲥⲩⲛⲅⲉⲛⲏⲥ ⲙ̄ⲙⲁⲣⲓⲁ ⲧⲙ̄ⲁⲁⲩ ⲙ̄ⲡϫⲟⲉⲓⲥ).

33 On foolishness and laughter in the Bible, cf. John Morreall, "Philosophy and Religion", in Victor Raskin (ed.), *The Primer of Humor Research* (Berlin/New York: De Gruyter, 2008), 211–242, esp. 212–213, cf. Luke 24:13–35 (the road to Emmaus) for an example of the Pauline admonition within the text of the Gospels.

34 *V. Sym.* 122–123: οἴδαμεν γὰρ ὅτι τοῖς ἀφρονεστέροις καὶ καταφρονηταῖς ἄπιστα δόξομεν λέγειν καὶ γελοίων ἄξια. εἰ δὲ ἤκουσαν τοῦ εἰπόντος· «ὁ θέλων σοφὸς εἶναι ἐν τῷ αἰῶνι τούτῳ μωρὸς γενέσθω, ἵνα γένηται σοφός», καὶ πάλιν· «ἡμεῖς μωροὶ διὰ Χριστόν», καὶ πάλιν· «ὅτι τὸ μωρὸν τοῦ θεοῦ σοφώτερον τῶν ἀνθρώπων ἐστίν», οὐκ ἂν τοῖς ὑπὸ τούτου τοῦ ὄντως ἀθλητοῦ κατεργασθεῖσιν ὡς γελοίοις προσεῖχον, ἀλλ' ἢ μᾶλλον καὶ πλέον τῶν τὰς λοιπὰς τῆς ἀρετῆς πολιτείας μετελθόντων ἐθαύμαζον. Cf. also Ivanov, *Holy Fools*, 18–23.

> the achievements of this true athlete to be laughable; rather they would marvel again at those seeking the alternate ways to virtue.

But again, there is a difference between Macarius and Symeon: for the latter, the attribute 'fool' describes the specific way in which he works deeds for God. Foolishness is not one of many character traits of his personality, he simply *is* the fool; that is as the way in which he is recognised from the beginning of the text. For example, when he first joins a monastery, 'welcome fool' (καλῶς ἦλθες, Σαλέ)[35] is how the doorkeeper greets him without ever having seen him before. Symeon's foolishness, however, is not static: it gets increasingly extravagant, especially in Emesa, where, to quote from the *Vita*, 'he [really] pretended to be a fool' (ἔνθα καὶ τὸν σαλὸν προσεποιήσατο).[36] It should suffice to quote from Symeon's entry into this city, a description that is of course a parody of Christ's entry into Jerusalem:[37]

> When the famous Symeon found a dead dog on a dunghill outside the city, he loosened the rope belt he was wearing, and tied it to the dog's foot. He dragged the dog as he ran and entered to gate, where there was a children's school nearby. When the children saw him, they began to cry, 'Hey, a crazy abba (ἔ, ἀββᾶς μωρός)!' And they set about to run after him and box him on the ears.

3 Sanctity, Comedy, and Ridicule

It is a thin line dividing the comical from the ridiculous.[38] In his study on Symeon the Holy Fool, Derek Krueger suggested that most readers must have

---

35 *V. Sym.* 126. On similar phrases in the *Apophthegmata Patrum* and in the *Vitae* by John of Ephesus, cf. Ivanov, *Holy Fools*, 34–37.

36 *V. Sym.* 125.

37 *V. Sym.* 145: εὑρὼν ὁ ἀοίδιμος ἐπὶ τῆς κοπρίας τῆς ἔξω τῆς πόλεως κύνα νεκρόν, λύσας ὃ ἐφόρει ζωνάριον ἐκ σχοινίου καὶ δήσας τὸν πόδα αὐτοῦ ἔσυρεν αὐτὸν τρέχων καὶ εἰσερχόμενος διὰ τῆς πόρτης, ὅπου πλησίον ἐστὶν τὸ σχολίον τῶν παιδίων. ὡς τοῦτον οὖν ἐθεάσαντο οἱ παῖδες, ἤρξαντο κράζειν· 'ἔ, ἀββᾶς μωρός' καὶ ἔβαλον τρέχειν ὀπίσω αὐτοῦ καὶ κοσσίζειν αὐτόν. Cf. Ewald Kislinger, "Symeon Salos' Hund", *Jahrbuch der Österreichischen Byzantinistik* 38 (1988), 165–170, esp. 165–166. Again, there is a textual parallel with the *Apophthegmata Patrum* (*PG* 65, 240), when the disciple of Abba John, a certain Paul, catches a hyena. The elder reprimands his disciple that the latter, characterised as a fool, has brought a mad dog (Σαλέ, κύνα σαλὸν ἤνεγκας), probably hinting at the hyenas 'mad' laughter, cf. Ivanov, *Holy Fools*, 38–39.

38 Cf. Hans Jauss, "Zum Problem der Grenzziehung zwischen dem Lächerlichen und dem

enjoyed the text for its slapstick humour, and he refers to the *Vita* as a confirmation that late antique Christians did have a sense of humour.[39] We can detect this also from the writings of Anastasius of Sinai who was mocking the behaviour of Christians in Syria and Palestine—how people yawn during service or are making a pretence of falling asleep.[40] However, the question is whether the *Panegyricus on Macarius* was similarly intended to be funny, or whether it is only the modern reader that inevitably has to smile when she or he reads the unsuccessful deeds of a saint who eventually suffers martyrdom through a well-directed kick into his private parts.[41] Macarius is not a holy fool per se in the way that Symeon is styled as one by his hagiographer Leontius. Macarius is implicitly mocked by the compiler of the *Panegyricus*, where he appears as a fool against his will. Within the context of saintly simplicity, however, one may conclude that Macarius was a true hero, albeit of a very different kind when compared to a universally learned (alleged) contemporary such as Shenoute of Atripe, who had received an excellent education in Greek rhetoric[42] and never failed in any heroic endeavour.

In general, exploring the role of Shenoute (and the episodes connected to him) appears to be a fruitful direction for further research on the *Panegyricus*. So far the important role of Atripe, the White Monastery, in this text has

Komischen", in Wolfgang Preisendanz and Rainer Warning (eds.), *Das Komische* (Munich: Fink, 1974), 361–371. How we look at humour and laughter has changed over time, moreover, it is necessary to distinguish between e.g. official and unofficial laughter as well as between the objects of ridicule (in pre-modern times often the grotesque); cf. Jan N. Bremmer and Herman Roodenburg, "Humor und Geschichte", in Jan N. Bremmer (ed.), *Kulturgeschichte des Humors von der Antike bis heute* (Darmstadt: Wissenschaftliche Buchgesellschaft, 1999), 9–17, esp. 10–11 and Triezenberg, "Humor", 523–524 as well as Gun-Britt Kohler (2012), "Karneval und kultureller Raum. Überlegungen zu Bachtins Konzept des Lachens", in Stefan Bießenecker and Christian Kuhn (eds.), *Valenzen des Lachens in der Vormoderne* (Bamberg: University of Bamberg Press, 2012), 29–52, esp. 29–31 and 43–44 with n. 43 (with similar examples from medieval Russia).

39 Cf. Krueger, *Symeon*, 47–48 and 126.

40 John Haldon, "Humour and the Everyday in Byzantium", in Guy Halsall (ed.), *Humour, History and Politics in Late Antiquity and the Early Middle Ages* (Cambridge: Cambridge University Press, 2004), 48–71, esp. 62–63. On Byzantine survivals of the mimus, cf. Ludwig, *Sonderformen*, 351–383.

41 *Pan. Mac.* 13.6. Macarius' way to die is introduced in a sensationalist fashion and only narrated properly later in order to make him appear more like a martyr and less undignified. The specific manner of death is, of course, connected with assertions of his virginity: Macarius dies by a kick into that body part which other people use for the worst of sins, while the saint himself remains without sin throughout his life.

42 Cf. Johannes Leipoldt, *Schenute von Atripe und die Entstehung des national-ägyptischen Christentums* (Leipzig: Hinrichs, 1903), 82.

only received little attention: we have encountered how Besa, Shenoute's successor, has to make an appearance to save the day at the temple of Kothos. Shenoute himself appears several times in the text, always in order to endorse Macarius—be it by giving guidance in theological matters or when he recognises the importance of this monk,[43] an importance which the *Panegyricus* itself dismantles on almost every page. If one casts an eye on the *Panegyricus on Macarius of Tkōou* reading it not so much as a text that aims at heaping praise on Macarius but rather on Shenoute, a much more central figure in late antique Egypt, many episodes make more sense. It has already been noted that the *Panegyricus* shares much content with the dossier of texts on and by Shenoute. Perhaps it is necessary to go one step further and see Macarius as the boorish alter ego of Shenoute.

Moreover, from what we know, the text was predominantly transmitted and circulated in the monastic foundations of Shenoute so one could go as far as to claim that the mere fact that Macarius belonged to the circle and to the successor generation of the famous abbot was sufficient to reassure the audience of the text that, despite Macarius' incapacities and misfortunes (from which those listening and reading the text might or might not draw entertainment), they will still be edified since all these misfortunes were presented in an edifying envelope which praises Macarius' simplicity and humility. Being a member of the circle of Shenoute or walking in his footsteps thus can be seen as just enough to survive in a dangerous world full of pagans, heretics, and frightening diseases.

4 The Art of Imitation

Almost a millennium before the compilation of the *Panegyricus* on Macarius, Xenophon in his *Symposium* had described the uninvited arrival of the jester Philippus. Initially, this man had unsuccessfully tried to elicit laughter in the guests. However, he only achieves this goal when he, who is described

43 The same phenomenon can be observed in the *Vita* of Moses of Abydos (cf. *V. Mos.* 9–10), in which Shenoute on his deathbed prophesises Moses' future fame. On the influence of texts by and on Shenoute in the *Panegyricus on Macarius* and the *Vita Mosis*, cf. David Brakke, *Demons and the Making of the Monk: Spiritual Combat in Early Christianity* (Cambridge, MA: Harvard University Press, 2006), 222–223 and David Brakke, "From Temple to Cell, from Gods to Demons: Pagan Temples in the Monastic Topography of Fourth Century Egypt", in Johannes Hahn, Stephen Emmel, and Ulrich Gotter (eds.), *From Temple to Church: Destruction and Renewal of Local Cultic Topography in Late Antiquity* (Leiden: Brill, 2008), 91–112, esp. 108–109, as well as Dijkstra, "Fate of the Temples", 399–400 and 400 with n. 40. On humour in the *Vita Mosis*, cf. also Ludwig, *Sonderformen*, 305.

as ridiculous to look at, starts dancing and doing impressions of the professional (and beautiful) dancers. Eventually, all guests praised Philippus' ability to 'compare' and 'imitate' other people.[44] Xenophon's literary description of the act of the jester has often been used to exemplify the differences between ancient and modern attitudes towards humour: Philippus is funny not because of his jokes, but (apart from his 'ridiculous existence') purely because of his talent to imitate. While this does not mean, of course, that the compiler of the *Panegyricus* was aware of Xenophon's writings, we might nevertheless detect a parallel, if we read this late antique text (or, at least, certain episodes in it) as a parody mimicking the genre of saints' lives.[45] According to Victor Raskin, what makes the comical aspect of a text successful is the overlap between two scripts which are each internally consistent but contradict each other.[46] Thus, within the relatively conventional script (i.e. form) of a saint's life (despite the *Panegyricus*' patchwork character) we find a second script inserted, that of the main protagonist refusing to fit into the expected stereotypes of his role. This leads to a humorous dichotomy between the anticipated and the actual behaviour of Macarius, resembling the characteristic traits of the *mimus* in late antiquity, which reduced ancient tragedies to the level of vulgar parodies. The success of the *mimus* may have resided in the audience's satisfaction at the failure of the main characters and at seeing all that was heroic being replaced by the grotesque and comic.[47] It is often doubted that humour is at all compatible with religion. Although its use has been demonstrated in Christian religious texts in a few instances,[48] comical genres faced a notice-

44 Xen. *Symp.* 2.21–23 as well as 6.8–10, cf. Jan N. Bremmer, "Witze, Spaßmacher und Witzbücher in der antiken griechischen Kultur", in Jan N. Bremmer (ed.), *Kulturgeschichte des Humors von der Antike bis heute* (Darmstadt: Wissenschaftliche Buchgesellschaft, 1999), 18–31, esp. 18–21 on Philippus and other jesters (*gelotopoioi*) who knew how to imitate not only dancers but athletes. Already in Roman times, *gelotopoioi* had a low standing and were often equated with the actors of the *mimus*, cf. Bremmer, "Witze", 23, Sotera Fornaro, "Philogelos", *DNP* 9 (Stuttgart: Metzler, 2000), coll. 828–829, esp. 829, and Elizabeth Rawson, "The Vulgarity of the Roman Mime", in H.D. Jocelyn (ed.), *Tria lustra* (Liverpool: Liverpool Classical Monthly, 1993), 255–260. On the difficulties of detecting actors in late antique documentary sources, cf. Roueché, "Spectacles", 59–60.

45 On parody, cf. Triezenberg, "Humor", 533.

46 Cf. Victor Raskin, *Semantic Mechanisms of Humor* (Dordrecht: Reidel, 1985), 99 with Triezenberg, "Humor", 534–535 and 538. The overlapping of scripts has later been called 'script opposition', cf. Salvatore Attardo and Victor Raskin, "Script Theory Revis(it)ed: Joke Similarity and Joke Representation Model", *Humor* 4 (1991), 293–341.

47 Cf. Furley, "Mimos", 204. On anti-heroes in hagiography, cf. Ludwig, *Sonderformen*, 3.

48 Cf. Morreall, "Philosophy and Religion", 229–230 and esp. 232, on how the Old Testament story of Jonah and the whale can be understood as a satire on a reluctant prophet. Cf.

able decline in late antiquity,[49] and one might wonder whether the audience was offended by this unusual form of hagiography. However, the large amount of manuscript witnesses and translations in different Coptic dialects as well as into Arabic prove these doubts wrong. Moreover, despite the shortcomings of the main character, the text displays an unwavering respect for the faith and religion. However, it is almost impossible to answer the question as to why the author or compiler may have chosen this perhaps unprecedented creation of a hagiographical script opposition. We can only speculate that the reason for Macarius' depiction as a highly unsuccessful saint has to be seen in connection with Shenoute, too: Macarius is the famous abbot's sacred sidekick, and therefore his shortcomings were no shortcomings at all, since they increased the fame of Shenoute. One holy man's failures underscored the other's triumphs.

Bibliography

Attardo, Salvatore and Victor Raskin, "Script Theory Revis(it)ed: Joke Similarity and Joke Representation Model", *Humor* 4 (1991), 293–341.

Bell, David N., *Besa: Life of Shenoute* (Kalamazoo, MI: Cistercian Publications, 1983).

Benz, Lore, "Pantomimos", *Der Neue Pauly* 9 (Stuttgart: Metzler, 2000), coll. 274–276.

Brakke, David, *Demons and the Making of the Monk: Spiritual Combat in Early Christianity* (Cambridge, MA: Harvard University Press, 2006).

Brakke, David, "From Temple to Cell, from Gods to Demons: Pagan Temples in the Monastic Topography of Fourth Century Egypt", in Johannes Hahn, Stephen Emmel, and Ulrich Gotter (eds.), *From Temple to Church: Destruction and Renewal of Local Cultic Topography in Late Antiquity* (Leiden/Boston, MA: Brill, 2008), 91–112.

Bremmer, Jan N., "Witze, Spaßmacher und Witzbücher in der antiken griechischen Kultur", in Jan N. Bremmer (ed.), *Kulturgeschichte des Humors von der Antike bis heute* (Darmstadt: Wissenschaftliche Buchgesellschaft, 1999), 18–31.

Bremmer, Jan N. and Herman Roodenburg, "Humor und Geschichte", in Jan N. Brem-

also Georg Luck, "Humor", *RAC* 16 (Stuttgart: Hiersemann, 1994), coll. 753–773, esp. 765–767 on parts of the Gospels which may derive from humorous folk tales and on Paul's use of sarcasm in 1 Cor. 4,6.

49 Cf. Bremmer, "Witze", 30–31, with convincing remarks that much of the late antique critique of laughter actually stems from older Pythagoraean models, and also Morreall, "Philosophy and Religion", 216–217 and Triezenberg, "Humor", 538. Luck, "Humor", 767–768 and 769–770 (on the hostile depiction of laughter in hagiography) and esp. 754, demonstrating that the amount of different terms which were used to name and distinguish humorous genres decreased in late antiquity.

mer (ed.), *Kulturgeschichte des Humors von der Antike bis heute* (Darmstadt: Wissenschaftliche Buchgesellschaft, 1999), 9–17.

Carrié, Jean-Michel, "Conclusion", in Christian Landes and Jean-Michel Carrié (eds.), *Jeux et spectacles dans l'Antiquité tardive = AntTard* 15 (2007), 215–219.

Corke-Webster, James, "Author and Authority: Literary Representations of Moral Authority in Eusebius of Caesarea's The Martyrs of Palestine", in Peter Gemeinhardt and Johan Leemans (eds.), *Martyrdom in Late Antiquity (300–400 AD): History and Discourse, Tradition and Religious Identity* (Berlin/Boston, MA: De Gruyter, 2012), 51–78.

Delehaye, Hippolyte, "Les Martyrs d'Égypte", *Analecta Bollandiana* 40 (1922), 5–154 and 299–364.

Déroche, Vincent, *Études Léontios de Néapolis* (Uppsala: Acta Universitatis Upsaliensis, 1995).

Dijkstra, Jitse, "The Fate of the Temples in Late Antique Egypt", in Luke Lavan and Michael Mulryan (eds.), *The Archaeology of Late Antique 'Paganism'* (Leiden/Boston, MA: Brill), 389–436.

Emmel, Stephen, "Immer erst das Kleingedruckte lesen. 'Die Pointe verstehen' in dem koptischen Panegyrikos auf Makarios von Tkōou", in Anke Blöbaum, Joachim Kahl, and Simon Schweitzer (eds.), *Ägypten—Münster. Kulturwissenschaftliche Studien zu Ägypten, dem Vorderen Orient und verwandten Gebieten* (Wiesbaden: Harrassowitz, 2003), 91–114.

Festugière, André-Jean (ed.), *Vie de Syméon le Fou et Vie de Jean de Chypre* (Paris: Geuthner, 1974).

Fornaro, Sotera, "Philogelos", *DNP* 9 (Stuttgart: Metzler, 2000), coll. 828–829.

Frankfurter, David, "Illuminating the Cult of Kothos: The *Panegyric on Macarius* and Local Religion in Fifth-Century Egypt", in James Goehring (ed.), *The World of Early Egyptian Christianity: Language, Literature, and Social Context* (Washington, DC: Catholic University of America Press, 2007), 176–188.

Furley, William, "Mimos", *DNP* 8 (Stuttgart: Metzler, 2000), coll. 201–207.

Gaudement, Jean, "La condamnation des praticques païennes en 391", in Jacques Fontaine and Charles Kannengiesser (eds.), *Epektasis: FS Jean Daniélou* (Paris: Beauchesne, 1972), 597–602.

Haldon, John, "Humour and the Everyday in Byzantium", in Guy Halsall (ed.), *Humour, History and Politics in Late Antiquity and the Early Middle Ages* (Cambridge: Cambridge University Press, 2004), 48–71.

Harries, Jill, "Constructing the Judge: Judicial Accountability and the Culture of Criticism in Late Antiquity", in Richard Miles (ed.), *Constructing Identity in Late Antiquity* (London: Routledge, 1999), 214–233.

Ivanov, Sergey, *Holy Fools in Byzantium and Beyond* (Oxford: Oxford University Press, 2006).

Jauss, Hans, "Zum Problem der Grenzziehung zwischen dem Lächerlichen und dem Komischen", in Wolfgang Preisendanz and Rainer Warning (eds.), *Das Komische* (Munich: Fink, 1974), 361–371.

Johnson, David, *A Panegyric on Macarius Bishop of Tkôw Attributed to Dioscorus of Alexandria* (Louvain: Secretariat du CorpusSCO, 1980).

Kislinger, Ewald, "Symeon Salos' Hund", *Jahrbuch der Österreichischen Byzantinistik* 38 (1988), 165–170.

Klein, Konstantin, "Invisible Monks, Human Eyes and the Egyptian Desert in Late Antique Hagiography", in Hans Barnard and Kim Duistermaat (eds.), *The History of the Peoples of the Eastern Desert* (Los Angeles: University of California Press, 2012), 298–311.

Klein, Konstantin, "Review of S. Moawad (2010), *Untersuchungen zum Panegyrikos auf Makarios*, Wiesbaden", *Plekos* 16 (2014), 55–77.

Kohler, Gunn-Britt, (2012), "Karneval und kultureller Raum. Überlegungen zu Bachtins Konzept des Lachens", in Stefan Bießenecker and Christian Kuhn (eds.), *Valenzen des Lachens in der Vormoderne* (Bamberg: University of Bamberg Press, 2012), 29–52.

Krueger, Derek, *Symeon the Holy Fool: Leontius's* Life *and the Late Antique City* (Berkeley: University of California Press, 1996).

Leipoldt, Johannes, *Schenute von Atripe und die Entstehung des national-ägyptischen Christentums* (Leipzig: Hinrichs, 1903).

Luck, Georg, "Humor", *RAC* 16 (Stuttgart: Hiersemann, 1994), coll. 753–773.

Ludwig, Claudia, *Sonderformen byzantinischer Hagiographie und ihr literarisches Vorbild: Untersuchungen zu den Viten des Äsop, des Philaretos, des Symeon Salos und des Andreas Salos* (Frankfurt: Peter Lang, 1997).

McKenzie, Judith, Sheila Gibson, and Andreas Reyes, "Reconstructing the Serapeum in Alexandria from the Archaeological Evidence", *JRS* 94 (2004), 73–121.

Moawad, Samuel, *Untersuchungen zum Paneygyrikos auf Makarios von Tkōou und zu seiner Überlieferung* (Wiesbaden: Reichert 2010).

Morreall, John, "Philosophy and Religion", in Victor Raskin (ed.), *The Primer of Humor Research* (Berlin/New York: De Gruyter, 2008), 211–242.

Puk, Alexander, *Das römische Spielewesen in der Spätantike* (Berlin/Boston: De Gruyter, 2014).

Raskin, Victor, *Semantic Mechanisms of Humor* (Dordrecht: Reidel, 1985).

Rawson, Elizabeth, "The Vulgarity of the Roman Mime", in Henry D. Jocelyn (ed.), *Tria lustra* (Liverpool: Liverpool Classical Monthly, 1993), 255–260.

Reymond, Eve and John Barns (eds.), *Four Martyrdoms from the Pierpont Morgan Coptic Codices* (Oxford: Clarendon Press, 1973).

Rochcau, Vsévolod, "Saint Syméon Salos, ermite palestinien et prototype des 'Fous-pour-le-Christ'", *Proche-Orient Chrétien* 28 (1978), 209–219.

Roldanus, Johannes, "Stützen und Störenfriede: mönchische Einmischung in die doktrinäre und kirchenpolitische Rezeption von Chalkedon", in Johannes van Oort and Johannes Roldanus (eds.), *Chalkedon: Geschichte und Aktualität: Studien zur Rezeption der christologischen Formel von Chalkedon* (Leuven: Peeters, 1998), 123–146.

Roueché, Charlotte, "Spectacles in Late Antiquity: Some Observations", in Christian Landes and Jean-Michel Carrié (eds.), *Jeux et spectacles dans l'Antiquité tardive* = *AntTard* 15 (2007), 59–64.

Triezenberg, Katrina, "Humor in Literature", in Victor Raskin (ed.), *The Primer of Humor Research* (Berlin/New York: De Gruyter; 2008), 523–542.

Wallis Budge, Ernest Alfred, *Coptic Texts v: Miscellaneous Coptic Texts in the Dialect of Upper Egypt* (London: Trustees of the British Museum, 1915).

CHAPTER 10

Disclosing Secret Chaste Marriages in Jerome's *Life of Malchus* and Stephen the African's *Life of Amator*

Klazina Staat

1 Introduction

This article focuses on the literary depictions of chaste marriage in two Latin *Lives* from late antiquity, namely Jerome's *Life of Malchus* (BHL 5190; from now on, *V. Malchi*)[1] and the lesser-known *Life of Amator*, written by Stephen the African (BHL 356, *V. Amat.*).[2] In a book on the constructed nature of saintly characters and their stories, it comes as no surprise that the hagiographers of the *Lives* of Malchus and Amator provide the readers with depictions of chaste marriages which are literary and stylised rather than historically reliable representations of reality. Although the stories reflect an ascetic practice common in late antiquity and the middle ages,[3] many elements are the product of

1 Unless stated otherwise, I use the Latin text and translation of the *Life of Malchus* provided by Christa Gray (ed.), *Jerome, Vita Malchi: Introduction, Text, Translation, and Commentary* (Oxford: Oxford University Press, 2015), which is the most complete study of the *Life* and contains an extensive bibliography. The *Life* is usually dated to around AD 391–392; see Gray, *Vita Malchi*, 5–6. For another recent edition and French translation, see Pierre Leclerc, Edgardo M. Morales, and Adalbert de Vogüé (eds.), *Jérôme: Trois vies de moines* (*Paul, Malchus, Hilarion*). Sources chrétiennes 508 (Paris: Les Éditions du Cerf, 2007).

2 The Latin text of the *Life of Amator* is taken from Louis-Maximilien Duru (ed.), "Saint Aunaire, éveque d'Auxerre, et Etienne Africain", in idem, *Bibliothèque historique de l'Yonne ou Collection de légendes, chroniques et documents divers* (Auxerre: Perriquet, 1850), 134–160, at 136–158; the translations are my own. The *Life* can be dated to the second half of the sixth century, during the bishopric of Aunarius of Auxerre (c. AD 561–603), who commissioned it. See Wolfert S. Van Egmond, *Conversing with the Saints: Communication in Pre-Carolingian Hagiography from Auxerre* (Turnhout: Brepols, 2006), 74–81 and 169–182, and Sylvie Joye, "Couples chastes à la fin de l'Antiquité et au haut Moyen Âge", *Médiévales* 65 (2013), 47–63 for recent discussions of the *Life*, including further references.

3 Chaste marriage is a form of 'syneisaktism', which is the designation commonly used for domestic relationships under which married or unmarried virgins of different sexes (*syneisaktoi* in the East or *subintroductae* in the West) live chastely together. The most important study of chaste marriage is still Dyan Elliott, *Spiritual Marriage: Sexual Abstinence in Medieval Wedlock* (Princeton, NJ: Princeton University Press, 1993); see also Hans Achelis, *Virgines subintro-*

 | DOI:10.1163/9789004421332_012

the hagiographers' invention or literary conventions, employed to idealise the depicted heroes and to contribute to the readers' active engagement with the text.[4] Accordingly, the *Lives* of Malchus and Amator play out the characteristic topical material found more generally in *Lives* of chaste couples: the couple is forced to marry by their masters (Malchus) or their parents (Amator), but decides on the wedding night—which is described in some detail—to live in a chaste union.[5] This paper primarily focuses on one element that also characteristically occurs in other *Lives* of chaste spouses, namely the notion of secrecy: the chaste marriage is often kept secret for specific characters in the story who may object to it. Thus, Malchus and his wife keep silent about their chaste marriage to their master, who had forced them to marry as a reward for Malchus' good service (*V. Malchi* 6.7), and Amator declines to inform his parents, who had betrothed him out of a desire for offspring (*V. Amat.* 2–4).[6]

Secrecy in the *Lives* of chaste spouses has mainly been considered from a historical perspective, as an indication of the anxieties surrounding chaste marriage in late antique and early medieval society. More specifically, scholars have argued, secrecy was the logical result of the fact that chaste marriage jeopardised the traditional function of marriage to ensure the permanence of both the family and the larger community by the production of offspring.[7] In addi-

---

ductae. Ein Beitrag zum 7. Kapittel des 1. Korinthierbriefs (Leipzig: Hinrichs, 1902); Kathleen C. Kelly, *Performing Virginity and Testing Chastity in the Middle Ages* (London: Taylor and Francis, 2000), 1–7; and Richard D. Finn, *Asceticism in the Graeco-Roman World.* Key Themes in Ancient History (Cambridge: Cambridge University Press, 2009), 86–112.

4 Joye, *Couples chastes*, 48 similarly notes the invented nature of the stories of chaste spouses, including the *Life of Amator*. For further discussion of literary stylisation in late antique hagiography, see Marc Van Uytfanghe, "L'origine et les ingrédients du discours hagiographique", *Sacris Erudiri* 50 (2011), 35–70; for fictionality, see the chapter by Van Pelt in this volume.

5 See Baudouin de Gaiffier, "*Intactam sponsam reliquens*: à propos de la Vie de St. Alexis", *AB* 65 (1947), 157–195, for these topoi in the stories of chaste spouses, including a list of texts featuring them. The most comprehensive list of texts about chaste spouses is provided in Elliott, *Spiritual Marriage*, 303–320 (appendices 1–7).

6 Malchus was forced to marry earlier as well, which was his reason for fleeing the parental house (*V. Malchi* 3.1).

7 For this explanation of secrecy, see Elliott, *Spiritual Marriage*, 4–5, 10, 60–62, 65–66, 70, 73, and 86; and Anne P. Alwis, *Celibate Marriages in Late Antique and Byzantine Hagiography* (London: Bloomsbury, 2013), 88–90. The rejection of marriage and its procreative function in Christian discourse seems to be motivated by a changed view on chastity. While chastity traditionally denoted the self-mastery of husband and wife within marriage which was necessary for the production of legitimate offspring, Christianity related it more closely to virginity, the complete abstinence of sexuality; see Kate Cooper, *The Virgin and the Bride: Idealized Womanhood in Late Antiquity* (Cambridge, MA: Harvard University Press, 1996).

tion, chaste marriage and other forms of chaste cohabitation were not commonly accepted among ecclesiastical authorities, who argued that the practices easily raised questions concerning the physical and spiritual integrity of the ascetics.[8] My focus on the *Lives* of Malchus and Amator is motivated by the observation that the secrecy is not merely a historical aspect characterising the couples' chaste marriages, but, as I will argue, part of a larger rhetorical strategy that invites the readers' active involvement in the texts.[9]

These literary aspects of secrecy in the descriptions of chaste marriages in *Lives* of chaste spouses have received little attention. Most importantly, in her study of some Greek *Lives* of chaste spouses, Anne Alwis observes that secrecy has a significant narrative function, as it can operate as a 'catalyst' of the plot and contributes to the readers' active participation:

> Secrecy … confers a sense of control and also legitimization upon the holy figure but yet places the onus back onto the recipient/audience. For the latter, salvation can only be attained if s/he can penetrate what lies right in front of them. Thus the worshippers adopt the role of an initiate, learning to infiltrate what lies beneath the mask.[10]

8 Elliott, *Spiritual Marriage*, 32–33. See 16–50 for a detailed discussion of the various views of late antique authors on chaste marriage, as well as Liesbeth Van der Sypt, "Are there Messalian Syneisakts in Gregory of Nyssa's *De Virginitate* 23.4?", in Johan Leemans and Matthieu Cassin (eds.), *Gregory of Nyssa: Contra Eunomium III: an English Translation with Commentary and Supporting Studies: Proceedings of the 12th International Colloquium on Gregory Of Nyssa (Leuven, 14–17 September 2010)*, Vigiliae Christianae Supplements 124 (Leiden: Brill, 2014), 704–717, at 706–709. Jerome also criticises *virgines subintroductae*, for instance, in *Ep.* 22.14 and 117.

9 The *Lives* of Malchus and Amator are not the only texts in which secrecy is an important aspect of the couple's chaste union. It also occurs, for instance, in the story of Martinianus and Maxima in Victor of Vita, *History of the Vandal Persecution* 1.30–38, Serge Lancel (ed.), *Victor de Vita: Histoire de la persécution vandale en Afrique, La passion des sept martyrs, Registre des provinces et des cités d'Afrique* (Paris: Belles Lettres, 2002), 110–114; the story of the 'Two Lovers' in Gregory of Tours' *History of the Franks* 1.47, Bruno Krusch and Wilhelm Levison (eds.), *Gregorius Turonensis: Historia Francorum (Libri historiarum X)*, MGH 1.1 (Hannover: Hahn, 1937–1951), 54–55, and *Glory of the Confessors* 31, Bruno Krusch (ed.), *Gregorius Turonensis, Liber in gloria confessorum*, MGH 1.2 (Hannover: Hahn, 1885), 317; the *Life of Julian and Basilissa* (BHL 4529), Robert K. Upchurch, *Aelfric's Lives of the Virgin Spouses* (Liverpool: Liverpool University Press, 2007), 114–171; and the *Life of Melanius of Troyes* (BHL 5895), Henri Moretus, "Catalogus codicum hagiographicorum latinorum Bibliothecae Scholae Medicinae in Universitate Montepessulanensi", *AB* 34–35 (1915–1916), 289–292. More research is needed to assess the narrative function of secrecy in these texts.

10 Alwis, *Celibate Marriages*, 89.

However, it has remained largely unasked through which specific narrative techniques this secrecy is created and how they play with and build on reader expectations in the development of the narrative plot.[11]

This paper aims to fill this gap, by exploring the narrative function of secrecy in the *Lives* of Malchus and Amator in relation to their narrative representation and the notion of reader reception. In the first two sections, I employ narratological tools and literary-historical concepts in order to elucidate how the *Lives* create secrecy through a sophisticated narrative plotting.[12] In addition, I explore the effects of this secrecy on the active engagement of the readers with the texts. Finally, I relate the question of secrecy to the more general communicative aims of the texts. It has often been argued that hagiographical discourse employs entertaining elements in order to support its educational function.[13] How, then, does secrecy in the descriptions of chaste marriages

11 Virginia Burrus, *The Sex Lives of Saints: An Erotics of Ancient Hagiography* (Philadelphia: University of Pennsylvania Press, 2004), 33–39 and Joëlle Soler, "La conversion chrétienne du récit de voyage antique dans les Vies de moines de Jérôme", *IJCT* 18.1 (2011), 1–18 address the function of secrecy for the dynamics of reading in Jerome's *Life of Malchus*, but do not focus on the literary construction of the motif. For a narratological reading of the Life, see Jiří Šubrt, "Hagiographic Romance: Novelistic Narrative Strategy in Jerome's *Lives* of Hermits", in Marília Futre Pinheiro, Gareth L. Schmeling, and Edmund P. Cueva (eds.), *The Ancient Novel and the Frontiers of Genre*. Ancient Narrative Supplementum 18 (Eelde: Barkhuis, 2014), 205–214.

12 This presumes that the *Lives* had an audience which understood this plotting. However, the question as to which audience was intended, is difficult to answer. The *Lives* of Malchus and Amator both provide indications for possible real audiences, respectively Jerome's female attendants and friend Evagrius of Antioch (Gray, *Vita Malchi*, 10–12) and Aunarius of Auxerre (which is implied by Stephen's dedication letter to Aunarius; see Duru, *Saint Aunaire*, 134–136). Nevertheless, given that the *Lives* were more circulated among a wider audience, I focus on what has been called the 'implied reader', which I understand in its Iserian meaning, designating no particular historical reader, but rather the actualisation of pre-structured meanings by the reader in the process of reading/listening. See Wolfgang Iser, *The Implied Reader: Patterns of Communication in Prose Fiction from Bunyan to Beckett* (Baltimore: John Hopkins University Press, 1983) [original publication: *Der implizite Leser. Kommunikationsformen des Romans von Bunyan bis Beckett* (München: Wilhelm Fink Verlag, 1972)].

13 See Gerlinde Huber-Rebenich, "Hagiographic Fiction as Entertainment", in Heinz Hofmann (ed.), *Latin Fiction: The Latin Novel in Context* (London: Routledge, 1999), 187–212 for a general discussion on entertainment in Christian narratives, with examples from the *Apocryphal Acts of the Apostles* and Latin hagiographical texts. For entertainment in the *Life of Malchus*, see Herbert Kech, *Hagiographie als christliche Unterhaltungsliteratur: Studien zum Phänomen des Erbaulichen anhand der Mönchsviten des hl. Hieronymus* (Göppingen: Kümmerle, 1977), 174–177; Christa Gray, "The Monk and the Ridiculous: Comedy in Jerome's Vita Malchi", *Studia Patristica* 69 (2013), 115–121, at 121, and Gray, *Vita Malchi*, 14.

accommodate these oft-attained effects of edification and reading pleasure in the *Lives* of Malchus and Amator?

2 Jerome's *Life of Malchus*: A Hermeneutic Quest

Although the *Lives* of Malchus and Amator both concentrate on the same question—is the couple united by a sexual or an asexual relationship?—they take different plot structures in order to give form to their contents. In the *Life of Malchus*, the plot is organised according to what Roland Barthes calls the 'hermeneutic code' in his *S/Z*: 'the various (formal) terms by which an enigma can be distinguished, suggested, formulated, held in suspense, and finally disclosed'.[14] Without discussing in detail Barthes' theory of hermeneutics in *S/Z*, we can observe that the couple's relationship is presented as a question in the beginning of the *Life*, while the remainder of the story raises the expectation of providing an answer. In fact, the question of the couple's union constitutes an important link between the frame story of the author-narrator Jerome and the embedded story of the narrator Malchus, as both ego-narrators play an important role in both revealing and withholding information relevant for answering the enigma.

In the prologue (*V. Malchi* 1–2), Jerome introduces the text and tells about his meeting with the monk Malchus, the main protagonist of the *Life*, in the early or mid 370s during his sojourn with Evagrius near Antioch.[15] According to Jerome, Malchus lives together with a woman in the Syrian village of Maronia: 'There was in that place a certain old man named Malchus, whom we can call "Rex" in Latin, a Syrian by birth and language, like a true native of the same place. There was also an old woman to be seen in his house (*in contubernio*), very withered and already close to death'.[16] The prologue is important for the hermeneutic code, as it presents the leading question of the work. Firstly, Jerome *thematises* the subject of his quest:[17] the two spouses, who are

14 Roland Barthes, *S/Z. Translated by Richard Miller. Preface by Richard Howard* (Malden, MA/Oxford: Blackwell, 2002), 19; for further discussion of the hermeneutic code and its various elements, see 75–76 and 209–210 in the same work [original French publication: *S/Z* (Paris: Seuil, 1970)].

15 For the dramatic date of the frame story, see Gray, *Vita Malchi*, 7.

16 *V. Malchi* 2.2: *erat illic senex quidam nomine Malchus, quem nos Latine 'Regem' possumus dicere, Syrus natione et lingua, ut re vera eiusdem loci indigens. anus quoque in eius contubernio valde decrepita et iam morti proxima visebatur*. Translation adapted.

17 See Barthes, *S/Z*, 209–210 for a discussion of the 'question' as one of the elements of the hermeneutic code.

of 'such religious devotion and wore out the threshold of the church to such an extent that you would have believed them to be Zechariah and Elizabeth from the Gospel, except that John was not in their midst'.[18] As Gray notes, this sentence is modelled on Luke 1:6–7, which describes the sterility of Zechariah's wife Elisabeth.[19] The Biblical paradigm conveys some important information about Malchus and his wife, namely that they are childless. This raises the curiosity of Jerome and, by extension, the readers: why do the spouses live without a child and what kind of relationship do they have? This enigma is *formulated* at the end of the prologue, which culminates in the depiction of the author-narrator eagerly asking the neighbours about the couple's relationship, and finally Malchus himself:[20]

> When I enquired with curiosity about them among their neighbours and asked what their relationship was—one of marriage, kinship, or spiritual—all replied with one voice that they were holy and pleasing to God, and they added some remarkable details. When I, spurred by desire as a result, approached the man and asked him with more curiosity about the truth of the matter, I heard the following story from him.[21]

Jerome formulates the text's leading question, namely how the relationship of Malchus and his wife can be described. Is it one between spouses, siblings, or spiritual companions? This raises the readers' curiosity as to how the question will be answered. The readers' curiosity is prefigured by Jerome's repeated references to his own curiosity. These, as well as his use of the first-person voice, enable the readers to connect to the narrator's desire to know.[22] Sub-

18 *V. Malchi* 2.2: *tam studiosi ambo religionis et sic ecclesiae limen terentes ut Zachariam et Elisabeth de Evangelio crederes, nisi quod Ioannes in medio non erat.*

19 Gray, *Vita Malchi*, 127.

20 See Barthes, *S/Z*, 209–210 for the 'formulation of the question' as part of the hermeneutic code.

21 *V. Malchi* 2.3: *de his cum curiose ab accolis quaererem quaenam esset eorum copula, matrimonii, sanguinis, an spiritus, omnes voce consona sanctos et Deo placitos et mira nescio quae respondebant. qua cupiditate illectus adorsus sum hominem et curiosius sciscitans rerum fidem haec ab eo accepi.*

22 Proposing a narrator who describes in the first-person his own curiosity, the *Life* inscribes itself in a larger literary tradition of ancient texts, such as Apuleius' *Metamorphoses* and Augustine's *Confessions*, in which curiosity is an important narrative drive; see Nancy J. Shumate, "The Augustinian Pursuit of False Values as a Conversion Motif in Apuleius' 'Metamorphoses'", *Phoenix* 42 (1988), 35–60; Alexander Kirichenko, "Satire, Propaganda, and the Pleasure of Reading: Apuleius' Stories of Curiosity in Context", *HSPh* 104 (2008), 339–371.

sequently, Jerome gives, in Barthes' terminology, the 'promise of an answer', announcing that the truth of the matter will be disclosed by Malchus himself in the following narrative (which describes Malchus' early adulthood to incipient old age and should be located in the AD 340s or early AD 350s).[23] The readers thus expect that Malchus' inserted tale, which immediately follows on the prologue, has an explanatory function, giving an answer to Jerome's leading question.[24]

However, the ensuing inserted narrative in fact has what Gérard Genette calls an 'obstructive' effect.[25] The narrator Malchus circumvents the question in the first part of his narration by not directly providing an answer and thus impedes the progressing of the frame story. Malchus first starts a detour in which he lingers on the events happening before his forced marriage: his escape from his parental home in order to evade his parents' wish to marry, his entrance into and subsequent escape from his monastic community in the Syrian desert, his kidnapping by Saracens during his travel back home, his life as a captive shepherd in the seclusion of the inner desert, and his forced marriage with a fellow slave (*V. Malchi* 3–6.6).[26] Moreover, Malchus employs the device of *paralipsis*, sidestepping certain information which is relevant for answering Jerome's question.[27] Although Malchus mentions the woman who will be his future wife, she is not yet introduced as such; only in retrospect the reader will realise that the 'other captive, a little woman' who 'came by lot into the servitude of the same master' eventually becomes Malchus' wife.[28] Even when Malchus finally comes to speak about his marriage, he provides nothing more

23 See Gray, *Vita Malchi*, 8 for the dramatic date of the inserted tale, and Barthes, *S/Z*, 209–210 for the theme of the 'promise of an answer'.

24 As Genette explains, explanation (making a causal relationship) is but one function of inserted tales, the others being thematic (establishing a relation of contrast or analogy with the frame story), and purely narrational (creating the effect of distraction or obstruction, as the inserted tale impedes the unfolding of the frame story). See Genette, *Narrative Discourse*, 232–234.

25 This is one of the effects which Genette allots to inserted tales; see n. 24. Barthes, *S/Z*, 209–210 discusses the 'circumvention of the answer' as part of the hermeneutic code.

26 For the detour as an anti-closural device in narrative, see Peter Brooks, *Reading for the Plot: Design and Intention in Narrative* (Cambridge, MA: Harvard University Press, 1992), 103–112 [original publication: Oxford: Oxford University Press, 1984], as well as the article of Zachary Yuzwa in this volume.

27 *Paralipsis* is defined by Genette as a 'lateral' *ellipsis*, as it 'does not skip over a moment of time, as in an *ellipsis*, but it sidesteps a given element', which is mentioned earlier or later in the story; Genette, *Narrative Discourse*, 52.

28 *V. Malchi* 4.3: *cum altera muliercula in unius eri servitutem sortitus venio.*

than what Barthes calls a 'partial answer':[29] he tells how he is forced to marry the woman with whom he was taken captive, as a reward from the Saracen master for his good service, but he does not yet elucidate the precise nature of his marital union, leaving open Jerome's question whether it is a carnal or a spiritual one (*V. Malchi* 6.1–2). In fact, he only comes back to the question at the end of the marriage episode (*V. Malchi* 6.8), as I will explain later. The detour heightens the readers' curiosity: how will Jerome's question, which motivated the inclusion of Malchus' embedded tale, eventually be answered?

The first half of Malchus' tale culminates in the proposal of Malchus' wife, with which she convinces him during the wedding night to enter into a sexless union in order to preserve their chastity. This passage is crucial for the development of the hermeneutic code, as it provides Jerome (as the addressee of the embedded tale) and through him the readers with the first and most complete answer to the question of the nature of Malchus' coupling. As Malchus' wife indicates, the couple's relationship partakes in all three aspects defined by Jerome:

> Therefore take me as your partner in chastity (*coniugem pudicitiae*), and love the bond of the soul more than that of the body (*magis animae copulam amato quam corporis*). Let the masters think you my husband (*maritum*), Christ will know that you are my brother (*fratrem*). We shall easily convince (*facile persuadebimus*) them of our marriage when they see this mutual love of ours.[30]

In a juridical sense, the spouses are united by the marital bond between *maritus* and wife; in a spiritual sense, they are one another's brother (*fratrem*) and sister, connected by a spiritual bond (*animae copulam*). The woman's reference to her husband as brother implies a subtle reinterpretation of the familial relationships to which Jerome referred in the prologue: rather than a blood tie, it symbolises the spiritual bond between the spouses as fellow believers.[31]

Giving an answer to Jerome's question, the woman provides for the readers a momentary relief from the tension created earlier in the narrative. Moreover,

29 See Barthes, *S/Z*, 210 for the partial answer as an element of the hermeneutic code.

30 *V. Malchi* 6.7: *habeto me ergo coniugem pudicitae et magis animae copulam amato quam corporis. sperent domini maritum, Christus noverit fratrem. facile persuadebimus nuptias cum nos viderint sic amare.*

31 This allegorical siblingship is reminiscent of the New Testament literature, the Pauline letters in particular; see Reidar Aasgaard, *My Beloved Brothers and Sisters: Christian Siblingship in Paul* (London: T&T Clark International, 2004).

asserting that the chaste union is known to God but kept secret from the masters, she also creates dramatic irony, as the readers are given the sense that they know more about the real nature of the couple's relationship than some of the story's characters. They may even conclude from the woman's words that they are equal to God in the knowledge of the truth, which is an effective way of inviting the readers to support the couple's secret arrangement. Nevertheless, the woman's proposal also again arouses the readers' curiosity. For instance, if the masters can be deceived in thinking that the couple lives together in a natural union, could this also work the other way around, meaning that the readers are invited to consider the spouses as chaste while they are not in reality? Significantly, strategies are employed to underline the sincerity of the couple's intentions against such objections. Claiming that Christ knows the truth about the couple's chaste marriage, the woman gives it an aura of truthfulness. Moreover, in the aftermath of the wedding episode, Malchus adds information which gives credence to the woman's statement: he never looked upon her naked body or touched her flesh (*V. Malchi* 6.8).

The information provided by the woman remains unsupported by Malchus in the second half of his narrative (*V. Malchi* 7–10). Mirroring the first half of the narrative, the narrator includes another detour, in which he refrains from giving further details concerning his marriage. Observing the busy ants, Malchus reflects on his former monastic life and recalls his earlier narrative about how he once entered and escaped from the monastery (*V. Malchi* 7). The subsequent narrative describing the couple's escape from the desert reflects Malchus' first detour in its spatial arrangement (the crossing of the river to leave the inner desert, the travel through the desert, and the arrival in Chalcis, *V. Malchi* 8–10) as well as its narrative detail (as in the wedding episode, the spouses hide in a cave, *V. Malchi* 9). Through these strategies of repetition, the second detour forms a doublet with Malchus' first one at the beginning of the narrative. However, it does not provide further information concerning Jerome's initial question, hence being a 'suspended answer' within the hermeneutic plot.[32]

Finally, Malchus' inserted tale results in what Barthes calls an 'equivocation' or a 'double understanding', in which the narrator undermines the information earlier provided by his wife:[33]

32 Barthes, *S/Z*, 209–210.

33 Barthes, *S/Z*, 145.

> [U]pon reaching this region I returned myself to the monks; the woman (*hanc*) I handed over to the virgins, loving her as a sister but not entrusting myself to her as a sister (*diligens eam ut sororem, non tamen ei me credens ut sorori*).[34]

Claiming that the spouses each enter a monastic community, Malchus seems most likely to indicate that he and his wife start to live separately, which challenges the information provided by his wife about their marital union. In addition, Malchus' claim that he does not entrust himself to his wife as a sister undermines the wife's earlier statement about the couple's bond as spiritual siblings. Yet, Malchus immediately destabilises his own undermining statements, making it thus a prime example of an 'equivocation'. First of all, saying that he still loves his wife as a sister, Malchus suggests that he shares with her the intimate bond between siblings—a suggestion which he simultaneously defies. Moreover, he undermines his claim about the couple's separation by using the pronoun *hanc* in order to refer to his wife. Since there is no direct antecedent, the deictic force of the pronoun suggests that the woman is present at the moment of narration, which implies that Malchus points to his wife at the precise moment when he tells about their separation in the past.[35] The pronoun thus signals the narrative discrepancy between the frame story and the inserted tale that scholars have often noted: Malchus' claim that he separated from his wife on their arrival in Chalcis contradicts Jerome's statement in the prologue that he found the couple living together 'in a house' (*in contubernio*) in Maronia (*V. Malchi* 2.2).[36] Thus, while Barthes' hermeneutic code ideally ends with the 'disclosure' of the enigma, Malchus fails to provide such a close.[37] This creates surprise for the readers, as no full answer is provided to Jerome's initial question about the couple's relationship, notwithstanding the promise of the author-narrator in the prologue that the embedded tale would explain the question. In addition, the absence of full disclosure arouses curiosity. Is the couple still together, or not? Moreover, if they are together, how were they then united after their separation in Chalcis?

In the epilogue of the work (*V. Malchi* 11), the author-narrator Jerome adds no further information which helps to elucidate his own question in the prologue.

34 *V. Malchi* 10.3: *ad haec delatus loca me monachis reddo; hanc trado virginibus, diligens eam ut sororem, non tamen ei me credens ut sorori.*

35 As pointed out by Alison Orlebeke, "Jerome, *Vita Malchi*: Introduction, Text, Translation, and Commentary by Christa Gray (review)", *JLA* 9, 2 (2016), 549–552, at 552.

36 See Gray, *Vita Malchi*, 125–126.

37 See Barthes, *S/Z*, 209–210.

Jerome does not include information about the couple's whereabouts between their separation in Chalcis and their life-together in Maronia—information which he *could* have known, either from hearsay, or because Malchus had told it to him personally (and Jerome, for one reason or another, did not let Malchus tell it himself in his frame story). Through this *ellipsis*, Jerome keeps intact the narrative discrepancy between his prologue and Malchus' inserted tale. In addition, Jerome gives a highly elliptic summary—'You for your part tell the story to future generations, so that they may know that amid swords, deserts, and wild beasts chastity is never taken captive, and that a man who is devoted to Christ may die but cannot be defeated'.[38] The summary captures most of the story, but omits what is perhaps its most important topic: the couple's chaste marriage. There is no single reference to the marriage or the woman (who remains anonymous anyway in the *Life*); nor does Jerome return to his question about the relationship between Malchus and his wife, which had been the motivation for the insertion of Malchus' tale. Just like Malchus, Jerome thus fails to contribute to a full disclosure of the enigma. The lack of a full disclosure creates the experience of surprise for the readers expecting the narrative to provide a full answer to Jerome's question. Moreover, it spurs the readers' imagination on to fill in the gap—a task which has been willingly taken up by scholars, who have put forward various solutions in order to remove the narrative discrepancy between the stories of Jerome and Malchus.[39]

Jerome's *Life of Malchus* indicates that the secrecy surrounding the couple's chaste marriage is not just a detail in the private life of the spouses, but also a concept which is played out on the level of the narrative plot, in which it is important for shaping the readers' expectations. On the one hand, the hermeneutic shape of the narrative raises the readers' curiosity, which is satisfied by the woman, as she discloses information relevant for the answering of the enigma. In this case, the readers are given the idea to penetrate the secret of the couple's chastity, which is an effective way of involving them in the narrative. On the other hand, the readers ultimately find themselves in a less informed position, since most of the information given by Malchus and Jerome is insufficient or ambiguous, and a full disclosure is missing in the end. This creates surprise, as the readers discover that full disclosure is lacking, despite Jerome's promise of an answer. Creating curiosity through the promise of disclosure, and surprise through the absence of a full revelation, the hermeneutic

38 *V. Malchi* 11: *vos narrate posteris, ut sciant inter gladios, inter deserta et bestias pudicitiam numquam esse captivam, et hominem Christo deditum posse mori, non posse superari.*

39 For the various solutions suggested for this discrepancy, see Gray, *Vita Malchi*, 125–126.

shape of the narrative actively involves the readers in the narrative by letting them experience the secret of the chaste marriage. However, as will be demonstrated in the next section, the effect can be achieved in different ways as well.

3 Stephen the African's *Life of Amator*: Suspense and Surprise

While the *Life of Malchus* employs the hermeneutic code in order to raise the readers' curiosity in various first-person narratives, the *Life of Amator* is told by an omniscient narrator, who arouses suspense by providing the readers with information about the described events (which should be located in the second half of the fourth century and the early fifth century) and the future course of the plot, which remains hidden for most of the story characters.[40] As the narrator tells us, Amator is secretly devoted to God, a fact which remains hidden to his parents, though not to bishop Valerian, who instructs him in the Holy Scriptures. Amator's Christian parents force their son to marry a Christian girl, Martha. Amator wants to keep his chastity, and the bishop comes to his aid during the wedding: he reads the Levitical ordination rite instead of the marital blessing, thus ordaining the couple as deacons ('Levites').[41] During the wedding night, the newly-weds take their unusual blessing as an encouragement to live in a chaste union. Subsequently, they both enter into a monastic community after the honeymoon, which they keep secret for the neighbours around them. The couple's secret chaste marriage becomes problematic, however, after Amator's ordination as bishop of Auxerre (which he was from AD 388 until AD 418).[42] The archdeacon Litinus is possessed by a bad spirit, who stirs him to see if the bishop is really chaste, in accordance with the request of celibacy. Litinus secretly occupies Amator's bedroom together with a throng of people, in order to catch the bishop red-handed. However, in a sudden turn of the narrative, Christ appears in the form of a radiant lamb, not in order to illuminate the couple, but rather the hidden intruders. Litinus is struck blind while the others lose their minds; they are only restored by Amator's prayers. Having survived this

40 Amator is bishop from AD 388 until AD 418; see Johannes Staub, "Amator von Auxerre", in Bruno Steimer and Thomas Wetzstein (eds.), *Lexikon der Heiligen und der Heiligenverehrung* (Freiburg in Breisgau: Herder, 2003), 79–80. The narrator remains further unidentified, but the reader is likely to conflate him with the person of Stephen, the author of the text.

41 Van Egmond, *Conversing*, 174–175, with 169–182 for further discussion of the wedding episode in *the Life of Amator*. See also Isabelle Réal, *Vies de saints, vie de famille. Représentation et système de la parenté dans le Royaume mérovingien (481–751) d'après les sources hagiographiques* (Turnhout: Brepols, 2001), 170–177.

42 See n. 40.

test of chastity, the bishop becomes an important miracle worker and powerful figure in the political and monastic scene of Gaul. Two narrative techniques are particularly important for stimulating the readers' active participation by raising suspense about the narrated events, namely focalisation and *prolepsis*. In what follows, I focus on two passages which illuminate these techniques. The first relates the events surrounding the marriage ceremony and the wedding night, which take place in the nuptial bedroom (*LA* 3–7); the second narrates the secret invasion of the couple's bedroom after Amator's ordination (*V. Amat.* 16–17).

The first bedroom episode is characterised by what Genette calls 'zero focalisation': the omniscient narrator tells more than most of the characters know, so that the reader is better informed than the figures in the story.[43] For instance, the narrator says that Valerian's teaching of Amator in the Scriptures 'is done secretly (*clam*), unknown to the parents',[44] while the couple's consecration as Levites remains largely unnoticed by the attendants of their wedding: 'none of the bystanders (*nullus astantium*) could understand the actions which were performed by the bishop, except for the ones who received the blessings'.[45] When the couple goes to the newly appointed bishop Eladius in order to be officially ordained as deacons, the bishop indicates that he is unaware of the saints' earlier ordination as Levites. He says to the couple that 'it would have been quite sufficient (*satis fuit*)' if they had been consecrated in the Levirate order immediately at their wedding and with the 'right formulas (*congruis precibus*)'.[46] The reader, of course, knows already that the couple had been ordained as Levites and thus appointed to a life in chastity. Consequently, the result of these instances of zero focalisation is that the reader is better informed about the represented events than most of the characters in the story. Beyond the creation of dramatic irony—the pleasure of knowing more than

43 Genette, *Narrative Discourse*, 188–189. Genette follows the Todorovian 'information-based' model of focalisation, in which focalisation is defined in terms of knowledge and the distribution of information among the narrator and characters; the other predominant model is based on the metaphors of perspective and point-of-view. For more discussion of these models, see Burkhard Niederhoff, "Focalization", § 2–6; Website *The Living Handbook of Narratology* (2011) http://www.lhn.uni-hamburg.de/article/focalization, updated 24 September 2013, accessed on 15 November 2019.

44 *V. Amat.* 2, p. 137: *Hœc autem omnia clam parentibus agebantur.*

45 *V. Amat.* 4, p. 139: *Sed nullus astantium, quae ab episcopo gesta fuerant, nisi tantum hi qui benedictionibus fruebantur, cognoscere potuerunt.*

46 *V. Amat.* 7, p. 141: *Nam vere, filii, satis fuit in vestra conjunctione prostratus episopus moeroribus, quando pro conjunctionis vestrae congruis precibus, ordinationis ac sanctificationis levitarum preces effudit.*

other characters—this form of focalisation supports the readers' involvement in the story: they are allowed to enter the story, as it were, and to know about the couple's secret life. In an unusual narratorial comment accompanying his description of the couple's vow of chastity on the wedding night, the narrator explicitly reminds the readers of this privileged position as a *témoin bien informé* ('well-informed witness'), as Hippolyte Delehaye calls it: 'you would see (*aspiceres*) not lovers of marriage (*coniugii amatores*), but of the divine Scriptures'.[47] Through the apostrophe, the reader is explicitly invited to see, as it were, the chaste characters in the story world.[48] Moreover, the pun on the hero's name (*coniugii amatores*) not only underlines the couple's chastity, but also mounts the dramatic irony, as only the readers understand its ambiguity: while the characters may think that the spouses live up to the hero's name as real lovers of the marriage, the readers know that they do not in reality. At the same time, the unequal distribution of knowledge among the readers and the characters also raises suspense: will the other characters be implicated in the knowledge about the couple's chaste union? Will they ever find out the truth?

Besides the use of focalisation, suspense is created in the first bedroom episode through the tool of anticipation, or *prolepsis*: the reference to future events before their time.[49] Specifically the Levitical consecration of the couple has proleptic force, as it foreshadows the future sexual continence and celibacy of the couple. Although liturgical texts from the time of the writing of the *Life of Amator* (between AD 561–603)[50] have not been transmitted, later Merovingian liturgies may elucidate with what kind of Levitical blessing the couple was ordained by bishop Valerian, as they preserve remnants of older liturgical traditions. Significantly, these more recent liturgies indicate a close connection between chastity and the deaconate. Particularly interesting are the ordination rites for female deaconesses, which characterise the deaconate as a form

47 *V. Amat.* 4, p. 139: *ut sacrarum scripturarum, non conjugii amatores aspiceres*. See Delehaye 1966: 182–183. See also the contributions of Van Pelt and Alwis in this volume, on the motif of the well-informed witness.

48 While in ancient rhetorical theory, apostrophe usually denotes the narrator's 'turning away' from the normal audience to another one, I use the term in the way it is also used in modern literary theory, as a reference to 'any solemn address'. See Irene J.F. De Jong, "Metalepsis in Ancient Greek Literature", in Jonas Grethlein and Antonios Rengakos (eds.), *Narratology and Interpretation: The Content of Narrative Form in Ancient Literature*, Trends in Classics 4 (Berlin: De Gruyter, 2009), 87–116, at 93 n. 16.

49 See Shlomith Rimmon-Kenan, *Narrative Fiction: Contemporary Poetics* (London: Routledge, 1999) 46–51 [original publication: London: Methuen, 1983] for anticipation as a function of Genette's category of order.

50 See n. 2 for the dating of the *Life of Amator*.

of spiritual marriage between the virgin and Christ.[51] For instance, the ordination blessing of deaconesses in the eight-century *Pontifical of Egbert of York* considers the female deaconate as a means of entering upon a spiritual marriage: 'The lamps of the sinners have been filled with the oil of virtue to such a degree that you can enter the bedroom of your heavenly spouse with them.'[52] Similarly, the tenth-century *Romano-Germanic Pontifical* states that the deaconess, when she is consecrated and takes the veil, is 'married to [the Lord]'.[53] As a result, the reader who had knowledge of the ordination rites of deacons could have seen the reference to the Levitical blessing in the *Life of Amator* as foreshadowing the couple's future sexual abstinence and spiritual union with Christ. To be sure, the expectations raised by the Levitical blessing are soon fulfilled: during the wedding night, the spouses interpret their curious blessing as a motivation to stay chaste for the rest of their lives.[54] The reader can conclude from their nocturnal conversation that the couple's chaste union, which was foreshadowed by the Levitical blessing, has become a reality.

The story finds a provisional climax in *V. Amat.* 16–17, which describes the invasion of the bishop's bedroom by Litinus and his followers. Zero focalisation is again important in the episode; one could even say that the episode is caused by the ignorance of Amator's fellow believers. This ignorance is most clearly expressed by Litinus, who presents himself as unaware of the couple's vow of chastity:

---

51 These rites were mostly used for the ordination of women married to clergy, although non-married women could be ordained too. For discussions of women performing clerical ministries, see Brian Brennan, "'Episcopae': Bishops' Wives Viewed in Sixth-Century Gaul", *ChHist* 54, 3 (1985), 311–323 and Gary Macy, *The Hidden History of Women's Ordination: Female Clergy in the Medieval West* (Oxford: Oxford University Press, 2008), 49–88. A discussion of the ordination rites of deaconesses is provided by Macy, *Hidden History*, 37–40 and 70–73.

52 *Quatenus virtutum oleo ita peccatorum lampades possint repleri, ut cum eis coelestis sponsi thalamum valeatis ingredi.* Edition: William Greenwell, "The Pontifical of Egbert, Archbishop of York, A.D. 732–766", *Surtees Society* 27 (1853), 94 (reprint in Macy, *Hidden History*, 133–134, 133); the translation is my own.

53 Edition: Cyrille Vogel and Reinhard Elze, *Le Pontifical Romano-Germanique du Dixième Siècle*. Studi e testi 226–228, 3 vols. (Vatican City: Biblioteca Apostolica, 1963), 10 (reprint in Macy, *Hidden History*, 134–137, 135); translation my own.

54 See *V. Amat.* 4, p. 139: Amator asks Martha if she understood the prayers of the bishop, which is answered positively by the virgin: 'I understood them, my beloved, and I am overwhelmed by a sense of great fear.' Amator then takes the blessing as the reason to agree upon a chaste marriage, to which the virgin consents: 'I beseech you therefore, if it is your will, to agree with my idea to keep intact this gift, which has been asked from and given by the mercy of God.'

> Priests are allowed to be united with virgins in their religious service, but when they have reached the highest order, they are no longer allowed to have spouses. However, our bishop does not only share his table [with his wife], but also his bed, which is not allowed.[55]

This creates dramatic irony, but also makes the readers aware of their informed position: they know more about the couple's chaste life than the other characters in the story. In addition, it raises suspense about the future development of the plot: how will Litinus and his throng be involved in the secret?

The readers' expectations are further raised by the adaptation of a typical stock scene which has been called the 'bedroom showdown', or the invasion of the bedroom by the cuckolded spouse and other intruders who want to catch the adulterous couple red-handed.[56] The stock scene typically describes the exposure of adulterers: Homer's description of the discovery of Aphrodite and Ares by Hephaistos is an early example (*Od.* 8.266–366), while the case of the murder of Eratosthenes in Lysias' *First Oration* is perhaps the most famous one. However, the *Life of Amator* adapts the motif in some important respects. Importantly, the focal object of the bedroom showdown is not the adulterous couple. Instead, Litinus and his throng hide in Amator's bedroom in order to see if the bishop shares the bed *with his legitimate wife*. Moreover, the stock figure of the 'third man' in the bedroom showdown—the adulterous lover who forms a love triangle with the wife and the cuckold—becomes the intruder in the *Life of Amator*.[57] These adaptations indicate the aim is not to reveal a possible case

55 *V. Amat.* 16, p. 146: *Sacerdotibus sancitum est, ut in clericatu virginibus socientur; postquam vero adepti fuerunt honoris praemium, non eis licet ulterius uxoribus jungi: hic autem noster episcopus, non solum particeps mensae, verum etiam lecti, quod nefas est, invenitur.* Litinus' words reflect contemporary concerns about the ideal of clerical celibacy in the Church in the West. From the fifth century onwards, chaste priesthood had become the main condition; hence, 'if anything was to be secret, it would be conjugal relations after ordination'; Elliott, *Spiritual Marriage*, 86. See also Van Egmond, *Conversing*, 173–174. See Robert Wiśniewski in this volume for the literary construction of clerical saints in hagiography from late antique Gaul.

56 See Saundra Schwartz, "From Bedroom to Courtroom: The Adultery Type-Scene and the *Acts of Andrew*", in Todd Penner and Caroline Vander Stichele (eds.), *Mapping Gender in Ancient Religious Discourses* (Leiden: Brill, 2007), 267–312 for a detailed discussion of the motif in various ancient literary traditions, for instance, the *Odyssey*, Greek tragedies, and specifically the Greek novels and the *Apocryphal Acts of the Apostles*.

57 In this respect, the Life diverts from other Christian narratives featuring bedroom showdowns, such as the *Apocryphal Acts of the Apostles*, in which the invasion of the bedroom by the Apostle (the 'third man') is a common motif; see Schwartz, "From Bedroom to Courtroom", 291–292 and Cooper, *Virgin and Bride*, 51–56, for discussions of examples

of adultery, but the *chastity* of the couple, ironically emphasising the 'properness' of their marital relationship. The irony is at the expense of the intruders, Litinus and his crowd, who appear as the ridiculous characters in a comical farce.

Lest the readers develop wrong expectations about the couple's chastity, the narrator foreshadows the outcome of the bedroom showdown in a proleptic comment:

> Christ ... who wanted to show to all people the chastity of his servants which is known to him but hidden for the people, who were secretly waiting for the right moment and adhering to the bedroom's walls ...[58]

Proclaiming that God himself will 'show' the chastity of the spouses 'to all people', the narrator indicates to the readers that, in contrast with the script of the bedroom showdown, the couple will not be caught in the act, and hence the expectation of disclosure will remain unfulfilled. This triggers suspense, raising the question as to how Litinus and his crowd will be informed about the couple's true relationship. The suspense is prefigured by the intruders, who are said to be 'waiting' to see what happens in the bedroom.

However, the reader will realise in retrospect that the passage just quoted is only partly proleptic. While the reader could interpret the narrator's remark that God wanted to show the couple's chastity as an implicit approval of their purity, the remainder of the episode describes a different outcome:

> ... look, then (*ecce tunc*) [Christ] occurred amid his servants in the appearance of a lamb, a present of God, in order to destroy the tricks of the proud people; miraculously shining in his splendour (*in tantum sui fulgoris coruscans miraculo*), so that even those who were hidden were bathed in the stream of the unknown light, as befits unworthy people.[59]

The ubiquitous reference to the visual indicates the climax of the bedroom showdown: the public display. Yet, contrary to what the readers possibly ex-

in the *Acts of Andrew*, the *Acts of Peter*, the *Acts of Thomas*, and the *Acts of Paul and Thecla*.

58 *V. Amat.* 17, p. 147: *Sed Christus, ... ut servorum suorum sibi quidem cognitam, populis vero latentem castitatem omnibus demonstraret, illis clam insidiantibus et lectuli lateribus adhaerentibus ...*

59 *V. Amat.* 17, p. 147: *ecce tunc, in specie agni, donum divinitatis, ad evacuandam machinationem superborum, in medio famulorum suorum irrepsit; in tantum sui fulgoris coruscans miraculo, ut etiam hi qui insidiabantur, licet indigni, luminis insoliti splendorem haurirent.*

pected on the basis of the narrator's earlier *prolepsis*, the bedroom showdown does not end with the display of the couple's chastity, but rather of the intruders hidden in the bedroom. It is as if the intruders become the adulterers, because they have betrayed their fidelity to their bishop. Nevertheless, Christ does not disclose information about the couple's chastity, and the narrator does not even refer to the couple's chastity anymore. The narrative thus ends with the absence of full disclosure, which creates surprise for the readers who expected a full disclosure of the chastity of the couple. This is prefigured by the use of *ecce*, as well as by the reference to Christ's appearance as a 'miracle' (*miraculo*), which both encompass the surprise experienced by the witnesses of the unexpected event.[60] While in the previous sections the readers were provided with more information than most of the story characters, they now find themselves on the same level as the ignorant intruders, discovering that the secret of the couple's chastity is not fully exposed to them.

Evidently, in the *Life of Amator*, the secret of the couple's chaste union is first played out through a difference in knowledge. In the first part of the narrative, the readers know about the couple's chastity and future events through zero focalisation and *prolepsis*, while most of the story characters are ignorant. The readers are thus given the sense of being implicated in the secret of the couple's chastity, which is an effective strategy of immersion. It also creates suspense, raising the question as to whether and how the others will be included in the secret. Later in the story, however, the readers discover that their expectations about the revelation of the couple's chaste union are not satisfied, because full disclosure is lacking. Just as the *Life of Malchus*, the *Life of Amator* thus ends with the surprising discovery that the secret of the couple's chaste union remains a secret.

4 Concluding Remarks: Secrecy, Edification, and Entertainment

In the *Lives* of Malchus and Amator, the secrecy surrounding the chaste marriages has an important narrative function, not only defining their narrative plot, but also contributing to the readers' active engagement with the texts. The *Life of Malchus* appeals to the readers' desire to know, while the *Life of Amator* lets the readers initially share in the omniscience of the narrator. Finally, both

60 See Caroline Kroon, *Discourse Particles in Latin: A Study of nam, enim, autem, vero and at* (Amsterdam: Gieben, 1995), 330 n. 76 for *ecce* as a particle which characteristically encompasses the sense of surprise of the speaker and audience at the occurrence of unexpected events.

Lives end in surprise, as they do not provide full insight into the narrated events. It follows that both texts play out the notion of secrecy in their own unique ways. This opens room for further exploration of other texts about chaste couples in which secrecy is important.[61]

Finally, it is worthwhile to consider the importance of secrecy for the more general goals of hagiography. As our readings of the *Lives* of Malchus and Amator indicate, the literary descriptions of secret chaste marriages move the readers by arousing their curiosity and suspense: the two 'master strategies' as they have been called, which, through the reconfiguration of expectations about past and future events respectively, stimulate the readers' active involvement in the text.[62] One could say that the effect of secrecy in the *Lives* is the readers' immersion: the aesthetic pleasure of imaginatively engaging with the represented world.[63] On the one hand, the immersion is 'temporal', since the reader is taken along in a represented world located in the past (in the *Life of Malchus*) or one unfolding in the present (in the *Life of Amator*). What is more, thematising the readers' desire to know the secret, the immersion is 'epistemic': the reader is invited to enter the world of the spouses, as it were, and to have the pleasurable feeling of discovering the secret of their chaste union.[64] The effect is most clearly played out in the *Life of Malchus*, by its employment of the hermeneutic code; nevertheless, it is present in the *Life of Amator* as well, as the text gives the readers the pleasurable experience of knowing more about the couple's secret chaste union than most of the story characters. In both *Lives*, secrecy thus has a mystagogical function, inviting the readers to enter into the

61 See n. 9 for examples.

62 Meir Sternberg, "Telling in Time (II): Chronology, Teleology, Narrativity", *PT* 13.3 (1992), 463–541.

63 For the connection between immersion and reading pleasure, see Werner Wolf, "Illusion (Aesthetic)", §1; Website *The Living Handbook of Narratology* (2011) http://www.lhn.uni-hamburg.de/article/illusion-aesthetic, updated 17 January 2014, accessed on 15 November 2019.

64 The language of mystery is common in late antique Christian discourse, as a way of initiating believers in the paradoxes and inexpressible aspects of the Christian doctrine; see Averil Cameron, *Christianity and the Rhetoric of Empire: The Development of Christian Discourse* (Berkeley: University of California Press, 1991), 47–48, 158–159, and 214–219, and Peter Turner, *Truthfulness, Realism, Historicity: A Study in Late Antique Spiritual Literature* (Farnham/Burlington, VT: Ashgate, 2012), 68–69. This may be informed by ancient rhetorical theory, in which mystery language is used for describing the initiation in *paideia* and the art of rhetoric; see C. Andrew Ballard, "The Mysteries of Paideia: "Mystery" and Education in Plato's Symposium, 4QInstruction, and 1 Corinthians", in Karina M. Hogan, Matthew Goff, and Emma Wasserman (eds.), *Pedagogy in Ancient Judaism and Early Christianity* (Atlanta: SBL Press, 2017), 243–282, at 244–252, and Huber-Rebenich, "Hagiographic Fiction", 188.

mystery.[65] This ties in with the often-encountered claim that hagiographical discourse employs entertaining strategies to achieve its edifying goal.

However, things are different for the third master strategy which we have detected: the surprise which is created through the unexpected absence of full disclosure in the *Lives*.[66] How can this be connected to the *Lives*' aim of education? In modern theory, surprise is often connected to the notion of estrangement, as the unforeseen frustration of expectations is believed to have a defamiliarising effect, deranging the readers' views on literature and life.[67] At first sight, this effect of estrangement does not seem to be in line with the dynamics of immersion in hagiography we just described. However, there may be some mileage in considering the idea that the lack of complete immersion is what is searched for in the *Lives* of Malchus and Amator, constituting a crucial element in their educational program. With respect to the *Life of Malchus*, it has been noted that the narrative discrepancy between the two narrative levels has an important informative function, reflecting the undefinable aspect of chaste marriage as 'a secret which remains fundamentally inexplicable, a mystery'.[68] Such a reading could pertain to the *Lives* of Malchus and Amator in general, which, through the use of ambiguities, the sidestepping and the withholding of information, as well as the absence of full disclosure, let the reader experience the ambiguous nature of the phenomenon of chaste marriage, being a bond between spouses which is legal and publicly acknowledged on the one hand,[69] but which remains a secret on the other, because it is based on the secret and invisible abstinence from sexuality. If this reading holds, the surprising absence of full disclosure can be considered as having an educational function, providing the readers with the lesson that a chaste union cannot fully be demonstrated and hence evades full understanding.

What is more, it teaches the readers to take a humble reading posture. Scholars have argued that hagiographers conceived of their task as an ascetic prac-

65 For temporal and epistemic immersion, see Marie-Laure Ryan, "From Narrative Games to Playable Stories: Toward a Poetics of Interactive Narrative", *Storyworlds: A Journal of Narrative Studies* 1 (2009), 43–59, at 53–57.

66 Surprise is created through frustrated expectations about the plot; see Sternberg, "Telling in Time (II)".

67 The connection between surprise and estrangement is a central tenet in Russian Formalism and various other aesthetic theories, although it has been criticised; see Meir Sternberg, "Telling in Time (III): Chronology, Estrangement, and Stories of Literary History", *PT* 27.1 (2006), 125–235, especially 130.

68 Gray, *Vita Malchi*, 125, paraphrasing Burrus, *Sex Lives*, 38.

69 See Gray, *Vita Malchi*, 40.

tice: their own self-humiliation in the presence of the saint's greatness.[70] I would suggest that, in the *Lives* of Malchus and Amator, reading hagiography is as ascetic as writing, since the absence of full disclosure makes the readers aware of their limitations of knowledge. If asceticism implies the imitation of the saint in his humility, ascetic reading and its accompanying effect of estrangement could paradoxically be the final step towards the reader's imitation of the saints in reality. The lack of knowledge could be the motivation for the reader to try the ascetic life themselves, and even emulate the saints, discovering through the full immersion in the ascetic practice the mysteries surrounding chastity in married life.

Modern literary theory indicates that such a form of ascetic reading, created by the absence of full disclosure, does not come without pleasure. Resisting the full revelation of the secret of the couples' chaste marriage, the *Lives* of Malchus and Amator not only create surprise, but also invite the readers to experience the joy of providing new interpretations in an attempt to solve narrative discrepancies and to overcome their ignorance.[71] The *Lives* thus resemble the type of 'writerly' (*scriptable*) texts which, according to Barthes, constitute the greatest 'bliss' (*jouissance*) for the readers by making them producers of narrative in order to bridge the gaps in the narrative: 'what pleasure wants is the site of a loss, the seam, the cut, the deflation, the dissolve which seizes the subject in the midst of bliss.'[72] In case of the *Lives* of chaste spouses, this implies that the texts' aims go beyond mere edification. Their educational purpose cannot be seen apart from the readers' pleasurable experience of actively engaging with the secret of the inexplicable chaste marriage.

70 See, for instance, Turner, *Truthfulness, Realism*, 71 and Derek Krueger, *Writing and Holiness: The Practice of Authorship in the Early Christian East* (Philadelphia: University of Pennsylvania Press, 2004), 94–109.

71 This is, after all, what all scholars do when interpreting literary texts.

72 Roland Barthes, *The Pleasure of the Text*. Translated by Richard Miller, with a Note on the Text by Richard Howard (New York: Hill and Wang, 1975), 7 [original publication: *Le plaisir du texte* (Paris: Seuil, 1973)]. See Barthes, *S/Z*, 3–4 for more discussion on 'writerly' texts. See Marco Formisano, "Perpetua's Prisons: Notes on the Margins of Literature", in Jan N. Bremmer and Marco Formisano (eds.), *Perpetua's Passions: Multidisciplinary Approaches to the Passio Perpetuae et Felicitatis* (Oxford: Oxford University Press, 2012), 329–347 for a similar reading of the *Passion of Perpetua* (BHL 6633).

Acknowledgments

This chapter was written within the ERC project 'Novel Saints: Ancient novelistic heroism in the hagiography of Late Antiquity and the early Middle Ages' (Grant Agreement 337344) at Ghent University. I thank Koen De Temmerman, Marco Formisano, Danny Praet, and Wim Verbaal, as well as the editors and other contributors to this volume for their feedback.

Bibliography

Aasgaard, Reidar, *My Beloved Brothers and Sisters: Christian Siblingship in Paul* (London: T&T Clark International, 2004).

Achelis, Hans, *Virgines subintroductae. Ein Beitrag zum 7. Kapittel des 1. Korinthierbriefs* (Leipzig: Hinrichs, 1902).

Alwis, Anne P., *Celibate Marriages in Late Antique and Byzantine Hagiography* (London: Bloomsbury, 2013).

Ballard, C. Andrew, "The Mysteries of Paideia: "Mystery" and Education in Plato's Symposium, 4QInstruction, and 1 Corinthians", in Karina M. Hogan, Matthew Goff, and Emma Wasserman (eds.), *Pedagogy in Ancient Judaism and Early Christianity* (Atlanta: SBL Press, 2017), 243–282.

Barthes, Roland, *The Pleasure of the Text*. Translated by Richard Miller, with a Note on the Text by Richard Howard (New York: Hill and Wang, 1975). Original publication: *Le plaisir du texte* (Paris: Seuil, 1973).

Barthes, Roland, *S/Z*. Translated by Richard Miller; Preface by Richard Howard (Malden, MA/Oxford: Blackwell, 2002). Original publication: *S/Z* (Paris: Seuil, 1970).

Brennan, Brian, "'Episcopae': Bishops' Wives Viewed in Sixth-Century Gaul", *ChHist* 54.3 (1985), 311–323.

Brooks, Peter, *Reading for the Plot: Design and Intention in Narrative* (Cambridge, MA: Harvard University Press, 1992) 103–112. Original publication: Oxford: Oxford University Press, 1984.

Burrus, Virginia, *The Sex Lives of Saints: An Erotics of Ancient Hagiography* (Philadelphia: University of Pennsylvania Press, 2004), 33–39.

Cameron, Averil, *Christianity and the Rhetoric of Empire: The Development of Christian Discourse* (Berkeley: University of California Press, 1991).

Cooper, Kate, *The Virgin and the Bride: Idealized Womanhood in Late Antiquity* (Cambridge, MA: Harvard University Press, 1996).

de Gaiffier, Baudouin, "*Intactam sponsam reliquens*: à propos de la Vie de St. Alexis", *AB* 65 (1947), 157–195.

de Jong, Irene J.F., "Metalepsis in Ancient Greek Literature", in Jonas Grethlein and

Antonios Rengakos (eds.), *Narratology and Interpretation: The Content of Narrative Form in Ancient Literature*, Trends in Classics 4 (Berlin: De Gruyter, 2009), 87–116.

Delehaye, Hippolyte, *Les passions des martyrs et les genres littéraires*. (Brussels: Société des Bollandistes, 1921; 2nd edition Brussels: Subsidia Hagiographica, 1966).

Duru, Louis-Maximilien (ed.), "Saint Aunaire, éveque d'Auxerre, et Etienne Africain", in idem, *Bibliothèque historique de l'Yonne ou Collection de légendes, chroniques et documents divers* (Auxerre: Perriquet, 1850).

Elliott, Dyan, *Spiritual Marriage: Sexual Abstinence in Medieval Wedlock* (Princeton, NJ: Princeton University Press, 1993).

Finn, Richard D., *Asceticism in the Graeco-Roman World* (Cambridge: Cambridge University Press, 2009).

Formisano, Marco, "Perpetua's Prisons: Notes on the Margins of Literature", in Jan N. Bremmer and Marco Formisano (eds.), *Perpetua's Passions: Multidisciplinary Approaches to the Passio Perpetuae et Felicitatis* (Oxford: Oxford University Press, 2012), 329–347.

Genette, Gérard, *Narrative Discourse: An Essay in Method*. Translated by Jane E. Lewin, Foreword by Jonathan Culler (Ithaca, NY: Cornell University Press, 1983). Original publication: "Discours du récit" in *Figures III* (Paris: Seuil, 1972).

Gray, Christa, "The Monk and the Ridiculous: Comedy in Jerome's *Vita Malchi*", *Studia Patristica* 69 (Leuven: Peeters, 2013), 115–121.

Gray, Christa, *Jerome, Vita Malchi: Introduction, Text, Translation, and Commentary* (Oxford: Oxford University Press, 2015).

Greenwell, William (ed.), "The Pontifical of Egbert, Archbishop of York, A.D. 732–766", *Surtees Society* 27 (1853).

Huber-Rebenich, Gerlinde, "Hagiographic Fiction as Entertainment", in Heinz Hofmann (ed.), *Latin Fiction: The Latin Novel in Context* (London/New York: Routledge, 1999), 187–212.

Iser, Wolfgang, *The Implied Reader: Patterns of Communication in Prose Fiction from Bunyan to Beckett* (Baltimore/London: Johns Hopkins University Press, 1983). Original publication: *Der implizite Leser. Kommunikationsformen des Romans von Bunyan bis Beckett* (München: Fink, 1972).

Joye, Sylvie, "Couples chastes à la fin de l'Antiquité et au haut Moyen Âge", *Médiévales* 65 (2013), 47–63.

Kech, Herbert, *Hagiographie als christliche Unterhaltungsliteratur: Studien zum Phänomen des Erbaulichen anhand der Mönchsviten des hl. Hieronymus*. Göppinger Arbeiten zur Germanistik (Göppingen: Kümmerle, 1977).

Kelly, Kathleen C., *Performing Virginity and Testing Chastity in the Middle Ages* (London: Routledge, 2000).

Kirichenko, Alexander, "Satire, Propaganda, and the Pleasure of Reading: Apuleius' Stories of Curiosity in Context", *HSPh* 104 (2008), 339–371.

Kroon, Caroline, *Discourse Particles in Latin: A Study of nam, enim, autem, vero and at* (Amsterdam: Gieben, 1995).

Krueger, Derek, *Writing and Holiness: The Practice of Authorship in the Early Christian East* (Philadelphia: University of Pennsylvania Press, 2004).

Krusch, Bruno (ed.), *Gregorius Turonensis, Liber in gloria confessorum*, MGH 1.2 (Hanover: Hahn, 1885).

Krusch, Bruno and Wilhelm Levison (eds.), *Gregorius Turonensis: Historia Francorum (Libri historiarum X)*, MGH 1.1 (Hannover: Hahn, 1937).

Lancel, Serge (ed.), *Victor de Vita: Histoire de la persécution vandale en Afrique, La passion des sept martyrs, Registre des provinces et des cités d'Afrique* (Paris: Belles Lettres, 2002).

Leclerc, Pierre, Edgardo M. Morales and Adalbert de Vogüé (eds.), *Jérôme: Trois vies de moines (Paul, Malchus, Hilarion)*. Sources chrétiennes 508 (Paris: Les Éditions du Cerf, 2007).

Macy, Gary, *The Hidden History of Women's Ordination: Female Clergy in the Medieval West* (Oxford: Oxford University Press, 2008).

Moretus, Henri (ed.), "Catalogus codicum hagiographicorum latinorum Bibliothecae Scholae Medicinae in Universitate Montepessulanensi", *AB* 34–35 (1915–1916), 289–292.

Niederhoff, Burkhard, "Focalization", Website *The Living Handbook of Narratology* (2011) http://www.lhn.uni-hamburg.de/article/focalization, updated 24 September 2013, accessed on 15 November 2019.

Orlebeke, Alison, "Jerome, *Vita Malchi: Introduction, Text, Translation, and Commentary* by Christa Gray (review)", *JLA* 9.2 (2016), 549–552.

Réal, Isabelle, *Vies de saints, vie de famille. Représentation et système de la parenté dans le Royaume mérovingien (481–751) d'après les sources hagiographiques* (Turnhout: Brepols, 2001).

Rimmon-Kenan, Shlomith, *Narrative Fiction: Contemporary Poetics* (London/New York: Routledge, 1999). Original publication: London: Methuen, 1983.

Ryan, Marie-Laure, "From Narrative Games to Playable Stories: Toward a Poetics of Interactive Narrative", *Storyworlds: A Journal of Narrative Studies* 1 (2009), 43–59.

Schwartz, Saundra, "From Bedroom to Courtroom: The Adultery Type-Scene and the *Acts of Andrew*", in Todd Penner and Caroline Vander Stichele (eds.), *Mapping Gender in Ancient Religious Discourses* (Leiden and Boston: Brill, 2007), 267–312.

Shumate, Nancy J., "The Augustinian Pursuit of False Values as a Conversion Motif in Apuleius' 'Metamorphoses' ", *Phoenix* 42.1 (1988), 35–60.

Soler, Joëlle, "La conversion chrétienne du récit de voyage antique dans les Vies de moines de Jérôme", *IJCT* 18.1 (2011), 1–18.

Steimer, Bruno and Thomas Wetzstein (eds.), *Lexikon der Heiligen und der Heiligenverehrung* (Freiburg im Breisgau: Herder, 2003).

Sternberg, Meir, "Telling in Time (II): Chronology, Teleology, Narrativity", *PT* 13.3 (1992), 463–541.

Sternberg, Meir, "Telling in Time (III): Chronology, Estrangement, and Stories of Literary History", *PT* 27.1 (2006), 125–235.

Šubrt, Jiří, "Hagiographic Romance: Novelistic Narrative Strategy in Jerome's *Lives* of Hermits", in Marília Futre Pinheiro, Gareth L. Schmeling, and Edmund P. Cueva (eds.), *The Ancient Novel and the Frontiers of Genre* (Eelde: Barkhuis, 2014), 205–214.

Turner, Peter, *Truthfulness, Realism, Historicity: A Study in Late Antique Spiritual Literature* (Farnham/Burlington, VT: Ashgate, 2012).

Upchurch, Robert K. (ed.), *Aelfric's Lives of the Virgin Spouses* (Exeter: University of Exeter Press, 2007).

van der Sypt, Liesbeth, "Are there Messalian Syneisakts in Gregory of Nyssa's *De Virginitate* 23.4?", in Johan Leemans and Matthieu Cassin (eds.), *Gregory of Nyssa: Contra Eunomium III: an English Translation with Commentary and Supporting Studies: Proceedings of the 12th International Colloquium on Gregory of Nyssa (Leuven, 14–17 September 2010)*. Vigiliae Christianae Supplements 124 (Leiden: Brill, 2014), 704–717.

van Egmond, Wolfert S., *Conversing with the Saints: Communication in Pre-Carolingian Hagiography from Auxerre* (Turnhout: Brepols, 2006).

Van Uytfanghe, Marc, "L'origine et les ingrédients du discours hagiographique", *Sacris Erudiri* 50 (2011), 35–70.

Vogel, Cyrille and Reinhard Elze (eds.), *Le Pontifical Romano-Germanique du Dixième Siècle*. Studi e testi 226–228, 3 vols. (Vatican City: Biblioteca Apostolica, 1963).

Wolf, Werner, "Illusion (Aesthetic)", Website *The Living Handbook of Narratology* (2011) http://www.lhn.uni-hamburg.de/article/illusion-aesthetic, updated 17 January 2014, accessed on 15 November 2019.

CHAPTER 11

The Hagiographer's Craft: Narrators and Focalisation in Byzantine Hagiography

Anne Alwis

This article redefines the craft of Byzantine hagiographers by using the narratological tools of voice and focalisation. Its appearance is timely as sustained discussions on narratology in Byzantine texts and images are just beginning, although Margaret Mullett has long called for action.[1] A 2018 edited volume on storytelling is the first to even use narratology in its title.[2] Until recently, then, the importance of these devices for understanding the complex interplay of motivations for (re)writing hagiography has been overlooked, although they have long been employed in western medieval literature and in the field of classics.[3] Although the recent flurry of brilliant scholarship on Byzantine

1 Margaret Mullett, "Dancing with Deconstructionists in the Gardens of the Muses: New literary history vs ?", *BMGS* 14 (1990), 258–275; Mullett, "The Madness of Genre", *DOP* 46 (1992), 233–243; Mullett, "New Literary History and the History of Byzantine Literature: A Worthwhile Endeavour?", in Paolo Odorico and Panagiotis A. Agapitos (eds.), *Pour une "nouvelle" histoire de la literature byzantine* (Paris: École des Hautes Études en Sciences Sociales, 2002), 37–60.

2 Charis Messis, Margaret Mullett, and Ingela Nilsson, *Storytelling in Byzantium: Narratological Approaches to Byzantine Texts and Images* (Uppsala: Acta Universitatis Upsaliensis, 2018).

3 Evelyn Birge Vitz, *Medieval Narrative and Modern Narratology. Subjects and Objects of Desire* (New York: New York University Press, 1989) and Irene de Jong, *Narratology and Classics: A Practical Guide* (Oxford: Oxford University Press, 2014) are good places to start. For late antiquity and Byzantium, the activities in the research centres of Uppsala, Paris, and Ghent and their affiliated projects are the central hive for the study of narratology. For the centres, see http://www.grekiska.net/byzantine-narrative/. For late antiquity, see the papers in this volume and Christa Gray, "'Holy and Pleasing to God': A Narratological Approach to Hagiography in Jerome's *Lives* of Paul and Malchus", *Ancient Narrative* 14 (2017), 103–128. Narratology has been used successfully in Byzantine literature, but mainly for the novel and historiography. Three excellent overviews of Byzantine literature are provided by Panagiotis A. Agapitos, "Literary Criticism", in Elizabeth Jeffreys, John Haldon, and Robin Cormack (eds.), *The Oxford Handbook of Byzantine Studies* (Oxford: Oxford University Press, 2008), 77–85; Margaret Mullett, "Imitatio—aemulatio—variatio", in Andreas Rhoby and Elisabeth Schiffer (eds.), *Imitatio—Aemulatio—Variatio* (Vienna: Austrian Academy of Sciences Press, 2010), 279–282; and Emmanuel C. Bourbouhakis and Ingela Nilsson, "Byzantine Narrative: The Form of Storytelling in Byzantium", in Liz James (ed.), *A Companion to Byzantium* (Oxford: John Wiley and Sons, 2010), 263–274. The latter focuses on historiography, hagiography (briefly), and 'extended fiction'. For individual studies on the novel, see Panagiotis A. Agapitos, *Nar-*

 | DOI:10.1163/9789004421332_013

rhetoric has been vital to help us understand some of the strategies utilised by authors,[4] this work has focused mainly on the showing (mimesis) and not the telling (narrative).[5] Narratology theorises the human capacity to generate and process narratives in a variety of communicative practices and forms. In the telling of how and why certain women, men, and children are led to a life of alterity and eventual sanctity, a hagiographer makes a series of narrative choices for his/ her eventual audience.[6] Recognising and articulating the inextricable nexus that binds narratology, communication, and hagiography is thus crucial to further our comprehension of hagiographic discourse because these forms of narratives impart agency: they are designed to be read and to be heard because they intend to instruct, entertain, mediate, reveal, and edify an audience of, theoretically, the entire Greek-speaking Eastern Orthodox Church, since hagiography became an integral part of Church liturgy as early as the seventh century. Moreover, for those texts translated into the myriad languages of the Byzantine Empire—Latin, Slavonic, Coptic, Ethiopic, Syriac, Armenian, or Georgian (and later, Russian), to name just a few—the composition might reach most, if not all, of Christendom; a demographic comprising a multiplicity of ethnicities and ages, social stations, and genders. This article, therefore,

---

rative Structure in the Byzantine Vernacular Romances: A Textual and Literary Study of Kallimachos, Belthandros and Libistros (Munich: Institut für Byzantinistik und Neugriechische Philologie der Universität, 1991) and Agapitos, "Narrative, Rhetoric, and 'Drama' Rediscovered: Scholars and Poets in Byzantium Interpret Heliodorus", in Richard Hunter (ed.), *Studies in Heliodorus* (Cambridge: Cambridge Philological Society, 1998), 125–156. Paolo Odorico, Panagiotis A. Agapitos, and Martin Hinterberger's *L'écriture de la mémoire: le littératuré de l'historiographie* (Paris: de Bocard, 2006) discusses narrative features in historiography as do several of the articles in Ruth Macrides (ed.), *History as Literature* (Farnham: Ashgate, 1988); for example, Elizabeth Jeffreys (73–91), Tessa Shawcross (93–111), Athanasios Angelou (289–305), and Stephanos Efthymiadis (169–185). Emmanuel Bourbouhakis, "'Political' personae: the poem from prison of Michael Glykas: Byzantine literature between fact and fiction", *Byzantine and Modern Greek Studies* 31.1 (2007), 53–75 focuses on poetry when he discusses Glykas's 'alter-ego' (71–74) and *persona* in the 'poem from prison'.

4 Dimiter Angelov, *Imperial Ideology and Political Thought in Byzantium, 1204–1330* (Cambridge: Cambridge University Press, 2007); Stratis Papaioannou, *Michael Psellos: Rhetoric and Authorship in Byzantium* (Cambridge: Cambridge University Press, 2013); and Floris Bernard, *Writing and Reading Byzantine Secular Poetry, 1025–1081* (Oxford: Oxford University Press, 2014). The initial groundwork was laid by the excellent collection of articles in Elizabeth Jeffreys (ed.), *Rhetoric in Byzantium* (Aldershot: Ashgate, 2003).

5 Mullett, "Imitatio", 281. For example, Martin Hinterberger, in the same volume, writes about mimesis and intertextuality whilst Ingela Nilsson focuses on transtextuality.

6 Although the number of female hagiographers in Byzantium is currently in single digits, I prefer to remain optimistic with regard to pronouns. For communication in early hagiography, see Claudia Rapp, "Storytelling as Spiritual Communication in Early Greek Hagiography: The Use of *Diegesis*", *JECS* 6.3 (1998), 431–448.

revaluates the hagiographer's artistry. In doing so, it contributes new possibilities for the evaluation of authorship and reception in Byzantium, which can obviously extend beyond hagiography.

Part I examines the metaphrasis of Tatiana of Rome (*BHG* 1699b), an adapted martyrdom, to show how its reviser becomes an author by constantly appending evaluative judgements on his characters and by adding psychological emphasis. This passion has never been studied before and I have also produced its first translation and commentary, as well as a series of studies that are forthcoming.[7] Metaphrasis itself was an exercise that involved stylistic rewriting, the use of erudite Greek—in terms of grammar, syntax, and vocabulary—, and accurate employment of rhetorical devices. By applying the idea of 'voice' and the concept of focalisation, our understanding of this rhetorical mainstay is expanded and its 'literary' aspects are demonstrated as well.[8] I further contend that a sophisticated literary structure can be incorporated into this antecedent by dividing 'style' and 'literary technique'.

In Part II, I provide a new approach to reading the famed *vita* of Mary of Egypt, which is reconceptualised using the same narratological tools. I demonstrate that in this particular iteration of the story, the author's concern lies with one of hagiography's central issues: the tentative balance between fiction and reality.

1 Part I: Tatiana of Rome

At first glance, Tatiana's story reads as a conventional virgin martyr account: a virtuous, young, and beautiful Christian girl valiantly refuses to sacrifice to the gods during a time of persecution, argues successfully with her persecutor, endures vicious tortures, and willingly forfeits her life. However, the revised version, which occurred at some point between the seventh and eleventh centuries, with some indications pointing to the ninth, discloses consistent thematic additions that indicate specific intent for the rewriting.[9] Moreover,

7 Anne P. Alwis, *Narrating Martyrdom: Rewriting Late-Antique Virgin Martyrs in Byzantium* (Liverpool: Liverpool University Press, forthcoming); Alwis, "Listen to Her: Rewriting Virgin Martyrs as Orators in the Byzantine Passions of St. Tatiana and St. Ia", in Koen De Temmerman (ed.), *Holy (He)roines* (Cambridge: Cambridge University Press, forthcoming); and Alwis, "The Shape of Water: Rewriting Iconoclasm, Islam, and Deleuze", in Stavroula Constantinou and Christian Høgel, (eds.) *Metaphrasis: A Byzantine Concept of Rewriting and Its Hagiographical Products* (Leiden: Brill, forthcoming).

8 For rethinking metaphrasis/'paraphrase', see Alwis, *Narrating Martyrdom*.

9 See Alwis, "The Shape of Water". The *passio* was composed between the third and seventh

Tatiana is also reconceived as an erudite orator.[10] This fascinating layered composition has much to offer.

The form of the adapted narrative was carefully chosen. Centuries after her alleged death, an anonymous author elected to resurrect this virgin martyr by adapting her passion (*BHG* 1699) as a metaphrasis (hereafter the *MT*). A variety of options were available to hagiographers. The metaphrast could have chosen to rewrite *Tatiana* as an encomium or *logos*, a *vita*, another *passio*, an edifying story, or as an epitome; instead, he chose to write a metaphrasis.[11] As noted above, in this rhetorical exercise, a reviser (known as a metaphrast) rewrites a text in an elevated style.[12] The *MT* is a particularly useful text for investigation of the practice because the metaphrast unquestionably used the extant *passio* as his model since it is meticulously revised, sentence by sentence. This allows us the luxury of tracking the metaphrast's literary choices and focus.[13]

---

centuries though it may have coincided with the flourishing of Tatiana's cult in Rome in the seventh century, see Alwis, *Narrating Martyrdom*. For the ideological aspects of metaphrasis, see Symeon Paschalides, "Παρατηρήσεις στὶς 'μεταφράσις' τῶν Βυζαντινῶν ἁγιολογικῶν κειμένων", *Βυζαντινά* 33 (2013–2014), 373–386, esp. 377–380, and Martin Hinterberger, "*Hagiographical Encomia as* Metaphrasis *in the 14th Century: Some Preliminary Observations*", in Stavroula Constantinou and Christian Høgel (eds.), *Metaphrasis* (Leiden: Brill, forthcoming). I am very grateful to Martin Hinterberger for the opportunity to see his paper in advance.

10 Alwis, "Listen to Her".

11 For the varying genres of hagiography, see Martin Hinterberger, "Byzantine Hagiography and its Literary Genres", in Stephanos Efthymiadis (ed.), *The Ashgate Research Companion to Byzantine Hagiography*, vol. 2 (Farnham: Ashgate, 2014), 25–60 with metaphrasis at 40.

12 Resh provides an extensive overview of metaphrasis and its development over time with recent bibliography: Daria Resh, "Toward a Byzantine Definition of Metaphrasis", *Greek, Roman, and Byzantine Studies* 55 (2015), 754–787. See also Martin Hinterberger, "Hagiographische Metaphrasen. Ein möglicher Weg der Annäherung an die Literarästhetik der frühen Palaiologenzeit", in Rhoby and Schiffer, *Imitatio*, 137–151. 'Metaphrasis' can also connote a 'paraphrase'. 'Paraphrase (*paraphrasis*) consists of changing the form of expression while keeping the thoughts; it is also called metaphrase': "The *Exercises* of Aelius Theon", ch. 15 (in the Armenian translation) in George A. Kennedy, *Progymnasmata: Greek Textbooks of Prose Composition and Rhetoric* (Atlanta: Society of Biblical Literature, 2003). Kennedy also cites other examples in Seneca, *Suasoriae* 1.12, and Plutarch, *Demosthenes* 8.2.

13 Metaphrasis should not be confused with the tenth-century *oeuvre* of Symeon Metaphrastes and his team, whose works are also known as 'metaphrastic' after their nominal head. This group was responsible for a programmatic campaign of rewriting hagiography by imperial command. The metaphrastic (as it became known) menologion (a liturgical calendar) of 148 revised saints' *vitae* is the largest corpus of hagiographic work from Byzantium and survives in over 700 manuscripts, attesting to its widespread popularity. For Symeon, see "Symeon (27504)" in *Prosopographie der mittelbyzantinische Zeit: Zweite*

Until very recently, the rewriting of hagiography in Byzantium has been most commonly understood as a stylistic exercise that occurred when the language of an original text was regarded as too simplistic or crude, requiring a stylistic update.[14] The converse also occurred, so that the story better corresponded to the humble origins of the protagonist.[15] Rapp outlines other reasons for rewriting, such as the need to eliminate objectionable content and to elevate the content with additional material.[16] Finally, there is also evidence that a personal experience, such as a healing miracle bestowed upon the reviser, his relative, or a friend, stimulated the reappearance of a saint. This primarily seems to apply in the Palaeologan period (the thirteenth to fourteenth centuries).[17] Liturgical motives are another explanation. In late Byzan-

Abteilung (868–1025), vol. 6 (Berlin: De Gruyter, 2013), 228–233. For the best overview of the Metaphrast, see Christian Høgel, *Symeon Metaphrastes: Rewriting and Canonization* (Copenhagen: Museum Tusculanum Press, 2002), and Høgel's later account, "Symeon Metaphrastes and the Metaphrastic Movement", in Efthymiadis, *Research Companion*, vol. 2, 161–180. These types of texts are referred to as a genre ('metaphrastic' texts). Thus, confusingly, especially to a non-Byzantinist, in modern scholarship 'metaphrastic' connotes texts by Symeon Metaphrastes and also texts rewritten using the rhetorical principles of metaphrasis. Stylistically, the *MT* does actually have much in common with the work of Symeon and his team. For some of Symeon's work, see Elisabeth Peyr Schiffer, "Zur Umarbeitung rhetorischer Texte durch Symeon Metaphrastes", *Jahrbuch der Österreichischen Byzantinistik* 42 (1992), 143–155; Schiffer, "Metaphrastic Lives and Earlier *Metaphráseis* of Saints' Lives" in Christian Høgel, *Metaphrasis: Redactions and Audiences in Middle Byzantine Hagiography* (Oslo: The Research Council of Norway, 1996), 22–41; Henrik Zilliacus, "Zur stilistischen Umarbeitungstechnik des Symeon Metaphastes", *Byzantinische Zeitschrift* 38 (1938), 333–350; and Laura Franco, "A Study of the Metaphrastic Process", Ph.D. diss., Royal Holloway, London (2009). For example, optative, perfect, and pluperfect forms are used, as are μι-verbs, illustrating an elevated style. Periphrasis, participial clauses, wordplay on names, and reduction of biblical citation are also features. Other characteristics include shifting dialogue into different modes: paraphrase, partial elimination, or transferral from direct to indirect speech. The *MT*'s most obvious differences from Symeon's team are the lack of a prologue and the inclusion of Latin loan words. Details are in Alwis, *Narrating Martyrdom*.

14 Martin Hinterberger, "Between Simplification and Elaboration: Byzantine Metaphraseis Compared", in Juan Signes Codoñer and Immaculada Pérez Martin (eds.), *Textual Transmission in Byzantium* (Turnhout: Brepols, 2014), 33–60 gives a succinct overview on 40. See also Stephanos Efthymiadis, "The Byzantine Hagiographer and his Audience in the Ninth and Tenth Centuries", in Høgel, *Metaphrasis*, 59–80, referring to Sabas' *vita* of Peter of Atroa and Methodius' *vita* of Euthymios of Sardis at 68–70.

15 Claudia Rapp, "Byzantine Hagiographers as Antiquarians, seventh to tenth centuries", *Byzantinische Forschungen* 21 (1995), 31–44, at 36–37.

16 Rapp, "Byzantine Hagiographers", 38.

17 Alice-Mary Talbot, "Old Wine in New Bottles: The Rewriting of Saints' Lives in the Palaeologan Period", in Alice-Mary Talbot (ed.), *Women and Religious Life in Byzantium* (Aldershot: Ashgate, 2001), 15–26, at 18.

tium especially, a text may have been rewritten to complement the renewal of a church or the resurrection of a cult, or to exhibit pride in a monastery.[18] Whilst these motives certainly apply to much rewritten hagiography, I believe that although the *MT* technically falls into the first category (linguistic elevation), there is certainly more to this metaphrasis than a mere upgrade.

1.1 *Identifying the Metaphrast's Technique*

The only definition of metaphrastic technique appears in the *progymnasmata*, the rhetorical handbooks that form the basis of Byzantine higher education. One of the authors, Aelius Theon, states: 'there are four main kinds (of paraphrase)'.[19] He goes on to state that it is 'variation in syntax, by addition, by subtraction, and by substitution, plus combinations of these'.[20]

The anonymous author carries out each of these directives but seizes the opportunity to expand and develop the basic instructions. Tatiana is adorned with positive epithets, which, unsurprisingly, elevate the protagonist, and possibly help justify the rewriting. The most frequent revision is the change from 'Tatiana', 'saint', 'Saint Tatiana', or simply 'her', to various forms of 'martyr', pointing to the story's emphasis.[21] Thematic alterations include heightened resilience[22] and endurance.[23]

---

18 Talbot, "Old Wine", 19 and Talbot, "Hagiography in Late Byzantium (1204–1453)", in Stephanos Efthymiadis, *The Ashgate Research Companion to Byzantine Hagiography*, vol. 1 (Farnham; Ashgate, 2011), 173–195, at 176–179.

19 Malcolm Heath, "Theon and the History of the *Progymnasmata*", *Greek, Roman, and Byzantine Studies* 43 (2002–2003), 129–160 examines the debate around Theon's identity.

20 "The *Exercises* of Aelius Theon", ch. 15.

21 *MT* 6, 7, 9, 10, 12, 13, 16, 17, and 18.

22 In the face of extended torture in the *MT*, Tatiana displays a corresponding defiance. For example, when Tatiana's body is hacked to pieces, the *passio* relates, 'the sword's downward stroke reached her bone' (καὶ κατῆλθεν ἡ καταφορὰ ἕως τῶν ὀστέων αὐτῆς, 17: 716–717). The *MT* retaliates with: 'While her flesh was being cut into pieces so horrifically, she uttered no cry of distress nor did she groan with pain but with courageous endurance and magnanimous strength, she resiliently offered the Saviour a grateful doxology from the psalms of David. While the hands of the blood-sucking executioners mercilessly hewed her into pieces …' (ἡ δὲ δεινῶς τὰς σάρκας κατατεμνομένη οὐ φωνὴν ἀλγυνομένων ἀφῆκεν, οὐ στεναγμὸν ὀδυνωμένων ἀνέδωκεν, ἀλλ' εὐφύχῳ καρτερίᾳ καὶ μεγαλοψύχῳ στερρότητι τὴν εὐχάριστον δοξολογίαν ἐκ τῆς δαυϊτικῆς ὑμνῳδίας τῷ σωτῆρι φερεπόνως προσέφερεν. ἀφειδῶς δὲ κατακρεουργημένη τῶν αἱμοβόρων δημίων χερσί …, 17: 657–662). Constantinou has written on the contradictory experiences of the saint's body under torture: Stavroula Constantinou, "The Saint's Two Bodies: Sensibility Under (Self-)Torture in Byzantine Hagiography", *Classica et Mediaevalia* 66 (2017), 1–36.

23 Her suffering is intensified and, conversely, increases her worth in Christian eyes. For instance, the *MT* adds that her torturers inflict punishments on her 'for many hours' (ἐπὶ πολλὰς τὰς ὥρας, 6: 163), emphasising the horror. In 9: 334–336, the public executioners,

The *MT*'s additions may be initially categorised as heightened characterisation. Thus, for example, when referring to the emperor, Alexander Severus, the metaphrast replaces 'Alexander' with 'tyrant',[24] 'brutish tyrant',[25] 'harshest tyrant',[26] 'bloodthirsty tyrant',[27] 'maddened tyrant',[28] or 'foolish tyrant'.[29] Instances of amended detail also occur. After Apollo's temple explodes, the demon who appears is now 'caked in dust';[30] Tatiana's hair, we later learn, is 'curly'.[31] Location and movement are also specified, which increase visualisation. An illustration of this comes when the lion, bounding out of its cage, now lands in 'the middle' of the theatre.[32] These fragments of *enargeia* (vividness) enhance the story and engage the audience. They allow the latter to visualise the unfolding narrative more easily.

'Subtraction' mainly occurs in speeches. When these types of discourse are analysed with dialogues, subtraction devolves into three separate actions: paraphrase; the deliberate elimination of words; and the omission of words during the transition from direct to indirect speech.[33]

An instance of paraphrase appears in a prayer, where twenty-four lines of the printed edition are condensed to eight.[34] The restatement launches directly into the prayer's rationale: the castigation of idols and those who worship them. Tatiana asks for unambiguous results in short phrases, namely, for God to provide a clear sign refuting idol worship that simultaneously affirms His followers; for idol worshippers to 'be filled with shame and humiliation' and for the

---

'eight in number, did not stop cudgelling her harshly, in rotation' (οὐκ ἐπαύσαντο οἱ ταύτην ῥαβδίζοντες ἀπηνῶς ἐν παραλλαγῇ δήμιοι, τὸν ἀριθμὸν ὀκτώ). See also 13: 528–529, where originally 'the eparch ordered her to be hanged from wood and to be flogged' (κελεύει δὲ ὁ ἔπαρχος ἀναρτηθεῖσαν αὐτὴν ἐπὶ ξύλου σπαθίζεσθαι). The *MT* revises this to 'Immediately, the eparch of evil commanded that she be suspended from the punishing wood and struck mercilessly with a sword' (καὶ ταύτην παραχρῆμα προστάττει τῆς πονηρίας ὁ ἔπαρχος ἀναρτηθεῖσαν ἐπὶ τοῦ κολαστηρίου ξύλου σπαθίζεσθαι ἀφειδῶς, 13: 494–496). 'Evil' (πονηρίας) is added, the wood is described as 'punishing' (κολαστηρίου) and she is now struck 'mercilessly' (ἀφειδῶς).

24 6: 177–178; 9: 337; 10: 348; 11: 406; 12: 446; 15: 562; 18: 728.

25 9: 292 θηριότροπος τύραννος; 315 θηρίωδους τυράννου.

26 9: 341 ἀπηνέστατος τύραννος.

27 9: 347 μιαιφόνου τύραννου.

28 12: 423 μαινόμενος τύραννος.

29 12: 431 ἀνόητε τύραννε.

30 5: 116 κονιζόμενος.

31 18: 688–689 θριξὶ … βοστρύχοις.

32 15: 546–547.

33 For full details on speeches, see Alwis, *Narrating Martyrdom*.

34 *Passio Tat.* 4: 97–121; cf *MT* 4: 90–98.

destruction of an offending statue.[35] Seven lines of Tatiana's praise to God expressed in a litany of epithets,[36] three invocations to her Saviour,[37] and three citations from the Septuagint are omitted,[38] as well as a focus on 'wily Alexander'.[39] These actions eliminate repetition. The *passio* also favours an extended description of the idol in question, describing it as 'immovable, blind and mute … a fraud of the emperor, armed with a breastplate and it gulps down those who believe in it …'.[40] The metaphrast greatly simplifies and focuses Tatiana's message.

Eliminated speech also occurs in situations other than paraphrase. For example, the account of the emperor's henchman overpowering Tatiana and taking her to the emperor is shortened from five to two lines.[41] What is subtracted is the reiteration of known information from the previous chapter: praise for Alexander, repeated notice of Tatiana's distinguished family, and the purpose of her summons (to sacrifice). The metaphrast also rejects obvious comments: 'he sends for you, while you are being guarded …'.[42] In so doing,

35 'She appealed to heaven to help her so that she could clearly refute the deceptive worship of idol maniacs. She appealed for confirmation of the devout religion of those who loved piety, so that the faces and hearts of those who leant on meaningless hopes and lifeless idols might be filled with shame and humiliation while the statue itself, which attracts the unspeakable crowd of idol maniacs to destruction, might shatter swiftly and disappear' (… τὴν ἐκεῖθεν βοήθειαν ἐπικαλεσαμένη παρασχεθῆναι αὐτῇ πρὸς ἔλεγχον μὲν σαφῆ τῆς ἀπατηλῆς λατρείας τῶν εἰδωλομανούντων, βεβαίωσιν δὲ τῆς θεοσεβοῦς θρησκείας τῶν φιλευσεβούντων, ὡς ἂν αἰσχύνης καὶ ἐντροπῆς τὰ πρόσωπα καὶ τὰς καρδίας ἐμπλησθήσωνται οἱ ματαίαις ἐλπίσιν ἐπερειδόμενοι καὶ τοῖς ἀψύχοις εἰδώλοις προστετηκότες, αὐτὸ δὲ τὸ πρὸς ἀπώλειαν ἕλκον ἄγαλμα τὸ ἀμύθητον πλῆθος τῶν εἰδωλομανούντων συντριβῇ τὸ τάχος καὶ ἀφανισθῇ, 4: 91–98).

36 *Passio Tat.* 4: 100–105: 'Glory to you, father Jesus Christ, most glorified God, undefiled, ungrudging provider with the Holy Spirit, full of sanctity and knowledge, always existing, eternal emperor, the God of mercies and Lord of all visible and invisible things, Who, in the grace of Your compassion, has mercy for those who confess the name of Your divine Christ …' (δόξα σοι, πάτερ καὶ Ἰησοῦ Χριστέ, δεδοξασμένε θεέ, σὺν ἁγίῳ πνεύματι, ἁγιωσύνης πλήρης καὶ γνώσεως ἄφθονε χορηγέ, ἄσπιλε, ἀεὶ ὤν, αἰώνιε βασιλεῦ, ὁ θεὸς τῶν οἰκτιρμῶν καὶ κύριος πάντων ὁρατῶν τε καὶ ἀοράτων, ὁ ἐλεῶν ἐν χάριτι τῆς σῆς εὐσπλαγχνίας τοὺς τὸ ὄνομα τῆς θεότητος τοῦ Χριστοῦ σου ὁμολογοῦντας …).

37 *Passio Tat.* 4: 105–108: 'I call upon You Who exists, is present, and Who waits eternally, I call You, begging, and I supplicate You to fulfil the completeness of my confession to You …' (σὲ ἐπικαλοῦμαι τὸν ὄντα καὶ παρόντα καὶ μένοντα εἰς τοὺς αἰῶνας, ὃν καὶ παρακαλῶ δεομένη καὶ ἱκετεύω τὴν τελειότητα τῆς εἰς σὲ ὁμολογίας πληρῶσαί με …).

38 Psalm 134:16–17, Deuteronomy 32:39, Wisdom 10:19.

39 *Passio Tat.* 4: 116 κακότεχνος.

40 *Passio Tat.* 4: 109–111.

41 *Passio Tat.* 2: 40–45.

42 *Passio Tat.* 2: 43.

our author distils the essence of the menacing context into the following: 'The impious servants overpowered her, just as if they had found some mighty prey, and hastened to the emperor'.[43]

Thus, a framework of subtraction is set in place, which clarifies an overall motivation. We can ascertain part of the metaphrast's literary choices and focus. He trims the majority of biblical citation, any negative characteristics ascribed to Tatiana by her enemies, extended epithets for Christ, and the bulk of references to the Devil. Furthermore, antiquated roles and locations are also specified for a later audience. References to 'praetorians' or 'centurions' are changed to 'executioners'[44] and the archaic 'Galileans' is eliminated.[45] When the author locates Tatiana's burial in the 'sixth region', using Augustan terminology, the reviser adds 'of the city', clarifying the layout of late antique Rome for his audience.[46]

These omissions and amendments can be placed into three clusters. When it comes to narrative, Theon stipulates three requirements: clarity, concision, and credibility.[47] Thus, the call for clarity would account for the explanations and for the modernising terminology. Omissions would occur for the sake of concision. This could pertain to the elimination of biblical citation, praise for Christ, and mention of the Devil. Given the stimulus for credibility (on which, see Part II), the diminution of the Devil as a physical entity makes sense since he was no longer such a visceral presence in Byzantine daily life.[48] But there is more. Working within these stipulations, the metaphrast is able to manipulate the mandate to further his own interests, as we shall now see.

1.2 *Literary Technique I: Story, Plot, and Narration*

Strikingly, careful comparison of the model with the product further reveals that the metaphrast also introduces a great deal of what might be termed liter-

43 *MT* 2: 42–44.

44 Praetorians: ch. 6 (also eliminated in ch. 18); centurions: ch. 9. Latin loan words are used here: see Alwis, *Narrating Martyrdom*.

45 Eliminated from *Passio Tat.* 1: 8.

46 *MT* 19: 797–798.

47 Theon 79. See also Nicolaus the Sophist 3: 'brevity, clarity, persuasiveness, charm, grandeur'; John of Sardis, commenting on Aphthonius, also cites Theon 19 but also adds 'Hellenism', which Kennedy assumes is 'pure Greek'.

48 To some extent, he became assimilated with *phthonos* (envy/jealousy): Martin Hinterberger, "Emotions in Byzantium", in James, *A Companion to Byzantium*, 123–134, at 131; Cyril Mango, "Diabolus Byzantinus", *Dumbarton Oaks Papers* 46 (1992), 215–223, at 222; and Enrico Maltese, *Dimensioni bizantine: Donne, angeli e demoni nel Medioevo greco* (Alessandria: Edizioni dell'Orso, 2007), 47–64.

ary technique in the process. By this, I refer to the structural elements underpinning the crafting of a text, such as narrative structure, framing techniques, and the use of literary devices such as simile and/or metaphor, which is where technique and style begin to overlap. Thus, a distinction may be imposed between style and literary technique where style is more akin to tone. By tone, I mean the choices an author makes in terms of literary elements such as diction and syntax as well as his/her appeal to the senses, use of facts, and figurative language.[49]

This position challenges current notions in scholarship since such distinctions did not explicitly exist in Byzantium or classical antiquity, especially in the ostensible absence of comprehensive, overt Byzantine literary criticism in the vein of Horace or Longinus. But the situation is improving, for example with the most welcome recent translation of a collection of Psellos' writings.[50] Pertinently, Agapitos points out that there are 'momentary glimpses into issues of literary taste' by authors on individual works[51] and scholia, commentaries, essays, and lectures that interpret ancient Greek literature also provide valuable insights.[52]

Nevertheless, as Papaioannou observes, 'we are dealing with various registers of discourse, operating for different audiences and with different objectives', and thus sweeping statements are futile.[53] However, as he, in particular, has successfully illustrated, it is possible to see how the Byzantine *literati* utilised rhetoric to produce multiple discourses.[54] The subsequent unveiling of

49 With huge thanks to Kelli Rudolph for elucidating and refining my thoughts (pers. comm).

50 Charles Barber and Stratis Papaioannou (eds.), *Michael Psellos on Literature and Art: A Byzantine Perspective on Aesthetics* (Notre Dame, IN: University of Notre Dame Press, 2017).

51 Agapitos, "Literary Criticism", 78. In his comprehensive overview of the state of Byzantine literary criticism, Agapitos selects Constantine Akropolites' comments on the twelfth-century *Timarion*; Nikephoros Basiliakes' detailed explanations of his own work, also in the twelfth-century; Michael Italikos' observation of how his facility of recitation relates to his letter's literary qualities; and also Metochites' remarks on Dio Chrysostom and Synesius (79). For Photios' view on hagiography, see Tomas Hägg, "Photius as a Reader of Hagiography: Selection and Criticism", *Dumbarton Oaks Papers* 53 (1999), 43–58.

52 For scholia, see Ole L. Smith, "Medieval and Renaissance Commentaries in Greek on Classical Greek texts", *Classica et Medievalia* 47 (1996), 391–405. Agapitos, "Literary Criticism", 79–80 also shows how far modern scholarship has come in identifying changes in literary taste and genre.

53 Stratis Papaioannou, "Byzantine *Enargeia* and Theories of Representation", *Byzantinoslavica* 69.3 (2011), 48–60, and Papaioannou, *Michael Psellos*. The set of articles in Jeffreys, *Rhetoric* is an excellent start.

54 On a micro level, between the ninth and twelfth centuries, *enargeia* ('vividness'), for example, which is related to the concept of ekphrasis, not only indicated truth but was also associated with metaphor and discursive dramatisation. For *enargeia* denoting truth in

'meta-culture and meta-language' invites the use of modern literary theory.[55] Where this article diverges from previous studies is its interest in the substrata of metaphrasis and rhetoric more generally: the framing components pertaining to rhetorical processes and devices. Style and literary technique are generally merged when discussing concepts such as *pathos*, *phantasia*, *ethiopoeia*, or *ekphrasis*, for example. But if the various constituting elements are disentangled, their individual application enhances our understanding of some texts as literary narratives.

The starting point is Hermogenes' observation that 'a narrative (*diēgēma*) differs from a narration (*diēgēsis*)'.[56] His separation of the two concepts underpins modern narratology where 'narrative' is understood as the representation of events and 'narration' is the process of telling. In Kennedy's translation, *diēgēma* ('narrative') is 'an exposition of something that has happened or as if it happened'. Hermogenes continues: 'The *History* of Herodotus is a *diēgēsis*, as is that of Thucydides, but the story of Arion (Herodotus 1.23) or of Alcmeon (Thucydides 2.102) is a *diēgēma*'.[57] John of Sardis clarifies further: 'a *diēgēsis* is exposition that is comprehensive of many things, whereas *diēgēma* is an exposition of one thing'.[58] Recognising and employing these distinctions allows us to change the way we view hagiography and to appreciate the hagiographer's artistry.

However, matters are complicated since narratology also includes 'story' and 'plot', which themselves are often confused in informal discourse. 'Story' is a chronological sequence of events, whilst 'plot' can be used in the sense of a

the ninth to twelfth centuries, see Papaioannou, "Byzantine *Enargeia*", 50–52; for the other ideas proposed by the Byzantines, see 53–60. An illuminating analysis of ekphrasis in the early periods is Ruth Webb, *Ekphrasis, Imagination and Persuasion in Ancient Rhetorical Theory and Practice* (Farnham: Ashgate, 2009). See also, for example, Koen De Temmerman, "Ancient Rhetoric as a Hermeneutical Tool for the Analysis of Characterization in Narrative Literature", *Rhetorica* 28.1 (2010), 23–51. On a wider level, Papaioannou, *Michael Psellos* illustrates how Psellos used rhetoric as self-presentation, which evolved into nascent literary writing.

55 Agapitos, "Literary Criticism", 80.

56 Hermogenes ch. 4 in Kennedy, *Progymnasmata*. Hermogenes of Tarsus' rhetorical treatises were very influential in the Byzantine period.

57 Hermogenes ch. 4; Nicolaus the Sophist chs. 11–12; John of Sardis chs. 15–16. Kennedy, *Progymnasmata*, 73 explains the vexed question of attribution and authorship of Hermogenes' work. Hermogenes' conceptions are more compressed than Theon's, who breaks narrative ('language descriptive of things that have happened or as though they had happened') into six elements: person, action, place, time, manner, and cause (Theon 78). See also Agapitos, *Narrative Structure*, 144 for a modern application of these terms to the late-Byzantine novels.

58 John of Sardis ch. 16.

story-type; Porter Abbott refers to the 'revenge plot or marriage plot'.[59] Correlating the two Greek terms to the four modern concepts of 'narrative', 'narration', 'story', and 'plot' is tricky but using Hermogenes and John of Sardis' explanations and a very English early modern exemplar, we can say that in Austen's *Pride and Prejudice* the *diēgēma* (here, also, 'narrative' and 'story') comprises the changing feelings of Elizabeth Bennet towards Fitzwilliam Darcy. The intricate *diēgēsis* (here, 'narration' and 'plot') would involve, at the very least, the heralded arrival of Mr Bingley, the attraction between Jane Bennet and Bingley, Mr Collins' maladroit courtship of Elizabeth, Mr Darcy's stilted first proposal, Elizabeth's attraction to Mr Wickham, Elizabeth's revelatory visit to Pemberley, Lydia Bennet's elopement with Wickham, and Lady Catherine visiting Elizabeth at Longbourn. The narration is led by the voice of the author, which at this point, we will call the third person. However, the narration would be very different if, for example, it were to be led by Elizabeth, Darcy, or Mr Collins.

Applying these initial distinctions to the *MT* would mean that its *diēgēma* concerns Tatiana, a deaconess and daughter of a consul, who is martyred during the rule of Alexander Severus (reigned c. AD 222–235). At this stage, I will say that the *MT*'s narration is led by the anonymous author; a third-person narrator. The *diēgēsis* comprises the following details, chosen specifically and in that order by the author.[60]

After she is ordered to sacrifice to Apollo, Tatiana appears to acquiesce, lulling the emperor into a false sense of security. However, rather than submit to the emperor, the future martyr unexpectedly unleashes chaos and violent death by inflicting a terrifying earthquake upon the temple and those in its proximity. Apollo's sanctuary is destroyed and its residing demon banished. As punishment, Alexander orders the first of many excruciating tortures: Tatiana is to be beaten on the eyes and blinded with iron hooks—but, simultaneously, the torturers miraculously receive the identical punishment. Incensed by their complaints, Alexander goads them to strike potsherds on the girl's face. However, intervention by the voice of God prompts the torturers to convert, increasing Alexander's ire and resulting in their subsequent decapitation.

After further altercation with an implacable Tatiana, the infuriated Alexander orders her to be stripped to her undergarment and hewn to pieces. Spec-

59 H. Porter Abbott, *The Cambridge Introduction to Narrative* (Cambridge: Cambridge University Press, 2008), 40–54 devotes a chapter to the 'masterplot', which he finds a more useful category than 'plot'.

60 Since metaphrasis is a paraphrase, the story would remain constant. However, some elements do occasionally disappear or the modification might produce a different interpretation. For further discussion, see Alwis, "The Shape of Water".

tacularly, milk, not blood, flows from her body as a beautiful scent permeates the air. Undeterred, the emperor commands his men to stretch out her mangled body and to cudgel her relentlessly. But yet again, her eight new torturers are weakened when invisible angels simultaneously strike them with iron rods. Tatiana is subsequently imprisoned whilst plans are made to immerse her in boiling animal fat as a form of purification.

When Limenius, a tribune, is dispensed to fetch her, he notices light blazing from her prison. Entering, he witnesses Tatiana seated on a throne, encircled by beauteous beings clad in white. On hearing Limenius' account of this wonder, Alexander orders a trial during which thunder, lightning, and heavenly fire erupt, destroying Artemis' temple and her priests. As retribution, Tatiana is then attached to a wheel whilst Justin, an eparch, is commanded to slice her with a sword and to shred her breasts with the points of iron nails. Tatiana's silence during this further torment leads the perplexed Justin to command that she be borne once again to prison, carried on a pallet. However, defiantly (and practically) binding the pieces of her body with her hair, Tatiana jumps off and sprints to the prison, outracing the pursuing eparch, who is on horseback.

As retribution, she is thrown to a ravenous lion, but to no avail. The beast bows before her and licks her gently before mauling the unfortunate Limenius to pieces. Tatiana is then hanged from a scaffold, flogged, shackled, and finally tossed into a fire. Her head is also shaved because the persecutors fear her powers are infused in her curly hair. Undaunted and resolutely alive, she is confined in a temple of Zeus. The following day, the dumbfounded emperor finds her enthroned once again, surrounded by four radiant angels whilst the cult statue of Zeus lies in smithereens. At his wits' end, Alexander condemns Tatiana to decapitation on 12 January. Her broken body is retrieved by the bishop of Rome, his clergy, and the populace, and she is laid to rest in an alabaster coffin that is buried in a garden that resembles Paradise. Alexander suffers a heart attack and repents. Nonetheless, he is escorted to the eternal fire of Gehenna, leaving behind 2,300 souls who now believe in Christ.

1.3 *Literary Technique II: Voice and Narrators*

At the core of formulating a narrative text lie Gérard Genette's two questions, 'who speaks?' (voice) and 'who sees?' (focalisation). This is a contentious binary, which, for now, I will follow.[61] At its simplest level, voice manifests in

61 In *Narrative Discourse Revisited*, Genette changed 'Who sees?' to 'Who perceives?', based on Bal's work: Gérard Genette, *Narrative Discourse Revisited*. Translated by Jane E. Lewin (Cornell: Cornell University Press, 1990); Mieke Bal, *Narratology: Introduction to the Theory of Narrative* (2nd edition Toronto: University of Toronto Press, 1997). Jahn, in particular,

two forms: author and narrator.[62] Thus, Dorothy L. Sayers and Hermann Hesse are the authors of *Gaudy Night* and *Siddhartha* respectively. Both these novels also include an 'omniscient' (anonymous) third-person narrator.[63] By contrast, a 'limited' third-person narrator is one who knows only what the main character(s) know, building suspense, such as the narrator of Orwell's *1984*. First-person narration is another possibility. The person who opens the pages of *Jane Eyre* knows that Charlotte Brontë is the author but discovers fairly soon that Jane is the narrator (and protagonist), and she is technically distinct from the author.[64] The rarest form is the second-person narrator, found in Italo Calvino's *If on a Winter's Night a Traveller*, where the reader is addressed directly in the first lines.[65]

Hagiography prefers two options. First-person narrators are favoured when the author, named or otherwise, drives the account. An example is Athana-

---

shows how seeing and speaking need not be construed as a binary: Manfred Jahn, "Windows of Focalization: Deconstructing and Reconstructing a Narratological Concept", *Style* 30.2 (1996), 241–267.

62 Agapitos, *Narrative Structure*, 74–95 also distinguished between author and narrator in his study of the Byzantine novels. For his distinctions between authorial 'intervention' and 'interjection', see 78–84 and 84–90, respectively.

63 The first lines of each are as follows: 'Harriet Vane sat at her writing table and stared out into Mecklenburg Square. The late tulips made a brave show in the Square garden, and a quartet of early tennis players were energetically calling the score of a rather erratic and unpractised game' (Dorothy L. Sayers, *Gaudy Night* (London: Victor Gollancz Ltd, 1935), 1). *Siddhartha*'s first lines are: 'In the shade of the house, in the sunshine of the riverbank near the boats, in the shade of the Sal-wood forest, in the shade of the fig tree is where Siddhartha grew up, the handsome son of the Brahman, the young falcon, together with his friend Govinda, son of a Brahman' (Hermann Hesse, *Siddhartha* (1922). Translated by Hilda Rosner (London: Picador, 1998), 1). Both novels utilise other characters as focalisers: Sayers uses Harriet whilst Hesse uses Govinda and Kamala.

64 'There was no possibility of taking a walk that day. We had been wandering, indeed, in the leafless shrubbery an hour in the morning; but since dinner (Mrs. Reed, when there was no company, dined early) the cold winter wind had brought with it clouds so sombre, and a rain so penetrating, that further out-door exercise was now out of the question.' (Charlotte Brontë, *Jane Eyre*, London: Smith, Elder, and Co, 1847), 1.

65 When the narrator refers to at least one character as 'you', suggesting that the audience is a character within the narrative: 'You are about to begin reading Italo Calvino's new novel, *If on a winter's night a traveler*. Relax. Concentrate. Dispel every other thought. Let the world around you fade. Best to close the door; the TV is always on in the next room. Tell the others right away, "No, I don't want to watch TV!" Raise your voice—they won't hear you otherwise—"I'm reading! I don't want to be disturbed!" Maybe they haven't heard you, with all that racket; speak louder, yell: "I'm beginning to read Italo Calvino's new novel!" Or if you prefer, don't say anything; just hope they'll leave you alone.' (Italo Calvino, *If on a Winter's Night a Traveller* (1979). Translated by William Weaver (London: Everyman, 1993), 1).

sius' *vita* of Antony. These narrators may overlap into the so-called 'eye-witness' accounts, where often, the technical author is anonymous.[66] The second alternative for a hagiographer, who is sometimes a member of the elite or otherwise anonymous, is to employ a disembodied omniscient third-person narrator, such as those found in *Gaudy Night*, *Siddhartha*, or *Pride and Prejudice*. Into the former camp fall the illustrious names of, for example, Gregory of Nyssa, John Chrysostom, Jerome, Constantine Akropolites, or Nikephoros Gregoras.[67] Hagiography never recognises alternative, named, fully-realised personalities, like Jane Eyre, Huck Finn, or Humbert Humbert. This enables the narrative to be related in its entirety by a narrator who is not, nor likely to be, equated with the author. The reason is clear: since it colours the story it narrates, 'voice' is of prime interest when thinking about reliability and veracity, as we shall see below, in Part II, for the *vita* of Mary of Egypt and its various narrators. Nabokov masters these concepts with Humbert and *Lolita*. In addition, authors can then play with ideas and constructs relating to memory as Sebald fathoms, particularly with *Austerlitz*.[68]

The grammatical first-person lends the most 'reality' to a saint, whether or not the claim bears historical credence, and since so much of authored hagiography is anonymous, voice is a means of authentication.[69] In the case of third-

66 Lennart Rydén, "Fiction and Reality in the Hagiographer's Self-Presentation", *Travaux et Mémoires* 14 (2002), 547–552. For example, Eutolmios for Galaktion and Episteme (Anne Alwis, *Celibate Marriages in Late-Antique and Byzantine Hagiography: the Lives of Saints Julian and Basilissa, Andronikos and Athanasia, and Galaktion and Episteme* (London: Bloomsbury, 2011)); Alexius for Florus and Laurus (*Analecta Bollandiana* 51 (1933) and *Acta Sanctorum*, Aug. 3: 521); Anthimus for Philetaerus and Eubiotus (*Acta Sanctorum*, May 4: 312–328); and Florentius for Cassiodorus and his companions (*Analecta Bollandiana* 16 (1897), 301 n. 5 and *Analecta Bollandiana* 23 (1904), 36 n. 6). See also Hippolyte Delehaye, *Les passions des martyrs et les genres littéraires* (Brussels: Société des Bollandistes, 1966), 182–183. Kleinberg explains how the eyewitness account is as much a personal revelation as straightforward narrative, using Peter of Dacia's account of Christina of Stommeln: Aviad Kleinberg, *Prophets in Their Own Country: Living Saints and the Making of Sainthood in the Later Middle Ages* (Chicago: University of Chicago Press, 1993), 55.

67 Alexander Kazhdan (ed.), *The Oxford Dictionary of Byzantium*, 3 vols. (Oxford: Oxford University Press, 1991) provides introductions to these authors.

68 Humbert is a notorious unreliable narrator. See, for example, James Phelan, "Estranging Unreliability, Bonding Unreliability, and the Ethics of *Lolita*", *Narrative* 15.2 (2007), 222–238. Boese gives a highly nuanced perspective on Sebald: Stefanie Boese, "'Forever Just Occurring': Postwar Belatedness in W.G. Sebald's *Austerlitz*", *Journal of Modern Literature* 39.4 (2016), 104–121.

69 See also Julie Van Pelt in this volume and Charis Messis, "Fiction and/or Novelisation in Byzantine Hagiography" in Efthymiadis, *Ashgate Research Companion*, vol. 2, 313–341, discussing first-person narrative at 328–329.

person omniscient narrators, their status validates their authority and provides the stamp of legitimacy.[70] Saints could be a problem. Many hagiographers had to grapple with the extraordinary and outlandish alterity of their subjects.[71] Conceptions of voice therefore provide another mode with which to analyse 'fictional' work—hagiography, conceived broadly ('that which does not correspond to truth-judgement')—rather than 'fictive' work (a falsehood), concepts that Van Pelt explains in this volume.[72]

Even more useful than distinguishing between first- and third-person narration is Genette's corresponding homo- and heterodiegetic narrators. These appellations refer to actual characters in the story (homo-) or those who stand outside (hetero-). Thus, a homodiegetic/internal narrator would be Nelly Dean from *Wuthering Heights* or Eutolmios in the *vita* and *passio* of Galaktion and Episteme.[73] *Pride and Prejudice*'s narrator is heterodiegetic/external, as is Constantine Akropolites, for example, or the anonymous author of the *MT*. Because she is telling her own story, Jane Eyre is called an autodiegetic narrator; so too are Humbert Humbert and Huck Finn.

The author of the *MT* is not a character in the story and, accordingly, not allotted a life or personality of his own but, as a heterodiegetic narrator, he shows awareness of his role. An example is when he directly addresses an audience when he attempts to describe angelic beings: 'Words cannot express the sight of their beauty';[74] or when he declares, 'It is not easy to describe the beauty of the brilliance of these men nor the sweet fragrance of incense'.[75] Most pertinently for my argument, he evaluates and comments on the events he relates, as we shall see.

1.4 *Focalisation in the* MT

As we expand our notion of narrative voice, we must discuss focalisation, also known as orientation, point of view, or perspective.[76] The story the narrator,

---

70 All these narratorial modes direct attention to the narrator as opposed to the narration and can be thus used accordingly.

71 Paul Magdalino, "The Byzantine Holy Man in the Twelfth Century", in Sergei Hackel (ed.), *The Byzantine Saint* (London, The Fellowship of St Alban and St Sergius, 1981), 51–66, and Anthony Kaldellis, "The Hagiography of Doubt and Scepticism", in Efthymiadis, *Ashgate Research Companion* vol. 2, 453–477.

72 Van Pelt in this volume and Rydén, "Fiction and Reality".

73 Alwis, *Celibate Marriages*, 72; 293–294.

74 ὧν οὐκ ἔστιν ἱστορῆσαι λόγῳ τὴν θέαν τῆς καλλονῆς 10: 381–382.

75 ὧν τὴν καλλονὴν τῆς λαμπρότητος οὐκ ἔστιν εὐχερὲς διηγήσασθαι 18: 724–725.

76 Michael Toolan, *Narrative: A Critical Linguistic Introduction* (London: Routledge, 2001), 59–63; Jahn, "Windows of Focalization"; Don Fowler, "Deviant Focalisation in Virgil's *Aeneid*", *The Cambridge Classical Journal* 36 (1990), 42–63, at 42 and n. 3.

here the metaphrast, tells is his version/focalisation of a series of events that are either supposed to have taken place (the 'suspension of disbelief') or that have really taken place (historiographical/biographical narratives). Although no narrator can ever tell the whole 'truth', if the reader/audience is aware of the variety of orientations that may be present, then focalisation contributes to a richer involvement in terms of how s/he thinks, feels, and thus reacts. Nünlist has illustrated how focalisation was implicit in Homeric scholia in the practice of *lusis ek tou prosõpou* ('solving contradictions') as critics tried to explain why the poet and his characters could hold opposing positions.[77]

Post-Genettean critique, initiated by Bal, expanded the scope of 'who sees?' to the widening of the perceptual modes of psychology, cognition, emotion, and ideology, which leads to the blanket term of 'apperception'.[78] Essentially, a modern critic needs to decide whether to take a broad or narrow view. In the case of hagiography, it is necessary to approach with wide eyes and see what the texts reveal and what might work with each, since they are all so different.

A clear example of the *MT*'s heterodiegetic focalisation is the manner in which the narrator refers to Tatiana's antagonist, Alexander Severus. Rarely is an opportunity missed to denigrate the emperor. Unquestionably, the persecutor is always maligned in passions but now this archetype is hugely magnified, viewed through a lens of devastating authorial comment. It is not merely a question of the metaphrastic 'addition' style.

'Emperor' is no longer sufficient; it is pre-empted with a scathing 'impious'[79] or 'irrational'.[80] Other epithets include 'delighting in blood',[81] 'bloodythirsty',[82] 'unjust and extremely wicked',[83] 'all-abominable',[84] 'villainous',[85] 'vengeful',[86]

---

77 René Nünlist, "The Homeric Scholia on Focalization", *Mnemosyne* 56.1 (2003), 61–71 shows how the practice of focalisation existed in antiquity by 'allowing two sides to hold contradicting opinions' (λύσις ἐκ τοῦ προσώπου).

78 A useful overview is given by Manfred Jahn, "Focalization", in David Herman (ed.), *The Cambridge Companion to Narrative* (Cambridge, Cambridge University Press, 2007), 94–108, at 100–102. See also Toolan, *Narrative*, 62–63, and Shlomith Rimmon-Kenan, *Narrative Fiction: Contemporary Poetics* (London: Methuen, 1983).

79 ἀσεβεία 10: 386.

80 ἀλογία 12: 469; 16: 613; 17: 646; highly irrational (ἀλογώτατος) 12: 451; 15: 573.

81 αἱμοχαρῆ 13: 506.

82 μιαιφόνος 6: 166; 7: 243; 8: 276; 9: 347.

83 ἀδίκου καὶ πονηροτάτου 1: 2.

84 παμμίαρος 7: 224, 232; 8: 266.

85 πανοῦργος 15: 549.

86 ἀλάστορος 16: 602, 633.

'champion of error',[87] 'superstitious and God-fighting',[88] and 'more shameless than a dog and more savage than every beast'.[89] Alexander is also ascribed a new series of emotional responses such as 'helpless',[90] 'frantic',[91] and 'astounded'.[92]

On one level, Alexander's enhanced reactions add variety and tone whilst further underscoring Tatiana's impact, since they occur in response to the martyr's feats. These heightened responses are extended beyond adjectival or adverbial accessories. For example, when Alexander sees Tatiana triumphant after she has blasted Zeus' statue to smithereens, the *passio* details his reaction minimally: 'The emperor was astounded at such exultation …'.[93] However, the narrator-focaliser expands: 'Terror overwhelmed the thunderstruck tyrant at such glory and the sheer joy of the gloriously triumphant martyr …'.[94] After Alexander, in the words of the *passio*, orders 'her to be hung up again and to be flogged',[95] the metaphrast seizes the opportunity to rewrite as follows: 'Seized by reckless anger, diabolical madness, and inflamed, Alexander commanded that the manly-minded martyr be hanged from a scaffold and scraped mercilessly'.[96]

An alternative facet of focalisation that appears in the *MT* transpires when the narrator alerts the audience to the inner workings of Alexander's personality, further intensifying characterisation. This is enforced by auxiliary commentary, which has no equivalent in the *passio*. For example, after Tatiana produces a particularly rhetorical flourish, he writes: 'The martyr's oratorical skills struck the heart of the bestial tyrant with a heavy blow, as if they were a sword, and he was reduced to greater madness'.[97] Another striking example (amongst many) comes after Tatiana has survived a vicious flogging and the repeated slicing of her body. In reaction, Alexander states: 'her deception has worked because of

87 πλάνης πρόμαχος 18: 716.

88 δεισιδαίμων καὶ θεομάχος 20: 802.

89 ἀναιδέστερος ὑπάρχων κυνὸς καὶ παντὸς θηρίου ἀγριώτερος 8: 267.

90 ἀμηχανία 9: 341; 13: 515; 16: 633; 18: 741.

91 ἐμμανῶς 9: 342.

92 καταπλαγεὶς (3: 52); 'greatly astounded' (πάνυ καταπληττόμενος) 11: 408.

93 *Passio Tat.* 18: 772–773.

94 *MT* 18: 727–729.

95 *Passio Tat.* 17: 711–712.

96 *MT* 17: 654–657. See also when the *passio* states, 'He [Alexander] ordered her to be handed over to fire' (κελεύει δὲ αὐτὴν πυρὶ παραδοθῆναι, 17: 726), which the *MT* amends to, 'Alexander, the heir of darkness and fire, aflame with anger and kindled by madness, commanded that the undefiled martyr be handed over into a fire' (ὁ δὲ τοῦ σκότους καὶ τοῦ πυρὸς κληρονόμος Ἀλέξανδρος ἐμπιπρώμενος θυμῷ καὶ μανίᾳ ἀναπτόμενος προστάττει πυρὶ παραδοθῆναι τὴν ἀμίαντον μάρτυρα, 17: 672–674).

97 *MT* 9: 313–316.

witchcraft …'.[98] True to form, the narrator-focaliser expands significantly and evaluates: 'The lawless emperor neither wished to understand the action of divine power nor was he able to admire the magnitude of the incredible marvels as he ought. He [was] more savage than wild beasts.'[99]

Although the amplified characterisation of the brutal persecutor and the heroic martyr has been well-documented, for instance, in the work of Symeon Metaphrastes,[100] in this text we are concerned with something subtly different. In the *MT*, the heterodiegetic narrator-focaliser renovates his characters not only by labelling them explicitly but by appraising them. He manipulates their words and actions to portray their sentiments and reactions, effectively directing a response and creating a moral judgement.

Revisions also serve a different purpose: to provide motivations for Alexander's actions and thus momentum for the story. For instance, after one of the saint's defiant speeches, the *passio*'s simple 'Alexander ordered the saint to go back to the prison' is altered to '… the vengeful one, full of helplessness and speechlessness, commanded that she be carried off to prison'.[101] Tatiana is subsequently thrown to a ravenous lion. Here, the metaphrast/narrator-focaliser emphasises Alexander's frustration and impotence, and generates the stimulus for the saint's next punishment. A further example occurs when Tatiana has been brought to the theatre to be devoured by the lion. As she enters, 'an astonishing sound swelled from heaven causing everyone to become scared and cry out'.[102] The *passio*'s simple response, 'And the emperor said …', is altered to, 'The villainous emperor, full of deceit in his manner and by inclination, tried, in a certain way, to beguile the resolute soldier of Christ by using deceitful flattery'.[103] At this juncture, the narrator explains why Alexander continues with the punishment instead of (perhaps) reacting in fear and saving Tatiana.

A psychological dimension is also present. Most obviously, this occurs at the apex of the plot—Tatiana's final punishment, which will lead to inevitable death. At this significant moment, the narrator-focaliser dwells at great length on Alexander's reasons for the ultimate punishment, expanding the *passio*'s functional details. Thus, 'Then he [the emperor] ordered her to be led away

---

98 *Passio Tat.* 14: 572–573.

99 *MT* 14: 532–536.

100 Christian Høgel, "The Redaction of Symeon Metaphrastes: Literary Aspects of the Metaphrastic Martyria", in Høgel, *Metaphrasis*, 7–21, at 16.

101 *Passio Tat.* 16: 693–694; cf. *MT* 16: 633–634.

102 *MT* 15: 547–548.

103 *Passio Tat.* 15: 605; cf. *MT* 15: 548–551.

outside the city and put under the sword'[104] is modified to 'Treacherous and deceitful Alexander now had serious doubts concerning all the practices of his extravagant schemes and manifold devices. He was disgraced and at a loss from every side. Driven to a state of extreme discomfiture and helplessness, he could no longer bear to see his personal superstition made a laughing stock nor could he endure the shame of the destruction of those whom he revered. And so he gave the sentence against the holy martyr—the sword would be her punishment'.[105]

Alexander Severus is not a semiotic representation functioning within the narrative realm. He is not a typical symbol of personified evil. His internal dilemmas are of importance rather than embodying an archetype assigned a place within the contextual framework. Nor is the reviser/author/narrator-focaliser merely fulfilling the perceived stylistic criteria of metaphrasis. Although we could speculate that the narrator's auxiliary commentary on Alexander's mental capabilities may be present for credibility, as prescribed by Theon, there are so many detailed examples that whilst this may indeed be the case or whilst the additions may demonstrate *amplificatio*, for example, it is also clear that the metaphrast is psychologising and adding his own comment. In so doing, this author prompts his audience how to feel with emotional colouring; how to think; how to respond. In a sense, then, he is providing another level of instruction. This indicates a sophisticated level of engagement with the audience.[106]

Interestingly, these facets of focalisation rarely apply to Tatiana herself. Only one comment appears to express what she is feeling. At this juncture, Alexander has recently misunderstood her intentions: he believes that she will sacrifice to Apollo and the narrator-focaliser wishes to emphasise the emperor's ignorance. Thus, the *passio*'s 'As she went in [to the temple], the saint turned and said to the emperor with a charming face ...' is altered to 'She was delighted by this. With a cheerful face, she elegantly says to the emperor ...'.[107] This sole example of focalisation for Tatiana, and the use of the present tense, occurs at a key moment, just before the martyr displays her power for the first time by annihilating Apollo's temple and all those inside, thereby underscoring the event. The narrator may have chosen this one occasion to capture the full extent of Tatiana's power. There is no need to continue to

104 *Passio Tat.* 18: 779–780.

105 *MT* 18: 737–744.

106 See Alwis, "The Shape of Water".

107 *Passio Tat.* 4: 87–88; cf. *MT* 4: 79–80.

focalise since Alexander's rewritten reactions perpetuate the idea. It is also possible that the metaphrast did not wish to presume that he knew the mind of a saint.

I have written elsewhere how Tatiana and also Ia of Persia are rewritten as skilful orators, and acclaimed for their facility for rhetorical discourse. It is as rhetors that these women defy and overwhelm those in consummate authority.[108] Furthermore, the women's voices are raised to further their revisers' interests during times of particular conflict: the *MT*, for example, may have been read within the context of iconoclasm, or as a reaction to continual Islamic threat.[109] If so, the narrator's determined engagement with his audience gains additional traction. This author used the framework of metaphrastic techniques to manipulate holiness to express his personal concerns and persuade an audience. This is the very essence of rhetoric.

2 Part II: Mary of Egypt

The early Byzantine *vita* of Mary of Egypt (hereafter the *V. Mar.*) presents a contrasting case study, since two main voices perform the narration: the anonymous author/narrator, who may be Sophronius, but who does not identify himself; and Mary herself.[110] By the use of direct speech, we also hear the voice of Zosimus, the monk who encounters Mary in the wilderness.[111]

108 Alwis, "Listen to Her".

109 Alwis, "The Shape of Water".

110 Mary's limited bibliography can be found in Maria Kouli, "Mary of Egypt", in Alice-Mary Talbot, *Holy Women of Byzantium* (Washington DC: Dumbarton Oaks, 1996), 69. In addition, Bernard Flusin, "Le serviteur Caché ou Le saint sans Existence", in Paolo Odorico and Panagiotis A. Agapitos (eds.), *Les vies des saints à Byzance. Genre littéraire ou biographie historique?* (Paris: Centre d'études byzantines, néo-helléniques et sud-est européennes, 2004), 59–71 positions Zosimus as narrator (at 67 and 70–71) whilst Virginia Burrus, *The Sex Lives of Saints: An Erotics of Ancient Hagiography* (Philadelphia: University of Philadelphia Press, 2004), 147–155 interprets the text as 'an author bent on exposing what has been concealed' (148).

111 As Maria Kouli has stated, the earliest version dates to the sixth century. This brief account appears in the *vita* of Kyriakos by Cyril of Skythopolis (Richard Price, *Lives of the Monks of Palestine* (Kalamazoo, MI: Cistercian Publications, 1991), 256–258; Kouli, "Mary of Egypt", 65). The narrative discussed here has been attributed to Sophronios, Patriarch of Jerusalem (634–638) although there are doubts (see Kouli, "Mary of Egypt", 66 for bibliography). The *terminus ante quem* is around the seventh century, since it was cited by John of Damascus in the eighth century (*Patrologia Graeca* 94: 1416–1417) and translated into Latin (for example, by Paul the Deacon) in the same century. A proper Greek edition is still required.

In narratological terminology, the *V. Mar.*'s story comprises the transformation of a rampantly sexual woman into a God-fearing desert hermit. The plot encompasses, amongst many other elements, Zosimus' spiritual disenchantment; his decision to leave his monastery; his arrival at the monastery by the river Jordan, where the rule is that each monk lives as a solitary in the desert; Zosimus' first encounter with Mary as a consequence; Mary's account of her former life, which in itself includes several episodes; Mary's miraculous qualities (levitation, omniscience); Zosimus' return to the monastery; the pair's second encounter, when Mary walks on water; Zosimus' third visit where he finds Mary's corpse; the arrival of the lion who helps him to dig a grave; and finally, Zosimus' return to the monastery and the dissemination of his adventures.

2.1 *Internal and External Focalisation in the* Vita *of Mary of Egypt*

Like the *MT*, the *V. Mar.*'s author chooses to use an (external) heterodiegetic narrator but, unlike the *MT*, the narrative also features an (internal) homodiegetic narrator, Mary herself. This text also contains internal focalisation, which stems from both Mary and Zosimus. The varied voices and their orientations reveal an author who openly shoulders the burden tacitly acknowledged by many other hagiographers, namely that 'normal' society is asked to believe in implausible circumstances and fantastical beings.[112] More to the point, he attempts to redress the balance with the use of voice and focalisation. The *status quo* is declared during the prologue:

> If there are some people who happen to read this account and, allegedly because of their amazement at the extraordinary [aspects] of the story ... refuse to believe it readily, may the Lord be merciful to them, because they, too, thinking in terms of the weakness of human nature, find it hard to believe extraordinary tales told about human beings.[113]

The heterodiegetic narrator is on a quest to disabuse these sceptics and uphold his creation. His pursuit monopolises the prologue. First, biblical authority operates as justification for the telling. Although it is common for quotations to typify the story they instigate, the *V. Mar.*'s citation is also accompanied by

---

112 Peter Turner, *Truthfulness, Realism, Historicity: A Study in Late Antique Spiritual Literature* (Farnham, Ashgate: 2012) makes the case for late antiquity; Kaldellis, "The Hagiography of Doubt", for Byzantium.

113 *V. Mar.* 1.

a defensive exegesis, which essentially avows that if the narrator did not relate this fantastical story, his soul would be endangered and he would be belittling God.[114]

This theme of authenticity continues as the story progresses. Before the audience meets Zosimus, the narrator-focaliser provides a background check by supplying a catalogue of his every conceivable virtue.[115] Since it will be Zosimus who engages with Mary, and Zosimus whose story the narrator is utilising for his own purposes, the monk's trustworthiness must be ascertained to an (assumed) audience of sceptics. Such cynicism is inevitable when a monk meets any woman, let alone one who is unrestrainedly promiscuous.

When Zosimus is first named, the narrator-focaliser unexpectedly halts a conventional third-person narrative about the Palestinian monk's life and switches to the first person to clarify his identity: 'One must not assume that I am talking of the Zosimus who was once accused of being a heretic, simply because of the name'.[116] Trust must be maintained and voice is used to do so. The abrupt changing of voice to the first person in order to substantiate dubious information continues when Zosimus espies Mary for the first time and is chasing after the vision. The pair are 'running toward[s] a place where a dry streambed had left its traces'. At this exciting moment, the narrator interjects to ruminate over an implausible landscape: 'I do not think that a torrent ever existed there (for how could a torrent appear in that land?) but the place happened to have such a setting'.[117] He seems to anticipate critique.

Another narratological device the *V. Mar.*'s heterodiegetic narrator employs is various speech modes: direct and indirect speech (also referred to as 'discourse' or 'style') and direct thought. Whilst these may function to provide variety and tone, it is also possible they relate to the concern for authenticity. A striking example where all three are conveyed together appears when the audience learn why Zosimus had to leave his monastery (and thus meet Mary). The chapter commences with reported speech: 'Zosimus told [us] then that he was given to this monastery …'.[118] This statement has the effect of corroborating the monk's background. The narrator then moves to indirect speech: 'After that he was disturbed, as he said, by certain thoughts …'. Here, Zosimus' internal process justifies his possibly hazardous spiritual restlessness. Since indirect speech indicates a faithful quotation of someone's words, it is another authen-

114 *V. Mar.* 1.
115 *V. Mar.* 2.
116 *V. Mar.* 2.
117 *V. Mar.* 11.
118 *V. Mar.* 3.

ticating tactic. Then, in a lightning stroke, the narrator progresses from further indirect speech to a series of direct thoughts: 'For, as he said, he thought to himself, "Is there a monk on earth who can teach me anything new …?"'. 'As he said' again specifies that the narrator is accurately reporting Zosimus' thoughts and further endorses the objective by then presenting those direct thoughts. The audience are taken directly into Zosimus' mind and 'truth'.[119]

Using indirect speech in the form of 'as he [Zosimus] said' or 'as he told [us]',[120] or even 'He swore [to us]',[121] is another tactic for authentication at principal moments. We see it when Zosimus experiences spiritual dissatisfaction, thus initiating the plot;[122] after Mary unexpectedly hails Zosimus by his name, and thus first reveals her inexplicable characteristics;[123] or just before Mary levitates, an undoubtedly miraculous event.[124] A final validation occurs during Zosimus and Mary's final encounter. It is late in the evening and Mary is late for their assignation. Zosimus is beleaguered by doubt but suddenly spots her on the opposite bank of the Jordan. The narrator-focaliser continues: 'Then he saw her making the sign of the holy cross over the Jordan—for, as he told us, there was a full moon that night …'.[125] The implication is that an audience would disbelieve that Zosimus could see anything at night and so this is countered.

Not only does the diversity of modes provide for a more interesting text but the audience is assailed by a barrage of authenticating strategies. Basically, the variation of voice that manifests throughout promotes the narrative's validity. As Margaret Atwood has said, 'fiction has to be something that people would actually believe'.[126]

Enhancing the author's endeavours further is the presence of internal focalisation, that is, focalisation from the perspective of a character in the story who is not the narrator, in this case, Zosimus. Mary's first appearance heralds its first use, which can hardly be a coincidence. Thus, the audience's first view of the protagonist as an eerie figment coincides with Zosimus' initial glimpse: '… he saw the shadowy illusion of a human body appear to the right of where he was

119 For a modern variation on how this can be played with, see Sebald's *Austerlitz*. An example is, 'From time to time, so Vera recollected, said Austerlitz, Maximilian would tell the tale of how once …' (Winfried Georg Sebald, *Austerlitz*. Translated by Anthea Bell (London: Penguin, 2013), 166).

120 *V. Mar.* 5, 9, 12.

121 *V. Mar.* 15.

122 *V. Mar.* 3.

123 *V. Mar.* 12.

124 *V. Mar.* 15.

125 *V. Mar.* 35.

126 Rebecca Mead, "The Prophet of Dystopia", *New Yorker*, April 17 (2017), 38.

standing ...'.[127] After he makes the sign of the cross, he looks once more and then the audience again sees with his eyes: 'What he saw was a naked figure whose body was black, as if tanned by the scorching of the sun. It had on its head hair white as wool, and even this was sparse as it did not reach below the neck of its body'.[128] Internal focalisation is repeated when Zosimus revisits a year later: 'Then he saw her making the sign of the holy cross over the Jordan ... and at the same time she set foot on the water and walked on it, approaching him'.[129]

Mary too is allocated focalisation in her extended homodiegetic narrative, which spans nine chapters. Her focalised narrative, which is reported as direct speech, vitalises her story: 'I saw some young men standing at the seashore, about ten or more, vigorous in their bodies as well as in their movements ...'.[130] Her perspective enables an audience to sense her carnality, which is so important to the story. Later, when an invisible force physically restrains her from entering a church repeatedly, her point of view allows the audience to struggle with her: 'So I mingled with other people and pushed with all my strength, shoving with my elbows and forcing myself inside'.[131] Internal focalisation in the *V. Mar.* seems to function to animate the figure of Mary. Zosimus' focalisation vividly brings this curious otherworldly individual to life whilst Mary's own orientation invites her audience to participate in, empathise with, and, ultimately, understand her extreme life.

Mary also intermittently disrupts her own discourse to address Zosimus directly, much like the *V. Mar.*'s heterodiegetic narrator-focaliser: 'please forgive me';[132] 'I swear';[133] 'forgive me, my father';[134] 'I warned you';[135] 'for it happened that I had it in my hands at the time' (when referring to a distaff);[136] 'How can I possibly describe to you what followed, my dear man?'.[137] The outcome of this communicative strategy seems to be both for authentication and to vary the pace of the narrative. Since the events of her life are so extreme, Mary's intru-

127 *V. Mar.* 10.
128 *V. Mar.* 10.
129 *V. Mar.* 35.
130 *V. Mar.* 20.
131 *V. Mar.* 22.
132 *V. Mar.* 18.
133 *V. Mar.* 18.
134 *V. Mar.* 19.
135 *V. Mar.* 19.
136 *V. Mar.* 20.
137 *V. Mar.* 21. She also intersperses her narrative with direct speech, recounting the conversations she had (19, 20).

sions serve to validate the situations. Moreover, Mary's discourse is very long, spanning chapters 17–30, and although the details are occasionally salacious and thus might help to retain an audience's attention, Mary's (and Zosimus') brief interruptions help break the extended speech. Furthermore, given that the text was ultimately viewed as a call to repentance—we know that the text must have been read aloud or even sung during Lent[138]—the narrator-focaliser must have wanted to engage his viewers and listeners in as many ways as possible. The varying dialogue also allows for performance as the reader would take on the different roles and also have to enact Mary's character development. Once again, we have an author who is acutely aware of his audience and who wishes to steer them according to his wishes.[139]

3 Conclusions

Narratology has faced criticism—that it limits interpretation by becoming an end in itself;[140] that its premises and practices lack perspectives from feminist[141] and cultural historical angles;[142] and that it fails to describe the actual experience of reading.[143] The rise of cognitive theory in the disciplines of Classics and Late Antiquity is one way to counter the latter.[144] Yet whilst these points are certainly valid and a variety of approaches are always advisable for interpreting texts, it is also evident that narratology does have much to offer hagiography and Byzantine literature in general. Only two of its devices are

138 During the fifth week on Thursday: Antonia Giannouli, *Die beiden byzantinischen Kommentare zum Großen Kanon des Andreas von Kreta* (Vienna: Verlag der Österreichischen Akademie der Wissenschafte, 2007), 34. With many thanks to Martin Hinterberger for this reference.

139 Mary Cunningham has also rightly pointed out to me the *V. Mar.*'s 'sophisticated irony' in highlighting how the outwardly pious figure of Zosimus is shown true humility by a transgressive woman and 'why this virtue is essential to genuine holiness' (pers. comm.).

140 Jonas Grethlein and Antonios Rengakos (eds.), *Narratology and Interpretation. The Content of Narrative Form in Ancient Literature* (Berlin/New York: De Gruyter, 2009), 3.

141 For example, Susan Sniader Lanser, *Fictions of Authority: Women Writers and Narrative Voice* (Ithaca, NY: Cornell University Press, 1992).

142 For example, Monika Fludernik, "'When the Self is an Other'. Vergleichende erzähltheoretische und postkoloniale Überlegungen zur Identitäts(de)konstruktion in der (exil)indischen Gegenwartsliteratur", *Anglia* 117.1 (1999), 71–96.

143 Tim Whitmarsh, "An I for an I. Reading Fictional Autobiography", in Anna Marmodoro and Jonathan Hill (eds.), *The Author's Voice in Classical and Late Antiquity* (Oxford: Oxford University Press, 2013), 233–250, at 244.

144 https://cognitiveclassics.blogs.sas.ac.uk/.

explored here, namely voice and focalisation, but it is clear that their application substantiates the place of hagiography amongst the literary productions of Byzantium while also making clear the fraught nature of the contested dialogue that hagiography maintains with 'truth'.[145] The passions of martyrs and the *Lives* of saints are indeed a fictional truth, of the type posited by Aristotle; one of meaning rather than fact.[146] Above all, it is evident that a hagiographer utilises a multitude of processes when crafting his/her opus. He/she has to engage with a set of certain cognitive processes. The metaphrast, more than a general reviser in some senses, has to actively engage with each word and its function within its linguistic domain and make decisions about the text he/she wishes to create. Each choice determines the thought the author wishes to commit. Ultimately, the explorations of the *MT* and the *V. Mar.* clearly illustrate that both authors wished to move their audiences, to tell them what to think and how to feel; in effect, the hagiographer's craft enabled a rhetoric of sanctity.

Acknowledgments

I would like to thank the editors of this volume as well as Mary Cunningham, Laura Franco, Martin Hinterberger, Lucy O'Meara, and Kelli Rudolph for their invaluable comments and corrections.

Bibliography

Agapitos, Panagiotis A., *Narrative Structure in the Byzantine Vernacular Romances: A Textual and Literary Study of Kallimachos, Belthandros and Libistros* (Munich: Institut für Byzantinistik und Neugriechische Philologie der Universität, 1991).

Agapitos, Panagiotis A., "Narrative, Rhetoric, and 'Drama' Rediscovered: Scholars and Poets in Byzantium Interpret Heliodorus", in Richard Hunter (ed.), *Studies in Heliodorus* (Cambridge: Cambridge University Press, 1998), 125–156.

145 Other narratological devices used to frame Zosimus and Mary's encounters include a temporal narratological change. The action is decelerated by the use of the present tense, direct speech, and dialogue. The effect allows the audience the luxury of time: to see events through the eyes of both protagonists and thus engage more fully in their narratives.

146 Aristotle, *Poetics*. Translated by Anthony Kenny (Oxford: Oxford University Press, 2013), 9 (1451b).

Agapitos, Panagiotis A., "Literary Criticism", in Elizabeth Jeffreys, John Haldon, and Robin Cormack (eds.), *The Oxford Handbook of Byzantine Studies* (Oxford: Oxford University Press, 2008), 77–85.

Alwis, Anne P., *Celibate Marriages in Late-Antique and Byzantine Hagiography* (London: Bloomsbury, 2011).

Alwis, Anne P., *Narrating Martyrdom: Rewriting Late-Antique Virgin Martyrs in Byzantium* (Liverpool: Liverpool University Press, forthcoming).

Alwis, Anne P., "Listen to Her: Rewriting Virgin Martyrs as Orators in the Byzantine Passions of St. Tatiana and St. Ia", in Koen De Temmerman (ed.), *Holy Hero(in)es* (Cambridge: Cambridge University Press, forthcoming).

Alwis, Anne P., "The Shape of Water: Rewriting Iconoclasm, Islam, and Deleuze", in Stavroula Constantinou and Christian Høgel (eds.), *Metaphrasis: A Byzantine Concept of Rewriting and Its Hagiographical Products* (Leiden: Brill, forthcoming).

Angelov, Dimiter, *Imperial Ideology and Political Thought in Byzantium, 1204–1330* (Cambridge: Cambridge University Press, 2007).

Bal, Mieke, *Narratology: Introduction to the Theory of Narrative* (2nd edition Toronto: University of Toronto Press, 1997).

Barber, Charles and Stratis Papaioannou, *Michael Psellos on Literature and Art: A Byzantine Perspective on Aesthetics* (Notre Dame, IN: University of Notre Dame Press, 2017).

Bernard, Floris, *Writing and Reading Byzantine Secular Poetry, 1025–1081* (Oxford: Oxford University Press, 2014).

Boese, Stefanie, "'Forever Just Occurring': Postwar Belatedness in W.G. Sebald's *Austerlitz*", *Journal of Modern Literature* 39.4 (2016), 104–121.

Bourbouhakis, Emmanuel C., "'Political' Personae: The Poem from Prison of Michael Glykas: Byzantine Literature between Fact and Fiction", *Byzantine and Modern Greek Studies* 31.1 (2007), 53–75.

Bourbouhakis, Emmanuel C. and Ingela Nilsson, "Byzantine Narrative: The Form of Storytelling in Byzantium", in Liz James (ed.), *A Companion to Byzantium* (Oxford: Oxford University Press, 2010), 263–274.

Brontë, Charlotte, *Jane Eyre* (London: Smith, Elder, and Co. 1847).

Burrus, Virginia, *The Sex Lives of Saints: An Erotics of Ancient Hagiography* (Philadelphia: University of Pennsylvania Press, 2004).

Calvino, Italo, *If on a Winter's Night a Traveller* (1979), tr. W. Weaver (London: Vintage Classics, 1993).

Constantinou, Stavroula, "The Saint's Two Bodies: Sensibility Under (Self-)Torture in Byzantine Hagiography", *Classica et Mediaevalia* 66 (2017), 1–36.

de Jong, Irene J.F., René Nünlist, and Angus Bowie (eds.), *Narrators, Narratees, and Narratives in Ancient Greek Literature* (Leiden: Brill, 2004).

de Jong, Irene J.F., *Narratology and Classics: A Practical Guide* (Oxford: Oxford University Press, 2014).

De Temmerman, Koen, "Ancient Rhetoric as a Hermeneutical Tool for the Analysis of Characterization in Narrative Literature", *Rhetorica* 28.1 (2010), 23–51.

Delehaye, Hippolyte, *Les passions des martyrs et les genres littéraires* (Brussels: Société des Bollandistes, 1966).

Demoen, Kristoffel, "John Geometres' Iambic Life of Saint Panteleemon", in Bart Janssens, Bram Roosen, and Peter van Deun (eds.), *Philomathestatos* (Leuven/Paris: Orientalia Louvaniensia Analecta, 2005), 165–184.

Efthymiadis, Stephanos, "John of Sardis and the *Metaphrasis* of the *Passio* of St. Nikephoros the Martyr (*BHG* 1334)", *Rivista di studi bizantini e neoellenici* 28 (1991), 23–44.

Efthymiadis, Stephanos, "The Byzantine Hagiographer and his Audience in the Ninth and Tenth Centuries", in Christian Høgel (ed.), *Metaphrasis: Redactions and Audiences in Middle Byzantine Hagiography* (Oslo: The Research Council of Norway, 1996), 59–80.

Fisher, Elizabeth A., *Michaelis Pselli orationes hagiographicae* (Stuttgart/Leipzig: Teubner, 1994).

Fludernik, Monika, *The Fictions of Language and the Languages of Fiction* (London: Routledge, 1993).

Fludernik, Monika, "'When the Self is an Other'. Vergleichende erzähltheoretische und postkoloniale Überlegungen zur Identitäts(de)konstruktion in der (exil)indischen Gegenwartsliteratur", *Anglia* 117.1 (1999), 71–96.

Flusin, Bernard, "Le serviteur caché ou le saint sans existence", in Paolo Odorico and Panagiotis A. Agapitos (eds.), *Les vies des saints à Byzance. Genre littéraire ou biographie historique?* (Paris: Centre d'études byzantines, néo-helléniques et sud-est européennes, 2004), 59–71.

Fowler, Don, "Deviant Focalisation in Virgil's *Aeneid*", *The Cambridge Classical Journal* 36 (1990), 42–63.

Franco, Laura, "A Study of the Metaphrastic Process", Ph.D. diss., Royal Holloway, London (2009).

Genette, Gérard, *Narrative Discourse Revisited.* Translated by Jane E. Lewin (Cornell: Cornell University Press, 1990).

Genette, Gérard, *Palimpsests: Literature in the Second Degree.* Translated by Channa Newman and Claude Doubinsky (Lincoln/London: University of Nebraska Press, 1997).

Giannouli, Antonia, *Die beiden byzantinischen Kommentare zum Großen Kanon des Andreas von Kreta* (Vienna: Verlag der Österreichischen Akademie der Wissenschaften, 2007).

Gray, Christa, "'Holy and Pleasing to God': A Narratological Approach to Hagiography in Jerome's *Lives* of Paul and Malchus", *Ancient Narrative* 14 (2017), 103–128.

Grethlein, Jonas and Antonios Rengakos (eds.), *Narratology and Interpretation: The Content of Narrative Form in Ancient Literature* (Berlin/New York: De Gruyter, 2009).

Hägg, Tomas, "Photius as a Reader of Hagiography: Selection and Criticism", *Dumbarton Oaks Papers* 53 (1999), 43–58.

Halkin, François, *Légendes grecques de 'martyres romaines'* (Brussels: Société des Bollandistes, 1973).

Heath, Malcolm, "Theon and the History of the *Progymnasmata*", *Greek, Roman, and Byzantine Studies* 43 (2002–2003), 129–160.

Hesse, Hermann, *Siddhartha* (1922). Translated by Hilda R. Rosner (London: Picador, 1998).

Hinterberger, Martin, *Autobiographische Traditionen in Byzanz* (Vienna: Wiener Byzantinische Studien, 1999).

Hinterberger, Martin, "Autobiography and Hagiography in Byzantium", *SO* 75 (2000), 139–164.

Hinterberger, Martin, "Hagiographische Metaphrasen. Ein möglicher Weg der Annäherung an die Literarästhetik der frühen Palaiologenzeit", in Andreas Rhoby and Elisabeth Schiffer (eds.), *Imitatio—Aemulatio—Variatio* (Vienna: Verlag der Österreichischen Akademie der Wissenschaften, 2010), 137–151.

Hinterberger, Martin, "Emotions in Byzantium", in Liz James (ed.), *A Companion to Byzantium* (London: Wiley and Sons, 2010), 123–134.

Hinterberger, Martin, "Phthonos: A Pagan Relic in Byzantine Imperial Acclamations", in Alexander Beihammer, Stavroula Constantinou, and Maria Parani (eds.), *Court Ceremonies and Rituals of Power in Byzantium and the Medieval Mediterranean* (Leiden: Brill, 2013), 51–66.

Hinterberger, Martin, "Between Simplification and Elaboration: Byzantine Metaphraseis in Comparison", in Juan Signes Codoñer and Immaculada Perez Martin (eds.), *Textual Transmission in Byzantium* (Turnhout: Brepols, 2014), 33–60.

Hinterberger, Martin, "Byzantine Hagiography and its Literary Genres", in Stephanos Efthymiadis (ed.), *The Ashgate Research Companion to Byzantine Hagiography*, vol. 2 (Farnham: Ashgate, 2014), 25–60.

Hinterberger, Martin, "The Byzantine Hagiographer and his Text", in Stephanos Efthymiadis (ed.), *The Ashgate Research Companion to Byzantine Hagiography*, vol. 2 (Farnham: Ashgate 2014), 211–235.

Hinterberger, Martin, "Hagiographical Encomia as Metaphrasis in the 14th Century: Some Preliminary Observations", in Stavroula Constantinou and Christian Høgel (eds.), *Metaphrasis: A Byzantine Concept of Rewriting and Its Hagiographical Products* (Leiden: Brill, forthcoming).

Høgel, Christian, "The Redaction of Symeon Metaphrastes: Literary Aspects of the Metaphrastic Martyria", in idem (ed.), *Metaphrasis: Redactions and Audiences in Middle Byzantine Hagiography* (Oslo: The Research Council of Norway, 1996), 7–21.

Høgel, Christian, "Literary Aspects of Greek Byzantine Hagiography: A Bibliographical Survey", *SO* 72 (1997), 164–171.

Høgel, Christian, *Symeon Metaphrastes. Rewriting and Canonization* (Copenhagen: Museum Tusculanum Press, 2002).

Høgel, Christian, "Symeon Metaphrastes and the Metaphrastic Movement" in Stephanos Efthymiadis (ed.), *The Ashgate Research Companion to Byzantine Hagiography*, vol. 2 (Farnham: Ashgate, 2014), 161-–180.

Jahn, Manfred, "Windows of Focalization: Deconstructing and Reconstructing a Narratological Concept", *Style* 30.2 (1996), 241–267.

Jahn, Manfred, "Focalization", in David Herman (ed.), *The Cambridge Companion to Narrative* (Cambridge: Cambridge University Press, 2007), 94–108.

Jeffreys, Elizabeth (ed.), *Rhetoric in Byzantium* (Aldershot: Ashgate, 2003).

Kaldellis, Anthony, "The Hagiography of Doubt and Scepticism", in Stephanos Efthymiadis (ed.), *The Ashgate Research Companion to Byzantine Hagiography*, vol. 2 (Farnham: Ashgate, 2014), 453–477.

Kazhdan, Alexander (ed.), *The Oxford Dictionary of Byzantium*, 3 vols. (Oxford: Oxford University Press, 1991).

Kennedy, George A., *Progymnasmata: Greek Textbooks of Prose Composition and Rhetoric* (Atlanta: Society of Biblical Literature, 2003).

Kenny, Anthony, *Aristotle, Poetics* (Oxford: Oxford University Press, 2013).

Kleinberg, Aviad, *Prophets in Their Own Country: Living Saints and the Making of Sainthood in the Later Middle Ages* (Chicago: University of Chicago Press, 1993).

Kouli, Maria, "Mary of Egypt", in Alice-Mary Talbot (ed.), *Holy Women of Byzantium* (Washington DC: Dumbarton Oaks, 1996), 65–93.

Lanser, Susan Sniader, *Fictions of Authority: Women Writers and Narrative Voice* (Ithaca, NY: Cornell University Press, 1992).

Macrides, Ruth (ed.), *History as Literature* (Farnham: Ashgate, 1988).

Magdalino, Paul, "The Byzantine Holy Man in the Twelfth Century", in Sergei Hackel (ed.), *The Byzantine Saint* (London: Fellowship of St Alban and St Sergius, 1981), 51–66.

Maltese, Enrico, *Dimensioni bizantine: Donne, angeli e demoni nel Medioevo greco* (Alessandria: Edizioni dell'Orso, 2007).

Mango, Cyril, "Diabolus Byzantinus", *Dumbarton Oaks Papers* 46 (1992), 215–223.

Mead, Rebecca, "The Prophet of Dystopia", *New Yorker*, April 17th (2017).

Messis, Charis, "Fiction and/or Novelisation in Byzantine Hagiography", in Stephanos Efthymiadis (ed.), *The Ashgate Research Companion to Byzantine Hagiography*, vol. 2 (Farnham: Ashgate, 2014), 313–341.

Messis, Charis, Margaret Mullett, and Ingela Nilsson (eds.), *Storytelling in Byzantium: Narratological Approaches to Byzantine Texts and Images* (Uppsala: Acta Universitatis Upsaliensis, 2018).

Mullett, Margaret, "Dancing with Deconstructionists in the Gardens of the Muses: New literary history vs ?" *BMGS* 14 (1990), 258–275.

Mullett, Margaret, "The Madness of Genre" *DOP* 46 (1992), 233–243.

Mullett, Margaret, "New Literary History and the History of Byzantine Literature: A Worthwhile Endeavour?" in Paolo Odorico and Panagiotis A. Agapitos (eds.), *Pour une "nouvelle" histoire de la literature byzantine* (Paris: École des Hautes Études en Sciences Sociales, 2002), 37–60.

Mullett, Margaret, "Imitatio—aemulatio—variatio", in Andreas Rhoby and Elisabeth Schiffer (eds.), *Imitatio—Aemulatio—Variatio* (Vienna: Verlag der Österreichischen Akademie der Wissenschaften, 2010), 279–282.

Nünlist, René, "The Homeric Scholia on Focalization", *Mnemosyne* 56.1 (2003), 61–71.

Odorico, Paolo, Panagiotis, A. Agapitos, and Martin Hinterberger (eds.), *L'écriture de la mémoire: le littératuré de l'historiographie* (Paris: Centre d'études byzantines, néo-helléniques et sud-est européennes, 2006).

Papaioannou, Stratis, "Byzantine *Enargeia* and Theories of Representation", *Byzantinoslavica* 69:3 (2011), 48–60.

Papaioannou, Stratis, *Michael Psellos: Rhetoric and Authorship in Byzantium* (Cambridge: Cambridge University Press, 2013).

Paschalides, Symeon, "Παρατηρήσεις στὶς μεταφράσις τῶν Βυζαντινῶν ἁγιολογικῶν κειμένων", *Βυζαντινά* 33 (2013–2014), 373–386.

Phelan, James, "Estranging Unreliability, Bonding Unreliability, and the Ethics of *Lolita*", *Narrative* 15.2 (2007), 222–238.

Porter Abbott, H., *The Cambridge Introduction to Narrative* (Cambridge: Cambridge University Press, 2008).

Price, Richard, *Cyril Scythopolis: Lives of the Monks of Palestine* (Kalamazoo, MI: Cistercian Publications, 1991).

Rapp, Claudia, "Byzantine Hagiographers as Antiquarians, Seventh to Tenth Centuries", *Byzantinische Forschungen* 21 (1995), 31–44.

Rapp, Claudia, "Figures of Female Sanctity: Byzantine Edifying Manuscripts and Their Audience", *Dumbarton Oaks Papers* 50 (1996), 313–344.

Rapp, Claudia, "Storytelling as Spiritual Communication in Early Greek Hagiography: The Use of *Diegesis*", *JECS* 6:3 (1998), 431–448.

Resh, Daria, "Toward a Byzantine Definition of Metaphrasis", *Greek, Roman, and Byzantine Studies* 55 (2015), 754–787.

Rimmon-Kenan, Shlomith, *Narrative Fiction: Contemporary Poetics* (New York: Methuen, 1983).

Rydén, Lennart, "Fiction and Reality in the Hagiographer's Self-Presentation", *Travaux et Mémoires* 14 (2002), 547–552.

Rydén, Lennart, "Literariness in Byzantine Saints' Lives", in Paolo Odorico and Panagiotis A. Agapitos (eds.), *Les vies des saints à Byzance: Genre littéraire ou biographie historique* (Paris: Centre d'études byzantines, néo-helléniques et sud-est européennes, 2004), 49–58.

Sayers, Dorothy L., *Gaudy Night* (London: Victor Gollancz, 1935).

Schiffer, Elisabeth Peyr, "Zur Umarbeitung rhetorischer Texte durch Symeon Metaphrastes", *Jahrbuch der Österreichischen Byzantinistik* 42 (1992), 143–155.

Schiffer, Elisabeth Peyr, "Metaphrastic Lives and Earlier *Metaphráseis* of Saints' Lives", in Christian Høgel (ed.), *Metaphrasis: Redactions and Audiences in Middle Byzantine Hagiography* (Oslo: The Research Council of Norway, 1996), 22–41.

Smith, Ole L., "Medieval and Renaissance Commentaries in Greek on Classical Greek Texts", *Classica et Medievalia* 47 (1996), 391–405.

Talbot, Alice-Mary, *Holy Women of Byzantium* (Washington DC: Dumbarton Oaks, 1996).

Talbot, Alice-Mary, "Old Wine in New Bottles: The Rewriting of Saints' *Lives* in the Palaeologan Period" in eadem, *Women and Religious Life in Byzantium* (Aldershot: Ashgate, 2001), X: 15–26.

Talbot, Alice-Mary, "Hagiography in Late Byzantium (1204–1453)" in Stephanos Efthymiadis (ed.), *The Ashgate Research Companion to Byzantine Hagiography*, vol. 1 (Farnham: Ashgate, 2011), 173–195.

Toolan, Michael, *Narrative: A Critical Linguistic Introduction* (London: Routledge, 2001).

Turner, Peter, *Truthfulness, Realism, Historicity: A Study in Late Antique Spiritual Literature* (Farnham: Ashgate, 2012).

Vitz, Evelyn Birge, *Medieval Narrative and Modern Narratology. Subjects and Objects of Desire* (New York: New York University Press, 1989).

Webb, Ruth, "Imagination and the Arousal of the Emotions in Greco-Roman Rhetoric", in Susanna Morton Braund and Christopher Gill (eds.), *The Passions in Roman Thought and Literature* (Cambridge: Cambridge University Press, 1997), 112–127.

Webb, Ruth, *Ekphrasis, Imagination and Persuasion in Ancient Rhetorical Theory and Practice* (Farnham: Ashgate, 2009).

Whitmarsh, Tim, "An I for an I. Reading Fictional Autobiography", in Anna Marmodoro and Jonathan Hill (eds.), *The Author's Voice in Classical and Late Antiquity* (Oxford: Oxford University Press, 2013), 233–250.

Zilliacus, Henrik, "Zur stilistischen Umarbeitungstechnik des Symeon Metaphastes", *Byzantinsche Zeitschrift* 38 (1938), 333–350.

CHAPTER 12

Postscript

Lucy Grig

We meet a whole cast of saints in this volume, from the hapless, ill-dressed, and linguistically inferior Macarius of Tkōou to the urbane 'gentleman amateur' Paulinus of Nola. We consider a variety of types of text—certainly bound more by a 'family resemblance' than by any formal limitations. Where we might expect to find certainty and closure we often find openness and even 'polyphony'. We encounter the satirical, the agonistic, and the (mildly) comic, and a wide variety of intertexts. Early in their introduction, James Corke-Webster and Christa Gray posit a 'liminal' position for hagiography in scholarship: from derision, through Bollandist rigour, to social history, interest in hagiographical texts *qua* literature has been a long time coming. However, it is fair to say that with the collection of articles assembled here, a fully-pronged *literary* approach to hagiography can be said—finally!—to have arrived. This brief final essay will pick up on some of the key themes dealt with in the collection, and finish by suggesting questions and ideas for future studies. It is offered as a personal response—more as a postscript than a conclusion, embracing the collection's spirit of openness rather than closure.

While the editors rightly assert that this collection is not intended as a linear history of hagiography, but as 'a study of development rather than of origins',[1] it takes us on a journey from our earliest surviving (and lost!) *Lives* from the fourth century through to texts from middle Byzantium. From the very beginning we see hagiographic texts engaged in dialogue and debate with each other—in agonistic and occasionally even antagonistic relationship. For instance, James Corke-Webster offers a new perspective on the *Life of Antony*, viewing it as a rival to Eusebius' lost *Life of Pamphilus*, showing that a debate on the nature of sanctity was already in existence at this seemingly early date. Jerome's explicitly agonistic claim that Paul the Hermit was the *real* first hermit is well-known, but Alan J. Ross shows how Jerome's use of satirical intertexts plays a crucial role in making this claim. The strikingly intertextual quality of Jerome's *Lives* is shown further by Christa Gray's analysis of scenes of supplication.

Literary experimentation remains a consistent feature of hagiographical texts. Indeed, the demonstration here of the experimentalism of our hagiographic authors is striking, in notable contrast to traditional notions of the tired

1 See the Introduction to this volume, 9.

 | DOI:10.1163/9789004421332_014

repetitiveness of hagiography as a genre. It is one of the most important contributions of this collection to demonstrate this feature. The writings of Paulinus of Nola, for instance, can certainly be seen as experimenting with genre in several ways; Michael Stuart Williams examines one particular aspect of his letter writing, as introducing 'a kind of autohagiography' playing with the conventions of the epistolary genre. While biographical closure is expected by the reader of the saint's *Life*, Zachary Yuzwa explores a case which confounds this expectation: Sulpicius Severus' *Life of Martin*, written *before* the saint's death. Martin's life goes beyond his *Life*, however, being narrated across a number of different texts and indeed genres: Sulpicius Severus, Yuzwa argues, continues to experiment with 'the manifold possibilities of genre and narrative in the context of a still nascent and constantly developing literary project of hagiographical remembering'.[2] That this experimentalism continued over the *longue durée* is shown by Anne Alwis in her analysis of the mid Byzantine metaphrastic *Life* of Tatiana of Rome, demonstrating how the metaphrast engages actively with each aspect of the text.

Removing hagiography from its scholarly cul-de-sac into the much wider domain of literary studies enables new approaches, which draw on key trends in current classical scholarship. For instance, the importance and impact of narratological approaches to ancient literature is clear in this collection, with several papers focusing on key narratological elements or concepts, such as focalisation (as in the contributions of Klazina Staat and Anne Alwis). An interest in the question of fiction, meanwhile, prominent in some of the most recent scholarship on late antiquity,[3] proves another highly fertile theme for exploration. The question of the fictive qualities of hagiography is raised by Julie Van Pelt, who focuses in particular on holy fools, who choose in their *Lives* to play a part, and thus to deceive onlookers, while at the same time leading them towards a larger truth. This proves to be a fruitful metaphor for the role of the hagiographer, who aims to rouse in his or her audience[4] 'a different kind of belief, which is a belief in the religious rather than the historical truth of his narration.' This brings to mind Peter Turner's notable recent discussion of 'hagiographical realism',[5] discussed by several contributors, but also clearly

2 See Yuzwa in this volume, 170.

3 Note (inter alia) Anders Cullhed, *The Shadow of Creusa. Negotiating Fictionality in Late Antique Latin Literature*. Translated by Michael Knight (Berlin: De Gruyter, 2015); Koen De Termmerman and Kristoffel Demoen (eds.), *Writing Biography in Greece and Rome: Narrative Technique and Fictionalisation* (Cambridge: Cambridge University Press, 2016).

4 I take heart from Anne Alwis' optimism as regards the existence of female hagiographers.

5 As discussed by several contributors: Peter Turner, *Truthfulness, Realism, Historicity: A Study in Late Antique Spiritual Literature* (Farnham: Ashgate, 2012).

bears wider resonance for a volume unashamedly concerned with hagiography as literature. Indeed, rather than trying to extract the historical or 'truthful' core from hagiographical texts we should instead seek to understand 'fictive' elements as essential aspects in themselves, and to appreciate hagiography's 'fictiveness' as constitutive.[6] Exploring ideas of fiction and the fictive, as well as late antique critiques of fiction, will enable us to consider further questions about the nature of hagiographical texts and their place in late antique culture.

This place, as already suggested, is shaped by the interaction of diverse genres, including biography, epistolography, and the novel. While the relationship between hagiography and the ancient novel is currently the focus of the innovative 'Novel Saints' project at Ghent, now is perhaps the time to range more widely in terms of relevant literary models, intertexts, and milieux. In his analysis of the *Paneygric of Macarius of Tkōou*, Konstantin Klein comments that the comic elements in the text recall aspects of the ancient mime, with Macarius himself bearing clear similarities to the mime's *stupidus*. Klein's observation opens up a number of potentially fruitful areas for exploration. It reminds us that hagiographic discourse interacts with a wide range of influences and intertexts, not all of which are preserved in textual form. Mime, despised by the elite of the Roman world as a 'low' form, shows signs of persistence well into the period represented in our hagiographic texts. This is significant because the mime arguably offers a site for 'unauthorised' or even 'popular' culture and thus again is telling of the ideological and cultural location of—at least—some hagiographic texts.

Broader questions about the *ideological* nature of hagiographical texts here arise and more formal literary analysis enables us to see not just what ideological positions our texts expound, but *how* they do it. Previously scholars (including myself) have written about hagiographical narratives as particularly suitable vehicles for ideological exposition. Martyr texts in particular are 'centripetal', based on strict binary oppositions and moving in a straight line towards a single, clear climax, leaving is no room for ambiguity or impartiality.[7] Such an analysis highlights the strongly didactic nature of hagiographic narrative, exploring how different strategies work to fix the meaning of the story. In

6 See here the useful reflections of one of this volume's contributors: Klazina Staat, "Late Antique Latin Hagiography, Truth and Fiction: Trends in Scholarship", *L'Antiquité Classique* 87 (2018), 209–224.

7 See Lucy Grig, *Making Martyrs in Late Antiquity* (London: Duckworth, 2004), 39, building on the work of e.g. Charles F. Altman, "Two Types of Opposition and the Structure of Saints' Lives", *Medievalia et Humanistica* n.s. 6 (1987), 1–11, and Alison Goddard Elliott, *Roads to Paradise: Reading the Lives of the Saints* (Hanover/London: New England University Press, 1987).

this way, we might see hagiographical texts as *lisible* ('readable', in the terms of Roland Barthes), as highly redundant, as working to restrict the possible number of readings and fix just one, authoritative reading.[8] However, it is interesting that several authors in this collection, by contrast, see openness as equally characteristic of hagiographical texts, openness that admits a real possibility of alternate readings. Indeed, rather than seeing hagiographical narratives as *lisible*, Klazina Staat, in her analysis of the motif of secret chaste marriages across the *Life of Malchus* and that of Amator, argues that we can see them as instead as *scriptable*/writable. That is, these texts offer opportunities to their readers to engage directly with the text themselves and to bridge the narrative plots. A *lack* of narrative closure is again at issue. Instead of seeing hagiographical texts as monolithic and closed, several of the chapters instead highlight a broader kind of openness. Todd E. French discusses the inherent polyphony of hagiographical collections in particular, arguing that hagiographical stories could 'take on a life of their own as they are received, interpreted, and reimagined by the author, and eventually by the reader.'

The question remains: who and what are hagiographic texts *for*? If they are models, who are they models for? And how are these models supposed to work? The question of the audience is not one considered in any detail by most of our papers. However, Robert Wiśniewksi does offer an important corrective to usual commonplaces that regard clerical *Lives* unproblematically as models for members of the clergy—particularly bishops. Wiśniewksi points out that episcopal hagiography in fact has very little to say about specifically *episcopal* sanctity, with priestly aspects being downplayed across the majority of *vitae*. This reminds us that the notion of hagiographical texts working as models is always a complex issue. Compilations such as those discussed by French would certainly offer potentially rich opportunities to explore these questions.

Where (else) next? I shall use the privilege of this postscript position to dare to offer some final, brief—and subjective—suggestions as to directions future scholars in the field might wish to take.

Firstly, there is the question of diversity. This volume has brought together hagiographical texts in Latin, Greek, Syriac, and Coptic: undoubtedly more remains to be done to consider a broader range of languages and traditions, as the editors themselves acknowledge. The range of languages and traditions incorporated into the literature of late antiquity goes far beyond the competency of any individual, and so collaborative projects will be needed for

8 First expounded in Roland Barthes, *S/Z* (Paris: Seuil, 1970); see too Grig, *Making Martyrs*, 5.

examining hagiography comparatively. While scholars have for some time now been making a case for a more diverse or even global late antiquity, real structural and financial challenges, incorporating continuing biases and hierarchies, work against such projects. However, research that looked at 'hagiographic discourse' in broad perspective, including texts from non-Christian traditions—for instance incorporating of Islamic martyrology—would enable significant advances.

Next, the question of the identity of the hagiographic audience is a crucial one that deserves more work, from a variety of angles. Work with manuscripts and manuscript traditions is one aspect of this but consideration of the hagiographic *reader* alongside the hagiographic author (on whom stimulating work has already been done) is also called for. Connected to the question of audience is an attention to a broader range of literary and para-literary texts and fragments of culture with which hagiography interacted. A focus on 'openness' has arisen at several points and it has been widely recognised that this openness (comprising, but going beyond, 'textual fluidity') is a notable characteristic of 'popular literature'.[9] While it has been an important advance to show that hagiography has literary qualities (to put it crudely), that it engages in often sophisticated ways with other classical literature, now we can explore ways in which it engages with other types of literary culture.

More speculatively: since the linguistic turn in late antique studies has borne real dividends for the literary study of hagiography, other more recent trends could be equally fruitful. The spatial turn has been very influential in late antique cultural history: the construction of space is obviously a constitutive element in the construction of the holy and more thought about how this operates in hagiography could well offer new insights.[10] Secondly, the material turn is now in full flow. Is it implausible to suggest that we could we also think about the materiality of hagiography—for instance thinking about the role of objects in hagiographic texts, or indeed the materiality of the manuscripts themselves (thus linking back to the question of the hagiographic audience)?

Finally, Anne Alwis acknowledges in her chapter that narratological approaches to literature have faced criticisms: in particular, around the danger that such readings can become an end in themselves and can seem to lack other important perspectives—such as the lens of gender, or a cultural-historical

9 William Hansen (ed.), *An Anthology of Ancient Greek Popular Literature* (Bloomington/Indianopolis: Indiana University Press, 1998), xxi–xxiii.

10 See Juliette Day, Raimo Hakola, Maijastina Kahlos, and Ulla Tervahauta (eds.), *Spaces in Late Antiquity: Cultural, Theological and Archaeological Perspectives* (London/New York: Routledge, 2016).

approach. From the point of view of *this* hagiographical scholar, while literary approaches have been a very long time coming, future studies of hagiography should be able to incorporate as many different methodologies as possible, in order to develop ever richer readings.

Bibliography

Altman, Charles F., “Two Types of Opposition and the Structure of Saints' Lives”, *Medievalia et Humanistica* n.s. 6 (1987), 1–11.

Barthes, Roland, *S/Z* (Paris: Seuil, 1970).

Cullhed, Anders, *The Shadow of Creusa: Negotiating Fictionality in Late Antique Latin Literature*. Translated by M. Knight (Berlin/Boston: De Gruyter, 2015).

Day, Juliette, Raimo Hakola, Maijastina Kahlos, and Ulla Tervahauta (eds.), *Spaces in Late Antiquity: Cultural, Theological and Archaeological Perspectives* (London/New York: Routledge, 2016).

De Temmerman, Koen and Kristoffel Demoen (eds.), *Writing Biography in Greece and Rome: Narrative Technique and Fictionalisation* (Cambridge, Cambridge University Press, 2016).

Elliott, Alison Goddard, *Roads to Paradise: Reading the Lives of the Saints* (Hanover/London: New England University Press, 1987).

Grig, Lucy, *Making Martyrs in Late Antiquity* (London: Duckworth, 2004).

Hansen, William (ed.), *An Anthology of Ancient Greek Popular Literature* (Bloomington/Indianopolis: Indiana University Press, 1998).

Staat, Klazina, “Late Antique Latin Hagiography, Truth and Fiction: Trends in Scholarship”, *L'Antiquité Classique* 87 (2018), 209–224.

Turner, Peter, *Truthfulness, Realism, Historicity: A Study in Late Antique Spiritual Literature* (Farnham: Ashgate, 2012).

Index

Printed in the United States
By Bookmasters